**Herkimer County
Community College Library**
Herkimer, New York
13350

1. Books may be kept for three weeks and may be renewed once, except when otherwise noted.

2. Reference books, such as dictionaries and encyclopedias are to be used only in the Library.

3. A fine is charged for each day a book is not returned according to the above rule.

4. All injuries to books beyond reasonable wear and all losses shall be made good to the satisfaction of the Librarian.

5. Each borrower is held responsible for all books drawn on his card and for all fines accruing on the same.

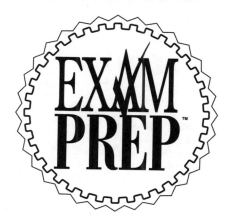

MCSD Visual Basic
6 Desktop

Michael Ekedahl

The Coriolis Group, LLC
14455 N. Hayden Road, Suite 220
Scottsdale, Arizona 85260

480/483-0192
FAX 480/483-0193
http://www.coriolis.com

Library of Congress Cataloging-in-Publication Data
Ekedahl, Michael
        MCSD Visual Basic 6 Desktop exam prep / Michael Ekedahl.
        p.   cm.
Includes index.
ISBN 1-57610-260-2
        1. Electronic data processing personnel--Certification.   2. Microsoft software--Examinations--Study guides.   3. Microsoft Visual BASIC
I. Title.
QA76.3.E36   1999
005.26'8--dc21
                                                        99-38513
                                                        CIP

President, CEO
Keith Weiskamp

Publishers
Kristen Duerr
Steve Sayre

Acquisitions Editor
Jeff Kellum

Marketing Managers
Susan Ogan
Cynthia Caldwell

Product Managers
Margarita Donovan
Tom Lamoureux

Production Editors
Elena Montillo
Kim Eoff

Editorial Assistant
Tricia Coia

Cover Design
Jesse Dunn

Layout Design
April Nielsen

CD-ROM Developer
Robert Clarfield

 CORIOLIS

Printed in the United States of America
10   9   8   7   6   5   4   3   2   1

14455 North Hayden Road, Suite 220 • Scottsdale, Arizona 85260

Coriolis: The Training And Certification Destination™

Thank you for purchasing one of our innovative certification study guides, just one of the many members of the Coriolis family of certification products.

Certification Insider Press™ has long believed that achieving your IT certification is more of a road trip than anything else. This is why most of our readers consider us their *Training And Certification Destination*. By providing a one-stop shop for the most innovative and unique training materials, our readers know we are the first place to look when it comes to achieving their certification. As one reader put it, "I plan on using your books for all of the exams I take."

To help you reach your goals, we've listened to others like you, and we've designed our entire product line around you and the way you like to study, learn, and master challenging subjects. Our approach is *The Smartest Way To Get Certified*™.

In addition to our highly popular *Exam Cram* and *Exam Prep* guides, we have a number of new products. We recently launched Exam Cram Live!, two-day seminars based on *Exam Cram* material. We've also developed a new series of books and study aides—*Practice Tests Exam Crams* and *Exam Cram Flash Cards*—designed to make your studying fun as well as productive.

Our commitment to being the Training And Certification Destination does not stop there. We just introduced *Exam Cram Insider*, a biweekly newsletter containing the latest in certification news, study tips, and announcements from Certification Insider Press. (To subscribe, send an email to **eci@coriolis.com** and type "subscribe insider" in the body of the email.) We also recently announced the launch of the Certified Crammer Society and the Coriolis Help Center—two new additions to the Certification Insider Press family.

We'd like to hear from you. Help us continue to provide the very best certification study materials possible. Write us or email us at **cipq@coriolis.com** and let us know how our books have helped you study, or tell us about new features that you'd like us to add. If you send us a story about how we've helped you, and we use it in one of our books, we'll send you an official Coriolis shirt for your efforts.

Good luck with your certification exam and your career. Thank you for allowing us to help you achieve your goals.

Keith Weiskamp
President and CEO

Look For These Other Books From The Coriolis Group:

MCSD Architectures Exam Cram
Donald Brandt

MCSD Architectures Exam Prep
Keith Morneau

MCSD VB6 Core 3 Exam Cram Pack
Certification Insider Press Author Team

MCSD Visual C++ 6 Desktop Exam Cram
James Lacey

MCSD Visual C++ 6 Distributed Exam Cram
James Lacey

ABOUT THE AUTHOR

Michael Ekedahl spent five years as the Senior Systems Analyst for the National Supercomputing Center for Energy and the Environment at the University of Nevada Las Vegas. He is an Adjunct Faculty member at UNLV, teaching advanced MIS seminar classes and advanced Visual Basic. He presently has a consulting business that supplies Visual Basic and Visual C++ solutions to complex business problems.

ACKNOWLEDGMENTS

I would like to thank the reviewers Melinda White, John Schoeberlein, Cherie Ann Sherman, Dawn Craig and Mary Amundson-Miller, as well as the team at Course Technology for making this book possible. I would also like to thank Dr. William A. Newman for his support and giving me the confidence that I could create this book. Thanks also to Brian Munroe for creating the test bank and his assistance with the instructor's guide.

I would especially like to thank Jill Batistick, for her quality work as developmental editor. I would also like to thank Kristen Duerr and Margarita Donovan for keeping the process on track and all their support along the way.

Finally, I would like to thank my dog Rio. His constant companionship and amusing distractions made those long nights bearable.

Contents At A Glance

TABLE OF CONTENTS

INTRODUCTION

MCSD *Visual Basic 6 Desktop Exam Prep* was written to provide the
Visual Basic programmer with the tools to create Visual Basic programs
that conform to well-adopted Windows standards. Where possible, existing
Visual Basic tools are used. In some cases, Windows libraries are used to extend
the functionality of Visual Basic. The intent is to provide the reader with a rich
set of tools to create programs that satisfy the demands of today's business
environment.

ORGANIZATION AND APPROACH

This book presumes a familiarity with Visual Basic syntax and use of intrinsic
controls. Chapters 1 and 2 are a review of the basics of the Visual Basic
development environment, language syntax, and programming in an event-
driven environment. Depending upon the reader's level of experience, these
chapters may be skipped.

The book is relatively modular in design. Some readers may be interested in
database-related topics, while others may want specific information about class
modules and object-oriented programming. As such, some chapters are
functionally related and others are not.

Chapters 3 and 4 cover database topics. Creators of business applications will
find these chapters useful. The database coverage uses the new ADO object
model.

Chapters 5 and 6 cover the Windows Common controls. These chapters are
applicable to anyone who is creating a user interface that uses common
Windows metaphors. Chapter 7 discusses MDI programming.

Chapter 8 contains a discussion of component-based design techniques and
provides a foundation for Chapters 9 through 13. Chapter 9 introduces class
modules. Chapter 10 is an extension of Chapter 9 and discusses abstract classes
and creating object hierarchies using collections.

Chapters 11 and 12 discuss the creation of ActiveX controls, and Chapter 13
covers ActiveX documents.

Chapter 14 is an independent chapter that covers Internet related controls.
Chapter 15 discusses Dynamic HTML programs and how to create HTML
Help.

Chapter 16 covers the Windows Application Programming Interface, and how to perform asynchronous processing using both events and callbacks. Chapter 17 covers the program Visual Component Manager and program deployment and maintenance.

Appendix A is intended to demonstrate how to use the Visual Basic Integrated Development Environment to locate program errors, and how to correct them.

MCSD Visual Basic 6 Desktop Exam Prep is designed to provide the necessary skills to pass the Developing Applications with Microsoft Visual Basic 6.0 Certification Exam.

FEATURES

Chapter Organization

Each chapter includes a programming-related problem that you could expect to encounter in business, as well as a demonstration of an application that could be used to solve the problem. Showing the completed application before learning how to create it is motivational and instructionally sound. By allowing you to see the type of application you will be able to create after completing the chapter, you will be more motivated to learn because you can see how the programming concepts can be used and, therefore, why the concepts are important. Each chapter includes the following features:

➤ **Chapter Case and Application** Each chapter includes a programming-related problem that the reader could expect to encounter in business, and a demonstration of an application that could be used to solve the problem.

➤ **Step-by-Step Methodology** This methodology keeps you on track. The text reinforces where you are in the development process and emphasizes how each phase relates to the others. You also learn development concepts and techniques in the context of creating a contemporary application.

➤ **Objectives** The Objectives call out the main concepts that will be presented in the chapter.

➤ **Syntax Windows** Syntax for statements, functions, objects, and so on, is presented as it appears in online Help so you will not have difficulty identifying them. Syntax is then "dissected," with a complete definition of each keyword and variable in the statement. Notes regarding peculiarities of the syntax, properties, methods, and events, code examples, and an explanation of the code example are also provided. These Syntax Windows gather important information about programming constructs and objects in an easy-to-reference format.

➤ **Code Examples** In addition to code examples included with the syntax, actual code is used within the text of the chapter to provide additional examples of a concept or illustrate further peculiarities. The completed application that accompanies each chapter is fully commented and will often contain additional code beyond the code entered in the step-by-step instructions included in the chapters. The intent is to demonstrate a reasonably robust example.

➤ **Tips** Tips supply additional information, such as references to materials to enhance the learning experience.

➤ **Chapter Summary** Following each chapter is a section highlighting the programming concepts, commands, and controls covered in the chapter.

➤ **Review Questions** Each chapter concludes with meaningful, conceptual review questions that test the reader's understanding of the material presented in the chapter.

➤ **Hands-On Projects** The Review Questions are followed by exercises that test the user's understanding of how to complete business-related programs pertaining to the chapter. The Projects provide additional practice of skills and concepts presented in the chapter.

CD-ROM Tools

Many tools are included on the CD-ROM, including:

➤ **Answer Files** Reveal answers to all of the Review Questions.

➤ **Solution Files** Contain possible solutions to all the problems you are asked to create or modify in the chapters and cases. (Due to the nature of software development, your solutions might differ from these solutions and still be correct.)

➤ **Data Files** Contain all data that you will use for the chapters and exercises in this textbook, and are provided on the CD-ROM.

➤ **Practice Exams** Two practice exams enable you to test your knowledge and score and graph your exam results.

Preparing For Microsoft Certification

Microsoft offers a program called the Microsoft Certified Professional (MCP) program. Becoming a Microsoft Certified Professional can open many doors for you. Whether you want to be a network engineer, product specialist, or software developer, obtaining the appropriate Microsoft Certified Professional credentials can provide a formal record of your skills to potential employers. Certification can be equally effective in helping you secure a raise or promotion.

The Microsoft Certified Professional program is made up of many courses in several different tracks. Combinations of individual courses can lead to certification in a specific track. Most tracks require a combination of required and elective courses. One of the most common tracks for beginners is the Microsoft Certified Product Specialist (MCPS). By obtaining this status, your credentials tell a potential employer that you are an expert in a specialized computing area, such as Microsoft Technologies.

Want To Know More About Microsoft Certification?

There are many additional benefits to achieving Microsoft Certified status. These benefits apply to you as well as to your potential employer. As a Microsoft Certified Professional (MCP), you will be recognized as an expert on Microsoft products, have access to ongoing technical information from Microsoft, and receive special invitations to Microsoft conferences and events. You can obtain a comprehensive, interactive tool that provides full details about the Microsoft Certified Professional program online at **www.microsoft.com/ train_cert/programs/prog_mcp.htm**.

When you become a Certified Product Specialist, Microsoft sends you a Welcome Kit that contains:

➤ An 8-1/2 × 11" Microsoft Certified Product Specialist wall certificate. Also, within a few weeks after you have passed any exam, Microsoft sends you a Microsoft Certified Professional Transcript that shows which exams you have passed.

➤ A Microsoft Certified Professional Program membership card.

➤ A Microsoft Certified Professional lapel pin.

➤ A license to use the Microsoft Certified Professional logo. You are licensed to use the logo in your advertisements, promotions, proposals, and other materials, including business cards, letterheads, advertising circulars, brochures, yellow page advertisements, mailings, banners, resumes, and invitations.

➤ A Microsoft Certified Professional logo sheet. Before using the camera-ready logo, you must agree to the terms of the licensing agreement.

➤ A one-year subscription to Microsoft Certified Professional Magazine, a career and professional development magazine created especially for Microsoft Certified Professionals.

➤ A Certification Update subscription. Certification Update is a bimonthly newsletter from the Microsoft Certified Professional program that keeps you informed of changes and advances in the program and exams.

➤ Invitations to Microsoft conferences, technical training sessions, and special events.

➤ Eligibility to join the Network Professional Association, a worldwide association of computer professionals. Microsoft Certified Product Specialists are invited to join as associate members.

A Microsoft Certified Systems Developer receives all the benefits mentioned above as well as the following additional benefits:

➤ Microsoft Certified Systems Developer logos and other materials to help you identify yourself as a Microsoft Certified Systems Developer to colleagues or clients.

➤ A one-year subscription to the Microsoft TechNet Plus Technical Information Network. Subscribers to TechNet Plus will receive all evaluation beta products on CD-ROM along with 12 monthly TechNet issues.

An MSDN Online Certified Membership which is a free program exclusively for MCPs, sponsored by MSDN Online. MSDN Online Certified Membership helps you tap into the best technical resources, connect to the MCP community, and gain access to valuable resources and services. (Some MSDN Online benefits may be available in English only or may not be available in all countries.) See the MSDN Web site for a growing list of certified member benefits.

Certify Me!

So you are ready to become a Microsoft Certified Professional. The examinations are administered through Sylvan Prometric (formerly Drake Prometric) and are offered at more than 700 authorized testing centers around the world. Microsoft evaluates certification status based on current exam records. Your current exam record is the set of exams you have passed. To maintain Microsoft Certified Professional status, you must remain current on all the requirements for your certification.

Registering for an exam is easy. To register, contact Sylvan Prometric, 2601 West 88th Street, Bloomington, MN, 55431, at (800) 755-EXAM (3926). Dial (612) 896-7000 or (612) 820-5707 if you cannot place a call to an 800 number from your location. You must call to schedule the exam at least one day before the day you want to take the exam. Taking the exam automatically enrolls you in the Microsoft Certified Professional program; you do not need to submit an application to Microsoft Corporation.

When you call Sylvan Prometric, have the following information ready:

➤ Your name, organization (if any), mailing address, and phone number.

➤ A unique ID number (e.g., your Social Security number).

➤ The number of the exam you wish to take (Designing and Implementing Desktop Applications with Microsoft Visual Basic 6.0 Certification Exam #70-176).

➤ A payment method (e.g., credit card number). If you pay by check, payment is due before the examination can be scheduled. The fee to take each exam is currently $100.

CHAPTER ONE

INSTALLING AND CONFIGURING VISUAL BASIC FOR THE DESKTOP

AFTER READING THIS CHAPTER AND COMPLETING THE EXERCISES, YOU WILL BE ABLE TO:

➤ Install and configure Visual Basic for use on the desktop

➤ Install and configure the Microsoft Developer Network Library

➤ Learn about the features of the Visual Basic development environment

➤ Understand the files that constitute a Visual Basic program

➤ Learn about properties

➤ Learn how to use the Code window

➤ Learn the purpose of Visual SourceSafe

➤ Configure Visual SourceSafe

➤ Manage projects with Visual SourceSafe

INSTALLING VISUAL BASIC FOR THE DESKTOP

Installing Visual Basic

Visual Basic must be installed on your computer before you can use it to create applications. The installation you perform will configure Visual Basic so that you can later develop and deploy Visual Basic applications. Because the Visual Basic programming environment has changed considerably since its inception in 1991, growing in both size and complexity, you as the programmer have several options as to which Visual Basic software components you install on your system. In this chapter, you will examine the different components associated with Visual Basic. The available components will vary depending on which edition of Visual Basic you use. Before beginning the installation process, consider the three different editions of Visual Basic distributed by Microsoft:

➤ **Learning Edition**   Contains the basic features necessary to learn how to use Visual Basic. It contains templates, a limited set of ActiveX controls, Application and Setup Wizards, and the MSDN Library.

➤ **Professional Edition**   Contains a native code compiler, integrated database tools, and additional ActiveX controls. It also includes the Data Environment Designer and many other tools.

➤ **Enterprise Edition**   Primarily designed for program development carried out by large programmer teams. Its features include Visual SourceSafe, Visual Modeler, SQL Server, Microsoft Transaction Server, and Internet Information Server.

You can complete most of the Hands-On Projects shown in this book by using the Professional Edition of Visual Basic. A few topics, however, require use of the Enterprise Edition. For example, the last section of this chapter discusses Visual SourceSafe, which is not included with the Professional Edition of Visual Basic. In situations where the Enterprise Edition is required to complete a section, it will be clearly identified that the Enterprise Edition is necessary. If you do not have the Enterprise Edition, you will not be able to complete hands-on steps discussed in the section.

The Visual Basic software package contains four CD-ROMs. Two of the CDs contain the Visual Basic program itself. The other two CDs hold the Microsoft Developer Network (MSDN) Library, which contains the Help system and associated files accompanying Visual Basic.

In this section, you will learn about the various components that constitute the Visual Basic development environment. You will also install those components on your computer in preparation for developing applications. To complete the steps in this section, you must have all access to four Visual Basic CD-ROMs shipped with either the Professional Edition of Visual Basic 6.0 or the Enterprise Edition of Visual Basic 6.0. Although the steps and figures in this chapter assume the use of the Enterprise Edition of Visual Basic, most of the differences you will encounter if you are installing the Professional Edition will be identified.

As you install Visual Basic, you can decide whether to install particular components of the Visual Basic system depending on your own needs. A thorough discussion of each Visual Basic component lies beyond the scope of this chapter, however. As you use the various components throughout the course of this book, each will be described in more detail. This chapter presents only a brief overview of a component's purpose.

Note that depending on the existing software installed on your computer, and whether Visual Basic 5.0 was previously installed, the dialog boxes that appear in the steps may vary slightly.

To begin the installation process, insert the first Microsoft Visual Basic 6.0 CD-ROM into your computer. Depending on the configuration of your computer, it may recognize the insertion of the CD-ROM into the drive and start the Installation Wizard automatically. Figure 1.1 shows the first dialog box pertaining to the Installation Wizard.

 If your system does not start the Installation Wizard automatically, click on Start on the Windows taskbar, then click on Run. When the Run dialog box appears, enter "D:\Setup". Replace the drive designator with the drive designator assigned to the CD-ROM on your computer.

The Installation Wizard guides you through the Visual Basic installation process by having you complete a series of dialog boxes. To move forward to the next dialog box, click on the Next button. To move backward to the previous dialog

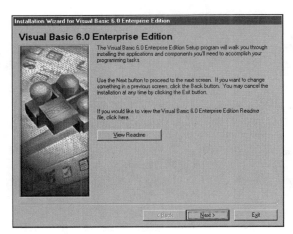

Figure 1.1   Visual Basic 6.0 Installation Wizard dialog box.

box, click on the Back button. You can move backward and forward through the various dialog boxes until you are satisfied that all installation options are specified correctly. The dialog box following the introductory dialog box is the End User License Agreement.

To accept the End User License Agreement:

1. Click on Next to view the End User License Agreement dialog box, as shown in Figure 1.2.

2. Read the End User License Agreement displayed in the text box. Use the scroll bars to read any text that does not initially appear in the window.

3. To accept the terms and conditions of the End User License Agreement, click on the option button having the caption I Accept The Agreement. You must click on this option button to proceed with the installation.

4. Click on Next to activate the Product Number and User ID dialog box, as shown in Figure 1.3.

The Product Number and User ID dialog box contains three items of information:

➤ **ID Number** You must enter the product's ID number. This number appears on the back of the Visual Basic 6.0 CD-ROM case. Do not lose this number, as you must enter it every time you install Visual Basic.

➤ **Your Name** In the Your Name field, you should enter the name of the software owner.

➤ **Your Company** In the Your Company's Name field, you should enter the name of the company, if applicable, that purchased the software.

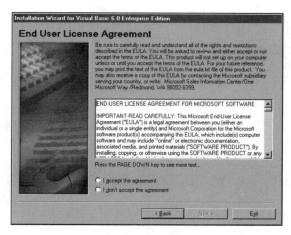

Figure 1.2   End User License Agreement dialog box.

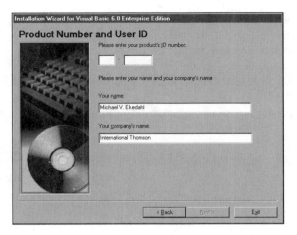

Figure 1.3   Product Number and User ID dialog box.

Note that default values may be supplied for the Your Name and Your Company's Name fields. The system retrieves this information from existing configuration files. You can change these values if desired.

To complete the Product Number And User ID dialog box:

1. Enter the product number, which is found on the back of the Visual Basic CD-ROM.

2. Enter your name and, if applicable, a company name.

3. Note that the Next button remains disabled until you enter the product number.

4. Click on the Next button to activate the Visual Basic 6.0 Enterprise Edition dialog box, as shown in Figure 1.4.

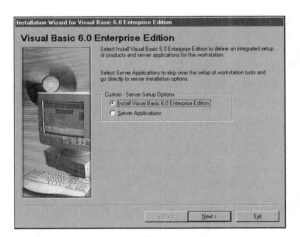

Figure 1.4   Custom-Server Setup Options dialog box.

If you enter the product ID number incorrectly, a dialog box will appear, indicating that the ID number is incorrect. Click on OK to close the dialog box, and then reenter the correct number. Depending on the existing software installed on your computer, the Installation Wizard may require DCOM 98 to be installed and the computer to be restarted. In such a case, install DCOM 98. After restarting the computer, the dialog box shown in Figure 1.4 will reappear. DCOM, or Distributed COM, allows objects to communicate over a network.

The dialog box shown in Figure 1.4 contains two options. The first installs the Enterprise Edition of Visual Basic 6.0. The second installs the following server applications:

➤ The NT Option Pack (for Windows 95 and Windows 98)

➤ Microsoft FrontPage 98 Server Extensions

➤ Data Access Components 2.0

➤ Application Performance Explorer

➤ Visual SourceSafe Server

The last two items are available only with the Enterprise Edition of Visual Basic. The first three options are supplied with both the Professional and Enterprise Editions.

To install the Visual Basic 6.0 Enterprise Edition:

1. Click on Install Visual Basic 6.0 Enterprise Edition.

2. Click on Next to activate the Setup program. A dialog box will appear, indicating that the Setup program is loading. Once loaded, the Visual Basic 6.0 Enterprise Setup dialog box will appear, as shown in Figure 1.5.

 Depending on the configuration of your computer, a dialog box may appear requesting that you choose a common folder. If this dialog box appears, accept the default option, and then click on Next to continue.

3. Click on Continue to activate the Product ID dialog box, as shown in Figure 1.6.

 Write down the product ID number. You will need this number if you ever need to contact Microsoft to obtain technical support. In Figure 1.6, the product ID has been blanked out to prevent unauthorized software duplication.

4. Click on OK to activate the next dialog box. When you click on this button, the Installation Wizard will display a dialog box with the message

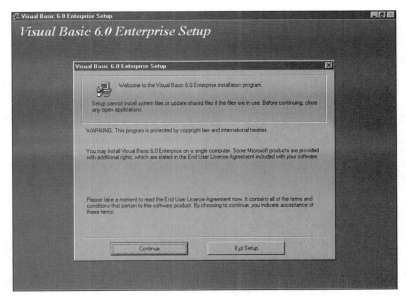

Figure 1.5   Visual Basic 6.0 Enterprise Setup dialog box.

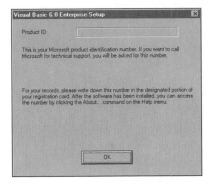

Figure 1.6   Product ID dialog box.

Setup Is Searching For Installed Components. If you have previously installed Visual Basic 6.0 on your computer and are now adding or removing options, the Installation Wizard will detect the software currently installed on your computer. After searching for installed components, the Installation Wizard displays the dialog box shown in Figure 1.7.

The dialog box shown in Figure 1.7 contains four buttons:

➤ **Typical** Installs Visual Basic with the most commonly used components.

➤ **Custom** Allows you to explicitly select which components to install. In this chapter, you will select this option to learn about the different components that make up the Visual Basic system.

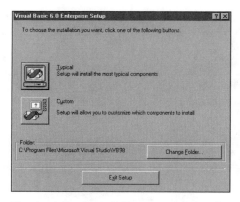

Figure 1.7 Installation type dialog box.

➤ **Change Folder** Allows you to change the drive and folder where Visual Basic is installed. By default, Visual Basic is placed in the folder named C:\Program Files\Microsoft Visual Studio\VB98, but you can change this folder if desired. You may want to change the drive if you have insufficient disk space on the default disk drive.

➤ **Exit Setup** Allows you to cancel the Visual Basic installation.

To examine the components that constitute the Visual Basic system, you will perform a custom installation. To begin a custom installation, click on Custom to activate the Custom dialog box, as shown in Figure 1.8.

The Custom dialog box contains several vital pieces of information related to the Visual Basic components to be installed:

➤ **Options list** Contains checkboxes allowing you to select or deselect a particular component. Some components have subcomponents. The Data

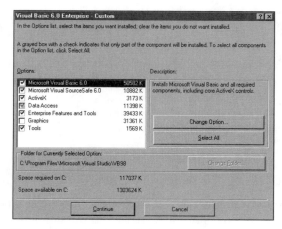

Figure 1.8 Custom dialog box.

Access component shown in Figure 1.8 is shaded, indicating that only certain subcomponents are selected.

➤ **Change Option button** Becomes enabled only when a component has subcomponents. Clicking the Change Option button will display a dialog box in which you can select or deselect subcomponents for the component currently selected in the Options list.

➤ **Select All button** Selects all subcomponents pertaining to the selected component.

In addition to these buttons, the dialog box indicates the disk space required by the selected component as well as the disk space currently available on the selected drive.

Some components must be installed if other components are to work properly. If you attempt to deselect a component that is an integral part of the Visual Basic environment, a warning dialog box will appear, indicating that Visual Basic may not run properly without that particular component.

The Options list shown in Figure 1.8 lists seven components:

➤ **Microsoft Visual Basic 6.0** This option contains the core part of the Visual Basic system.

➤ **Microsoft Visual SourceSafe 6.0 (VSS)** This option installs the source code control system that is used in conjunction with Visual Basic and other languages.

➤ **ActiveX** This option installs additional ActiveX controls.

➤ **Data Access** This option installs various database drivers and providers, including ActiveX Data Objects (ADO), Remote Data Service (RDS), and OLE DB. It is also used to install Remote Data Objects (RDO) and the Data Environment designer.

➤ **Enterprise Features and Tools** This option installs the Visual Component Manager and Repository.

➤ **Graphics** This option installs the various Windows metafiles, bitmaps, cursors, icons, and limited video clips.

➤ **Tools** This option installs MS Info, which is a tool used to gather system configuration information, and the API Text Viewer. The API Text Viewer tool allows you to obtain function prototypes for most Windows application program interface (API) functions.

If you are installing the Professional Edition of Visual Basic, the Microsoft Visual SourceSafe option will not be available. Also, the Enterprise Features and Tools item will be replaced by the Professional Features and Tools option.

To begin selecting the installation components:

1. In the options list, click on the line containing the Data Access checkbox. The line will appear highlighted.

2. Click on the Change Option command button to activate the Data Access dialog box, as shown in Figure 1.9.

Visual Basic 6.0 supports many ways to access different types of data. Many of these options are new to this version of Visual Basic. In the Data Access dialog box, you can configure the options to access different types of data, as described in the following list:

➤ **Universal Data Access**   Allows applications to access data wherever the data resides (as part of Microsoft's strategy to improve the flexibility of programs that access data). Data may reside on a local computer, network computer, or the Internet. Furthermore, Universal Data Access allows access to data without conversion. In Visual Basic, Universal Data Access is made a reality by ADO, RDS, and OLE DB.

➤ **Open Database Connectivity (ODBC)**   Represents an older way of accessing heterogeneous data formats. You can access SQL Server, Oracle, Access, Excel, FoxPro, dBase, and Paradox databases via ODBC drivers. ADO and OLE DB have superceded most of the functionality of ODBC.

➤ **Jet IISAM drivers**   Provide another way to access Excel, Exchange, Lotus 1-2-3, Paradox, and Xbase data.

➤ **RDO**   An object model used to access SQL Server, Oracle, and other databases. ADO has largely superceded its functionality.

➤ **Data Environment**   A development tool designed to assist you, the programmer, in developing applications that operate with a database.

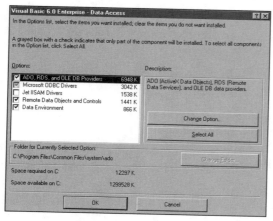

Figure 1.9   Data Access dialog box.

To select the Data Access options:

1. Make sure that the ADO, RDS, and OLE DB Providers checkbox is checked and not dimmed. Make sure that the Data Environment checkbox is checked as well.

   You will not use the other options in this book. If you intend to use Oracle or another database via ODBC, however, you should add the necessary ODBC driver.

2. Click on OK to return to the Custom dialog box.

3. Click on the Enterprise Features and Tools list item, and then click on Change Option to view the Enterprise Features And Tools dialog box, as shown in Figure 1.10.

The Enterprise Features And Tools dialog box lists five tools:

➤ **Application Performance Explorer** Helps you analyze your programs so you can obtain peak performance from them.

➤ **Visual Basic Enterprise Components option** Installs the Connection Designer and RemAuto Connection manager. These tools help you to establish database connections with ADO.

➤ **Visual Component Manager tool** Enables you to share and reuse your own software components. As you develop ever more programs, you will likely create utilities that will prove beneficial to many programs and potentially many other programmers. The Visual Component Manager helps you organize and make these components available to other programmers.

➤ **Repository** Stores and maintains the structure of Visual Basic projects.

➤ **Microsoft Visual Modeler** Helps you to analyze the structure of applications.

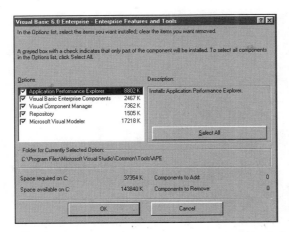

Figure 1.10   Enterprise Features and Tools dialog box.

If you are installing the Professional Edition of Visual Basic, only the Visual Component Manager and Repository options will be available.

To select the Enterprise Features And Tools options:

1. Make sure that all the options are selected.

2. Click on OK to return to the Custom dialog box.

3. Click on the Graphics list item, and then click on Change Option to view the Graphics dialog box, as shown in Figure 1.11.

Visual Basic supplies myriad graphic files that you can use in your applications. These graphic files are organized by type as follows:

➤ **Metafiles** Visual Basic supplies approximately 80 metafiles. Metafiles have the file suffix of ".wmf".

➤ **Bitmaps** Approximately 250 bitmaps having the extension of ".bmp" can be used with forms, toolbars, and with other controls.

➤ **Cursors** Approximately 100 cursors are available with which to change the mouse pointer as necessary in your applications.

➤ **Icons** The icon library contains more than 450 icons that you can use on forms, toolbars, and other controls.

➤ **Video** The Video option provides AVI files with which you can add animation to your applications.

When developing production-quality applications, you will commonly use the graphic files discussed in the previous list. These graphic files consume about 31 megabytes of disk space. Thus, if your computer has only limited disk space, you may want to omit these files from your installation. Note that the graphic files required to complete the exercises in this book appear on the CD-ROM

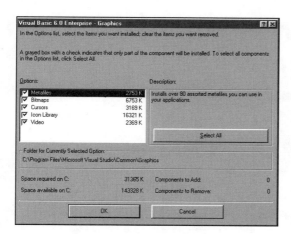

Figure 1.11   Graphics dialog box.

accompanying this book. Thus you can complete the chapter exercises without installing the Visual Basic graphic files.

To select the graphic files:

1. Click on Select All to select all of the graphic files. If the disk space on your computer is limited, do not select the graphic files.

2. Click on OK to return to the Custom dialog box.

3. Click on the Tools list item, if necessary, and then click on Change Option to activate the Tools dialog box, as shown in Figure 1.12.

   The Tools dialog box contains two options: Ms Info and API Text Viewer. You will use both tools in the exercises in this book, so both must be installed. The Ms Info application gathers information about your system. The API Text Viewer utility helps you declare function prototypes so as to call functions contained by the Windows API.

4. Be sure that both options are selected, and then click on OK to return to the Custom dialog box.

   You have now finished specifying the software to install. At this point, you can install the software to your hard disk by clicking the Continue button.

5. Click on Continue to begin installing Visual Basic 6.0. As Visual Basic and the corresponding components are placed on your hard disk, a progress bar appears indicating the relative status of the installation. When the process is complete, the dialog box shown in Figure 1.13 will appear, requesting that you restart Windows before continuing.

6. Click on Restart Windows to update your system configuration and restart Windows.

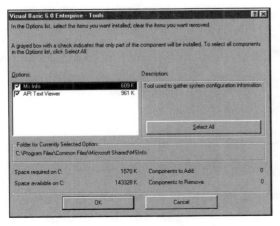

Figure 1.12 Tools dialog box.

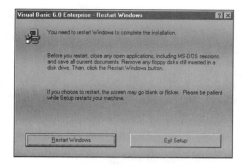

Figure 1.13 Restart Windows dialog box.

 If Visual Basic 5.0 or another OLE tool was previously installed on your computer, a dialog box will appear. Respond as necessary to install OLE for Visual Basic 6.0. Because you chose to install VSS, a dialog box will appear asking if you want to upgrade VSS clients. Click on Yes.

After Windows restarts, the Installation Wizard will reactivate, allowing you to install the MSDN Library. This library contains all the Visual Basic reference documentation. The MSDN Library consumes more than 800 megabytes of disk space.

To install the MSDN Library:

1. When Windows restarts, the Installation Wizard will display the Install MSDN dialog box, as shown in Figure 1.14.

 If you are working in a networked environment, you may be requested to enter a network login and password. If the dialog box shown in Figure 1.14 does not appear, run the Setup program again.

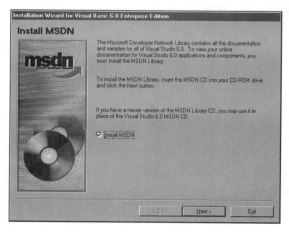

Figure 1.14 Install MSDN dialog box.

2. Click on Next to display the Visual Studio 6.0 Setup dialog box.

3. Insert the Microsoft Developer Network Disk 1 into the CD-ROM drive, and then click on OK when prompted to do so.

4. The Setup dialog box will appear. Click on Continue.

5. The dialog box listing the Product ID will appear. Write down the product ID number, and then click on OK to display the License Agreement dialog box.

6. If you agree to the license agreement, click on I Agree. The Setup dialog box appears, as shown in Figure 1.15.

The Setup dialog box provides three installation options:

➤ **Typical** Installs the core components and leaves the actual documentation on the CD-ROM so as to minimize disk space usage. If you select this option, you must insert the MSDN Library CD-ROM(s) in the drive whenever you want to view the Help files.

➤ **Custom Installation** Allows you to select which MSDN Library components to install. This process is identical to the process for selecting the Visual Basic components. The MSDN Library contains the documentation not only for Visual Basic, but also for other Visual Studio products.

➤ **Full** Copies all library documentation to the hard disk to improve performance. This option requires that you have at least 800 megabytes of disk space available on your computer.

If you have used previous versions of Visual Basic, you will notice a significant difference between the MSDN Library and the previous

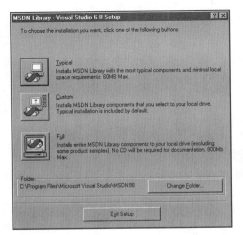

Figure 1.15 MSDN Library Setup dialog box.

versions of Help. First, the MSDN Library is much more complete than the Help system provided with previous versions of Visual Basic. Furthermore, the MSDN Library is based on HTML rather than Win32 Help. When developing complex applications, you will find this vast library of technical information to be a valuable resource.

The MSDN Library contains much more than simple Visual Basic documentation. The following list summarizes some of the topics found in this library:

➤ **MSDN, Books and Periodicals**   Contains selected Microsoft books and published technical articles.

➤ **MSDN, Knowledge Base**   Contains more than 40,000 technical articles and sample programs created and maintained by Microsoft Technical Support.

➤ **Software development kits (SDK)**   Contain a vast array of technical papers.

➤ **MSDN Library**   Provides documentation for other Visual Studio components.

To install the MSDN Library:

1. If your computer has limited disk space, click on the Typical button. If you have 800 or more megabytes of available disk space, click on the Full option. If you click on Full, you will not need the MSDN CD-ROMs to view the Help files. Note that, depending on the speed of your CD-ROM and computer, installing the Help files may take between 5 minutes and 1 hour.

2. Change the CD when requested, if necessary.

3. Complete the remaining dialog boxes to finish the installation.

4. Restart the computer if requested to do so. Depending on your system configuration, the Server Setups dialog box may automatically appear.

At this point, you have installed the client components required to run Visual Basic on your computer. You can now proceed to install the server components that will be used in the later chapters of this book.

Installing Server Components

After installing the Visual Basic software, you can install the server components. These components are used to implement a Personal Web Server (PWS) and FrontPage 98 Server extensions, as well as to add Data Access Components that provide access via OLE DB and ODBC to Oracle and other databases. In this book, you will develop intranet applications, so you must install the Personal Web Server.

To install the Personal Web Server:

1. Reinsert the first Visual Basic CD-ROM. Again, your computer may recognize the insertion of the CD-ROM. If it does not, click on Start on the taskbar, click on Run, then enter "D:\Setup". Replace the drive designator as necessary.

2. Depending on the state of your system, the initial installation dialog box may appear. If it does, click on Server Applications And Tools, and then click on Next to activate the Server Setups dialog box, as shown in Figure 1.16.

3. Click on NT Option Pack (For Windows 9x), and then click on Install. Insert the appropriate CD-ROM, if requested, to activate the dialog box shown in Figure 1.17.

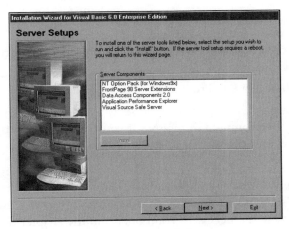

Figure 1.16   Server Setups dialog box.

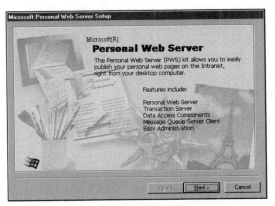

Figure 1.17   Microsoft Personal Web Server Setup dialog box.

4. Click on Next to begin the installation.

5. Read and accept the license agreement.

 Depending on the software currently installed on your computer, you may be prompted to update MS Web Server to a newer version.

6. Click on the Typical button to install the default software and activate the Setup dialog box.

   By default, server extensions for Microsoft FrontPage 98 and data access components are installed. These components allow you to author and administer Web sites with Microsoft FrontPage 98 and Visual InterDev. Microsoft Data Access Components are also installed. In addition, the Personal Web Server and Transaction Server are installed.

7. Accept the default options shown in the dialog box, and then click on Next to complete the installation. As the installation progresses, a progress bar indicates the overall progress of the installation.

8. Click on Finish when requested to complete the installation.

9. Restart the computer when requested to do so. After restarting the computer, you may be prompted to register. If you are connected to the Internet, you can register the software now.

In addition to the software installed using the Installation Wizard, the Visual Basic CD-ROM contains software components that are not installed automatically. Some of these components are needed to complete the exercises in this book. You will install the necessary components in the chapter that uses the needed component. The following list identifies these components, their location on the Visual Basic CD-ROM, and their purpose:

➤ **SQDB_SS folder** Contains the SQL Server Debugging program. This program requires Windows NT.

➤ **HTMLHelp folder** Contains the HTML Help Workshop software. This program is used to create Help files for use with Visual Basic and other applications.

This book does not use the many other tools supplied with Visual Basic. At this point, the Visual Basic installation is complete. You have installed all of the components required to complete the exercises in this book. Visual Basic and the MSDN Library options should now appear on the Start menu.

THE BASICS OF VISUAL BASIC

A Review Of Visual Basic

This book discusses the advanced Visual Basic programming topics that you must know to successfully complete Microsoft certification exam number 70-176. It assumes that you are familiar with Visual Basic essentials. The following list summarizes the topics reviewed in this section:

➤ Creating instances of the intrinsic controls from the toolbox

➤ Essential properties, events, and methods supported by those intrinsic controls

➤ Using the Code window to create event procedures for intrinsic controls

➤ Understanding the concepts of variables, procedures, and scope

A Visual Basic program consists of instructions called *statements*. Statements are grouped together into procedures, which perform well-defined tasks. This book refers to a group of statements as code. Visual Basic is an event driven programming language—that is, the statements in a program execute in response to a user action, such as a mouse click. This user action produces an event. The code you write executes in response to specific events. An event-driven program cannot predict which procedure will execute next, because it cannot predict the user's next action.

The programmer uses a visual designer to create the visual part of a program, which consists of a series of forms. A form is a window having a rectangular area, an optional title bar, and a border. It can be resized, maximized, minimized, and closed.

The user interacts with a form by using visible objects created on the form. The programmer creates these objects from controls, and each different type of control performs a specific type of task, as described here:

➤ **CheckBox** Works like an on/off switch. The box can be either checked or not checked.

➤ **ComboBox** and **ListBox** Allow the user to select an item from a list.

➤ **CommandButton** Performs an action when the user clicks it.

➤ **Frame** Acts as a container for other objects, typically option buttons.

➤ **Label** Displays textual information.

➤ **OptionButton** Indicates that an item is selected from among a group of items.

➤ **ScrollBar** Stores an Integer value that lies within a specified range.

➤ **TextBox** Is used for input and output of textual information.

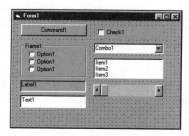

Figure 1.18   Intrinsic control instances.

Figure 1.18 shows a form that includes nine types of intrinsic control instances.

Visual Basic supports most of the characteristics of an object-oriented programming language. An object can be envisioned as a representation of an everyday tool. For example, some objects work like on/off switches. When the user clicks the object, the switch is turned on. When the user clicks it again, the switch is turned off. An object integrates data with the procedures that act on the data. This coupling of data and procedures is called *encapsulation*.

In Visual Basic, an object's data are represented as properties. An object's properties define its behavior and appearance. The procedures that act on the data are implemented using methods. The methods pertaining to an object define the tasks and actions that the object can perform. Functionally, methods resemble procedures in that they execute code to perform a task.

Some objects can respond to events. The concept of an event extends far beyond Visual Basic. As you know, Windows can run several programs simultaneously. Each Windows program includes buttons and other objects, and the user interacts with a program by clicking buttons, selecting items from lists, and so on. The operating system views every button, every list box, and any visible object on the screen—no matter to which program it belongs—as a window. When the user clicks a button (window), Windows recognizes that the button was clicked and sends a message to your program; code then executes. This process is known as an event.

Events can occur as the result of a user action, such as typing a key on the keyboard or clicking the mouse button. Different objects respond to different events, and most objects respond to several events. For example, a button generates a **Click** event when the user clicks it. Additional events occur when the mouse passes over the button or the user presses down or releases a mouse button. The **MouseMove** event occurs as the mouse passes over a control instance. The **MouseDown** event occurs when the user presses the mouse button, and the **MouseUp** event occurs when the user releases the mouse button. The properties, methods, and events pertaining to an object make up its interface. Note that the term *interface* has a different meaning here than when used as part of the concept of a user interface.

The user interface pertains to how the user interacts with a program. An object's interface relates to how the programmer interacts with an object.

A program can interact with an object only through its interface—that is, by setting properties, calling methods, and responding to events. Some objects, such as buttons and boxes, are visible to the user; others, such as timers, remain hidden. Using object-oriented terminology, every object is created from a class, which serves as a blueprint or template for an object. When an object is created from its class, an instance of the class is created. *Class instances* are objects that are identical copies of their class. Once an instance has been created from its underlying class, it is possible to set the object's properties and call its methods. Visual Basic supports several types of classes:

➤ A form is a class. One or many instances of the same form can be created from a form's class.

➤ A control is a type of class. Each different control performs a well-defined task. Drawing a control instance on a form causes an object to be created. Most control instances are visible on the form when the program runs, but some are not. For example, the Label and TextBox controls are visible when the program runs, while the Timer control remains hidden from the user at run time.

➤ Some classes and objects can be accessed only programmatically. For example, the Printer object sends data to the printer by executing code, but the Printer object has no visible component.

➤ ActiveX controls are created from the **UserControl** class.

The preceding list defines but a few of the classes accessible to a Visual Basic program. You will use many other classes throughout the course of this book.

Having defined the general characteristics of Visual Basic, and recognizing how it differs from procedural languages, you are ready to see how Visual Basic stores the files that make up a program and to review the structure of those files.

The Structure Of A Visual Basic Program

Every Visual Basic program has a common structure:

➤ **Module files** A program contains one or more module files. A module file stores a particular type of program element. Unique module types exist to store the visual forms seen by the user and ActiveX controls. Other module types allow you, the programmer, to create your own objects. Each type of module has a suffix to denote its type.

➤ **Project files** The project file defines the general characteristics of a program and identifies the name of the program, its title, and its compilation method. The project file also contains a reference to the different modules that make up the project. Visual Basic supports several types of projects. For example, stand-alone executable files and ActiveX controls are each created using a different project type as defined in the project file.

➤ **Project groups** For debugging purposes, you can execute projects by using a project group. Rather than operating in a stand-alone mode, some Visual Basic programs are designed to operate with other Visual Basic programs. For example, you can create controls from Visual Basic using the ActiveX control project type. As you develop the ActiveX control, you can use another project to debug it.

Every module file is of a distinct type. Each module type serves a particular purpose. In this book, the terms *module file* and *module* are used synonymously. Each module is stored as a separate file on the disk. Some of the module types supported by Visual Basic are as follows:

➤ **Form** Consists of two parts. The first part contains the information related to the visible objects (control instances) drawn on the form and the form itself. The second part contains variable declarations and procedures. Each form module represents a unique class. When a program is run, Visual Basic creates one or more instances of the form class. Each instance of the form's class corresponds to a visible copy of the form on the screen. Form modules have a file extension of ".frm".

➤ **Standard** Contains variable declarations and procedures. Standard modules (also known as bas modules) commonly contain procedures that must be shared between modules. That is, the procedures and variables declared in a standard module can be exposed to other modules or invisible to other modules. Standard modules have the extension of ".bas".

➤ **Class** Contains user-defined classes. In addition to creating objects from existing classes, you may also create your own classes and objects from those classes. Class modules carry a file extension of ".cls".

➤ **User control**, **user document**, and **property page** You use these modules to create your own controls. The suffixes for these modules are ".ctl", ".dob", and ".pag", respectively.

➤ **Data environment designer** An interactive visual interface that allows you, the programmer, to simplify the process of writing programs to perform database operations. Its file extension is ".Dsr".

➤ **Data report designer** Enables you to build reports. It also carries the ".Dsr" file extension.

The preceding list presents just a few of many Visual Basic module types. All module files are stored as text files. Thus you could edit a module file using any word-processing program, such as Notepad or WordPad. Visual Basic allows you to add and remove individual modules in a project as necessary. Listing 1.1 illustrates the anatomy of a form file.

Listing 1.1   Anatomy of a module file.

```
VERSION 6.00
Begin VB.Form Form1
    Caption        =   "Form1"
    ClientHeight   =   3195
    ClientLeft     =   60
    ClientTop      =   345
    ClientWidth    =   4680
    LinkTopic      =   "Form1"
    ScaleHeight    =   3195
    ScaleWidth     =   4680
    StartUpPosition =  3  'Windows Default
End
Attribute VB_Name = "Form1"
Attribute VB_GlobalNameSpace = False
Attribute VB_Creatable = False
Attribute VB_PredeclaredId = True
Attribute VB_Exposed = False
```

The first line of Listing 1.1 identifies the version of the module. Note that this version may differ from your computer's version of Visual Basic.

Consider carefully the second line in the form file:

```
Begin Vb.Form Form1
```

This line identifies the class name of the module (**Vb.Form**), followed by the name of the module as it is known to your program (**Form1**). The statements to define the properties of the form appear between the Begin and End lines. For example, the caption that appears in the form's title bar is "Form1."

Different types of modules support different types of attributes. For example, standard modules support the one attribute (**VB_Name**), while a form module supports five attributes.

```
Attribute VB_Creatable = False
Attribute VB_Exposed = False
```

These attributes define whether other programs can create an instance of the module. Visual Basic creates and defines the attributes automatically, based upon the type of module and the module-related properties that you set.

The project file groups all general program information. It contains a reference to each module file that is part of the project. In addition, it stores references to ActiveX controls. ActiveX controls can be included in a project in addition to intrinsic controls. Visual Basic supports several types of projects, a sample of which is described in the following list:

➤ **Standard EXE** Used to build a stand–alone executable program. This type of executable program can be run directly by the user.

➤ **ActiveX DLL** Creates an executable file that is called by another program.

➤ **ActiveX Control** Used to create controls from Visual Basic. These controls are then referenced from another project, typically a standard EXE project.

In addition to these project types, other project types include Internet Information Servers and dynamic HTML projects. No matter the type of project, each has the same general structure.

Listing 1.2 shows a segment of a project file.

Listing 1.2   Project file segment.

```
Type=Exe
Reference=*\G{00020430-0000-0000-C000-
000000000046}#2.0#0#..\WINDOWS\SYSTEM\STDOLE2.TLB#OLE Automation
Form=Form1.frm
Form=Form2.frm
Class=Class1; Class1.cls
Module=Module1; Module1.bas
Startup="Form1"
Command32=""
Name="Project1"
HelpContextID="0"
CompatibleMode="0"
MajorVer=1
MinorVer=0
RevisionVer=0
```

A project file consists of lines containing a key followed by a value. The key and value are separated by an equals sign. The following line—the first line of the project file—denotes the project's type:

```
Type=Exe
```

The following lines define the modules that make up the project:

```
Form=Form1.frm
Form=Form2.frm
Class=Class1; Class1.cls
Module=Module1; Module1.bas
```

This code segment lists two form module files (**Form1.frm** and **Form2.frm**), one class module (**Class1.cls**), and one standard module (**Module1.bas**).

In addition to containing a reference to the project's modules, the project file stores general program information, like that shown in the following:

```
MajorVer=1
MinorVer=0
RevisionVer=0
```

These lines define the version information pertaining to the project.

Visual Basic manages the information in the project file. As a result, the programmer does not usually need to edit this file directly.

You create all project files and modules using the Visual Basic integrated development environment.

The Visual Basic Integrated Development Environment

Visual Basic programs are created using an integrated development environment (IDE). That is, you add new and existing form modules and create control instances on a form to build the user interface. Standard and class modules can be added and removed from a project as needed. You can create and edit all of the code pertaining to the different modules using the IDE. In addition, programs can be debugged, tested, and compiled into executable (.exe) files from this environment. The Visual Basic IDE consists of several windows in which you can perform these tasks, as shown in Figure 1.19.

Figure 1.19 shows the Visual Basic IDE with the most common windows open. The windows that open initially, as well as their position and size, will vary based on

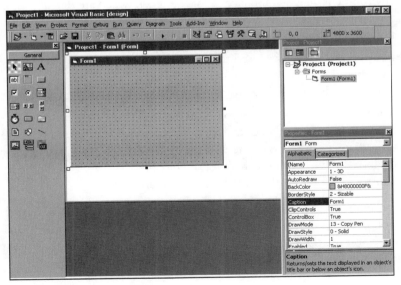

Figure 1.19   Visual Basic windows.

the configuration of Visual Basic when it was last used. If more than one person uses Visual Basic on your computer, you may need to open, close, and position windows each time you start Visual Basic. These windows have the following purpose:

➤ **Menu bar**   Contains the commands used to design, test, and compile Visual Basic programs.

➤ **Toolbar**   Contains buttons to provide quick access to menu commands. Visual Basic can display several standard toolbars, and you can create custom toolbars as well. To change the toolbars that appear on the Visual Basic menu bar, click on Toolbars on the View menu, then select the toolbars you want to appear.

➤ **Form window**   Shows a form and the control instances created on that form as the user will see them. One instance of the Form window can be open for each form module in the project.

➤ **Code window**   Used to declare variables and create procedures for a module. One instance of the Code window can be open for each module in a project. Note that the Code window is not shown in Figure 1.19.

➤ **Project Explorer**   Displays a hierarchical list of all modules in a project. Modules can be organized into folders, which can then be expanded and collapsed. The Project Explorer contains three buttons. The View Code button opens the Code window for the selected module. The View Object button opens the Form window. This button is not applicable to class modules or standard modules. Clicking the Toggle Folders button will display the modules in folders organized according to the module category. Note that Visual Basic groups some module types into a single category. For example, the data environment designer and data report designer, which are different module types, both appear in the Designers category. When the Toggle Folders button is not clicked, all modules appear as a flat alphabetical list.

➤ **Properties window**   Used to assign and display values to the properties of a form and the control instances created on a form. Unlike with the Code window, only one instance of the Properties window can be open at a time.

➤ **Toolbox**   Contains all controls available to the currently loaded project. To create an instance of a control, you click on the control on the toolbox and then draw an instance of the control on a form. The intrinsic controls in the toolbox shown in Figure 1.19 represent only a small subset of the many controls available to the Visual Basic programmer.

The programmer can customize the configuration of the Visual Basic user interface. The following list describes some of the settings that define the behavior of this interface. You use the Tools | Options menu selection to define these configuration settings.

➤ **Editor tab** Primarily designed to control the behavior of the Code window. The Code Settings frame enables or disables options pertaining to automatic syntax checking and the automatic displaying of tips.

➤ **Editor Format tab** Defines the colors for text in the Code window and the font of the text in the Code window.

➤ **General tab** Used to specify whether a rectangular grid appears in the Form window at design time, how errors are handled, and how the project runs while executing inside the IDE.

➤ **Docking tab** Enables or disables docking for specific IDE windows. Docking allows you to attach, or dock, the border of a window to the borders of other windows. This feature can also be enabled or disabled for specific windows by right-clicking the mouse button in a window and checking or unchecking the docking option.

➤ **Environment tab** Controls what happens when Visual Basic first starts, as well as what happens when you add modules to a project. When Visual Basic starts, you can cause it to create a new default project or to prompt you to specify a project type. When switching from design mode to run mode, you can configure Visual Basic to automatically save all files in the project. Visual Basic also supports templates for various types of modules. Templates contain prewritten, commonly used modules. For example, Visual Basic provides predefined templates for startup screens and login dialog boxes.

➤ **Advanced tab** Controls how the windows in the IDE appear to you, when you act as the programmer. The IDE can operate as a multiple document interface (MDI) program or as a single document interface (SDI) program. MDI programs, like Microsoft Word and Excel, display windows inside a parent or container window. In contrast, the windows in an SDI program can appear anywhere on the screen. The change will take effect the next time Visual Basic starts. The choice of whether to use Visual Basic in SDI or MDI mode is a matter of personal preference. If you have worked with older versions of Visual Basic, such as version 3.0 or 4.0, the SDI interface may be more familiar to you.

You can also customize the Visual Basic toolbars. Depending on whether you are debugging a program or creating a form, you can display or hide toolbars by clicking Toolbars on the View menu. A feature new to Visual Basic 6.0 allows the programmer to align multiple control instances drawn on a form. To align multiple control instances, select the control instances to be aligned, and then select the desired option from the Format menu.

Opening And Saving Projects

Visual Basic does not automatically save the modules in a project, and the project file itself, to disk. Rather, you must explicitly save these files using the

File menu or the corresponding toolbar buttons. Six commands on the File menu enable you to open and save project and module files:

➤ **New Project** and **Open Project**   Create a new project and open an existing project, respectively. The New Project command displays the New Project dialog box, in which you specify the type of project that should be created. The Open Project command displays a dialog box allowing you to navigate through different folders to locate an existing project file.

➤ **Save Project** and **Save Project As**   Used to save a project and its module files using the current file name or to assign a new file name, respectively. If any module files remain unsaved, the Save Module As dialog box will appear; you must assign a name to the unsaved module before saving it. (In this case, the word "Module" is replaced with the actual module name on the menu bar). If the project has never been saved, the Save Project As dialog box then appears, requesting that you specify a new file name for the project.

➤ **Save Module** and **Save Module As**   Used to save the active module. In these commands, the word *Module* is replaced with the actual module name, which will vary depending on which module is active. For example, when a form has not been saved, the commands will read Save Form1 and Save Form1 As, respectively; if the form's name is frmCh1, the commands will read Save frmCh1.frm and Save frmCh1.frm As, respectively. When you save a form or other module for the first time, the Save *Module* As dialog box appears, requesting that you specify a name for the module.

Once saved, a project and its module files can be opened by starting Visual Basic and clicking the Open Project command on the File menu. The Open Project dialog box allows you to select a folder and project file. Module files pertaining to the project file need not be opened one by one. Rather, they are loaded into the project because of the references in the project file.

To create a new project and save it:

1. Start Visual Basic. The New Project dialog box appears, as shown in Figure 1.20.

   Depending on your Visual Basic configuration, the New Project dialog box may not appear, and a new project will be created automatically. If this is the case, skip Step 2.

2. Make sure that the Standard EXE icon is selected, and then click on Open to create a new project. The new project is created with a single form module.

3. Use the View menu to open the Project Explorer, select the form, and then click on the View Object button to open the form, if necessary.

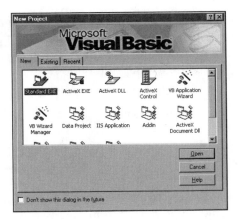

Figure 1.20   New Project dialog box.

4. Click on File, and then click on Save Form1 As. Save the form in the folder named Chapter.01\Startup using the name frmCh1.frm.

This book will specify relative path names when you load and save files. You may store projects and files on either the hard disk or the floppy disk. You should therefore set the drive designator appropriately depending where you have copied the files contained on the CD-ROM that accompanies this book. Most chapters in this book include a completed program and a startup program that you can complete by following the chapter's hands-on steps. The folder name for the completed program is Complete, and the program used with the hands-on steps appears in the Startup folder. This chapter lacks a completed program, so no Complete folder is provided for Chapter 1.

5. Click on File, and then click on Save Project As. Save the project in the folder named Chapter.01\Startup, using the project name Ch1.vbp.

6. If you installed the Enterprise Edition of Visual Basic, a dialog box appears, asking if you want to add this project to SourceSafe. If this dialog box appears, click on No. You will configure and use Visual SourceSafe later in this chapter.

The new file names appear in the Project Explorer. Note that if you saved the project without first saving the form, Visual Basic would have displayed the dialog boxes for you to save both the form and the project, because neither had ever been saved.

The Project menu enables you to add and remove modules and references to object libraries. When you add a module to a project, a dialog box appears through which you can create new modules and insert existing modules into the project.

The Add Form command on the Project menu is used to insert new empty forms, forms created from templates, and existing forms into the current project. Similarly, the Add Module command is used to insert a new or existing standard module into the current project. The other Add options on the Project menu pertain to modules discussed in subsequent chapters of this book.

Both the Add Form and Add Module commands cause Visual Basic to display a dialog box with two tabs. The New tab enables you to insert a new empty form or standard module. The Existing tab allows you to locate a form or standard module file and add it to the project. To remove a module from a project, you activate the module, then click on the Remove command on the Project menu. When you take a module out of a project, only the reference is deleted from the project file. That is, the module file is not deleted from the disk. As modules are added and removed, the content of the Project Explorer is updated accordingly. It is a good idea to save the project whenever you have added or removed a module.

Understanding Properties

Each object, including a form, supports a fixed set of properties. Each property, in turn, possesses a well-defined set of values. For example, the valid values for some properties are the Boolean values True and False. Other properties support a finite list of constant values. Still others can accept textual descriptions or numbers as values.

The properties can also be set to specific values. Every form supports properties that define the general characteristics of the form, including its position on the screen and the characteristics of its border and title bar. Likewise, every visible control instance created on a form supports several properties to define the position and appearance of that instance.

The following properties pertain to a form:

➤ **BorderStyle** Defines how the border appears around the form and whether the form can be resized. If set to 0 - None, no border is drawn around the form. If set to 1 - Fixed Single, the only way to resize the form is via the Maximize and Minimize buttons on the form's control box. If set to 2 - Sizable (the default), the user can also resize the form by dragging the mouse over the border. The setting 3 - Fixed Dialog box applies to dialog boxes; the window for dialog boxes can neither contain Maximize and Minimize buttons nor be resized. The settings 4 - Fixed ToolWindow and 5 - Sizable ToolWindow are used to create Tool windows. These windows do not appear on the taskbar when minimized, and the text on the title bar appears in a smaller font size.

➤ **Caption** Defines the text that appears on the title bar.

➤ **ControlBox** Can be either True or False. If set to True (the default), a control box appears on the upper-right corner of the title bar. If set to False, no control box appears. The control box always contains a Close button; if you set the options appropriately, it can also contain Maximize and Minimize buttons.

➤ **MaxButton** and **MinButton** Can be set to True or False to specify whether the Maximize and Minimize buttons, respectively, appear on the control box.

➤ **Enabled** Determines whether the user can interact with an object; it can be either True or False. When the **Enabled** property of a form or control instance is set to False, neither the form nor control instance will respond to events, respectively. If set to True (the default), the form or control instance can respond to events.

➤ **ShowInTaskbar** Can be either True or False. If set to True, the form will appear on the taskbar when minimized. If set to False, the form will not appear on the taskbar.

➤ **StartUpPosition** Can have one of three constant values, as shown in the Properties window. If set to 0 – Manual (the default), no initial position is specified. If set to 1 – CenterOwner, the form appears centered in the parent form. If set to 2 – CenterScreen, it is centered on the entire screen. If set to 3 – WindowsDefault, the form is positioned in the upper-left corner of the screen.

➤ **Top** and **Left** Define the position of a form's upper-left corner relative to the screen, or, in the case of a control instance, the instance's upper-left corner relative to the form.

➤ **Height** and **Width** Specify the size of the control instance or form.

➤ **ScaleMode** Defines the unit of measure applied to control instances. By default, the unit of measure is a twip, a screen-independent unit of measure. There are approximately 1440 twips per inch.

➤ **ScaleHeight** and **ScaleWidth** Enable you to create custom coordinates for an object.

➤ **Visible** Determines whether an object is visible on the screen. If set to True, the form or object on the form is visible. If set to False, the form or object remains hidden, and the user cannot interact with it. It is possible, however, to reference an invisible object with code.

The **Name** Property

Every form and control instance supports a **Name** property. Each time you add a form class to a project or create a control instance on a form, Visual

Basic assigns a unique name to the object. The default name for the first form created in a project is Form1. The default name for a control instance works the same way. For example, the first Label control instance created on a form has the name Label1, the second Label2, and so on.

An object's name is significant for two reasons. First, the name of a form and the control instances drawn on the form provide the means for Visual Basic and Windows to locate the code associated with a specific event pertaining to the control instance. Second, you use the name of an object to reference it with code.

Selecting appropriate names for the objects you create will greatly improve the readability of the resulting program. A common strategy for assigning names to objects is to use a three-character prefix that denotes the object's type, followed by a name that describes the object's purpose. When a name contains multiple words, capitalize the first letter of each word. Also, avoid obscure abbreviations. The standard prefix for a form is "frm".

The **Name** property of a form must satisfy several constraints:

➤ It must begin with a letter.

➤ It can consist of only letters, numbers, or the underscore character (_).

➤ It cannot contain punctuation or special characters such as the period (.) or dash (-).

➤ It must be 40 characters or less.

Table 1.1 lists the Visual Basic intrinsic controls and gives examples of valid object names.

Properties—Design Mode Vs. Run Mode

You have seen that an object supports properties, and that those properties can be set by the programmer. Whether Visual Basic is in design mode or run mode affects an object's properties as well. For example, certain properties can be changed both at run time and design time. The **Text** property pertaining to a text box, for instance, is read-write both at run time and design time. Certain other properties can be changed at design time, but not at run time. In other words, these properties are read-only at run time. For example, a form's **BorderStyle** property can be set at design time but is read-only at run time. Finally, other properties have meaning only at run time—that is, they cannot be set at design time. For example, most controls support the **hWnd** property, which contains a Long Integer number that the Windows operating system assigns to uniquely identify the window. As the programmer, you cannot change

Table 1.1   Object naming conventions.

Control	Prefix	Example
CheckBox	chk	chkPrint
ComboBox	cbo	cboSelectItem
CommandButton	cmd	cmdExit
Data	dat	datMainDatabase
DirListBox	dir	dirCurrent
DriveListBox	drv	drvCurrent
FileListBox	fil	filCurrent
Frame	fra	fraGroup
hScrollBar	hsb	hsbPosition
Image	img	imgStartup
Label	lbl	lblPrompt
Line	lin	linHorizontal
ListBox	lst	lstItems
OLE	ole	oleObject
OptionButton	opt	optSelect
PictureBox	pic	picStartup
Shape	shp	shpBox
TextBox	txt	txtFirstName
Timer	tmr	tmrSeconds
vScrollBar	vsb	vsbPosition

its value, and the value does not exist at design time. Other properties are entirely read-only. That is, they can never be set either at design time or at run time; they can be read only at run time. To set properties at design time, you use the Properties window.

Using The Properties Window

The Properties window works with an active module (form, standard, or class) at design time, but remains unavailable at run time. If no module is active, the Properties window remains blank. When used with a form module, the Properties window displays the currently selected object (form or control instance) in its title bar, as shown in Figure 1.21.

You can apply several techniques to select an object in the Properties window. For example, you can use the list arrow in the Object box to select the current object. The Object box contains the name of the control instance or form followed by the name of the class from which the instance was derived.

Figure 1.21   Properties window.

Alternatively, you can right-click on the mouse button on a form or control, and then click on Properties on the pop-up menu to activate the Properties window for a specific object. The Properties window contains two tabs:

➤ **Alphabetic**   Displays the properties for the selected object in alphabetical order.

➤ **Categorized**   Displays properties based on the property's purpose. The Categorized tab employs a drill-down interface very similar to the Windows Explorer program. At the top level, the property category can be expanded or collapsed to view the properties pertaining to the selected category.

The list section of the Properties window contains two columns. The first column—the Property column—identifies the name of the property. The second colum—the Value column—contains the current value of the property. To assign properties that support a fixed set of values, you click on the Properties button at the right side of the Value column and select a value from the drop-down list box. If the Properties button appears with three dots, clicking it will activate a dialog box in which you can set the property. The description pane appears at the bottom of the Properties window, giving a brief description of the selected property's purpose. Right-clicking the mouse button in the Properties window and deselecting the Description checkbox will hide the description pane and allow you to view more properties at one time in the Properties window.

Like many other programming environments, Visual Basic allows you to apply different techniques to accomplish the same task. For example, you may desire to display a form on the center of the screen when the program starts. You can either explicitly set both the **Top** and **Left** properties of a form or change the value of the form's **StartUpPosition** property. To change the size of a form, you may either drag the border of the form at design time or set the **Height** and **Width** properties in the Properties window. Which technique you use largely depends on your preferences as a programmer.

To set the form's design-time properties for your client, follow these steps. Your client in this chapter will be Diverse Products, a company that sells household products throughout the United States. The company will be using Visual Basic as its primary programming language for application development.

1. Activate the form named Form1 by clicking the form name in the Project Explorer, and then clicking the View Object button, if necessary. Note that both Form1 and frmCh1.frm appear in the Project Explorer. Form1 is the value of the form's Name property, and frmCh1.frm is the file name stored on the disk.

2. Activate the Properties window for the form by clicking the right mouse button while the cursor is positioned over the form, and then clicking Properties.

3. Set the **Name** property to **frmCh1**.

4. In the Properties window, locate the **StartUpPosition** property using the scroll bars. Set its value to 2 – CenterScreen.

5. Set the **Caption** property to Diverse Products – Demo. As you change the characters in the Properties window, note that the caption on the title bar is updated.

6. Set the **Height** and **Width** properties to 2385 and 6045, respectively. The size of the form changes accordingly.

7. On the Visual Basic menu bar, click on File, and then click on Save Project. The form and project file are saved to the disk. You should save the module and project files regularly in case you make an error or the computer fails for some reason. You will then be able to recover your work from the last time you saved the project.

The effect of setting the properties of a form or control instance is interactive. As you modify the value of a property that affects the visual part of a form or control instance, the change appears in the Form window. For example, when you set a property to change the position of control instances, its font, or color, the change appears immediately, providing you with feedback on the change.

To illustrate the fundamental elements of a Visual Basic program, you will create a simple program that displays the current date on the form. This program uses an instance of the Label control to display the date. It determines the date by querying the system date. The value appears in the label when the program is run. Note that this task will be performed in response to an event.

The Label Control

The primary purpose of the Label control is to display a prompt or message. This prompt typically describes the contents of another field. The text in the prompt is stored in the **Caption** property of the label.

➤ **Alignment**   Controls the alignment of the text inside the region of the label. It can be set to the values 0 – Left Justify (the default), 1 – Right Justify, and 2 – Center.

➤ **Caption**   Specifies the text that appears in the label.

➤ **BorderStyle**   If set to 0 – None (the default), will cause no border to be displayed. If set to 1 – Fixed Single, a single line is drawn around the control.

The standard prefix for the Label control is "lbl".

In this example, you will create two labels. The date label, which displays the current date, will be used for program output. The other label will display a descriptive prompt.

To create a control instance and set its design-time properties:

1. Click on the Label control on the toolbox. Create an instance of the control to display the current date, as shown in Figure 1.22. Position and size the label to match the label shown in Figure 1.22.

2. Activate the Properties window for the newly created label. Set the **BorderStyle** property to 1– Fixed Single, and set the **Name** property to **lblDate**. Remove the text from the **Caption** property.

3. Create another label to display the date prompt, as shown in Figure 1.22. Set the **Caption** property to **Date**. Set the Alignment to 1 – Right Justify. Note that you did not explicitly set the **Name** property of this label, because it contains a descriptive prompt and will not be referenced with code. This book will follow the convention of using default names for objects when those objects will never be referenced with code.

4. Click on the Value column of the **Font** property, then click on the Properties button at the right side of the Value column to open the Font dialog box. Click on Bold in the Font Style list box, and then click on OK. The finished form should resemble Figure 1.22.

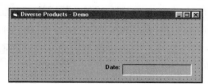

Figure 1.22   Completed labels drawn on form.

Responding To An Event

If you are accustomed to writing programs in a procedural language, you know that a main procedure typically executes automatically when the program first begins. In this example, the date will not be displayed in the label because a statement executes in the main procedure. Rather, the statement will execute in response to an event. Remember that a form is an object and that an object can respond to events. When a form is loaded into memory, an event occurs. You will now write the statement to display the date in the label you just created. In writing code that responds to an event, you create a procedure called an *event procedure*. An event procedure has a specific syntax, as illustrated in Figure 1.23.

Figure 1.23 also illustrates that the procedure begins with the keywords **Private Sub** and ends with the keywords **End Sub**. These keywords mark the beginning and end of the event procedure. (They also mark the beginning and end of other procedures.) Between these lines is the code that executes in response to the event. This event procedure has the name **Form_Load( )**. This name consists of two parts: a part indicating that the event procedure pertains to the form, and the name of the particular event. An underscore character (_) separates these two parts. Typically, you would refer to this event as the **Form Load** event. The following list summarizes the processing that takes place in a typical event driven Visual Basic program:

1. When a program starts, a form called the startup form loads and is displayed on the screen. Any event procedures pertaining to initializing the startup form also execute.

2. At this time, the program waits for an event to occur and no code executes. The code that will execute next cannot be predicted, because it is impossible to determine which event will occur next, and to which object. That is, the program does not know whether the user will click on a command button or enter characters into a text box.

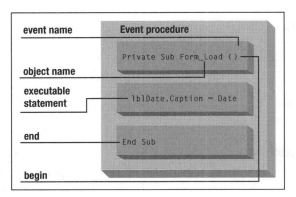

Figure 1.23   Form_Load event procedure.

3. When the user enters a keystroke, clicks a mouse button on an object, or performs some other action, an event occurs. The code in the event procedure corresponding to this event then executes. When the procedure finishes, the program waits for the next event to occur. If no code has been written for the event procedure, the event occurs but no code executes in response to the event.

4. Events also occur to a form when the program ends or the form unloads.

In addition to the syntax for the event procedure, consider carefully the assignment statement inside the event procedure. An assignment statement contains a left-hand side, followed by an equals sign (=), followed by the right-hand side. During the execution of this statement, the expression on the right-hand side is evaluated and the result is stored in the left-hand side. In this example, the expression on the right-hand side obtains the date from the system. The expression on the left-hand side refers to the **Caption** property of the Label object named lblDate. When you reference the property of an object using code, the following syntax is used.

Syntax
objectname.propertyname

Dissection

➤ The *objectname* is the name of a form or control instance on a form.

➤ The *propertyname* is the name of a property supported by the object.

➤ The *objectname* and *propertyname* are separated by a period (.).

Code Example
```
lbldate.Caption = Date
```

Code Dissection
This statement obtains the system date and stores it in the **Caption** property of the label. The label then displays the current date.

To create the code for an event procedure, or write any other statements, you use the Code window.

The Code Window

The Code window is an intelligent text editor designed specifically for writing Visual Basic programs. One instance of the Code window can be open for each module in a project. Thus, if a program has two form modules, two separate instances of the Code window could be open—one for each form. The Code window supports features to select event procedures and other parts of a module. By default, it will capitalize keywords and use a consistent case for all procedure and variable names. It also supports a technology called IntelliSense. As you write statements in the Code window, this text editor will display ToolTips describing the syntax for procedure calls. In addition, it indicates the valid properties and methods that pertain to the objects and variables. Figure 1.24 depicts the components of the Code window.

The Code window contains two list boxes, as shown in Figure 1.24. You use the Object list box to select an object drawn on the form, the form itself, or the general procedures. You use the Procedure list box to select an event procedure pertaining to the selected object or a general procedure. In addition to using the Object and Procedure boxes to select a procedure, you can press the Page Up and Page Down keys to scroll through the procedures in the module. If you click on the Procedure View button, the Code window will display one procedure at a time. If you click on the Full Module View button, it will show several procedures simultaneously. Which mode you use is a matter of personal preference.

Also, as shown in Figure 1.24, a ToolTip displays a list of properties pertaining to the Label control. Visual Basic then recognizes that lblName is an instance of the Label control. When you type the period character, Visual Basic tries to help you with the next step by displaying the list of properties. You can use the scroll bars to select a property from the list or continue to type characters.

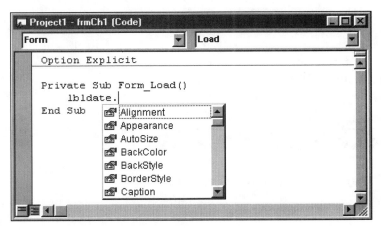

Figure 1.24   The Code window.

Selecting An Event Procedure

All executable code must reside inside a procedure. For your program, you need to write the statement that will display the current date on the form when the form loads. This statement must reside in the **Form_Load** event procedure.

To enter code into an event procedure:

1. Make sure that the Form window is active. To open the Code window for the form, click on Code on the View menu or double-click on the form.

2. Select the Form object and the Load procedure. On the blank line below the line that begins with the word "Private," enter the following statement into the event procedure:

```
lblDate.Caption = Date
```

3. Save the project, and then run it. The date should appear in the label. By default, when the year is 1999 or less, only the last two digits are displayed. Dates including 2000 or subsequent years, however, are displayed with all four digits.

4. End the program to return to design mode.

5. Exit Visual Basic.

 In this book, you will follow the convention of saving your work, then testing it. You will save and test the program at regular intervals throughout the chapter. For brevity, this book uses the phrase "Test the program" to mean "Save the project and all of its files, and then run the program."

The Label control is merely one control employed in Visual Basic programs. As this textbook takes an advanced look at Visual Basic, it will not discuss the specific features of each intrinsic control. If you are not familiar with the use of intrinsic controls, refer to an introductory Visual Basic text.

CONFIGURING VISUAL SOURCESAFE

The Purpose Of Visual SourceSafe

Visual SourceSafe (VSS) is a utility program designed to help manage software development projects. In this book, VSS will be used only with Visual Basic projects; it can also be used with other programming languages, such as Visual C++, however. Note that VSS is not supplied with the Professional Edition of Visual Basic. To install, configure, and use VSS, you must have the Enterprise Edition of Visual Basic. Without the Enterprise Edition, you will not be able to complete the steps in this section.

Development of a large software package typically requires the services of teams of programmers. VSS satisfies this need by allowing team members to share files across a network and control the changes made to those files. The most important VSS capabilities relate to version control and are as follows:

➤ **Team coordination** Assures that only one programmer is modifying a file at any given time. This capability prevents programmers from overwriting each other's changes.

➤ **Version tracking** Allows multiple software versions to be cataloged and archived. This feature allows programmers to reverse previous changes if necessary.

➤ **Multiple-platform development** Allows the development team to track code maintenance for software that will be deployed on multiple hardware or software environments.

➤ **Tracking of reusable code** Enables the development team to readily determine which programs use which software modules.

To implement these features, VSS groups files together into a project. Note that the term *project* in VSS differs from the term in Visual Basic. The files that make up a VSS project are stored in a database. VSS supports projects having as many as 8,000 files. A VSS project can contain many files in addition to a Visual Basic project. The following list identifies the types of files you would likely maintain using VSS:

➤ Help files

➤ Bitmaps and icons

➤ Text and database files

➤ Internal documentation

VSS categorizes files into two types: text and binary. This distinction is significant, because the different operations can be performed on the different file types. With text files, VSS can keep track of exactly how a file has changed. With a binary file, VSS can determine that a file has changed but cannot display the nature of those modifications. To determine the file type, VSS scans the file for null bytes (bytes with the value 0). If it finds a null byte, it categorizes the file as a binary file. If no null byte is found, the utility categorizes the file as a text file. Because of the way VSS automatically classifies files, a binary file could potentially be called a text file. In this situation, you can explicitly tell VSS that a file is a text or binary file.

Visual SourceSafe is implemented using a client/server model. Under this model, the VSS server takes responsibility for maintaining the VSS database(s). The VSS database, in turn, serves as the repository for the projects created by the development team. Each programmer who is part of the team uses a VSS client. VSS retrieves files from the VSS database and stores them on the client computer. The area on the client computer in which files are stored is called the *working folder.* VSS also sends files from the client computer back to the server-based VSS database. Note that VSS can be used on a single computer with both client and server components installed.

Installing Visual SourceSafe

You can apply any of four techniques to install Visual SourceSafe:

1. You can perform a client installation from a local disk. This task is typically carried out after completing a server installation. When you perform a client installation, only VSS is installed; that is, the database files and support files are not installed.

2. You can perform a client installation from a network. NetSetup enables you to accomplish such a client installation.

3. The custom installation option allows you to tailor VSS to the needs of your particular environment. This technique provides you with the ability to install both the client and server components, create a VSS database, and install optional conversion utilities.

4. The VSS administrator uses the server installation option to set up a VSS server that should be accessible to multiple users.

By default, VSS is installed along with the Enterprise Edition of Visual Basic. This default installation adds both the client and server utilities to your computer. It also creates a database file to store the projects maintained by VSS. If you have not installed VSS, you can place it on your computer by using the Visual Basic installation CD-ROM. By default during this process, VSS creates the following folders in C:\Program Files\Microsoft Visual Studio\Common\Vss:

➤ **\Data**   Contains the database file used to store all projects and the files belonging to those projects

➤ **\Users**   Contains initialization files

➤ **\Temp**   Contains temporary files

➤ **\Template**   Contains configuration information

➤ **\Win32**   Contains the application files used by Windows NT, Windows 95, and Windows 98

➤ **\Setup**   Contains the files used by Setup.exe

➤ **\Netsetup**   Contains the files necessary to install VSS on a client computer over a network

Note that the \Setup and \Netsetup folders may not be present, depending on how VSS is configured. Microsoft Access uses a much different type of database than that used by VSS. Microsoft Access stores a database in a single file with an extension of ".mdb." In contrast, a VSS database is not stored in a single file, but rather contains several folders and files that in turn store projects.

Configuring Visual SourceSafe

1

Even though VSS is installed along with Visual Basic, an administrator must configure it before team programmers can take advantage of the software. The VSS administrator plays a significant role, taking responsibility for performing the following tasks:

➤ Creating VSS databases

➤ Granting and revoking access to the VSS database

➤ Locking and unlocking databases

➤ Archiving database and restoring projects

The VSS administrative tasks are performed using the Visual SourceSafe Administrator program. This stand-alone program operates independently of Visual Basic.

To activate the Visual SourceSafe Administrator program, click on Start on the taskbar, highlight Programs, highlight Microsoft Visual SourceSafe, and then click on Visual SourceSafe 6.0 Admin.

When you first install VSS, the administrator does not have a password. VSS will display a dialog box warning you that, without a password, any user on the network can gain access to the VSS Administrator program. Click on OK to close this dialog box. As a general rule, the Administrator password should be tightly controlled and knowledge of it should remain limited to a single person or a small group of people.

The VSS Administrator program should appear, as shown in Figure 1.25.

Figure 1.25 shows the Visual SourceSafe Administrator program with two users, Admin and Guest. These users are automatically added when you create a new SourceSafe database.

The administrator takes charge of adding users to the VSS database. These users typically include the team members who are part of a development project. Adding, changing, and deleting users is accomplished by using the options on

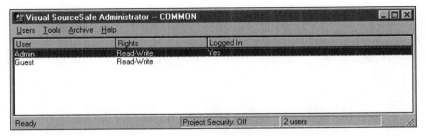

Figure 1.25   Visual SourceSafe Administrator.

the Users menu and changing a user's password appropriately. When you add a user, you specify a required user name, an optional password, and the VSS access rights. In this section, you will add two users to the VSS database. You will assume the role of Mary Deems later in the chapter to help illustrate the capabilities of VSS.

To add a user to the VSS database:

1. Click on Users, and then click on Add User. The Add User dialog box appears, as shown in Figure 1.26.

2. Enter a user name of Tom Smith. Do not enter a password.

3. Click on OK to add the user and close the dialog box.

4. Enter a second user with the name of Mary Deems.

5. Exit the VSS Administrator program.

By default, during the installation of VSS, a single VSS database named COMMON was created. Using the Administrator program, you can create additional databases by completing the following steps:

1. Click on Tools, and then click on Create Database. The Create New VSS Database dialog box will appear.

2. Click on Browse to specify the folder where the new database will reside.

3. Click on OK to begin database creation. VSS will display various windows as it generates the new database.

VSS offers considerable flexibility in managing the rights and privileges granted to VSS users. The administrator can grant and revoke four rights and privileges:

➤ **Read access** Allows a team member to read–view a VSS project but prohibits this user from performing any other action on the project.

➤ **Check Out/Check In access** Allows a team member to copy files from the VSS database to a working folder and copy working folder files back to the database.

➤ **Add/Rename/Delete access** Allows a team member to add new files to a project, change file names, and remove files.

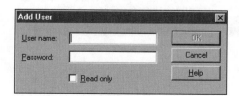

Figure 1.26   Add User dialog box.

➤ **Destroy access** Similar to delete access, but it ensures that destroyed files cannot be recovered. In contrast, deleted files and projects can be recovered.

The Tools menu contains two menu items to manage user rights. The Project Rights dialog box allows the administrator to select a VSS project, then grant or revoke specific rights for various users. Thus some users may have read–write access for a particular project, while other users have read–only access. Figure 1.27 shows this dialog box.

The Assignments dialog box performs essentially the same task as the Project Rights dialog box. Project rights, however, are granted or revoked on a project for a particular user. Figure 1.28 shows this dialog box.

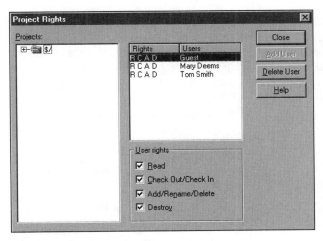

Figure 1.27   Project Rights dialog box.

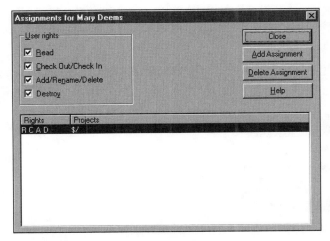

Figure 1.28   Assignments dialog box.

At this point, you as the administrator have created two users in addition to the Admin and Guest users that were automatically created during the installation of VSS. These users have full access rights. That is, they can create new projects, add, rename, and delete files, check in and check out files, and destroy files. Next, you need to learn how to use the VSS database when acting as a team member.

As a Visual Basic programmer, you can use VSS directly from Visual Basic by way of an Add-In. You can also access VSS as a stand-alone program. To practice using VSS as a programmer, you will use the project you completed previously in this chapter. Here you will check a project module in and out of VSS and change the module.

The VSS Add-In should be started and loaded by default. If it does not appear on the Tools menu, click on Add-Ins on the Visual Basic menu bar, and then click on Add-In Manager to activate the Add-In Manager dialog box. In the Available Add-Ins list, locate the item named Source Code Control. In the Load Behavior frame, make sure that the Loaded/Unloaded checkbox is checked. Also, verify that the Load on Startup checkbox is checked.

To add a project to VSS:

1. Start Visual Basic and open Chapter.01\Startup\Ch1.vbp, the project you created previously in this chapter.

2. On the Visual Basic menu bar, click on Tools, and then highlight SourceSafe. Click on Add Project To SourceSafe. The Visual SourceSafe Login dialog box appears, as shown in Figure 1.29.

3. Be sure that the database COMMON is selected. If it is not, click on the Browse button to locate the database.

4. Enter Mary Deems as the Username. It is the name of the VSS user you added earlier in the section.

5. Click on OK to activate the Add to SourceSafe Project dialog box, as shown in Figure 1.30.

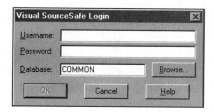

Figure 1.29   Visual SourceSafe Login dialog box.

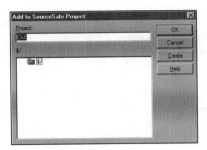

Figure 1.30   Add to SourceSafe Project dialog box.

6. By default, the VSS project name is the same as the Visual Basic project name, although having matching names is not a requirement. Click on OK to add the Visual Basic project to VSS. A dialog box will appear, indicating that the project does not exist. Click on Yes to activate the Add Files to SourceSafe dialog box, as shown in Figure 1.31.

 If you inadvertently added the project to SourceSafe in Section B, a dialog box with the following text will appear: "All available files have already been added to source code control."

7. As shown in Figure 1.31, all files making up the project appear in the dialog box. You can click on specific files to prevent them from being added to the VSS database. The command buttons at the right of the dialog box allow you to select or deselect the files. Typically, you want to add all of the Visual Basic files to the VSS project. Note that you can write a comment to describe your actions and that this information will be stored in the VSS database. Enter the text "Project initially added to VSS" as a comment, and then click on the OK button to add the files to VSS.

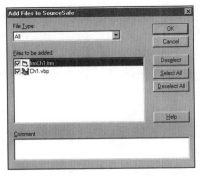

Figure 1.31   Add Files to SourceSafe dialog box.

At this point, the Visual Basic project file and Visual Basic form file have been added to the VSS project. Thus VSS now takes charge of these files. Figure 1.32 shows the Project Explorer with the form and project file.

The icons to the left of the project and form files appear with a small padlock, which indicates that the files are marked as read-only and locked by VSS. If you attempt to change and then save either the Visual Basic project or form file, you will receive a message indicating that the files are read-only. Before editing it, you must check out the file.

 When you save a project for the first time, the dialog box Add Project to Visual SourceSafe will appear. Responding "yes" to this dialog box adds the project to VSS, allowing you to complete the same dialog boxes mentioned in the previous steps.

As noted earlier, you can interact with the VSS features with Visual Basic by means of an Add-In. By default, this Add-In is loaded when Visual Basic starts. To make the functionality of this Add-In available, click on Tools, and then highlight Visual SourceSafe on the menu bar. This menu contains the following options:

➤ **Get Latest Version** Retrieve the most current version of the file from the VSS database and place it in the working folder.

➤ **Check Out** Copy the most current version of the file from VSS to the working folder. The file is made available for editing and locked so that other users cannot edit it until you check the file back in.

➤ **Check In** Copy the file from the working folder to the VSS database. The file in the working folder becomes read-only, and other team members can check out the file in the VSS database.

➤ **Undo Check Out** The file just checked out is checked back in, the version information is not updated.

➤ **Show History** The changes made to the file since it was created appear in a dialog box.

➤ **Show Differences** The differences between two versions of the same file are displayed.

Figure 1.32   Project Explorer with locked icons.

➤ **Source Safe Properties** The properties pertaining to the VSS project are set using this dialog box.

➤ **Add Files to SourceSafe** This option adds a new file to a VSS project. This new file is locked by VSS and must be checked out before you can edit it.

➤ **Share Files** Checked out files can be shared by multiple team members.

➤ **Create Project from SourceSafe** This option creates a working copy of a project in the VSS database.

➤ **Run SourceSafe** The stand-alone VSS user interface becomes activated. This interface has a functionality that is similar to the VSS Add-In.

➤ **Options** Sets general options pertaining to the VSS options.

➤ **Refresh File Status** This option synchronizes a working file with the file stored in the VSS database.

To illustrate that the files are locked by VSS, you will now try to edit them.

To view the locked files:

1. Open the form window for the form named frmCh1.

2. Try to create another label on the form. A dialog box appears, indicating that the file is read-only.

3. Click on OK to close the dialog box.

At this point, two copies of the files that constitute your Visual Basic project exist: one in the VSS database, and another in your working folder. The working folder is named Chapter.01\Startup. To edit the files in your working folder, you must check out the files from the VSS database. While a file remains checked out, no other programmer can edit it. When the file is checked back in to the database, it becomes available for editing by other team members. Note that you can check out a single file or many files.

To check out files from the VSS database:

1. On the Visual Basic menu bar, click on Tools, highlight SourceSafe, then click on Check Out to activate the Check Out Files from SourceSafe dialog box.

2. The dialog box allows you to check out as many files as necessary. As a general rule, you should check out only those files that you want to edit, leaving the other files available for editing by other team members. Verify that the file named frmCh1.frm is checked and that the project file is not checked.

3. In the Comment box, enter the following comment: Adding additional control instances to form.

4. Click on OK to check out the file.

   When you check out the file, it is copied to the working folder and becomes available for editing. Because you checked out only the form file, it is the only file that you can edit and save. The project file has not been checked out, so it remains locked.

To see that you can edit the form file but not the project file, you will now create an additional label instance on the form and attempt to save both the form and project file back to the disk.

To edit a file from the working folder:

1. Make sure that the form window is open.

2. Create an instance of the Label control on the form. Note that you do not receive the same read-only error message that you saw a moment ago.

3. Click on File, and then click on Save frmCh1.frm. The form is saved to the working folder.

4. Click on File, and then click on Save Project. You will receive an error message, indicating that the project cannot be saved.

5. Click on OK to close the dialog box. The Save Project As dialog box will appear. Click on Cancel to close the dialog box.

After changing the form, you should check the form back in to the VSS database so that it can be edited by the other members of the development team. This process is similar to that used to check out a file from the VSS database.

To check a file back in to the VSS database:

1. Click on Tools, highlight SourceSafe, and then click on Check In.

2. When the Check In Files to SourceSafe dialog box appears, make sure that only the form file is selected, and then click on OK to check the form back into the VSS database. This file should be the only one available, because it is the only file checked out. At this point, your working copy of the file is marked as read-only and cannot be edited until someone checks it out again. You can determine that the file is read-only by opening the Project Explorer and noting that the file appears with the locked icon.

As multiple team members edit the files belonging to a VSS project, your working copies of various files may become outdated. For example, assume that the programmer Tom Smith checked out the form file, modified it, and checked the file back into the VSS database. At this point, your working copy of the file is not synchronized with the VSS database. To reconcile this problem, you can use the Get Latest Version option to keep your working folder files up-to-date with the VSS database files.

To synchronize the working copy files with the VSS database:

1. Click on Tools, highlight SourceSafe, and then click on Get Latest Version to activate the dialog box.

2. Select all files in the dialog box, and then click on OK. Now the copies of the database files are copied into your working folder and the files are synchronized.

VSS enables you to view the change history related to a particular file. The information recorded includes when a file was checked in and checked out, the modifications made to that file, and the identity of the programmer who made the changes. You can print reports containing this information.

To view the changes to a VSS file:

1. Click on Tools, highlight SourceSafe, and then click on Show History to display the History Options dialog box, as shown in Figure 1.33.

2. As illustrated in Figure 1.33, this dialog box offers several options for viewing the descriptive labels pertaining to a file. SourceSafe labels are different from the toolbox's Label control. They store descriptive, historical information. Other options allow you to view only those changes made between a particular range of dates. Finally, you can view the changes made by a particular user. Click on OK to accept the default options. The History dialog box appears, as shown in Figure 1.34.

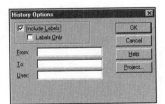

Figure 1.33   History Options dialog box.

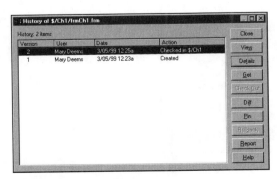

Figure 1.34   History dialog box.

As shown in Figure 1.34, the History dialog box contains several options that enable you to analyze the changes that have been made to a particular file.

➤ **View** Will activate an editor in which you can view the version of the file as maintained by VSS.

➤ **Details** Displays a dialog box containing detailed descriptive information pertaining to the selected revision of the file. These data include any label information, the names of team members who have checked the file in or out, and any associated comments.

➤ **Get** Retrieves the latest version of the file from the VSS database.

➤ **Report** Allows you to print a report to a file, to the Windows Clipboard, or to the printer.

To review the file information recorded by VSS, you will preview a printed report of the changes to the form file with which you have been working in this chapter.

To view the changes to a file:

1. In the History dialog box, select the form file that was just checked in.
2. Click on Report to view the History Report dialog box.
3. Check the Include Details and Include Differences checkboxes.
4. Click on the Preview button to open the dialog box shown in Figure 1.35.
5. Close all the dialog boxes.
6. Exit Visual Basic.

Figure 1.35 File report.

In addition to using VSS from the Visual Basic Add-In, you can use VSS as a stand-alone application. While the interface differs slightly for the latter choice, from the perspective of the team member using VSS, the effect is the same.

The VSS Interface

The VSS interface is a stand-alone program that operates independently of Visual Basic. Using this interface, team members can check files in and out of VSS, create new projects, add files to projects, and perform all of the other tasks that you accomplished in this chapter using the VSS Add-In.

To start the VSS interface:

1. Click on the Start button on the Windows taskbar. Highlight Programs, highlight Microsoft Visual SourceSafe, and then click on Microsoft Visual SourceSafe 6.0. The same login dialog box appears that you saw previously in the chapter.

2. Login with the user name of Mary Deems, then click on OK to display the Visual SourceSafe Explorer window, as shown in Figure 1.36.

3. Exit Visual SourceSafe.

As shown in Figure 1.36, the project you added to VSS now appears in the All projects list. This list works much like the Windows Explorer program. That is, you can click on the plus and minus signs in the window to open and close VSS folders. The files in the folders appear in the right pane of the window, just as they do in the Windows Explorer program. The menu items in the program enable you to check in and check out files and perform all other tasks that can be accomplished with the Add-In.

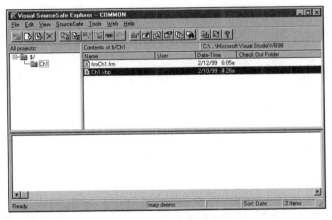

Figure 1.36   Visual SourceSafe Explorer.

CHAPTER SUMMARY

This chapter discussed three significant topics: installation of Visual Basic, Visual Basic fundamentals, and use of Visual SourceSafe for team development.

To install Visual Basic:

➤ Make sure you have the Visual Basic CD-ROMs available.

➤ Insert the first CD-ROM into the disk drive and run the Setup.exe program, if necessary.

➤ Complete the dialog boxes to enter the user name, company name, and product ID number.

➤ Select the software components you want to install.

➤ Copy the software components to the hard disk.

➤ When the installation is complete, restart your computer.

➤ Install the MDSN Library.

To create a new Visual Basic project:

➤ Click on File, and then click on New Project.

➤ Select the project type from the New project dialog box.

➤ Save the project by clicking File, and then Save Project As. You will be requested to assign folder and file names to the modules belonging to the project.

To set design-time properties for a project:

➤ Select the desired object in the Form window.

➤ Activate the Properties window by pressing F4 or by clicking the right mouse button and selecting Properties.

➤ Locate the desired property.

➤ Click on the Value column and enter the desired value for the property.

To create an event procedure:

➤ In the Form window, select the object for which you want to create an event procedure.

➤ Double-click on the object to activate the Code window.

➤ Select the event for which you want to create a procedure.

➤ Enter the code in the event procedure.

To configure Visual SourceSafe:

➤ Start the VSS Administrator program.

➤ Add the desired team members to the VSS database. Specify user names and passwords as necessary. (In this chapter, you did not explicitly set passwords for the new users.)

➤ Set the access rights for each user that is added.

➤ Note that the administrator should have a tightly controlled password.

To add a project to VSS:

➤ Open the project in Visual Basic.

➤ Click on Tools, highlight SourceSafe, and then click on Add Project to SourceSafe.

➤ When the login dialog box appears, enter the user name and password, and then select the desired database.

➤ When the Add Files to SourceSafe dialog box appears, select the files to add.

➤ Newly added files are controlled by VSS, and the file copies stored in the working folder are marked as read-only.

To check out a file from the VSS database:

➤ On the Visual Basic menu bar, click on Tools, highlight SourceSafe, and then click on Check Out.

➤ Select only the files you plan to edit, and then check them out of the VSS database and store a read-write copy in the working folder.

To check a file in to the VSS database:

➤ In the Project Explorer, select the desired file.

➤ Click on Tools, highlight SourceSafe, and then click on Check In.

➤ The Check In Files to SourceSafe dialog box appears. Verify that the desired file is selected, and then click on OK.

To synchronize the working folder the with the VSS database:

➤ Click on Tools, highlight SourceSafe, and then click on Get Latest Version.

➤ Select the desired files in the dialog box, and then click on OK.

To view the changes made to a VSS file:

➤ Click on Tools, highlight SourceSafe, and then click on Show History to display the History Options dialog box.

➤ Click on OK to accept the default options.

➤ When the History dialog box appears, click on Details to view specific information about the change file.

➤ Click on report to print a report containing the history of the changed files.

REVIEW QUESTIONS

1. What are the valid editions of Visual Basic 6.0?
   a. Learning Edition
   b. Professional Edition
   c. Enterprise Edition
   d. All of the above.
   e. None of the above

2. What is the name of the program used to access Help files?
   a. MSDN Library
   b. Windows Help
   c. Learn
   d. HelpTools
   e. None of the above

3. What is the name of the program used to install Visual Basic?
   a. Install
   b. Configure
   c. Installation Wizard
   d. Deploy
   e. None of the above

4. Which of the following is a valid Visual Basic server installation option?
   a. Microsoft FrontPage 98 Server Extensions
   b. Data Access Components 2.0
   c. Application Performance Explorer
   d. All of the above.
   e. None of the above

5. Which of the following Visual Basic installation options are valid?
   a. Typical, Configure
   b. Typical, Custom
   c. Normal, Custom
   d. Normal, Configure
   e. None of the above

6. What is the default path name of the Visual Basic installation folder?
   a. C:\Program Files\Visual Basic
   b. C:\Program Files\Microsoft Visual Studio\VB98
   c. C:\Program Files\Microsoft Visual Basic
   d. C:\Program Files\VB\VB98
   e. None of the above

7. Which of the following statements regarding a custom installation is true?
   a. You can elect to install either selected components or the entire Visual Basic system.
   b. Some components are required and others are not.
   c. The Graphics component installs bitmaps, icons, and cursors.
   d. All of the above.
   e. None of the above.

8. Which of the following is a valid Visual Basic tool?
   a. Application Performance Explorer
   b. Visual Component Manager
   c. Microsoft Visual Modeler
   d. Repository
   e. All of the above.

9. Which of the following are valid MSDN Library installation options?
   a. Typical, Custom, Full
   b. Common, Custom, Full
   c. Minimal, Custom, Full
   d. Partial, Custom, Complete
   e. None of the above

10. Which of the following statements regarding the MSDN Library are true?
    a. The Help files can be copied to the hard disk.
    b. The Help files can be used from the MSDN CD-ROM.
    c. The Help files consume about 800 megabytes of disk space.
    d. All of the above.
    e. None of the above.

11. Which of the following statements is true regarding objects?

    a. An object may have properties.

    b. An object may have methods

    c. An object may support events.

    d. An object has a well-defined interface.

    e. All of the above.

12. Which of the following statements is true?

    a. A form module has code and a visual interface.

    b. A standard module contains code.

    c. Form and standard modules are stored in separate files.

    d. None of the above.

    e. All of the above.

13. Which of the following statements is false?

    a. At design time, you write code and create instances of controls on a form.

    b. You can open only one instance of the Code window.

    c. You can open multiple copies of the Properties window.

    d. All of the above.

    e. None of the above.

14. Which are the valid file extensions for project, form, and standard modules?

    a. .vbp, .frm, .bas

    b. .prj, .frm, .bas

    c. .prj, .frm, .std

    d. .vbp, .for, .bas

    e. .vbp, .for, .std

15. Which properties are used to determine the location and size of the form and its objects?

    a. **Size, Top, Left**

    b. **Height, Width, Top, Left**

    c. **Height, Width, Top, Left, Bottom, Right**

    d. **Width, Length, Top, Left**

    e. **Width, Length, Bottom, Right**

16. The _____ window is used to set an object's properties at design time.

17. The _____ control typically is used to display output.

18. Write a statement to store the caption "Perfect Products" in the title bar of the form named **frmDemo**.

19. Write a statement to assign the contents of the label named **lblDemo** to the contents of the label named **lblDemo1**.

20. Write statements to set the **Height** and **Width** properties of the label named **lblDemo** to 100 and 500, respectively.

21. Which of the following statements regarding version control is true?

    a. Only one programmer in a team should be able to modify a file at any given time.

    b. Multiple software versions can be cataloged and archived.

    c. The team can track code maintenance for software that will be deployed on multiple platforms.

    d. All of the above.

    e. None of the above

22. Which of the following statements about a VSS project is true?

    a. A VSS project is analogous to a Visual Basic project.

    b. VSS projects can store only Visual Basic project and form files.

    c. A VSS project is limited to 100 files.

    d. All of the above.

    e. None of the above

23. What are the two categories of VSS files?
    a. Source files, Binary files
    b. Source files, Destination files
    c. Text files, Binary files
    d. Text files, Destination files
    e. None of the above

24. What is the name of the area in which VSS files are stored on the client computer?
    a. Temporary folder
    b. Working folder
    c. Dummy folder
    d. Scratch folder
    e. None of the above

25. Which VSS tasks does the VSS administrator perform?
    a. Creating VSS databases
    b. Checking project files in and out
    c. Adding users
    d. Both a and b
    e. Both a and c

26. Which of the following statements about the VSS administrator program is true?
    a. It is called from Visual Basic.
    b. It is a stand-alone program.
    c. It is run on the client machine.
    d. All of the above.
    e. None of the above.

27. Which of the following statements about a VSS user is true?
    a. A user has a required user name.
    b. A user has an optional password.
    c. A user has access rights, which permit the user to check files in and out, add and remove files, and read files.
    d. All of the above.
    e. None of the above.

28. How do you add a Visual Basic project to VSS?

   a. Use the Add Project to SourceSafe option from the Visual Basic Add-In.

   b. Use the VSS Explorer program.

   c. Use the Windows Explorer program.

   d. Both a and c.

   e. Both a and b.

29. By default, how many team members can check out a file from the VSS database?

   a. 1

   b. 2

   c. 3

   d. 5

   e. Any number of team members

30. Which of the following statements regarding the information maintained by VSS is true?

   a. All changes are tracked and can be viewed.

   b. Changes can be viewed that occur within a particular time range.

   c. Changes expire after one year.

   d. Both a and b.

   e. All of the above.

HANDS-ON PROJECTS

Project 1

In this project, you will use the VSS Administrator program to create users and grant access rights.

   a. Create a directory on the hard disk.

   b. Start the VSS Administrator program.

   c. Use the Tools menu to create a new database. Set the database name to Demo. Save the database in the root directory you created in step a.

   d. In the new database, create a user named Harkin Smith.

   e. Modify the access rights for the user so that he can read projects but not check them in and out. Make sure that the user cannot write changes.

f. Create another user named Emma Bates. Set the permissions so that she can read projects, and check them in and out. This user should not be able to either add files to the VSS database or destroy them.

g. Create a third user named Nevil Morshed. This user should have full access privileges.

h. Exit the VSS Administrator program.

Project 2

In this project, you will create a new Visual Basic project, and then check it in to the VSS database. You will then practice checking the project in and out of the database, and adding files to the project.

a. Start Visual Basic and create a new project. Set the Name property of the form to "frmEx2". Save the form in the Chapter.01\Exercise folder using the file name "frmEx2.frm". Save the project using the name "frmEx2.vbp".

b. Add the project to VSS, using the database that you created in exercise and Nevil Morshed as the user name.

c. Check out all files in the project to the working folder.

d. Create two labels on the form.

e. Write the code to display the date in one of the labels when the form loads.

f. Check the project back in to the VSS database.

g. Check the form out of the VSS database.

h. Set the caption of one of the labels to "Date". This label should appear as a prompt for the other label.

i. Check the form back in to the VSS database.

j. Exit Visual Basic.

k. Start the VSS Explorer program.

l. Print a report documenting the changes made to the form file.

m. Exit the program.

CHAPTER TWO

FUNDAMENTALS OF EVENT DRIVEN PROGRAMMING

AFTER READING THIS CHAPTER AND COMPLETING THE EXERCISES, YOU WILL BE ABLE TO:

➤ Review the structure of a Visual Basic program

➤ Learn about keyboard and mouse events

➤ Learn about form events and how to display and hide forms

➤ Learn the basics of control arrays

➤ Add a menu to an application

➤ Add a pop-up menu to an application

➤ Display standard dialogs using the InputBox and MsgBox functions

➤ Dynamically modify the appearance of a menu

➤ Add and delete menus at run time

➤ Use the Controls collection

➤ Learn how to handle run-time errors

CREATING AND DESTROYING CONTROL INSTANCES AT RUN TIME

Understanding Visual Basic Syntax

The format of this chapter differs slightly from the format of Chapter 1. This chapter, like subsequent chapters in this book, includes a completed program that duplicates the code that you will write during the chapter's hands-on steps. You will preview this completed program, which will allow you to visualize the end result of the program you will create. The completed program also serves as a tool to help you discover errors made while completing the hands-on steps. Consider printing the code for the completed program and using it as a reference as you complete the hands-on steps.

The completed program for this chapter is much more complex than the program you created in Chapter 1. Nevertheless, most of the concepts presented should already be familiar to you. To help you understand the program you will create later in this chapter, the completed program contains numerous comments that document how it works. Carefully review this program and its comments as you complete the steps in the chapter.

As you enter code in the hands-on steps in this chapter, you will not duplicate the comments of the completed program. This approach minimizes the volume of typing that you are required to perform.

To preview the completed application:

1. Start Visual Basic and load the project named Chapter.02\Complete\ Ch2_C.vbp. As mentioned in Chapter 1, this book uses relative path names. Set the path and drive designator as necessary depending upon where you have installed the student files corresponding to this chapter. The completed program has a name suffix of "_C", which denotes "complete." Startup programs have a suffix of "_S", which denotes "startup."

2. Open the Form window for the form named **frmCh2**. Figure 2.1 shows this form at design time.

    As shown in Figure 2.1, the form contains a menu. It also contains three control instances: a line, a shape, and a label.

3. Run the program. The program allows the user to draw lines, shapes, and labels on the form by using the mouse. When the program first starts, the control instances are invisible.

4. Click on Object on the menu bar. These menu items operate such that only one item is active at a time. When the items on the Object menu are

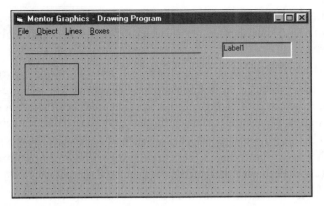

Figure 2.1   Completed main form at design time.

visible, a check mark appears to the left of the Line menu item, indicating that it is the active menu item. The type of object created by the user at run time differs depending upon the active menu item. Click on Box.

5. You will now draw a box at run time by positioning the mouse at the upper-left corner of the intended position of the box, then pressing the left mouse button. Finally, you will move the mouse and release the mouse button. First, position the mouse pointer on the form and hold down the left mouse button. Next, move the mouse down and to the right, then release the mouse button. A box should appear on the form.

6. Repeat the process in Step 5 to create a second box. This time, however, draw the box by starting at the lower-right corner of the box and moving the mouse to the upper-left corner of the box. A dialog box called a message box appears, indicating that you must draw boxes down and to the right. Figure 2.2 shows this message box.

7. Click on OK to close the message box.

8. Click on Object, and then click on Line. In this step, you will draw a line. Position the mouse pointer at the starting point of the line. Move the mouse to the line's endpoint, then release the mouse button. A line should appear on the form.

9. You will now draw a label on the form. Click on Object, and then click on Label. Again, position the mouse pointer at the upper-left corner, where

Figure 2.2   Message box.

the label should appear. Press the left mouse button, move the mouse down and to the right, and then release the mouse button. A descriptive label will appear.

10. This chapter illustrates the dynamic creation of control instances at run time. As you create the lines and shapes, references are added to Lines and Boxes menus, respectively. Click on Lines, and then click on the single item listed on the menu. This item contains the position of the line you drew in Step 8. After clicking the menu, another form will appear, as shown in Figure 2.3. The positional values in the text boxes will vary depending on where you drew the line on the form.

11. The text boxes on this form contain the position of the line you drew earlier. Change the position of the line slightly by editing the contents of the text boxes, then clicking the OK button. When you click on the OK button, the dialog box will close, the line will move to its new position, and the menu item under the Lines menu title will be updated accordingly to indicate the line's new location.

12. Click on the right mouse button on the label you drew in Step 9. A pop-up menu appears. Click on Delete to remove the instance of the Label control. When the dialog box appears requesting confirmation, click on Yes.

13. End the program and exit Visual Basic.

This chapter is not designed to be an introduction to Visual Basic. Rather, it is merely a refresher and review of key concepts. It is assumed that you already understand the following concepts:

➤ The basic properties of the Line, Shape, and Label controls

➤ Fundamental Visual Basic syntactical elements, including string concatenation and decision making using both **If** and **Select Case** statements

➤ Techniques to work with multiple forms

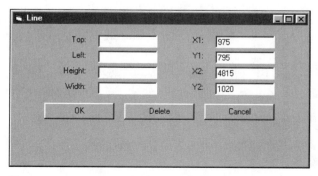

Figure 2.3 Positional properties form.

➤ The syntax to create and call procedures

➤ The **With** statement

If you are not familiar with these topics, refer to an introductory Visual Basic text or consult the MSDN Library as necessary.

2

The Structure Of A Visual Basic Program

Every Visual Basic program contains one or more modules, including the form, standard, and class modules. Each module has a well-defined, similar structure. The first part of a module is known as the general declarations section. The general declarations section contains variable, constant, and type declarations used by the procedures in the module. Procedures follow the general declarations section; they may contain additional variable declarations and executable statements.

Visual Basic programs can include two types of procedures: event and general. As Chapter 1 discussed, an event procedure executes in response to a specific event supported by an object. A general procedure executes when it is explicitly called by an event procedure or another general procedure. The order in which the procedures appear relative to one another in the Code window is not significant, although alphabetizing the procedure names can improve the program's readability.

The arguments for procedures, the return values for procedures, and the variables declared in a module all have a specific data type. This syntax is consistent with that followed by most languages. Visual Basic supports several predefined data types called *intrinsic data types* to store numbers, strings of characters, Boolean information, and so on. Object properties and variables also have specific data types.

Adopting a standard convention for naming variables and procedure arguments will make your code more readable. In this book, variables will have a three-character prefix denoting the variable's data type. This format is consistent with the notion of a three-character prefix for objects. In addition to the three-character prefix to identify a variable's type, a single character will precede the prefix to denote a variable's scope. For global variables, the character "g" is used as the prefix. For module-level variables, the character "m" is used, and for local (procedure-level) variables, the character "p" is used. Table 2.1 shows each intrinsic data type, its prefix, the amount of memory used to store a variable of that type, and the valid values.

Note that these prefixes are merely a naming convention designed to help the programmer; they are not required by Visual Basic. Consider the following valid declaration statements:

```
Dim pintName As String
Dim pstrCounter As Integer
```

Table 2.1   Intrinsic data types.

Data Type	Prefix	Size	Values
Byte	byt	1 byte	0 to 255
Boolean	bln	2 bytes	True or False
Integer	int	2 bytes	32,768 to 32,767
Long	lng	4 bytes	-2,147,483,648 to 2,147,483,647
Single	sng	4 bytes	-3.402823E38 to -1.401298E-45 for negative values; 1.401298E-45 to 3.402823E38 for positive values
Double	dbl	8 bytes	-1.79769313486232E308 to -4.94065645841247E for negative values; 4.94065645841247E-324 to 1.79769313486232E308 for positive values
Currency	cur	8 bytes	-922,337,203,685,477.5808 to 922,337,203,685,477.5807
Date	dat	8 bytes	January 1, 100 to December 31, 9999
Object	obj	4 bytes	Any object reference
String (variable length)	str	10 bytes + string length	0 to approximately 2 billion
String (fixed length)	str	Length of string	1 to approximately 65,400
Variant (with numbers)	vnt	16 bytes	Any numeric value up to the range of a Double
Variant (with characters)	vnt	22 bytes + string length	Same range as for variable-length String

Although these declarations are valid, the prefix used is not consistent with the actual data type. Thus a programmer reading statements that use these variables would likely be confused as to the actual data types.

Procedures

Procedures can contain local variable declarations and executable statements. All executable statements in a program must reside inside a procedure. Visual Basic does not allow procedures to be nested—that is, a procedure cannot be created inside another procedure. Like a variable, a procedure has a defined scope. The scope of a procedure is defined using the **Public** and **Private** keywords. **Public** procedures are visible to other modules; **Private** procedures are not.

Unlike event procedures, general procedures do not execute in response to an event. Rather, they must be called explicitly from an event procedure or another general procedure. Visual Basic supports two types of general procedures: **Function** procedures, which return a value of a specific data type, and **Sub** procedures, which do not return a value. Both **Function** and **Sub** procedures have descriptive names by which they are known. Also, a procedure may accept zero or more arguments. These arguments comprise a list of names separated by commas and communicate information to the procedure.

Understanding Call By Reference And Call By Value

Procedure arguments are passed in one of two ways: by reference or by value. When an argument is passed by reference (the default), the memory address of the variable is passed as the argument. The called procedure can therefore change the actual value of the argument. When an argument is passed by value, the current value of the variable is determined, and the procedure receives only a copy of the variable. Thus, if the procedure changes the value of the variable, only the copy is modified; the value of the actual variable remains unchanged. The keywords **ByRef** and **ByVal** indicate that an argument is passed by reference and by value, respectively. If the keyword is omitted, the argument is passed by reference. For example, consider the following **Function** and **Sub** procedures:

```
Public Sub SquareSub(ByRef plngResult As Long, _
    ByVal pintArg As Integer)
    plngResult = pintArg * pintArg
End Sub

Public Function SquareFn(ByVal pintArg As Integer) As Long
    SquareFn = pintArg * pintArg
End Function
```

These two procedures illustrate different approaches to computing the square of a number. In the **Sub** procedure, the result (plngResult) is passed as an argument. Using this approach, the result is declared by reference so that it can be communicated back to the calling procedure. In the **Function** procedure, the function returns the result.

When a procedure returns a single value, a **Function** procedure is generally considered preferable because the code is more intuitive. A procedure that must return multiple values, however, must be implemented as a **Sub** procedure. Each value to be returned must take the form of a **ByRef** argument.

The following statements could be used to call the two procedures. The statements assume that txtInput and txtOutput are text boxes, and that txtInput contains a valid **Integer** number.

```
SquareSub txtOutput.Text, txtInput.Text
Call SquareSub(txtOutput.Text,txtInput.Text)
txtOutput = SquareFn(txtInput.Text)
```

The first two statements illustrate equivalent techniques to call a **Sub** procedure. If you omit the **Call** statement, the procedure's arguments must be separated by commas, but the parentheses are omitted. If you use the **Call** statement, parentheses must surround the arguments.

Scope

Variables can be declared in the general declarations section of a module or inside a procedure. A variable declared in the general declarations section of a standard module exists for the life of the program. A variable declared in the general declarations section of a class or form module exists for as long as an instance of the form or class exists; a unique copy of the variable exists for each form or class instance. In contrast, a variable declared inside a procedure is allocated from the stack and exists only while the procedure is executing (unless you use the **Static** keyword). The stack is an area of memory used to store local variables and keep track of procedures called.

Variables have a defined scope. The scope of a variable determines both how long the variable remains in existence and whether a variable can be referenced by other procedures in a module or by procedures in other modules. The scope of a variable depends on where in the module the variable is declared and which statement is used to declare the variable. Variables are declared explicitly with **Public**, **Private**, **Static**, or **Dim** statements. Figure 2.4 details the scope of variables in two separate modules.

In Figure 2.4, the variable **gstrName** is a global variable visible to both the standard module and the form module. Changing its value in one module affects its value in all other modules. In contrast, the variable **mintName** is a module-level variable that is visible only to the standard module. Attempting to use this variable in the form module will generate a syntax error, assuming that the module includes the **Option Explicit** statement. The general procedure named **PrivateProcedure** (because it is declared as **Private**) can be called only by procedures in the standard module. Attempting to call this procedure from the form module will generate a syntax error. Also in Figure 2.4, the **Static** variable **pintCount** is local to **PrivateProcedure**. Because it is declared as **Static**, however, the variable's value persists while the program continues to run. The next statement in the procedure adds one (1) to the variable **pintCount**. Thus **pintCount** will have a value of one (1) after the procedure is called the first time, a value of two (2) the second time it is called, and so on. **PublicProcedure** is visible to both the standard module and form module.

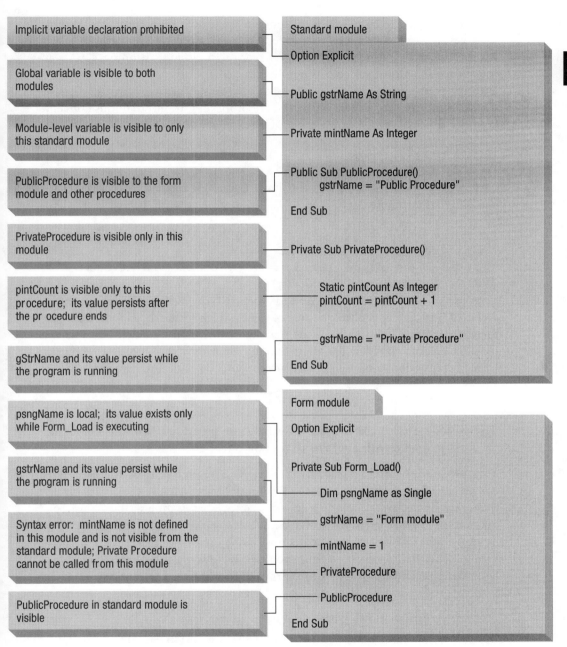

Figure 2.4   Variable and procedure scope.

Finally, the variable **psngNam**e is local to the event procedure named
Form_Load. Memory for this variable is allocated when the procedure starts
and deallocated when the procedure ends.

Public variables declared in a form module are treated differently than **Public** variables declared in a standard module. When declared in a standard module, a **Public** variable continues to exist whenever the program is running. That is, it is considered a global variable. When declared in a form module, however, a **Public** variable is treated as a property of the form, because a form is a class and **Public** variables declared in a class are properties. To illustrate this concept, consider the following example using a label named **lblDemo**:

```
lblDemo.Caption = "Prompt"
```

Assume that you have declared the following variable in the form module named **frmProperties**:

```
Public ControlType As String
```

The variable **ControlType** is treated as a property of the form **frmProperties**. Thus, to reference the variable (property) from another form, you would use the same syntax as needed to read or write a property. Note that the variable is named **ControlType**, which violates the rule of using a three-character prefix to denote the variable's type. This variable name was chosen intentionally. Public variables in a form module are considered properties, so the variable name conforms to the naming conventions for properties. Property names do not utilize a prefix.

```
frmProperties.ControlType = "Label"
```

The preceding statement sets the **ControlType** property (**Public** variable) for the form named **frmProperties** to the value "Label".

Your program requires several variables that will be used only by the main form named **frmCh2**. As multiple procedures on the form will use these variables, they must be declared as module-level variables. That is, the variables must be declared as **Private** variables in the general declarations section of the form module. Other variables must be declared to be used by both the form named frmCh2 and the form named frmProperties. Technically, these variables could be declared as **Public** in either form. You will declare them in the form named frmProperties, however, because the variables pertain to that form.

To declare **Public** and **Private** variables in a form module:

1. Start Visual Basic and open the project file named Chapter.02\Startup\ Ch2_S.vbp. Activate the Code window for the form module named **frmCh2**. (To open the Code window for a module, highlight the desired module in the Project Explorer, then click on the View Code button.) Make sure that you activate the Code window for the correct form.

2. Enter the following statements in the general declarations section of the form module after the **Option Explicit** statement. The Object list box

should display the text (General), and the Procedure list box should display the text (Declarations). Note that the module contains the words "Option Explicit." This statement requires that variables be explicitly declared before they are used. This practice helps you avoid hard-to-locate errors that result from improper typing of a variable name. All modules described in this book will use the **Option Explicit** statement.

```
Private mintStartX As Integer
Private mintEndX As Integer
Private mintStartY As Integer
Private mintEndY As Integer
Private mintMaxLine As Integer
Private mintMaxBox As Integer
Private mintMaxLabel As Integer
Private mintCurrentLine As Integer
Private mintCurrentBox As Integer
Private mintCurrentLabel As Integer
```

The variables **mintStartX**, **mintStartY**, **mintEndX**, and **mintEndY** will store the *x,y* coordinates of the mouse pointer as the user draws lines and shapes on the form. As the user draws additional lines, shapes, and labels, your code will create additional instances of these different controls. The variables **mintMaxLine**, **mintMaxBox**, and **mintMaxLabel** will store the current count of each type of control. The remaining variables—**mintCurrentLine**, **mintCurrentBox,** and **mintCurrentLabel**—will identify the current control instance during editing.

3. Activate the Code window for the form module named **frmProperties**, then enter the following statements in the general declarations section of the module after the **Option Explicit** statement:

```
Public ControlType As String
Public ControlIndex As Integer
```

Once again, because you have declared these variables as Public within a form module, they are considered properties of the form and do not utilize a prefix denoting the data type. The first variable will store a string identifying a particular type of control. The second variable will store an index to identify a particular control instance in a control array. You will learn about control arrays later in this chapter.

Understanding Mouse And Keyboard Events

Although you have likely worked with common events like **Click** and **Change**, you may not have written code to respond to events that deal directly with individual keyboard characters or mouse actions. As the user presses and releases the mouse button, code must respond to these events, identifying which mouse button was pressed. In addition, you will create an event procedure that will execute as the user types individual characters at the keyboard. To accomplish these tasks, you must learn about the **MouseDown**, **MouseUp**, and **MouseMove** events.

Syntax

Private Sub Form_MouseDown(*button* As Integer, *shift* As Integer, *x* As Single, *y* As Single)

Private Sub *object*_MouseDown([*index* As Integer,]*button* As Integer, *shift* As Integer, *x* As Single, *y* As Single)

Private Sub Form_MouseUp(*button* As Integer, *shift* As Integer, *x* As Single, *y* As Single)

Private Sub *object* _MouseUp([*index* As Integer,]*button* As Integer, *shift* As Integer, *x* As Single, *y* As Single)

Dissection

➤ The **MouseDown** event occurs when the user presses a button on the mouse. The **MouseUp** event occurs when the user releases the button on the mouse.

➤ The *button* argument identifies which mouse button was pressed or released. The button can be represented by the following constant values: **vbLeftButton**, **vbRightButton**, or **vbMiddleButton**. Most PCs use a two–button mouse that has no middle button.

➤ The *shift* argument is commonly used with the *button* argument to detect the state of the Shift, Ctrl, and Alt keys. The following masks represent these values: **vbShiftMask**, **vbCtrlMask**, and **vbAltMask**.

➤ The *x* and *y* arguments specify the current location of the mouse pointer. These values correspond to the coordinate system established by the **ScaleHeight**, **ScaleWidth**, **ScaleLeft**, and **ScaleTop** properties of the object.

➤ The *index* argument is used if the object is a member of a control array.

Code Example

```
Private Sub Form_MouseDown(Button As Integer, _
    Shift As Integer, X As Single, Y As Single)
    Select Case Button
        Case vbLeftButton
            Debug.Print "Left mouse button"
        Case vbMiddleButton
            Debug.Print "Middle mouse button"
        Case vbRightButton
            Debug.Print "Right mouse button"
    End Select
```

```
        If Shift = vbShiftMask Then
            Debug.Print "Shift"
        End If

        If Shift = vbCtrlMask Then
            Debug.Print "Ctrl"
        End If

        If Shift = (vbCtrlMask + vbShiftMask) Then
            Debug.Print "Ctrl and Shift"
        End If
    End Sub
```

Code Dissection

The **MouseDown** event procedure executes when the user presses a mouse button. It occurs for the form itself or for a control instance on the form. The **Select Case** statement uses constants to determine which mouse button was pressed. The **If** statements determine whether the Shift, Ctrl, or Shift + Ctrl keys were pressed at the time of the event.

In addition to the **MouseDown** and **MouseUp** events, you can detect the **MouseMove** event, which occurs when the mouse moves to a new position on the form.

Syntax

Private Sub Form_MouseMove(*button* As Integer, *shift* As Integer, *x* As Single, y As Single)

Private Sub *object*_MouseMove([*index* As Integer,] *button* As Integer, *shift* As Integer, *x* As Single, *y* As Single)

Dissection

➤ The **MouseMove** event occurs repeatedly whenever the user moves the mouse. This event occurs for either the form or the control instance where the insertion point is positioned. If the user holds down the mouse button and moves the mouse, the MouseMove event continues to apply to the same object, even if the mouse pointer is moved off that object.

➤ The *button* argument is used to detect whether the user pressed one or more buttons on the mouse.

➤ The *shift, x*, and *y* arguments have the same purpose as they do with the **MouseDown** and **MouseUp** events.

➤ The *index* argument is used if the object is a member of a control array.

Code Example
```
Private Sub Form_MouseMove(Button As Integer, _
    Shift As Integer, X As Single, Y As Single)
    Debug.Print "Form cursor at X,Y"; X, Y
End Sub
```

Code Dissection

The code for the **MouseMove** event prints the X and Y coordinates of the form as the user moves the mouse. These events occur repeatedly as the mouse changes its location.

In addition to writing code that responds to specific mouse events, you can write code that responds to keyboard events. Two techniques to process keyboard events exist: responding to the **KeyPress** event and responding to the **KeyDown** and **KeyUp** events.

The logic of the **KeyPress** event utilizes the character set used by Windows. This 8-bit character set was formalized by the American National Standards Institute (ANSI); it is commonly referred to as ASCII or ANSI. The character set consists of 256 characters. The first 128 characters represent the letters and symbols on the keyboard; the second 128 characters represent special characters and international characters. The digits 0 through 9 have corresponding ASCII values of 48 through 57. The lowercase letters a through z have ASCII values of 97 through 122, and the uppercase letters A through Z have ASCII values of 65 through 90. These **Integer** values are referred to as ASCII character codes. To review the complete list of the ASCII characters and their corresponding character codes, access the ASCII Help topic in the MSDN Library.

The **KeyPress** event interprets the state of the keyboard and returns an ASCII character every time the user presses a key on the keyboard. That is, the **1** event determines the state of certain keys before returning a character. For example, lowercase and uppercase letters are recognized as separate characters. As such, the **KeyPress** event will interpret whether the user has pressed the Shift key and return an uppercase or lowercase letter accordingly.

Syntax

Private Sub Form_KeyPress(*keyascii* As Integer)
Private Sub *object*_KeyPress([*index* As Integer,] *keyascii* As Integer)

Dissection

➤ The **KeyPress** event occurs each time the user types a character at the keyboard.

➤ *Object* is the name of a control instance created on a form.

➤ The *keyascii* argument contains an **Integer** representing the ASCII character that was pressed. If the value of the argument is set to zero (0) in the event procedure, then the keystroke is canceled and the object will not return the character.

➤ If *object* is a member of a control array, *index* contains an **Integer** value that uniquely identifies a control instance.

Code Example

```
Private Sub txtID_KeyPress(KeyAscii As Integer)
    If KeyAscii <> 8 And _
        (KeyAscii > 57 Or KeyAscii < 48) Then
        KeyAscii = 0
    End If
End Sub
```

Code Dissection

These statements determine whether the ASCII character is a digit between 0 and 9 or the backspace character (ASCII code of 8). The ASCII character codes are used because the **KeyAscii** argument contains **Integer** values. If the input character does not fall within the correct range, then **KeyAscii** is set to zero (0) and the keystroke is therefore ignored.

Some characters used by Windows—and most computers for that matter—are not part of the ANSI character set. For example, most keyboards contain keys like Home, End, Page Up, and Page Down. To process these characters, you use the **KeyDown** and **KeyUp** event procedures.

 As a general rule, it is more complex to process **KeyDown** and **KeyUp** events than to handle the **KeyPress** event. When you are programming ASCII characters, you should therefore use the **KeyPress** event. When you are programming function keys and other special keys, use the **KeyDown** or **KeyUp** events.

The **KeyDown** and **KeyUp** events do not return a character. Rather, they return the state of the keyboard. For example, if the user typed an uppercase "C", the **KeyDown** event returns a result indicating that the Shift key has been pressed plus the key code for the letter "c."

Syntax

Private Sub Form_KeyDown(*keycode* As Integer, *shift* As Integer)
Private Sub *object*_KeyDown([*index* As Integer,] *keycode* As Integer, *shift* As Integer)

Private Sub Form_KeyUp(keycode As Integer, *shift* As Integer)
Private Sub *object*_KeyUp([*index* As Integer,] *keycode* As Integer, *shift*
As Integer)

Dissection

➤ The **KeyDown** event occurs when the user presses a key, and the **KeyUp**
event occurs when the user releases the key.

➤ *object* is the name of a control instance created on the form.

➤ The *keycode* argument contains a constant value for the pressed key. (See the
Help topic "Keycode constants" for a list of these constants.)

➤ The *shift* argument contains a bit field indicating whether the user has
pressed the Shift, Ctrl, or Alt key. Bit 0 represents the Shift key, bit 1
indicates the Ctrl key, and bit 2 identifies the Alt key. These arguments are
treated as bit fields in the same way as in the **MouseDown** and **MouseUp**
events.

➤ The *index* is used when the *object* is a member of a control array.

Code Example

```
Private Sub txtAddress_KeyDown(Index As Integer, _
    KeyCode As Integer, Shift As Integer)
    If KeyCode = vbKeyHome And (Shift And vbAltMask) Then
        txtAddress.SetFocus
    End If
End Sub
```

Code Dissection

This event procedure determines whether the Home key and Alt key were
pressed simultaneously. If so, then the text box named txtAddress(0) on the
form receives focus.

Normally, keyboard events occur for the control instance on the form that has
focus. Sometimes, however, the form should be able to intercept keyboard
events. For example, consider the previous situation, in which the Alt + Home
key combination sets the focus to a text box. In this case, the code in the
KeyDown event pertains to a text box rather than the form. Thus, if a different
object than the text box has focus, the keyboard sequence would have no effect.

Two solutions to this problem exist. First, you can duplicate the code for the
KeyDown event for all objects on the form. Alternatively, the form can
intercept the keyboard events before they are processed by a specific control
instance. To cause a form to intercept keyboard events, you set the **KeyPreview**

property of a form to True. The keyboard events still occur for the control instance that has focus, but they occur for the form first, and then for the control instance with focus.

In the following steps, you will utilize the **KeyPress** event to validate input. The end user will use the form named **frmProperties** to enter either a new position or a new size for a particular line, shape, or label. In each case, the input must be an **Integer** number. One possible input validation technique involves the IsNumeric classification function. You can also use the **KeyPress** event to dispose of all characters except for the characters zero (0) through nine (9). Using this event, you could write an event procedure for each text box on the form. Because all input objects on this form are text boxes and all text boxes must contain **Integers**, however, you can preview the characters in the form and write code for only one event procedure.

To validate input using the **KeyPress** event:

1. Activate the Code window for the form named frmProperties, if necessary. Activate the **Form_KeyPress** event procedure, and then enter the following statements:

```
If KeyAscii <> 8 And _
    (KeyAscii > 57 Or KeyAscii < 48) Then
    KeyAscii = 0
End If
```

2. Activate the Properties window for the form named frmProperties.

3. Set the **KeyPreview** property to True, if necessary. The keystrokes will be intercepted by the form before being passed to the text boxes.

Consider carefully the code you just wrote. The **If** statement determines whether the character entered at the keyboard has an ASCII character code of 8 or is between 48 and 57. The key having an **Integer** value of 8 allows the backspace key to be passed to the text boxes. The character codes 48 through 57 represent the digits 0 through 9. If the character typed is not one of these keys, then it is discarded—that is, the value of **KeyAscii** is set to zero. The passing of the backspace key to the text boxes is significant. If the program discarded this key, then the user could not press the backspace key to remove a character. This event procedure executes each time the user types a character on the form because you set the **KeyPreview** property to True.

The Basics Of Form Events

In any application that operates with multiple forms, you must know how to display and hide forms and respond to the events that occur as these forms are displayed and hidden. When a form appears on the screen, it is displayed in one of two ways. A form can appear as a modeless form, meaning that the other forms in the program can receive input focus while this form remains active. Alternatively, a form can appear as a modal form, meaning that no other form in the program can receive input focus while it remains active. That is, the user cannot type characters or click on buttons on other forms until the modal form is closed or hidden. A form can be explicitly displayed and hidden using the **Show** and **Hide** methods.

Syntax

object.**Show** [style] [, ownerform]
object.**Hide**

Dissection

➤ The optional *object* must be a valid instance of a form.

➤ The **Show** method causes the form referenced by *object* to appear on the screen and receive focus.

➤ The **Hide** method causes the form referenced by *object* to become invisible. The memory allocated to the form and its objects still exist, however, and can be referenced with code.

➤ The optional *style* argument determines whether the form is displayed as modal or modeless form. The constants **vbModal** and **vbModeless** display the form as a modal or modeless form, respectively. If you omit this argument, the form appears as a modeless form.

➤ The optional *ownerform* identifies which form owns the new form.

Code Example

```
Form1.Show vbModal
Me.Hide
```

Code Dissection

The first statement displays the form named Form1 as a modal form, which receives focus. Until the modal form is closed, no other form in the program can receive focus. The second statement hides the current form. The form remains loaded, and you can reference it with code.

Note the use of the **Me** keyword, which provides a reference to the active form instance. The **Me** keyword will be discussed in future chapters when you create multiple instances of the same form.

In addition to the **Show** and **Hide** methods, the **Load** and **Unload** statements load and unload a form, respectively.

Syntax
Load object
Unload object

Dissection

➤ The **Load** statement loads a form into memory. The form does not appear on screen until the program calls the **Show** method. Even though the form is not visible, its objects can still be referenced with code.

➤ Calling the **Unload** statement removes the form from the screen and memory. Once unloaded, the Form object no longer exists and cannot be referenced. Unloading all the forms from a program has the effect of ending the program.

➤ The *object* placeholder must be a valid instance of a Form object.

Code Example

```
Load Form1
Unload Me
```

Code Dissection

The first statement loads the form named Form1. The second statement unloads the current form.

Several events occur to a Form object as it is loaded and unloaded. It is possible to write code for these events that performs initialization tasks when the form loads and housekeeping tasks when the form unloads. The following list summarizes the events that occur to a form as it is loaded:

1. The **Initialize** event occurs first, when an instance of a form is created initially. Remember that a form instance is created from a class. This event is commonly used to initialize data before the form loads.

2. The Load event occurs after the **Initialize** event. The code in this event procedure is also used to initialize the value of control instances and data.

3. The Activate event occurs after the **Load** event, when the form becomes the active form.

The **Initialize** and **Load** events occur when a form is loaded into memory. They do not occur repeatedly as a form receives and loses focus, however. Each time a form receives focus, the **Activate** event occurs. Each time it loses focus, the Deactivate event occurs. When a form is unloaded, three events occur:

1. The **QueryUnload** event occurs before a form is unloaded from memory.

2. After the **QueryUnload** event occurs, the **Unload** event occurs.

3. The **Terminate** event occurs after the **Unload** event.

In this chapter, you will work with multiple forms. In subsequent chapters, you will work more with these different form events.

Control Arrays

It is possible to create multiple instances of a control in such a way that each control instance has the same name and shares the same event procedures. For example, it is possible to create five instances of a Label control, all with the same name. In this situation, each label would execute the same code in response to the same event. A control array is a group of controls that share the same name and class (that is, they are all created from the same type of control). Conceptually, a control array is identical to any other array. It has multiple elements of the same type (control) and individual elements are referenced using an index (subscript).

A unique copy of the properties exists for each control instance in a control array. The **Index** property identifies each specific control instance in a control array. When an event procedure is called, the **Index** property of the active object is passed as an argument to the event procedure. This value is used to determine which control in the control array is active.

In Figure 2.5, three labels are defined in the control array named lblArray. The elements have Index values of zero (0), one (1), and two (2). Each element has a

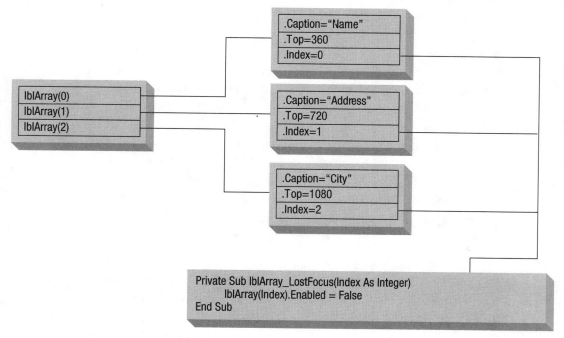

Figure 2.5   Control array.

unique copy of its properties. Its **Index** property identifies each particular element (control instance) in the control array. When an event procedure executes for an element in a control array, the index of the pertinent control is passed as an argument to the event procedure. Figure 2.5 illustrates this process.

Control arrays are useful for several reasons:

➤ They improve program efficiency by reducing the number of event procedures and the amount of code. The resulting modules are smaller in size, which reduces the load time.

➤ Performance is improved because a control array uses fewer resources than do multiple instances of the same control.

➤ Control arrays allow you to create and delete control instances at run time. When a new instance of a control array member is created at run time, the new control instance inherits the properties of the first element in the control array. That is, the new control instance has the same properties as the first element in the control array. Note, however, that the **Visible** property of the new control instance is initially set to False (the control instance is invisible).

Although you can add a control instance to a control array at run time, control arrays must be created at design time. You can apply three techniques to create a control array:

➤ Changing the **Name** property of a control instance to the same name as another control instance will cause a dialog box to appear. Depending upon your response to the dialog box, a control array will be created or the **Name** property will be reset to its original value.

➤ Changing the **Index** property to a value that is not Null will create a control array.

➤ When copying and pasting a control instance using the Windows Clipboard, a dialog box appears asking whether you want to create a control array. If no control array is created, Visual Basic assigns a default name to the object.

 Index values typically begin at zero (0) and are incremented by one (1) for each element in the control array. It is possible, however, to assign nonsequential index values. The maximum index for a control array is 32,767, although this limitation seldom poses a problem. Typically, control arrays are used with option buttons and menus. When labels must serve as descriptive prompts, consider using a control array for these labels, as the control array is slightly more efficient.

Mentor Graphics is developing a prototype for a drawing program. The drawing program must allow the user to draw lines and boxes on a form along with descriptive text stored in a label control instance. The user must also be able to change the position of existing lines, boxes, and labels and delete them as necessary. Finally, the user should be able to create, edit, and delete descriptive prompts.

The user will click on buttons, causing your code to create additional control instances at run time. You must therefore implement these control instances as control arrays. Remember that a control array cannot be created at run time; it is created at design time. You need to create Line, Shape, and Label control arrays.

To create a control array:

1. Activate the form named frmCh2.

2. Using the Shape control button, create an instance of the Shape control on the form. Set the Name property to **shpArray**, and set the **Index** property to 0. Set the **Visible** property to False so that the control instance will not appear at run time. Note that the three-character prefix for the Shape control is "shp".

3. Using the Line control button, create an instance of the Line control on the form. Set the **Name** property to **linArray**, and set the **Index** property to 0. Set the **Visible** property to False. Note that the three-character prefix for the Line control is "lin".

4. Using the Label control button, create an instance of the Label control on the form. Set the **Name** property to **lblArray**, and set the **Index** property to 0. Again, set the **Visible** property to False. Also, set the **BorderStyle** to 1 − Fixed Single.

Once a control array has been created at design time, the **Load** and **Unload** statements can be used to add and remove elements from the control array at run time. Note that these statements differ from the form methods of the same name.

Syntax
Load object(index–value)
Unload object(index–value)

Dissection

➤ The **Load** statement creates a new control instance in a preexisting control array. The properties of the new control array instance are inherited from the first element in this control array. Note that the new control instance is initially invisible.

➤ The **Unload** statement unloads a control array instance. It can be used only on elements created at run time with the **Load** statement.

➤ The *object* must be an element of an existing control array.

➤ The *index-value* contains an Integer number identifying the object location in the control array. When you seek to add an element to a control array, the *index-value* must not already be in use.

2

Code Example

```
Load lblArray(1)
lblArray(1).Caption = "Demo"
Unload lblDemo(1)
```

Code Dissection

Assuming that there is a control array named lblDemo, the **Load** statement creates a second element in the control array with an index of one (1), and the last statement destroys the control array instance created by this Load statement. The syntax to reference an element in a control array matches that used for arrays. In this code example, lblDemo(1) provides a reference to a particular element, and Caption references the **Caption** property for that element. A control array supports the **UBound** and **LBound** run-time properties to determine the largest and smallest index values, respectively, in a control array. Assuming that there is a control array named lblArray, the following statements will reference the lower and upper bounds in the control array, respectively.

```
Debug.Print lblArray.LBound
Debug.Print lblArray.Ubound
```

Ultimately, your drawing program will create additional instances of Line, Shape, and Label controls. So that you can see how to create control array instances at run time, you will now create a simple prototype that will create additional instances of the Label control. The code will work as follows:

➤ When the user presses the left mouse button, the starting *x,y* coordinates will be recorded. You will save these coordinates in the **mintStartX** and **mintStartY** variables that you declared earlier in the chapter.

➤ When the user releases the mouse button, the ending *x,y* coordinates will be recorded. You will save these coordinates in the **mintEndX** and **mintEndY** variables.

➤ Then, calling the **Load** statement will create a new instance of the Label control.

➤ Next, the position of the label will be set.

➤ Finally, you will keep track of the number of elements in the control array in the variable **mintMaxLabel**.

To create control array instances at run time:

1. Activate the Code window to the **Form_MouseDown** event procedure for the form named frmCh2, and then enter the following statements:

```
If Button = vbLeftButton Then
    mintStartX = X
    mintStartY = Y
End If
```

2. Activate the Code window to the **Form_MouseUp** event procedure in the same form, and then enter the following statements:

```
If Button <> vbLeftButton Then
    Exit Sub
End If
mintEndX = X
mintEndY = Y
mintMaxLabel = mintMaxLabel + 1
Load lblArray(mintMaxLabel)
With lblArray(mintMaxLabel)
    .Top = mintStartY
    .Left = mintStartX
    .Width = mintEndX - mintStartX
    .Height = mintEndY - mintStartY
    .Visible = True
End With
```

The code in the **Form_MouseDown** event procedure saves the starting x and y coordinates to the variables **mintStartX** and **mintStartY**, respectively. The code in the **Form_MouseUp** event procedure saves the ending x and y coordinates to the variables **mintEndX** and **mintEndY**, respectively. Consider carefully the following statements:

```
mintMaxLabel = mintMaxLabel + 1
Load lblArray(mintMaxLabel)
```

The first time the program calls this procedure, the variable **mintMaxLabel** has a value of zero (0). Remember, you already created one instance of the Label control also having an index value of zero (0). The variable **mintMaxLabel** is incremented by one (1), and the value of the variable serves as the argument to the **Load** statement. Thus, the first time this statement executes, the new instance of the Label control has an index value of one (1). The second time the procedure executes, the index is 2, and so on. Note that the original control instance is never actually used. Rather, this instance serves as a template for creating additional control instances. This technique simplifies the program considerably.

```
With lblArray(mintMaxLabel)
    .Top = mintStartY
    .Left = mintStartX
    .Width = mintEndX - mintStartX
    .Height = mintEndY - mintStartY
    .Visible = True
End With
```

The preceding statements set the positional properties of the newly created label and make it visible. The **Top** and **Left** properties are set to the variables **mintStartY** and **mintStartX**, respectively. To calculate the **Width** and **Height** properties, the code subtracts the ending x coordinate from the starting x coordinate. Note that this program has a flaw—the user must draw the label from the upper-left corner to the lower-right corner or an error will occur. This problem arises because the code attempts to set the **Height** and **Width** properties to a negative value. You will overcome this deficiency later in the chapter. Note also that the preceding code uses the With statement as a shorthand notation to reference the same object repeatedly. If you are not familiar with the **With** statement, refer to the MSDN Library.

You can now test your work to ensure that the program is working correctly.

To test the label control array:

1. Test the program. That is, save the program and then run it.

2. When the main form appears, hold down the left mouse button and move the mouse to the position where the lower-right corner of the label should appear. Release the mouse button. The label should appear on the form.

3. Repeat Step 2 to create an additional label.

4. End the program to return to design mode.

You have now completed the programming for this section, which showed you how to work with keyboard and mouse events and how to create control arrays.

Working With Menus

Adding A Menu To An Application

In Visual Basic, menus are implemented as objects contained by a form. As such, each form can have a distinct menu. In Figure 2.6, each menu title, menu, submenu, and separator bar is considered a distinct menu item. Each of these objects has properties and can respond to a **Click** event. This behavior is analogous to that of a command button.

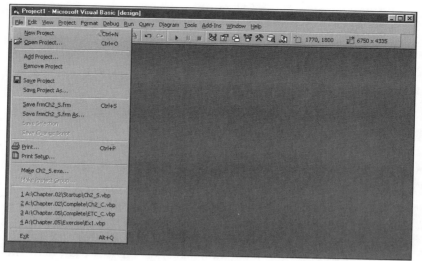

Figure 2.6 Anatomy of a menu.

Figure 2.6 identifies the different components of a menu, listed here:

➤ **Menu bar** Appears across the top of a form, just below the title bar.

➤ **Menu titles** Appear horizontally on the menu bar. A menu title contains menus.

➤ **Menu** May contain a combination of submenus, separator bars, and commands (also known as menu items). Selecting a menu item executes a command, much like clicking a command button. A menu can have a submenu.

➤ **Submenu** A menu item that displays another menu, rather than executing code in an event procedure.

➤ **Separator bar** A horizontal line that visually groups related menu items, thereby making the interface easier to use. Like all components of a menu, a separator bar must have a unique name or be a member of a control array. To create a separator bar, you set a command's **Caption** property to a hyphen (-).

➤ **Shortcut key** A function key (such as F5) or a key combination (such as Ctrl + A or Ctrl + X) that executes a command. Menu commands support shortcut keys; you cannot create a shortcut key for a menu title.

➤ **Hot Key** Also known as an access key, this is a key that the user presses while holding down the Alt key to open a menu or carry out a command. For example, Alt + F opens the File menu in most Windows applications.

➤ **Checked menu item** Works like a two-state control; that is, it can be checked or unchecked.

Several style guidelines will help you create menus that have a look and feel similar to those of menus in other Windows programs:

➤ A menu's caption should be short enough to appear on one line, but can contain multiple words to convey its purpose. In fact, a caption will not appear on multiple lines.

➤ When a menu's caption contains multiple words, the first letter of each word should be capitalized. Each word should be separated from the preceding and following words by a space.

➤ If a menu item displays a dialog box or requires the user to input other information, its caption should be followed by an ellipsis (...).

➤ To group related commands on a menu, use a separator bar.

➤ All menu titles, menus, and menu items should have access keys, as some users prefer to use the keyboard instead of the mouse.

➤ Create shortcut keys for the more frequently used commands. Such keys minimize the number of keystrokes needed to activate a command. When selecting characters for a shortcut key, use the same characters as employed in other programs. For example, many programs use Ctrl + P as the shortcut key for printing. Using the first character of the menu caption is also a common choice.

You write the code for a menu's **Click** event procedure in the same way as you would for a command button. That is, you can locate the object and event procedure in the Code window. Menus, like other objects, have standard prefixes and naming conventions. Use the following guidelines for menu naming:

➤ Menu names should begin with the prefix "mnu".

➤ A descriptive name should follow the prefix. This name should be the same as the menu title, but with the spaces removed.

➤ For menus and commands, the name should consist of the command preceded by the menu title, preceded by the menu prefix.

➤ To save typing, consider abbreviating the name if it exceeds 20 characters.

Using The Menu Editor

In Visual Basic, menus are created at design time using the Menu Editor. They can also be modified at run time. Each Menu object (menu title or command) supports a number of properties. Some of these properties can be set only by using the Properties window and are not available through the Menu Editor.

Syntax

   *Object.***Menu**

Properties

➤ The **Caption** property contains the text that appears on the menu.

➤ The **Name** property has the same purpose as it does with any other control instance. You use this name to reference the object at run time with code.

➤ The **Checked** property is used to create two-state menu items. A two-state menu item is similar to a checkbox—that is, its value either can be either True or False.

➤ The **Enabled** property can be either True or False. If set to True, the menu will respond to a **Click** event. If set to False, the menu appears grayed and will not respond to the **Click** event.

➤ The **Index** property is used to create a menu control array. A menu control array has the same characteristics as control arrays pertaining to other objects.

➤ The **Visible** property, when set to True, causes the menu to appear. If this property is set to False, the menu remains invisible. In this case, any submenus will not appear on the menu either.

➤ The **WindowList** property is used with multiple-document interface (MDI) programs. When set to True, the menu will list all open MDI child forms. Only one Menu object on a form can have the **WindowList** property set to True.

Events

Like a command button, Menu objects respond to the **Click** event.

The Menu Editor is an intelligent interface that you use to create instances of menu controls and set design-time properties. As a modal dialog box, it must be closed before you can interact with other windows in the project. This dialog box consists of two main sections: a properties section, which is used to set the properties of a menu control, and a list section, which displays the commands available and explains their relationship to one another. Figure 2.7 shows the Menu Editor with an already-created menu system.

As shown in Figure 2.7, some Menu objects are indented but others are not. The order of the menus in the list section has significance. For example:

➤ A menu that is not indented is considered a menu title.

➤ A menu that is indented once appears when the menu title is selected.

➤ Indenting a command more than once causes the command to appear as a submenu title.

➤ For menus in the list section, names indented at the same level appear on the same menu in the order that they appear in the Menu Editor.

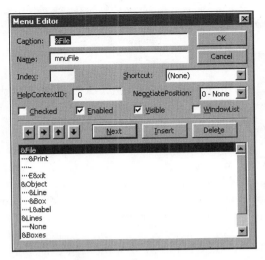

Figure 2.7   Menu Editor.

The Left and Right Arrow buttons on the Menu Editor decrease and increase, respectively, the indenting of the currently selected menu. Similarly, the Up and Down Arrow buttons move the currently selected menu up or down with respect to the previous or next menu displayed in the list section. The Next button either activates the next menu in the list section or adds a new menu if the last menu is currently selected. The Insert button inserts a menu just before the currently selected menu, and the Delete button removes the selected menu.

When the user clicks a menu item, the code that you wrote executes in response to its **Click** event procedure. The Print menu item on the File menu should print the control instances on the form. The Exit menu item should exit the program. Although you will write the code for the Print menu item later in this chapter, you already have the tools needed to write the code for the Exit menu item. The most common way to exit a program is to unload all of the program's forms. The **Unload** statement removes a form from memory. To reference the current form, you use the **Me** keyword. The following statement unloads the current form:

```
Unload Me
```

You can now write the code to unload the current form when the user clicks the Exit menu item on the File menu.

To code the **Click** event procedure for a menu item:

1. Activate the form named frmCh2, and make sure that Visual Basic is in design mode. On the form's menu, click on File, and then click on Exit on the menu bar. This approach offers the easiest way to activate the **Click** event procedure for a menu item.

2.   Enter the following statement in the **mnuFileExit_Click** event procedure:

```
Unload Me
```

3.   Test the program. On the main form's menu bar, click on File, and then click on Exit. Visual Basic should return to design mode.

The Object menu contains menu items named Line, Box, and Label. These menu items behave differently than the items on the File menu, instead working in a manner similar to an option group. That is, only one menu item from the list of menu items should be selected (marked with a checkbox) at any given time. To cause these three menu items to operate as checked menus, their **Checked** property was set to True during the creation of the menu system. You will now write the code to cause only one of the three menu items to be checked at any given time. This code will ensure that the user can check only one of the three menu items, and then create an instance of the desired control. When the form first loads, the **Checked** property should be set so that only one of the three menu items is checked. Although this decision is an arbitrary one, you will check the Line menu item initially. When the user checks a different menu item, the other items should be unchecked.

To create the check list of menu items:

1.   Activate the Code window for the form named **frmCh2**, select the **Form_Load** event procedure, and then enter the following statements:

```
mnuObjectLine.Checked = True
mnuObjectBox.Checked = False
mnuObjectLabel.Checked = False
```

2.   Activate the Code window for the **mnuObjectLine_Click** event procedure, and then enter the following statements:

```
mnuObjectBox.Checked = False
mnuObjectLabel.Checked = False
mnuObjectLine.Checked = True
```

3.   Enter the following statements in the **mnuObjectBox_Click** event procedure:

```
mnuObjectLine.Checked = False
mnuObjectLabel.Checked = False
mnuObjectBox.Checked = True
```

4. Enter the following statements in the **mnuObjectLabel_Click** event procedure:

```
mnuObjectBox.Checked = False
mnuObjectLabel.Checked = True
mnuObjectLine.Checked = False
```

2

5. Test the program and click on the Object menu. The Line menu item should appear checked. Next, click on the Box menu item.

6. Click on the Object menu again. The Box menu item should appear checked. Click on the Label menu item.

7. Click on the Object menu again. The Label menu item should appear checked.

8. End the program to return to design mode.

In addition to creating menus that appear on the menu bar, you can create menus that appear on various parts of the form when the user clicks the right mouse button on the form or on a particular control instance.

Adding A Pop-Up Menu To An Application

Visual Basic supports another type of menu, called a pop-up menu or shortcut menu. This menu does not appear automatically at the top of the form, but rather when the user right-clicks on the form or on a specific control instance on the form. Pop-up menus are useful for displaying different menus based on the active object or current state of the program. Only one pop-up menu can be displayed at a time.

Syntax
object.**PopupMenu** menuname, [flags] [, x, y] [,boldcommand]

Dissection

➤ The **PopupMenu** method displays the menu associated with the object.

➤ The optional *object* is typically a form. If you omit the *object* argument, then the program uses the form that has focus.

➤ The required *menuname* argument specifies which menu to display. The menu must have at least one submenu to be displayed as a pop-up menu.

➤ The optional *flags* argument controls the alignment of the menu around the insertion point or *x* and *y* coordinates. It also determines whether a **Click** event will be generated when the user clicks the left or left and right mouse buttons.

➤ The optional *x* and *y* arguments specify the *x,y* coordinates where the pop-up menu appears on the form. If omitted, the menu appears at the current insertion point position.

➤ The optional *boldcommand* indicates that the name of a menu control in the pop-up menu should display its caption in bold text. If omitted, no controls in the pop-up menu appear in bold.

Code Example

```
frmCh2.PopupMenu mnuPopUpLabel
```

Code Dissection

The preceding statement assumes that a menu named mnuPopUpLabel exists on the form named frmCh2. When this statement executes, the pop-up menu will appear.

In this example, you will create a pop-up menu that appears when the user clicks the right mouse button over an existing label. This pop-up menu contains three menu items: one item to delete the current label, a second to display a dialog box that enables the user to reposition the label, and a third that allows the user to change the label's caption. When creating a pop-up menu, you use the Menu Editor just as you would with other menu items. To ensure that the menu does not appear at run time, you can set the **Visible** property of the menu title to False.

To create a pop-up menu:

1. Activate the form named frmCh2.

2. Click on Tools, and then click on Menu Editor to activate the Menu Editor.

3. Use the scroll bars to locate the last line of the menu.

4. Click on the blank line following the None menu item on the Boxes menu.

5. Set the **Caption** property to **&mnuPopupLabel**, set the **Name** property to **mnuPopUpLabel**, and then remove the check from the *Visible* checkbox.

6. Click on the Next button to create a new menu item.

7. Set the **Caption** property to **&Delete**, and then set the **Name** property to **mnuPopUpLabelDelete**.

8. Click on the right arrow button to indent the menu. The menu should appear with four leading dots.

9. Create another menu. Set its **Caption** property to **&Properties** and its Name property to **mnuPopUpLabelProperties**. Make sure that the menu is indented with four leading dots.

10. Create a third menu. Set its **Caption** property to **&Caption** and its **Name** property to **mnuPopUpLabelCaption**. Make sure that the menu is indented with four leading dots. When complete, the menu and its menu items should appear in the Menu Editor as shown in Figure 2.8.

11. Click on OK to close the Menu Editor.

Now that the pop-up menu exists, you need to write the code that will execute when the user right-clicks an existing label. The control array of labels that you created earlier in the chapter is named lblArray. You can write the code to detect when the user clicks the mouse on one of the Label control instances in either the **MouseDown** or **MouseUp** event procedure. In this case, you will use the **MouseDown** event procedure, although the choice is arbitrary.

To display a pop-up menu:

1. In the form named frmCh2, activate the Code window for the **lblArray_MouseDown** event procedure, and then enter the following statements into the event procedure:

```
If Button = vbRightButton Then
    mintCurrentLabel = Index
    frmCh2.PopupMenu mnuPopUpLabel
End If
```

2. Test the program. Click and hold down the left mouse button. Move the mouse down and to the right to create an instance of the label.

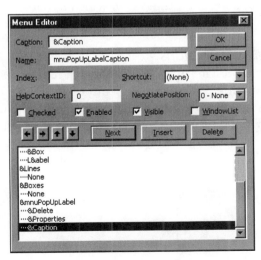

Figure 2.8   Menu Editor with pop-up menu created.

3. Right-click on the new label to display the pop-up menu. The pop-up menu should appear at the current mouse position.

4. End the program to return to design mode.

Consider carefully the statements you just wrote:

```
If Button = vbRightButton Then
    mintCurrentLabel = Index
    frmCh2.PopupMenu mnuPopUpLabel
End If
```

The **If** statement tests whether the user clicked the right mouse button. The pop-up menu should appear only if this button was clicked. Remember that a control array element is uniquely identified by its **Index** property. This value is passed as an argument to the event procedure. The value is saved to the variable **mintCurrentLabel**, enabling the program to identify which label control instance was selected; you will use this value shortly. Finally, the pop-up menu is displayed at the current cursor position.

Although the pop-up menu now exists, you have not yet written any code that will execute when the user clicks any of its menu items. When the user clicks the Delete menu item, the selected Label control instance should be deleted. The program can accomplish this task by unloading the selected control array element. When the user clicks the Properties menu item, a dialog box should appear, allowing the user to change the size and position of the label. When the user clicks the Caption menu item, he or she should be able to change the label's caption. Visual Basic supports two dialogs with which to obtain information from the user.

The InputBox And MsgBox Functions

The InputBox function displays a standard dialog box, which returns a **String** data type entered by the user. An input box has two buttons. If the user clicks the OK button, the text string entered as input will be returned. If the user clicks the Cancel button, an empty string is returned. In addition, the programmer can control the position of the input box on the screen. Figure 2.9 shows the parts of an input box.

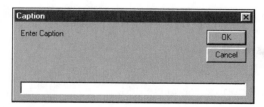

Figure 2.9 Input box.

Syntax

> **InputBox**(prompt [, title] [, default] [, xpos] [, ypos] [, helpfile, context])

Dissection

➤ The required *prompt* argument is a string expression displayed in the message portion of the dialog box. This string can span multiple lines using the carriage return or linefeed characters.

➤ The optional *title* argument is a string expression displayed in the title bar of the dialog box.

➤ The optional *default* argument places a default string expression in the text box portion of the dialog box.

➤ The optional *xpos* and *ypos* arguments specify the horizontal and vertical distance, in twips, from the left and top of the screen, respectively. If omitted, the dialog box is centered horizontally and the top of the box appears about one-third of the way down from the top of the screen.

➤ The optional *helpfile* and *context* arguments display a help message.

Code Example

```
Dim pstrFileName As String
pstrFileName = InputBox("Enter file name.", "Enter")
If pstrFileName = vbNullString Then
    Exit Sub
End If
```

Code Dissection

These statements call the InputBox function with the prompt "Enter file name." and the title "Enter". The **If** statement determines whether the user clicked the Cancel button by testing the string returned by the InputBox function. If this string is empty, then the user clicked the Cancel button; the **Sub** procedure therefore exits. Otherwise, the procedure continues to execute.

In addition to the input box dialog box, Visual Basic supports another standard dialog box for displaying a message to the user. This message box dialog can contain a message, title, icon, and buttons. Figure 2.10 shows a sample message box.

The message box shown in Figure 2.10 contains a prompt, an icon, a title bar, and two buttons. When the user clicks one of the buttons, the message box closes. The next statement in the program can then determine which button was clicked and perform the appropriate action.

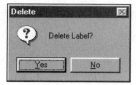

Figure 2.10   Message box.

Syntax

MsgBox(prompt[, buttons] [, title] [, helpfile, context])

Dissection

➤ The required *prompt* argument is a string expression displayed in the message portion of the dialog box. This string can span multiple lines using the carriage return or linefeed characters.

➤ The optional *title* argument is a string expression displayed in the title bar of the dialog box.

➤ The optional *helpfile* and ***context*** arguments display a help message.

➤ The optional *buttons* argument is a Long Integer value that defines the run-time characteristics of the dialog box. These characteristics are divided into six groups, with each group being represented as four bits in a **Long** Integer value. To set one value from each group, you can add a constant value from each group in an expression.

➤ The first group specifies how many buttons appear on the screen and sets the caption of each button. The value is determined through the following constants: **vbOKOnly**, **vbOKCancel**, **vbAbortRetryIgnore**, **vbYesNoCancel**, **vbYesNo**, and **vbRetryCancel**.

➤ The second group indicates the icon displayed in the message box. The valid icon constants are **vbCritical**, **vbQuestion**, **vbExclamation**, and **vbInformation**.

➤ The third group specifies a default button, which has the same effect as setting the **Default** property to True for a command button. The valid button constants are **vbDefaultButton1**, **vbDefaultButton2**, **vbDefaultButton3**, and **vbDefaultButton4**.

➤ The fourth group is used to make the dialog box application modal or system modal. If the dialog box is application modal, the user can interact with other applications while the dialog box appears on the screen. If the dialog box is system modal, all applications are suspended until the user closes the message box. The valid constants are **vbApplicationModal** and **vbSystemModal**.

➤ The fifth group adds a Help button and specifies the message box as the foreground window. The valid constants are **vbMsgBoxHelpButton** and **vbMsgBoxSetForeground**.

➤ The sixth group right-aligns the text and specifies the appearance of the text in right-to-left reading on Hebrew and Arabic systems. The valid constants are **vbMsgBoxRight** and **vbMsgBoxRtlReading**.

Code Example
```
Dim pintReturn As Integer
pintReturn = MsgBox("Delete Label?", vbYesNo + vbQuestion, _
    "Delete")
```

Code Dissection

The call to the MsgBox function creates a box with Yes and No buttons, as well as a question mark icon. If the user clicks the Yes button, the function returns the constant **vbYes**; otherwise, it returns the constant **vbNo**. The MsgBox function returns an **Integer** value indicating which button was clicked. Typically, an **If** or **Select Case** statement uses this value to determine which button was clicked and then executes code accordingly.

Table 2.2 lists the valid return constants, their values, and their descriptions.

To illustrate the use of constant values versus the underlying values, consider the following equivalent statements to display a message box:

```
pintReturn = MsgBox("Delete Label?", vbYesNo + vbQuestion, _
    "Delete")
pintReturn = MsgBox("Delete Label?", 4 + 32, _
    "Delete")
```

Table 2.2   MsgBox return values.

Constant	Value	Description
vbOK	1	OK
vbCancel	2	Cancel
vbAbort	3	Abort
vbRetry	4	Retry
vbIgnore	5	Ignore
vbYes	6	Yes
vbNo	7	No

The constant value for **vbYesNo** is 4, and the constant value for **vbQuestion** is 32. Thus the value of the button's argument is 36. Using the constants is much more intuitive for the programmer, however, because the purpose of the button is clearly defined in the call to the MsgBox function.

You now have the tools required to write the code for the Caption and Delete menus.

To write the code for a pop-up menu and to display an input box:

1. Activate the Code window for the form named frmCh2, and select the **mnuPopUpLabelCaption_Click** event procedure. Enter the following statements:

```
Dim pstrCaption As String
pstrCaption = InputBox("Enter Caption", "Caption")
lblArray(mintCurrentLabel).Caption = pstrCaption
```

2. Activate the Code window for the **mnuPopUpLabelDelete_Click** event procedure, and then enter the following statements:

```
Dim pintReturn As Integer
pintReturn = MsgBox("Delete Label?", vbYesNo _
    + vbQuestion, "Delete")
If pintReturn = vbYes Then
    Unload lblArray(mintCurrentLabel)
End If
```

3. Test the program. Click and hold down the left mouse button, move it down and to the right, and then release the mouse to create a new instance of the Label control.

4. Click the right mouse button while the cursor is positioned over the newly created label, and then select Caption to display the input box. Set the caption to Testing, and then click on OK. The new caption should appear in the label.

5. Click the right mouse button again, and select Delete to remove the control instance from the form. The message box should appear. Click on Yes to delete the Label control instance.

6. End the program to return to design mode.

Consider carefully the statements you just wrote to set the label's caption:

```
Dim pstrCaption As String
pstrCaption = InputBox("Enter Caption", "Caption")
lblArray(mintCurrentLabel).Caption = pstrCaption
```

First, you declared the variable named **pstrCaption** to store the new caption of the label. Next, you called the InputBox function to display the input box. The string entered by the user was then stored in the variable **pstrCaption**. Finally, you stored the variable's value into the **Caption** property of the currently selected label. Remember that you set the value of the module-level variable **mintCurrentLabel** to the currently selected label in the **lblArray_MouseDown** event procedure.

```
Dim pintReturn As Integer
pintReturn = MsgBox("Delete Label?", vbYesNo + vbQuestion, _
    "Delete")
If pintReturn = vbYes Then
    Unload lblArray(mintCurrentLabel)
End If
```

These statements display a message box to obtain user confirmation before deleting the Label control instance. If the user clicks the Yes button in the message box, pintReturn contains the constant value **vbYes**; otherwise, it contains the value **vbNo**. The If statement tests the return value, deleting the control instance only if the user clicked the Yes button.

At this point, you have written the code to create and destroy additional instances of Label controls, as well as to set their properties. In addition, you must write the code to create instances of Shape and Line controls. Before performing this task, consider carefully the technique employed to delete and change the caption of a label. In the case of the Label control, you displayed a pop-up menu when the user clicked the right mouse button. This technique will not work with the Line and Shape controls, however, because these controls neither respond to events nor receive input focus.

To solve this problem, you will use dynamic menus. On those menus, you will display the size and position of each label and shape instance. Two menus have already been created for this purpose. The Lines menu will list all lines drawn on the form, and the Boxes menu will display all shapes drawn by the user. Because these menus will be created and destroyed at run time, you must add and remove them as the control instances are created and destroyed.

To assist you with this process, the Lines and Boxes menus have already been created with one menu item. Each menu item is a control array with the caption None, indicating that no lines or boxes have been created. To add a menu to a control array, you call the Load function, just as you did with the Label control instance. To remove a menu from a control array, you call the Unload function to delete the control array element. Again, the process is the same as the one you used to destroy a Label control instance. The task to create the Line and Shape objects should take place in the **Form_MouseUp** event procedure—the same procedure that you used to create the Label control instances.

To create the Line and Shape control instances:

1. Activate the Code window for the **Form_MouseUp** event procedure for the form named frmCh2, and then enter the following statements

```
If Button <> vbLeftButton Then
    Exit Sub
End If
mintEndX = X
mintEndY = Y
    If mnuObjectLine.Checked Then

        mintMaxLine = mintMaxLine + 1
        Load linArray(mintMaxLine)
        With linArray(mintMaxLine)
            .X1 = mintStartX
            .Y1 = mintStartY
            .X2 = mintEndX
            .Y2 = mintEndY
            .Visible = True
        End With

        Load mnuLinesArray(mintMaxLine)
        mnuLinesArray(0).Visible = False
        With mnuLinesArray(mintMaxLine)
            .Visible = True
            .Caption = "From " & mintStartX & _
                "," & mintStartY & " To " & _
                mintEndX & "," & mintEndY
        End With
    End If
    If mnuObjectBox.Checked Then
        mintMaxBox = mintMaxBox + 1
        Load shpArray(mintMaxBox)
        With shpArray(mintMaxBox)
            .Top = mintStartY
            .Left = mintStartX
            .Width = mintEndX - mintStartX
            .Height = mintEndY - mintStartY
            .Visible = True
        End With
    Load mnuBoxesArray(mintMaxBox)
    mnuBoxesArray(0).Visible = False
```

2

```
With mnuBoxesArray(mintMaxBox)
    .Visible = True
    .Caption = "Top=" & _
        shpArray(mintMaxBox).Top & _
        " Left=" & shpArray(mintMaxBox).Left & _
        " Height=" & _
        shpArray(mintMaxBox).Height & _
        " Width=" & shpArray(mintMaxBox).Width
End With
End If
If mnuObjectLabel.Checked Then
    mintMaxLabel = mintMaxLabel + 1
    Load lblArray(mintMaxLabel)
    With lblArray(mintMaxLabel)
     .Top = mintStartY
     .Left = mintStartX
     .Width = mintEndX - mintStartX
     .Height = mintEndY - mintStartY
     .Visible = True
End With
End If
```

2. Test the program. Press the left mouse button, and then move the cursor down and to the right. Release the left mouse button to create a line.

3. Click on Object, and then click on Box. On the form, press and hold down the left mouse button. Move the mouse down and to the right, and then release the mouse button to create the shape on the form.

4. End the program to return to design mode.

Consider carefully the following code:

```
If Button <> vbLeftButton Then
    Exit Sub
End If
```

The **If** statement tests whether the user has clicked the left mouse button. If not, the procedure exits. The code consists of three **If** statements that determine which menu item on the Object menu is clicked.

```
If mnuObjectLine.Checked Then

    mintMaxLine = mintMaxLine + 1
    Load linArray(mintMaxLine)
    With linArray(mintMaxLine)
        .X1 = mintStartX
```

```
            .Y1 = mintStartY
            .X2 = mintEndX
            .Y2 = mintEndY
            .Visible = True
        End With

        Load mnuLinesArray(mintMaxLine)
        mnuLinesArray(0).Visible = False
        With mnuLinesArray(mintMaxLine)
            .Visible = True
            .Caption = "From " & mintStartX & _
                "," & mintStartY & " To " & _
                mintEndX & "," & mintEndY
        End With
End If
```

The first **If** statement executes when the user selects Line on the Object menu. The program increments the variable **mintMaxLine** to keep track of the number of Line control instances drawn on the form. The variable serves as the argument to **linArray** when the code calls the **Load** statement. The next four statements position the control instance on the form. The variables **mintStartX** and **mintStartY** were set in the **Form_MouseDown** event procedure, and the variables **mintEndX** and **mintEndY** were set at the beginning of this event procedure. Finally, the code makes the control instance visible.

The second block of statements adds a control instance to the menu control array named mnuLinesArray. Again, **mintMaxLine** serves as the index into the control array. First, the new instance is created when the code calls the **Load** statement. Next, the **Visible** property of control array element zero (0) is set to False, which hides the control array element with the caption None. Next, the **Visible** property of the new control array element is set to True. Finally, the **Caption** property is set to indicate the control's position on the form.

Consider the next block of code:

```
If mnuObjectBox.Checked Then
    mintMaxBox = mintMaxBox + 1
    Load shpArray(mintMaxBox)
    With shpArray(mintMaxBox)
        .Top = mintStartY
        .Left = mintStartX
        .Width = mintEndX - mintStartX
        .Height = mintEndY - mintStartY
        .Visible = True
    End With
    Load mnuBoxesArray(mintMaxBox)
```

```
    mnuBoxesArray(0).Visible = False
    With mnuBoxesArray(mintMaxBox)
        .Visible = True
        .Caption = "Top=" & _
            shpArray(mintMaxBox).Top & _
            " Left=" & shpArray(mintMaxBox).Left & _
            " Height=" & shpArray(mintMaxBox).Height & _
            " Width=" & shpArray(mintMaxBox).Width
    End With
End If
```

This **If** statement works with the Shape control instance rather than the Line control instance. Its structure is nearly identical to that of the **If** statement that works with the Line. The first block of statements creates a new instance of the Shape control and sets its properties. Instead of setting the **X1**, **X2**, **Y1**, and **Y2** properties, however, it specifies the **Top**, **Left**, **Width**, and **Height** properties. Finally, the **Visible** property for the new shape is set to True.

The second block of statements creates an instance of a menu control. As before, the only difference between this group of statements and the previous group is that the position indicators stored in the **Caption** property use the **Top**, **Left**, **Height**, and **Width** properties.

The final group of statements match the statements that you wrote at the beginning of the chapter. They operate on the Label control instance.

As you will recall from running the completed program, the Properties form enables the user to change the position of the control instances on the form. This form must appear on the screen when the user selects a line on the Lines menu, a shape on the Boxes menu, or Properties on the pop-up menu. You must therefore write the code for the following event procedures: **mnuBoxesArray_Click**, **mnuLinesArray_Click**, and **mnuPopUpLabelProperties**.

To display the Properties form:

1. For the form named frmCh2, activate the Code window for the **mnuBoxesArray_Click** event procedure, and then enter the following statements:

```
    If mnuBoxesArray(Index).Caption = "None" Then
        Exit Sub
    End If
    mintCurrentBox = Index
    With frmProperties
        .ControlType = "Shape"
        .ControlIndex = Index
        .txtHeight.Text = shpArray(mintCurrentBox).Height
```

```
      .txtLeft.Text = shpArray(mintCurrentBox).Left
      .txtTop.Text = shpArray(mintCurrentBox).Top
      .txtWidth.Text = shpArray(mintCurrentBox).Width
      .Caption = "Box"
      .Show vbModal
   End With
```

2. Activate the Code window for the **mnuLinesArray_Click** event procedure, and then enter the following statements:

```
If mnuLinesArray(Index).Caption = "None" Then
    Exit Sub
End If
mintCurrentLine = Index
With frmProperties
    .ControlType = "Line"
    .ControlIndex = Index
    .txtX1.Text = linArray(mintCurrentLine).X1
    .txtY1.Text = linArray(mintCurrentLine).Y1
    .txtX2.Text = linArray(mintCurrentLine).X2
    .txtY2.Text = linArray(mintCurrentLine).Y2
    .Caption = "Line"
    .Show vbModal
End With
```

3. Activate the Code window for the **mnuPopUpLabelProperties_Click** event procedure, and then enter the following statements:

```
With frmProperties
    .ControlType = "Label"
    .ControlIndex = mintCurrentLabel
    .txtHeight.Text = lblArray(mintCurrentLabel).Height
    .txtLeft.Text = lblArray(mintCurrentLabel).Left
    .txtTop.Text = lblArray(mintCurrentLabel).Top
    .txtWidth.Text = lblArray(mintCurrentLabel).Width
    .Caption = "Label"
    .Show vbModal
End With
```

Consider carefully the code that you just wrote for the **mnuBoxesArray_Click** event procedure, which displays the Properties form.

```
If mnuBoxesArray(Index).Caption = "None" Then
    Exit Sub
End If
mintCurrentBox = Index
```

These statements first check whether the Caption of the selected box is None. If so, this menu item represents the control instance created at design time and cannot be deleted. Thus, if the Caption is None, the procedure exits. The final statement sets the variable **mintCurrentBox**, which represents the current Index of the selected menu in the menu control array.

```
With frmProperties
    .ControlType = "Shape"
    .ControlIndex = Index
```

These statements set the **Public** variables on the form named **frmProperties**. The variable **ControlType** is set to the string "Shape" indicating the type of control to which the properties apply. The **ControlIndex** variable stores the control array index of the selected control. The form will use these two variables when the positional properties are reset. Again, the **With** statement was used to reduce typing.

```
.txtHeight.Text = shpArray(mintCurrentBox).Height
.txtLeft.Text = shpArray(mintCurrentBox).Left
.txtTop.Text = shpArray(mintCurrentBox).Top
.txtWidth.Text = shpArray(mintCurrentBox).Width
```

The Properties form contains four text boxes named txtHeight, txtLeft, txtTop, and txtWidth. These text boxes store the current position of the currently selected control instance.

```
 .Caption = "Box"
    .Show vbModal
End With
```

In the first statement, the form's caption is set to the string "Box", indicating the type of control that is being set. The next statement displays the form as a modal form, which prevents other forms in the program from receiving input focus until the modal form closes.

Ultimately, the Properties form will alter the positional properties of the selected control instance. The caption of the menu control array must therefore change to reflect the new position. Remember that the value of the variable **mintCurrentBox** is identical to the index of the Shape control instance to be modified. This index, in turn, is the same as the index for the menu control array.

```
If mnuLinesArray(Index).Caption = "None" Then
    Exit Sub
End If
mintCurrentLine = Index
```

These statements serve the same purpose as the nearly identical statements you wrote for the Shape control instance. They verify that the control array contains more than one element (line) before proceeding.

```
With frmProperties
    .ControlType = "Line"
    .ControlIndex = Index
```

These statements set the **Public** variables on the form named **frmProperties**. The variable **ControlType** is set to the string "Line", indicating the type of control instance to which the properties apply. The **ControlIndex** variable stores the control array index of the selected control instance. The form will use these two variables when resetting the positional properties.

```
.txtX1.Text = linArray(mintCurrentLine).X1
.txtY1.Text = linArray(mintCurrentLine).Y1
.txtX2.Text = linArray(mintCurrentLine).X2
.txtY2.Text = linArray(mintCurrentLine).Y2
```

The Index of the menu control array has the same value as the control array index of the control instance whose positional properties will be set. The current control array index is therefore stored in the variable **mintCurrentLine**. The Properties form contains four text boxes—txtX1, txtY1, txtX2, and txtY—that store the current position of the currently selected control instance.

```
    .Caption = "Line"
    .Show vbModal
End With
```

The form's caption is set to the string "Line", indicating the type of control that is being set. The next statement displays the form as a modal form.

The final event procedure executes when the user clicks the Properties pop-up menu.

```
With frmProperties
    .ControlType = "Label"
    .ControlIndex = mintCurrentLabel
```

These statements set the control type and the index of the selected control instance on the form named frmProperties. You will use these properties on the Properties form shortly.

```
.txtHeight.Text = lblArray(mintCurrentLabel).Height
```

```
.txtLeft.Text = lblArray(mintCurrentLabel).Left
.txtTop.Text = lblArray(mintCurrentLabel).Top
.txtWidth.Text = lblArray(mintCurrentLabel).Width
```

2

Like the statements in the previous two event procedures, the preceding statements read the positional properties of the currently selected Label control instance and store them in the text boxes on the form named frmProperties.

```
    .Caption = "Label"
    .Show vbModal
End With
```

Finally, the form's caption is set and then displayed as a modal form.

Next, you must write the code in the Properties form to update the value of the selected control instance. Figure 2.11 shows the Properties form at design time. Note that this form already includes control instances.

In Figure 2.11, one group of text boxes sets the x, y coordinates for Line control instances, and another group of text boxes sets the positional properties for both the Shape and Label control instances. In addition, the form contains descriptive prompts describing the text boxes and three command buttons. By clicking the OK command button, the user sets the positional properties of the selected control instance. Clicking the Cancel command button causes the changes to be ignored. The dialog box will close when the user clicks either command button. Finally, the Delete command button enables the user to remove the currently selected control instance.

When setting the properties for the Shape or Label controls, the user must work with the first column of text boxes. When setting the properties for the Line control, the second group of text boxes must be used. To ensure that the user cannot set the wrong control instances, you will enable and disable the appropriate text boxes depending upon the currently selected control instance. In the event procedures you just wrote to display the Properties form, you set

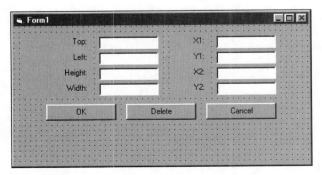

Figure 2.11   Properties form.

the variable **ControlType** to indicate the type of the currently selected control instance. This value will be employed to enable or disable the text boxes at run time. To enable or disable a control instance, you set the **Enabled** property to either True or False. Consider the following statements:

```
txtX1.Enabled = False
txtX1.Enabled = True
```

When the **Enabled** property for a control instance is set to False, it cannot receive focus or respond to events. When this property is set to True, the control can receive focus and respond to events. In addition to enabling and disabling a control instance, you can make it visible or invisible by setting the **Visible** property, as shown in the following statements:

```
txtX1.Visible = False
txtX1.Visible = True
```

These statements resemble those statements used for the **Enabled** property. The first statement makes the text box named txtX1 invisible, and the second statement makes the text box visible. Whether to enable or disable a control instance or make it visible or invisible is often a subjective choice. In this example, you will enable and disable the text boxes.

To enable and disable a control instance at run time:

1. Activate the Code window for the form named **frmProperties**, and then enter the following statements in the **Form_Load** event procedure:

```
Select Case ControlType
    Case "Label"
        Call SetupControls("HWTL")
    Case "Line"
        Call SetupControls("XY")
    Case "Shape"
        Call SetupControls("HWTL")
End Select
```

2. Create the following general procedure named **SetupControls**:

```
Private Sub SetupControls(pstrType As String)
    Select Case pstrType

        Case "HWTL"
            txtHeight.Enabled = True
            txtLeft.Enabled = True
            txtTop.Enabled = True
```

```
            txtWidth.Enabled = True
            txtX1.Enabled = False
            txtX2.Enabled = False
            txtY1.Enabled = False
            txtY2.Enabled = False
       Case "XY"
            txtHeight.Enabled = False
            txtLeft.Enabled = False
            txtTop.Enabled = False
            txtWidth.Enabled = False
            txtX1.Enabled = True
            txtX2.Enabled = True
            txtY1.Enabled = True
            txtY2.Enabled = True
      End Select
   End Sub
```

Consider carefully the code you just wrote.

```
Select Case ControlType
    Case "Label"
        Call SetupControls("HWTL")
    Case "Line"
        Call SetupControls("XY")
    Case "Shape"
        Call SetupControls("HWTL")
End Select
```

When the form loads, the type of the selected control instance is stored in the variable **ControlType**. The Sub value contains the string "Label", "Line", or "Shape". If the control type is a Shape or a Label, then the procedure **SetupControls** is called with the argument "**HWTL**". This is an arbitrary string meaning HeightWidthTopLeft. If the control is a Line, then the same **Sub** procedure is called with the argument "**XY**". Again, this is an arbitrary string indicating that *x,y* coordinates are being set.

The code for the **SetupControls** procedure is very simple. A **Select Case** statement determines the type of control passed in the argument named **pstrType**. If the type is "**HWTL**", then the text boxes in the left column are enabled and the text boxes in the right column are disabled. If the type is "**XY**", then the text boxes in the right column are enabled and the text boxes in the left column are disabled.

Now that you have set the necessary properties that will appear during the display of the Properties form, you must write the code that sets the positional properties if the user clicks the OK button or that abandons the changes if the user clicks the Cancel button. Remember that the current index of the control array is stored in the variable **ControlIndex** and that the control type is stored in the variable **ControlType**. You can use this information to set the positional properties of the current control.

To set the positional properties of the current control:

1. Activate the Code window for the form named frmProperties, and then select the **cmdOK_Click** event procedure. Enter the following statements in the event procedure:

```
Select Case ControlType
    Case "Label"
        With frmCh2.lblArray(ControlIndex)
            .Height = txtHeight.Text
            .Left = txtLeft.Text
            .Top = txtTop.Text
            .Width = txtWidth.Text
        End With
    Case "Line"
        With frmCh2.linArray(ControlIndex)
            .X1 = txtX1.Text
            .Y1 = txtY1.Text
            .X2 = txtX2.Text
            .Y2 = txtY2.Text
            frmCh2.mnuLinesArray(ControlIndex).Caption = _
                "From " & .X1 & "," & .Y1 & " To " & _
                .X2 & "," & .Y2
        End With
    Case "Shape"
        With frmCh2.shpArray(ControlIndex)
.Height = txtHeight.Text
.Left = txtLeft.Text
.Top = txtTop.Text
.Width = txtWidth.Text
frmCh2.mnuBoxesArray(ControlIndex).Caption = _
    " Top=" & .Top & _
    " Left=" & .Left & _
    " Height=" & .Height & _
    " Width=" & .Width
        End With
End Select

Unload Me
```

2. Activate the Code window for the **cmdCancel_Click** event procedure, and then enter the following statement:

```
Unload Me
```

3. Activate the Code window for the **cmdDelete_Click** event procedure, and then enter the following statements:

```
Dim pintReturn As Integer
pintReturn = MsgBox("Do you really want to delete?",_
    vbYesNo + vbQuestion, "Delete")
If pintReturn = vbNo Then
    Exit Sub
End If

Select Case ControlType
    Case "Label"
        Unload frmCh2.lblArray(ControlIndex)
    Case "Line"
        Unload frmCh2.lblArray(ControlIndex)
        Unload frmCh2.mnuLinesArray(ControlIndex)
    Case "Shape"
        Unload frmCh2.shpArray(ControlIndex)
        Unload frmCh2.mnuBoxesArray(ControlIndex)
End Select

Unload Me
```

Consider carefully the code you just wrote for the **cmdOK_Click** event procedure.

```
Select Case ControlType
    Case "Label"
        With frmCh2.lblArray(ControlIndex)
            .Height = txtHeight.Text
            .Left = txtLeft.Text
            .Top = txtTop.Text
            .Width = txtWidth.Text
        End With
```

This code determines the type of control by working with the **ControlType** variable. In the case of the label, you use the index of the currently selected control instance (stored in the variable **ControlIndex**) to save the data in the text boxes back to the control array. This action repositions the label on the main form. Note the syntax of the following statement fragment:

```
frmCh2.lblArray(ControlIndex)
```

The Label control instance appears on the form name frmCh2. Thus you must specify the form name followed by the control instance name. Because the label is a member of a control array, you used an index.

Consider the following code:

```
Case "Line"
 With frmCh2.linArray(ControlIndex)
        .X1 = txtX1.Text
        .Y1 = txtY1.Text
        .X2 = txtX2.Text
        .Y2 = txtY2.Text
           frmCh2.mnuLinesArray(ControlIndex).Caption = _
               "From " & .X1 & "," & .Y1 & " To " & _
               .X2 & "," & .Y2
 End With
```

The code to change the position line differ—but only slightly—from the code to reposition the label. The positional properties for the line are X1, X2, Y1, and Y2. In addition to resetting these positional properties, the code updates the text in the menu control array element. As a result, the menu item on the Lines array will contain the correct position.

The code to save the Shape control instance properties is essentially the same as the code to save the Line and Label control instance properties.

The code for the **cmdDelete_Click** event procedure also requires analysis.

```
Dim pintReturn As Integer
pintReturn = MsgBox("Do you really want to delete?", _
    vbYesNo + vbQuestion, "Delete")
If pintReturn = vbNo Then
    Exit Sub
End If

Select Case ControlType
    Case "Label"
        Unload frmCh2.lblArray(ControlIndex)
    Case "Line"
        Unload frmCh2.linArray(ControlIndex)
        Unload frmCh2.mnuLinesArray(ControlIndex)
```

```
    Case "Shape"
        Unload frmCh2.shpArray(ControlIndex)
        Unload frmCh2.mnuBoxesArray(ControlIndex)
End Select
```

2

These statements first request confirmation from the user to delete the selected element. If the user answers No, the procedure exits. Otherwise, it determines the control type and removes the control instance from the control array via an Unload statement. In the case of the Line and Shape controls, the menu item is removed as well. You should now test that the code you have written works correctly.

To test the properties form:

1. Test the program.

2. Create two instances of each control type.

3. Change the position of each control type.

4. Delete one of the Shape and Line control instances using the Properties form. Note that if you delete the last Line or Shape, an error will occur. This problem does not pertain to the Label control instances. You will correct this error in the next section.

At this point in the program's development, you have written the code that allows the user to add and delete control instances at run time. Furthermore, using the Properties form, the user can change the position of those control instances.

Working With Collections Of Controls And Handling Errors

Collections

An integral part of programming with objects in Visual Basic involves using a collection. A collection is similar to an array but supplies greater functionality. A brief review of arrays illustrates this concept. Arrays can store intrinsic data types, like **Integers** and **Strings**, and references to objects. For example, an array may reference command buttons, forms, or any other object. The use of an array, however, requires searching the array for a particular item. Also, if you do not know the size of an array at design time, it is necessary to redimension the array at run time to accommodate the addition of new elements. If an array element is deleted, the programmer must also take responsibility for tracking the deleted element.

Collections solve many of the problems associated with arrays. A collection can be envisioned as an object-based implementation of an array. It supports properties and methods to keep track of the number of members in the collection. In addition, a collection provides a mechanism to access a collection member—using a unique string key that avoids having to search each individual collection member. Methods to add and delete members from a collection are provided as well. The following list describes the properties and methods of most collections. Note, however, that some collections are more robust than others and supply additional properties and methods.

Syntax

    Collection

Properties

> ➤ The **Count** property contains the number of items in the collection.

Methods

➤ The **Add** method adds a new member to a collection.

➤ The **Item** method uses either a numeric index or a string key to locate a specific item in a collection. It is typically the default method of a collection.

➤ The **Remove** method deletes an item from a collection.

Visual Basic supports several intrinsic collections that keep track of the control instances on a form and the forms themselves. It is possible to iterate through the items in a collection in the same way as an array. Remember that arrays are, by default, zero-based—that is, the first element in an array has an index of zero (0). Using the Option Base statement, you can change the default lower bound of an array to one (1). Although collections are also zero-based or one-based, the lower bound of a collection cannot be changed. Whether a collection is zero-based or one-based depends on the collection itself. Collections created in earlier versions of Visual Basic generally are zero-based. Collections created in newer versions of Visual Basic, on the other hand, tend to be one-based, reflecting the general belief that one-based collections are more intuitive. Before using a collection, refer to the MSDN Library to determine whether a specific collection is one-based or zero-based.

The **Controls** collection, because it has been around since the beginning of Visual Basic, is zero-based. It contains a reference to each control instance drawn on a form and it is useful for setting the properties of several control instances simultaneously. To examine each element in an array or each member of a collection, you can use a **For** loop. Consider the following statements:

```
Dim pintCurrent As Integer
For pintCurrent = 0 to Controls.Count - 1
    Debug.Print Controls.Item(pintCurrent).Name
Next
```

2

These statements print the **Name** property of each control instance drawn on a form by using a **For** loop. The loop is initialized to 0, the first member of the **Controls** collection, and incremented to the value of the Count property –1. This approach is similar to referencing a zero-based array. The **Controls** collection, like other collections, supports the Item method to examine a specific element in the collection.

Because the **Item** method represents the default method for the **Controls** collection, you usually abbreviate the statement inside the previous For Loop as follows:

```
Debug.Print Controls(pintCurrent).Name
```

A collection does not store the objects managed by the collection. Rather, it stores a reference to the individual objects or, in other words, pointers to the objects. The statement fragment **Controls(pintCurrent)** provides a reference to a specific control instance. Using that reference, you can access any property or method, just as if the control instance name had been used.

Although the **For** loop works well for iterating through the members of a collection, Visual Basic supports a variation of a **For** loop—the **For Each** loop—that is designed specifically to examine all members of a collection.

Syntax
For Each *element* **In** *group*
            [*statements*]
        [**Exit For**]
            [*statements*]
        Next [*element*]

Dissection

➤ The required *element* must be an object variable of the same type as the objects in the collection, a general Object, or a Variant. That is, if you want to examine each Control object in the Controls collection, you must declare *element* as a Control object type, a Variant data type, or an Object data type.

➤ The required *group* defines the collection to examine.

➤ The optional *statements* execute until no more *elements* remain in the collection.

➤ The **Exit For** statement has the same effect here as it does in an ordinary **For** loop. When executed, the **For Each** loop terminates and the statement following the **Next** statement executes.

Code Example
```
Dim pctlCurrent As Control
For Each pctlCurrent In Controls
    Debug.Print pctlCurrent.Name
Next
```

Code Dissection

This **For Each** loop performs the same task as the previous For loop. You need not create a variable to count expressly the members of the collection. The statement works by storing in the variable **pctlCurrent** a reference to a control instance in the **Controls** collection. Each time through the loop, **pctlCurrent** references the next control instance in the collection.

The **TypeOf** keyword is frequently employed in conjunction with collections. It can help you by identifying the underlying type of any object variable commonly used in an **If** statement.

Syntax
If TypeOf *objectname* **Is** *objecttype* **Then** ...

Dissection

➤ The *objectname* can be any valid object variable reference.

➤ The *objecttype* can be any object class.

Code Example
```
Dim pctlCurrent As Control
For Each pctlCurrent In Controls
    If TypeOf pctlCurrent Is TextBox Then
        pctlCurrent.FontSize = 12
    End If
Next
```

Code Dissection

➤ These statements use the **Controls** collection to examine each control instance on a form. If the type of the control is a TextBox (the class name for a text box), then the **FontSize** property is set to 12 points. As you can see, this approach offers a useful way to set the same properties for several control instances simultaneously.

In addition to the **Controls** collection, Visual Basic supports the **Forms** collection. One **Forms** collection exists for each project; it lists each of the loaded forms. You will work with the **Forms** Collection when using multiple instances of the same form.

In this chapter, you will use the **Controls** collection to print the positional properties for the drawn objects created by the user on the form. These objects include the Line, Shape, and Label controls on the main form. To illustrate the use of the **Controls** collection, you will print the information to the Immediate window. You could, however, just as easily print a formatted report with the Printer object. In addition, you could save the information to the text file using a well-defined format and then read the file and write code to dynamically re-create the control instances based upon the information contained in the file.

To examine the controls in the **Controls** collection:

1. Activate the Code window for the form named frmCh2, and locate the **mnuFilePrint_Click** event procedure. Enter the following statements into the event procedure:

```
Dim ctlCurrent As Control
For Each ctlCurrent In Controls
    Debug.Print "Name: "; ctlCurrent.Name
    If TypeOf ctlCurrent Is Line Then
        Debug.Print "X1: "; ctlCurrent.X1
        Debug.Print "Y1: "; ctlCurrent.Y1
        Debug.Print "X2: "; ctlCurrent.X2; ""
        Debug.Print "Y2: "; ctlCurrent.Y2; ""
    ElseIf TypeOf ctlCurrent Is Shape Or _
        TypeOf ctlCurrent Is Label Then
        Debug.Print "Name: "; ctlCurrent.Name
        Debug.Print "Top: "; ctlCurrent.Top
        Debug.Print "Left: "; ctlCurrent.Left
        Debug.Print "Height: "; ctlCurrent.Height
        Debug.Print "Width: "; ctlCurrent.Width
    End If
Next
```

2. Test the program. Create multiple instances of each object on the form, click on File on the form's menu bar, and then click on Print.

3. Click on View, and then click on Immediate Window on the Visual Basic menu bar. The positional properties of the control instances should appear.

4. End the program to return to design mode.

Creating An Error Handler

The current version of your program has a major flaw. The user can commit actions that will generate a run-time error—that is, the program will end unexpectedly. Well-written programs should not crash, no matter what input they receive. In the drawing program example, if the user attempts to draw a box by starting at the lower-right corner of the box and ending at the upper-left corner of the box, a runtime error will occur because the code will attempt to set the positional properties to a negative number. One solution to this problem relies on an error handler.

The process of developing an error handler involves three steps:

1. Enable error handling for a procedure by creating an error trap with the **On Error** statement. The **On Error** statement identifies the location of the error-handling code.

2. Create the error-handling code that executes when a run-time error occurs.

3. Write the statements that specify where execution should continue when the error-handling code completes.

To establish an error handler or error trap, you use the **On Error** statement. This statement typically appears as the first statement in any general or event procedure that may possibly generate a run-time error. Consider the following **On Error** statement:

```
On Error GoTo DrawError
```

This statement enables an error trap and should appear as the first statement in a procedure. If a run-time error occurs, execution will continue with the block of statements following the line label named DrawError. These statements constitute the error-handling code. To illustrate, consider the following statements:

```
Private Sub Form_MouseUp(Button As Integer, _
    Shift As Integer, X As Single, Y As Single)
On Error GoTo DrawError
    ' Statements in a procedure that may cause an error.
    Exit Sub
DrawError:
    Call MsgBox("You must draw down and to the right.", _
        vbOKOnly + vbInformation, "Error")
End Sub
```

If no error occurs, the event procedure reaches the **Exit Sub** statement and exits without executing the code in the error handler. If an error occurs, however, execution continues at the statement following the line label named

DrawError. Note that line labels must appear in column one (1) and end with a full colon (:). Thus, if an error occurs in this procedure, the procedure displays the message box and then exits.

In addition to exiting a procedure if an error occurs, you can change the flow of execution with the **Resume** statement.

Syntax

```
Resume
Resume Next
Resume [line, label]
```

Dissection

➤ The **Resume** statement causes execution to continue at the statement that caused the run-time error to occur.

➤ The **Resume Next** statement causes execution to continue at the statement following the statement that caused the run-time error to occur.

➤ The **Resume** *line,label* statement causes execution to continue at a specific line or label.

To illustrate the use of the three variations of the **Resume** statement, examine the following procedures.

```
Private Sub ErrorDemo()
On Error GoTo OverflowError
Dim pint1 As Integer, pint2 As Integer, pintResult As Integer
    pint1 = 12345
    pint2 = 12345
    pintResult = pint1 * pint2
    Exit Sub
OverFlowError:
    pint1 = 0
    pint2 = 0
    Resume
End Sub
```

In this procedure, a numeric overflow error will occur when pint1 is multiplied by pint2, thereby activating the error handler. The error handler corrects the problem by setting the values of both pint1 and pint2 to zero. Because it uses the **Resume** statement with no options, the multiplication statement executes again. No error is produced, and the procedure exits when it reaches the **Exit Sub** statement.

Now consider a variation of the preceding procedure:

```
Private Sub ErrorDemo()
On Error GoTo OverflowError
Dim pint1 As Integer, pint2 As Integer, pintResult As Integer
    pint1 = 12345
    pint2 = 12345
    pintResult = pint1 * pint2
    Exit Sub
OverFlowError:
    Resume Next
End Sub
```

In this procedure, the statement that causes the error to occur does not execute again. Rather, the statement following the error executes, causing the procedure to exit.

Another way to handle errors is to apply a technique called inline error handling. With this technique, statements that deal with any possible errors appear immediately after the statement that could potentially generate the error. Creating an inline error handler requires that you know how to use the Err object.

Syntax

    Err

Properties

➤ The **Number** property contains the numerical value of the error. If no error has occurred, the value of **Number** is zero (0).

➤ The **Source** property contains the name of the current Visual Basic project.

➤ The **Description** property contains a **String** data type corresponding to the error number if one exists. If not, the description contains a string like "Application-defined or object-defined error".

Methods

➤ The **Clear** method resets the error.

➤ The **Raise** method generates a run-time error inside an application. Raising an error is common in class modules and ActiveX controls.

To illustrate the use of an inline error handler, consider yet another variation of the preceding procedure.

```
Private Sub ErrorDemo()
On Error Resume Next
Dim pint1 As Integer, pint2 As Integer, pintResult As Integer
    pint1 = 12345
    pint2 = 12345
    pintResult = pint1 * pint2
    If Err.Number <> 0 Then
        Call MsgBox("Overflow Error")
        Err.Clear
    End If
End Sub
```

You can now modify your program by adding error handlers that will prevent
run-time errors from occurring.

To create an error handler:

1. Activate the Code window for the form named frmCh2, and then activate
    the **Form_MouseUp** event procedure. Enter the following statements into
    the procedure:

```
On Error GoTo DrawError
    mintEndX = X
    mintEndY = Y
    . . .
    If mnuObjectLabel.Checked Then
        mintMaxLabel = mintMaxLabel + 1
        Load lblArray(mintMaxLabel)
        With lblArray(mintMaxLabel)
            .Top = mintStartY
            .Left = mintStartX
            .Width = mintEndX - mintStartX
            .Height = mintEndY - mintStartY
            .Visible = True
        End With
    End If
    Exit Sub
DrawError:
    Call MsgBox("You must draw down and right.", _
        vbOKOnly + vbInformation, "Error")
```

2. Activate the Code window for the form named **frmProperties**, and then
    select the **cmdDelete_Click** event procedure. Enter the following
    statements (shown in bold) into the procedure:

```
On Error GoTo LastElement
    Dim pintReturn As Integer
```

```
        . . .
    Select Case ControlType
        Case "Label"
            Unload frmCh2.lblArray(ControlIndex)
        Case "Line"
            Unload frmCh2.linArray(ControlIndex)
            Unload frmCh2.mnuLinesArray(ControlIndex)
        Case "Shape"
            Unload frmCh2.shpArray(ControlIndex)
            Unload frmCh2.mnuBoxesArray(ControlIndex)
    End Select
    Unload Me
    Exit Sub
LastElement:
    Select Case ControlType
        Case "Line"
            frmCh2.mnuLinesArray(0).Visible = True
            Unload frmCh2.mnuLinesArray(ControlIndex)
        Case "Shape"
            frmCh2.mnuBoxesArray(0).Visible = True
            Unload frmCh2.mnuBoxesArray(ControlIndex)
    End Select
    Unload Me
```

3. Test the program. Attempt to draw a box up and to the left. Instead of a run-time error occurring, the error should be trapped and a message box should appear. Click on OK to close the message box. End the program.

The code you just wrote will trap a run-time error if the user draws a Line or Shape control instance incorrectly. It will also trap a run-time error that occurs when the code tries to delete the only element in the mnuLinesArray or mnuShapes control arrays. Note that the Line property will not generate a run-time error.

CHAPTER SUMMARY

This chapter discussed several major topics. First, it presented a brief review describing the structure of a Visual Basic program. This discussion covered the fundamental Visual Basic data types, **Function** and **Sub** procedures, and passing arguments to procedures. The scope of a variable was discussed as well. Second, you learned how to process keyboard and mouse events. Third, you learned how to work with control arrays. Fourth, you created menus and dynamic menus. Finally, you learned how to use the **Controls** collection to examine the control instances created on a form.

To respond to an event when the mouse is pressed:

➤ To respond to either **MouseDown** or **MouseMove** events:

Private Sub Form_MouseDown(*button* As Integer, *shift* As Integer, *x* As Single, *y* As Single)

Private Sub *object*_MouseDown([*index* As Integer,]*button* As Integer, *shift* As Integer, *x* As Single, *y* As Single)

Private Sub Form_MouseUp(*button* As Integer, *shift* As Integer, *x* As Single, *y* As Single)

Private Sub *object* _MouseUp([*index* As Integer,]*button* As Integer, *shift* As Integer, *x* As Single, *y* As Single)

To respond to an event when the mouse moves:

➤ To respond to the **MouseMove** event:

Private Sub Form_MouseMove(*button* As Integer, *shift* As Integer, *x* As Single, y As Single)

Private Sub *object*_MouseMove([*index* As Integer,] *button* As Integer, *shift* As Integer, *x* As Single, *y* As Single)

To respond to an event when the user presses a key at the keyboard:

➤ To respond to the **KeyPress** event:

Private Sub Form_KeyPress(*keyascii* As Integer)

Private Sub *object*_KeyPress([*index* As Integer,] *keyascii* As Integer)

To get the state of the keyboard:

➤ To respond to the **KeyDown** or **KeyUp** events:

Private Sub Form_KeyDown(*keycode* As Integer, *shift* As Integer)

Private Sub *object*_KeyDown([*index* As Integer,] *keycode* As Integer, *shift* As Integer)

Private Sub Form_KeyUp(keycode As Integer, *shift* As Integer)

Private Sub *object*_KeyUp([*index* As Integer,] *keycode* As Integer, *shift* As Integer)

To create a control array:

➤ Create an instance of a control.

➤ Set the **Index** property to an **Integer** value.

➤ Create additional control instances and set their index values.

➤ Note that multiple elements in a control array share the same name and have unique index values.

To create an instance of a control at run time using a control array:

➤ Call the **Load** statement with the following syntax. Note that the object must be an existing control array.

Load *object*(*index–value*)

To destroy a control array instance at run time:

➤ Call the **Unload** statement with the following syntax. Note that the object must be an existing control array and the index value must be the index of a control array element created at run time.

Unload *object*(*index–value*)

To create the menu for a program:

➤ Activate the desired form, then activate the Menu Editor.

➤ For each menu title or menu item, set the **Name** and **Caption** properties. Define shortcut keys and hot keys as desired.

➤ Set the **Checked**, **Visible**, and **Enabled** properties as necessary.

➤ Create separator bars by using a dash (-) for the **Caption** property.

➤ Indent a menu item to cause it to appear as a submenu of the menu appearing above it in the Menu Editor.

To create and use a pop-up menu in an application:

➤ Create a menu title and its menu items. Generally the menu title should be invisible, as it appears only when the pop-up menu becomes activated.

➤ Display the menu by calling the **PopupMenu** method.

object.PopupMenu *menuname* [, *flags*] [, *x*, *y*][, *boldcommand*]

To display an input box:

➤ Call the InputBox function with the following syntax:

InputBox(*prompt*[, *title*] [, *default*] [, *xpos*] [, *ypos*] [, *helpfile*, *context*])

To examine the **Controls** Collection:

➤ Create a **For Each** loop.

```
For Each element In group
    [ statements ]
    [ Exit For ]
    [ statements ]
Next [element]
```

To determine the type of a particular control:

➤ Use the TypeOf statement.

  If TypeOf *objectname* Is *objecttype* Then …

To create an error handler:

➤ Add an On Error statement to a procedure.

➤ Add the error-handling code to the end of the procedure.

➤ Use the Resume statement to indicate where execution should continue.

  Resume
  Resume Next
  Resume [*line, label*]

REVIEW QUESTIONS

1. Which of the following is a valid type of procedure?
   a. **Function**
   b. **Sub**
   c. **Call**
   d. Both a and b
   e. Both a and c

2. Which of the following statements regarding variables is true?
   a. **Public** variables are visible to all modules.
   b. **Private** variables are visible only to the module in which the variable is declared.
   c. Variables have a data type.
   d. All of the above.
   e. None of the above.

3. What events occur when the user presses and releases the mouse button?
   a. **MousePress, MouseRelease**
   b. **Up, Down**
   c. **MouseDown, MouseUp**
   d. **Press, Release**
   e. None of the above

4. Which of the following are valid keyboard events?

   a. **Press, Up, Down**

   b. **KeyBoardPress, KeyboardUp, KeyBoardDown**

   c. **KeyPress, KeyUp, KeyDown**

   d. **KeyBoardActivity**

   e. None of the above

5. Which of the following statements pertaining to control arrays is true?

   a. Each control array element has the same name and class.

   b. The **Index** property uniquely identifies each element.

   c. The maximum index is 32,767.

   d. All of the above.

   e. None of the above.

6. Which statements are used to create and destroy a control array instance at run time?

   a. **ControlArray**

   b. **Load, Unload**

   c. **Create, Destroy**

   d. **NewInstance, DestroyInstance**

   e. **CreateControl, UnloadControl**

7. Write the necessary statements to display in the text boxes named txtX and txtY the position of the mouse when the user presses the left mouse button on a form.

8. Write the statement to create an instance of a label assuming that you have a control array named lblArray. Use an index value of 2.

9. Destroy the control array instance you created in Question 8.

10. Write the statement to determine the maximum index value for the control array named lblArray and store the value in the **Integer** variable named **intMax**.

11. Which of the following statements about collections is true?

    a. They are similar to an object-based implementation of an array.

    b. They store references to objects.

    c. You can write code that will add and delete members from most collections.

    d. All of the above.

    e. None of the above.

12. Which of the following methods is supported by the Collection object?
    a. **Add**
    b. **Delete**
    c. **Change**
    d. All of the above.
    e. None of the above.

13. Which of the following is a valid Visual Basic collection?
    a. **Controls**
    b. Forms
    c. **Windows**
    d. Both a and b
    e. Both a and c

14. What type of loop is used to examine all members of a collection?
    a. **For Collection**
    b. **For Each**
    c. **Do**
    d. **Do Each**
    e. None of the above

15. Which statement is used to determine the class name of an object?
    a. **ClassName**
    b. **Type**
    c. **TypeOf**
    d. **Class**
    e. None of the above

16. What is the name of the statement used to create an error handler?
    a. **Error**
    b. **On Error**
    c. **ErrorOccured**
    d. **Err**
    e. None of the above

17. Which of the following statements continues execution after an error handler has completed?

    a. **Resume**

    b. **Resume Next**

    c. **Resume Function**

    d. Both a and b

    e. Both a and c

18. Write a loop to examine all of the control instances on the current form. If the type of the control is a text box, print the contents of the **Text** property to the Immediate window.

19. Create a general **Function** procedure named **SquareSub** that accepts one argument, **pintArg1**. The **Function** procedure should compute the square of the argument (multiply the argument by itself). Create an error handler that will return the value 21 if an error occurs.

20. Re-create the **Function** procedure described in Question 9, but create an inline error handler.

21. Which of the following statements about menus is true?

    a. The menu bar appears above the form's title bar.

    b. Menu titles appear vertically.

    c. A shortcut key is also known as an access key.

    d. All of the above.

    e. None of the above.

22. Which of the following statements pertaining to menu design is true?

    a. The first letter of a menu's caption should be capitalized.

    b. Menu captions must be one word.

    c. Menu captions can contain multiple words.

    d. Both a and b.

    e. Both a and c.

23. A menu item that responds to the event procedure.

    a. Click

    b. MenuClick

    c. Item

    d. MenuItem

    e. None of the above

2

24. Which of the following properties is supported by a menu?
    a. **Caption**
    b. **Checked**
    c. **Enabled**
    d. Visible
    e. All of the above

25. What is the name of the method to display a pop-up menu?
    a. **Menu**
    b. **Show**
    c. **Popup**
    d. **PopupMenu**
    e. None of the above

26. Write the statement to display an input box with a prompt of "Enter your name." and a title of "Name". Store the text entered by the user in the variable pstrName.

27. Write the statements to display a message box with a title of "Demo" and a prompt of "Do you want to continue?". The message box should include a question mark icon and Yes/No buttons. Store the return value of the message box in the variable pintResult.

28. Write the code to display a pop-up menu named mnuPopup on the form named frmMain. Display the menu at the current *x, y* coordinates.

29. Write the code to add an element to the menu control array named mnuControlArray. Add the menu with an index value of 4.

30. Write the statements to enable and make visible the control instance named txtCurrent.

HANDS-ON PROJECTS

Project 1

In this project, you will create a financial calculator that computes the present value of a lump sum, the future value of a lump sum, and a payment. As shown in Figure 2.12, the completed form contains a menu, descriptive prompts, and text boxes to store input and output. The File menu contains one menu item to exit the program. The Calculate menu contains three menu items capable of being checked or unchecked, though only one menu item should be checked at any given time. These menu items have captions of Payment, Future Value,

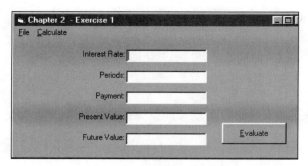

Figure 2.12   Exercise 1 completed form.

and Present Value. Depending on which menu item is checked, the code in the program should enable the text boxes necessary for input and disable the text box that will store the output. To compute the output, you will use the PV, FV, and PMT functions supported by Visual Basic. These functions have the following syntax:

Syntax

$\textbf{PV}(rate, nper, pmt[, fv[, type]])$

$\textbf{FV}(rate, nper, pmt[, pv[, type]])$

$\textbf{Pmt}(rate, nper, pv[, fv[, type]])$

The *rate* argument represents an interest rate, and the *nper* argument represents the number of periods. The *pmt* argument represents the payment, if any. The *pv* and *fv* arguments define the present value and future value, respectively. The *type* argument indicates whether payments are made at the beginning or end of the period.

a. For each exercise in this book, a completed executable program is provided to illustrate one possible solution to the exercise. You can run this executable file as an aid to guide you through the process of writing the program. Run the executable file named Chapter.02\Exercise\Ex1Demo.exe. Relative path names are used, so you will need to set the drive designator. On the menu bar, click on Calculate. Note that Payment is checked. Enter an interest rate of .10, a period of 10, and a present value of 1000. These input values represent the annual payment over 10 years at an interest rate of 10%. The initial amount is $1000.00. Enter 0 for the future value. Click on the Evaluate button to calculate the payment, which will appear in the Payment text box. The payment amount is $-162.74. For brevity, the output has not

2

been formatted. Also note that the Payment text box is disabled because it holds the output value. When you select other options on the Calculate menu, the other text boxes will be enabled and disabled as necessary. Exit the program.

b. Start Visual Basic, and create a new project with a single form. Set the **Name** property of the form to frmEx1. Save the form as Chapter.02\Exercise\frmCh1.frm and the project as Chapter.02\Exercise\Ex1.vbp.

c. Create the menu for the form. The File menu should have one menu item named Exit, which should exit the program. The Calculate menu should have three checked menu items with captions of Payment, Future Value, and Present Value.

d. Only one option on the Calculate menu should be checked at any time. Write the necessary code to check the Payment menu item when the form loads. Write the code to check and uncheck the other menu items as the user clicks each menu item. Consider creating a general procedure to accomplish this task.

e. Depending on which menu item is checked, some text boxes will hold output and others will contain input. If the Payment option is checked, the Payment text box will hold output and should be disabled. If the Future Value option is checked, the Future Value text box should be disabled. If the Present Value option is checked, the Present Value checkbox should be disabled. All other text boxes should be enabled. Write the necessary code to enable and disable the text boxes depending on which menu item is checked.

f. Next, you should write the code for the Evaluate command button. Note that run-time errors can occur for several reasons. If the user enters text into a field, a type conversion error will occur. If the user enters invalid numeric values, numeric overflow or underflow errors may occur. You should, therefore, write an error handler for the procedure that will display the message "Cannot evaluate" in the event of a run-time error. Taking into account the currently selected option on the Calculate menu, write the code to compute the Payment, Present Value, or Future Value based upon the values in the text boxes. Display the result in the output text box.

g. Save and test the program to verify that only one checked menu item is checked at any time. Also, verify that a run-time error does not cause the program to crash, but instead causes a message box to appear. Finally, evaluate all three formulas to check their results, and ensure that the text boxes are enabled and disabled correctly.

Project 2

In this exercise, you will work with multiple forms. The first form will serve as a test form for the second form. It will contain two buttons to test the second form and a third button to exit the program. On the second form, you will implement a form similar to a message box. The form will display between one and four buttons based on the test form's settings. The test form's settings will also determine the format of the buttons. The form will be displayed as a modal dialog box. The buttons on the dialog form will be created dynamically at run time using control arrays.

  a. Run the executable file named Chapter.02\Exercise\Ex2Demo.exe.
  Figure 2.13 shows the form at run time.

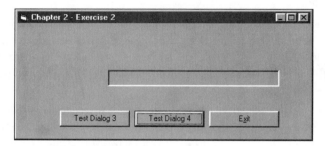

Figure 2.13   Exercise 2 completed form.

In Figure 2.13, two of the buttons have the captions Test Dialog 3 and Test Dialog 4. These buttons display a dialog box with three and four buttons, respectively. Click on the Test Dialog 3 button to display the dialog box shown in Figure 2.14.

On the dialog box shown in Figure 2.14, click on the button with the caption Button 0 to close the dialog box. The button that was clicked appears in the label on the main form. Click on the Test Dialog 4 button to display the same dialog box with four buttons. Click on the button with the caption Button 0 to close the dialog box. On the test form, click on the Exit button to exit the program.

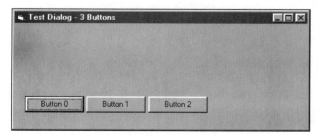

Figure 2.14   Exercise 2 completed form.

b. Start Visual Basic, and create a new project with a single form. Set the **Name** property of the form to **frmEx2**. Save the form as Chapter.02\ Exercise\frmEx2.frm and the project as Chapter.02\Exercise\Ex2.vbp. Add a second form to the project. (You can click on Project, and then click on Add Form to add a second form to a project.) Set the **Name** property of the form to **frmDlg** and save it as Chapter.02\Exercise\frmDlg.frm.

c. Create a command button on the form named frmDlg and name it cmdButton. This button must be a member of a control array.

d. Create two **Public** variables in the general declarations section of the form named Buttons and ButtonClicked. Both of these variables should be of type **Integer.** Because they are **Public** variables in a form module, these variables are treated as properties of the form.

e. In the **Form_Load** event procedure, write the code to read the value of the **Buttons** variable that you created in Step D. For the purposes of this exercise, you can assume that the value of this variable that has been set correctly. Write the statements to create additional instances of the control array of buttons. Thus, if the value of the **Buttons** variable is 4, then control array of buttons should have four elements.

f. In the same event procedure, write the code to make each control array element visible, and move the control array instances so that they appear as shown in Figure 2.14. To accomplish this task, reset the **Left** property of the buttons.

g. Create a general **Function** procedure named **SetCaption**. This procedure should accept two arguments, an **Integer** and a **String**. The first argument will identify a button in the control array of buttons. The second will set the caption of the selected button.

h. In the **Function** procedure created in Step G, set the caption of the selected button. For this procedure, assume that the user can pass an invalid value as an argument. That is, the user can input a nonexistent control array element. Create an inline error handler such that if the button exists, the function will return the value 0. If the button does not exist, the function will return the value 21.

i. Next, you will write the code and create the objects on the main form so that you can test the dialog box. On the main form, create three command buttons having the captions shown in Figure 2.13.

j. For the button with the caption Test Dialog 3, write the code to set the **Buttons** variable (property) for the form named frmDlg to 3. Call the Load statement to load the form, then set the caption of the dialog box to "Test Dialog – 3 Buttons". Next, call the SetCaption function you created to set the caption for the three buttons. Show the dialog form as a modal form.

k. Read the value of the **ButtonClicked** property on the dialog form and display it on the main form's label, then unload the dialog form by calling the **Unload** statement.

l. Create the code for the button Test Dialog 4. Use the same procedure as before, but create four buttons instead of three.

m. Write the code for the Exit command button.

n. Save and test the project. Make sure that the number of buttons appearing on the dialog box is correct. Also verify that their captions are set correctly. Try passing an invalid argument to the SetCaption function. The error handler should execute, and a run-time error should not occur.

Project 3

In this project, you will create a pop-up menu and change the properties of control instances at run time. The properties you will modify are the font-related properties that pertain to all visible controls, including **FontBold**, **FontItalic**, and **FontUnderline**. You will also set the **FontSize** property. The ability to change fonts dynamically at run time is important, as different users prefer different typefaces and font sizes. For example, some users have impaired vision and require a larger font. To test your ability to use the **Controls** collection and determine the type of control, you will set the fonts independently for the labels and text boxes drawn on the form.

a. Run the executable file named Chapter.02\Exercise\Ex3Demo.exe. Figure 2.15 shows the completed form.

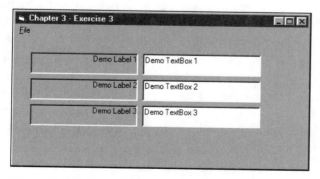

Figure 2.15   Exercise 3 completed form.

As shown in Figure 2.15, the form contains three labels and three text boxes with sample text. Click the right mouse button while the cursor is positioned over one of the label control instances. A pop-up menu appears with two font sizes (8 point and 10 point) and three font attributes (Bold, Italic, and Underline). Select different font sizes and

2

attributes. They are applied to the labels. Repeat the process for the text boxes on the form. To activate the pop-up menu for the text boxes, click the left mouse button. Exit the program.

b. Start Visual Basic, and create a new project with a single form. Set the **Name** property of the form to **frmEx3**. Save the form as Chapter.02\ Exercise\frmCh3.frm and the project as Chapter.02\Exercise\Ex3.vbp.

c. You have several options for implementing this program. Consider carefully how you create the general procedures to apply the formatting attributes. You can simplify the code for the program considerably by making the right choices.

d. Create the three labels and three text boxes on the form. The labels should be members of a control array. The text boxes should be members of another control array.

e. Create the menu system for the program. The File menu should have one menu item: Exit, to exit the program. The other menu, Font, should be invisible because it will appear as a pop-up menu. This menu should have the following options: 8 Point Font, 10 Point Font, Bold, Italic, and Underline.

f. Write the code to display the pop-up menu when the user right-clicks one of the labels.

g. Write the code to display the pop-up menu when the user left-clicks one of the text boxes.

h. Write the code for each of the menu items on the pop-up menu. For this task, careful planning will simplify the code considerably. The code you write must accomplish the following:

➤ When the user sets the font size, the program should set the font of all labels or text boxes (depending on which control type is selected) accordingly. You must therefore examine the **Controls** collection and use a **TypeOf** statement to examine the type of control. If the control is of the correct type, set the **FontSize** property.

➤ For the Bold, Italic, and Underline formatting attributes, the code you write should change the formatting for the labels or the text boxes, but not both. If the selected formatting attribute is applied, remove it. If the formatting attribute is not applied, set it. That is, if the user is setting the bold attribute, check the value of the **FontBold** property for the selected control group. If it is True, then set it to False. If it is False, then set it to True.

i. Test the program. Test each of the formatting attributes for both the labels and text boxes to verify that they are applied correctly.

Project 4

In this project, you will extend Mentor Graphics' drawing program created earlier in the chapter by adding functions to change the thickness of a line or shape. This task is accomplished by setting the **BorderWidth** property. In addition, you will write code to set the border color of a line or shape. This task is accomplished by setting the **BorderColor** property. Finally, you will add a feature so that the user can set the **Shape** property—for example, changing the shape to a circle.

a. Run the executable file named Chapter.02\Exercise\Ex4Demo.exe. On the menu bar, click on Object, and then click on Box. Create a box on the form. Click on Boxes, and select the instance of the Shape control you just created. In the Box dialog, set the Shape Style to 2, the Border Width to 3, and the Border Color to Red. Click on OK to apply the changes. Next, create a line on the form. On the menu, click on Lines, and then select the line you just created. Notice that the Shape Style text box does not appear—this property does not apply to the line. Change the Border Width and Border Color, and click on OK to apply the changes. Figure 2.16 shows a completed Properties form. Exit the program.

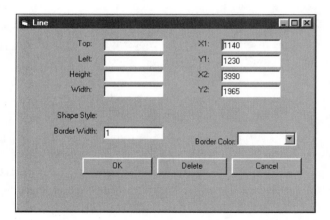

Figure 2.16   Exercise 4 completed Properties form.

b. Start Visual Basic, and create a new project with a single form. Set the **Name** property of the form to **frmEx4**. Save the form as Chapter.02\Exercise\frmCh4.frm and the project as Chapter.02\Exercise\Ex4.vbp. Create a second form having a name of frmProperties. Save this form as Chapter.02\Exercise\frmProp.frm.

c. The code presented in the hands-on steps provides a foundation for this exercise. Consider making a copy of the Form modules and using them as the starting point for this exercise.

d. On the Properties form, create the additional objects. You need two text boxes to store the shape style and border width. You also need to create an instance of the ComboBox control. (You should already be familiar with the basic use of the ComboBox control). For this control, set the **List** property so that it contains the following values: Red, Blue, Green, Yellow, and Black.

e. Modify the program to support the **BorderColor** property. Note that this property pertains only to the Shape and Line controls. Thus, when the user is editing a Label control instance, these controls should be invisible. Use the same techniques presented in the chapter to initialize the value of these text boxes to the current value of the selected control. When the user clicks the OK button, apply the changes.

f. Modify the program to support the **BorderWidth** property pertaining to both the Line and Shape controls.

g. Modify the program to support the **Style** property. This property pertains only to the Shape control, so the user should be able to set this property only when a Shape control instance is selected for editing.

h. Test the program to verify that you can set the shape's style, the border width of both the shape and line, and the color of both the shape and line. Save the project again, if necessary, and exit Visual Basic.

CHAPTER THREE

CREATING DATA SERVICES USING ADO

AFTER READING THIS CHAPTER AND COMPLETING THE EXERCISES, YOU WILL BE ABLE TO:

➤ Become familiar with fundamental database concepts

➤ Learn the concept of ActiveX Data Objects (ADO)

➤ Learn about ActiveX controls

➤ Use the ADO Data control to establish a connection to a database

➤ Use bound controls

➤ Learn about the Recordset object

➤ Program a Recordset object and understand the interaction between the recordset and the ADO Data control

➤ Locate records using a recordset

➤ Add, change, and delete records using a recordset

ACCESSING A DATABASE BY USING CONTROLS AND BY PROGRAMMING OBJECTS

Using Visual Basic Controls To Interact With A Database

You can load and execute the completed project for this chapter, using it for reference as you work through the hands-on steps. The data for the program are stored in a database file. The completed program consists of three forms through which a user can add, change, and delete records stored in the database file. A main form displays two other forms that illustrate two different techniques to manage database data:

➤ The form named frmADODC takes advantage of the ADO Data control along with text boxes bound to the ADO Data control to display database information.

➤ The form named frmADO is visually similar to frmADODC, but all functionality is accomplished programmatically rather than by using the ADO Data control.

To preview the completed program:

1. Start Visual Basic, and load the project named Chapter.03\Complete\ Ch3_C.vbp. Note that this program was developed using ADO 2.0. You may receive errors if you use ADO 2.1.

2. Run the program. Figure 3.1 shows the main form for the running program.

The form contains three Command buttons. The first two buttons are used to display the forms that view and edit database data. The third button exits the program.

3. Click on the Command button with the caption ADO Data Control to display the form shown in Figure 3.2.

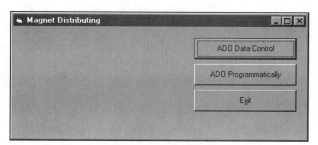

Figure 3.1 Completed main form.

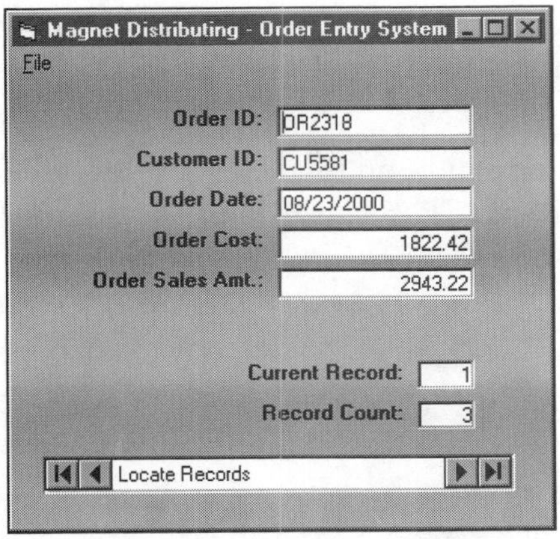

Figure 3.2 Completed ADO Data control form.

Depending on the short date format used on your computer, the date will appear with either two-digit years or four-digit years. You can change the short date format from the Control Panel of your computer.

4. On the ADO Data control, click on the Move Last button to locate the last record in the database. Click on the Move First button to locate the first record in the database. Click on the Move Next button and then the Move Previous button to locate the next and previous records, respectively. Click on File, and then click on Close to close the form.

5. Click on the Command button with the caption ADO Programmatically to display the form shown in Figure 3.3.

This form is very similar to the one that you just viewed. The form in Figure 3.3, however, contains a menu to perform all database navigation and does not utilize the ADO Data control.

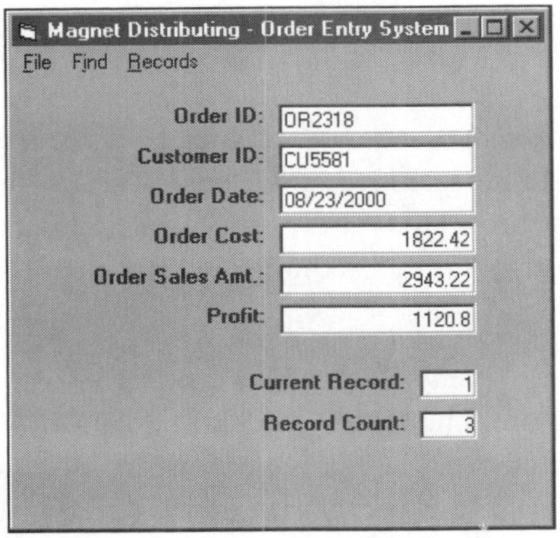

Figure 3.3 Completed form without the ADO Data control.

6. On the form's menu bar, click on Find, and then click on Last to locate the last record. On the Find menu, test the Next, Previous, and First menu items.

7. On the form's menu bar, click on Find, and then click on By Order ID. Enter "OR9943" in the input box. Click on OK. The program locates the record and displays it in the form's text boxes.

8. On the form's menu bar, click on Records, and then click on Add to create a new record. The text boxes are cleared. Enter the value "OR9999" for the Order ID and the value "CU9999" for the Customer ID. Use the current date for the order date. Enter positive numbers for the order cost and order sales amount.

9. Click on Records, and then click on Update to save the new record to the database. Whenever the user saves the record to the database, the program updates the current record and record count fields.

10. Click on Records, and then click on Delete to remove the record you just added.

11. Click on File, and then click on Close to close the form.

12. On the main form, click on Exit to end the program, and then exit Visual Basic.

Fundamental Database Concepts

Prior to the advent of database management systems, programs that manipulated data worked via a traditional file-processing system in which separate data files existed for each application. This approach resulted in inconsistent data being stored in different files. For example, a customer's name in one file might differ from the name found in another file. In addition, redundant data were stored in different files. For example, a customer's address might exist in an accounts payable file as well as a sales file. To solve the limitations of traditional file processing, many organizations now use database management systems.

Current business and scientific applications often process large volumes of data. Frequently, this information must be reorganized and viewed dynamically. The complex data requirements of most programs require sophisticated data-processing capabilities beyond those provided by traditional file-processing systems.

In a database management system, the database contains a set of information related to a particular topic or purpose. The data is stored in a database inside a table. Most databases contain several tables. Each table consists of rows and columns. The column defines the name for, and characteristics of, the stored information. The columns in a table are called fields, and the rows in a table are called records. By using a query, you can view multiple tables as if they were all part of a single table. In this chapter, you will work with tables. In Chapter 4, you will work with queries.

A variety of software companies—such as Microsoft, Informix, Oracle, and Sybase—manufacture database management programs. Visual Basic can operate with many of these programs. It is particularly well suited to operate the Microsoft Jet database engine (also known as Jet or the Jet engine), the database management program used by Microsoft Access. Although Visual Basic operates with several different databases, this chapter describes only how to use Visual Basic with a Jet database.

Properly designing the structure of a database requires an understanding of several key concepts:

➤ The tables in a database should be created to eliminate data redundancy. For example, a customer's address should be stored in a database once and only once. This stage of the design process is commonly called *normalization*. If you are unfamiliar with the concept of database design and normalization, consider reviewing *Fundamentals of Database Systems*, by Shamkant B. Navthe and Ramez A. Elmasri, or *Database Management*, by Fred R. McFadden and Jeffrey A. Hoffer.

➤ Each row (record) in a table should have a unique index, enabling the code that you write to locate the row. The unique index may consist of one or more fields. The unique index for a table is referred to as the *primary key*.

➤ The data stored in a table is often related to another table in some way. For example, consider a situation where customer information is stored in one table and a unique customer ID (primary key) identifies a customer. Assume that orders pertaining to customers are stored in a different table. Under this scenario, the customer ID is stored in both tables and a relationship is defined between the two fields in the two different tables. The customer ID in the second table is known as the *foreign key*.

This chapter focuses on the use of Visual Basic with an existing Jet database. It does not attempt to cover the topic of proper database design. If you have never used a database like Microsoft Access, consider starting Microsoft Access and reviewing the Help topic About Designing A Database with the Microsoft Office Assistant. The database for the program of this chapter's client, Magnet Incorporated, has already been defined, and Figure 3.4 shows its structure. Magnet Incorporated distributes floppy disks, magnetic tapes, and other removable media. The company needs a program to manage customer orders. The order information is stored in a database file. Magnet Incorporated needs a program to add, change, and delete the orders found in this file. In addition, the program should allow users to locate and display specific orders.

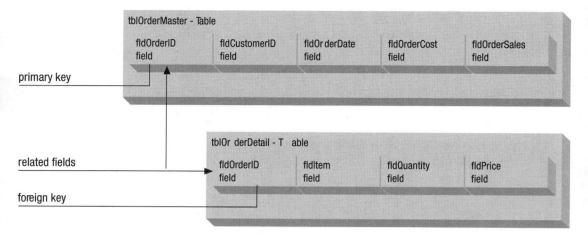

Figure 3.4 Database structure.

As shown in Figure 3.4, the database has two tables: tblOrderMaster and tblOrderDetail. These tables share a common field named fldOrderID. In the table tblOrderMaster, the field fldOrderID is unique and is referred to as the primary key. In the second table, this field is considered to be the foreign key. Like other objects that you have created, database objects should contain a three-character prefix denoting the object's type. The three-character prefix for a table is "tbl". Each table contains several fields, each of which has a standard prefix of "fld". In this case, information about a sales order is stored in the table named tblOrderMaster. In the chapter's hands-on steps, you will use only tblOrderMaster.

A Conceptual Overview Of ActiveX Data Objects And OLE DB

The previous section outlined file-processing technology as it has evolved from traditional file-processing techniques to databases. Database technology has evolved considerably over the past few years in response to today's demand for data access over heterogeneous computing platforms and networks. Several years ago, the database management systems used on personal computers operated in a stand-alone mode. That is, multiple computers did not share the data over a network. As computers were networked together, however, users wanted to share data between computers. They also needed to store different kinds of data in their databases. For example, instead of merely storing textual strings and numeric values, it became necessary to store formatted data, images, audio files, and even video files. To meet this need, many vendors designed and implemented a universal database. Under the universal database model, each database vendor supports a wide variety of data types, including graphics, audio, and video. All of these data are then stored in the vendor's monolithic database system and can be shared by all users within an organization.

Although the universal database allowed an organization to store heterogeneous data, that data had to be stored in a single database. In addition, it was often necessary to convert the format of specific data types before storing to make the data compatible with the underlying database. To solve this problem, Microsoft embarked on a strategy that allowed software developers to create enterprise applications that could provide users with access to diverse data sources, including database files, text files, and data stored on intranets or the Internet. The strategy, called *universal data access*, enables applications to access data without requiring storage of the information in a standardized format. That is, an application can access data from a spreadsheet or text file as easily as it can access data from a relational database. In addition, the universal data access model does not require that data be replicated or converted in any way.

To implement the universal data access model, a multitiered programming interface based upon Component Object Modules (COM) was implemented. The concept of COM will be discussed in more detail throughout this book. For now, consider COM as a contract by which different objects communicate.

At the core of universal data access is the OLE DB object interface. The OLE DB interface provides a standardized interface for accessing information stored in different formats. That is, through OLE DB, an application can use data stored in a spreadsheet and data stored in a database just as if they were both stored in the same format.

The universal data access model defines three layers of database components:

➤ **Data providers** Are analogous to data sources. Data sources include spreadsheets, text files, and database files.

➤ **Data services** Consume data from data providers and present that data to data consumers. Data services typically consist of query and cursor engines. A cursor engine retrieves rows from a database, enabling a data consumer to access those rows.

➤ **Data consumers** Consist of business applications that use the data retrieved from data services.

Figure 3.5 illustrates the universal data access model.

As shown in Figure 3.5, data providers consist of database programs, spreadsheets, text files, and other files. The OLE DB interface retrieves data from a provider. OLE DB can send data either through a data service or directly to ADO. Ultimately, the data will be presented to a data consumer such as a Visual Basic program. Fortunately, Visual Basic and ADO insulates you, the programmer, from the technical intricacies of OLE DB.

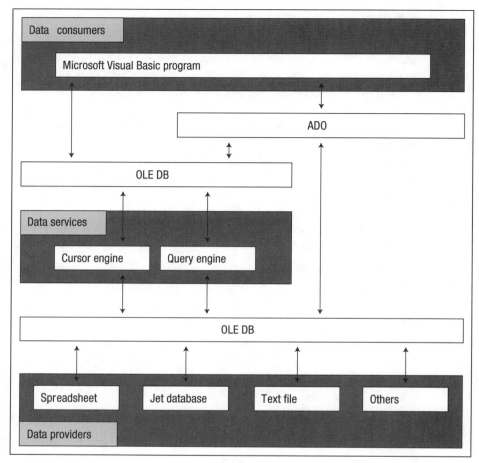

Figure 3.5 Universal data access model.

In Visual Basic, you gain access to OLE DB by using ActiveX Data Objects (ADO). ADO comprises a group of objects and Visual Basic controls, such as the ADO Data control. Before you begin using ADO, a brief introduction to ActiveX technology is in order.

Introducing ActiveX Controls

Visual Basic supports two types of controls: intrinsic controls and ActiveX controls. Consider the intrinsic controls (command buttons, labels, text boxes, and so on) that you used in Chapters 1 and 2. These controls are not unique to Visual Basic. Rather, Visual Basic uses the underlying controls supported by the Windows operating system. When you compile a program, the code to call the underlying Windows controls becomes embedded in the executable file produced by Visual

Basic. Refer to Chapter 16 on the Windows Application Programming Interface for more information on the interaction between Visual Basic and its intrinsic controls.

An ActiveX control differs from an intrinsic control in many ways. For example, the code containing the methods and events for an ActiveX control is not stored in the executable file produced by Visual Basic; instead, it is stored in a separate file with the file extension ".ocx". To execute a program that uses an ActiveX control, this .ocx file must reside on the computer running the program. Figure 3.6 illustrates this distinction.

Because an ActiveX control remains independent of Visual Basic itself, this type of control can be used with many different programming languages. Active X controls are also suitable for use over the Internet. You can, for example, create ActiveX controls that are downloaded over the Internet to a Web browser and then executed. ActiveX controls can operate with multiple languages because the mechanism that enables a program to interact with an ActiveX control is clearly defined. That is, ActiveX is built upon COM, a contract that defines a standard interface by which objects communicate.

ActiveX controls also support Property Pages. Property Pages provide you, the programmer, with a way of setting properties other than through the Properties window. In many cases, you can set a property by using either an ActiveX control's Property Pages or the Properties window. In some cases, however, you must use the Properties window to set a particular property. In still other circumstances, you must use the control's Property Pages to set a property.

Some languages, such as PowerBuilder, take advantage of ActiveX controls but do not support the Properties window. With these languages, Property Pages provide the only means to set design-time properties.

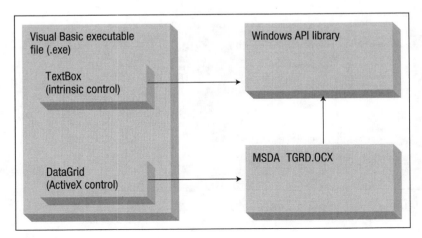

Figure 3.6   Intrinsic and ActiveX controls.

The Professional and Enterprise Editions of Visual Basic are distributed with several ActiveX controls in addition to the intrinsic controls you used in Chapters 1 and 2. In this chapter, you will use the ADO Data control—an ActiveX control—to establish a connection with a database. Before a program can use an ActiveX control, you must explicitly add a reference to the control to the project file. To accomplish this task, you use the Components dialog box, as shown in Figure 3.7.

The list of controls displayed on your system will likely differ from those shown in Figure 3.7. Different ActiveX controls can be purchased from third-party vendors to implement facsimile machines, electronic mail, and to perform many other tasks. When you add an ActiveX control to a project, the project file is updated to indicate that the project requires the ActiveX control.

To add an ActiveX control to the project file:

1. Start Visual Basic, and open the project named Chapter.03\Startup\ Ch3_S.vbp.

2. Click on Project, and then click on Components to open the Components dialog box.

3. Use the scroll bars to locate the Microsoft ADO Data Control 6.0 (OLEDB). Click on the checkbox to the left of this name, and then click on OK to close the dialog box.

4. The ADO Data control should appear in the toolbox. Save the project to record the reference to the control in the project file.

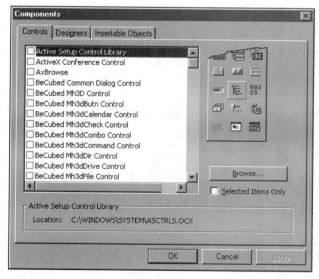

Figure 3.7 Components dialog box.

In addition to adding ActiveX control references to a project using the Components dialog box, you can add another type of COM object using the References dialog box. Many programs including Microsoft Word and Excel can be used in a way that does not utilize the visual interface with which you are likely accustomed. For example, you can use both Word and Excel by referencing their respective object libraries, then writing code to manipulate their objects. Before referencing a program's objects with code, you must make the object library accessible to your program. This task is accomplished via the References dialog box on the Project menu.

Instead of using the ADO Data control, you can work with ADO programmatically. To do so, you must use the References dialog box and add a reference to the ADO object library.

The ADO Data Control

Now that a reference to the ADO Data control exists in the project file and consequently on the toolbox, you can create an instance of this control on the form, just as you would with any other control. After creating an instance of the ADO Data control, you set its properties so that the control instance can establish a connection with a database at run time. The following syntax presentation summarizes the properties, events, and methods supported by the ADO Data control. The use of these properties, events, and methods will be discussed in more detail as you work through the remainder of the chapter.

Syntax

> ADO Data control

Properties

➤ The **BOF** and **EOF** properties signify the beginning and end of file, respectively. When the current record position is before the first record, **BOF** is **True**; otherwise, it is False. When the current record position is after the last record, **EOF** is **True**; otherwise, it is False.

➤ The **BOFAction** property defines the behavior of the current record when beginning of file is reached. If set to the constant value **adDoMoveFirst**, then the first record becomes the current record. If set to the constant value adStayBOF, beginning of file is **True** and no current record exists.

➤ The **ConnectionString** property is used to establish a connection with a provider (data source). You can set this property by using the Property Pages pertaining to the ADO Data control, by using the Properties window, or by writing code to build a variable representing the connection string.

➤ Once the ADO Data control establishes a connection to a database, this control can execute commands. These commands in turn return records, which your program can then manipulate. The **CommandType** property defines the kind of command that the ADO Data control will execute.

➤ The **EOFAction** property defines the behavior of the current record when end of file is reached. If set to the constant value adDoMoveLast, the last record becomes the current record. If set to adDoAddNew, a new record is added. If set to adStayEOF, end of file has been reached and no current record exists.

➤ The **MaxRecords** property specifies the maximum number of records returned when a command executes. The default is zero (0), indicating that an infinite number of records can be returned.

➤ When the ADO Data control returns records as a result of executing a command, it does so in a Recordset object. The **Recordset** property pertaining to the ADO Data control stores a reference to this object. The **Recordset** property and Recordset object will be discussed in more detail later in this chapter.

➤ The **RecordSource** property stores the command that will execute. It defines the table name or query that returns a recordset.

➤ The **CausesValidation** property contains a Boolean value indicating whether a second control will generate a **Validate** event.

Methods

➤ The **UpdateControls** method retrieves the fields from recordset's current record and displays the information in the bound controls.

Events

➤ The **EndOfRecordset** event occurs when the user attempts to move past the last record in the recordset.

➤ Just before an operation changes a field in a recordset, the **WillChangeField** event occurs. Your program can cancel the event by setting the status argument to the constant value **adStatusCancel.** Just after an operation changes a field in a recordset, the **FieldChangeComplete** event occurs.

➤ The **WillMove** and **MoveComplete** events, respectively, occur just before and just after the current record is repositioned.

➤ The **WillChangeRecord** and **RecordChangeComplete** events occur before the current record is updated and after the contents of the current record are updated, respectively.

As you work through the steps in this chapter, these properties, events, and methods will be explained in further detail. You now have the necessary tools to create an instance of the ADO Data control.

To create an instance of the ADO Data control:

1. Activate the form named **frmADODC**.

2. Click on the ADO Data control, then create an instance of the control across the bottom of the form.

3. Activate the Properties window for the form and set the **Name** property to **adMagnet**. This book will use "ad" as the standard prefix for the ADO Data control. Although only two characters long, this prefix is consistent with the prefix attached to the constants pertaining to the ADO Data control.

4. Set the **Caption** property to **Locate Records**. The caption appears inside the visible region of the ADO Data control.

Once you have created an instance of the ADO Data control, you must set its properties to establish a connection with a database.

Connecting To A Database With The ADO Data Control

Several different groups of objects and controls allow a Visual Basic program to interact with a database. If you have worked with previous versions of Visual Basic, you have likely used the Data control and other controls, such as text boxes, that are bound to an instance of the Data control. Additionally, you may have written code to reference objects in the Data Access Objects (DAO) or Remote Data Objects (RDO) hierarchy. Although Visual Basic 6.0 supports these object hierarchies, they are no longer the preferred mechanism for database access. Instead, Visual Basic 6.0 provides a new object model called ActiveX Data Objects (ADO). The following list of features makes ADO a more flexible data access tool than DAO and other older database access technologies:

➤ ADO works with several different database management systems, which increases flexibility.

➤ ADO is well suited to networked environments. (RDO can still be used in networked environments, however.)

➤ The ADO object model is much simpler than older object models like DAO and RDO.

➤ ADO tends to be faster than programs such as Jet DAO.

If you are familiar with the intrinsic Data control, you will recognize some similarities when working with the ADO Data control. The two controls perform roughly the same tasks. Both establish a connection to a database, create and load records into a Recordset object, and operate with bound controls, such as text boxes. If you are accustomed to using the intrinsic Data control, setting the properties of the ADO Data control to establish a database connection may appear to be a more complex task. This complexity arises because the ADO Data control is capable of establishing connections to many more data types in many different ways. This book uses the latest OLE DB technology supported by Microsoft to establish a connection with a database.

The first step in establishing a connection to a database is to build a connection string. A connection string is built using the General tab on the ADO Data control's Property Pages, which is shown in Figure 3.8.

As shown in Figure 3.8, three options exist to define the source of the connection:

➤ Connection information can be stored in a separate file known as a connection file or data link file. This file has a suffix of ".udl". You can build connection files from the Control Panel.

➤ Another option is to use an existing ODBC data source or to create a new one. With this option, you can establish a connection to multiple types of databases using the Open Database Connectivity (ODBC) standards. ODBC employs a software driver to act as an interface between your application and a database. Most database vendors support ODBC. Prior to the advent of OLE DB and ADO, ODBC was the preferred—and sometimes only—way for a Visual Basic application to access a database.

➤ The third option is to build a connection string. This option takes advantage of OLE DB and ADO. As the OLE DB and ADO technologies are much newer than ODBC, fewer vendors support OLE DB. As ADO will likely supplant the ODBC standard, however, this book will cover the newest technology.

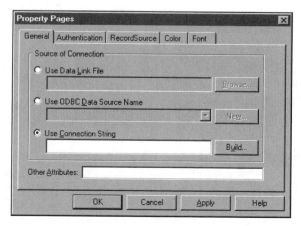

Figure 3.8 General tab of the Property Pages.

The easiest way to build a connection string is via the ADO Data control's Property Pages. With the Property Pages, you interactively specify the parameters that make up the connection string. It is also possible to set the **ConnectionString** property by entering the connection string into the Properties window or by writing code.

To build a connection string:

1. Activate the form named frmADODC, then activate the Properties window for the ADO Data control, if necessary.

2. Locate the **ConnectionString** property. Click on the Value column, and then click on the Properties button   to activate the control's Property Pages. The General tab on the Property Pages appears. If you right-click on the control instance and then click on Properties, all the tabs appear. Alternatively, you can right-click on the control and select ADODC Properties.

3. The General tab of the Property Pages contains three options for defining a connection. To create a connection string, click on Use Connection String, if necessary, and then click on Build to activate the Data Link Properties dialog box and begin creating the connection string. Figure 3.9 shows this dialog box .

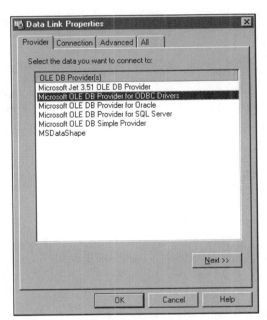

Figure 3.9   Data Link Properties dialog box Provider tab.

As shown in Figure 3.9, the Data Link Properties dialog box contains four tabs.

➤ **Provider** You specify which data provider to use. As shown in Figure 3.9, data providers are supported for Jet, SQL Server, Oracle, and others. This list of data providers may vary depending on the configuration of your system.

➤ **Connection** The options will vary depending on the provider selected. These options assist you in building the string stored into the ConnectionString property.

➤ **Advanced** The contents will also vary depending upon the provider selected. This tab contains other options to configure the data link.

➤ **All** Allows you to manually set each of the options pertaining to the data link.

Connection strings rely on OLE DB. The first step in building the connection string is to define the OLE DB provider. Certain providers exist for Microsoft Access databases (Jet); other providers supply an interface to ODBC. Still other providers are defined for both ORACLE and SQL Server. In this example, you will use a Microsoft Jet database, so you will select the Microsoft Jet 3.51 OLE DB Provider.

To select the OLE DB provider:

1. Make sure that the Provider tab on the Data Link Properties dialog box is active.

2. Select Microsoft Jet 3.51 OLE DB Provider, and then click on Next to activate the Connection tab, as shown in Figure 3.10.

On the Connection tab, you define the database to which you want to connect and specify any login or password information required to make this connection.

3. Click on the Properties button to the right of the text box named Select or enter a database name. An Open dialog box appears, allowing you to select a database file to open.

4. Locate and select the file Chapter.03\Startup\Magnet.mdb, and then click on Open. The full path name of the database should appear in the text box.

5. To verify that the ADO Data control can establish a connection with the database, click on the Test Connection command button. If the connection is successful, a message box will indicate that the test connection succeeded. Click on OK to close this dialog box. If the connection fails, a dialog box will describe the cause of the error.

6. Click on the Advanced tab to view advanced option—that is, the options pertaining to network connections and those pertaining to sharing the open database. Select the default access permission of Share Deny None, if necessary, and then click on OK to close the dialog box.

7. Reactivate the Property Pages for the ADO Data control. Note that the Property Pages may have been obscured as you set the Connection string. The connection string you created should appear in the Use Connection String text box.

8. Click on OK to close the Property Pages. The Connection string should appear in the Properties window.

The connection string should appear in the ConnectionString property in the Properties window. This value is a string of characters. As such, you could declare a variable, build the connection string by writing code, and then store the value into the ADO Data control's ConnectionString property. Alternatively, you could have entered this value manually into the Properties window. Consider carefully the value of the ConnectionString property (the following string appears on multiple lines in this text but is actually a continuous string of characters):

```
Provider=Microsoft.Jet.OLEDB.3.51;Persist Security Info=False;Data
Source=A:\Chapter.03\Startup\Magnet.mdb
```

A connection string adheres to a standard syntax. First, the string consists of key/value pairs. Each key/value pair is separated by a semicolon (;). In the preceding connection string, Provider is a key, and Microsoft.Jet.OLEDB.3.51 is a value. Note that an equals sign separates the key and value.

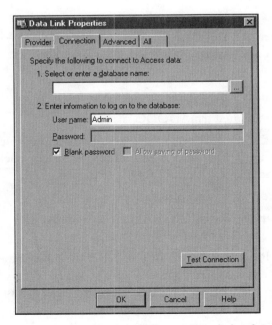

Figure 3.10   Data Link Properties dialog box Connection tab.

If you are accustomed to using the intrinsic Data control, you will recognize that the steps to establish the connection string are analogous to setting the Data control's **Connect** and **DataSource** properties. In essence, you have established a connection to a database but you have not specified the information to which you want to connect. With the intrinsic Data control, you set the **RecordSource** property to the name of a database table or query. With the ADO Data control, the process becomes a bit more complex because you must specify multiple items of information. One object in the ADO model is the Command object. This object can either operate as a stand-alone object or be dependent upon an existing connection string. In the example you are creating, the latter is true.

You can specify four types of commands in the Properties window:

➤ The command type is initially set to **adCmdUnknown**, indicating that the type of command is unknown.

➤ When set to **adCmdTable**, the **RecordSource** property consists of the name of a database table.

➤ When set to **adCmdText**, the **RecordSource** property is viewed as a text string. This string typically contains an SQL statement. You will learn about SQL statements in Chapter 4.

➤ When set to **adCmdStoredProc**, the command type is a stored procedure. A stored procedure is used with an SQL server and contains a precompiled SQL statement.

In this chapter, you will use the ADO Data control to establish a connection with a database table. Therefore, you will set the **CommandType** to **adCmdTable** and the **RecordSource** property to the name of the database table.

To build the ADO command:

1. Make sure that the form named frmADODC is active.

2. Activate the ADO Data control named adMagnet, and open the Property Pages. To open the Property Pages for the control instance, right-click on the control instance, and then click on ADODC Properties.

3. Select the RecordSource tab, as shown in Figure 3.11.

4. Set the **Command Type** to **2 – adCmdTable**. The underlying **CommandType** property will be set.

5. In the Table or Stored Procedure Name list box, select the table named tblOrderMaster. The **RecordSource** property will be set. Note that the ADO Data control uses the **ConnectionString** property to establish a connection with the database. It then looks up the available tables and displays them in the list box.

6. Click on OK to close the Property Pages.

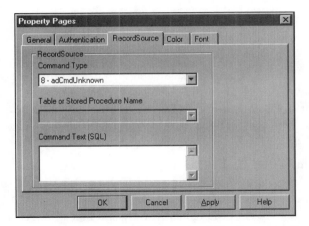

Figure 3.11 RecordSource tab of the Property Pages.

When you set the **CommandType** and **RecordSource** properties, the ADO Data control is able to execute a command on the connection that you built in the previous steps. When this command executes, it returns records in the form of a Recordset object. Although the Recordset object is discussed more fully later in this chapter, you must have a basic understanding of its purpose to comprehend how the ADO Data control locates records at run time. When the program runs, the ADO Data control creates an instance of the Recordset object. Only one record can be active at any given time. The current record pointer indicates this active record. You do not write code to access the current record pointer explicitly; rather, the ADO Data control moves the current record pointer indirectly by using the Recordset object's methods. When the user clicks the buttons on the ADO Data control, the current record pointer changes automatically.

Although the previous steps allow the ADO Data control to establish a connection with the database named Magnet.mdb, no information will be displayed in the form's text boxes. This situation occurs because you have not set the necessary properties pertaining to the form's text boxes.

Creating Bound Controls

A *bound control* (also known as a *data-aware control*) displays a field from the current record as identified by the ADO Data control. Many different controls that can hold text (such as the Label or ListBox controls) and graphics (such as the ImageBox or PictureBox controls) can be bound to a field in an ADO Data control. When a text box or label is bound to an instance of the ADO Data control, changes in the current record are reflected in the bound control (text box, label, and so on). Each bound control corresponds to a field in a table or query.

The process of binding a control instance to an instance of the ADO Data control requires that you set two additional design-time properties:

➤ **DataSource** Is set to an instance of the ADO Data control. If the properties of the ADO Data control have been set, clicking the list arrow for this property will display all of the instances of ADO Data controls created on the form. If a form must interact with multiple tables or queries, you can create multiple instances of the ADO Data control on a form, then select the desired ADO Data control.

➤ **DataField** Identifies the field in a table or query displayed in the bound control instance. When you select a field with the list arrow, Visual Basic uses the DataSource property to determine the appropriate ADO Data control instance, then looks in the table or query and lists all relevant fields.

The text boxes in Magnet Incorporated's program have already been created. However, you must set the necessary properties to establish a link between the text boxes drawn in the form and the newly created ADO Data control instance.

To create bound controls:

1. Activate the Text Box objects, as shown in Figure 3.12. To select multiple objects, hold down the Shift key and click on each object. You can also use the pointer tool in the toolbox to draw a rectangle around the desired objects.

2. Set the **DataSource** property to **adMagnet** for each of the text boxes. Selecting all of the text boxes and then setting the **DataSource** property causes the property to be set for all controls simultaneously.

3. Click on the form to deselect the control instances.

4. For each of the text boxes, set the **DataField** property to **fldOrderID**, **fldCustomerID**, **fldOrderDate**, **fldOrderCost**, and **fldOrderSales**, as

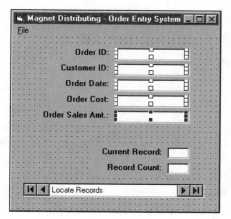

Figure 3.12 Selecting multiple TextBox control instances.

shown in Figure 3.12. Because you have already identified the ADO Data control instance and set the necessary properties for it to establish a connection to the data source, you can set the DataField by using the list arrow and selecting a field from the list.

5. Test the program. Click on the ADO Data Control command button to display the form. Data from the database should appear, as shown in Figure 3.13. Nothing appears in the unbound objects—you have not written any code to display the current record or record count.

6. Click on the buttons on the ADO Data control instance. The Move First button locates the first record. The Move Next button locates the next record. The Move Previous and Move Last buttons locate the previous and last records, respectively.

7. End the program to return to design mode.

In addition to locating different records, the ADO Data control allows you to modify existing records and create new ones. To create a new record, you must set the **EOFAction** property pertaining to the ADO Data control. By default, this property's value is **adDoMoveLast**; that is, attempting to locate a record beyond the last record will cause the ADO Data control to reload the last record instead of allowing EOF to become True. Setting this property to **adDoAddNew** will add a new record upon such an attempt. To illustrate this concept, you will modify the **EOFAction** property to add new records, and see how to modify records.

To add and modify records using the ADO Data control:

1. Activate the form named **frmADODC**.

2. Activate the Properties window for the ADO Data control instance named **adMagnet**.

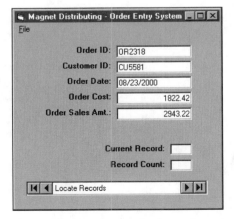

Figure 3.13   Testing the bound controls.

3. Set the **EOFAction** property to **2 – adDoAddNew**.

4. Test the program. Click on the ADO Data Control command button on the main form.

5. Click on the Move Last button to locate the last record.

6. Click on the Move Next button. Because you set this property to **adDoAddNew**, the ADO data control instance adds a new record and clears the contents of the bound text boxes.

7. Enter an Order ID of "N9999", a customer ID of "CU5584", an order date of "8/23/2001", an order cost of "2933.81", and an order sales amount of "3984.22".

8. Click on the Move Previous button on the ADO Data control. The record is updated and the previous record is located.

If you enter invalid data, a dialog box will appear similiar to the one shown in Figure 3.14, indicating that the change was canceled during notification. The ADO Data control generates this message because it cannot save the changes to the database. Click on OK to close the dialog box.

9. Click on the Move Next button to locate the newly added record.

10. Modify the values for the order cost and order sales amount. Locate the previous record. The data are updated.

At this point, your program will generate an error if you attempt to update a field to an invalid value. For example, the order date must be a valid date and the order cost and order sales amounts must be numeric.

11. Locate the record you created in Step 6. Update the date to an invalid date, and enter a character in the order cost field and the order sales amount field. Locate the previous record to record the changes. A run-time error will occur and a dialog box will appear, as shown in Figure 3.14.

12. Click on OK to close the dialog box.

13. End the program to return to design mode.

To remedy the problem of errors occurring when the user enters invalid data, the ADO Data control supports several events that occur before a field or record is updated. The **WillChangeRecord** event takes place just before a record is updated. Several arguments are passed to this event procedure,

Figure 3.14 Locate Records error dialog box.

enabling your code to determine the cause of the change and cancel it if it detects invalid data.

Syntax

Private Sub *object*_WillChangeRecord(ByVal *adReason* As ADODB.EventReasonEnum, ByVal *cRecords* As Long, *adStatus* As ADODB.EventStatusEnum, ByVal *pRecordset* As ADODB.Recordset)

Dissection

➤ The *object* is an instance of the ADO Data control.

➤ The **WillChangeRecord** event occurs just before a record in the underlying recordset is changed.

➤ The *adReason* argument contains a constant value indicating the reason for the event (a complete list will be provided later). For example, if a new record was added, the *adReason* argument would be set to the constant value **adRsnAddNew**.

➤ The *cRecords* argument contains a Long Integer value indicating the number of records affected.

➤ The *adStatus* argument contains a constant value indicating the status of the method that caused this event to occur. It is usually set to **adStatusOK**. To cancel the method that caused this event, you can write code to set this argument to **adStatusCancel**.

➤ *pRecordset* contains a reference to the recordset involved in the operation.

The **WillChangeRecord** event occurs for many reasons. The following list indicates some of the possible constant values for the **adReason** argument:

➤ The constant value **adRsnAddNew** indicates that a new record will be added.

➤ The constant value **adRsnDelete** indicates that the current record will be deleted.

➤ The constant value **adRsnUpdate** indicates that the current record will be updated.

To illustrate the use of the **WillChangeRecord** event, you will write code to validate the input fields. If the input fields are valid, the update should continue; otherwise, it should be canceled. This code will use the IsDate and IsNumeric classification functions to determine whether the input is valid. If any field is invalid, a message box alerts the user about the problem and that the update should be canceled.

To prevent run-time errors from occurring when updating records:

1. Activate the Code window for the form named frmADODC, and locate the **adMagnet_WillChangeRecord** event procedure.

2. Enter the following code in the event procedure:

```
Dim pstrMsg As String
Dim pblnError As Boolean

If adReason = adRsnAddNew Then
    Exit Sub
End If

If Not IsDate(txtOrderDate) Then
    pstrMsg = pstrMsg & _
        "Order date not a valid date." _
        &Chr(13)
    pblnError = True
End If

If Not IsNumeric(txtOrderSales) Then
    pstrMsg = pstrMsg & "Sales must be numeric." & Chr(13)
    pblnError = True
End If

If Not IsNumeric(txtOrderCost) Then
    pstrMsg = pstrMsg & "Cost must be numeric." & Chr(13)
    pblnError = True
End If

If pblnError Then
    Call MsgBox(pstrMsg, vbOKOnly)
    adStatus = adStatusCancel
End If
```

Consider this code carefully. The **WillChangeRecord** event procedure executes just before changes are applied to the current record. This event can occur because a new record is being added or the contents of an existing record are being changed.

```
Dim pstrMsg As String
Dim pblnError As Boolean
```

The preceding statements declare two local variables. The variable **pstrMsg** stores a string that will be displayed to the user via a message box. This string will describe the invalid input fields. The second variable will be set to True if an input field is invalid and False otherwise.

```
If adReason = adRsnAddNew Then
   Exit Sub
End If
```

The preceding **If** statement is very important. When you first add a new record, the **WillChangeRecord** event occurs and the bound text boxes are cleared. The event will occur again when you attempt to save the changes. Thus, upon the addition of the record, this event procedure should exit without validating the input, because the user has not yet supplied any input in the text boxes. The argument **adReason** is therefore tested to determine whether the cause of the event was the **AddNew** procedure. If so, the event procedure exits.

```
If Not IsDate(txtOrderDate) Then
    pstrMsg = pstrMsg & _
      "Order date not a valid date." _
      &Chr(13)
  pblnError = True
End If
```

This **If** statement checks whether the text box **txtOrderDate** contains a valid date value. If it does not, a message is concatenated to the string variable and the error flag **pblnError** is set to **True**, indicating that the user entered invalid data.

```
      If Not IsNumeric(txtOrderSales) Then
    pstrMsg = pstrMsg & "Sales must be numeric." & Chr(13)
    pblnError = True
End If
```

In the preceding code, the validation process continues by checking that the field **txtOrderSales** contains a valid number. If it does not, then the string **"Sales must be numeric"** is appended to the message, and the error flag is set to **True**.

```
If Not IsNumeric(txtOrderCost) Then
    pstrMsg = pstrMsg & "Cost must be numeric." & Chr(13)
    pblnError = True
End If
```

The preceding **If** statement has the same effect as the **If** statement to validate the text box named **txtOrderSales**. Again, a string is appended to the message and the error flag is set to **True** if the text box does not contain numeric data.

```
If pblnError Then
    Call MsgBox(pstrMsg, vbOKOnly)
    adStatus = adStatusCancel
End If
```

The final **If** statement checks the value of **pblnError**. If the value is **True**, then an error occurred. A message box appears, advising the user of the error. Assigning the constant value **adStatusCancel** to the argument **adStatus** cancels the event causing the update.

Note that when you referenced the Text Box and Label control instances, you did specify a property name explicitly. Nearly every control or object supports a default property or a default method. A default property or method executes when no property or method name is specified. The default property for the text box is Text, and the default property for the label is Caption. Table 3.1 lists the default properties for specific Visual Basic intrinsic controls.

From this point forward, default properties will be used.

In addition to saving typing, statements that take advantage of default properties will execute approximately 25 percent faster than those that specify a default property explicitly by name. This difference in execution occurs because different code is used.

You can now test the program to verify that the validation code works correctly.

To test the validation code:

1. Test the program. Click on the ADO Data Control command button.

2. Modify the first record displayed so that the date is invalid.

3. Try to locate a different record. The message box should appear, as shown in Figure 3.15.

4. Click on OK to close the dialog box. End the program to return to design mode.

At this point in your program's development, the ADO Data control will establish a connection to the database and execute a command to load records into the bound controls you created. The user can click on the buttons on the

Table 3.1 Default properties.

Control	Default Property
CommandButton	Value
Label	Caption
Line	Visible
Shape	Shape
TextBox	Text
ScrollBar	Value

Figure 3.15   Message box.

3

ADO Data control to locate, edit, and add new records. You have also developed validation code that will execute when the user changes a record's contents.

The Recordset Object

The ADO Data control works by using the already-set design-time properties to create, at run time, an object called a recordset. The Recordset object is created as a result of executing an ADO command. The ADO Data control then uses the underlying methods and properties of the Recordset object to locate different records and to modify data. Both the ADO Data control and the Recordset object support a set of properties and methods that interact with each other. The properties and methods of the Recordset object will now be described.

Syntax

Recordset

Properties

➤ The **AbsolutePosition** property is a Long Integer between 1 and the number of records in the recordset. It can also contain one of the three possible constant values: **adPosUnknown, adPosBOF,** or **adPosEOF.** The constant **adPosUnknown** indicates that the current position in the recordset is unknown. **adPosBOF** and **adPosEOF** signify that the current record position is at the beginning and end of the recordset, respectively.

➤ The **BOF** and **EOF** properties store Boolean values indicating whether the current record pointer is at the beginning or end of the recordset, respectively. When **BOF** or **EOF** is **True**, no current record exists.

➤ The **BookMark** property allows you to create variables with which to locate and identify an individual record in the recordset.

➤ The **CursorLocation** property determines how the cursor engine creates the recordset.

➤ The **CursorType** property specifies the kind of recordset that will be created. It indirectly defines the operations that can be performed on the recordset.

➤ The **EditMode** property can assume one of four constant values. The value **adEditNone** indicates the current record is not being edited. The value

adEditInProgress indicates that the current record has been modified but not yet saved. The value **adEditAdd** indicates that a new record has been added by calling the **AddNew** method; the new record has not been saved, however. The constant value **adEditDelete** indicates that the current record has been deleted.

➤ The **LockType** property determines how records are locked while being edited. This property is useful only in multiuser situations.

➤ The **MaxRecords** property contains the maximum number of records that the recordset will return.

➤ The **RecordCount** property returns the number of records in a Recordset object.

Methods

➤ The **AddNew** method creates a new blank record in the edit buffer. The record is not written to the database until you call the **Update** method.

➤ The **Cancel** method cancels the execution of an asynchronous command. Most commands execute synchronously—that is, execution of the command must complete before the next command or Visual Basic statement can execute. Some commands execute asynchronously—that is, other commands or statements can execute before the execution of an asynchronous command completes.

➤ The **CancelUpdate** method cancels the update operation initiated by the **AddNew** or **Edit** method. If you called and then canceled the **AddNew** method, the record that was current prior to calling the **AddNew** method becomes current again.

➤ The **Clone** method duplicates a recordset from an original recordset. The new recordset has its own current record pointer, and each recordset has its own edit buffer.

➤ The **Delete** method either deletes the current record from the recordset or deletes a group of records based upon the value of the **Filter** property. After you call this method, no current record exists. Thus it is advisable to call the **MoveNext** method after calling the **Delete** method to ensure that a current record exists.

➤ The **MoveFirst**, **MoveNext**, **MovePrevious**, and **MoveLast** methods locate the first, next, previous, and last records in the recordset, respectively.

➤ The **Requery** method re-executes the query on which the recordset is based.

➤ The **Update** method writes any changes made to a record in the edit buffer to the database.

If you have worked with previous versions of Visual Basic, you are likely familiar with the Recordset object. The Recordset object created by the intrinsic Data control and used by the DAO hierarchy is not the same Recordset object used by ADO, however. That is, the two objects support different sets of properties and methods. When this book refers to a Recordset object, it means the Recordset object pertaining to ADO, rather than the Recordset object pertaining to DAO.

3

A recordset supports specific methods to add new records and to apply the changes to a record once editing is complete. The ADO Data control implicitly calls these methods for you. When you change the contents of a data-aware control and then locate a different record using the buttons on the ADO Data control, this control automatically enables editing on the recordset. In addition, the ADO Data control updates the current record and then locates the next record. You can also perform these same actions by calling the methods of the recordset explicitly.

It is possible to use the ADO Data control along with bound controls and never reference the underlying recordset directly, even though it always exists. Alternatively, you can use the ADO Data control and the underlying recordset simultaneously. Finally, you can create recordsets and display data in unbound controls without the aid of the ADO Data control. Figure 3.16 illustrates these various methods of processing Jet data.

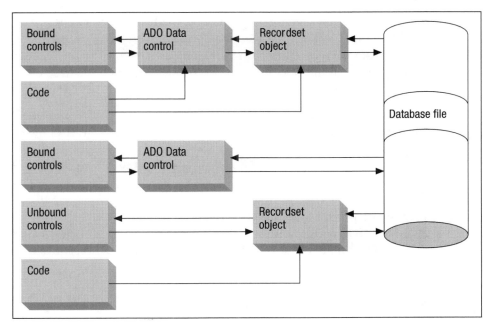

Figure 3.16   ADO Data control and Recordset relationship.

A reference to the Recordset object is stored in the Recordset property pertaining to the ADO Data control at run time. Recordsets differ from other objects you have created in that they have no visible component. Thus, the only way to interact with a recordset is programmatically. Describing the ADO Data control and the underlying recordset presents a "chicken and egg" problem, because the two objects are so closely interrelated. When the recordset is bound to an ADO Data control, any changes made to the recordset are reflected in both the ADO Data control and its bound controls.

In working with the ADO Data control and the recordset referenced by it, you need to recognize the effects they have on one another. When the user clicks the buttons on the ADO Data control instance, this control enables a record for editing and saves the changed record back to the database. When you program the recordset directly, however, you expressly call methods to record or discard changes. Thus, if the user executes menu commands that expressly call the methods pertaining to a recordset and the user has the capability to click on the buttons on the ADO Data control, the code in your program must keep track of the edit state of a record. Otherwise, run-time errors are likely.

To reference the Recordset object created by the ADO Data control, you use the Recordset property. Consider the following statement:

```
lblRecordCount = adMagnet.Recordset.RecordCount
```

This statement references the **Recordset** property pertaining to the ADO Data control named adMagnet. This property is itself an object. The Recordset object, in turn, supports the **RecordCount** property. This property contains a **Long Integer** variable indicating the number of records in the recordset. The result is stored in the label **lblRecordCount**. Again, note that the code used the default Caption property pertaining to the label.

On the ADO Data control form you have been working with, two labels have already been created to store the current record and the number of records. You can now write the code to display values in these control instances. To accomplish this task, you can rely on the ADO Data control's **MoveComplete event**.

Syntax
Private Sub *object*_MoveComplete(ByVal *adReason*
As ADODB.EventReasonEnum, ByVal *pError* As ADODB.Error, *adStatus* As
ADODB.EventStatusEnum, ByVal *pRecordset* As ADODB.Recordset)

Dissection

➤ The *object* must be an instance of the ADO Data control.

➤ The **MoveComplete** event occurs when the current record is repositioned.

➤ The *adReason* argument contains a constant value indicating why the MoveComplete event occurred.

➤ If the *adStatus* argument is set to adStatusErrorsOccured, then the *pError* argument describes the error. The *adStatus* argument contains one of two constant values. If set to **adStatusOK**, then the operation causing the event was successful. If the operation failed, then the value is set to **adStatusErrorsOccurred**.

➤ The *pRecordset* argument contains a reference to the affected recordset.

The **MoveComplete** event occurs after the current record has been repositioned. You can update the value of the two labels in this event procedure:

To respond to the **MoveComplete** event:

1. Activate the Code window for the form named frmADODC, and then enter the following statements in the **adMagnet_MoveComplete** event procedure:

```
lblRecordCount = adMagnet.Recordset.RecordCount
lblCurrentRecord = adMagnet.Recordset.AbsolutePosition
```

Note that the preceding statements used label's default **Caption** property.

2. Test the program. Click on the ADO Data Control command button to activate the appropriate form.

3. When the form first loads, the current record and number of records appear in the labels. Click on the buttons on the ADO Data control instance to locate different records. As you access various records, the current record is updated to reflect the currently selected record.

4. End the program to return to design mode.

At this point, your program uses the ADO Data control to establish a connection with a database and then executes a command to retrieve data. These tasks are performed automatically by the ADO Data control. The only code you wrote performed validation, displayed the current record, and displayed the number of records.

Using The Recordset Object To Manipulate Data

Using ADO Programmatically

In the previous section, you used the ADO Data control in conjunction with the properties of the Recordset object to locate and edit database records. You also saw the interaction that takes place between the ADO Data control and the underlying recordset object. It is also possible to create a Recordset object by writing code, without the aid of the ADO Data control. In this section, you will use menus on a form rather than the buttons on the ADO Data control; this approach will allow you to see the techniques used to create and manipulate the Recordset object with code. To prevent the user from selecting options that would otherwise cause run-time errors, certain menu commands and control instances will be enabled or disabled depending on the edit state of the current record. The Recordset object is but one member of a group of objects collectively referred to as the ADO Object model or ADO objects.

 Prior to the inception of ADO, Data Access Objects (DAO) was the preferred method of accessing Jet databases. Visual Basic 6.0 continues to support DAO, but the flexibility of ADO and the simplicity of its object hierarchy make it the preferred interface to a database's data. Remove Data Objects (RDO) provides another mechanism to access remote data over a network. Although the latest version of Visual Basic still supports RDO, ADO supplies the same functionality.

To perform ADO operations without the aid of the ADO Data control, you typically follow these steps:

1. Establish a connection to a data source.

2. Define a command.

3. Execute the command.

4. Commands may or may not return records. If they do, create a recordset.

5. Manipulate the records in the recordset as desired.

The objects in DAO and the objects in ADO form an object hierarchy. An object hierarchy consists of collections and objects, which in turn can reference other collections and objects. Figure 3.17 shows the ADO object model. This entire object model will be examined in the course of this section and in Chapter 4.

As shown in Figure 3.17, the Connection object appears at the top of the hierarchy, with the Error, Command, and Recordset objects all depending on the Connection object. You can also create specific ADO objects independently without explicitly creating a Connection object. This variation of the object hierarchy is shown in Figure 3.18.

ADO differs significantly from DAO in several ways. For instance, the ADO object model is considerably simpler than the DAO object model. Figure 3.19 shows part of the DAO object model.

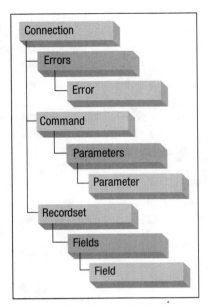

Figure 3.17   ADO object hierarchy (1).

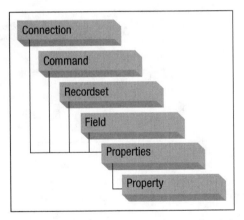

Figure 3.18   ADO object hierarchy (2).

As shown in Figure 3.19, the DAO root object is the DBEngine. This object is predefined; that is, you as the programmer do not create an instance of this object. The **Workspaces** collection and Workspace objects manage a session. When you write code to open a database, a reference to the open database is added to the **Databases** collection. The **Databases** collection contains the **TableDefs** collection, which in turn contains the **Fields** collection. These collections store references to the database tables and the fields in those tables.

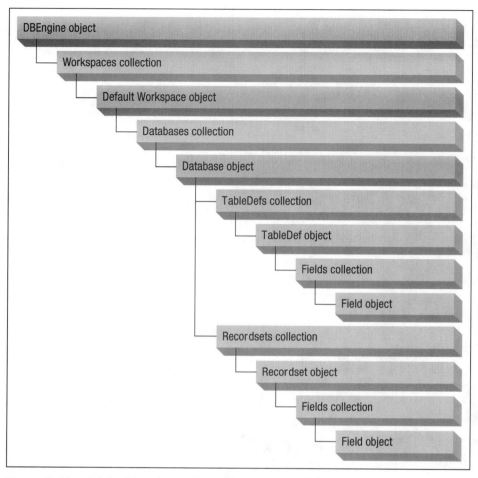

Figure 3.19 DAO object hierarchy.

The Database object also contains the **Recordsets** collection, which includes a Recordset object for each open recordset in the database. This book uses the new ADO object model rather than DAO; DAO is mentioned in this section only for comparison and reference.

When you used the ADO Data control and built the **ConnectionString** property using the control's Property Pages, the ADO Data control built the Connection object for you. When the program was run, the ADO Data control built and created an instance of the Command object and created a Recordset object. It performed both of these tasks automatically.

You can also create a Connection object without the aid of the ADO Data control.

Syntax

Connection

Properties

➤ The **ConnectionString** property is used to establish a connection with a provider. To build the string, you specify a key, followed by an equals sign (=), followed by a value that is assigned to the argument. Each key/value pair is separated by a semicolon (;).

➤ The **ConnectionTimeout** property contains a Long Integer value indicating the number of seconds to wait for a connection to open. The default is 15 seconds. This property is particularly important when establishing connections over a network.

➤ The **CommandTimeout** property contains a Long Integer value indicating the number of seconds to wait for a command to execute. The default value is 30 seconds.

➤ The **Mode** property defines the permissions applied to the data retrieved through the connection.

➤ The **Provider** property defines the name of the provider for the Connection object. You can also set this property by using the Provider key when setting the **ConnectionString** property.

Methods

➤ The **Open** method opens and establishes a connection with a data source.

➤ The **Close** method closes an open connection and any dependent objects. Calling this method frees the resources associated with this object.

➤ The **BeginTrans** method begins a new transaction. Transactions are used to group multiple database statements together such that all the statements must complete successfully or they will all be aborted.

➤ The **CommitTrans** method saves the changes made by the current transaction.

➤ The **RollbackTrans** method cancels any changes made during the current transaction and then ends the transaction. Chapter 4 discusses transactions in more detail.

In this example, you will set the necessary properties to establish a database connection without the aid of the ADO Data control. Thus you must build the Connection object programmatically. To accomplish this task, you must be able to set the necessary arguments for the **ConnectionString** property and to call the **Open** method.

The **ConnectionString property** is a string with which you specify a data source. This string defines connection information in the form of *argument = value* pairs separated by semicolons (;). ADO supports seven connection arguments:

➤ **Provider** Identifies the name of the provider that will establish the connection.

➤ **Data Source** Identifies the name of the data source for the connection.

➤ **User ID** and **Password** Identify the user name and password for the connection, respectively, if they are required.

➤ **File Name** A connection string can be stored in a file. The **File Name** property contains the name of the file containing the connection string or persisted data.

➤ **Remote Provider** and **Remote Server** Apply when you use Remote Data Service (RDS) to establish a client server connection. These arguments identify the provider name and server name, respectively. This book will not use RDS.

One further item of information is necessary before you can programmatically establish an ADO connection. Most ADO objects are created externally. That is, you must create an instance of a particular ADO object before you can use it.

 When programming DAO objects, the object instances are created when you call specific methods. For example, the **OpenDatabase** method creates an instance of a Database object and the **OpenRecordset** method creates an instance of the Recordset object. You, as the programmer, never explicitly create an instance of a DAO object. With ADO, however, the opposite is true. When using ADO objects, you must explicitly create an instance of each desired object.

When assigning object references, you must include a **Set** statement in the assignment statement. To create a new instance of an object, you must use the **New** keyword either when declaring the object variable or when calling the **Set** statement to assign an object reference. Carefully consider the following three statements:

```
Dim pconMagnet As New ADODB.Connection
Dim pconMagnet1 As ADODB.Connection
Set pconMagnet1 = pconMagnet
```

The object ADODB acts as the root ADO object. One object supported by ADO is the Connection object. Thus the statement fragment **ADODB.Connection** refers to an ADO Connection object. Note that the first statement applies the **New** keyword when declaring the variable **pconMagnet**. The **New** keyword causes two actions to occur. First, it creates an object of type Connection. Second, it stores a reference to that object in the object variable **pconMagnet**. This variable is of type Connection. Execution of this statement therefore creates an instance of a Connection object. Note that the necessary properties have not yet been set to open a connection and that the connection has not been opened.

The second statement differs significantly from the first. It omits the **New** keyword, so Visual Basic does not create an instance of the Connection object. Rather, it declares an object variable that can reference a Connection object, but the variable currently references Nothing. The third statement assigns an object reference. After this statement executes, the variable **pconMagnet1** references the same object as **pconMagnet**.

The important concept to understand is that when you declare a variable of an intrinsic data type, that information becomes stored in the memory address of the variable. The memory address of an object variable is a Long Integer number; it represents the memory address of the actual object. You use this reference to an object variable to call methods and to read and write the properties of the underlying object. Figure 3.20 illustrates this difference.

As this book is not intended as an introductory Visual Basic text, you may want to refer to such a text or to the MSDN Library if you are unfamiliar with the **New** keyword or the Set statement.

You now have the tools necessary to create an instance of an ADO Connection object and to establish a connection to a data source.

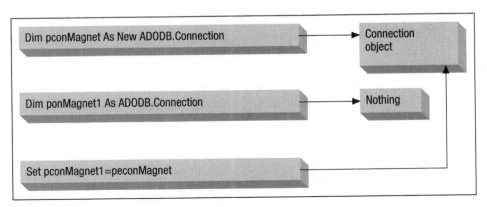

Figure 3.20   Object references.

To establish a connection with a data source:

1. Start Visual Basic and open the project Chapter.03\Startup\Ch3_S.vbp, if necessary. Click on Project, and then click on References to open the References dialog box. Note that the project includes a reference to the Microsoft ActiveX Data Objects 2.0 Library. Depending on the Visual Basic patch level, the ADO version may be 2.1. This situation arises because the ADO Data control was already added. If you did not use the ADO Data control in this project, you would need to manually add this reference. Click on OK to close the dialog box.

2. Activate the Code window for the form named **frmADO**, and then enter the following statements in the **Form_Load** event procedure:

```
Dim pconMagnet As New ADODB.Connection
Dim pcmdMagnet As New ADODB.Command
pconMagnet.Mode = adModeShareDenyNone
pconMagnet.CursorLocation = adUseClient
pconMagnet.Provider = "Microsoft.Jet.OLEDB.3.51"
pconMagnet.ConnectionString = _
    "Persist Security Info=False;" & _
    "Data Source=A:\Chapter.03\Startup\Magnet.mdb"
pconMagnet.Open
```

Be very careful to enter the connection string exactly as it appears here. If you omit the required spaces, the connection string will be invalid. Also, remember to change the drive designator as necessary.

Consider carefully the statements you just wrote.

```
Dim pconMagnet as New ADODB.Connection
Dim pcmdMagnet As New ADODB.Command
```

The first statement creates a new instance of a Connection object and stores a reference to that object in the variable **pconMagnet**. The second statement creates a new instance of a Command object and stores a reference to the Command object in the variable **pcmdMagnet**. You will use this object in a moment. Note that the three-character prefix for the Connection object is "con" and the three-character prefix for the Command object is "cmd".

```
pconMagnet.Mode = adModeShareDenyNone
pconMagnet.CursorLocation = adUseClient
```

The first statement defines the connection mode. The mode determines the sharing options in multiuser environments. The next statement creates a client cursor. Cursors will be defined in more detail in a moment.

```
pconMagnet.Provider = "Microsoft.Jet.OLEDB.3.51"
```

This statement defines the provider for the connection. In this case, you specified the OLE DB interface to the Microsoft Jet engine as the provider. Alternatively, you could have set this property using the **Provider** argument pertaining to the **ConnectionString** property.

```
pconMagnet.ConnectionString = _
    "Persist Security Info=False;" & _
    "Data Source=A:\Chapter.03\Complete\Magnet.mdb"
```

This statement builds the connection string by setting the necessary arguments. Note the argument named "Persist Security Info". It is not directly supported by ADO, but rather is passed to the provider (in this case, the Jet database engine). The Data Source argument indicates the data file name used to establish the connection. The final statement, shown below, opens the connection to the data source.

```
pconMagnet.Open
```

After defining a connection to a data source, you can define the command that should execute on the open connection. To accomplish this task, you create an instance of a Command object. Like the Connection object, the Command object supports properties and methods to define the command and to execute it.

Syntax

> Command

Properties

➤ The **ActiveConnection** property sets or returns an object reference to a Connection object. You can also set this property to a valid connection string.

➤ The **CommandText** property contains a string defining the command that should execute. This property can contain an SQL statement, table name, or any other command recognized by the provider.

➤ The **CommandTimeout** property contains a Long Integer value indicating the number of seconds that the Command object will wait for the command to execute.

➤ The **CommandType** property defines the type of command that the provider will execute. If set to the constant value **adCmdText**, the **CommandText** property is assumed to contain a textual command such as an SQL query. If set to **adCmdTable**, **Command Text** is assumed to contain a table name. If set to ad**CmdStoredProc**, **Command Text** is assumed to be a stored procedure name. If set to **adCommandFile**, it is assumed to be the file name of a persisted recordset. Finally, if set to **adExecuteNoRecords**, the command should not return any records.

Methods

> ➤ The **Cancel** method cancels the execution of an asynchronous Execute call that has not yet completed. (Recall that an asynchronous command is a command that does not have to complete before other commands or statements can execute.)

> ➤ The **Execute** method uses the **CommandType** and **CommandText** properties to execute the specified command. If the command returns any records, they are returned in a recordset.

Earlier, you wrote the necessary code to establish a connection to a data source. Next, you will define the properties for the Command object and then execute it. This command will return rows that will be stored in a Recordset object. If you are familiar with DAO programming, you will find use of the Recordset object to be somewhat different. With ADO, you must create an instance of the Recordset with the **New** keyword. With DAO, you create the Recordset instance by calling the **OpenRecordset** method.

To create an ADO command:

1. Activate the Code window for the form named frmADO, if necessary. Enter the following statement in the general declarations section of the form module:

```
Private mrstCurrent As New ADODB.Recordset
```

2. Select the Form_Load event procedure, and then enter the following statements (shown in bold) at the end of the procedure:

```
pconMagnet.Open
Set pcmdMagnet.ActiveConnection = pconMagnet
pcmdMagnet.CommandType = adCmdTable
pcmdMagnet.CommandText = "tblOrderMaster"
```

The statement you wrote in the general declarations section of the form module declares an object variable of type Recordset. The statements in the **Form_Load** event procedure define the properties for a command. Note that you did not explicitly execute the command. You will write the code to execute the command after you open the Recordset object.

Consider in more detail the code that you just wrote.

```
Private mrstCurrent As New ADODB.Recordset
```

Like the Recordset object created by the ADO Data control in the previous section, this Recordset object will be used by multiple modules. Thus, you declare it as a module-level variable so that all modules on the form can use it. Because you included the **New** keyword, the statement creates a new instance of the Recordset object.

```
Set pcmdMagnet.ActiveConnection = pconMagnet
```

The object variable **pconMagnet** contains a reference to the connection that you opened in the previous steps. This statement tells the Command object which connection to use by setting the **ActiveConnection** property pertaining to the Command object to the open connection. Note that the **Set** statement is used because the code is assigning object references.

```
pcmdMagnet.CommandType = adCmdTable
```

This statement sets the **CommandType** property to indicate that a table is being opened.

```
pcmdMagnet.CommandText = "tblOrderMaster"
```

This statement sets the **CommandText** property to the name of the table that will be opened.

In the next step in the program's development, you will set the properties pertaining to the recordset, then open the recordset based upon the open connection and the just defined command. These properties will control how the recordset is opened. That is, they determine the operations that your code can perform, such as adding new records, updating them, and so on. Before opening the recordset, however, you need to understand the concept of a cursor.

Remember that ADO is designed to operate in networked environments. That is, a program may browse and edit data using one computer even though the data physically reside on another computer. Manipulating data across a network poses several problems:

➤ **Data must be kept current.** When data change on a client computer, these changes must be propagated to the server where the data reside.

➤ **Network traffic should be kept to a minimum.** Copying entire tables or databases from one computer to another is a time-consuming and impractical operation.

➤ **Data must be synchronized.** When multiple clients access data on a server, changes made by one client should be made known to other clients.

To implement this type of functionality, you use a cursor. A cursor caches data on a client, provides synchronization mechanisms, and provides tools to minimize network traffic. A cursor is not an exposed object like a Recordset,

Command, or Connection. Rather, the ADO model implements cursors transparently. You, as the programmer, define how a cursor is created by using the **CursorLocation** and **CursorType** properties pertaining to the Recordset object. You must set these properties before opening the recordset.

The **CursorLocation** property specifies the location of the cursor engine and can be set to one of two constants:

➤ **adUseClient** If set to this, the program uses a local client cursor. Local client cursors tend to support additional functionality beyond that supported by server cursors.

➤ **adUseServer** (the default) If set to this, the program uses the cursor supplied with the data provider.

The **CursorType** property defines the kind of cursor that will be opened, according to the following constant values:

➤ **adOpenStatic** Creates a static cursor. A static copy of the data is created and stored in the Recordset object. Changes made to this static copy do not become visible to other users.

➤ **adOpenForwardOnly** Creates a cursor that is identical to a static cursor, but can only scroll forward through the records. In situations when you need to scroll through a group of records only once to print a report or perform a similar task, forward-only cursors represent the optimal choice because they improve performance.

➤ **adOpenDynamic** Creates a dynamic cursor. Additions, changes, and deletions will then be valid and visible to other users.

➤ **adOpenKeyset** Creates a keyset cursor. A keyset cursor is identical to a dynamic cursor, but records added by other users are not reflected in the open recordset. If a user deletes a record, that record is not accessible in your recordset. Changes to existing records made by other users are visible to your recordset.

In this example, you will work with a keyset cursor (the most flexible option). Because you are operating in a single-user environment, however, a dynamic cursor will function almost identically. You will also use a client cursor location.

After defining the cursor properties, you can open the recordset in one of two ways: by using the **Execute** method pertaining to the Command object or by calling the **Open** method pertaining to the Recordset object. In this case, you will use the Recordset's **Open** method, although the choice is arbitrary.

Syntax

recordset.**Open** [Source] [, ActiveConnection] [, CursorType] [, LockType] [, Options]

Dissection

➤ *recordset* must be an instance of an ADO Recordset object.

➤ The **Open** method opens a cursor (recordset).

➤ The optional *Source* argument is the name of a command object. It can also be an SQL statement or table name.

➤ The optional *ActiveConnection* argument can be an instance of a Connection object or a string containing a valid connection string.

➤ The optional *CursorType* argument defines the type of cursor used by the provider when opening the recordset.

➤ The optional *LockType* argument defines the type of record locking that will be applied to the recordset. Record locking will be discussed shortly.

➤ The optional *Options* argument defines how the provider should interpret the contents of the Source argument.

In this section, you have already created a Connection object as well as a Command object. You can set the various properties of the recordset and use the Command object as an argument to the **Open** method.

In multiuser environments, more than one user may access the same database simultaneously. Furthermore, multiple users may attempt to edit the same record or group of records at the same time. To resolve the conflicts that may arise when two users try to change the same record or groups of records, database providers support locking. To specify the type of locking, you set the **LockType** property to one of the following constants:

➤ **adLockReadOnly** If the property is set to this constant (the default), the provider creates a read-only recordset—that is, the contents of the recordset cannot be modified.

➤ **adLockPessimistic** If the property is set to this, the provider applies pessimistic locking. With pessimistic locking, a record is locked when editing begins and unlocked after the record is updated. While the record remains locked, other users cannot edit the record.

➤ **adLockOptimistic** If the property is set to this, the provider applies optimistic locking. With optimistic locking, the record remains locked only from the time the **Update** method is called to the time the update finishes.

➤ **adLockBatchOptimistic** If the property is set to this, the provider applies optimistic locking for batch updates. Batch updates are not discussed in this chapter.

To open a recordset:

1. Activate the Code window for the form named frmADO, and locate the **Form_Load** event procedure, if necessary.

2. Enter the following statements (shown in bold) at the end of the procedure:

```
pcmdMagnet.CommandText = "tblOrderMaster"
mrstCurrent.LockType = adLockOptimistic
mrstCurrent.CursorLocation = adUseClient
mrstCurrent.CursorType = adOpenKeyset
mrstCurrent.Open pcmdMagnet
```

Consider carefully the code you just wrote.

```
mrstCurrent.LockType = adLockOptimistic
```

The preceding statement sets the type of locking used for the recordset.

```
mrstCurrent.CursorLocation = adUseClient
```

This statement indicates that the newly created recordset uses a client-side cursor. Alternatively, you could specify this value as an argument to the Recordset object's Open method.

```
mrstCurrent.CursorType = adOpenKeyset
```

This statement establishes the cursor type for the recordset as a keyset. Again, you could specify this value as an argument to the recordset's **Open** method.

```
mrstCurrent.Open pcmdMagnet
```

The final statement opens the recordset. The only argument supplied is the Command object that you created earlier. You need not specify the Connection object as an argument to the **Open** method, because a reference to this Connection object is already stored in the **ActiveConnection** property of the Command object.

At this point in the program's development, you have written the necessary statements to create an instance of a Recordset object populated with records. This code accomplishes the same task as setting the properties of the ADO Data control. Now that you have seen how to create a recordset programmatically, you can call its methods to implement a program that is capable of adding, changing, and deleting records. This program should also locate records using various criteria.

Before writing this code, however, note that the user will locate, add, change, and delete records by using menu items. Some of these menu items should remain available only while the program exists in a specific state. For example, if a user adds a new record, he or she should either commit the changes or abandon them before attempting to locate a different record or add another new record. In this chapter, you prevent the user from attempting an invalid action by enabling and disabling menu items based upon the program's current state. An enumerated type has already been declared and a **Sub** procedure created to disable and enable these menu items.

```
Private Enum EditState
    Editing
    NotEditing
End Enum
```

This enumerated type declares two named constants, **Editing** and **NotEditing**, that serve as arguments in the **EditState Sub** procedure. If you are not familiar with enumerated types, refer to the MSDN Library.

```
Private Sub EditState(State As EditState)
    Dim ctlCurrent As Control

    If State = Editing Then

        ' Examine each control instance on the form.
        For Each ctlCurrent In Controls
            ' Lock only the text boxes.
            If TypeOf ctlCurrent Is TextBox Then
                ctlCurrent.Locked = False
            End If
        Next

        mnuRecordsEdit.Enabled = False
        mnuRecordsAdd.Enabled = False
        mnuRecordsUpdate.Enabled = True
        mnuRecordsAbandon.Enabled = True
        mnuRecordsDelete.Enabled = False
        mnuFind.Enabled = False
    Else

        For Each ctlCurrent In Controls
            If TypeOf ctlCurrent Is TextBox Then
                ctlCurrent.Locked = True
            End If
        Next

        mnuRecordsEdit.Enabled = True
```

```
            mnuRecordsAdd.Enabled = True
            mnuRecordsUpdate.Enabled = False
            mnuRecordsAbandon.Enabled = False
            mnuRecordsDelete.Enabled = True
            mnuFind.Enabled = True
        End If

    End Sub
```

The **EditState** procedure performs two tasks. First, it enables or disables specific menu items, depending on whether the user is adding a new record or editing a record. Second, it locks or unlocks the text boxes on the form using the **Controls** collection. (The **Controls** collection was discussed in Chapter 2.)

Now that you have written the code to open the Recordset objects and to set the edit state properly, you can write the code to call the methods supported by the recordset.

Programming The Recordset Object

In this section, you will develop the same program features that you developed with the ADO Data control; the only difference is that now you will provide those features by writing code. Thus, instead of using bound text boxes that automatically display a field from the current record, you will use the same text boxes in an unbound mode. You must therefore write code to load the current record into the various text boxes when the current record changes, as well as code to save the contents of the text boxes when the user attempts to save the current record.

Determining A Recordset's Functionality

Different types of recordsets support different functionality. That is, some recordsets may be updatable, while others may not. To determine whether a recordset supports a particular function, you call the **Supports** method.

Syntax

      object.**Supports**(CursorOptions)

Dissection

➤ The **Supports** method returns a Boolean value indicating whether the recordset supports a particular function.

➤ The *CursorOptions* argument contains a constant value.

➤ The **Supports** method uses constant values to determine whether the recordset supports a particular function.

3

➤ The constant value **adAddNew** tests whether you can add new records with the AddNew method.

➤ The constant value **adApproxPosition** tests whether you can call the **AbsolutePosition** and **AbsolutePage** properties to determine the position of the current record in the recordset.

➤ The constant value **adBookmark** tests whether you can read and write the **Bookmark** property.

➤ The constant value **adDelete** tests whether you can call the **Delete** method to remove records from the recordset.

➤ The constant value **adHoldRecords** tests whether you can retrieve additional records without committing the pending changes.

➤ The constant value **adMovePrevious** tests whether you can locate records by calling the **MoveFirst** and **MovePrevious** methods.

➤ The constant value **adResync** tests whether you can update the recordset by calling the **Resync** method.

➤ The constant value **adUpdate** tests whether you can call the **Update** method to modify existing data.

➤ The constant value **adUpdateBatch** tests whether you can call the **UpdateBatch** or **CancelBatch** methods.

Code Example

```
If mrstCurrent.Supports(adBookmark) Then
    ' Recordset supports bookmarks.
Else
    ' Recordset does not support bookmarks.
End If
```

Code Dissection
The preceding **If** statement tests whether the recordset named **mrstCurrent** supports bookmarks. If it does, the **Supports** method returns True; otherwise, it returns False.

In your program, you will exploit several additional capabilities supported by the Recordset object. The form named frmADO contains a menu with Find items that mimic the functionality of the buttons on the ADO Data control. Additionally, the menu contains menu items to find a specific record by an order ID and to add, edit, and delete records.

The first step in implementing this version of the program is to add the Find capabilities. In the past, you wrote code to create a Recordset object named mrstCurrent. You can therefore call the methods to locate records. In this section, however, the form's text boxes are not bound to an instance of the ADO Data control. You must therefore create a procedure to load the fields in the current record into the form's text boxes. The Recordset object supports the **Fields** collection, which contains a reference to all fields in the recordset. As mentioned in Chapter 2, you can reference a member of a collection through either a numeric index or a string key. The recordset named mrstCurrent contains the records for the table named tblOrderMaster. The table (and corresponding recordset) has fields, one of which is named fldOrderID. Consider the following statement to reference the contents of the field named fldOrderID:

```
txtOrderID = mrstCurrent.Fields("fldOrderID")
```

In the preceding statement, mrstCurrent.Fields references the **Fields** collection of the recordset. The string key for each field matches the field name. Thus the string key for the field named fldOrderID is "fldOrderID". The right-hand side of the assignment statement returns the contents of the field named fldOrderID, with this value being stored in the **Text** property of the text box named **txtOrderID**.

Earlier in this chapter, you learned that most objects support a default method or property. The default property for the recordset is the **Fields** collection. Consequently, you could abbreviate the preceding statement as follows:

```
txtOrderID = mrstCurrent("fldOrderID")
```

In this code section, you must load the current record into the text boxes whenever the current record changes. Because several different actions can alter the current record position, you will write a general procedure and call that procedure as necessary.

To read the fields for the current record:

1. Activate the Code window for the form named frmADO, if necessary.

2. Create a general procedure named **LoadCurrentRecord**, and then enter the following statements:

```
Private Sub LoadCurrentRecord()
    txtOrderID = mrstCurrent("fldOrderID")
    txtCustomerID = mrstCurrent("fldCustomerID")
    txtOrderDate = mrstCurrent("fldOrderDate")
    txtOrderCost = mrstCurrent("fldOrderCost")
```

```
        txtOrderSales = mrstCurrent("fldOrderSales")
        txtOrderProfit = txtOrderSales - txtOrderCost
        lblCurrentRecord = mrstCurrent.AbsolutePosition
        lblRecordCount = mrstCurrent.RecordCount
    End Sub
```

3

3. Enter the following statement (shown in bold) as the last statement in the
   Form_Load event procedure:

```
mrstCurrent.Open pcmdMagnet
Call LoadCurrentRecord
```

4. Test the program. On the main form, click on ADO Programmatically.
   When the form appears, the first record should load and the text boxes
   should become populated with data.

5. End the program to return to design mode.

The statements you just wrote load the five fields from the recordset into the
text boxes. Consider carefully the following statement:

```
txtOrderProfit = txtOrderSales - txtOrderCost
```

This statement computes the order profit by subtracting the order cost from the
order sales amount. This information is not stored in the database, however. You
could also use the recordset fields in the right-hand side of this statement.

```
lblCurrentRecord = mrstCurrent.AbsolutePosition
lblRecordCount = mrstCurrent.RecordCount
```

The preceding statements store the current record and number of records into
the labels drawn on the form.

You have now written the code to display the current record as it changes.
Next, you can write the code to locate different records. Here you will use the
same technique as that employed earlier in the chapter, except that you will not
use the ADO Data control.

To locate records without the ADO Data control:

1. Activate the Code window for the form named frmADO, if necessary.
   Locate the **mnuFindFirst_Click** event procedure, and then enter the
   following statements:

```
mrstCurrent.MoveFirst
Call LoadCurrentRecord
```

2. Locate the **mnuFindNext_Click** event procedure, and then enter the following statements:

```
mrstCurrent.MoveNext
If mrstCurrent.EOF Then
    mrstCurrent.MoveLast
End If
Call LoadCurrentRecord
```

3. Locate the **mnuFindPrevious_Click** event procedure, and then enter the following statements:

```
mrstCurrent.MovePrevious
If mrstCurrent.BOF Then
    mrstCurrent.MoveFirst
End If
Call LoadCurrentRecord
```

4. Locate the **mnuFindLast_Click** event procedure, and then enter the following statements:

```
mrstCurrent.MoveLast
Call LoadCurrentRecord
```

5. Test the program. On the main form, click on ADO Programmatically. Test each of the menu items on the Find menu, except for the menu item with the caption "By Order ID". You have not written the code for this menu item yet.

6. End the program to return to design mode.

The code that you just wrote mimics the buttons on the ADO Data control. That is, when you call the methods pertaining to the Recordset object that locate different records, the program automatically repositions the current record pointer. The **LoadCurrentRecord Sub** procedure is then called to display the current record in the unbound text boxes. The code to locate the first and last records is straightforward; it calls the **MoveFirst** and **MoveLast** methods, respectively. The code to locate the previous or next records requires more careful analysis.

```
mrstCurrent.MovePrevious
If mrstCurrent.BOF Then
    mrstCurrent.MoveFirst
End If
Call LoadCurrentRecord
```

One problem that can arise when locating the previous record occurs when the first record is the current record. In this situation, locating the previous record will cause **BOF** (beginning of file) to become **True**. As a result, no current record would exist. To alleviate this problem, the previous code uses an **If** statement to test whether **BOF** is **True**. If it is, then the code locates the first record. The code to locate the next record performs essentially the same test, but in reverse—that is, it tests the **EOF** property.

Locating Specific Records

In addition to navigating through the entire recordset, you may write code to locate records using specific criteria. You accomplish this task with the **Find** method, which pertains to the Recordset object.

Syntax

object.**Find** (criteria [, SkipRows] [, SearchDirection] [, start])

Dissection

➤ *object* must be an instance of the Recordset object.

➤ The **Find** method pertains to the Recordset object; it searches for the first record that matches the specified criteria. If it finds a record, the current record pointer is set to the found record. If no record is found, the **Find** method sets the current record to the end of the recordset (**EOF** is **True**).

➤ The *criteria* argument contains a string that determines how the search is performed. It must contain a column name, a comparison operator, and a value to use in the search. This argument takes the form of an SQL WHERE clause, but omits the word WHERE. When specifying the criteria, you must enclose dates in pound signs (#) and strings in single quotation marks ('). Numeric values should not be enclosed by any special characters. Chapter 4 discusses SQL statements in more depth.

➤ The optional *SkipRows* argument specifies the offset from the current row or *start* bookmark where the search will commence.

➤ The optional *SearchDirection* argument specifies the direction of the search. If set to the constant value **adSearchForward**, then the search is performed in a forward direction. If set to the constant value **adSearchBackward**, the search takes place in a backward direction.

➤ The optional *start* argument contains a variant bookmark used to indicate the starting position for the search. Bookmarks are discussed later in this chapter.

Code Example

```
Dim pstrName As String
pstrName = "John Smith"
mrstCurrent.Find "fldID = 123"
mrstCurrent.Find "fldName = 'John Smith'"
mrstCurrent.Find "fldName = " & "'" & pstrName & "'"
```

Code Dissection

These statements assume that **mrstCurrent** references an open recordset. The first statement assumes that **fldID** is a numeric field. After this statement executes, the first record having a fldID of 123 becomes the current record. The second statement locates the first record where **fldName** contains the value **"John Smith"**. Because this value is a string, you enclose it in single quotation marks. The final statement performs the same task. Instead of working with a literal value, however, it uses the variable containing the string. The string concatenation operator builds the criteria, and the single quotes are inserted.

The difficult part of using these methods is creating the criteria. Consider the following statements:

```
mrstCurrent.Find "fldOrderID = 'OR9441'"
mrstCurrent.Find _
    "fldOrderDate > #9/18/2000#"
mrstCurrent.Find "fldOrderCost <= 3000"
```

These statements use string, date, and numeric criteria based on the underlying data type of the database field. That is, **fldOrderID** is a String, **fldOrderDate** is a date, and **fldOrderCost** is numeric. Note that the String is enclosed in single quotes and the date is enclosed in pound signs. Conditions are applied much in the same way that the conditions are applied in an If statement, and the syntax is much the same as well. You can use both logical and relational operators in a criteria expression.

To use the **Find** method:

1. Activate the Code window for the form named frmADO, and then enter the following statements in the **mnuFindByOrderID_Click** event procedure:

```
Dim pstrOrderID As String
pstrOrderID = InputBox("Enter Order ID")
If pstrOrderID = vbNullString Then
    Exit Sub
```

```
Else
    mrstCurrent.Find "fldOrderID = " _
        & "'" & pstrOrderID & "'"
    If mrstCurrent.EOF = True Then
        Call MsgBox("Cannot find record.", vbOKOnly)
        mrstCurrent.MoveFirst
        Call LoadCurrentRecord
    Else
        Call LoadCurrentRecord
    End If
End If
```

2. Test the program. Click on the Command button named ADO Programmatically.

3. Click on Find, and then click on By Order ID. When the input box appears, enter the Order ID OR9943, and then click on the OK button. The corresponding record should appear in the text boxes.

4. Try to find the Order ID number ZZZZ. Because this record does not exist, the code you wrote displays a dialog box indicating that the desired record cannot be found. Click on OK to close the dialog box. The code you wrote then locates the first record in the recordset.

5. End the program to return to design mode.

This event procedure uses an input box to get an Order ID from the user. If the Order ID is blank, then the event procedure terminates; otherwise, it calls the FindFirst method.

```
mrstCurrent.Find "fldOrderID = " _
    & "'" & pstrOrderID & "'"
```

Because the **field fldOrderID** is a string, you must enclose the value in single quotation marks. To accomplish this task, you manually concatenate quotes around the variable **pstrOrderID**. For example, if the variable **pstrOrderID** contained the value "ABC123", then the string would be evaluated as follows:

```
fldOrderID = 'ABC123'
```

The **If** statement then tests to determine whether **EOF** is True. If so, then no record was found. The program displays a message box and then locates the first record.

In addition to locating records based upon specific criteria, you can use bookmarks.

Understanding Bookmarks

Rather than using the **AbsolutePosition** property to identify a specific record, it often is considered preferable to use a bookmark to locate or identify a specific record. An ADO bookmark works much like a bookmark used to mark the pages of a book. As with a physical bookmark, you can create multiple bookmarks. In this process, you set bookmarks and then locate a record by its bookmark. Every record in a recordset contains a bookmark stored in its **Bookmark** property. Some types of recordsets support bookmarks; others do not.

To create a bookmark, you assign the **Bookmark** property to a **Variant** data type. The following statements set a bookmark to the first record in a recordset:

```
Dim mvntBookmark As Variant
mrstCurrent.MoveFirst
mvntBookmark = mrstCurrent.Bookmark
```

To locate a record by its bookmark, you set the **Bookmark** property to the **Variant** variable containing the bookmark, as shown in the following statement. This statement changes the current record to the bookmarked record.

```
mrstCurrent.Bookmark = mvntBookmark
```

Although these statements illustrate the process of creating and locating a bookmark, they create only a single bookmark. The statements in the following steps can be used with dynamic arrays to create several bookmarks. They assume that you are familiar with dynamic arrays, the UBound function, and redimensioning dynamic arrays.

To create the necessary code for the bookmarks:

1. Activate the Code window for the form named frmADO, and then enter the following statement in the general declarations section of the form:

   ```
   Private mvntBookmarks() As Variant
   ```

This statement declares a dynamic array named **mvntBookmarks** of type Variant.

2. Enter the following statement at the end of the **Form_Load** event procedure:

   ```
   ReDim mvntBookmarks(1)
   ```

This statement changes the size of the array to 1.

3. In the Code window for the form named frmADO, locate the event procedure named **mnuRecordsNewBookmark_Click**, and then enter the following code:

```
ReDim Preserve mvntBookmarks(UBound(mvntBookmarks) + 1)
mvntBookmarks(UBound(mvntBookmarks)) = _
    mrstCurrent.Bookmark
```

4. Activate the Code window for the event procedure that is named **mnuRecordsRestoreLastBookmark_Click**, and then enter the following code:

```
If UBound(mvntBookmarks) > 1 Then
    mrstCurrent.Bookmark = _
        mvntBookmarks(UBound(mvntBookmarks))
    ReDim Preserve _
        mvntBookmarks(UBound(mvntBookmarks) - 1)
    Call LoadCurrentRecord
End If
```

5. Test the program. Click on the ADO Programmatically button to activate the correct form. Click on Records, and then click on New Bookmark to set a bookmark. Locate a different record. Click on Records, and then click on Restore Last Bookmark. The program should locate the record identified by the bookmark you just created.

6. End the program to return to design mode.

These event procedures operate using a **Variant** module-level array named **mvntBookmarks.** Opening the form initializes the **Variant** array.

Consider the code that you just wrote.

```
ReDim Preserve mvntBookmarks(UBound(mvntBookmarks) + 1)
mvntBookmarks(UBound(mvntBookmarks)) = _
    mrstCurrent.Bookmark
```

Each time a bookmark is added, the array size is increased by one element, and the new bookmark is stored in the newly created array element. Thus the array can store an indefinite number of bookmarks.

The code to restore or to use the existing bookmarks is a bit more complicated:

```
If UBound(mvntBookmarks) > 1 Then
    mrstCurrent.Bookmark = _
```

```
        mvntBookmarks(UBound(mvntBookmarks))
    ReDim Preserve _
        mvntBookmarks(UBound(mvntBookmarks) - 1)
    Call LoadCurrentRecord
End If
```

This **If** statement determines whether a bookmark exists and whether the upper bound of the array is greater than 1. It locates a record corresponding to a bookmark, from the most current bookmark to the least current bookmark. To find the most current bookmark, it locates the array element with the largest subscript and stores that value in the recordset's **Bookmark** property. After setting the **Bookmark** property, it decrements the size of the array and calls the **LoadCurrentRecord** procedure to display the current record in the unbound text boxes.

Looping Through The Records In A Recordset

In addition to locating a specific record, it often is necessary to create a loop to iterate through the records in a recordset to print a report or to accumulate totals. You can accomplish this task with a **Do** loop. The condition in the **Do** loop typically uses the **BOF** and **EOF** properties to determine when the recordset reaches the beginning of file or the end of file. These properties are False when a current record exists. Inside the **Do** loop, you can reference the individual fields programmatically in addition to using bound controls. Another way to reference a field in a recordset is through the following syntax.

Syntax

> object![fieldname]
> object("fieldname")

Dissection

➤ The *object* must be a valid instance of a recordset object.

➤ The *fieldname* must be a field in the recordset.

Code Example

```
    Do Until mrstCurrent.EOF
' The following two statements are equivalent.
Debug.Print mrstCurrent![fldOrderID]
Debug.Print mrstCurrent("fldOrderID")
mrstCurrent.MoveNext
Loop
```

Code Dissection

These statements use a **Do** loop to examine each record in a recordset. The **MoveNext** method is called on the recordset inside the **Do** loop. If it were not, the loop would examine the first record of the recordset indefinitely. For each record, the loop prints the field named fldOrderID in the Immediate window.

3

Making Changes To Data

The AddNew, Update, and Delete methods are used to add, change, and delete data in a database table referenced by a recordset, respectively. Before calling these methods, three caveats require explanation:

➤ The **AddNew** method creates a new record in the edit buffer. The data are not actually written to the underlying database table until you call the **Update** method.

➤ If you are editing a record, the **CancelUpdate** method will restore the contents of the current record to the values that existed before editing began.

➤ When you call the **Delete** method, the current record is removed. Thus, no current record exists. Typically, the **MoveNext** method is called so that a current record will exist.

Adding Data

The Recordset object allows you to add new records to a recordset—and therefore a table—in the database. The **AddNew** method accomplishes this task by creating a new blank record in the edit buffer. Before writing the changes to the database, you should call the **Update** method explicitly on the recordset. If you update records manually by calling the **Update** method, then the code in the menu command or button that calls the method could perform the necessary validation. Again, pay attention to the interaction between the ADO Data control and the recordset when using the ADO Data control. As you call the methods pertaining to the recordset, events occur to the ADO Data control. Of course, if you do not use the ADO Data control, then no events occur. Note that some recordsets can be updated, but others cannot. Furthermore, some fields in a recordset may be updatable and others may not. For example, a database field can be read-only, in which case you cannot update it. Refer to the Help topic "Recordsets, updating" for more information on this subject.

To add a new record to the database using the recordset's methods:

1. On the form named frmADO, activate the Code window for the event procedure named **mnuRecordsAdd_Click**, and then enter the following statements:

```
Call EditState(Editing)
mrstCurrent.AddNew
txtOrderID = vbNullString
txtCustomerID = vbNullString
txtOrderDate = vbNullString
txtOrderCost = vbNullString
txtOrderSales = vbNullString
txtOrderProfit = vbNullString
```

2. Activate the Code window for the event procedure that is named **mnuRecordsUpdate_Click** event, and then enter the following statements:

```
If IsDate(txtOrderDate) And IsNumeric(txtOrderCost) _
    And IsNumeric(txtOrderSales) Then
    Call EditState(NotEditing)
    mrstCurrent("fldOrderID") = txtOrderID
    mrstCurrent("fldCustomerID") = txtCustomerID
    mrstCurrent("fldOrderDate") = txtOrderDate
    mrstCurrent("fldOrderCost") = txtOrderCost
    mrstCurrent("fldOrderSales") = txtOrderSales
    mrstCurrent.Update
    txtOrderProfit = txtOrderSales - txtOrderCost
    lblCurrentRecord = mrstCurrent.AbsolutePosition
    lblRecordCount = mrstCurrent.RecordCount
Else
    Call MsgBox("Invalid input", vbOKOnly _
        + vbInformation, "Error")
End If
```

3. Test the program. Click on the Command button named ADO Programmatically to display the form.

4. Click on Records, and then click on Add to store a new record in the edit buffer. Enter an Order ID of "O9341", and then a Customer ID of "CU722". Enter the current date for the order date, and enter valid numeric values in the cost and sales fields. Finally, click on Records, and then click on Update to record the new record to the database.

5. End the program to return to design mode.

In addition to calling the **AddNew** and **Update** methods, these event procedures enable and disable the appropriate menu commands so that the user cannot attempt to perform an impossible action.

```
Call EditState(Editing)
mrstCurrent.AddNew
```

The preceding statements execute when the user adds a new record. First, the edit state is set to enable and disable the appropriate menu commands. Next, the code calls the AddNew method. Note that the remaining statements in this event procedure clear the contents of the input text boxes. This code is required because you are working with unbound text boxes. Thus these text boxes are not cleared automatically.

Consider the code to update the current record:

```
If IsDate(txtOrderDate) And IsNumeric(txtOrderCost) _
    And IsNumeric(txtOrderSales) Then
    Call EditState(NotEditing)
    mrstCurrent("fldOrderID") = txtOrderID
    mrstCurrent("fldCustomerID") = txtCustomerID
    mrstCurrent("fldOrderDate") = txtOrderDate
    mrstCurrent("fldOrderCost") = txtOrderCost
    mrstCurrent("fldOrderSales") = txtOrderSales
    mrstCurrent.Update
    txtOrderProfit = txtOrderSales - txtOrderCost
    lblCurrentRecord = mrstCurrent.AbsolutePosition
    lblRecordCount = mrstCurrent.RecordCount
Else
    Call MsgBox("Invalid input", vbOKOnly + vbInformation, _
        "Error")
End If
```

First, this code validates the numeric and date fields. If the input fields are valid, then the code resets the edit state. Next, the code stores the contents of the text boxes in the corresponding recordset fields. Then, the **Update** method is called. Finally, the statements recompute the profit and update the current record and total number of records.

Changing Data

The **Update** method causes modifications made to the current record to be recorded to the recordset. If changes have been made and you do not want to record them, you can call the **CancelUpdate** method.

If you are familiar with the DAO recordset, you know that the **Edit** method had to be called before the current record became available for editing. This requirement no longer holds true for the ADO recordset.

To program the Abandon menu item, activate the Code window for the form named frmADO, and enter the following statements in the **mnuRecordsAbandon** event procedure:

```
Call EditState(NotEditing)
mrstCurrent.CancelUpdate
Call LoadCurrentRecord
```

The first statement calls the **EditState** procedure, thereby enabling and disabling the appropriate menu items. Then, the **CancelUpdate** method is called on the current record. Finally, the current record is loaded back into the text boxes. Remember, because you are not using bound text boxes, you must implement this process manually with code.

Deleting Data

To delete data from a database, you call the **Delete** method pertaining to the recordset. This action causes the record identified by the current record pointer to be deleted from the database. After you call this method, the current record pointer no longer references the current record. As a result, the **MoveNext** method is commonly called after the **Delete** method to locate a different record.

To delete the current record, activate the Code window for the form named frmADO, and enter the following statements into the **mnuRecordsDelete_Click** event procedure:

```
Call EditState(NotEditing)
mrstCurrent.Delete
mrstCurrent.MoveNext
If mrstCurrent.EOF Then
    mrstCurrent.MoveLast
End If
Call LoadCurrentRecord
```

These statements first set the menu items to indicate that the current record is not being edited. Next, they delete the current record. No current record then exists, so the **MoveNext** method is called to locate the next record. Calling this method could cause **EOF** to be **True**, so the If statement tests for that condition. If **EOF** is **True**, then the last record is located.

Validating Field Input

Earlier in this chapter, you used the **WillChangeRecord** event pertaining to the ADO Data control as a means to validate user input. In this situation, you validated all necessary fields at once. In this section, you are not using the ADO Data control, so you need another means to validate data. Fortunately, most objects support the **Validate** event. This event occurs just before an object loses focus, but only if the **CausesValidation** property is set to **True**. The **Validate** event supports one argument, named **Cancel.** If the code you write in the **Validate** event procedure sets the value of the **Cancel** argument to **True**, then the focus will not change to the next object in the Tab order. Instead, input focus will return to the object that initiated the **Validate** event.

3

To program the **Validate** event:

1. Activate the Code window for the form named frmADO, and enter the following code into the **txtOrderDate_Validate** event procedure:

```
If Not IsDate(txtOrderDate) Then
    Cancel = True
End If
```

2. Enter the following code into the **txtOrderCost_Validate** event procedure:

```
If Not IsNumeric(txtOrderCost) Then
    Cancel = True
Else
    If txtOrderCost < 0 Then
        Cancel = True
    End If
End If
```

3. Enter the following statement into the **txtOrderSales_Validate** event procedure:

```
If Not IsNumeric(txtOrderSales) Then
    Cancel = True
Else
    If txtOrderSales < 0 Then
        Cancel = True
    End If
End If
```

4. Test the program. Click on the ADO Programmatically button. Attempt to change the information in the cost field to a nonnumeric value, and then press the Tab key. When you press the Tab key to change input focus to

another control instance, the **Validate** event occurs. If the input is invalid, focus is restored to the control instance containing invalid data. From the user's perspective, however, the control instance never appears to lose or regain focus.

5. Repeat Step 4 for the sales amount and order date fields.

6. End the program to return to design mode.

The program is now complete. By programmatically creating a Connection, Command, and Recordset objects, it emulates all of the functionality supplied by the ADO Data control. Your program adds, changes, and deletes records. It also validates user input before attempting to commit changes to the database.

CHAPTER SUMMARY

This chapter presented techniques to manage database information via ActiveX Data Objects (ADO). In the first section, you used the ADO Data control. In the second section, you explicitly used the objects in the ADO hierarchy to create a recordset and to manipulate the records in the recordset programmatically.

To add an ActiveX control to a project:

➤ Click on Project, and then click on Components on the Visual Basic menu bar to activate the Components dialog box.

➤ Select the desired ActiveX controls, and then click on OK to close the dialog box. The ActiveX controls will appear in the toolbox.

To connect the ADO Data control to a database:

➤ Activate the Property Pages for an instance of the ADO Data control.

➤ On the General tab of the Property Pages, make sure that the Use Connection String option is selected, then click on Build to activate the Data Link Properties dialog box.

➤ Set the Provider to Microsoft Jet 3.51 OLE DB Provider to connect to a Jet database.

➤ On the Connection tab, select the desired database.

➤ In the Properties window or Property Pages, set the **CommandType** as necessary.

➤ Set the **RecordSource** to the name of a table or an SQL statement.

To create a bound control:

➤ Set the **DataSource** property to the name of an ADO Data control instance created on the form.

➤ Set the **DataField** to a field in the table.

To validate user input using the ADO Data control:

➤ Write code for the **WillChangeRecord** event.

➤ In the event procedure, test the **adReason** argument as necessary to determine why the event occurred.

➤ Create the validation code as necessary. If a field is invalid, set the **adStatus** argument to **adStatusCancel**.

To create a recordset without the ADO Data control:

➤ Establish a connection to a data source.

➤ Define a command.

➤ Execute the command.

➤ Commands may or may not return records. If they do, create a recordset.

➤ Manipulate the records in the recordset as desired.

To open a recordset programmatically, call the **Open** method using the following syntax:

```
        recordset.Open [ Source ] [, ActiveConnection ] [, CursorType]
[, LockType]
 [, Options]
```

To determine the functionality of a particular recordset:

➤ Call the **Supports** method using the following syntax:

```
object.Supports(CursorOptions)
```

To locate records programmatically:

➤ Call the **MoveFirst** method to locate the first record in the recordset.

➤ Call the **MoveNext** method to locate the next record in the recordset.

➤ Call the **MovePrevious** method to locate the previous record in the recordset.

➤ Call the **MoveLast** method to locate the last record in the recordset.

To locate a record having specific criteria:

➤ Call the **Find** method using the following syntax:

```
object.Find (criteria, SkipRows, searchDirection, start)
```

To add, update, or delete records in a recordset:

➤ To add a new recordset, call the **AddNew** method. After the user has entered all data necessary, call the **Update** method.

➤ To update a record, call the **Update** method.

➤ To remove the current record, call the **Delete** method. After deleting the current record, call the **MoveNext** method so that a current record will exist.

To validate field input:

➤ Respond to the **Validate** event. Set the **Cancel** argument to **True** if invalid input is detected.

REVIEW QUESTIONS

1. Which of the following statements about a database is true?
   a. A table consists of rows and columns.
   b. The columns in a table are known as records.
   c. The rows in a table are known as fields.
   d. All of the above.
   e. None of the above.

2. Which layers does the universal data access model support?
   a. Data providers
   b. Data services
   c. Data consumers
   d. All of the above
   e. None of the above

3. Which of the following statements about ActiveX controls is true?
   a. They are added to a project using the Components dialog box.
   b. The file containing the code for the ActiveX control is stored in a separate file with the extension .ocx.
   c. They can be used by multiple programming languages.
   d. All of the above.
   e. None of the above.

4. What is the name of the ADO Data control property used to establish a link to a data provider?
   a. **DataLink**
   b. **ConnectionString**
   c. **ProviderString**
   d. **ProviderLink**
   e. None of the above

5. What ADO Data control properties do you set to build a Command object that creates a recordset?
   a. **DataCommand, RecordType**
   b. **Link**
   c. **Command, Record**
   d. **CommandType, RecordSource**
   e. None of the above

6. What properties do you use to create a bound control?
   a. **Database, Table, Field**
   b. **Table, Field**
   c. **DataSource, DataField**
   d. **DatabaseName, DataField**
   e. None of the above

7. What is the name of the event pertaining to the ADO Data control that occurs just before the contents of the current record are updated?
   a. **RecordChange**
   b. **ChangingRecord**
   c. **RecordWillChange**
   d. **WillChangeRecord**
   e. None of the above

8. Which of the following methods pertain to the Recordset object?
   a. **First, Next, Previous, Last**
   b. **LocateFirst, LocateNext, LocatePrevious, LocateLast**
   c. **MoveFirst, MoveNext, MovePrevious, MoveLast**
   d. **All of the above.**
   e. None of the above

9. Assume that an instance of the ADO Data control exists and that it is named adQuestion. Write the statements to read the current record number and the total number of records and then store the values in the labels named **lblCurrent** and **lblTotal**, respectively.

10. Assume that an instance of the ADO Data control exists and that it is named adQuestion. Write the statements to cancel the **WillChangeRecord** event when the reason for the event is the addition of a new record.

11. Which of the following are valid ADO objects?

   a. Connection, Errors, Command, Recordset
   b. Database, Errors, Command, Recordset
   c. Database, Table, Field
   d. All of the above
   e. None of the above

12. Which of the following properties does the Connection object support?

   a. **String**
   b. **Timeout**
   c. **ConnectionMode**
   d. All of the above
   e. None of the above

13. Which of the following statements is true?

   a. A Command object can be created based upon the active connection.
   b. The **BeginTrans**, **CommitTrans**, and **RollbackTrans** methods pertain to the Command object.
   c. To open a Connection, you can call the **OpenConnection** method.
   d. A Command object can be bound to multiple active connections at the same time.
   e. All of the above.

14. Which of the following statements pertaining to cursors is true?

   a. They are created using the Cursor object.
   b. The Recordset object supports client- and server-side cursors.
   c. The **CursorType** property defines the type of cursor and indirectly the operations that can be performed on the recordset.
   d. Both a and c.
   e. Both b and c.

15. Which of the following methods is supported by the Recordset object?
    a. Add
    b. Change
    c. Delete
    d. All of the above
    e. None of the above

16. Write the statements to open a recordset named mrstCurrent. Declare the Connection and Command object variables as necessary. Use the Jet engine as the provider. Connect to the table named tblDemo, and open the recordset such that client-side cursor is used. Open a Keyset type recordset.

17. Write an **If** statement to determine whether the recordset named prstDemo supports both the **AddNew** and **Delete** methods. If it does, print the text "Supported" in the Immediate window.

18. Write four statements to locate the first, next, previous, and last records in the recordset named prstDemo.

19. Write a statement to store a bookmark to the current record (use the recordset named prstDemo) in the variable mvntBookmark. Write a second statement to set the current record to the bookmark you created in the previous statement.

20. Write a statement to delete the current record from the recordset named mrstCurrent.

HANDS-ON PROJECTS

For the following exercises, use the database named Chapter.03\Exercise\ Inventory.mdb. This database has the structure shown in Table 3.2.

Table 3.2   Structure of Chapter 3 database.

tblSales		tblCustomers	
fldSalesID	Integer	fldCustomerID	Integer
fldSalesAmount	Single	fldName	Text
fldSalesCost	Single	fldAddress	Text
fldSalesDate	Date	fldCity	Text
		fldState	Text
		fldZipCode	Text
		fldDateModified	Date
		fldDateAdded	Date
		fldEstSalesAmount	Single

Project 1

In this project, you will use the ADO Data control to display each of the different fields in the table named tblSales. The program should update existing records, but you do not need to provide support for record addition or record deletion. Figure 3.21 shows the completed form for the program.

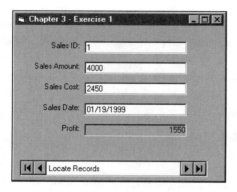

Figure 3.21 Exercise 1 Completed form.

a. Run the executable file named Chapter.03\Exercise\Ex1Demo.exe. Use the ADO Data control to locate different records. As you locate the various records, note that the bound text boxes are updated and the profit is also updated. Exit the program.

b. Start Visual Basic and create a new project. Set the **Name** property of the form to **frmEx1**. Save the form as Chapter.03\Exercise\ frmEx1.frm and the project as Chapter.03\Exercise\Ex1.vbp.

c. Create an instance of the ADO Data control on the form. Remember that you must add this ActiveX control to the project before you can use it. Set the necessary properties so that the ADO Data control will connect to the database named Chapter.03\Exercise\Inventory.mdb and to the table named tblSales.

d. Create text boxes to display the fields in the table named tblSales. Set the properties as necessary to make the text boxes work as bound controls. Note that the profit is stored in an instance of the Label control, because the user will not edit this value directly. Use Figure 3.22 as a template.

e. Create a prompt for each text box and label.

f. Write the code for the ADO Data control's **MoveComplete** event to compute the sales profit. You can calculate the sales profit by subtracting the sales amount from the sales cost.

g. Write the code for the **WillChangeRecord** event to validate the fields before writing changes to the database. That is, the sales date must be a valid Date value and the other fields must contain numbers.

h. Test the program. As you will change the database while testing it, you may want to make a copy of the database file Inventory.mdb before proceeding.

i. Exit Visual Basic.

Project 2

In this project, you will use the ADO Data control to locate and change existing records in a database. You will also write code to display the current record, to show the number of records, and to validate user input.

a. Run the executable file named Chapter.03\Exercise\Ex2Demo.exe. Figure 3.22 shows the completed form for the program. Locate different records in the database. Try to change the date added or date modified to an invalid date. A message box will appear. Try to change the estimated sales amount to an invalid number. A message box will also appear. Exit the program.

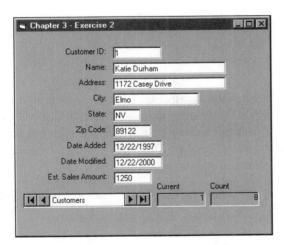

Figure 3.22 Exercise 2 Completed form.

b. Start Visual Basic, and create a new project. Set the **Name** property of the form to **frmEx2**. Save the form as Chapter.03\Exercise\ frmEx2.frm and the project as Chapter.03\Exercise\Ex2.vbp.

c. Create an instance of the ADO Data control on the form. Remember that you must add the ActiveX control to the project before you can use it. Set the necessary properties so that the ADO Data control will connect to the database named Chapter.03\Exercise\Inventory.mdb and the table named tblCustomers.

d. Create the text boxes to display the fields in the table named tblCustomers. Set the properties to make the text boxes work as bound controls. Use Figure 3.23 as a template.

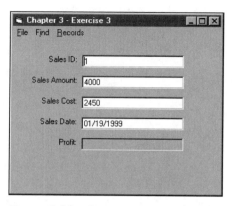

Figure 3.23   Exercise 3 Completed form.

e. Create a prompt for each text box.

f. Create labels to the right of the ADO Data control to display the current record and number of records.

g. Write the code for the ADO Data control's **MoveComplete** event to display the current record and number of records in the labels to the right of the ADO Data control instance.

h. Write the code for the **WillChangeField** event to verify that the field contains valid data. That is, the date added and date modified must be valid dates. The estimated sales amount must be a valid number. The state must be exactly two characters long, and the ZIP code must be five characters long and a number.

i. Test the program. As you will change the database while testing it, you may want to make a copy of the database file Inventory.mdb before proceeding.

j. Exit Visual Basic.

Project 3

In this project you will explicitly create an instance of the Recordset object using ADO. You will write code to locate, add, change, and delete records, and to validate user input.

a. Run the executable file named Chapter.03\Exercise\Ex3Demo.exe. As shown in Figure 3.23, the form contains a menu. The File menu contains one menu item, which exits the program. The Find menu contains options to locate records. The Records menu contains options to add, change, and delete records. Click on the options on the Find menu to locate different records. On the Records menu, click on Add, enter valid amounts into the text boxes, click on Records, then click on Update to add a new record. Note that when you add a new record, the Find menu becomes disabled, along with the invalid options on the Records menu. Locate and delete the record you just added. Exit the program.

b. Start Visual Basic, and create a new project. Set the **Name** property of the form to **frmEx3**. Save the form as Chapter.03\Exercise\ frmEx3.frm and the project as Chapter.03\Exercise\Ex3.vbp.

c. Use the References dialog box to establish a connection to the Microsoft ActiveX Data Objects 2.0 Library. Because you are not using the ADO Data control, you must explicitly establish this reference. Note that depending on the Visual Basic patch level, the version of the ADO object library may be 2.1.

d. Create the control instances shown in Figure 3.23. Note that in this exercise, you are using unbound controls.

e. In the general declarations section of the form module, create an enumerated type named **EditState** with two members named **Editing** and **NotEditing**. You used this enumerated type earlier in the chapter.

f. Also in the general declarations section of the form module, declare an object variable of type **ADODB.Recordset**. In your declaration, create a new instance of the object.

g. In the **Form_Load** event procedure, write the necessary statements to open the recordset so that all of the records in the table named tblSales appear. You will need to create instances of the Connection and Command objects. The command type should be a table command. Set the **LockType**, **CursorLocation**, and **CursorType** properties so that you can locate records forward and backward as well as add, change, and delete records.

h. Create the menu system for the program. The File menu should contain one item named Exit. The Find menu should have options to locate the first, next, previous, and last records. The Records menu should have options to add, edit, update, delete, and abandon changes.

i. Write the code for the options on the Find menu. Make sure that you write the necessary code so that BOF and EOF conditions will not generate an error. Because this program uses unbound controls, each time you locate a new record, you must display the current record in the text boxes. You may want to create a general procedure to accomplish this task.

j. Create a general procedure named **EditState**. This procedure should disable and enable the form's menu items using the same technique presented in this chapter. Also, lock and unlock the text boxes as necessary.

k. Write the code for the menu items on the Records menu. When the user adds a new record, clear the contents of the text boxes. When the user updates a record, save the changes to the recordset. If the user abandons the changes, restore the current record in the text boxes. If the user deletes the current record, locate and display the last record in the text boxes.

l. Save and test the program to verify that the Find and Edit menus work correctly.

m. Exit Visual Basic.

Project 4

In this project you will use the Recordset object without the aid of the ADO Data control.

a. Run the executable file named Chapter.03\Exercise\Ex4Demo.exe. As shown in Figure 3.24, the form contains a menu. The File menu contains one menu item, which exits the program. The Find menu contains options to locate records and use bookmarks. The Records menu contains options to add, change, and delete records. Click on the options on the Find menu to locate different records. On the Records menu, click on Add, enter valid values into the text boxes, click on Records, then click on Update to add a new record to the database. Note that when you add a new record, the Find menu becomes

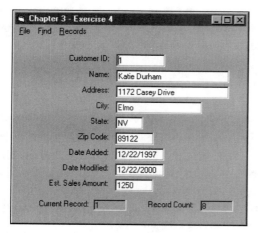

Figure 3.24   Exercise 4 Completed form.

disabled, along with the invalid options on the Records menu. Locate and delete the record you just added. Exit the program.

b. Start Visual Basic and create a new project. Set the **Name** property of the form to **frmEx4**. Save the form as Chapter.03\Exercise\ frmEx4.frm and the project as Chapter.03\Exercise\Ex4.vbp.

c. Use the References dialog box to establish a connection to the Microsoft ActiveX Data Objects 2.0 Library. Because you are not using the ADO Data control, you must explicitly establish this reference. Again, the object library version may be 2.1.

d. Create the control instances shown in Figure 3.24. Note that in this exercise, you are using unbound controls.

e. In the general declarations section of the form module, create an enumerated type named **EditState** with two members named **Editing** and **NotEditing**. You used this same enumerated type earlier in the chapter.

f. Also in the general declarations section of the form module, declare an object variable of type **ADODB.Recordset**. In your declaration, create a new instance of the object.

g. In the **Form_Load** event procedure, write the necessary statements to open the recordset so that all of the records in the table named tblCustomers appear. You will need to create instances of the Connection and Command objects. The command type should be a table command. Set the **LockType**, **CursorLocation**, and **CursorType** properties so that you can locate records forward and backward as well as add, change, and delete records.

h. Create the menu system for the program. The File menu should contain one item named Exit. The Find menu should have options to locate the first, next, previous, and last records. It should also include options to add and restore bookmarks. The Records menu should have options to add, edit, update, delete, and abandon changes.

i. Write the code for the options on the Find menu. Make sure that you write the necessary code so that BOF and EOF conditions will not generate an error. Because this program uses unbound controls, each time you locate a new record, you must display the current record in the text boxes. You may want to create a general procedure to accomplish this task.

j. Also on the Find menu, write the necessary code to add and restore bookmarks. You will also need to declare a Variant array to store these bookmarks.

k. Create a general procedure named **EditState**. This procedure should disable and enable the form's control instances using the same technique presented in this chapter. Also, lock and unlock the text boxes as necessary.

l. Write the code for the menu items on the Records menu. When the user adds a new record, clear the text boxes. When the user updates a record, save the changes to the recordset. If the user abandons the changes, restore the current record in the text boxes. If the user deletes the current record, locate and display the last record in the text boxes.

m. Create the necessary objects to display the current record and number of records. Write the code to display the current and total records in these objects.

n. Write the code to validate the text boxes as the user changes their contents. The State text box should contain exactly two characters. The Date Added and Date Modified text boxes should be valid dates. The estimated sales amount should be a number.

o. Save and test the program to verify that the Find and Edit menus work correctly.

p. Exit Visual Basic.

ACCESSING A DATABASE WITH SQL AND ACTIVEX CONTROLS

AFTER READING THIS CHAPTER AND COMPLETING THE EXERCISES, YOU WILL BE ABLE TO:

➤ Use SQL

➤ Create a recordset using a **SELECT** statement

➤ Handle database errors

➤ Add, change, and delete data using the **INSERT**, **UPDATE**, and **DELETE** statements

➤ Use unbound controls with a database

➤ Group database statements into transactions

➤ Program a type of list box and combo box called the DataList and DataCombo controls

➤ Program the DataGrid control, which displays multiple rows and columns

➤ Use **SELECT** statements to change the rows contained in these controls dynamically

INTRODUCTION TO THE SQL PROGRAMMING LANGUAGE

Previewing The Completed Application

IGA Travel is a travel agency with offices in 37 states. Its existing payroll system is no longer adequate for the size of the business. In this chapter, you will help IGA create a new program to manage its payroll processing. The tasks for this project include computing the payroll, updating the salaries of employees, and deleting obsolete payroll records. The system also includes functions to select employees and view their corresponding payroll records.

The completed payroll application for IGA Travel utilizes three ActiveX controls that you have not encountered before: DataGrid, DataList, and DataCombo. These controls work like other bound controls. The DataList and DataCombo controls, however, display multiple rows from a single field in a table, and the DataGrid control displays multiple rows and columns from a specific table. In addition, the program uses the Structured Query Language (SQL) to perform options on the records in a table. SQL is a language specifically designed to manipulate database information. You can use SQL statements to add, update, and to delete records. In addition, SQL statements can be used to select records from a table and return them in the form of a recordset.

1. Start Visual Basic, and open the project named Chapter.04\Complete\Ch4_C.vbp.

2. View the main form named frmIGA. Figure 4.1 shows this form at design time.

3. Run the program. Click on the list arrow on the DataCombo control instance to display the different employment categories. Note that the ADO Data control instance that connects to the Category table was coded to be invisible at run time, because the user will not interact with it. Select

Figure 4.1   IGA main form.

one of the descriptions in the DataCombo control instance. Although not visually apparent, the program retrieves the numeric Category ID from the Category ADO Data control instance and saves it in the payroll master table via the ADO Data control instance that is connected to the payroll master table.

4. Click on the buttons on the Payroll Master ADO Data control to locate different payroll master records. Note that the corresponding information appears in the Payroll Master DataCombo control instance. For brevity, error handlers have been omitted for BOF and EOF conditions.

5. Click on View, and then click on Payroll Detail to view the Payroll Detail form. In the DataList control, click on the employee named Wilson, Andy. Figure 4.2 shows the Payroll Detail form with this employee selected and the detailed payroll records for Andy Wilson appearing in the DataGrid control instance.

As shown in Figure 4.2, the form contains two new types of control instances. The rows in the DataList control instance correspond to the rows in a database field. The DataList control instance obtains these rows from a field in the database. The DataGrid control instance displays the payroll detail records corresponding to the name currently selected in the DataList control instance. Note the formatting and alignment of the data in the DataGrid control instance. The Hours Worked field is formatted to one decimal place. The Gross Pay, Withholding, and Net Pay columns are right-justified and formatted as currency values. The DataGrid control supports all of these capabilities. The DataGrid and DataList control instances are each bound to a separate instance of the ADO Data control. Because the user will not need to interact with the ADO Data control instances at run time, the **Visible** property has been set to False.

6. Select a different name in the DataList control instance by clicking on that name. The records corresponding to the selected name appear in the DataGrid control instance. Close the form by clicking Window, and then clicking Close.

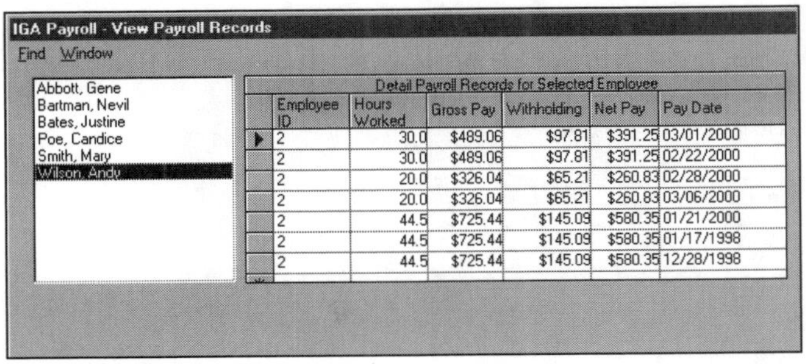

Figure 4.2   Payroll detail form.

7. You can link together the data found in multiple DataGrid control instances. On the main form's menu bar, click on View, and then click on Linked DataGrids. Figure 4.3 shows this form.

As shown in Figure 4.3, two instances of the DataGrid control appear on the form. The first DataGrid control instance displays all employee master records. When the user selects an employee master record, the payroll detail records corresponding to the selected employee appear in the second DataGrid control instance. For brevity, the column titles on the DataGrid control instances of this form are not formatted.

8. Click on the different rows in the DataGrid control instance at the top of the form. As you select different employees, the corresponding payroll records are displayed in the DataGrid control instance at the bottom of the form.

9. The DataGrid control instances are bound to ADO Data control instances. Click on the buttons on each of the ADO Data control instances. As you click on each button, the current record in the corresponding DataGrid control instance is repositioned.

10. Close the form.

11. End the program and exit Visual Basic.

The database for this program contains three tables: tblPayrollMaster, tblCategory, and tblPayrollDetail.

➤ **tblCategory**   Can be envisioned as a lookup table. The field fldCategoryID in the table tblPayrollMaster contains an Integer value corresponding to a description stored in the field fldCategoryDescription in the table tblCategory.

➤ **tblPayrollMaster**   Contains the name, hourly wage, and other information pertaining to an employee. One record exists in this table for each employee.

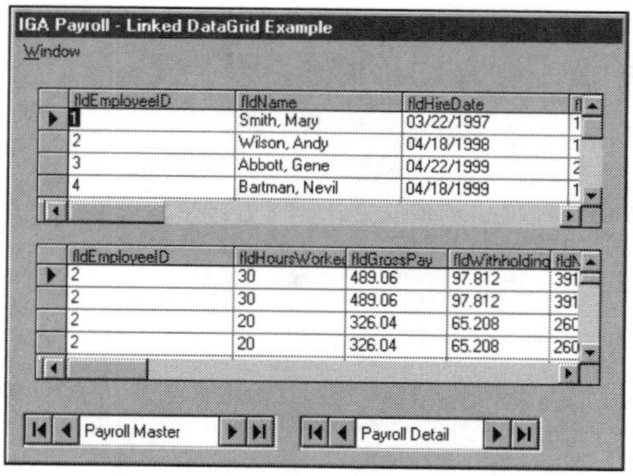

Figure 4.3   Linking DataGrid controls.

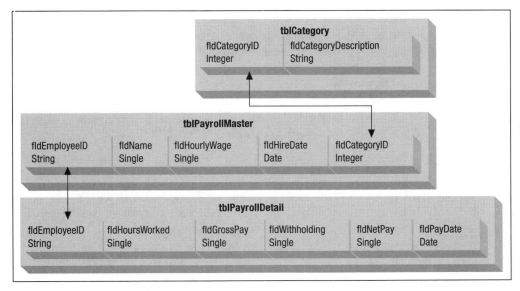

Figure 4.4   Database structure.

➤ **tblPayrollDetail** Contains multiple records for one employee. That is, it contains a record for each employee for each time that the employee was paid.

Figure 4.4 illustrates the relationships among tblCategory, tblPayrollMaster, and tblPayrollDetail in the database.

THE SQL LANGUAGE

In Chapter 3, you learned how to use the ADO Data control along with bound controls to view the records in a table and to navigate through them. You also saw how to programmatically create a recordset from an underlying table using ADO objects. To accomplish record insertion and modification, you used either bound control instances combined with an instance of the ADO Data control or the Recordset object coupled with unbound control instances. In each case, the resulting program added, changed, and deleted data one record at a time. Furthermore, you located a specific record by moving from one record to the next.

This type of interface works well for tasks that operate on a single record. Performing the same task repeatedly for several records would require a loop, however. For example, imagine a payroll table in which each employee needs to receive a 10 percent salary increase. Using a recordset, it would be necessary to examine each record via a **Do** loop and to write statements inside the Do loop that would update the appropriate field. Consider a similar situation in which you need to delete or archive obsolete information like old sales or accounts payable history. Again, it would be necessary to examine each record via a **Do** loop. Inside the **Do** loop, an **If** statement would determine whether the current record should be deleted. In each situation, performing the same operations on multiple records requires a **Do** loop to examine all records, as well as statements inside the **Do** loop to perform a specific task on each record. This form of database access commonly is referred to as the *navigational model* or *navigational access*, because you write code to navigate from record to record and to perform tasks on each record, one record at a time.

As an alternative to using the navigational model, you can create a single statement that will modify the contents of several database records simultaneously, based on some criteria. In other words, you can write a single statement to update the salary field of the payroll table for all records or to perform the same task on specific records, such as those having a specific pay date. That is, only one statement is needed to update records where the length of employment is greater than five years or records that meet some other criteria that you specify. Record deletion can be performed in a similar manner. That is, you can write a statement to delete all payroll records with a pay date that is five years old or older. This method of data access is called *relational access* or the *relational model*. To utilize the relational model, you use SQL.

IBM developed SQL in the early 1970s. Since that time, SQL has evolved into the de facto standard language for manipulating database information. Today, nearly every manufacturer of database management systems provides support for SQL, and Visual Basic allows you to tap into the power of SQL using the same ADO objects presented in Chapter 3.

When creating programs that operate with the ADO, you must decide when to use the ADO Data control coupled with bound controls, when to write SQL statements, and when to combine the two techniques. In situations where the user needs to navigate through different records and edit those records one at a time, using the ADO Data control and bound controls is suitable. In other situations, where the user must perform the same task on many records at the same time, using SQL statements may be more appropriate. Using SQL statements does not preclude using the ADO Data control, or vice versa. In fact, the two techniques can complement one another.

In Chapter 3, you set the ADO Data control's **RecordSource** property to the name of an existing table or query. SQL statements can be built dynamically at run time, however. For example, you can set the **CommandType** property to **adCmdText** and the **RecordSource** property to a valid SQL statement. In this situation, the ADO Data control will cause the provider to execute the SQL statement, and the recordset will be created based on the results of the SQL statement. Any changes to the recordset are then reflected in any control instances bound to an instance of the ADO Data control. SQL statements are executed from Visual Basic without the aid of the ADO Data control in a similar fashion. That is, all SQL statements execute by using the **Open** or **Execute** methods pertaining to the Recordset or Command objects, respectively.

The following guidelines will help you determine when use of the ADO Data control is preferable, when use of SQL statements is desirable, and when either option is suitable:

➤ When using bound controls (including instances of text boxes, DataList, DataCombo, or DataGrid controls), you must use an instance of the ADO Data control. You can replace the ADO Data control's active recordset by changing the **RecordSource** property at run time.

➤ When the rows selected in a recordset need to be changed dynamically at run time, you should use an SQL statement. In this situation, you can take advantage of an instance of the ADO Data control or create the recordset programmatically.

➤ When performing the same operation on a number of rows, you should use an SQL. In this situation, no instance of the ADO Data control is used.

➤ It is possible to use control instances such as text boxes in an unbound mode. To copy data from a recordset into the text boxes, you may write code. With this technique, however, you must write statements to retrieve the information from the recordset and display it in the contents of the text boxes when the current record changes. Furthermore, it becomes necessary to write code to locate, add, change, and delete records. This option is most suitable when you want more control over recordset processing than the ADO Data control provides. Using unbound controls without the aid of the ADO Data control was discussed in Chapter 3.

Visual Basic supports two techniques to execute SQL statements. The first technique is to create an instance of the ADO Data control and then set the **RecordSource** property to a valid SQL statement instead of to a table name. After setting the **RecordSource** property, you should write code to call the ADO Data control's **Refresh** method to execute the SQL statement and recreate the recordset. The second technique is to use the **Open** and **Execute** methods supported by the **Recordset** and **Command** objects. The **Open** method, which was described in Chapter 3, is typically used when the command returns records. The **Execute** method is used when the command does not return records.

Two types of SQL statements exist. One type of statement, called an *action query*, performs an action such as updating or deleting records but does not return any records. You use an action query to insert, update, or delete records. The other type of query, called a *select query* or *selection query*, executes an SQL statement and returns a reference to a Recordset object. This Recordset object can be manipulated in the same way as the recordsets created implicitly by an ADO Data control instance at run time. A select query is suitable when you want to display records in bound control instances, in unbound control instances, or process records individually via a loop.

SQL statements are classified into two groups. Statements used to modify the structure of a database are referred to collectively as *Data Definition Language (DDL) statements*. This book does not discuss DDL statements. To modify the structure of a database, you call DDL statements in the same way that you call other SQL statements. In addition, depending on the type of database involved, you can use the VisData program supplied with Visual Basic (it appears on the Visual Basic Add-Ins menu). Finally, you can use the provider to change the structure of a database. For example, to modify the structure of a Jet database, you can use Microsoft Access.

The second group of SQL statements retrieves, inserts, updates, and deletes the data contained in a database. These statements are referred to as *Data Manipulation Language (DML) statements*. SQL supports four DML statements, as shown in Table 4.1.

 The four DML statements appear in uppercase characters. This convention is common when writing any SQL statement. This book will follow the convention of capitalizing SQL statements and clauses.

The following section describes each DML statement and its use with ADO. The material presented in this chapter provides an overview of the SQL language. You can create much more complex and sophisticated statements than those presented in this book. For further information on the SQL language, refer to *A Guide to SQL,* by Philip J. Pratt, or *A Guide to the SQL Standard,* by C. J. Date and Hugh Darwen.

One common task supported by the SQL language is the selection of records from a database and the subsequent display of their contents in visible control instances or on a report. Although you can accomplish this task by setting the

Table 4.1   DML statements.

Statement	Description
INSERT	Inserts rows into a table
UPDATE	Updates rows in a table or query
DELETE	Deletes rows from a table
SELECT	Selects rows from a table or query

ADO Data control's **RecordSource** property to a table in the database at design time, this technique does not allow records to be selected dynamically or allow specific records to be selected. Consider the payroll example: A user may want to select only those records for a given pay period, which can change. This scenario requires that the user select specific rows from a table, rather than all of the rows. Selecting only specific rows from a table can be accomplished with an SQL SELECT statement.

Retrieving Data With The SELECT Statement

The **SELECT** statement retrieves one or more records from a database and can retrieve records from multiple tables or queries. When a **SELECT** statement is used with a database program like Microsoft Access, you can type the statement into one window and view the results of the statement in another window. When you use the **SELECT** statement with Visual Basic, the statement is typically stored in a **String** variable and in the **CommandText** property pertaining to the ADO Command object. In addition, an SQL statement can be stored in the **RecordSource** property pertaining to the ADO Data control. When the program calls the recordset's **Open** method, the provider executes the **SELECT** statement and the resultant rows are retrieved and stored in a Recordset object. The same **SELECT** statement can be stored in the ADO Data control's **RecordSource** property and executed by calling the ADO Data control's **Refresh** method. When the ADO Data control is involved, the command type must be set to adCmdText. You can scroll through the records and change a recordset by calling the recordset's methods, just as you have done in the past.

Syntax

SELECT ★ FROM *tablename*

Dissection

➤ The **SELECT** statement retrieves records from a table or query.

➤ The **FROM** clause defines the source (table or query) from which the records will be retrieved.

➤ The *tablename* indicates the name of a table or query in the database.

Code Example

```
SELECT * FROM tblPayrollMaster
```

Code Dissection

This simple form of the **SELECT** statement is roughly equivalent to setting the **RecordSource** property pertaining to the ADO Data control to a table in the database. That is, it selects all records from the table named tblPayrollMaster. Although the preceding statement represents a valid SQL statement, it is not a valid Visual Basic statement. You will see in a moment how to execute SQL statements from Visual Basic.

To illustrate the use of a **SELECT** statement without the aid of the ADO Data control, the following code has already been written in the **Click** event procedure for the Select Records command button. This code uses the same technique to create a recordset that you used in Chapter 3. To review the critical concepts, examine the code in detail.

```
Dim pconCurrent As New ADODB.Connection
Dim pcmdCurrent As New ADODB.Command
```

The preceding statements create instances of the Connection and Command objects used by the event procedure.

```
Set mrstCurrent = Nothing
```

The object variable **mrstCurrent** is declared as ADODB.Recordset. This statement destroys the existing Recordset object if one exists. The Recordset object will be recreated in this event procedure.

```
pconCurrent.ConnectionString = _
    "Provider=Microsoft.Jet.OLEDB.3.51;" & _
    "Persist Security Info=False;" & _
    "Data Source=" & App.Path & "\IGA.mdb"
pconCurrent.Open
pcmdCurrent.ActiveConnection = pconCurrent
pcmdCurrent.CommandType = adCmdText
```

These statements establish the connection and set the type of command to adCmdText. This constant value indicates that the command will contain an SQL statement.

```
pcmdCurrent.CommandText = _
    txtSelect
```

This statement sets the **CommandText** property. The actual SQL statement will be entered by the user and stored in the text box named txtSelect. It is in this text box that the user will execute an SQL statement. Note that you could also use a string variable containing an SQL statement.

```
mrstCurrent.LockType = adLockOptimistic
mrstCurrent.CursorLocation = adUseClient
```

```
mrstCurrent.CursorType = adOpenKeyset
mrstCurrent.Open pcmdCurrent
```

These statements set the recordset-related properties and open the **Recordset**.

```
mrstCurrent.MoveLast
lblRecordCount = mrstCurrent.RecordCount & _
    " Records Selected"
Call LoadCurrentRecord
```

4

These final statements call the **MoveLast** method to locate the last record in the recordset. The next statement displays the number of records in the label named **lblRecordCount**. The final statement displays the recordset's current record in the unbound control instances. Note that the **LoadCurrentRecord** Sub procedure contains code to load the current record into the form's unbound text boxes.

In addition to the preceding code, an error handler exists. Thus, if the user enters an invalid SQL statement, a dialog box will appear indicating the cause of the error. This error handler will be discussed later in this section.

To use the ADO Data control with a **SELECT** statement:

1. Start Visual Basic, and open the project named Chapter.04\
   Startup\Ch4_S.vbp.

2. Run the program. Click on View, and then click on Select Form.

3. Enter the following statement into the text box, as shown in Figure 4.5, and then click on the Select Records command button:

   ```
   SELECT * FROM tblPayrollMaster
   ```

   The label at the bottom of the screen displays the number of records selected. Furthermore, the current record is loaded into the unbound text boxes on the form. Click on the menu items on the Find menu to locate different records in the unbound text boxes.

4. The code has been designed to display an error message if you do not enter the **SELECT** statement correctly. Delete the previous **SELECT** statement, enter the following invalid statement, and then click on the Select Records command button:

   ```
   SELECT * FROMZ tblPayrollMaster
   ```

5. A dialog box will appear indicating that the statement is invalid. Click on OK to close the dialog box.

6. Click on Window, and then click on Close to close the form.

7. End the program to return to design mode.

Although this simple form of the **SELECT** statement is useful, it can be expanded to return rows in a specific order, to select specific rows from a table, or to select only specific fields. Expanding the **SELECT** statement requires that you add more clauses. The previous **SELECT** statement returned all rows from the table, but it returned them in the same order that the records originally were added to the table. Typically, however, you should sort the records. For example, it is common to order records by name. For a sales report, you may want to order the records by the sales amount. In other situations, records may be ordered by date. To accomplish this goal, you add an **ORDER BY** clause to the **SELECT** statement.

Syntax

> **SELECT ★ FROM** *tablename*
> > [**ORDER BY** *field1* [**ASC** | **DESC**][*,field2* [**ASC** | **DESC**][*,fieldn*
> [**ASC** | **DESC**]]

Dissection

➤ The optional **ORDER BY** clause causes the selected rows to be returned in a specific order. The order is determined by the field names specified in *field1, field2, fieldn,* and so on.

➤ The optional **ASC** keyword causes the records to be returned in ascending order. If you omit this keyword, the ascending–order option is the default.

➤ The optional **DESC** keyword causes the records to be returned in descending order. The **ASC** and **DESC** keywords cannot be applied to the same field simultaneously.

➤ To sort multiple fields, you may specify multiple field names separated by commas. Sorting a Date value in ascending order will return the records

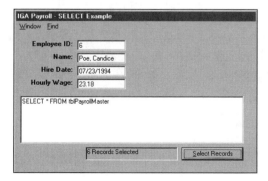

Figure 4.5 Select form.

ordered from the oldest date to the newest date. Sorting a numeric value in ascending order will order records from the smallest value to the largest value.

Code Example

```
SELECT * FROM tblPayrollMaster ORDER BY fldName
SELECT * FROM tblPayrollMaster ORDER BY fldName, fldCategoryID
SELECT * FROM tblPayrollMaster ORDER BY fldHireDate DESC
```

4

Code Dissection

The first **SELECT** statement returns the same records as shown in the previous steps, but sorts them in ascending order by name. The second **SELECT** statement has the same effect as the first unless two records have the same name. In that situation, records with the same name will be further sorted by category. The final **SELECT** statement returns the records from the most current date to the least current date. Use caution when entering the **SELECT** statements, being careful to place spaces between keywords and spell the keywords correctly. If you enter a statement incorrectly, a dialog box will appear indicating the possible cause of the error.

To select records in a specific order:

1. Test the program. On the startup form's menu bar, click on View, and then click on Select Form to display the Select form. Enter the **SELECT** statement shown below into the text box, and then click on the Select Records command button. Use the menu items on the Find menu to navigate through the records to verify that the sort order is correct.

```
SELECT * FROM tblPayrollMaster ORDER BY fldName DESC
```

2. Replace the first **SELECT** statement with the **SELECT** statement shown below, and then click on Select Records. Although the second statement appears on multiple lines here, you should enter the statement without pressing the Enter key—that is, the SQL statement should appear as a contiguous string of characters.

```
SELECT * FROM tblPayrollMaster ORDER BY fldHourlyWage
     DESC, fldName
```

3. Exit the program to return to design mode.

The first statement selects all six records and orders them by name, and the second statement orders the records by hourly wage in descending order. If two records have the same hourly wage, the records are further sorted by name.

The **SELECT** statements used here selected all records from the table. You can also restrict which rows are selected by inserting the **WHERE** clause.

 When you sort records with the **ORDER BY** clause, you can considerably improve the statement's performance by indexing the underlying field names. You can use Microsoft Access to create indexes interactively, or use DAO objects to create indexes programmatically.

Restricting The Rows Returned With The **WHERE** Clause

One of the most powerful capabilities of the **SELECT** statement is the ability to select only those rows that match specific criteria. In Chapter 3, you used a limited form of this type of functionality by working with the **Find** method pertaining to the **Recordset** object. In that situation, the underlying recordset contained all of the rows in a specific table, and you used methods to search through the recordset and find a specific record. A **SELECT** statement with a **WHERE** clause produces a similar result, but the recordset includes only those records matching the criteria, regardless of how many records exist in the underlying table. This capability enables the user to perform complex queries like selecting only those payroll records having a specific date paid or selecting only those employees with an hourly wage greater than some number.

The **WHERE** clause restricts the rows returned by an SQL statement. In the case of the **SELECT** statement, it restricts the rows returned in the recordset. The **WHERE** clause consists of the keyword **WHERE** followed by a condition list.

Syntax

> **SELECT * FROM** *tablename*
> > **WHERE** *conditionlist*
> > **[ORDER BY** *field1* **[ASC | DESC][,***field2* **[ASC | DESC][,***fieldn***]**
> **[ASC | DESC]]**

Dissection

➤ The optional **WHERE** clause typically follows the **SELECT** statement and precedes the **ORDER BY** clause. It consists of the keyword **WHERE** followed by the *conditionlist*.

➤ The *conditionlist* is a condition that evaluates to True or False and is syntactically similar to the condition in an **If** statement. The *conditionlist* consists of individual conditions separated by logical operators such as And and Or, among others. It is applied to each row in *tablename*. If the *conditionlist* is True, the record matches the criteria and is returned by the **SELECT** statement. If it is False, the record is ignored and not returned by the **SELECT** statement. In other words, it will not appear in the recordset.

Code Example

```
SELECT * FROM tblPayroll WHERE fldEmployeeID = 'A32'
SELECT * FROM tblPayroll WHERE fldHireDate > #3/22/2001#
SELECT * FROM tblPayroll WHERE fldHourlyWage < 10.22
```

Code Dissection

These three **SELECT** statements all use a **WHERE** clause to restrict the number of rows returned. The condition looks just like a condition in an **If** statement. The Employee ID is enclosed in single quotes because it is a **String** data type, and the Hire Date is enclosed in pound signs because it is a Date data type. Because the hourly wage contains a numeric value, you do not surround it with either quotation marks or pound signs.

The first statement selects only those records having an Employee ID of A32. The second statement selects only those records where the date hired is more recent than 3/22/2001. The final statement selects only those records where the hourly wage is less than $10.22.

4

The syntax for the **WHERE** clause is identical to the syntax you used in Chapter 3 with the **Find** method pertaining to the Recordset object. When the data type of a field is a **String**, you must enclose the value in single quotation marks. When the data type is a **Date** or **Time**, you must enclose the value in pound signs. No such special characters surround numeric values.

The **WHERE** clause is very powerful and flexible. In addition to using relational operators like < or >, you can use logical operators to create more complex expressions. Logical operators in a **WHERE** clause follow the same syntax as they do in an **If** statement. Consider the following statements:

```
SELECT * FROM tblPayrollMaster
    WHERE fldHireDate > #3/22/1990# And fldHourlyWage > 12.00
SELECT * FROM tblPayrollMaster
    WHERE fldHireDate > #3/22/1990# Or fldHourlyWage > 12.00
    ORDER BY fldName
```

The first **SELECT** statement selects only those records for which both the date hired is more recent than 3/22/1990 and the hourly wage is greater than $12.00. The second **SELECT** statement selects those records for which either of the conditions is True. Although these statements appear on multiple lines in this book, each should be entered as a contiguous string of characters on the screen.

To restrict the records selected using a **WHERE** clause:

1. Test the program. On the startup form's menu bar, click on View, and then click on Select Form.

2. Enter the following **SELECT** statement into the text box, and click on the Select Records command button to execute the statement. *Note:* The **SELECT** statement appears on multiple lines here, but should be entered as a single statement on screen. If you make a typographical error, a dialog box will appear indicating the cause of the error.

```
SELECT * FROM tblPayrollMaster
    WHERE fldHireDate > #3/23/1997#
```

The statement should retrieve four records.

3. Replace the previous **SELECT** statement with the following statement, and click on the Select Records command button:

```
SELECT * FROM tblPayrollMaster
    WHERE fldHireDate > #3/22/1999#
    Or fldHourlyWage > 23.00
    ORDER BY fldName
```

The **SELECT** statement should return three records.

4. End the program to return to design mode.

You can expand the functionality of the **WHERE** clause by using the Between and Like operators to select specific records.

Selecting Records Using Ranges And Patterns

The Like and Between operators enable you to create conditions in a **WHERE** clause. These operators allow a range of values to be selected or pattern matching to be used to select records.

Syntax

expression [**NOT**] **Between** value1 **And** value2

Dissection

➤ The *expression* typically contains the field name you want to evaluate.

➤ The NOT operator is a negation operator. When you use this operator, the values not between the range are selected.

➤ The **Between** operator is used as a condition in the **WHERE** clause's *conditionlist*. Multiple operations can be concatenated using logical operators.

➤ *value1* and *value2* are applied to the expression to determine whether *expression* is between *value1* and *value2*. If it is, then the value is True and the SELECT statement returns that record.

Code Example

```
SELECT * FROM tblPayrollMaster
    WHERE fldHireDate Between #3/22/1990# And #3/22/1991#
SELECT * FROM tblPayrollMaster
    WHERE fldHourlyWage Between 10.00 And 11.00 And
    fldHireDate Between #3/22/1990# And #3/22/1991#
```

Code Dissection

These **SELECT** statements use the Between operator to select records within a range of values. The first statement returns those records for which the date hired is between 3/22/1990 and 3/22/1991. The second statement returns those records for which the hourly wage is between $10.00 and $11.00 per hour and the date hired is between 3/22/1990 and 3/22/1991.

The Like operator is a pattern-matching operator that works with strings. That is, it assesses string fields to determine whether they contain a specific pattern. To perform pattern matching, a set of special characters is used as wildcard characters. Table 4.2 illustrates the different pattern-matching characters.

These characters can be combined to form complex patterns, as shown in Table 4.3.

Table 4.2   Pattern-matching operators.

Character	Operation
*	Matches multiple characters
?	Matches a single character
[a-b]	Matches a range of characters from a to b
![a-b]	Matched characters are excluded
#	Matches a single digit

Table 4.3   Pattern-matching examples.

Pattern	Will Match	Will Not Match
smi*	smith, smitty	smythe
th	the, then, smith	tih
the*	then, them	that than
1#3	123,133	1a3
[A-L]	A, B, L	M, N, Z
[!A-L]	M, N, Z	A, B, L
[S-T]?i*	This, Sting, Thin	The, Then

To test the **Between** clause:

1. Test the program. On the startup form's menu bar, click on View, and then click on Select Form. Enter the following **SELECT** statement into the text box. Click on the Select Records command button to execute the **SELECT** statement, and then use the menu items on the Find menu to view the selected records.

```
SELECT * FROM tblPayrollMaster
    WHERE fldHireDate Between #8/1/1997#
    And #12/22/2001# ORDER BY fldName
```

The **SELECT** statement returns four records.

2. End the program to return to design mode.

In addition to selecting records in a particular order and restricting the rows selected, SQL supports the selection of specific fields.

Selecting Specific Fields

The **SELECT** statements you have written so far have retrieved all fields from a table or query. In situations where only specific fields should be selected, however, you can improve the performance of the **SELECT** statement by selecting only a subset of those fields. This form of the **SELECT** statement has the following syntax.

Syntax
SELECT [*predicate*] ★ | *table.*★ | [*table.*]*field1* [**AS** *alias1*] [, [*table.*]*field2* [**AS** *alias2*] [, ...]]}
   FROM *tablename*
   WHERE *conditionlist*
   ORDER BY *field1* [**ASC** | **DESC**] [,*field2* [**ASC** | **DESC**] [,*fieldn*] [**ASC** | **DESC**]]

Dissection

➤ The *table* contains the name of the table containing the field.

➤ The asterisk (★) specifies that all fields from the specified table or tables are selected.

➤ The names of each field to be retrieved are represented by the variables *field1*, *field2*, and *fieldn*. Fields are retrieved in the order that they appear in the SELECT statement.

➤ The **As** *alias* clause assigns a name to a column that is different from the field name.

Code Example
```
SELECT fldEmployeeID AS ID, fldName AS FullName FROM
    tblPayrollMaster
```

Code Dissection

The preceding **SELECT** statement selects two fields from the table named tblPayrollMaster. The first field named fldEmployeeID is renamed ID in the recordset. The second field is renamed FullName in the recordset.

4

Consider a situation in which the user wants to add a **WHERE** clause to the **SELECT** statement and in which the user specifies the values for the **WHERE** clause, rather than the code contained in the **SELECT** statement. If a **WHERE** clause needs to contain **Date** or **String** values, you must insert the pound sign (#) or single quote (') characters, respectively, into the **SELECT** statement. In these situations, the code for **SELECT** statement can become extremely long. Instead of using several continuation lines, the code may be more readable if you create a separate variable for each clause making up the **SELECT** statement and then concatenate the individual variables into one variable representing the entire **SELECT** statement.

Assume that the user wants to select payroll records for a specific date. The user needs to specify different dates before running the query each time, however. Most likely, the value will be entered into a text box. This value will then be used to create and execute the proper **SELECT** statement. The following statements accomplish this task. Assume that the Connection object has been declared and opened, that the Command and Recordset objects have been declared, and that the names for these objects are pcmdCurrent and prstCurrent, respectively.

```
Dim pstrSQL As String, pstrSELECT As String, _
    pstrWHERE As String
' Statements to declare objects and open the
' Connection
pstrSELECT = "SELECT * FROM tblPayroll "
pstrWHERE = "WHERE fldPayDate = " & "#" [&] txtPayDate & "#"
pstrSQL = pstrSELECT & pstrWHERE
pcmdCurrent.CommandType = adCmdText
pcmdCurrent.CommandText = pstrSQL
prstCurrent.LockType = adLockOptimistic
prstCurrent.CursorLocation = adUseClient
prstCurrent.CursorType = adOpenKeyset
prstCurrent.Open pcmdCurrent
```

These statements perform a query that selects all records from **tblPayroll** for which the field named fldPayDate matches the value stored in the text box named txtPayDate. Pound signs were concatenated into the string. Thus, if txtPayDate contained the value 3/22/1999, the variable **pstrSQL** would contain the following string:

```
SELECT * FROM tblPayroll WHERE fldPayDate = #3/22/1999#
```

Use caution when building **String** variables for use with the SELECT statement. If you fail to separate the keywords with spaces, the SQL statement will be invalid and a run-time error will occur. In the previous statement, the first line of the assignment statement appends a space after the table named tblPayroll, and another space follows the equals sign.

 As a useful technique for debugging SQL statements, consider storing the statement in a variable. Just before executing the statement that opens the recordset, print the value of the variable to the Immediate window to verify the syntax.

Now that you have seen how to write SQL **SELECT** statements, you need to learn how to handle the errors that arise when the user enters an invalid **SELECT** statement.

Handling Database Errors

Database errors can occur for many reasons. A user might try to add a record with invalid information—for example, attempting to store character data in a numeric field. The user might also attempt to add or change records in such a way as to violate the underlying rules of the database. As a programmer, you must deal with the resulting errors. Handling such an error requires an understanding of its cause and the proper way to deal with it. As you saw in Chapter 3, the ADO Data control can handle some errors. When a Visual Basic statement generates an error, however, you must write an error handler to trap the error. As you saw in Chapter 2, when the execution of a Visual Basic statement causes a run-time error, you can create an error handler to trap the error. When the run-time error occurs, the **Number**, **Source**, and **Description** properties pertaining to the Err object are set. The code in the error handler uses this information to determine whether the program should continue processing, display a message to the user, or perform some other action.

If an invalid **SELECT** statement executes, the provider will generate a run-time error that can then be trapped. For each run-time error, several different database errors may have occurred. To enable the program to determine the specific database error that has occurred, the Errors collection and Error object pertaining to the active connection store each database error leading to a run-time error. The **Errors** collection contains one Error object for each database error. The last Error object in the **Errors** collection corresponds to the error value stored in the Visual Basic Err object. Note that the Error object and the Err object are different objects. When a database error occurs that pertains to objects in the ADO hierarchy, ADO creates an Error object in the **Errors** collection. After this process is complete, Visual Basic detects and raises an error. The trappable run-time error then occurs, and the properties of the Err object are set to the last error in the ADO **Errors** collection. The **Errors** collection is stored as a property of the Connection object. Thus, to reference the **Errors** collection and Error object, you must create an instance of the Connection object.

Syntax

> Error

Properties

➤ The **Description** property contains a string describing the error.

➤ The **Number** property contains a Long Integer identifying the error.

➤ The **Source** property contains the name of the object or program that generated the error.

➤ The **SQLState** and **NativeError** properties provide information from SQL data sources.

When a provider error occurs, Error objects are created in the **Errors** Collection. A single database operation may generate several errors. If you do not explicitly create an instance of the Connection object, you must retrieve the error information from the Err object, because neither the **Errors** collection nor the Error objects exist.

To prevent an invalid SQL statement from generating a run-time error, the code for the Select Records command button can be expanded to trap the error and display the errors in a message box. These statements have already been written for you. The new statements are shown in bold.

```
On Error GoTo cmdSelect_Error:
    Dim errSelect As ADODB.Error, pstrMessage As String
    Dim pconCurrent As New ADODB.Connection
    Dim pcmdCurrent As New ADODB.Command
    . . .
    mrstCurrent.Open pcmdCurrent
```

```
    mrstCurrent.MoveLast
    lblRecordCount = mrstCurrent.RecordCount & _
            " Records Selected"
    Exit Sub
cmdSelect_Error:
    pstrMessage = "You typed an invalid SQL statement" _
        & Chr(13)
    For Each errSelect In pconCurrent.Errors
        pstrMessage = pstrMessage & _
                errSelect.Description & Chr(13)
    Next
    Call MsgBox(pstrMessage, vbOKOnly + vbInformation, _
        "Database Error")
```

Examine these additional statements, which define an error handler for the event procedure.

```
cmdSelect_Error:
```

This statement defines the line label for the error handler. This line label appears at the end of the procedure.

```
pstrMessage = "You typed an invalid SQL statement" _
    Chr(13)
For Each errSelect In pconCurrent.Errors
pstrMessage = pstrMessage & _
        errSelect.Description & Chr(13)
Next
```

Like most collections, the **Errors** collection can be enumerated using a **For Each** loop. In the preceding case, the variable **errSelect** is declared as an Error object. Thus, each time through the loop, the object variable **errSelect** references the next error in the **Errors** collection. The error messages become concatenated into the message that will ultimately be displayed in the message box.

```
Call MsgBox(pstrMessage, vbOKOnly + vbInformation, _
    "Database Error")
```

After all errors have been examined, the message box is displayed.

The queries that you have performed with the **SELECT** statement returned records, so you used the **Open** method pertaining to the Recordset object. Other types of queries, however, enable you to add, change, and delete records.

Performing Action Queries

The action query is another type of SQL query. The primary difference between a select query and an action query is that an action query does not return records. Instead, action queries perform operations on data, such as inserting a new row, changing the records in a table, and deleting records. In each case, the action is performed without returning a recordset. Rather, the task is performed, and then the query returns a value indicating whether the operation completed successfully.

The **Execute** method pertains to the ADO Command object and executes an SQL statement that runs an action query. If the statement returns rows from a database table or query (a select query), you typically open a recordset using the **Open** method pertaining to the **Recordset** object.

Syntax

> object.**Execute** [RecordsAffected], [Parameters], [Options]

Dissection

➤ The *object* argument typically refers to the Command object that will execute the command.

➤ The **Execute** method executes an SQL statement. The optional *RecordsAffected* argument is a Long Integer. The provider will return the number of records affected in this argument.

➤ The optional *Parameters* argument is a **Variant** array. It contains a list of parameter values passed with an SQL statement.

➤ The optional *Options* argument contains a Long Integer value indicating how the provider should evaluate the **CommandText** property. This argument can contain the same constant values pertaining to the **CommandText** property as you saw in Chapter 3.

Code Example

```
Private mconCurrent As New ADODB.Connection
Private mcmdCurrent As New ADODB.Command
mconCurrent.ConnectionString = _
        "Provider=Microsoft.Jet.OLEDB.3.51;" & _
        "Persist Security Info=False;" & _
        "Data Source=A:\Chapter.04\Complete\IGA.mdb"
mconCurrent.Open
mcmdCurrent.ActiveConnection = mconCurrent
mcmdCurrent.CommandType = adCmdText
mcmdCurrent.CommandText = ActionQuery
mcmdCurrent.Execute
```

Code Dissection

These statements execute an SQL action query. In this example, the *ActionQuery* would be replaced with a valid INSERT, UPDATE, or DELETE statement. Unlike the previous statements, the **Execute** method pertaining to the Command object is used instead of the **Open** method pertaining to the Recordset object. If the method cannot be executed, the provider will raise a run-time error and store the error(s) in the **Errors** collection.

Regardless of whether you execute an **INSERT**, **UPDATE**, or **DELETE** statement, the program calls the Command object's **Execute** method. Now that you have learned how to call the **Execute** method, you can create an action query using the INSERT statement.

The INSERT Statement

Visual Basic supports two forms of the **INSERT** statement. The first appends a single record to a table, while the second appends multiple records based on the contents of some other table. Consider the syntax of the first form of the **INSERT** statement.

Syntax

> **INSERT INTO** *target* [(*field1*[, *field2* [, ...]])]
> **VALUES** (*value1*[, *value2* [, ...]])

Dissection

➤ The **INSERT INTO** statement inserts a row into a table.

➤ The *target* is the name of the table or query where the records will be appended (inserted).

➤ For each *field* in the target, the **INSERT** statement will store the corresponding *value* in the *field*. Parentheses enclose the list of fields, and a comma separates each *field*.

➤ The values stored in the fields are specified via the **VALUES** clause, which is followed by the values *value1*, *value2*, and so on. Each value is inserted such that *value1* corresponds to *field1*, *value2* corresponds to *field2*, and so on.

Code Example

```
Dim pstrSQL As String
pstrSQL = "INSERT INTO tblDemo (fldString, fldDate," & _
    "fldNumber) VALUES ('Marty Smith', #3/22/2001#," & _
    "3884.33)"
mcmdCurrent.CommandText = pstrSQL
mcmdCurrent.Execute
```

Code Dissection

These statements insert a record into the table named tblDemo. The inserted record has the fields named fldString, fldDate, and fldNumber, which have the values Marty Smith, 3/22/2001, and 3884.33, respectively. The newly built **INSERT** statement is stored in the String variable pstrSQL. In turn, this value is stored in the Command object variable's **CommandText** property and then executed.

4

The number of fields and values in the **INSERT** statement must match. Commas must separate each value, and values must be enclosed in parentheses. Text data must be enclosed by quotation marks, but no special characters surround numeric data. A pound sign (#) must enclose Date fields.

In reality, you will seldom insert records with literal values. Rather, you will use variables to store input values. Another common practice is to insert records into a database from a text file. In this case, a **Do** loop reads each record in the text file. Inside the **Do** loop, the code must create the string containing the proper input statement and then execute it for each record. For example, assume that the values in the previous statement are stored in the variables **pstrName, pstrDate,** and **psngValue.** The following statements would perform the same insert operation instead of using literal values:

```
' Statements to setup Connection and Command objects.
. . .
Dim pstrSQL As String
pstrSQL = "INSERT INTO tblDemo " & _
    "(fldString, fldDate, fldNumber) " & _
    "VALUES (" & "'" & pstrName & "'," & "#" & pstrDate & _
    "#," & psngValue & ")"
mcmdCurrent.CommandText = pstrSQL
mcmdCurrent.Execute pstrSQL
```

A run-time error will occur if you write code that attempts to insert invalid data into a database table. To avoid this problem, consider validating all input fields before writing code to insert those fields into the database. Also, write an error handler to trap any unavoidable run-time errors.

IGA Travel's payroll arrives at the Payroll office in the form of a text file containing two fields: Employee ID and Hours Worked. This information must be inserted into the database before processing of the payroll takes place. To accomplish this task, you will write a **Do** loop to read the text file. For each record in the text file, the information will be inserted into the table named tblPayrollDetail. Once this task is complete, the program can process the payroll.

Note that the following declarations have already been written in the general declarations section of the form named frmIGA:

```
Private mconCurrent As New ADODB.Connection
Private mcmdCurrent As New ADODB.Command
```

These statements create instances of the Connection and Command objects.

Furthermore, the following code has already been written in the **Form_Load** event procedure to establish a connection to a provider and to set up the essential properties for the Command object:

```
mconCurrent.ConnectionString = _
    "Provider=Microsoft.Jet.OLEDB.3.51;" & _
    "Persist Security Info=False;" & _
    "Data Source=" & App.Path & "\IGA.mdb"
mconCurrent.Open
mcmdCurrent.ActiveConnection = mconCurrent
mcmdCurrent.CommandType = adCmdText
```

These statements set the **ConnectionString** property and then open the connection. Next, the Command object's properties are set by defining ActiveConnection and CommandType. Note that the **CommandType** property is set to **adCmdText**, indicating that the **CommandText** property will contain an SQL statement rather than a table name. In the steps that follow, you will write the code to set the **CommandText** property and then execute the command.

To insert the payroll data into the database:

1. Locate the **mnuPayrollReadTextFile_Click** event procedure for the form named frmIGA, and enter the following statements into the event procedure:

```
Dim pstrFileName As String, pstrEmployeeID As String
Dim psngHoursWorked As String, pstrPayDate As String
Dim pstrSQL As String
pstrPayDate = CStr(Date)
pstrFileName = InputBox("Enter Payroll Filename")
Open pstrFileName For Input As #1
Do Until EOF(1)
    Input #1, pstrEmployeeID, psngHoursWorked
    pstrSQL = "INSERT INTO tblPayrollDetail " & _
```

```
            "(fldEmployeeID,fldHoursWorked,fldPayDate) " & _
            "VALUES " & "('" & pstrEmployeeID & "'," & _
            psngHoursWorked & "," & "#" & pstrPayDate & "#)"
        mcmdCurrent.CommandText = pstrSQL
        mcmdCurrent.Execute
    Loop
```

2. Test the program. Click on Payroll, and then click on Read Text File. When the input box appears, enter the name of the file Chapter.04\ Startup\Payroll.txt. Set the path name and drive designator as necessary. Click on OK. The file will open and the records will be inserted into the table.

3. End the program to return to design mode.

These statements open the text file, read the records into variables, and then insert the records into the database. The syntax for the **String** variable containing the **INSERT** statement requires careful analysis.

```
pstrSQL = "INSERT INTO tblPayrollDetail " & _
    "(fldEmployeeID,fldHoursWorked,fldPayDate) " & _
    "VALUES " & "('" & pstrEmployeeID & "'," & _
    psngHoursWorked & "," & "#" & pstrPayDate & "#)"
```

Building the **String** variable requires extensive string concatenation. Because you must enclose the **string pstrEmployeeID** in single quotation marks and the Date value in pound signs, you must embed these characters into the string expression by manually concatenating the characters. Thus, in the previous example, the variable **pstrEmployeeID** is evaluated and surrounded by quotation characters. Because **fldPayDate** is a **Date** data type, pound signs surround the variable **pstrPayDate**. In addition, the parentheses are inserted into the **VALUES** clause. Assuming that the EmployeeID contains the value 1A, the hours worked contains the value 32, and the current date contains the value 3/22/2001, the value of **pstrSQL** would contain the following text:

```
INSERT INTO tblPayrollDetail
    (fldEmployeeID,fldHoursWorked,fldPayDate)
    VALUES ('1A',32,#3/22/2001#)
```

The previous statement is stored as a string on one line, although it appears here formatted on multiple lines to improve readability.

In addition to adding new records to a table, SQL statements can be used to update existing records.

The **UPDATE** Statement

In Chapter 3 you updated records using the **Update** method pertaining to the Recordset object. With these methods, one record was updated at a time. To update all of the records in a recordset, you wrote a **Do** loop to examine each record and then to manually update each record. This updating task can be accomplished with the **UPDATE** statement as well, so that you can use the relational model to update several records in a table at one time.

Syntax

> **UPDATE** tablename
> > **SET** fieldname = newvalue [,fieldname = newvalue]
> > **WHERE** criteria

Dissection

➤ The **UPDATE** statement changes the contents of one or more fields from one or more rows in a database.

➤ The *fieldname* is a field from the table or query specified by *tablename*.

➤ The *newvalue* can be a literal value or expression. *fieldname* is set to *newvalue*.

➤ The **WHERE** clause follows the same syntax employed with the **SELECT** statement.

➤ The *criteria* expression determines which records will be updated.

Code Example

```
pstrSQL = "UPDATE tblPayrollDetail " & _
    "SET fldGrossPay = fldHourlyWage * fldHoursWorked"
mcmdCurrent.CommandText = pstrSQL
mcmdCurrent.Execute
```

Code Dissection

These statements update the Gross Pay field in the table named tblPayrollDetail. The value of the field fldGrossPay is set to the value of the field fldHourlyWage multiplied by fldHoursWorked. Once again, you store the SQL statement in a **String** data type, and then store the string variable in the **CommandText** property pertaining to the Command object. This command then executes.

You may create these statements dynamically using variables and/or literal values, as shown in the following statements:

```
pstrSQL = "UPDATE tblPayrollMaster " & _
    "SET fldHourlyWage = fldHourlyWage * 1.10"
```

```
mcmdCurrent.CommandText = pstrSQL
mcmdCurrent.Execute
```

The preceding statements increase the value of the column fldHourlyWage by 10 percent. To accomplish this task, they multiply the current value of the field by 1.10 and store the result in the same field. The statement executes for all rows in the database. To restrict the rows that are subject to updating, you can add a **WHERE** clause, as shown in the following statements:

```
pstrSQL = "UPDATE tblPayrollMaster " & _
    "SET fldHourlyWage = fldHourlyWage * 1.10 " & _
    "WHERE fldHourlyWage < 10.00"
mcmdCurrent.CommandText = pstrSQL
mcmdCurrent.Execute
```

This **WHERE** clause restricts the rows selected, ensuring that only those employees having an hourly wage of less than $10.00 per hour are updated.

IGA Travel's payroll must be computed for the newly added records. To accomplish this goal, you can perform the following tasks for the records having a date paid equal to the current date:

➤ The gross pay is computed by multiplying the hourly wage by the hours worked.

➤ The withholding tax is computed by multiplying the gross pay by 20 percent.

➤ The net pay is computed by subtracting the withholding tax from the gross pay.

To perform an action query with the **UPDATE** statement:

1. Locate the **mnuComputePayroll_Click** event procedure for the form named frmIGA, and enter the following statements into the event procedure:

```
Dim pstrSQL As String
Dim pstrWHERE As String
Dim pstrDate As String
pstrDate = InputBox("Enter Payroll Date", , Date)
pstrWHERE = " WHERE  fldPayDate = " & "#" & pstrDate & "#"
pstrSQL = "UPDATE qryPayroll " & _
    "SET fldGrossPay = fldHoursWorked * fldHourlyWage " _
    & pstrWHERE
mcmdCurrent.CommandText = pstrSQL
mcmdCurrent.Execute
```

```
pstrSQL = "UPDATE qryPayroll " & _
    "SET fldWithholding = fldGrossPay * .20" & pstrWHERE
mcmdCurrent.CommandText = pstrSQL
mcmdCurrent.Execute
pstrSQL = "UPDATE qryPayroll " & _
    "SET fldNetPay = fldGrossPay - fldWithholding" & _
    pstrWHERE
mcmdCurrent.CommandText = pstrSQL
mcmdCurrent.Execute
```

2. Test the program. Click on Payroll, and then click on Compute Payroll.

3. The input box appears, with the current date listed as the default value. Click on OK to select this default value. The payroll records for the current date are updated.

4. End the program to return to design mode.

The **UPDATE** statements created in the preceding steps compute the gross pay, the withholding amount, and the net pay. This set of statements executes three separate **UPDATE** statements rather than creating a single **UPDATE** statement that sets all three fields. In this case, three **UPDATE** statements were required because of the order in which the **UPDATE** is performed. Rather than computing the value for the first field and then using that result in the second computation, the **UPDATE** statement reads the values only once. That is, fldGrossPay serves as the result in the first **UPDATE** statement. The code must compute this result before using it as an operand to compute the gross pay in the second **UPDATE** statement. Each **UPDATE** statement contains a **WHERE** clause to change only those records having a specific date paid.

In addition to inserting and updating records using the relational model, it is also possible to delete records.

Deleting Database Records

The **DELETE** statement allows you to remove one or more rows from a table. Again, you could create a recordset and call the **Delete** method for each record to be deleted. On the other hand, you can call the **DELETE** statement once to remove several records, just as you can call the **UPDATE** statement once to update several records. The syntax of the **DELETE** statement is as follows:

Syntax

> **DELETE** ⋆
> > **FROM** *table*
> > **WHERE** *criteria*

Dissection

➤ The **DELETE** statement removes one or more rows from a table or query.

➤ The *table* is the name of the table from which records are deleted.

➤ The *criteria* is an expression that determines which records to delete. It has the same format as the **WHERE** clause in the **UPDATE** and **SELECT** statements. That is, the expression contained in *criteria* must evaluate to True or False. If True, the record is deleted; if False, the record is ignored.

Code Example

```
Dim pstrSQL As String
pstrSQL = "DELETE * FROM tblPayroll " & _
    "WHERE fldPayDate < #3/10/1995#"
cmdCurrent.CommandText = pstrSQL
cmdCurrent.Execute
```

Code Dissection

These statements delete the payroll records from the table named tblPayroll where the date paid is less than the value 3/10/1995. Again, it is common for the user to specify the values employed in the **WHERE** clause.

This section on SQL described only the most fundamental concepts of the language. You can write much more complicated SQL statements to join multiple tables, group together and summarize the contents of specific fields in a record, and perform many other tasks. As you develop your SQL queries, be careful to consider the database engine involved, as each vendor supplies a slightly different version of SQL.

When using the relational model to add, change, or delete records, situations may arise in which multiple SQL statements should be treated as a group. Transactions allow you to handle this requirement.

Transactions

In the previous examples using the **UPDATE** statement, you executed multiple **UPDATE** statements to compute IGA Travel's payroll. One statement executed to compute the gross pay, another to compute the withholding, and another to compute the net pay. All of these **UPDATE** statements had to be carried out successfully to ensure accurate payroll processing. That is, if one of the **UPDATE** statements executed and then the power failed or some other system error occurred, thereby preventing the remaining **UPDATE** statements from completing, the payroll would not have been correct and the database would have been left in an inconsistent state. This problem becomes magnified as the number and complexity of statements that collectively perform a task grow. Grouping multiple statements into a transaction can solve this problem.

A series of database statements, such as the three **UPDATE** statements you just wrote, can be considered a single transaction. The ADO Connection object enables you to view a group of statements as a unit through the use of transactions. You implement transactions by using three methods pertaining to the Connection object.

Syntax

> *object*.BeginTrans
> *object*.CommitTrans
> *object*.RollbackTrans

Dissection

➤ The *object* must be an instance of the Connection object.

➤ The code should call the **BeginTrans** method before the first action query. This method identifies the start of the transaction.

➤ The **CommitTrans** method saves (commits) the action queries performed between the **BeginTrans** and **CommitTrans** methods to the database. Once you call the **CommitTrans** method, you cannot undo the changes.

➤ The **Rollback** method reverses the changes made by any action query up to the last **BeginTrans** method.

Code Example

```
mconCurrent.BeginTrans
' Statements
mconCurrent.CommitTrans

mconCurrent.BeginTrans
' Statements
mconCurrent.RollbackTrans
```

Code Dissection

The first statement block illustrates the use of a transaction that becomes committed to the database. The second block illustrates the use of a transaction that is rolled back. In the later case, the changes are not written to the database.

When you create a transaction, it is possible to embed multiple action queries in the transaction. For example, a transaction may consist of one or more **INSERT**, **UPDATE**, and **DELETE** statements.

This section presented a fundamental discussion of the database relational model and the use of SQL statements. SQL statements and the relational model can complement the use of the ADO Data control and even replace it.

USING THE DATALIST, DATACOMBO, AND DATAGRID CONTROLS

4

The DataList And DataCombo Controls

The DataList and DataCombo controls work much like the intrinsic ListBox and ComboBox controls, but support several additional properties that allow you to read and write data from and to a database table. Both are bound controls that, like a text box, will display information obtained from a Data control's recordset.

The DataList control displays information in the same manner as a list box; that is, multiple lines always remain visible on the screen. If the size of the object, as it is drawn on the form, cannot display all of the lines, scroll bars will appear. The DataCombo control works like a combo box, supporting a drop-down combo box from which the user can select an item.

Like other bound controls you have used, the DataCombo control obtains its information from a Recordset object created by an instance of the ADO Data control. Thus you set properties to identify an instance of the ADO Data control and to identify a field name. Each row in the field is displayed in the list automatically when you run the program. In addition to displaying a field from a single ADO Data control instance, two ADO Data control instances may be created to perform lookup operations. That is, by selecting an item from the list, you can look up another record in a second ADO Data control instance. The standard prefix for the DataList control is "dbl"; the standard prefix for the DataCombo control is "dbc". The following list summarizes the properties pertaining to the DataCombo and DataList controls.

Syntax

> DataCombo
> DataList

Properties

➤ The **DataSource** property, which contains the name of an ADO Data control instance, specifies the recordset to be updated.

➤ The **DataField** property works with the **DataSource** property, specifying the field in the **DataSource** that will be updated. Typically, the **DataField** and **BoundColumn** properties refer to the same field name in two different ADO Data control instances.

➤ The **RowSource** property identifies the ADO Data control instance whose records will appear in the list.

➤ The **ListField** property identifies the field in a recordset that will be displayed. As noted above, the **RowSource** property identifies the desired recordset.

➤ The **BoundColumn** property identifies a second field in the ADO Data control instance indicated by **RowSource**. This field instance typically supplies a value to a second ADO Data control instance. The second ADO Data control instance and field are specified via the **DataSource** and **DataField** properties, respectively.

➤ When the user selects an item in the list, the **BoundText** property becomes updated to the value of the **BoundColumn** property.

➤ The **Text** property contains the text of the currently selected item in the control instance.

➤ The **MatchEntry** property determines how the search is performed as the user types characters. If it is set to the constant **dblBasicMatching**, then typing a character will search the list for the first item that matches the character typed by the user. If it is set to **dblExtendedMatching**, then the search becomes increasingly more refined as the user types each character.

➤ The **MatchedWithList** property returns True if the current contents of the **BoundText** property match one of the records in the list portion of the control.

➤ The **SelectedItem** property specifies the bookmark of the selected item in the Recordset object identified by the **RowSource** property.

➤ The **VisibleCount** property contains a number indicating the number of items appearing in the visible region of the control.

➤ The **VisibleItems** property specifies an array of bookmarks with a maximum number of items equal to the **VisibleCount** property.

Methods

➤ Calling the **Refill** method refreshes the list and repaints the control instance.

Events

➤ The **Click** event occurs when the user clicks on and selects an item from the control instance.

➤ The **Validate** event occurs just before the control instance loses focus. This event occurs only if the **CausesValidation** property is set to True.

In the following simple example, you will use the DataList and DataCombo controls to display a list of rows from a field in a recordset. Each row from the underlying recordset created by the ADO Data control instance appears on a single line in the DataList and DataCombo controls. To connect the DataList or DataCombo controls to a recordset, you use the **RowSource** and **ListField** properties. In IGA Travel's payroll program, the DataCombo control instance will be used to display the employee category description pertaining to an employee. The first step is to display a list of valid employee categories.

4

To create a bound DataCombo control instance:

1. Start Visual Basic and open the project Chapter.04\Startup\Ch4_S.vbp, if necessary.

2. Using the DataCombo button on the toolbox, create an instance of the control on the form named frmIGA, as shown in Figure 4.6, and set the following properties: **RowSource** to **adCategory**, **ListField** to **fldCategoryDescription**, **Name** to **dbcCategory**, and **Style** to **2 – dbcDropdownList**. The ADO Data control instance related to the DataCombo control instance has already been created.

3. Test the program. The rows should appear in the DataCombo control instance when you click on the list arrow.

4. End the program to return to design mode.

Although this example displays a list of items, the DataCombo control is most commonly used to look up a value from one table and update a value in another table. For IGA Travel's program, consider that each employee has a Category ID assigned in the table named tblPayrollMaster. This value—an **Integer** data type—corresponds to a description stored in the table named tblCategory. Although you can display the Category ID in a bound text box, the user interface would be more intuitive if the descriptive text appears. This goal can be accomplished with the DataCombo control. As the user selects different employee records, the category description corresponding to the numeric Category ID can be displayed in an instance of the DataCombo control. In addition, by selecting a different category description in the DataCombo control, the numeric Category ID in the payroll

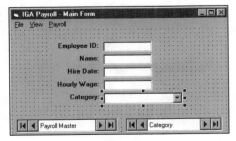

Figure 4.6   Creating a DataCombo box.

record will be updated. To achieve this functionality, you must set the **BoundColumn**, **DataSource**, and **DataField** properties. The **BoundColumn** property will be set to the field named fldCategoryID. When the user selects a different record in the DataCombo box, the **BoundColumn** property is used to set the **BoundText** property. In addition, the **DataSource** property is set to the ADO Data control instance for the Payroll Master table, and the **DataField** property is set to the **Category ID**. Thus, when the user selects a different item from the list, the program updates the **BoundText** property to the new Category ID. The **DataField** and **DataSource** properties are then used to update the Category ID in the Payroll Master table.

Figure 4.7 illustrates the process of selecting the category description Manager in the list box. Assume that the Category ID corresponding to Manager is the value three (3).

To link two ADO Data control instances with a DataCombo control instance:

1. Activate the Properties window for the DataCombo control named dbcCategory. Set **BoundColumn** to **fldCategoryID**, **DataSource** to **adPayrollMaster**, and **DataField** to **fldCategoryID**.

2. Test the program. Using the buttons on the ADO Data control instance for the table named tblPayrollMaster, select different records. The category description should be updated for the different payroll records as you select them.

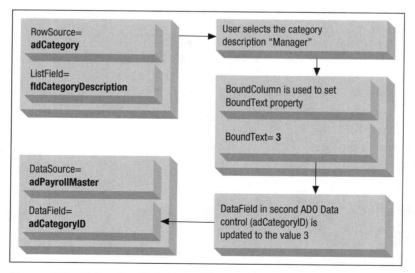

RowSource=
adCategory

ListField=
fldCategoryDescription

DataSource=
adPayrollMaster

DataField=
adCategoryID

User selects the category description "Manager"

BoundColumn is used to set BoundText property

BoundText= **3**

DataField in second ADO Data control (adCategoryID) is updated to the value 3

Figure 4.7 Using the DataList with two ADO Data controls.

3. Locate the first record. Change the category description to a different value. When a new record is selected, the record in the Payroll Master database should be updated with the new corresponding Category ID, because the **DataSource** and **DataField** properties change. Note that this change is not apparent from the program's visual interface.

4. End the program to return to design mode.

In addition to the DataList and DataCombo controls, Visual Basic supports another control that, instead of displaying multiple rows from a single field, can display multiple rows from multiple fields. This control is the DataGrid Control.

The DataGrid Control

The DataGrid control displays the records in a Recordset object associated with an instance of the ADO Data control as a grid containing multiple rows and columns. The standard prefix for the DataGrid control is "dg". Figure 4.8 shows the anatomy of the DataGrid control.

As shown in Figure 4.8, a caption typically describes the table or purpose of the control instance. Beneath the caption appears a row of column headers. By default, these values contain the column names in the table, though you can modify them to include more descriptive text. An instance of the DataGrid control can have a fixed number of columns and any number of rows. The DataGrid control can store as many as 32,767 columns; the number of rows possible will vary based on the configuration of your system. The intersection of a row and column in a DataGrid control is called a *cell*.

The left-hand column of the DataGrid control contains an icon that identifies the current row. If the record is being edited, a pencil icon appears. The last row of the control instance contains an asterisk if record addition is enabled. Editing this row will add a new record.

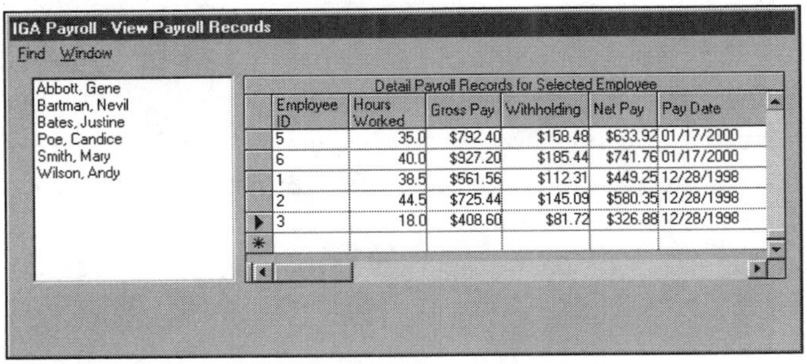

Figure 4.8 Anatomy of the DataGrid control.

To navigate through the individual cells at run time, you work with the arrow keys and other keyboard keys such as the PageUp, PageDown, Home, and End keys. The following list describes the default behavior of these keys:

➤ **Right Arrow** This key's behavior varies according to whether a cell is being edited. When a cell receives focus, all characters in the cell are selected. Pressing the Right Arrow key will move the focus to the next field (column). If the current field (column) is the last visible field, pressing the Right Arrow key has no effect. If a cell is being edited, the Right Arrow key will move forward one character position in the cell. If the insertion point is on the last character, the next field will receive focus.

➤ **Left Arrow** Works like the Right Arrow key, but the operations pertain to the previous column instead of the next column. That is, pressing the Left Arrow key while editing the first character in a cell will cause the previous field to be selected.

➤ **Up** and **Down Arrow** Locate the previous and next rows, respectively. If the first or last row is the current row, then pressing these keys has no effect.

➤ **Home** Will locate the first field in the current row if the current cell is not being edited; it will locate the first character in the cell if the cell is being edited.

➤ **End** Will locate the last field in the current row if the current cell is not being edited; it will locate the last character in the cell if the cell is being edited.

➤ **Tab** Will change focus to the next object in the tab order. You can change the default behavior of the Tab key if necessary.

➤ **Clicking** Clicking on the left-hand column selects an entire row. This row can then be deleted and other operations can be performed.

To load the rows and columns appearing in a DataGrid control instance at run time, the program connects the DataGrid control instance to an instance of the ADO Data control. Setting the **DataSource** property for the DataGrid control instance associates the DataGrid control instance with the ADO Data control instance. Taking this approach has the same effect as setting the **DataSource** property for a text box. No property exists to specify a specific field—that is, the DataGrid control does not support an equivalent **DataField** or **ListField** property, because the DataGrid control operates on all fields in the recordset at the same time. Note that the Column object pertaining to the DataGrid control supports this property, as Column objects display fields.

To create an instance of the DataGrid control and navigate through the rows and columns:

1. Activate the form named frmPayrollDetail. Create an instance of the DataGrid control, as shown in Figure 4.9, and set the properties as follows: **DataSource** to **adPayrollDetail** and **Name** to **dgPayrollDetail**. The instance of the DataList control has already been created and its properties set.

2. Test the program. On the form's menu bar, click on View, and then click on Payroll Detail. The DataGrid control instance becomes populated with the records retrieved by the underlying ADO Data control instance.

3. Click on the DataGrid control instance so that it receives the focus. Press the Right and Left Arrow keys. The focus changes to the next and previous cells, respectively. Press the Home and End keys to locate the first and last fields in the row, respectively.

4. Press the Up and Down Arrow keys to locate the next and previous rows, respectively. As the focus moves from row to row, the current record pointer changes. The scroll bars also can be used to change which rows and columns are visible.

5. End the program to return to design mode.

The DataGrid control provides very flexible editing capabilities. You can set properties and write code to modify the general editing behavior of a control instance.

Changing The Behavior Of The Arrow And Tab Keys

Setting the **AllowArrows** and the **TabAction** properties modifies the behavior of the Arrow and Tab keys, respectively.

➤ If you set the **AllowArrows** property to False, pressing an Arrow key will change the focus to the next control instance on the form. If you set it to True, pressing the Arrow keys will navigate through the cells in the DataGrid. Focus will not change to another control instance.

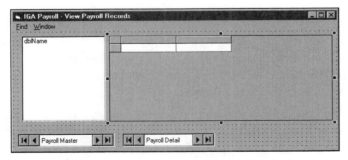

Figure 4.9 Creating an instance of the DataGrid control.

➤ By default, pressing the Tab key changes the focus to the next control instance. You can set the **TabAction** property to cause the Tab key to navigate through the different cells in the DataGrid.

➤ If the **TabAction** property is set to grid navigation, and the **WrapCellPointer** property is True, pressing the Tab key will change the active cell to the first column in the next row when the last column is current. If the **Wrap CellPointer** property is set to False, pressing the Tab key will have no effect.

The **TabAction** property supports three settings. You can use the following constants at run time or use the Property Pages to set **TabAction** property at design time:

➤ If the **Tab Action** property is set to the constant **dbgControlNavigation** (the default), pressing the Tab key will cause the next control instance on the form to receive focus.

➤ If the **Tab Action** property is set to the constant **dbgColumnNavigation**, pressing the Tab key will move the focus to the cell in the next or previous column. If the last column in the DataGrid control is active, pressing the Tab key will change the focus to the next control instance on the form.

➤ If the **Tab Action** property is set to the constant **dbgGridNavigation**, pressing the Tab key will move the current cell to the next or previous column. What happens when you press the Tab key while the last column is active depends on the setting of the **WrapCellPointer** property.

 Note that the prefix for the DataGrid constants is "dbg" and the prefix for the DataGrid control is "dg". The reason is historical. The DataGrid control replaced the DataBound Grid control. The DataBound Grid control worked with the intrinsic Data control. To maintain compatibility with existing programs, most of the constant names for the DataGrid control are the same as the constant names for the DataBound Grid control.

To see the effects of the **TabAction** property:

1. Activate the Property Pages for the DataGrid control on the form named frmPayrollDetail. Activate the Keyboard tab on the Property Pages.

2. Check the WrapCellPointer checkbox, and then click on 2 – dbgGridNavigation from the TabAction combo box. Click on OK to apply the changes and close the Property Pages.

3. Test the program. Display the Payroll Detail form, activate the DataGrid control instance, and press the Tab and Shift + Tab keys. When you press the Tab key, the cell focus moves to the next cell. When you press the Shift + Tab keys, the focus moves to the previous cell. When the last column has

focus and you press the Tab key, focus changes to the first column in the next row.

4. End the program to return to design mode.

In addition to providing sophisticated editing capabilities, the DataGrid control offers considerable flexibility in terms of the formatting applied to its contents.

Formatting The DataGrid Control

When an instance of the DataGrid control is created, by default it displays two rows and three columns at design time. Each column has an empty column header that can store a descriptive prompt. When you run the program, the field names appear automatically in the column headers. The Property Pages define both the general appearance of the DataGrid control and the appearance of each column. The General tab on the Property Pages defines properties that apply to all columns in the DataGrid control.

Syntax

    DataGrid

Properties

➤ If the **AllowAddNew** property is set to True, the DataGrid control will display an asterisk in the last row of the grid and allow new records to be added. If the underlying recordset is not updatable, new records cannot be added even when the **AllowAddNew** property is True.

➤ If the **AllowDelete** property is set to True, records can be deleted from the DataGrid control; otherwise, records cannot be deleted. Again, if the underlying recordset is not updatable, records cannot be deleted and a trappable error occurs when the user tries to remove a record.

➤ If the **AllowUpdate** property is set to True, the user can modify rows in the DataGrid control; otherwise, data cannot be modified. The Recordset object may not enable updates even if the **AllowUpdate** property is set to True for the DataGrid control.

➤ The **BorderStyle** property, if set to **1 - dbgFixedSingle**, draws a border around the region of the DataGrid control. If set to **0 - dbgNoBorder**, no border is drawn.

➤ The **Caption** property causes a caption to be displayed in the DataGrid control on its own line just above the column headers.

➤ The **Col** and **Row** properties are used to set or return the current cell in the grid.

➤ The **DataSource** property is typically set to an instance of the ADO Data control. Although you can use the intrinsic Data control, you cannot set this property dynamically at run time.

➤ The **HeadLines** property, which must contain a value between 0 and 10, identifies the number of lines displayed in the column headers.

➤ The **RowDividerStyle** property describes the characteristics of the line separating each row and column. For a description of the valid settings, see the Help topic "RowDividerStyle property."

Events

➤ The **BeforeDelete** event occurs just before the selected record is removed from the database. If the cancel argument is set to True, the deletion will be canceled and the **AfterDelete** event will not occur. Displaying a message box in this event procedure that asks the user to confirm deletion is a common practice. The **AfterDelete** event occurs immediately after the removal of the record.

➤ The **BeforeInsert** event occurs just before a new record is added to the DataGrid control, and the **AfterInsert** event occurs after a new record is added.

➤ The **BeforeUpdate** event occurs before the current record is updated, and the **AfterUpdate** event occurs after the record is updated.

Remember that the Recordset object supports a **Fields** collection containing one Field object for each field in the recordset. When you ran the program, it determined the number of columns and the contents of each column by using the Recordset object of the underlying ADO Data control instance.

Just as the Field object and **Fields** collection identify the fields in a recordset, so too does the Column object and **Columns** collection identify the columns in the DataGrid control. The **Columns** collection is a zero-based collection containing one Column object for each column in the DataGrid control. Each Column object in the **Columns** collection supports the properties that pertain to an individual column. These properties include the column's caption, the field in a table or query to be displayed, a default value (if any), and formatting for the data displayed in the column.

 The **Columns** collection contains a numeric index for each Column object in the collection. It does not support a string key to identify a specific column, unlike the other collections you have used to this point.

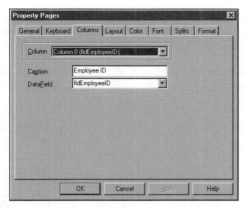

Figure 4.10   Property Pages Columns tab.

The Columns Property Page defines the title, format, and field of each column displayed in the DataGrid control. You use the Column list box to select a column. Figure 4.10 shows the Columns tab on the Property Pages.

The Layout tab on the Property Pages works like the Columns tab. You select a column through the Column list box and then set the properties that define the layout of the column.

Syntax

Column

Properties

➤ The **DataField** property works like the **DataField** property that applies to a text box. It identifies the field for a table or query. The **DataField** property is set automatically when the fields are retrieved.

➤ The **DefaultValue** property is a placeholder in which you can program an event that sets a default value of a column.

➤ The **NumberFormat** property defines how numeric data in a column are displayed. The formats are the same as the named formats used in the **Format** statement.

➤ The **Split** object splits the region of the DataGrid control into multiple panes, much as you might split a spreadsheet in Microsoft Excel.

➤ If the **AllowSizing** property is set to True, the mouse pointer changes to a double-headed arrow when positioned over the row or column divider. The user can resize the rows and columns by dragging them at run time.

➤ The **Alignment**, **Locked**, and **Width** properties work like the properties of the same names for the other controls you have used.

➤ The **Visible** property, if set to False, causes a column to be invisible. Even though the user cannot see the column, the data in the column can still be accessed programmatically.

➤ The **Text** property pertains to a Column object and contains a formatted version of the data. The formatting reflects the value of the **NumberFormat** property.

➤ The **Value** property also pertains to a Column object and contains the raw data stored as a **Variant** data type.

To change the caption for a column, you must load the field names from the ADO Data control at design time. To accomplish this task, you click the right mouse button while the insertion point is positioned over the DataGrid control instance and then click on Retrieve Fields. The fields from the table identified by the ADO Data control instance will be loaded into the column headings for the DataGrid control. You can then use the Property Pages to change the caption and size of each individual column.

In addition to setting the caption and formatting for each column, you can adjust the column width at design time by making the DataGrid control instance user interface (UI) active. To accomplish this goal, you activate the pop-up menu for the DataGrid control and then click on Edit. After you click on Edit, the mouse pointer will change to a double-headed arrow when it is positioned over a row divider or column divider. Dragging the mouse at this time will increase or decrease the size of the row or column, respectively.

To change the column titles and sizes:

1. Click on the DataGrid control instance on the form named **frmPayrollDetail** to activate it.

2. Click the right mouse button, and then click on Retrieve fields to load the fields into the DataGrid control instance. Click on Yes in the dialog box that appears.

3. Click the right mouse button, and then click on Properties to activate the Property Pages for the control instance. Click on the General tab on the Property Pages, and set the **HeadLines** property to 2. The column headers will be displayed on two lines. Set the **Caption** property to **Detail Payroll Records for Selected Employee**.

4. Click on the Columns tab on the Property Pages, and then select each column using the Column list box. Change the caption to remove the "fld" prefix and separate the words with spaces.

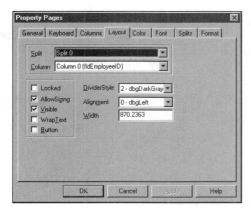

Figure 4.11   Property Pages Layout tab.

5. Click on the Layout tab on the Property Pages, as shown in Figure 4.11.

6. Select each of the different columns using the list box. The alignment should be set based on whether the data type is **String** or **Numeric**. For the fields named fldHoursWorked, fldGrossPay, fldWithholding, and fldNetPay, set the alignment to 1–dbgRight.

7. Click on OK to save the changes and to close the Property Pages.

 Be careful to click on the OK or Apply buttons on the Property Pages to record any changes. Clicking on the Close button on the control box will cause any changes to be lost.

In addition to setting the column captions and column layout, you can format the data in the individual cells using the Format tab on the Property Pages. Figure 4.12 shows the Format tab on the Property Pages.

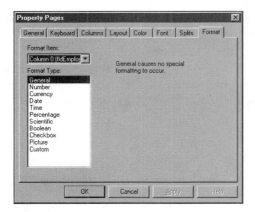

Figure 4.12   Property Pages Format tab.

To use the Format tab on the Property Pages, you select the desired column and then set the format type. As you select a format type, different options will appear on the Property Pages pertaining to that format type.

To format the DataGrid columns:

1. Activate the form named frmPayrollDetail, and then activate the Property Pages for the DataGrid control instance.

2. Activate the Format tab on the Property Pages.

3. Select Column1 (fldHoursWorked) in the Column list box. Set the Format Type to Number. Additional information appears on the Format tab.

4. Set the Decimal Places to 1.

5. For the fields named fldGrossPay, fldWithholding, and fldNetPay, set the format to Currency and the number of decimal places to 2. Click on OK to apply the changes and close the Property Pages.

6. Test the program. Activate the Payroll Detail form. The columns should be formatted such that the hours worked information has one decimal place, and the gross pay, withholding, and net pay columns appear with a leading dollar sign and two decimal places.

7. End the program to return to design mode.

In addition to binding an instance of the DataGrid control to a static recordset, it is possible to select records dynamically.

Selecting Records Dynamically

Another common task is to link two DataGrid control instances or to link a DataCombo or DataList control with the DataGrid control. Currently, the DataGrid control instance on the Payroll Detail form displays all of the rows. You can easily modify the program to display in the DataGrid control instance only those records matching the currently selected employee. To select employees by name, you use the DataList control instance already created on the form. When a record is selected, the code in the **Click** event can create a **SELECT** statement and re-create the recordset so that it contains only those records having the Employee ID matching the selected name. To accomplish this task, you set the **BoundText** property for the DataList control to the Employee ID field and then use this field in a **SELECT** statement to select the matching payroll detail records.

The properties pertaining to the ADO Data control instance named adPayrollDetail have been set such that **CommandType** is **adCmdText**. This approach allows you to set the **RecordSource** property to an SQL statement. If the **CommandType** property had been set to **adCmdTable**, then setting the **RecordSource** property to an SQL statement would generate an error, because the provider would attempt to interpret the property as a table name.

To display the payroll detail records for one employee in the DataGrid control instance:

1. Open the Payroll Detail form, select the DataList control named dblName, and then activate the Properties window.

2. Make sure that the **BoundColumn** property is set to **fldEmployeeID**.

3. Locate the **dblName_Click** event procedure in the Code window, and enter the following statements:

```
Dim pstrSQL As String
pstrSQL = "SELECT * FROM tblPayrollDetail " & _
    "WHERE fldEmployeeID = " & "'" & _
        dblName.BoundText & "'"
adPayrollDetail.RecordSource = pstrSQL
adPayrollDetail.Refresh
```

4. Test the program. Open the Payroll Detail form. Click on each employee. The recordset is updated, meaning that the records pertaining to the selected employee appear in the DataGrid control instance.

5. End the program to return to design mode.

The preceding statements declared a local variable named **pstrSQL** to store a **SELECT** statement. The **SELECT** statement is built by using the **BoundText** property pertaining to the DataList control. This field is set to the fldEmployeeID. Once built, the **RecordSource** property pertaining to the ADO Data control is set to the string variable containing the SQL statement. Next, the program refreshes the recordset. Because the DataGrid control is synchronized with the ADO Data control, the newly selected records appear in the ADO Data control.

When you used bound controls like text boxes and labels, explicitly calling the methods of the underlying recordset to navigate records updated the current record. This change was reflected in the ADO Data control and the bound controls. The same holds true for the DataGrid control—that is, you can call the methods of the recordset to locate records and the changes will be reflected in the DataGrid control instance. The following event procedures exist for the Find menu commands on the Payroll Detail form:

```
Private Sub mnuFindNext_Click()
    adPayrollDetail.Recordset.MoveNext
End Sub

Private Sub mnuFindPrevious_Click()
    adPayrollDetail.Recordset.MovePrevious
End Sub
```

When the program is run, these methods are called on the recordset affecting the current row.

To locate the records in the recordset:

1. Test the program. Open the Payroll Detail form.

2. Click on the Find, Next and Find, Previous menu items to locate different records. The current record pointer in the DataGrid control becomes updated as the current record changes. For brevity, this program omits error handlers for these procedures that would account for BOF and EOF conditions.

3. End the program to return to design mode.

In addition to formatting data and selecting data dynamically using the DataGrid control, the control supports modification of existing data.

Modifying Data With The DataGrid Control

The DataGrid control enables the user to add, change, and delete records. Changes made to the current record are stored in the DataGrid control's edit buffer. Remember that the DataGrid control reads and writes data to the recordset; also recall that the ADO Data control and its recordset have their own edit buffer. Data is manipulated within the DataGrid control's internal edit buffer before being passed to the edit buffer used by the ADO Data control and the recordset.

Three properties pertaining to the DataGrid control determine whether records can be added, changed, or deleted: the **AllowAddNew**, **AllowUpdate**, and **AllowDelete** properties.

Much as the ADO Data control responds to events and allows you to verify input before writing data to a table in the database, the DataGrid control supports several events that occur when the user moves from field to field or from one row to another. Some of these events occur for actions involving an entire record or row in the DataGrid control. Other events are generated for actions involving a specific column. When the user locates a different record, the fields in the DataGrid control's edit buffer become written to the ADO Data control. In fact, events for the ADO Data control occur because of actions caused by the DataGrid control. You can write code to respond to these events as necessary.

To allow record addition, changes, and deletion:

1. Activate the form named frmPayrollDetail.

2. Activate the General tab of the DataGrid control's Property Pages.

3. Click on the AllowAddNew and AllowDelete checkboxes, apply the changes, and then click on OK to close the Property Pages.

4. Test the program. Activate the Payroll Detail form. Locate and click on the first cell in the row containing the asterisk. A new row should be added in the DataGrid control's internal edit buffer. Enter a payroll record in the row with an Employee ID of 1.

5. Locate a different row. The new record is added to the underlying recordset.

6. Click on the border to the left of the field you just added to select the entire record, and press the Delete key to remove the record.

7. End the program to return to design mode.

When the user attempts to add, change, or delete records, your code should validate that input. User input is typically validated via the events pertaining to the DataGrid control.

Events Pertaining To The DataGrid Control

As the user enters information into cells and changes focus from row to row or from column to column, several different events occur. Some events pertain to the entire record, while others pertain to individual cells. You can respond to these events to validate user input and possibly cancel an action such as updating a record. Consider the following scenario, in which the user updates two fields in the DataGrid control. The user changes the first field, modifies a second field, and finally locates a new row. Several events occur as the user performs these tasks:

1. The **BeforeColEdit** event occurs when the user makes the first change to the contents of a specific cell. An Integer representing the column is passed as an argument to the event procedure. This Integer contains the index of the Column object in the **Columns** collection. If the cancel argument is set to True, the editing of the cell is canceled and the original contents of the cell are restored.

2. Immediately after the **BeforeColEdit** event occurs, the ColEdit event takes place only if the **BeforeColEdit** event was not canceled.

3. When the focus changes to another cell in the same row or to another row, editing is complete for the column. Just before the data in the new cell is copied to the DataGrid control's internal edit buffer, the **BeforeColUpdate** event occurs. Typically, this event serves to validate the contents of the changed cell before continuing. If the contents of the cell are invalid, the event's two arguments can be used to restore the original data to the cell and cancel the update.

4. If the **BeforeColUpdate** event is not canceled, the **AfterColUpdate** event occurs. It takes place immediately after the new contents of the cell are copied to the DataGrid control's internal edit buffer.

5. The **AfterColEdit** event occurs next, indicating that editing is complete in the current cell. It takes place even if no changes were made to the current cell or if editing was canceled. The **BeforeColEdit** and **AfterColEdit** events are often used to update a status message or to change the insertion point while the record is being updated.

6. When the user locates a different row, the DataGrid control will attempt to update any changes in the record to the database. The **BeforeUpdate** event occurs in the DataGrid control just before the program copies the row to the ADO Data control's edit buffer. It can be used to validate the cells in the row before committing the changes. The event can be canceled by setting the cancel argument to True.

7. If the **BeforeUpdate** event is not canceled, the AfterUpdate event occurs, indicating the update is complete. It is common to recompute the values of any computed columns in this event.

The events pertaining to the ADO Data control also occur as a record is being updated. That is, when the data is copied from the DataGrid control's internal edit buffer to the Data control's edit buffer, the **WillChangeRecord** event occurs for the ADO Data control. Deciding whether to validate data in the ADO Data control's **WillChangeRecord** event or in the DataGrid control is a matter of choice for the programmer, as both solutions will work. Also, as different records are located in the DataGrid control, the **WillMove** event continues to occur to the ADO Data control. Performing the validation in the DataGrid control, however, ensures that error checks are carried out on each column as changes are made, instead of by validating the entire row in the Data control's **WillChangeRecord** event.

During the insertion of data into the DataGrid control, other events occur in a defined sequence:

1. When the user selects a new record in the DataGrid control (identified by an asterisk (★) in the status column) and begins editing, the **BeforeInsert** event occurs.

2. As cells are edited, the events shown in the previous list occur.

3. When editing is complete, the **AfterInsert** event occurs.

The DataGrid control supports two events pertaining to record deletion: the **BeforeDelete** event and the **AfterDelete** event. The next section discusses these events.

Validating Changes In The DataGrid Control

Before allowing the user to add, change, or delete database records, the program should check the validity of the user input. Using the same techniques as those introduced in Chapter 3 with the ADO Data control's **WillChangeField** and

WillChangeRecord events, you can validate input and request user confirmation by programming the change events pertaining to the DataGrid control. The following list summarizes the syntax of selected events.

Syntax

Private Sub *object*_BeforeColUpdate ([*index* As Integer,] *colindex* As Integer, *oldvalue* As Variant, *cancel* As Integer)

Private Sub *object*_BeforeUpdate ([*index* As Integer,] *cancel* As Integer)

Private Sub *object*_RowColChange ([*index* As Integer,] *lastrow* As String, *lastcol* As Integer)

Dissection

➤ The *index* identifies the control instance if DataGrid control instance is a member of a control array.

➤ The *colindex* contains an Integer value indicating the column that is being updated. Like the **Columns** collection, the first column has an index of zero (0), the second a value of one (1), and so on.

➤ The *oldvalue* contains the value of the column before editing began. This value commonly is used to restore the contents of the column when the user abandons the editing.

➤ If the *cancel* argument is set to True, editing is canceled on the field or row.

➤ The *object* must be a valid instance of the DataGrid control, and the *index* uniquely identifies the DataGrid control if it is a member of a control array.

➤ The *lastrow* argument is a **String** data type representing a bookmark. The concept of a bookmark here is the same as that introduced in Chapter 3. It is used to locate a record.

➤ The *lastcol* argument contains an Integer value that identifies the previously selected column. Using these two arguments, it is possible to restore the contents of a cell that previously had focus or to locate the previously selected row.

Code Example

```
Private Sub dgPayrollDetail_BeforeColUpdate(ByVal ColIndex As _
    Integer, OldValue As Variant, Cancel As Integer)

    If ColIndex = 0 Then
        If Not _
            IsNumeric(dgPayrollDetail.Columns(ColIndex)) Then
            Cancel = True
            dgPayrollDetail.Columns(ColIndex).Value = _
                OldValue
```

```
        End If
    End If
End Sub
```

Code Dissection
These statements examine the first column to make sure it contains numeric data. If not, they cancel the update and restore the value of the column to the value before editing began.

Because the index of the current column is passed as an argument to the **BeforeColUpdate** event, the following statement fragments can be used to reference the contents of the current cell. The following two statements are equivalent because the **Value** property is the default property for a Column object:

```
dgPayrollDetail.Columns(ColIndex).Value
dgPayrollDetail.Columns(ColIndex)
```

This syntax resembles the syntax you have used to reference an item in a specific collection. Columns(ColIndex) references the contents of the current column (the **Value** property). Both of these properties select the value of the column for the currently selected row.

To confirm deletion of records, you can write code that responds to the **BeforeDelete** event. Remember, this event is generated just before the record is deleted. Setting the *cancel* argument to True aborts the deletion.

To confirm record deletion:

1. Locate the **dgPayrollDetail_BeforeDelete** event procedure for the form named **frmPayrollDetail**, and enter the following statements:

```
Dim pintReturn As Integer
pintReturn = MsgBox("Delete current record?", _
    vbQuestion + vbYesNo)
If pintReturn = vbNo Then
    Cancel = True
End If
```

2. Test the program. Locate the Payroll Detail form. Select the first record by clicking the row containing the current record indicator. Press the Delete key to attempt to delete the record. The **BeforeDelete** event will occur, and the code you just wrote will execute. The message box should appear.

Click on No in the message box to cancel the deletion, and click on OK in the subsequent message box.

3. End the program to return to design mode.

In addition to creating columns statically at design time, it is possible to create them dynamically at run time.

Creating Columns At Run Time

Another feature offered by the DataGrid control is the capability to add and delete columns at run time. It is also possible to modify the appearance of individual columns at run time dynamically. In IGA Travel's program, the Net Pay is stored in a database column. Alternatively, you could compute this value in the DataGrid control and store the result in a column not bound to the database. Both implementations have advantages and disadvantages. Storing the Net Pay in a column in the database increases the physical size of the database, but the field need not be computed from the Gross Pay and Withholding each time the record is displayed. Computing the Net Pay has the reverse effect.

The mechanics of adding a column at run time are the same as those involved in adding an item to any collection. That is, you call the **Add** method pertaining to the **Columns** collection with one argument—the numeric index of the column indicating where the new column should be inserted. The following statement will insert a new column as the first column in the DataGrid control. The numeric indexes of the other columns are adjusted accordingly.

```
dbgPayrollDetail.Columns.Add 0
```

A newly added column is initially invisible, has no caption, and is not bound to a field in the recordset. Three properties must be set to make the column usable. To make the column visible, you must set the **Visible** property. To define the header appearing at the top of the column, you must set the **Caption** property. To bind the column to the recordset, the **DataField** property must be set. The code required to accomplish these tasks is shown here:

```
With dbgPayrollDetail
    .Columns.Add 0
    .Columns(0).Caption = "New Column"
    .Columns(0).Visible = True
    .Columns(0).DataField = "fldEmployeeID"
End With
```

These statements insert a new column as the first column in the DataGrid control, set the caption in the row header to the value New Column, make the column visible, and then bind the column to the field fldEmployeeID.

The form you have been using illustrated how to link an instance of the DataList control with an instance of the DataGrid control. It is also possible to link two instances of the DataGrid control together.

Linking Multiple DataGrid Controls

A master-detail relationship exists between the two payroll tables. Thus you might create a user interface in which selecting a row in one DataGrid control instance that displays the records for the master payroll table causes the detail records corresponding to the selected Employee ID to appear in a second DataGrid control instance. To accomplish this task, two ADO Data control instances are used on a form—one for each table. The DataGrid control instances are, in turn, bound to the ADO Data control instances. When the user selects a record, the **RowColChange** event occurs. In this event procedure, a **SELECT** statement can be used to re-create the recordset for the second ADO Data control, so that only the records corresponding to the selected Employee ID field are displayed in the second ADO Data control.

To link two DataGrid control instances:

1. Locate the **dgPayrollMaster_RowColChange** event procedure in the Code window for the form named frmLinked, and enter the following statements into the event procedure:

```
Dim pstrSQL As String
pstrSQL = "SELECT * FROM tblPayrollDetail " & _
    "WHERE fldEmployeeID = '" & _
    adPayrollMaster.Recordset![fldEmployeeID] & "'"
adPayrollDetail.RecordSource = pstrSQL
adPayrollDetail.Refresh
```

2. Test the program. Open the form by clicking View on the menu bar, and then click on Linked DataGrids. Select different master records in the first table. The detail records for the corresponding Employee ID field are displayed in the second DataGrid control.

3. End the program to return to design mode.

4. Exit Visual Basic.

This chapter has presented two important topics. First, you learned how to use SQL statements to select database records and to add, change, and delete records. Second, you learned how to use the DataGrid, DataCombo, and DataList controls.

CHAPTER SUMMARY

To select records from a table:

➤ Use the **SELECT** statement having the following syntax:

```
SELECT * FROM tablename
```

To select records in a particular order:

➤ Use the **SELECT** statement with the **ORDER BY** clause:

```
SELECT * FROM tablename
    [ORDER BY field1 [ASC | DESC][,field2 [ASC | DESC][,fieldn [ASC |
        DESC]]
```

To select specific records from a database table:

➤ Create a **SELECT** statement with a **WHERE** clause:

```
SELECT * FROM tablename
    WHERE conditionlist
    [ORDER BY field1 [ASC | DESC][,field2] [ASC | DESC][,fieldn]
        [ASC | DESC]]
```

To select records between two values:

➤ Use the between statement in a **WHERE** clause:

expression [NOT] Between *value1* And *value2*

To handle database errors:

➤ Create an instance of the Connection object.

➤ When a run–time error occurs, create an error handler and examine the Error objects in the Errors collection.

To perform an action query:

➤ Call the **Execute** method pertaining to the Command object:

object.Execute [*RecordsAffected*], [*Parameters*], [*Options*]

To call the **INSERT SQL** statement:

```
INSERT INTO target [(field1[, field2 [, ...]])]
    VALUES (value1[, value2[, ...]])
```

To call the **UPDATE SQL** statement:

```
UPDATE tablename
        SET fieldname = newvalue [,fieldname = newvalue]
        WHERE criteria
```

To call the **DELETE SQL** statement:

```
DELETE*
        FROM table
        WHERE criteria
```

To define a transaction:

➤ Call the **BeginTrans**, **CommitTrans**, or **RollBackTrans** methods pertaining to the **Connection** object:

```
object.BeginTrans
object.CommitTrans
obect.RollbackTrans
```

To use the DataList and DataCombo controls:

➤ Create an instance of the control on the form.

➤ Set the **RowSource** property to an instance of the ADO Data control.

➤ Set the **ListField** property to a field in the table specified by the ADO Data control. The **RowSource** and **ListField** properties determine which field appears in the visible portion of the control instance.

➤ Set the **DataSource** to a second instance of the ADO Data control. A field in this control instance will be updated.

➤ Set the **BoundColumn** to a field in the table specified by the second ADO Data control instance.

➤ Set the **DataField** to the same field as the Bound column.

To use the DataGrid control:

➤ Create an instance of the DataGrid control on the form.

➤ Set the **DataSource** property to the name of an ADO Data control instance created on the form.

➤ Using the Keyboard Property Page, set the **AllowArrows**, **TabAction**, and **WrapCellPointer** properties.

➤ To retrieve the fields into the control instance, right-click the mouse and click on Retrieve Fields. The fields appear in the control instance.

➤ Activate the Property Pages for the control instance. Use the Columns tab of the Property Pages to define the caption for each column. Use the Layout tab of the Property Pages to set a column's alignment and other column-related properties. Use the Format tab of the Property Pages to format each column.

To validate changes made to a cell in the DataGrid control:

➤ Respond to the **BeforeColUpdate** or **RowColChange** event.

REVIEW QUESTIONS

1. Which of the following statements are valid SQL DML statements?
   a. **SELECT, UPDATE, INSERT, DELETE**
   b. **SELECT, CHANGE, INSERT, REMOVE**
   c. **SELECT, CHANGE, INSERT, DELETE**
   d. **RECORDSET, UPDATE, INSERT, DELETE**
   e. None of the above.

2. When using a **WHERE** clause, some values must be enclosed in special characters depending on the data type: _____ variables are enclosed in single quotes, _____ variables are enclosed in pound signs, and _____ variables are not enclosed in any special characters.
   a. **Date, String, Numeric**
   b. **Numeric Date, String**
   c. **String, Date, Numeric**
   d. **Numeric, String, Date**
   e. None of the above

3. Which of the following sets of characters consists of pattern–matching characters that are used with the **Like** keyword?
   a. ★ [ ] # !
   b. ★ { } # !
   c. ★ [ ] ^ !
   d. & [ ] ^ !
   e. All of the above.

4. Write a **SELECT** statement to retrieve all of the rows from the table named tblPayrollMaster for which the hourly wage (fldWage) is greater than or equal to $5.50 and less than $10.00. Return the rows sorted in descending order by hourly wage.

5. Write a **SELECT** statement to retrieve all of the rows from the table named tblPayrollMaster for which the field named fldDatePaid is equal to 10/22/2001.

6. Write a **SELECT** statement to retrieve all of the rows from the table named tblPayrollMaster for which fldHireDate, a Date data type, is between 3/1/1990 and 3/1/1997.

7. Write a **SELECT** statement to retrieve all of the rows from the table named tblPayrollMaster for which the field named fldLastName begins with the character "C".

8. Write an **INSERT** statement to insert the value A10 into the field named fldEmployeeID, the value 7/17/2000 into the field named fldDate, and 2874.22 into the field named fldValue. The data should be inserted into the table named tblPayrollMaster.

9. Write an **UPDATE** statement to increase the value of fldHourlyWage by 5 percent where fldName is John Smith.

10. Write a **DELETE** statement to delete the row from tblCategory where the value of the field fldCategoryID is 3.

11. In which order do the following events occur when updating the contents of the DataGrid control?
    a. **BeforeColUpdate, BeforeColEdit, AfterColEdit, AfterColUpdate**
    b. **BeforeUpdate, BeforeColUpdate, AfterColUpdate, AfterUpdate**
    c. **BBeforeColEdit, BeforeColUpdate, AfterColUpdate, AfterColEdit**
    d. Both a and c.
    e. None of the above.

12. The _____ property contains the field displayed in the DataList and DataCombo controls. The table (Data control) used is specified by the _____ property.
    a. **DataSource, DataField**
    b. **ListField, BoundColumn**
    c. **ListField, RowSource**
    d. **DataField, BoundText**
    e. **DataSource, ListField**

13. Which properties are used to change the behavior of the tab and arrow keys in the DataGrid control?
    a. **TabKey, ArrowKey**
    b. **Tab, Arrow**
    c. **TabAction, ArrowKey**
    d. **TabAction, AllowArrows**
    e. **Tab, AllowArrows**

14. Which properties control whether records can be added, changed, and deleted from the DataGrid control?
    a. **AddNew, Update, Delete**
    b. **Add, Update, Delete**
    c. **AllowAdd, AllowUpdate, AllowDelete**
    d. **AllowAddNew, AllowUpdate, AllowDelete**
    e. **AllowNew, AllowUpdate, AllowDelete**

15. Write the necessary Visual Basic statements to open the database named A:\Chapter.04\Startup\IGA.mdb and create a recordset based on the following **SELECT** statement:

    SELECT * FROM tblCategory

16. Write the event procedure that will execute just before the deletion of the selected record in the DataGrid control named dgPayroll. The code in the event procedure should display a message box requesting confirmation and then cancel or complete the deletion, depending on the user's response.

17. Write a **For Each** loop that will examine the Error objects in the **Errors** collection. For each Error object, add the error description to the contents of the list box named lstErrors.

18. Write a **For Each** loop that will examine all of the Column objects in the **Columns** collection for the DataGrid control's object named dbgTest. For each column, set the **Alignment** property so that the text is centered in the column.

HANDS-ON PROJECTS

All of the following exercises use the database named Chapter.04\Exercise\ Inventory.mdb. Figure 4.13 illustrates the structure of this database.

Project 1

In this project, you will use SQL statements to change and delete different rows in the database. You will also use a DataGrid control.

a. Run the executable file named Chapter.04\Exercise\Ex1Demo.exe. The form appears as shown in Figure 4.14. Click on the option buttons on the form. As you click on each option button, the records corresponding to the selected category appear in the DataGrid control instance. Enter a value of

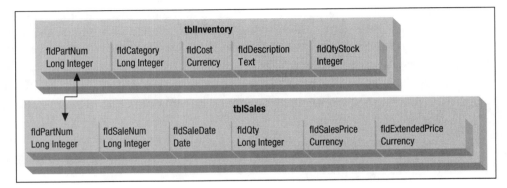

Figure 4.13   Database structure.

10 in the Price Increase % text box, and then click on the Update command button; the prices for the selected category are increased by 10 percent. Exit the program.

b. Start Visual Basic and create a new project. Set the **Name** property of the form to **frmEx1**. Save the form as Chapter.04\Exercise\frmEx1.frm and the project as Chapter.04\Exercise\Ex1.vbp.

c. Use the Components dialog box to add a reference to the DataGrid and ADO Data controls to the roject.

d. Create the control instances as shown in Figure 4.14. The option buttons should be members of a control array.

e. Set the properties of the ADO Data control instance to connect to the database named Inventory.mdb and the table named tblInventory. Do not use a table command type. Rather, use a Text command type and set the **RecordSource** property to a **SELECT** statement that selects all records from the table named tblInventory.

f. Bind the DataGrid control instance to the ADO Data control instance.

g. In the general declarations section of the form module, write statements to declare variables of type **Connection** and **Command**.

h. In the **Form_Load** event procedure, write the code to create an active connection to the database. Set the type of the Command object so that it will execute SQL statements.

i. In the **Click** event procedure for the option buttons, write the statements to determine which option button is selected. Using that information, build a **SELECT** statement to locate all records from the table named tblInventory having the selected category.

j. Using the **SELECT** statement you created in the previous step, refresh the recordset created by the ADO Data control instance.

k. Write the code for the Update command button. This code should update the field named fldCost by the amount specified in the form's text box. Thus, if the user entered the value 10 in the text box, the program should update the field named fldCost by 10 percent. Update only those records for the currently selected category. After updating the records, refresh the recordset as necessary.

l. Write the code for the Delete command button. Display an input box to obtain the part number from the user. Refresh the recordset after deleting the part number.

m. Set the properties of the DataGrid control instance so that the user cannot add, change, or delete records. Also, format the records as shown in Figure 4.14.

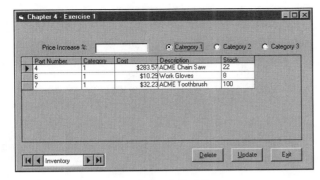

Figure 4.14   Exercise 1 Completed form.

n. Test the program to verify that the Update and Delete buttons work correctly. Also, verify that the recordset is refreshed when the user selects different categories.

o. Exit Visual Basic.

Project 2

In this project, you will use the DataList control linked to a DataGrid control.

a. Run the executable file named Chapter.04\Exercise\Ex2Demo.exe. The form appears as shown in Figure 4.15. Click on the descriptions in the DataList control instance. The corresponding part numbers appear in the DataGrid control. Exit the program.

b. Start Visual Basic, and create a new project. Set the **Name** property of the form to **frmEx2**. Save the form as Chapter.04\Exercise\frmEx2.frm and the project as Chapter.04\Exercise\Ex2.vbp.

c. Use the Components dialog box to add references to the DataList, DataGrid, and ADO Data controls to the project.

Figure 4.15   Exercise 2 Completed form.

   d. Create instances of the ADO Data control, DataList control, and DataGrid control on the form.

   e. Set the necessary properties so that the first ADO Data control connects to the table named tblInventory and the second ADO Data control connects to the table named tblSales. Use SQL statements to establish both connections.

   f. Create an instance of the DataList control on the form. The control instance should display the field named fldDescription from the table tblInventory.

   g. Create an instance of the DataGrid control on the form. Associate this control instance with the ADO Data control associated with the table tblSales. Format the control instance so that it is similar to the one shown in Figure 4.18.

   h. Set the necessary properties for the DataList control instance so that when the user clicks a description, the corresponding part number becomes stored in the **BoundText** property. Also, write the code in the **Click** event procedure that will display in the DataGrid control instance only those records having the same part number.

   i. Save and test the program. Verify that when the user clicks an item in the DataList control, the correct part numbers appear in the DataGrid control instance.

   j. Exit Visual Basic.

Project 3

In this project, you will link two DataGrid controls together.

   a. Run the executable file named Chapter.04\Exercise\Ex3Demo.exe. The form appears as shown in Figure 4.16. Click on the rows on the topmost DataGrid control instance. The corresponding rows appear on the other control instance. Exit the program.

   b. Start Visual Basic and create a new project. Set the **Name** property of the form to **frmEx3**. Save the form as Chapter.04\Exercise\frmEx3.frm and the project as Chapter.04\Exercise\Ex3.vbp.

   c. Add references to the ADO Data control and the DataGrid control to the project.

   d. Create two instances of the ADO Data control on the form. The first ADO Data control instance should reference the table named tblInventory, and the second should reference the table named tblSales.

   e. Create two instances of the DataGrid controls to display the data from the two ADO Data control instances.

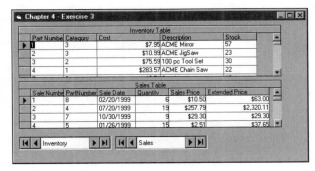

Figure 4.16   Exercise 3 Completed form.

f. Load the fields for each DataGrid control instance, and format the columns as shown in Figure 4.16.

g. Create a caption for both DataGrid control instances.

h. Write the statements that will execute when the user selects a row in the first DataGrid control instance. When a row is selected, only those sales records corresponding to the selected part number should appear in the second DataGrid control instance.

i. Write the code for the appropriate event procedure in the second DataGrid control instance that will verify that the fields fldQtySold, fldSalesPrice, and fldExtendedPrice all contain valid numbers as the fields are being edited. If a field contains invalid data, cancel the update and restore the contents of the fields to their previous values.

j. Test the program. Verify that the DataGrid control instances are synchronized.

k. Exit Visual Basic.

CHAPTER FIVE

THE WINDOWS COMMON CONTROLS (PART 1)

AFTER READING THIS CHAPTER AND COMPLETING THE EXCERCISES, YOU WILL BE ABLE TO:

➤ Use an instance of the ImageList control to store icons and bitmaps that will be used by other control instances on the form

➤ Understand the concept of a drill-down interface

➤ Create an instance of the TreeView control to display information hierarchically

➤ Program the Node object pertaining to the TreeView control

➤ Write code to navigate through the nodes in the TreeView control

➤ Understand the basics of the ListView control

➤ Distinguish the characteristics of the different views supported by the ListView control

➤ Program the ListView control

USING THE TREEVIEW AND LISTVIEW CONTROLS

The Tree View Control

The completed program for this chapter uses three new ActiveX controls: ImageList, TreeView, and ListView. The ImageList control stores graphic files for use by other control instances, including the TreeView and ListView controls. The program in this chapter takes advantage of the TreeView and ListView controls together to create a user interface similar to the interface used by the Windows Explorer program.

ETC Corporation needs a program to manage a telephone list for each of its offices around the world. This program will display in a hierarchical manner the names, telephone numbers, and telephone extensions of all employees in the organization.

To preview the completed application:

1. Start Visual Basic, and open the completed project named Chapter.05\Complete\Ch5_C.vbp.

2. Run the program. When the program starts, information is read from the database using ADO. The same techniques that you used in Chapters 3 and 4 are applied in this chapter to create the Connection, Command, and Recordset objects. That is, the code sets the **ConnectionString** property and then opens a connection. Once a connection exists, the properties pertaining to the Command object are set, and a recordset is opened. Figure 5.1 shows the program's main form at run time.

   As shown in Figure 5.1, two new control instances occupy the majority of the form. The TreeView control instance appears on the left side of the form, and the ListView control instance appears on the right side of the form.

3. Click on the + (plus sign) to the left of the item Buena Park California, as shown in Figure 5.1, to open the folder and display the departments pertaining to the selected regional office. The Buena Park, California, regional office has six departments.

4. Click on the folder named Finance to open the folder and display, in the ListView control instance, the employees working in the Finance department. Figure 5.2 shows these employees.

5. On the form's Display menu, click on Expand Nodes. The elements in the entire tree in the TreeView control instance appear.

6. On the form's Display menu, click on Collapse Nodes. When collapsed, only the Offices node appears.

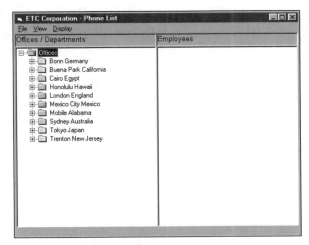

Figure 5.1   Completed main form at run time (1).

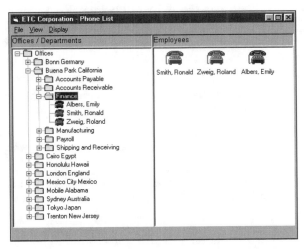

Figure 5.2   Completed main form at run time (2).

7. On the form's View menu, click on Small, Large, List, and Report. As you click on each menu item, the current view in the ListView control instance changes.

8. Make sure that Report view is selected. In the ListView control instance, click on the different column headers. Note that the data in the column are sorted in ascending order.

9. End the program, and then exit Visual Basic.

The ETC program is based on a hierarchical database. The company has 10 different offices, each having one or more departments. Each department includes employees who work only for that department. For each employee, a table in the database contains fields that list his or her phone number and extension and that indicate whether the employee is in the office.

Introducing The Windows Common Controls

The Windows operating system provides much more than just an interface for users. It also offers a rich set of software libraries for the programmer. Several groups of ActiveX controls allow the Visual Basic programmer to access the objects defined in these libraries. One such group of controls is commonly referred to as the Windows Common Controls. Three separate ActiveX libraries store the code for these controls. The Windows Common Controls include the following controls:

➤ A programmer uses the control to create buttons that display animations, such as .avi files, when clicked.

➤ The control works in a way that is similar to the Toolbar control. Unlike the Toolbar control, however, the CoolBar control supports a customizable toolbar that appears to the user much like the toolbar supported by Internet Explorer.

➤ The control provides the user with an easy way to select dates. It displays a formatted box in which the user enters a date. In addition, the user can drop down a box to select a date. This drop-down box resembles a calendar.

➤ The control displays a scroll bar that operates in a manner that is similar to the intrinsic horizontal and vertical scroll bar controls.

➤ The control operates in a manner that is similar to the intrinsic ComboBox control. Unlike the ComboBox control, however, the ImageCombo control can display an image adjacent to the list item.

➤ The control manages a collection of bitmap and icon images. You typically use it with another control, such as Toolbar, ListView, or TreeView.

➤ The control displays items in a list.

➤ The control displays a box containing the days in a month. The user can select different days, months, and years.

➤ The control indicates the relative progress of a time-consuming operation.

➤ The control is similar to a scroll bar, except that it displays a slider in a range of tick marks.

➤ The control typically appears at the bottom of a form and describes the current state of the program or selected keyboard keys, such as the Caps Lock key.

➤ The control contains tabs that work like the dividers in a notebook. Visual Basic implements Property Pages using an interface that looks like a TabStrip control.

➤ The control displays a toolbar containing buttons that the user can click on. The buttons on a toolbar typically mimic the most commonly used items on a menu.

➤ The control displays information hierarchically. Each item in the hierarchy consists of a text string and an optional icon.

➤ The control looks much like a scroll bar. You typically use it to increment or decrement the value of another control instance, such as a text box.

As with other ActiveX controls, the .ocx files corresponding to the Windows Common Controls must reside on the computer that is running the program that uses the particular control(s). The file mscomctl.ocx contains the code for the TabStrip, Toolbar, StatusBar, ProgressBar, TreeView, ListView, ImageList, Slider, and ImageCombo controls. The file mscomct2.ocx contains the code for the Animation, UpDown, MonthView, DTPicker, and FlatScrollBar controls. The file cmdct332.ocx contains the code for the CoolBar control.

 The Windows Common Controls supported by Visual Basic 5.0, or previous versions of Visual Basic, have been replaced by newer control versions. These new control versions support additional properties and methods not found in previous versions. Thus, when adding a project reference to the Windows Common Controls, use caution and make sure to select the correct control version.

As previously noted, the ETC program communicates with a database using the same ADO code that you wrote in Chapters 3 and 4. The startup application for this chapter contains several control instances and some code. The following Connection and Command objects appear in the startup program:

```
Private mconCurrent As New ADODB.Connection
Private mcmdCurrent As New ADODB.Command
```

The preceding statements create instances of the ADO Connection and Command objects. Because these object variables will be used throughout the program, they are declared in the general declarations section of the form.

The following statements already exist in the **Form_Load** event procedure:

```
mconCurrent.ConnectionString = _
    "Provider=Microsoft.Jet.OLEDB.3.51;" & _
    "Persist Security Info=False;" & _
    "Data Source=" & App.Path & "\ETC.mdb"
mconCurrent.Open
Set mcmdCurrent.ActiveConnection = mconCurrent
```

These statements define the connection string and then open the connection. Next, the code sets the Command object's **ActiveConnection** property in preparation for executing commands on the open connection.

This chapter is the first of two chapters that discusses the Windows Common Controls. Here, and in Chapter 6, you will utilize the Windows Common Controls to create programs with user interfaces that closely model the interfaces supplied by many Windows-based programs. As with other ActiveX controls, a reference to the Windows Common Controls must be added to the project before the controls can be used. You, as the programmer, can accomplish this task by using the Project Components dialog box.

You will now load the startup program and begin creating the program in this chapter.

To load the startup application:

1. Start Visual Basic, and the load the project file named Chapter.05\Startup\Ch5_S.vbp. Figure 5.3 shows the startup form at design time.

2. Click on on the Visual Basic menu bar, and then click on Components to activate the Components dialog box.

3. Locate the Microsoft Windows Common Controls 6.0 line, and verify that the checkbox is checked. Click on OK to close the dialog box. When the dialog box closes, a reference to the controls is added to the project and the controls appear in the toolbox.

4. Save the project.

In Figure 5.3, the form already contains a menu system and Label control instances. Your next step is to create the control instances that will store the graphic files used by the other control instances in the program.

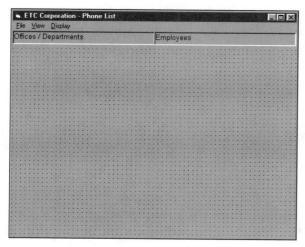

Figure 5.3   Startup form.

Storing Images In The ImageList Control

The ImageList control is not a visible control. Rather, it serves as a repository for graphic files such as bitmap (.bmp), icon (.ico), graphical interchange format (.gif), jpeg (.jpg), and cursor (.cur) files.

The ImageList control is rarely used by itself. Instead, it is used in conjunction with other controls that display icons. Consider the Visual Basic IDE, which contains a toolbar that displays several different images. Furthermore, the Project Explorer displays images indicating whether a folder is open or closed and images identifying the type of each module. All of these images could be stored in a single instance of the ImageList control. When a TreeView or ListView control instance displays images, the control instance itself does not store those images; rather, an instance of the ImageList control holds the images.

A good reason exists for separating images from the control instances that use them. Consider a program that contains both ListView and TreeView control instances. Assume that both of the control instances use many of the same graphic files. Rather than storing multiple copies of the same graphic file in the ListView and TreeView control instances, one ImageList control instance stores the actual graphic files that are shared by the multiple control instances that use them. Sharing the graphic files among multiple control instances conserves memory, thus improving program performance.

 An instance of the ImageList control tends to contain static information, so it is very uncommon for the images to change at run time. As a general rule, identify all images that your program might use, and load the images into the control instance at design time using the Property Pages. You, as the programmer, can modify the images in an ImageList control at run time. Several restrictions exist, however, regarding the changes that you can make to the images once they are used by other control instances. Because the bitmaps and other graphic files stored in the ImageList control are usually very small, the performance impact of inserting seldom or never-used graphic files is minimal. Thus, if you think you may need a graphic file, insert it at design time even if you are not certain that the graphic file will be used.

An ImageList control instance stores each graphic file as a ListImage object in a **ListImages** collection. A numeric index or a string key can be defined to reference ListImage objects. This concept is consistent with most collections. You insert the images in an ImageList control instance by using the Property Pages pertaining to the ImageList control. The Property Pages contains three tabs:

➤ **General** Used to set the size of the images. All images in an ImageList control instance must be of the same size. If your program will use images of different sizes, then create multiple ImageList control instances and change the size of the image that is contained in each control instance. Once an image has been added to an instance of the ImageList control, the image size cannot be changed. The only way to change the image size is to remove all images, change the size, and then re-create the images. Note that the ImageList control will resize the actual graphic files as necessary to ensure that the image stored in the control instance is the correct size.

➤ **Images** Used to add and delete images to and from the list. The corresponding ListImage objects are added or removed from the **ListImages** collection. You use this Property Page tab to assign a string key and a Tag to an image.

➤ **Color** Used to set the background color of the images.

For the ETC program, you will create the ImageList control instance that will be used by both the ListView and TreeView controls. The standard prefix for the ImageList control is "ils". The Chapter.05\Startup folder contains the images for ETC's telephone list form. If you installed the graphic files when you installed Visual Basic, the Graphics folder will also contain these files.

To create the ImageList control instance and set the size of the images:

1. Using the ImageList button on the toolbox, create an instance of the ImageList control on the form.

2. Set the **Name** property to **ilsSmallIcons** using the Properties window.

   Because the ImageList control instance is not visible on the form at run time, it does not matter where you place the control instance on the form. Note that you cannot change the visible size of the control instance. No matter which region you select on the form when you create the ImageList control instance, the control instance as it appears on the form will be adjusted to the same size—about a 1/2-inch square.

3. Activate the Property Pages for the ImageList control instance you just created, and make sure that the General tab on the Property Pages is active.

4. Set the size of the buttons to 16x16. Remember, once you add images, you cannot change the size.

After defining the size of the images, the images themselves can be added to the image list. This task is accomplished using the Images tab on the Property Pages, which is shown in Figure 5.4.

Figure 5.4 shows the images used in this example. The Images tab contains command buttons to insert and remove pictures from the image list. When the **Insert Picture** command button is clicked, the Select picture dialog box appears, allowing you to select an image to insert. Removing a picture is accomplished by clicking on an image in the Images window to select it, and then clicking on the **Remove Picture** command button. As you add and remove images using the

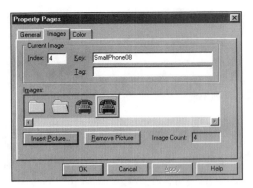

5

Figure 5.4   Property Pages Image tab.

Property Pages, the ImageList control adds and removes ListImage objects in the **ListImages** collection automatically.

Like most collections, the **ListImages** collection supports a numeric index and a string key that control instances use to reference a specific image in the collection. The numeric index is assigned automatically when you use the Images tab on the Property Pages. You must set the string key manually, however. The string key, which is case-sensitive, should be given a meaningful name that will help describe the image. Because a string key is typically more intuitive to other programmers reading your code, you should consider assigning a string key to each image that you create. The practice of assigning a string key to each image will be followed in this chapter.

To add images to the ImageList control:

1. Select the ilsSmallIcons ImageList control instance, if necessary, and open its Property Pages to the Images tab.

2. Click on the **Insert Picture** command button to activate the Select picture dialog box. Locate the Chapter.05\Startup folder, and select the icon named Clsdfold.ico. Click on the Open button in the dialog box to insert the picture into the Property Pages.

   After you insert the image, the Property Pages may lose focus and be obscured by the form. You may need to move the form and select the Property Pages again.

3. Set the **Key** property to **SmallClsdfold**. Because string keys are case-sensitive, make sure that you duplicate the uppercase and lowercase characters exactly.

4. Repeat Steps 2 and 3 to insert the following images: Openfold.ico, Phone07.ico, and Phone08.ico. As you add the images, set the case-sensitive **Key** properties to **SmallOpenfold**, **SmallPhone07**, and **SmallPhone08**, respectively.

5. Click on OK to close the Property Pages.

In addition to displaying 16x16 pixel images, the ListView control can display 32x32 pixel images. To show an image at this size, you must create a second instance of the ImageList control. The second control instance will utilize the same images, but resize those images to 32x32.

To create a second instance of the ImageList control:

1. Create a second instance of the ImageList control, and use the Properties window to set the **Name** property to **ilsLargeIcons**.

2. Activate the Property Pages for the ImageList control instance you just created, and set the image size to 32x32 pixels.

3. Into the second control instance, insert the same images (Clsdfold.ico, Openfold.ico, Phone07.ico, and Phone08.ico) and set the **Key** properties of the images to **LargeClsdfold**, **LargeOpenfold**, **LargePhone07**, and **LargePhone08**, respectively.

4. Click on OK to save the changes, and close the Property Pages.

In the second control instance, the word "Large" has replaced the word "Small" in the string key names. For example, LargePhone07 replaced SmallPhone07. The key names could be the same for the two control instances because each ImageList control instance contains its own **ListImages** collection. The code uses different names to clarify which ImageList control instance is being used.

Make sure that you create the ImageList control instance and define its images before creating ListView, TreeView, or other control instances that use the images. Once another control instance references an ImageList control instance, new images can be added to the ImageList but existing images cannot be modified or removed.

When you set the properties pertaining to each ListImage object using the Property Pages, you might notice that the ListImage object supports the **Tag** property. Visual Basic does not utilize the **Tag** property. Instead, it exists so that a programmer can store additional information about a control instance.

You can write code to reference a particular ListImage object by using the same syntax you have used to reference collections and the objects contained by a collection. Consider the following statement:

```
Debug.Print ilsLargeIcons.ListImages("LargeOpenfold").Tag
```

The statement fragment **ilsLargeIcons.ListImages** references the **ListImages** collection pertaining to the ImageList control instance named **ilsLargeIcons**. The string key **LargeOpenfold** is used to reference a particular ListImage object. Thus the statement prints to the Immediate window the value of the **Tag** property for the ListImage object named **ilsLargeIcons**.

Although the technique is seldom used, you can write code to call the **Add**, **Remove**, and **Clear** methods pertaining to the **ListImages** collection at run time so as to add or delete a ListImage object, or to remove all ListImage objects from the collection.

Now that you have created the ImageList control instances that will be used by the other control instances on the form, you can begin to create those other control instances.

Introduction To Drill-Down Interfaces

Many Windows programs utilize a drill-down user interface that supports hierarchically organized data. The Windows Explorer program shown in Figure 5.5 provides one example of a drill-down interface.

As shown in Figure 5.5, Windows Explorer consists of two separate panes. The left pane displays folders and files in a hierarchy. The interface allows individual folders to be expanded and collapsed. When a folder is expanded, the contents of the folder, including files and other folders, appear. The right pane displays the specific information pertaining to the files in the selected folder. As shown in Figure 5.5, it consists of several columns. Each column typically displays the same type of information in each line. For Windows Explorer, the first column contains the file name, the second column contains the size, and so on. Both panes can display an icon adjacent to each item.

In Visual Basic, the programmer uses two different controls to create the two parts of this drill-down user interface. The TreeView control supports properties and methods to create the hierarchical part of the user interface, which is displayed in the left pane of Windows Explorer. The ListView control supports

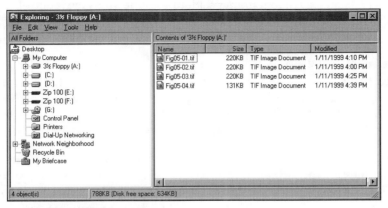

Figure 5.5   Windows Explorer.

properties and methods to create the part of the list that is displayed in the right pane of Windows Explorer.

Programmers commonly use the TreeView and ListView controls in tandem. For example, in Windows Explorer, the data displayed in the ListView control is synchronized with the selected folder in the TreeView control. The synchronization process is not automatic. Instead, you must write code to update the contents of the ListView control when a different element of the TreeView control is selected.

In the ETC program, you will use instances of the TreeView and ListView controls to display and locate the phone numbers for employees in the organization based on their geographic location and the department in which the employees work. In the remaining part of this section, you will create and program the instance of the TreeView control. In the next section, you will work with the ListView control.

The TreeView Control

The TreeView control displays information in a hierarchical format much like Windows Explorer. It could, therefore, be used to display a hierarchy of files stored on a physical disk. The standard prefix for the TreeView control is "tvw". In this chapter, you will use an instance of the TreeView control to navigate the hierarchical structure of the employees working for ETC Corporation.

The **Nodes** property provides the key to understanding the TreeView control. This property references a collection that, in turn, stores references to Node objects. Each Node object in the **Nodes** collection represents an element in the tree view hierarchy. That is, if you create a hierarchy of directories and files with the TreeView control, each directory or file is represented as a Node object in the hierarchy. Each Node object that appears in the TreeView control has a visual component consisting of a textual label, an optional bitmap, and an optional checkbox. A programmer seldom uses the TreeView control without Node objects, or vice versa, because the items are closely intertwined. This book will therefore discuss the TreeView control and the Node object together.

In the context of Visual Basic and the TreeView control, the term "Node" refers to a particular Node object in a **Nodes** collection. In contrast, the lowercase term "node" has a much more generic meaning; a "node" is used to define an element of a hierarchical data structure. In this chapter, the terms "node" and "Node" object are used interchangeably to refer to a Node object.

Relationships exist between individual nodes in any hierarchy. The hierarchy of relationships is expressed as an inverted tree structure that is similar in form to the ADO hierarchy introduced in Chapters 3 and 4. The terms used to describe hierarchical relationships mimic those used to describe genealogical relationships. For instance, the root node, appears at the top of the hierarchy (family tree) and can have zero or more children. All children having the same parent are siblings. A child node can have only one parent, but a parent can have multiple children. Child nodes can have children, who in turn can have their own children. The terms *grandchildren* and *great grandchildren* describe these additional relationships.

Figure 5.6 illustrates hierarchical relationships. In Figure 5.6, the root node has two children (Node1 and Node2). These two nodes are siblings. Node2 is the parent of three children: Node3, Node4, and Node5. Node3, Node4, and Node5 are siblings.

Before working with the Node objects themselves, you must understand the properties and methods pertaining to the TreeView control.

Syntax

TreeView

Properties

➤ The **CheckBoxes** property can be set to **True** or **False**. If set to **True**, checkboxes appear to the left of each node. If set to **False**, they do not.

➤ When the TreeView contains nodes that pertain to files, the **PathSeparator** and **FullPath** properties are typically used to specify the character separating the folder name and the full path for a particular file. The **PathSeparator** property is a string value typically set to the backslash (\ ) character because this character is used to separate DOS path names. When the **FullPath** property is read, it returns the fully qualified path. A fully qualified path includes the drive designator, followed by a colon, directories, and a file name.

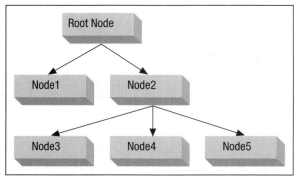

Figure 5.6   TreeView node representation.

➤ The **ImageList** property contains the images that appear in the TreeView control. This property should be set to the name of an ImageList control instance drawn on the form.

➤ The **Indentation** property defines how far the child nodes are indented when they appear below the parent node.

➤ The **LabelEdit** property determines how the user can edit the textual part of a node. If set to the constant **tvwAutomatic**, the user can click in the text portion of the node to edit the text. If set to **tvwManual**, the **StartLabelEdit** method must be called programmatically to initiate editing.

➤ The **LineStyle** property works in conjunction with the **Style** property. If set to the constant value **tvwTreeLines** (the default), the control instance draws lines between a node and its parent. If set to **tvwRootLines**, the control instance also draws lines back to the root node.

➤ The **Nodes** property contains a reference to the **Nodes** collection.

➤ The value in the **Scroll** property determines whether scroll bars appear. If set to **True**, scroll bars appear. If set to **False**, they do not.

➤ The **Sorted** property contains a Boolean value that pertains to both a TreeView control and a Node object. When the **Sorted** property of the TreeView control contains the value of **True**, the control instance sorts the child nodes of the current node. If the programmer adds child nodes after setting the **Sorted** property to **True**, the new child nodes will not be sorted until the **Sorted** property is set to **True** again. Thus the **Sorted** property must be set after the addition of all child nodes.

➤ The **Style** property contains the attributes that control the graphics, if any, that appear next to each node. It also controls whether plus and minus signs appear. These graphics indicate to the user whether the node is expanded or collapsed. Lines may or may not connect the different nodes visually.

Methods

➤ The **GetVisibleCount** method returns the number of Node objects that can appear in the visible region of the TreeView control. This property is commonly used to change the size of a TreeView control instance when a certain number of nodes should be visible.

➤ Calling the **StartLabelEdit** method manually initiates editing on a node.

Events

➤ The **BeforeLabelEdit** and **AfterLabelEdit** events occur when the user starts to edit a label and when the user completes editing, respectively. These events accept one argument—a reference to the node being edited. You typically write code in these events to save changes to data in a database or other file.

➤ The **Collapse** and **Expand** events occur when the user expands a node (its children become visible) or collapses a node (its children become invisible), respectively. As in the **NodeClick** event, the node being collapsed or expanded is passed as an argument to the event procedures.

➤ Two different events can occur when the user clicks the mouse inside the region of the TreeView control instance. If the user clicks the mouse when it is positioned over a node, a **NodeClick** event occurs. If the user clicks the mouse outside the region of a node, a **Click** event occurs. The **NodeClick** event pertains to the TreeView control rather than to a specific node. To determine which node received the **NodeClick** event, Visual Basic passes a reference to the node as an argument to the event procedure.

➤ If the **CheckBoxes** property contains the Boolean value of **True**, the **NodeCheck** event occurs when the user checks or unchecks the node.

The TreeView control expands and collapses nodes automatically. The programmer can also write code to expand and collapse them.

To create an instance of the TreeView control:

1. Using the TreeView button, create an instance of the TreeView control, as shown in Figure 5.7.

2. Using the Properties window, set the **Name** to **tvwETC**, **Indentation** to **200**, and **LabelEdit** to **1– tvwManual**.

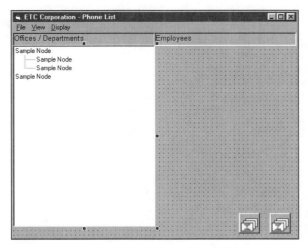

Figure 5.7   Creating an instance of the TreeView control.

3. Activate the Property Pages for the TreeView control instance that you just created. Figure 5.8 shows the Property Pages.

4. Set the **ImageList** property to **ilsSmallIcons**, and then click on OK to close the Property Pages.

By setting the **ImageList** property, you have associated the TreeView control instance with the instance of the ImageList control that you already created on the form. You also could have set this property at run time with the following statement:

```
Set tvwETC.ImageList = ilsSmallIcons
```

Because this statement assigns an object reference, the **Set** statement must be used.

Although several additional properties can be set using the Property Pages, you cannot see the effect of these properties until the TreeView control instance contains data. For the ETC program, you will first add data to the TreeView control instance and then set the properties that alter its visual appearance.

Once an instance of the TreeView control exists, you can write code to add nodes to the TreeView control instance at run time. Common sources for data include databases and text files. The Node object stores the data pertaining to the TreeView control.

The Node Object
The Node object supports several properties that determine the behavior of the node and its relationship to other nodes in the hierarchy. As you review the properties and methods pertaining to the TreeView control and Node object, you will see that the TreeView control and Node object share some of the same

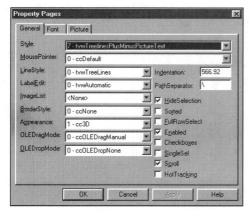

Figure 5.8   TreeView control Property Pages.

properties. For example, each supports the **Sorted** property. The **Sorted** property pertaining to the TreeView control is used to sort the immediate children of the TreeView control. The **Sorted** property pertaining to the Node object is used to sort the children of a particular node. Although both have nearly identical purposes and effects, these separate properties pertain to different objects.

Syntax

      Node

Properties

➤ The **Child** property contains a reference to the first child of a node, if one exists.

➤ The **Children** property returns a number indicating the number of children contained by the specified node. This property is commonly used in an **If** statement to determine whether child nodes exist.

➤ The **Expanded** property contains a Boolean value. If set to **True**, the children of the current node appear; otherwise, they do not. Double-clicking on a node toggles this property. That is, double-clicking on a node will cause its children to be displayed. Double-clicking on the node again will hide its children. The TreeView control performs this task automatically. You also can set the **Expanded** property by writing code. For example, you can write code to set the **Expanded** property for all nodes to **True**.

➤ Each node can display one of two icons, depending on whether the node is expanded. If the node is expanded, the image identified by the **ExpandedImage** property is displayed. If the node is collapsed, the image identified by the **Image** property is displayed.

➤ Nodes at the same level are siblings. The **FirstSibling** property contains a reference to the first node at that level of the hierarchy, and the **LastSibling** property contains a reference to the last node at the same level of the hierarchy.

➤ The **Index** and **Key** properties contain the numeric index and string key, respectively, to identify uniquely a Node object within the **Nodes** collection. The **Nodes** collection is a one-based collection. That is, the index of the first item in the collection has a value of 1. The string keys are case-sensitive.

➤ The **Next** and **Previous** properties contain a reference to the next and to the previous node (sibling) at the same hierarchical level, respectively.

➤ The **Parent** property contains a reference to a parent node, which is the node found one level up on the hierarchy.

➤ The **Root** property contains a reference to the root node.

➤ Each node can display a different image when clicked. The **SelectedImage** property identifies this image.

➤ The **Sorted** property can be set to **True** or **False**. If set to **True**, the child nodes at the same level in the hierarchy will be sorted alphabetically. If set to **False**, the child nodes will remain unsorted. If child nodes are added after setting the **Sorted** property, the new child nodes will not be sorted until the **Sorted** property is set again. Thus, you should set the **Sorted** property for a node after the addition of all child nodes.

➤ The **Text** property contains the text displayed in the node. This text appears to the right of the image, if one is defined.

Methods

➤ The **Add** method adds a node to the **Nodes** collection.

➤ The **Clear** method removes all nodes from the **Nodes** collection.

➤ The **EnsureVisible** method forces a node to become visible. The hierarchy is scrolled to accomplish this task.

➤ The **Remove** method removes a particular node from the **Nodes** collection.

Note that the Node object does not respond to events. Instead, the TreeView control itself handles all of the event processing. All event procedures contain a reference to the active node.

In the ETC program, the Root node will have a child node for each of the 10 different regional offices. The database table named tblOffices, which has fields named fldOfficeID and fldOfficeDescription, contains the relevant information. To display the information in the TreeView control instance, the database containing the information must be opened and the information in the table read. The startup program for this chapter already contains the code needed to establish a database connection. The code you write will use this connection to add a node to the TreeView control instance for each regional office.

 Although both the TreeView and ListView controls support editing of their textual contents, the programmer must decide how to handle the edited data. For example, if the code in this program permitted editing, changes must be recorded in the database by writing SQL statements or by writing data to a recordset.

Adding A Node To The TreeView Control

The code you will write calls the **Add** method pertaining to the **Nodes** collection to add a node to the **Nodes** collection. This process of adding items to a collection is consistent with the process for adding items to other collections. The **Add** method pertaining to the **Nodes** collection supports additional arguments to define the relationships of the node to the other nodes in the hierarchy, and the images displayed in it.

Syntax

object.Add([relative] [, relationship] [, key] [, text] [, image] [, selectedimage])

5

Dissection

➤ The required *object* must contain a reference to the **Nodes** collection in a TreeView control instance.

➤ The **Add** method adds a new node to the **Nodes** collection.

➤ The optional *relative* argument contains the index or string key of an existing Node object. Together with the *relationship* argument, the relative determines the placement of the new node in the hierarchy.

➤ The *relationship* argument contains a constant to define the relationship of the new node to the *relative* argument.

➤ The optional *key* contains a unique string key used to identify the node within the collection.

➤ The required *text* argument describes the text that appears to the right of the icon.

➤ The optional *image* argument identifies the image that is displayed to the left of the **text** argument.

➤ The *selectedimage* argument contains the image that is displayed when the node is selected.

Code Example

```
Dim nodExample As Node
Set tvwETC.ImageList = ilsView        ' ilsView is an ImageList
Set nodExample = tvwETC.Nodes.Add( )     ' Add the Root node
nodExample.Key = "Unique Value"
nodExample.Text = "Buena Park"
nodExample.Image = "Clsdfold"
nodExample.SelectedImage = "Openfold"
Set nodExample = tvwETC.Nodes.Add(, , "UniqueValue", _
    "Buena Park", "Clsdfold", "Openfold")
```

Code Dissection

The preceding statements illustrate two techniques for adding a Node object to the **Nodes** collection. The first technique calls the **Add** method with no arguments and sets the properties individually after adding the node. The second technique supplies the same values using the arguments supported by the **Add** method.

The first statement declares an object variable named **nodExample** to supply a reference to the Node. The three-character prefix "nod" will be used in this book to denote a Node object. The second statement identifies the ImageList control instance that contains the images used by the TreeView control instance. The **Set** statement is required because you are assigning object references. The next statement adds a new node. Consider the contents of that statement:

```
Set∫nodExample∫=∫tvwETC.Nodes.Add(∫)
```

The TreeView control supports the **Nodes** property. This property is itself a collection and, as such, supports the **Add** method. Because this statement calls the **Add** method with no arguments, the node is added to the top level of the hierarchy. If the top level of the hierarchy contains other nodes, the node would appear as the last node in the same hierarchy level. The object named nodExample stores a reference to the newly added node. Again, because the **assignment** statement involves an object reference, the **Set** statement is required. After your code adds the node, the text and images for the node are specified.

The statements given in the Syntax dissection illustrate a very important concept pertaining to the nodes used by the TreeView control. Although you have used object variables previously, you seldom used multiple object variables to reference the same object. In this chapter, object variables of type Node will be created frequently to reference the nodes in the hierarchy.

Another distinction should be made regarding the **Nodes** collection and other collections you have used. While Visual Basic considers all collections as mere lists of values, the TreeView control—and the code in your program—views the **Nodes** collection differently: as a hierarchically organized group of elements.

For the ETC program, you will create a root-level node. Each of the 10 offices will appear as children of this root-level node. Each of the 10 offices, in turn, will have its own children representing the departments, which will vary depending on the office. Each department, in turn, will have a specific number of employees. In other words, the employees are children of the department and grandchildren of the office.

The implementation developed in this chapter to create the nodes uses four general procedures. The first general procedure creates the root-level node and then calls a procedure to create a node for each of the 10 offices. For each office, this second procedure calls a third procedure to create the nodes for the departments pertaining to that office. The procedure to create the department nodes calls a fourth procedure to create the nodes representing the employees working in that particular department. Thus, a specific procedure performs the processing for each level of the hierarchy. Figure 5.9 illustrates these procedures and their organization.

5

Now that you have reviewed the general structure of the program, you will begin the process by creating the root-level node.

Creating The Root-Level Node

The **Sub** procedure to create the root level node is relatively simple. It creates the node and defines the node's text and icons. Then, the procedure calls another procedure to add the child nodes that represent the offices. After the

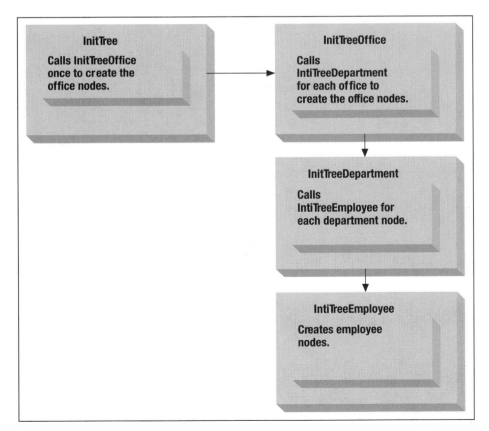

Figure 5.9   Processing the node hierarchy.

code in this second procedure adds the offices, it sorts the child nodes and expands the current node. The children are then displayed.

To create the root-level node:

1. Activate the general declarations section of the Code window, and declare the following variable to store a reference to the root-level node. Note that the prefix "nod" denotes the Node object.

```
Private mnodRoot As Node
```

2. Locate the **InitTree** general procedure, and enter the following statements:

```
Private Sub InitTree()
    Set mnodRoot = tvwETC.Nodes.Add _
        (, , "Root", "Offices", "SmallClsdfold", _
        "SmallOpenfold")
    Call InitTreeOffice(mnodRoot)
    mnodRoot.Expanded = True
    mnodRoot.Sorted = True
End Sub
```

3. Locate the **Form_Load** event procedure, and enter the following statement at the end of the procedure:

```
Call InitTree
```

4. Test the program. The root-level node with the caption "Offices" will appear with an open folder when the program is run. The procedure **InitTreeOffice** has been previously declared but contains no code. Thus the offices will not appear as child nodes until you complete the next group of steps.

5. End the program to return to design mode.

Consider carefully the code you just wrote.

```
Set mnodRoot = tvwETC.Nodes.Add _
    (, , "Root", "Offices", "SmallClsdfold", _
    "SmallOpenfold")
```

Calling the **Add** method creates a Node object in the **Nodes** collection. In the preceding statements, you set the properties through arguments to the **Add** method; you could have set them by writing the individual properties of the Node. Because the **relative** and **relationship** arguments contain no values, the code adds a root-level node. The node has the assigned string key of "Root".

This string—an arbitrary name—indicates the purpose of the node. At run time, the node contains the textual description "Offices". The ImageList control instance that you previously created in this section provided the string keys used to obtain the images. The string key for the image is "SmallClsdfold", and the string key for the selected image is "SmallOpenfold". As you can see, the string key provides greater program readability than does the numeric index value.

Consider the next statement:

```
Call InitTreeOffice(mnodRoot)
```

This statement calls the general procedure **InitTreeOffice**, which initializes the office-level nodes. The procedure accepts one argument: a reference to the root-level node. Although this procedure has been declared, it contains no code. You will write this code in the next set of steps.

```
mnodRoot.Expanded = True
```

The preceding statement expands the node, which causes the **Expanded** property for the node to be set to **True** and the expanded image to appear. No child nodes appear at this point, because they have not been added.

```
mnodRoot.Sorted = True
```

This last statement sorts the children. This statement has no effect at this point; it will become significant after the child nodes have been added to the root node. Adding the child nodes is the next part of the program you will complete.

Creating Child Nodes

Before you can add nodes that exist at different levels of the hierarchy, you need to understand how to create nodes relative to other nodes. To accomplish this task, you use the **relative** and **relationship** arguments supported by the **Add** method pertaining to the **Nodes** collection.

A newly added node appears at the top of the node hierarchy by default. If a Node object is specified in the **relative** argument, however, the position of the new node in the hierarchy is relative to the specified node. The **relationship** argument determines the relative placement of the new node. The following list describes valid arguments for the **relationship** argument:

➤ The constant **tvwFirst** causes the node to be added at the same level in the hierarchy as the node named in the **relative** argument and positioned before all other nodes at the same level.

➤ The constant **tvwLast** causes the node to be added as the last node at the same level in the hierarchy as the node named in the **relative** argument. Any subsequently added node will be positioned after all other nodes at the same level.

➤ The constant **tvwNext** causes the node to be placed at the same hierarchical level as, but positioned immediately after, the node named in the **relative** argument.

➤ The constant **tvwPrevious** causes the node to be placed at the same hierarchical level as, but positioned immediately before, the node named in the **relative** argument.

➤ The constant **tvwChild** causes the node to be placed below the node named in the **relative** argument, thus becoming a child of the current node.

In the previous set of steps, you created the root-level node. Now, you will create the child nodes that represent the offices. The **InitTreeOffice** general procedure, which is called by the **InitTree** procedure, performs this task. It creates a recordset to examine each of the different offices. For each office, a node is added as a child node of the Root node.

To add the root node's children to the TreeView control:

1. Locate the **InitTreeOffice** general procedure in the Code window, and enter the following statements. Note that the Root node is passed as an argument named **pnodRoot**.

```
Private Sub InitTreeOffice(pnodRoot As Node)
    Dim prstCurrent As New ADODB.Recordset
    Dim pnodCurrent As Node
    mcmdCurrent.CommandType = adCmdTable
    mcmdCurrent.CommandText = "tblOffices"
    Set prstCurrent = mcmdCurrent.Execute
    Do Until prstCurrent.EOF
        Set pnodCurrent = _
            tvwETC.Nodes.Add(pnodRoot, tvwChild)
        With pnodCurrent
            .Text = prstCurrent("fldOfficeDescription")
            .Image = "SmallClsdfold"
            .ExpandedImage = "SmallOpenfold"
        End With
        Call InitTreeDepartment(pnodCurrent, _
            prstCurrent("fldOfficeID"))
        pnodCurrent.Sorted = True
        prstCurrent.MoveNext
    Loop
End Sub
```

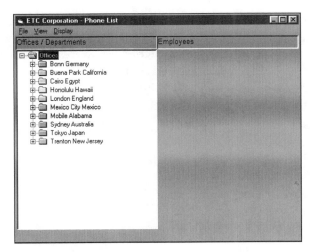

Figure 5.10   Offices displayed in the TreeView control instance.

2. Test the program. The offices should be displayed, as shown in Figure 5.10.

3. End the program to return to design mode.

These statements add all of the regional offices as children of the root node.

The code in the **Form_Load** event procedure established and opened the database connection. However, the properties for the Command object remain to be set and the Recordset object must still be opened, as shown in the following code:

```
Dim prstCurrent As New ADODB.Recordset
Dim pnodCurrent As Node
mcmdCurrent.CommandType = adCmdTable
mcmdCurrent.CommandText = "tblOffices"
Set prstCurrent = mcmdCurrent.Execute
```

The preceding statements declare the variable **prstCurrent** to store a reference to the Recordset object. The variable **pnodCurrent** will store a reference to each node as it is created in this procedure. Next, the code sets the **CommandType** and **CommandText** properties to open the table named tblOffices. Finally, the code opens the recordset.

Once the Recordset object is opened, a Do loop examines each record and adds each office node, as shown below:

```
Set pnodCurrent = _
    tvwETC.Nodes.Add(pnodRoot, tvwChild)
```

For each record in the table, the code adds a new node and stores a reference to that node in the variable **pnodCurrent**. These nodes become children of the root-level node. The **relative** argument, **pnodRoot**, references the root node. As you may remember, the root node is passed as an argument to this procedure. The **relationship** argument, **tvwChild**, indicates that the new node is added as a child of the root-level node.

Consider the following statements, which store the remaining values in the newly added office node:

```
With pnodCurrent
    .Text = prstCurrent("fldOfficeDescription")
    .Image = "SmallClsdfold"
    .ExpandedImage = "SmallOpenfold"
End With
```

The **Text** property of the node contains the office description. The recordset supplies the value stored in the **Text** property of the node. After setting the **Text** property, the code sets the Image and **ExpandedImage** properties to identify the images associated with the node. Remember that the image will be displayed when the node is collapsed, and the expanded image appears when the Node is expanded.

Instead of calling the **Add** method and then setting the properties, you could have used the following technique:

```
Set pnodCurrent = _
    tvwETC.Nodes.Add(pnodRoot, tvwChild, _
    prstCurrent("fldOfficeDescription"), _
    "SmallClsdfold")
pnodCurrent.ExpandedImage = "SmallOpenfold"
```

Instead of setting the properties via individual statements, the preceding call to the **Add** method sets the **Text** and **Image** properties.

Within each office, one or more different departments exist. Each time an office node is added, the departments for that office need to be added as child nodes of the current office. You can accomplish this task by creating a recordset containing the departments corresponding to an office. Then, using a **Do** loop, you can create a child node for each record in the recordset, set the text to the department description, and then set the pertinent image properties.

As you might expect, the structure of this procedure is similar to the structure of the **InitTreeOffice** procedure that you just wrote. This procedure, however, accepts two arguments—a reference to a node and an Office ID. Each department is associated with one office. Thus each department node will have an office node as its parent.

To add the departments as children of the appropriate office:

1. Locate the **InitTreeDepartment** general procedure, and insert the following statements. Note that the general procedure accepts two arguments. The first, **pnodParent**, is of type Node and provides a reference to the parent node. The second, **plngOfficeID**, is a **Long Integer** and contains the OfficeID of the parent node. You will write code that uses the argument **plngOfficeID** to look up the values pertaining to the office.

```
Private Sub InitTreeDepartment(pnodParent As Node, _
    plngOfficeID As Long)
    Dim pnodCurrent As Node
    Dim prstCurrent As Recordset
    mcmdCurrent.CommandType = adCmdText
    mcmdCurrent.CommandText = _
        "SELECT * FROM tblDepartments " & _
        "WHERE fldOfficeID = " & plngOfficeID
    Set prstCurrent = mcmdCurrent.Execute
    Do Until prstCurrent.EOF
        Set pnodCurrent = _
            tvwETC.Nodes.Add(pnodParent, tvwChild)
        With pnodCurrent
            .Text = prstCurrent _
                    ("fldDepartmentDescription")
            .Image = "SmallClsdfold"
            .ExpandedImage = "SmallOpenfold"
            .Tag = prstCurrent("fldDepartmentID")
        End With
        Call InitTreeEmployee(pnodCurrent, _
            prstCurrent("fldDepartmentID"))
        pnodCurrent.Sorted = True
        prstCurrent.MoveNext
    Loop
End Sub
```

2. Test the program. Double-click on the various offices to expand and collapse the different office nodes. The descriptions should appear under the expanded office node, as shown in Figure 5.11.

3. End the program to return to design mode.

The statements that you just wrote create a recordset containing the departments belonging to a specific office. A **Do** loop then creates nodes as children of the parent office node. Consider the following statements:

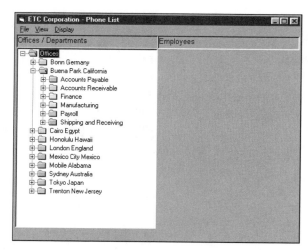

Figure 5.11   Departments displayed in the TreeView control instance.

```
Dim pnodCurrent As Node
Dim prstCurrent As Recordset
mcmdCurrent.CommandType = adCmdText
mcmdCurrent.CommandText = _
    "SELECT * FROM tblDepartments " & _
    "WHERE fldOfficeID = " & plngOfficeID
Set prstCurrent = mcmdCurrent.Execute
```

The variable **pnodCurrent** stores a reference to each department node as it is added. The code to create the recordset is similar to the code that you wrote to initialize the office. In this procedure, however, an SQL statement executes and retrieves only those departments pertaining to a particular office. Thus the statement sets the **CommandType** property to **adCmdText** and the **CommandText** statement to an SQL statement. Finally, the recordset is opened.

```
Set pnodCurrent = tvwETC.Nodes.Add(pnodParent, tvwChild)
```

The **relative** argument is set to **pnodParent**, which contains a reference to the corresponding office. Note that the following statements would have had the same effect, because both provide a reference to a node:

```
Set pnodCurrent = tvwETC.Nodes.Add(pnodParent.Key, _
    tvwChild)
Set pnodCurrent = tvwETC.Nodes.Add(pnodParent.Index, _
    tvwChild)
```

After adding the new node, the next statements set the properties pertaining to the newly added node:

```
With pnodCurrent
    .Text = prstCurrent("fldDepartmentDescription")
    .Image = "SmallClsdfold"
    .ExpandedImage = "SmallOpenfold"
```

The recordset supplies the value for the **Text** property. The code that you just wrote uses the same images as were used when you set the office node.

Consider carefully the following statement, which stores the current Department ID in the **Tag** property:

```
.Tag = prstCurrent("fldDepartmentID")
```

In this example, only departments have employees. Furthermore, when an end user selects a department, the ListView control instance will ultimately display all employees pertaining to that department. You can write code that checks the **Tag** property to see whether it contains a value when the user clicks on a node. If it does, the code should display the corresponding employees in the ListView control instance. If the property does not contain a value, the contents of the ListView control should be cleared.

```
Call InitTreeEmployee(pnodCurrent, _
    prstCurrent("fldDepartmentID"))
pnodCurrent.Sorted = True
prstCurrent.MoveNext
```

The preceding statements call the procedure to load the employees pertaining to the currently selected department and to sort the nodes.

The final step in the process of building the hierarchy of nodes adds the employees to the departments where they work. The process of adding the employees closely resembles the process of adding the departments. Every employee works for one—and only one—department. The **InitTreeDepartment** procedure passes the department node and department ID as arguments to the **InitTreeEmployee** general procedure.

To add the employees to their department:

1. Locate the **InitTreeEmployee** general procedure and insert the following statements. The general procedure passes the parent node (department) in the argument **pnodParent**.

```
Private Sub InitTreeEmployee(pnodParent As Node, _
    pintDepartmentID As Integer)
On Error GoTo No_Record
```

```
        Dim pnodCurrent As Node
        Dim prstCurrent As ADODB.Recordset
        mcmdCurrent.CommandType = adCmdText
        mcmdCurrent.CommandText = _
            "SELECT * FROM tblEmployees " & _
            "WHERE fldDepartmentID = " & pintDepartmentID
        Set prstCurrent = mcmdCurrent.Execute
        Do Until prstCurrent.EOF
            Set pnodCurrent = _
            tvwETC.Nodes.Add(pnodParent, tvwChild)
            pnodCurrent.Text = prstCurrent("fldName")
            If prstCurrent("fldInOut") = True Then
                pnodCurrent.Image = "SmallPhone07"
            Else
                pnodCurrent.Image = "SmallPhone08"
            End If
            prstCurrent.MoveNext
        Loop
No_Record:
End Sub
```

2. Test the program. Expand the offices and departments. Double-click on various departments and verify that the employees are listed with an icon. Note that employees do not appear for all the departments.

3. End the program to return to design mode.

The statements that you just wrote closely resemble the statements that add the departmental nodes, with a few exceptions. First, the new procedure uses an error handler to account for the scenario where a department has no employees. If a department has no employees, the procedure exits without adding any employee nodes.

```
Dim pnodCurrent As Node
Dim prstCurrent As ADODB.Recordset
mcmdCurrent.CommandType = adCmdText
mcmdCurrent.CommandText = _
    "SELECT * FROM tblEmployees " & _
    "WHERE fldDepartmentID = " & pintDepartmentID
Set prstCurrent = mcmdCurrent.Execute
```

The preceding code uses a **SELECT** statement to create a recordset containing the names of the employees who work for a specific department. The technique is the same as that used to add the department nodes. The code to set the properties for each node differs slightly.

```
Set pnodCurrent = _
    tvwETC.Nodes.Add(pnodParent, tvwChild)
pnodCurrent.Text = prstCurrent("fldName")
If prstCurrent("fldInOut") = True Then
    pnodCurrent.Image = "SmallPhone07"
Else
    pnodCurrent.Image = "SmallPhone08"
End If
```

Although the same code is used to add the node and to set the **Text** property, the code to set the icons differs. Because the employee nodes will never have children, you do not need to set the **ExpandedImage** property. Furthermore, the icon that appears indicates whether the employee is in or out of the office. If the employee is in the office, the value of **fldInOut** is **True**, and the **Image** is set to "**SmallPhone07**". If the employee is out of the office, the value of **fldInOut** is **False**, and the image is set to "**SmallPhone08**".

At this point in the program, you have written all of the code needed to initialize the TreeView control instance; the control instance itself expands and collapses nodes as necessary when the user clicks on a particular node. In addition to using this automated method of processing, you can write code to explicitly select nodes, expand and collapse them, and navigate through the hierarchy of nodes.

Navigating The Node Hierarchy

A Node object supports the following navigation properties: **Children**, **Child**, **FirstSibling**, **LastSibling**, **Next**, and **Previous**. These properties allow you to traverse the nodes in the tree and print the contents of individual nodes.

With these properties, you can use any of several techniques to examine the entire hierarchy of nodes. If you want to list all of the children (offices of the root node), you could generalize this concept and create a procedure to list all immediate children of a node:

```
Private Sub ListChildren(pnod As Node)
    Dim pintCount As Integer, pintCurrent As Integer
    Dim pnodCurrent As Node
    Set pnodCurrent = pnod.Child
    pintCount = pnod.Children
    For pintCurrent = 1 To pintCount
        Debug.Print pnodCurrent.Text
        Set pnodCurrent = pnodCurrent.Next
    Next
End Sub
```

This code illustrates the importance of using the **Set** statement with object references. The general procedure accepts one argument—a reference to a node. In this example, assume that the general procedure passes the root node for ETC as the argument. The reference **pnod.Children** contains the number of children in the node (in this case, the 10 offices or nodes). As a result, the **For** loop goes through 10 iterations. Inside the For loop, the code prints the contents of a node's **Text** property. The final statement holds special significance:

```
Set pnodCurrent = pnodCurrent.Next
```

Each node supports the **Next** property, which contains a reference to the next sibling. This assignment statement sets the object variable **pnodCurrent** so that it will reference the next sibling. The process continues until all nodes have been examined.

This example can be extended to examine multiple hierarchies. To accomplish this task, you can use nested **For** loops. For ETC's program, the code to print the hierarchy of nodes uses the navigational properties to print the **Text** property for each Node object in the tree. The children are printed in an indented fashion, similar to the way they appear on the form.

The code created in the following steps assumes that you are familiar with the basic usage of the Printer object.

To use the navigational properties to print the tree:

1. Locate the **mnuFilePrint_Click** event procedure, and enter the following statements:

```
Dim pnodOffice As Node, pnodDept As Node, _
    pnodEmp As Node
Dim pintRC As Integer, pintOC As Integer, _
    pintDC As Integer
Dim pintRCount As Integer, pintOCount As Integer, _
    pintDCount As Integer
Printer.Print mnodRoot.Text
Set pnodOffice = mnodRoot.Child
pintRC = mnodRoot.Children
For pintRCount = 1 To pintRC
    Printer.Print "    "; pnodOffice.Text
    Set pnodDept = pnodOffice.Child
    pintOC = pnodOffice.Children
    For pintOCount = 1 To pintOC
        Printer.Print "        "; pnodDept.Text
        Set pnodEmp = pnodDept.Child
        pintDC = pnodDept.Children
```

```
        For pintDCount = 1 To pintDC
            Printer.Print "                "; pnodEmp.Text
            Set pnodEmp = pnodEmp.Next
        Next
        Set pnodDept = pnodDept.Next
    Next
    Set pnodOffice = pnodOffice.Next
Next
Printer.EndDoc
```

2. Test the program. On the menu bar, click on File, and then click on Print. The report printed on the printer should appear similar to the tree, with all nodes expanded.

3. End the program to return to design mode.

The organization of these statements resembles the organization of the general procedures that you used to create the nodes hierarchy. That is, the new event procedure uses three nested For loops to process each level of nodes. The first For loop examines the offices, the second loop looks at the departments, and the inner loop examines the employees for a specific department.

All of the remaining **For** loops work in the same way. The **Children** property is used to determine whether a node has any children. If so, the statements in the loop execute. If the node has no children, they do not execute. Inside the loop, the text of the current node prints and then the next node is selected.

In addition to relying upon the TreeView control to expand and collapse individual nodes in the hierarchy, you can write code to accomplish the same task by manually setting the **Expanded** property. In the following set of steps, you will write code to expand and collapse all nodes in the hierarchy when the end user clicks on a menu item.

Consider the following code example, which expands all nodes in the hierarchy:

```
Dim pnodCurrent As Node
For Each pnodCurrent In tvwETC.Nodes
    pnodCurrent.Expanded = True
Next
```

The first statement declares an object variable to reference the current node. A **For Each** loop then examines each node in the hierarchy. Again, the **Nodes** collection uses the **For Each** loop in the same manner as does any other collection. For each node examined, the node expands, causing the children to appear.

To expand and collapse all nodes in the hierarchy:

1. Locate the **mnuDisplayCollapse_Click** event procedure, and enter the following statements:

```
Dim pnodCurrent As Node
For Each pnodCurrent In tvwETC.Nodes
    pnodCurrent.Expanded = False
Next
```

2. Locate the **mnuDisplayExpand_Click** event procedure, and enter the following statements:

```
Dim pnodCurrent As Node
For Each pnodCurrent In tvwETC.Nodes
    pnodCurrent.Expanded = True
Next
```

3. Test the program. Click on Display, and then click on Expand Nodes to expand the entire hierarchy. Click on Display, and then click on Collapse Nodes to collapse the entire hierarchy.

4. End the program to return to design mode.

At this point in the program's development, you have loaded the database information into the TreeView control instance. Furthermore, you have written the code needed to expand and collapse the nodes in the hierarchy. You also have created the code to print the hierarchy. In the next section, you will synchronize an instance of the ListView control with the instance of the TreeView control.

WORKING WITH THE LISTVIEW AND STATUSBAR CONTROLS

The ListView Control

The ListView control displays data in the form of lists or organized into columns. The view defines how the data are shown on the screen. In icon and small icon view, data appear with an icon and a short description. In list view and report view, data appear organized into columns. Depending on specific property settings, data can appear sorted and columns of data can be rearranged. The ListView control also allows the user to select one or multiple items. You can write code to examine and use selected items as part of other tasks. The standard prefix for the ListView control is "lvw".

Syntax

    ListView

Properties

➤ The **AllowColumnReorder** property stores a Boolean value. If set to **True,** the user can reorder the columns at run time. If set to **False,** the column order cannot be changed. This property is used only in report view.

➤ The **Arrange** property pertains to icon or small icon view only. If you set the property to the constant value **lvwNone** (the default), the items are not arranged. Setting the property to **lvwAutoLeft** vertically aligns the items along the left side of the control instance. Setting the property to **lvwAutoTop** horizontally aligns the items across the top of the control instance.

➤ The **CheckBoxes** property stores a Boolean value. If set to **True,** a checkbox appears adjacent to each item. If set to **False,** no checkboxes appear. The position of the checkbox depends on the view.

➤ The **ColumnHeaders** collection applies only in report view. The ListView control uses this collection to define which titles will appear across columns.

➤ The **GridLines** property stores a Boolean value. If set to **True,** gridlines divide the rows and columns in report view. If set to **False,** no gridlines appear.

➤ The **HideColumnHeaders** property stores a Boolean value. If set to **True,** the column header is invisible at run time. If set to **False,** the column header is visible at run time.

➤ The **HoverSelection** property stores a Boolean value. If set to **True,** the current item becomes automatically selected when the user moves the mouse over the item. When set to **False,** the item does not become automatically selected.

➤ The **Icons** property contains a reference to an ImageList control instance. These icons are displayed while the view is set to icon.

➤ The **LabelEdit** property can store one of two constant values. If set to **lvwManual,** the **StartLabelEdit** method must be called before the user can edit the list view's textual component. If set to **lvwAutomatic,** selecting the label will enable editing.

➤ The **ListSubItems** property contains a reference to the **ListSubItems** collection. The ListView control uses this collection to display information in columns when the view is set to report.

➤ The **SmallIcons** property contains a reference to an ImageList control instance. The ListView control displays these icons while the view is set to small icon, list, or report.

➤ The **SortKey** property contains an **Integer** value that determines how the rows are sorted in report view. If set to 0, the rows are sorted with the ListItem object's **Text** property. If set to a non-zero value, the index of the subitem corresponding to the **SortKey** property is used.

➤ The **SortOrder** property can have one of two constant values. If set to **lvwAscending** (the default), the rows are sorted in ascending order. If set to **lvwDescending**, the rows are sorted in descending order.

➤ The **Sorted** property contains a Boolean value indicating whether the rows will be sorted. If set to **True**, the rows are sorted based on the values of the **SortKey** and **SortOrder** properties. If set to **False**, the rows are not sorted.

Events

➤ The **ColumnClick** event occurs when the user selects a column header in report view. This event occurs when the user clicks on a ColumnHeader object. Visual Basic passes the column header that was clicked as an argument to the event procedure.

➤ The **ItemClick** event occurs when the user clicks on a ListItem object. Visual Basic passes a reference to the ListItem object as an argument to the event procedure.

Methods

➤ The **FindItem** method is used to locate a ListItem object.

➤ The **StartLabelEdit** method initiates editing on the selected label. The changes are recorded when the user presses the Enter key; they are abandoned when the user presses the Escape key.

The ListView control displays information in one of four different views, as determined by the setting of the **View** property. The view can be changed at run time or at design time. Each item of data contains two parts: a textual part and an associated icon.

➤ **Icon view** In icon view, each item appears with an icon and a textual description. The user can arrange the icons within the visible region of the ListView control. The user commonly performs drag-and-drop operations on the icons.

➤ **Small icon view** works like icon view but allows more ListItem objects to be viewed in the visible region of the ListView control.

➤ **List view** presents one item per line and with an optional icon appearing to the left of the icon. (Do not confuse list view with the ListView control.)

➤ **Report view** resembles list view, but displays each item with additional information called ListSubItems. The **ListSubItems** collection allows a columnar list of items to be displayed.

Programmers commonly use collections to manage the run-time objects pertaining to a control instance. For example, the DataGrid control uses the **Columns** collection and Column objects to keep track of the columns displayed in the grid. The ListView control works in a similar manner. The **ListItems** collection manages the data in the control instance. In icon and small icon view, each ListItem object appears with an icon and associated textual description. In list view, the same data appear, but data pertaining to each ListItem object appear in list form. In a moment, report view will be discussed.

Figure 5.12 illustrates the relationship between the ListView control and the **ListItems** collection.

Each item appearing in the ListView control is a ListItem object. Figure 5.12 shows an instance of the ListView control with three ListItem objects. Each

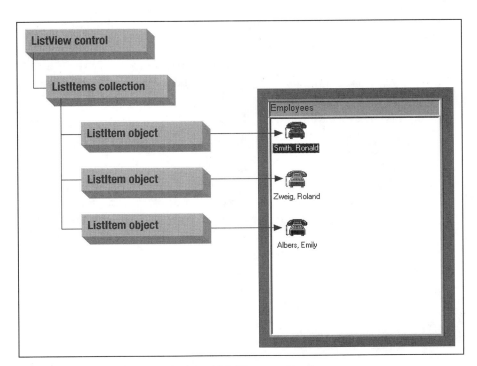

Figure 5.12   ListView control and **ListItems** collection.

ListItem object contains a textual description and an associated icon. The ListView control can be associated with multiple ImageList controls, whereas the TreeView control can be associated with only one. Remember that one ImageList control instance can contain only icons of the same size. When icon view is selected, the **SmallIcons** property determines which images appear at run time. With the other three views, an **Icons** property specifies which images appear at run time. Each of these properties references a particular ImageList control instance.

The text that accompanies the image is stored in the ListItem's **Text** property.

Syntax

    ListItem

Properties

➤ The **Icon** and **SmallIcon** properties contain the numeric index or string key of an image stored in a ListImage object. These properties cannot be set until the programmer associates the ListView control instance with an ImageList control instance.

➤ The **Index** and **Key** properties uniquely identify the ListItem object in the **ListItems** collection. They have the same purpose as the **Index** and **Key** properties pertaining to other collections.

➤ In icon view, text appears on multiple lines if the **LabelWrap** property is set to **True** and on one line if this property is set to False. When the **LabelWrap** property is set to **True**, the maximum width of a line is set using the Appearance tab on the Display control panel.

➤ The **Text** property identifies the text pertaining to the ListItem object.

➤ The **Ghosted** property can be **True** or **False**. When set to **True**, the ListItem object appears dimmed. When set to **False**, the ListItem object is available. This property is typically used with cut-and-paste operations.

➤ The ability to select multiple items (multiple ListItem objects) can prove useful in drag-and-drop operations. If the end user should be able to select multiple ListItem objects, set the **MultiSelect** property to **True**. Otherwise, set the property to **False**.

Methods

➤ You can use the **Add** and **Remove** methods to add and remove ListItem objects to and from the **ListItems** collection, respectively. These methods have the same purpose as the methods of the same name pertaining to other collections.

➤ The **Clear** method takes no arguments. It removes all ListItem objects from the collection, thereby removing all items from the list.

Loading the ListItem objects into the **ListItems** collection is the first step in using the ListView control. The programmer uses the **Add** method to add ListItem objects to the collection. Many viable sources for the data exist. A programmer could write code to read and display the contents of an ASCII-delimited file, for example. For each record in the ASCII-delimited file, the **Add** method would be called to insert the record in the **ListItems** collection. You could also write code to display the records in a database.

For the ETC program, you will display a list of names and phone numbers from a database. The usefulness of this list will become apparent during the discussion of report view.

Syntax

     object.Add([index] [, key] [, text] [, icon] [, smallIcon])

Dissection

➤ The required *object* must be a valid instance of the ListView control.

➤ The **Add** method adds a ListItem object to the **ListItems** collection.

➤ The optional *index* and *key* arguments uniquely identify a ListItem object. The *index* argument is a numeric value, and the **key** argument is a unique string key. String keys are case-sensitive.

➤ The optional *text* argument identifies the text associated with the ListItem object. The visual appearance of the ListItem object varies according to the current view.

➤ The optional *icon* and *smallIcon* arguments contain a string key or numeric index of an image in a corresponding ImageList control instance.

Code Example

```
lvwEmployees.Icons = ilsLargeIcons
lvwEmployees.SmallIcons = ilsSmallIcons
lvwEmployees.Add(1,"Item","String","SmallIcon", _
    "LargeIcon")
```

Code Dissection

This example assumes the existence of an instance of the ListView control named lvwEmployees. The first two assignment statements define the two image lists that will be used to display the normal and small icons, respectively. You could also have set the **Icons** and **SmallIcons** properties at design time.

The general procedure calls the **Add** method to add an item to the list. The arguments to the **Add** method define both the numeric index and the string key. The text "String" will appear in the ListItem object . The last two arguments specify the string keys of the icons in the two different ImageList control instances.

For the ETC program you will write code to create ListItem objects when the user double-clicks on a department in the TreeView control instance. This interface mimics the display of folders and files in the right-hand pane in Windows Explorer. Each ListItem object will eventually contain the name, phone number, and extension of the employee. For each employee in the list, the ListView control instance will display one of two icons to indicate whether the employee is in the office. You can see the appearance of the different views by examining the previously created menu items found on the View menu. In a moment, you will write the code for these menu items to set the **View** property to one of the four different views.

Integrating The ListView And TreeView Controls

Programmers commonly use the ListView control in conjunction with the TreeView control. When the user selects a department node from the TreeView control instance, the contents of the ListView control instance must be updated to display the contents pertaining to the selected node (department). In the completed program, the names, phone number, and extension for the employees in a department will appear when the user double-clicks on a department. You will begin here by displaying an icon and name in the ListView control instance.

When you created the nodes in the TreeView control instance, you set the **Tag** property for departments only. In the **NodeClick** event procedure pertaining to the TreeView control, you can create an **If** statement to determine whether the node's **Tag** property contains a value other than an empty string. If it does, the node represents a department and the employees should be displayed in the ListView control instance.

The logic used to initialize the list is similar to the procedure used to initialize the employees working for a department. The code for both the TreeView and ListView control instances initializes the same number of records. You will therefore create a recordset and then construct a loop to examine each record in the recordset. For each employee record, your code will add a ListItem object (an item in the list) to the **ListItems** collection and then set the **Text** and icon-related properties.

To create a ListView control instance and synchronize it with the TreeView control instance:

1. Using the ListView button in the toolbox, create an instance of the ListView control and place it on the right of the TreeView control instance. Using the Properties window, set the **Name** property to **lvwEmployees**.

2. Locate the **tvwETC_NodeClick** event procedure in the Code window, and enter the following statements:

```
If Node.Tag <> vbNullString Then
    Call InitializeList(Node.Tag)
Else
    Call ClearList
End If
```

3. Enter the following statement in the **ClearList Sub** procedure:

```
Private Sub ClearList()
    lvwEmployees.ListItems.Clear
End Sub
```

4. Enter the following statement in the **InitializeList** general procedure. Note that the **InitializeList** procedure receives the variable **pintID** as an argument; this argument contains the current **DepartmentID**.

```
Private Sub InitializeList(pintID As Integer)
    Dim pitmCurrent As ListItem
    Dim prstCurrent As New ADODB.Recordset
    mcmdCurrent.CommandType = adCmdText
    mcmdCurrent.CommandText = _
        "SELECT * FROM tblEmployees " & _
        "WHERE fldDepartmentID = " & pintID
    Set prstCurrent = mcmdCurrent.Execute
    lvwEmployees.Icons = ilsLargeIcons
    lvwEmployees.SmallIcons = ilsSmallIcons
    lvwEmployees.View = lvwIcon
    lvwEmployees.ListItems.Clear
    Do Until prstCurrent.EOF
        Set pitmCurrent = _
            lvwEmployees.ListItems.Add()
            pitmCurrent.Text = prstCurrent("fldName")
        If prstCurrent("fldInOut") = True Then
            pitmCurrent.SmallIcon = "SmallPhone07"
```

5

```
                    pitmCurrent.Icon = "LargePhone07"
            Else
                    pitmCurrent.SmallIcon = "SmallPhone08"
                    pitmCurrent.Icon = "LargePhone08"
            End If
            prstCurrent.MoveNext
        Loop
    End Sub
```

5. Test the program. Expand the folders until a folder at the office level appears, and then double-click on the icon for a particular office. This action generates a **NodeClick** event procedure, which in turn calls the **InitializeList** procedure. The ListView control should list the employees. In icon view (the default), the large icons are displayed. In small icon view, the other icons are displayed, which allows the display of more information in the visible area of the ListView control. In list view, the items appear in a columnar list. At this point in your program's development, however, only one view is used.

6. End the program to return to design mode.

The **NodeClick** event procedure tests to determine whether a value is stored in the **Tag** property. If so, it calls the procedure to list the employees. Only department-level nodes have a value stored in the **Tag** property. If no value is stored in the **Tag** property, the contents of the ListView control instance are cleared.

```
Dim pitmCurrent As ListItem
Dim prstCurrent As New ADODB.Recordset
mcmdCurrent.CommandType = adCmdText
mcmdCurrent.CommandText = _
    "SELECT * FROM tblEmployees " & _
    "WHERE fldDepartmentID = " & pintID
Set prstCurrent = mcmdCurrent.Execute
```

The **InitializeList** general procedure accepts one argument—the ID representing a department at a regional office. It uses this value in the **SELECT** statement. The resulting recordset, which is stored in **prstCurrent**, contains all employees who work in a specific department.

```
lvwEmployees.Icons = ilsLargeIcons
lvwEmployees.SmallIcons = ilsSmallIcons
lvwEmployees.View = lvwIcon
lvwEmployees.ListItems.Clear
```

The preceding statements initialize the ListView control instance. The first two statements associate the ListView control instance with the two ImageList control instances that you created on the form. You could have set these properties at design time as well, because they will never change. The third statement defines the view as icon view, ensuring that the large icons will appear at run time. The final statement removes any existing items from the control instance.

```
Do Until prstCurrent.EOF
    Set pitmCurrent = _
        lvwEmployees.ListItems.Add()
    pitmCurrent.Text = prstCurrent("fldName")
    If prstCurrent("fldInOut") = True Then
        pitmCurrent.SmallIcon = "SmallPhone07"
        pitmCurrent.Icon = "LargePhone07"
    Else
        pitmCurrent.SmallIcon = "SmallPhone08"
        pitmCurrent.Icon = "LargePhone08"
    End If
    prstCurrent.MoveNext
Loop
```

For each record, the **InitializeList** procedure adds an item to the list and stores the employee name in the **Text** property of the ListItem object. Depending on the value of the field named fldInOut, the code displays one of two different icons. The two ImageList control instances store large and small versions of the icons.

The first statement adds the new ListItem object to the collection. The numeric index of the item matches the Employee ID. ETC's implementation requires the use of unique Employee IDs so that the collection indexes will be unique. The **ListItems** collection uses a numeric index rather than a string key. The second statement stores the employee name in the **Text** property pertaining to the ListItem object. This value appears in the first column in report view; in the other three views, it will appear as the textual description.

Defining The View
The way in which the **View** property is set at run time or at design time defines the current view. The ListView control supports four different views as mentioned previously.

The View menu items already include four menu items that were created as a control array. The event procedure to set the current view must determine the index of the currently selected menu and then set the **View** property accordingly.

To set the **View** property:

1. Enter the following statements in the **mnuViewSet_Click** event procedure:

```
Select Case Index
    Case 0
        lvwEmployees.View = lvwIcon
    Case 1
        lvwEmployees.View = lvwSmallIcon
    Case 2
        lvwEmployees.View = lvwList
    Case 3
        lvwEmployees.View = lvwReport
End Select
```

2. Test the program. Select a department node having employees. Click on View, and then select Large, Small, List, and Report. As you select each view, the code that you wrote in Step 1 updates the ListView control instance. When you select report view, nothing appears, because you have not yet created the necessary objects to display information in report view.

3. End the program to return to design mode.

Although the program displays information properly in three of the four views, report view does not work. You need to create additional objects before report view will work correctly.

Arranging The Icons

In icon and small icon view, you can use the **Arrange** property to align the list items horizontally across the top of the control instance or vertically along the left side of the control instance. You can set the **Arrange** property by using the constants lvwAutoLeft and **lvwAutoTop**. Consider the following statements:

```
lvwEmployees.Arrange lvwAutoLeft
lvwEmployees.Arrange lvwAutoTop
```

The first statement aligns the items across the left side of the control instance, and the second statement aligns the items along the top of the control instance. Two menu items have already been created to perform alignment. You can now program these menu items.

To align the items in the ListView control instance:

1. Locate the code for the **mnuDisplayLeft_Click** event procedure, and enter the following statement:

```
lvwEmployees.Arrange = lvwAutoLeft
```

2. Activate the Code window for the **mnuDisplayTop_Click** event procedure, and enter the following statement:

```
lvwEmployees.Arrange = lvwAutoTop
```

3. Test the program. Open folders in the TreeView control instance for the Buena Park California Finance department, and display the employees in the ListView control instance. Click on Display, and then click on Left Align List. The items should align along the left side of the ListView control instance. Click on Display, and then click on Top Align List. The items should align across the top of the ListView control instance.

4. End the program to return to design mode.

Using Report View

Using the ListView control in report view adds considerable functionality beyond that available with the other three views. The additional functionality increases the programming complexity, however. Typically, report view displays records from a database or a text file as a columnar grid.

To support this functionality, you need a mechanism to store the column headers and the information in the rows under the column headers. The **ColumnHeaders** and **ListSubItems** collections perform this task. These objects are pertinent only in report view.

Figure 5.13 depicts the relationship between the ListView control and the collections and objects pertaining to it.

As shown in Figure 5.13, the name, phone number, and extension for each employee appear in columns. A column header identifies each column. Each row (item) in the ListView control is represented as a ListItem object, and each column is represented as a ColumnHeader object. The Text and icon that you assigned in the previous steps appear in the first column.

As presently implemented, your program causes the control instance to appear as empty in report view because you have defined no ColumnHeader object to display the column.

The ColumnHeader Object

The ListView control supports the **ColumnHeaders** collection. A ColumnHeader object in the **ColumnHeaders** collection represents each column. The **ColumnHeaders** property pertaining to the ListView control maintains a reference to this collection. The following syntax discussion summarizes the properties supported by the ColumnHeader object.

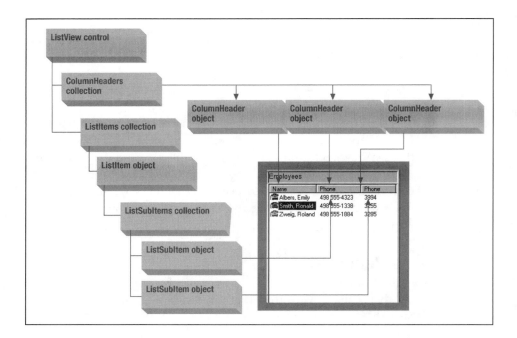

Figure 5.13   ListView and ListItems, ColumnHeaders, and ListSubItems.

Syntax

    ColumnHeader

Properties

➤ The **Index** and **Key** properties, respectively, contain the numeric index and string key of the ColumnHeader object in the **ColumnHeaders** collection.

➤ The **Text** property contains the caption that is displayed in the column header. Setting the **Alignment** property changes the justification of the text.

➤ Each column header corresponds to a subitem. The **SubItemIndex** property contains the numeric index of the subitem associated with the ColumnHeader object.

Column headers can be added at design time using the Property Pages, or at run time by calling the **Add** method, which has the following syntax.

Syntax
>   object.Add([index][, key][, text][, width][, alignment])

Dissection

➤ The required *object* must contain a reference to a **ColumnHeaders** collection.

➤ The optional *index* and *key* arguments, respectively, specify the numeric index and string key that identify a unique ColumnHeader object in the collection.

➤ The column header displays the value of the optional *text* argument.

➤ The optional *width* argument defines the width of the column header.

➤ The optional *alignment* argument is used to left-justify, right-justify, or center **text** in the column.

Code Example
```
lvwEmployees.ColumnHeaders.Add 1 "Column1", _
    "Description", 1500
```

Code Dissection
This statement adds a column header with the string key of "Column1". The text appearing in the column is "Description," and the column is 1500 twips wide.

For the ETC program, you need to create a column header for the name, phone number, and extension by using the **Add** method. For each column, the width of the column is set explicitly. Consider the following statements to add the column headers to the ListView control instance:

```
lvwEmployees.ColumnHeaders.Add , , "Name", 1400
lvwEmployees.ColumnHeaders.Add , , "Phone", 1500
lvwEmployees.ColumnHeaders.Add , , "Ext.",1000
```

The preceding statements add three columns to the list. The first column has a caption of Name and a width of 1400 twips. The second and third columns will have captions of "Phone" and "Ext.", respectively.

To create the column headers:

1. Locate the InitializeList general procedure, and enter the following statements:

```
lvwEmployees.ListItems.Clear
lvwEmployees.ColumnHeaders.Add , , "Name", 1400
lvwEmployees.ColumnHeaders.Add , , "Phone", 1500
lvwEmployees.ColumnHeaders.Add , , "Ext.", 1000
Do Until prstCurrent.EOF
```

2. Test the program. Double-click on the Buena Park California office, and then double-click on the Finance department. Click on View, and then click on Report. The column header, icon, and name appear in the list, but the telephone number and telephone extension do not. You will add these items in the next set of steps.

3. End the program to return to design mode.

In report view, the ListView control displays one ListItem object per line. The **ListSubItems** collection pertaining to the ListItem object defines the remaining columns.

To add the data for the remaining two columns (phone and extension), you must create two ListSubItem objects to represent the second and third columns in the view. The first column, which is already populated with the name and an icon, is represented by the ListView object itself.

You must repeat the task of adding the ListSubItem objects for each row. Consider the following statements:

```
pitmCurrent.ListSubItems.Add , "Phone", _
    prstCurrent("fldPhone")
pitmCurrent.ListSubItems.Add , "Extension", _
    prstCurrent("fldExtension")
```

Recall from the code that you wrote in the **InitializeList** procedure that **pitmCurrent** contains a reference to the current ListItem object being created. For each ListItem object (row), the preceding statements add two columns. In the first statement, the string key is set to "Phone" and the textual contents contain the value from the recordset's **fldPhone** field. The second statement adds the next column, which has a string key of "Extension" and the textual contents of the recordset's fldExtension field.

To create the ListSubItem objects:

1. Locate the InitializeList general procedure, and enter the following statements:

```
        pitmCurrent.Icon = "LargePhone08"
    End If
    pitmCurrent.ListSubItems.Add , "Phone", _
        prstCurrent("fldPhone")
    pitmCurrent.ListSubItems.Add , "Extension", _
        prstCurrent("fldExtension")
    prstCurrent.MoveNext
```

2. Test the program. Select Report view, and then select the Buena Park California Finance department. When the records appear in the ListView control instance, the data for the remaining two columns should appear as well.

3. End the program to return to design mode.

Visual Basic 5.0 and the corresponding version of the ListView control did not support the **ListSubItems** collection. Rather, the **SubItems** property referenced an array of string values. The ListView control is supported only by Windows 95, Windows 98, and Windows NT 3.51 or higher.

Column Selection

In report view, the user can click on a column header to generate a **ColumnClick** event. The **ColumnClick** event passes the column header that was clicked as an argument to the **ColumnClick** event procedure. Sorting rows by the values in the selected column is a common task performed in this event procedure. Sorting the rows in the ListView control is performed using the **SortKey** and **Sorted** properties. The **SortKey** contains an **Integer** value that determines the manner of sorting the rows. If **SortKey** is set to **zero (0)**, the rows are sorted using the **Text** property of the ListItem object. If **SortKey** is greater than zero, the rows are sorted by the ListSubItem object having the same Index value. Thus, if the value is **one (1)**, the rows are sorted by the first ListSubItem object. Before setting the **SortKey** property, the **Sorted** property should be set to **True**.

For the ETC program, you will write code for the **ColumnClick** event procedure to sort the rows by the column that was clicked.

To sort the columns:

1. Enter the following statements in the **lvwEmployees_ColumnClick** event procedure:

```
lvwEmployees.Sorted = True
lvwEmployees.SortKey = ColumnHeader.Index - 1
```

2. Test the program. Select the Buena Park California Finance office. Click on View, and then click on Report to select report view. Click on each column, noting that the data are sorted by the selected column.

3. End the program to return to design mode.

The new statements provide a generic way to sort the list by the column that was clicked and can be used with any ListView control instance to sort specific columns. Visual Basic passes a **ColumnHeader** object to the event procedure. Using the **Index** property of the ColumnHeader object, the column can be determined and assigned to the sort key.

You have now completed the drill-down interface for ETC's program, which takes advantage of the TreeView and ListView controls. This type of user interface is useful when data are hierarchically organized. For example, the same type of user interface would be useful to display an organization chart.

CHAPTER SUMMARY

This chapter discussed the following Windows Common Controls: ImageList, TreeView, and ListView.

To store images in the ImageList control:

➤ Make sure that a reference to the Windows Common Controls 6.0 has been added to the form.

➤ Create an instance of the ImageList control.

➤ Using the General tab on the Property Pages, set the image size.

➤ Using the Images tab on the Property Pages, add each image.

➤ For each image added, set the **Key** and **Tag** properties as necessary.

To create an instance of the TreeView control:

➤ Make sure that a reference to the Windows Common Controls 6.0 has been added to the project.

➤ Create an instance of the TreeView control.

➤ Using the General tab on the Property Pages, set the **ImageList** property to associate the TreeView control with an instance of the ImageList control. Alternatively, this task can be performed at run time.

To add a node to an instance of the TreeView control:

➤ Call the **Add** method with the following syntax:

```
object.Add([ relative ] [, relationship] [, key ] [, text] [, image]
[, selectedimage ] )
```

➤ When adding a root node, do not specify a relative or relationship.

➤ When adding a child node, specify the parent node in the relative argument, and use the constant value **tvwChild** in the relationship argument.

➤ Specify a string key, textual description, and images as necessary.

To navigate the child nodes for a node:

➤ Use the **Children** property of a node to specify the number of children pertaining to a node.

➤ Create a **For** loop that iterates from 1 to the number of children.

5

➤ As the last statement in the **For** loop, set the current node to the **Next** property of the current node.

To expand and collapse a node programmatically:

➤ Set a node's **Expanded** property to **True** to expand the node.

➤ Set a node's **Expanded** property to **False** to collapse the node.

To add ListItem object to a ListView control instance:

➤ Call the **Add** method having the following syntax:

```
object.Add([ index ] [, key] [, text] [, icon] [, smallIcon])
```

➤ Set the **Key** argument to define a string key for the ListItem object.

➤ Set **Icon** and **SmallIcon** properties to define the actual images that will appear in the ListItem object at run time.

To clear the contents of a ListView control instance:

➤ Call the **Clear** method pertaining to the **ListItems** collection. To change the current view in the ListView control:

➤ Set the **View** property to one of the following constant values: **lvwIcon**, **lvwSmallIcon**, **lvwList**, or **lvwReport**.

To create ColumnHeader objects:

➤ Call the **Add** method pertaining to the **ColumnHeaders** collection:

```
object.Add([index],[ key][, text][, width][, alignment])
```

➤ As with most collections, the ColumnHeader object supports a numeric index and string key.

➤ Set the text argument to define the text that will appear in the column. The width and alignment arguments set the width of the columns and align the text, respectively.

To create ListSubItem objects:

➤ Call the **Add** method pertaining to the **ListSubItems** collection.

To sort columns in report view:

➤ Set the **Sorted** property of the ListView control instance to **True**.

➤ To sort the first column (by ListItem), set the **SortKey** property to **0**.

➤ To sort by other columns, set the **SortKey** property to the **ColumnHeader.Index −1**.

➤ Note that this task is usually performed in the **ColumnClick** event procedure.

REVIEW QUESTIONS

1. The ImageList control stores images in the _____ object.
   a. ListItem
   b. Image
   c. ListImage
   d. ImageList
   e. List

2. Which of the following statements pertaining to the ImageList control is true?
   a. Images can have a numeric index or string key.
   b. Images must all be the same size.
   c. Both icons and bitmap images are supported.
   d. All of the above.
   e. None of the above.

3. Which properties are used to determine the images displayed in a TreeView control?
   a. **Image**, **ExpandedImage**, **SelectedImage**
   b. **Image**, **ListImage**, **SelectedImage**
   c. **Image**, **ListImage**, **CurrentImage**
   d. **Images** collection
   e. None of the above

4. Which of the following statements pertaining to the TreeView control is true?

   a. The TreeView control supports the **Node** collection.

   b. A node can have at most 10 children.

   c. A node must have at least one child.

   d. A node can support at most one image.

   e. None of the above.

5. A node object can have _____ parent(s), _____ child(ren), and _____ sibling(s).

   a. one, several, several

   b. several, one, one

   c. several, several, one

   d. zero, several, several

   e. zero, one, several

6. Which argument set pertaining to the **Nodes** collection's **Add** method determines where the node is added to the hierarchy?

   a. **Parent**, **Child**

   b. **Relative**, **Relationship**

   c. **Position**

   d. **Parent**, **Grandparent**, **Child**, **Grandchild**

   e. None of the above.

7. Assuming that the ImageList control instance has a ListImage object with a string key of "strDemo", write the statement to set the value of the **Tag** property to "This is a Tag".

8. Write the statements to add a Node object to the TreeView control instance named **tvwDemo**. Set the **Text** to **NewNode**. Add the object so that it appears as a child of the node referenced by the object variable **pnodRoot**.

9. Declare the necessary variables and write a loop to print the value of the **Text** property for all children of a Node object named pnodDemo.

10. Write the statements to create a Root node with 10 children. Each node should have a caption of 1, 2, 3, 4, and so on. (Hint: Use a **For** loop.)

11. Which of the following statements pertaining to the ListView control is true?

    a. Information is stored in a two-dimensional array.

    b. The ListSubItem and ColumnHeader subscripts reference the items in the collection.

    c. Each cell in the array is called a node.

    d. All of the above.

    e. None of the above.

12. Which of the following views is supported by the ListView control?

    a. icon

    b. small icon

    c. list

    d. report

    e. All of the above

13. Which properties are used to display multiple columns in the ListView control when report view is used?

    a. **ColumnHeader, ListSubItem**

    b. **Columns, Rows**

    c. **ListHeader, ListItem**

    d. All of the above

    e. None of the above

14. Which of the following properties are used when sorting the contents of the ListView control?

    a. **Sort, Key**

    b. **Sorting, Key**

    c. **Sorted, SortKey**

    d. **Sort, SortKey**

    e. None of the above

15. Which of the following events are supported by the ListView control?

    a. **Click, RowClick, ColumnClick**

    b. **Click, ItemClick, ColumnClick**

    c. **CellClick, RowClick, ColumnClick**

    d. **Click, GridClick**

    e. None of the above

16. Write the statements to create three column headers for a ListView control instance named **lvwDemo**. The column headers should have captions of First, Second, and Third, respectively. Set the width of each column to 1000 twips.

17. Assuming that lvwDemo is an instance of the ListView control, write the statements to store the text "One" in the ListItem object having a string key of "FirstItem".

18. Assume the same information from Question 7. Add two ListSubItem objects having string keys of "Second" and "Third", respectively. The text displayed in the ListSubItems should be "Second Column" and "Third Column", respectively.

19. Write the statements to clear the contents of the ListView control instance named **lvwDemo**. Clear both the list items and the column headers.

20. Write the statement to set the view of the ListView control instance named **lvwDemo** to report view.

HANDS-ON PROJECTS

Project 1

In this project, you will use the TreeView control to display the numbers 0–9 and the letters A–Z in a node hierarchy. This program does not require any data to run. Rather, the data are initialized using ASCII character codes.

    a. Run the completed program named Chapter.05\Exercise\ Ex1Demo.exe. The completed program is shown in Figure 5.14.

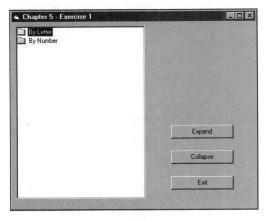

Figure 5.14 Exercise 1 Completed form.

As shown in Figure 5.14, the main form contains an instance of the TreeView control. It also includes command buttons to expand and collapse the child nodes and to exit the program. Double-click on the node having the caption of By Letter. The letters in the alphabet appear. End the program.

b. Start Visual Basic, and create a new project. Set the **Name** property of the form to **frmEx1**. Save the form with the name Chapter.05\Exercise\frmEx1.frm and the project with the name Chapter.05\Exercise\Ex1.vbp.

c. Add references to the TreeView and ImageList controls.

d. Create an instance of the ImageList control. Set the image size to 16x16. Add two images using the files named Clsdfold.ico and Openfold.ico. Assign string keys to the images as necessary.

e. Create an instance of the TreeView control. Set the necessary property to assign the newly created ImageList control to the TreeView control instance. When a node is expanded, the open folder icon should appear. When a node is collapsed, the closed folder icon should appear.

f. Create two root-level nodes having the captions By Letter and By Number.

g. Create a child node of the By Letter node for each letter of the alphabet. That is, there should be 26 Node objects, each having as its caption a letter of the alphabet. (Hint: Use a **For** loop and the Chr function.)

h. Create a child node of the By Number node for the numbers 0 through 9.

i. Create the command buttons on the form as shown in Figure 5.14. Write the code for the **Expand** command button to expand all nodes in the hierarchy.

j. Write the code for the **Collapse** command button to collapse all nodes in the hierarchy.

k. Write the code for the **Exit** command button to end the program.

l. Test the program. Verify that numbers and letter nodes appear in the proper locations in the hierarchy. Exit Visual Basic.

Project 2

In this project, you will read the contents of a text file into an instance of the ListView control. You will write code allowing the user to select different views. In addition, you will create the necessary objects for report view to function properly. That is, you will create report headers and list subitems. Note that this exercise assumes that you are familiar with reading sequential text files using the **Open**, **Input #**, and **Close** statements. The text file is named Inventory.txt and contains the following fields:

> ID (Integer)
> Description (String)
> Quantity (Integer)
> Price (Single)
> Extended Price (Single)

5

a. Run the completed program named Chapter.05\Exercise\ Ex2Demo.exe.

As shown in Figure 5.15, the program contains a menu and an instance of the ListView control. On the View menu, select each of the four different views. While report view is selected, click on each column in the ListView control instance. The column is sorted in ascending order. End the program.

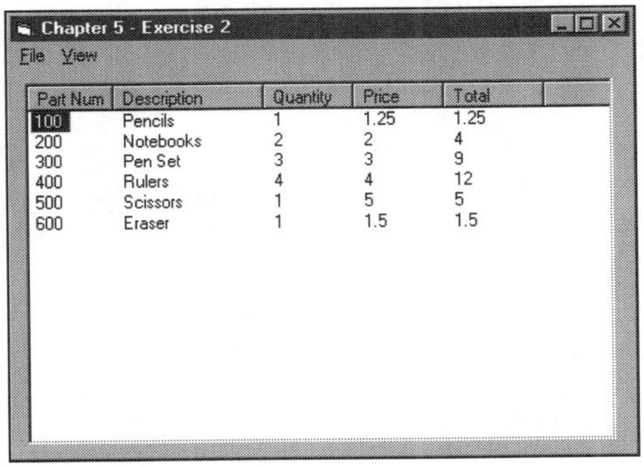

Figure 5.15   Exercise 2 Completed form.

b. Start Visual Basic, and create a new project. Set the **Name** property of the form to **frmEx2**. Save the form with the name Chapter.05\ Exercise\frmEx2.frm and the project with the name Chapter.05\ Exercise\Ex2.vbp.

c. Add a reference to the ListView control to the project.

d. Create an instance of the ListView control.

e. Create the menu system for the program. The File menu should have an Exit item. The View menu should have four items with captions of Small, Large, List, and Report.

f. Program the items on the View menu to display the information using each of the four different views.

g. Set the necessary properties and add the column headers to display the ListView control instance in report view. The columns should have titles of Part Num, Description, Quantity, Price, and Total.

h. Write the code to read the input file named Chapter.05\Exercise\inventory.txt. The description should be stored in a ListItem object. The remaining fields should be stored in ListSubItem objects.

i. Write the necessary code to sort each column in report view when the user clicks on a particular column.

j. Write the code for the Exit menu item.

k. Save and test the program. When started, six records should be read. Verify that each view works correctly. Also, verify that, while in report view, the user can sort the columns. Exit Visual Basic.

Project 3

In this project, you will use the TreeView and ListView controls in much the same way that they were used in the chapter. In this exercise, however, you will create a drill-down interface to look up a part number in inventory. This information is stored in the database file named Chapter.05\Exercise\Inv.mdb. This file contains a table named tblInventory that has the following fields: fldCategory (text), fldSubCategory (text), fldPartNumber (Integer), fldDescription (text), fldQuantity (Integer), and fldPrice (Single).

Even though this exercise will use control instances that are similar to the synchronized TreeView and ListView control instances created in the chapter, differences in the database will force you to change how the TreeView control instance is loaded. A single table stores all of the data. Thus multiple records will have the same category and subcategory. The Description field is unique. When you load the Category level of the hierarchy, you should therefore select unique records by using the **SELECT DISTINCT** statement. Consider organizing the procedures as shown in the chapter. One procedure should load the root node. This procedure, in turn, should call a second procedure to initialize each of the Category level nodes. For each category, this second procedure should call another procedure that initializes all of the subcategories pertaining to the current category.

a. Run the completed program named Chapter.05\Exercise\Ex3Demo.exe.

As shown in Figure 5.16, instances of the TreeView and ListView controls appear. Click on the nodes in the TreeView control. As you click on each node, the inventory items pertaining to the selected category or subcategory appear in the ListView control instance. Exit the program.

b. Start Visual Basic, and create a new project. Set the **Name** property of the form to **frmEx3**. Save the form with the name Chapter.05\

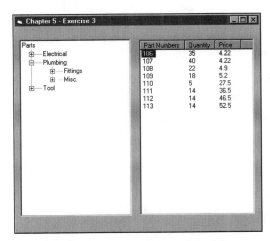

Figure 5.16   Exercise 3 Completed form.

Exercise\frmEx3.frm and the project with the name Chapter.05\ Exercise\Ex3.vbp.

c. Add a reference to the TreeView and ListView controls to the project.

d. Create instances of both the ListView and TreeView controls.

e. Declare the necessary variables, and write the code to establish a connection to the database and create Connection and Command objects.

f. Create a procedure to initialize the root node of the tree. The root node should have a caption of Parts.

g. Write the code to create the Category nodes. Because multiple descriptions for a particular category exist in the table, be sure to select distinct rows using the **SELECT DISTINCT** statement.

h. For each category created, the subcategory must be added. Create another procedure to accomplish this task. Use a **SELECT** statement with a **WHERE** clause to select specific categories and subcategories.

i. Write the code to manage the ListView control instance. When the user clicks on a category in the TreeView control instance, the program should display all records in that category. Note that multiple subcategories may be selected simultaneously. When the user selects a subcategory, select and display only the matching category and subcategory records in the ListView control.

j. Save and test the program. Verify that the data are loaded correctly and that the information appears in the TreeView and ListView controls property.

k. Exit Visual Basic.

THE WINDOWS COMMON CONTROLS (PART 2)

AFTER READING THIS CHAPTER AND COMPLETING THE EXERCISES, YOU WILL BE ABLE TO:

➤ Use the Toolbar control to mimic command buttons and the menu items found in a menu system

➤ Use the DTPicker control as a mechanism to allow the user to perform sophisticated processing on date values

➤ Use the UpDown control as a mechanism to increment and decrement values within a particular range of values

➤ Use the Slider control to allow the user to visualize a current value within a range of values

➤ Use the ImageCombo control to display items in a list coupled with a graphic image

➤ Use the FlatScrollBar control

➤ Display the relative completion status of a time-consuming operation using the ProgressBar control

➤ Display general information pertaining to the keyboard and the program using the StatusBar control

CREATING A CUSTOM USER INTERFACE

Using The Toolbar And DTPicker Controls

The completed application for this chapter demonstrates several ways to take advantage of the Windows Common Controls. It uses the UpDown, ImageCombo, DTPicker, Slider, ProgressBar, FlatScrollBar, Toolbar, and StatusBar controls. The data-oriented programs in Chapters 3 and 4 used a database. In contrast, the project in this chapter utilizes sequential text files—another technique for processing information.

To preview the completed application:

1. Start Visual Basic, and open the project named Chapter.06\Complete\ Ch6_C.vbp. Figure 6.1 shows the main form for the program at design time.

   As shown in Figure 6.1, the form includes several new types of controls. The ImageCombo control works like the intrinsic ComboBox control, but displays an image next to the list portion. The DTPicker control displays a formatted date and provides the user with sophisticated editing capabilities. The UpDown control works in conjunction with the TextBox control, allowing the user to change a numeric value by clicking on up and down buttons. The Slider control displays, or allows the user to select, a position within a range. Along the right side of the form can be seen an instance of the FlatScrollBar control. The flat scroll bar works like the intrinsic vertical and horizontal scroll bars, but has a two-dimensional visual appearance.

   At the bottom of the form, a progress bar appears. This control instance displays the relative completion of reading an input text file. The toolbar appears at the top of the form. This control instance works like the toolbars

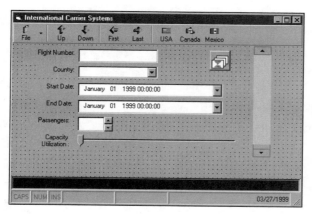

Figure 6.1   Completed form at design time.

supported by other Windows programs. The user clicks on its buttons to perform tasks. Finally, the status bar appears at the bottom of the form. It displays the state of specific keyboard keys and, after a file has been opened, the number of records in a file and the current record.

2. Run the program.

3. The program reads the contents of a text file into an array. The code in the program reads and writes elements from and to the array and displays the information into the control instances created on the form. Using the form's toolbar, click on the list arrow to the right of the File button, and then click on Open. When the input box appears, enter the file name Chapter.06\Complete\Demo.txt. Set the path name and drive designator as necessary. Click on OK to open the file.

As the text file loads, the progress bar appears across the bottom of the form, providing the user with visual evidence of the status of the loading file. After the file finishes loading, the progress bar becomes invisible and the first record appears in the control instances. The status bar at the bottom of the form also displays the number of records and the number of the current record.

Figure 6.2 shows the program at run time with the first record loaded and appearing in the control instances.

When you opened the file, the code in the **OpenFile** general procedure made additional buttons on the toolbar visible. These buttons allow the user to locate records. They are also used to display the country of origin of the currently selected record. In addition, the current record number and total number of records appear in the StatusBar control instance.

4. To view the features of these new control instances, click on the list arrow at the right side of the ImageCombo control instance. The list drops down,

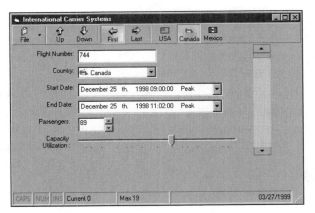

Figure 6.2   Completed form at run time.

and an icon appears to the left of each country name. When you click on another control instance, this drop-down list disappears.

5. The form contains two instances of the DTPicker control, which store and allow the user to edit the starting and ending date and time of the flight. Click on the list arrow to the right of the Start Date DTPicker control instance. A monthly calendar appears, allowing the user to easily select a date value. Clicking on the left and right arrows allows the user to select the previous and next month, respectively. Clicking on a day in the calendar selects that day, closes the calendar portion of the control instance, and updates the date in the text portion of the control instance. Clicking on the month causes a pop-up menu to appear, from which the user can select a month. Clicking on the year causes an up-down button to appear, with which the user can increment or decrement the year. Click on a day to close the calendar. The error-checking code for the control instance prevents it from losing focus unless the starting date and time is less than the ending date and time. That is, the starting date must be before the ending date. The date selected in the calendar appears in the text portion of the control instance.

6. To see the effect of the text portion of the DTPicker control instance, click on the month. Press the up and down arrows to decrement and increment the selected month. Each part of the date and time components functions the same way. Click on the hour of the flight, and press the up and down arrows to decrement and increment the value.

7. To see the effect of the UpDown control instance, click on the up and down buttons to the right of the Passengers text box. As you click on these buttons, the value of the text box is updated. In addition, as you change the value of the text box or click on the buttons on the UpDown control instance, the code updates the value of the capacity utilization Slider control instance.

8. Click on a region of the FlatScrollBar control instance appearing along the right side of the form. As you select different values, the current record pointer is updated and the information that pertains to the current record appears in the other control instances created on the form.

9. Click on the Up, Down, First, and Last buttons on the toolbar. These buttons locate the previous, next, first, and last records, respectively. As you select different records, a current record counter appears in the status bar at the bottom of the form. Additionally, the flag for the selected country appears recessed in the toolbar. While these measures are redundant, this program presents several techniques to display status information.

10. End the program, and exit Visual Basic.

Reviewing Fundamental Concepts

The case problem in this chapter focuses on several fundamental concepts with which you should already be familiar:

➤ user-defined types

➤ arrays

➤ sequential file processing

➤ control arrays

Each of these concepts will be illustrated in turn.

International Carrier Systems (ICS) audits the information pertaining to airline flights for multiple airlines. Each client airline records the information pertaining to each flight in a text file that must be audited. Each record includes a unique identification number, the date and time of the flight's departure and arrival, the number of passengers, the country of origin, and the capacity of the airplane. To ensure correctness, the contents of each text file must be compared with source documents. After a file is audited, the auditor records the number of errors detected. The staff members who perform the audits have limited computer expertise. ICS therefore requires the simplest and most intuitive user interface possible.

The first concept is the user-defined type. In the ICS program, a user-defined type groups the related information for each record that is stored in a sequential text file by using the following type declaration:

```
Private Type tFlightRecord
    FlightNumber As Integer
    FlightStart As Date
    FlightEnd As Date
    Passengers As Integer
    Country As Integer
    Capacity As Integer
End Type
```

The user-defined type shown in the previous code segment groups six related pieces of information pertaining to an airline flight into a single component. These pieces of information include an identification number, a flight's departure and arrival date, the number of passengers, the country of origin, and the capacity of the flight. Information from an ASCII file will be read into records that correspond to this user-defined type.

To store each of the records that will be read, an array of user-defined types is declared.

```
Private FlightRecord(5000) As tFlightRecord
```

The preceding statement declares an array containing 5000 elements. Each element has a user-defined type of **tFlightRecord**. To simplify the program's implementation, and to concentrate your development effort on the Windows Common Controls, this example uses a static array of 5000 elements. In reality, a dynamic array would likely be employed and redimensioned as each record is read. This technique would eliminate unused array elements and prevent error conditions from occurring if the program attempted to read more than 5000 records into the array.

The **Open** statement opens an input file that is read using the **Input #** statement.

```
Open pstrFileName For Input As #1
```

The Open statement opens a sequential file. In the ICS program, the file is opened For Input (reading). Every open file used by a program has an associated file number. The file number defined in the preceding statement is file #1. The name of the file that is opened is stored in the string variable **pstrFileName**.

In this example, after a file is opened, the code reads the file using the Input statement called from inside a **Do** loop:

```
Do Until EOF(1)
    Input #1, FlightRecord(pintCounter).FlightNumber, _
        FlightRecord(pintCounter).FlightStart, _
        FlightRecord(pintCounter).FlightEnd, _
        FlightRecord(pintCounter).Passengers, _
        FlightRecord(pintCounter).Country _
        FlightRecord(pintCounter).Capacity
pintCounter = pintCounter + 1
Loop
```

The statements in the preceding **Do** loop execute once for each record in the ASCII file. For each record read, the information is stored in the array of user-defined types. Each time that a record is read, the code increments the **Integer** variable **pintCounter** so that the next record is stored in the correct array element.

Once all of the records have been read, the code closes the sequential file using the following statement:

```
Close #1
```

A file that has been read should be explicitly closed using the **Close** statement.

```
Private mintMax As Integer
Private mintCurrent As Integer
```

The variables named **mintMax** and **mintCurrent** have already been declared. These variables store the number of records read and the current record, respectively. As you develop the code for the ICS program, you will use these variables to update the values of the various control instances that you create.

If you are not familiar with the review topics presented here, consider reviewing an introductory Visual Basic text or consult the MSDN Help library.

6

Improving A User Interface With The Toolbar Control

A toolbar typically contains a set of buttons that the user can click. Each button can contain text, a graphical image, or both. You can create several types of buttons. One type of button works like a command button. When clicked, it appears recessed while an event procedure is executing but returns to normal when the procedure ends. A button can also operate much like a checkbox. That is, a button can appear recessed or not recessed. In these situations, the button behaves much like a toggle switch. This type of button commonly displays status information, such as whether selected text is bolded.

Buttons can also work as a group. That is, you can set properties such that only one button can be selected from a group of buttons. For example, Word supports left-aligned, right-aligned, centered, and justified text. Only one justification setting is valid at any time, however. In this situation, a button group would be useful.

You can visually separate buttons from each other; separating buttons has much the same effect as using a separator bar on a menu. You can also place an empty region on the toolbar to hold other control instances, such as a drop-down combo box.

Microsoft introduced a new style of toolbar button with Visual Basic 6.0: the drop-down button. A drop-down button is similar to a menu. When it is clicked, a drop-down list appears. The user can then select an item from this list. Visual Basic 6.0 also supports a flat toolbar and button style. Many programs commonly use this style of button instead of raised buttons.

The purpose of every button, regardless of the type, is the same: When the user clicks on a button, code generally executes.

Figure 6.3 shows the anatomy of a toolbar and its buttons.

You create a toolbar by coupling one or more instances of the ImageList control with an instance of the Toolbar control. The ImageList control was

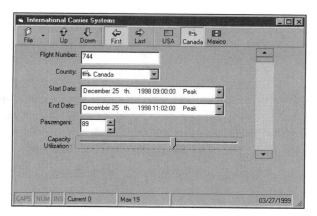

Figure 6.3   Anatomy of a toolbar.

introduced in Chapter 5. A programmer must create an ImageList control
instance before creating a toolbar; the ImageList control stores the graphical
images used in the toolbar.

A reference to the Windows Common Controls must be added to a project before
it becomes available to the project. In the startup program, the ImageList control
instance already exists, as does a reference to the Windows Common Controls.

Creating The Toolbar And Its Buttons

The Toolbar control is used to create a toolbar on a form. A toolbar is made up
of buttons. Each button on the toolbar is represented as a Button object in a
Buttons collection. A button can display text, images (stored in an ImageList
control instance), or both.

A programmer can use the Properties window or the Property Pages of a
toolbar to set the design-time properties of the toolbar. The process is similar to
setting the design-time properties of other ActiveX controls. The Property
Pages for the toolbar contains tabs that allow you to set the general properties
of the toolbar and the properties pertaining to the individual buttons.

➤ **General tab** Used to set the properties that define where the toolbar
   appears on the form, its size, and the name of the ImageList control
   instance(s) containing the images that will be displayed in the toolbar.

➤ **Buttons tab** Used to create and to set the properties for each of the
   toolbar's buttons, to define how the buttons behave, and to define which
   image from the ImageList control instance will appear in the button. In
   addition, the Buttons tab allows you to define the blank space, called a
   placeholder, that appears between the buttons.

Now that you understand the relationship between a toolbar and its buttons,
you can create instances of the toolbar and begin to set its properties.

Setting The General Characteristics Of The Toolbar

Typically, the programmer sets the general characteristics of the toolbar before creating the buttons. You set the general characteristics using the General tab of the Toolbar control's Property Pages, which is shown in Figure 6.4.

The Toolbar control is one of the Windows Common Controls; thus the Windows Common Controls must be added to the project and the file comctl32.ocx must be distributed with the program if the program is to run on a computer without the Visual Basic IDE. The three-character prefix for the toolbar is "tbr".

Syntax

> Toolbar

Properties

➤ The **Buttons** collection stores references to the Button objects created on the toolbar.

➤ The **DisabledImageList** property contains the name of an ImageList control instance created on the form. When a button is disabled, the image that appears in the button is pulled from this ImageList control instance.

➤ The **HotImageList** property contains the name of an ImageList control instance created on the form. When the cursor hovers over a button, the image appearing in the button is pulled from this ImageList control instance.

➤ The **ImageList** property contains the name of an ImageList control instance created on the form; it is the default image that appears in the button.

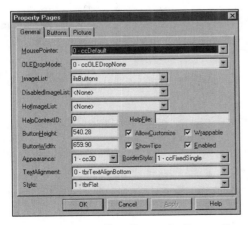

Figure 6.4   Toolbar Property Pages General tab.

➤ The **BorderStyle** property determines whether a single-line border appears around the region of the toolbar. If set to the constant value **ccFixedSingle**, a border appears. If set to **ccNone**, no border appears.

➤ The **Appearance** property can have one of two constant values. If set to **ccFlat**, the control instance appears flat on the form. If set to **cc3d**, the control instance appears as a three-dimensional bar raised off the form.

➤ The **ShowTips** property determines whether ToolTips appear for the buttons on the toolbar. If set to True, a ToolTip (if one is defined for the button) will appear when the user holds the mouse over a button.

➤ The **Enabled** property can be set to **True** or **False**. If set to **False**, the toolbar will not respond to events. If set to **True**, the toolbar responds to events when the user clicks on the toolbar's buttons.

➤ The **AllowCustomize** property can be set to **True** or **False**. If set to **True**, double-clicking on the toolbar at run time causes the Customize Toolbar dialog box to appear. This dialog box allows the user to change the characteristics of the toolbar.

➤ The **Style** property defines the format of the buttons appearing on the toolbar. If set to **tbrFlat**, the buttons appear flat on the toolbar. If set to **tbrStandard**, the buttons appear raised off the surface of the toolbar. Most newer applications—including Microsoft Word, Excel, Internet Explorer, and others—utilize flat toolbar buttons.

➤ The **TextAlignment** property determines where the text, if any, appears in the buttons. If set to **tbrTextAlignBottom**, the text appears at the bottom of the button below the graphic image, if one is defined. If set to **tbrTextAlignRight**, the text appears to the right of the graphic.

Events

➤ The **ButtonClick** event occurs when the user clicks on a button on the menu. Visual Basic passes a reference to the clicked button as an argument to the event procedure.

➤ The **ButtonDropDown** event occurs when the user clicks on a drop-down button.

➤ The **ButtonMenuClick** event occurs when the user clicks on a ButtonMenu object created on the toolbar.

This chapter's program already contains an ImageList control instance. The images, which are stored in the ImageList control instance, will appear in the toolbar control instance.

Once the **ImageList**, **DisabledImageList**, or **HotImageList** properties have been set, the images in the ImageList control instance
cannot be removed or changed. To change the images in the
ImageList control instance, the property must be cleared, the
ImageList control changed, and this property reset. It is still
possible, however, to add new images.

The first step in creating the toolbar control is to create the control instance
and set its general properties:

To create an instance of the Toolbar control and set its general properties:

1. Start Visual Basic, and open the project file Chapter.06\Startup\Ch6_S.vbp.

2. Open the Form window. Using the Toolbar button on the toolbox, create
   an instance of the Toolbar control on the form. Using the Properties
   window, set the **Name** property to **tbrICS**.

3. Activate the Property Pages for the control instance, and make sure that the
   General tab of Property Pages is active.

4. Set the **ImageList** property to **ilsButtons**.

5. Set the **Style** property to **1 – tbrFlat** and the **BorderStyle** to **1 –
   ccFixedSingle**.

6. Click on Apply to save the changes that you just made.

Once you have set the general properties for the control instance, you can
begin to create its buttons. Before creating the buttons, however, you must
understand the different types of buttons supported by the toolbar. In addition,
you must understand the purpose of the **Style** property pertaining to the
Button object as you insert buttons. The **Style** property can be set to one of the
constant values listed below. Note that the **Style** property pertaining to the
Button object differs from the **Style** property pertaining to the toolbar itself.

➤ **tbrDefault** When the **Style** property is set to this constant, the button
operates like an ordinary menu item. That is, code executes when the user
clicks on the button.

➤ **tbrCheck** When the **Style** property is set to this, the button operates in a
manner that is similar to a checked menu item. The button appears recessed
while checked and raised while not checked. You commonly use this button
style to display a **Boolean** status value, such as a formatting attribute being
applied or not applied.

➤ **tbrButtonGroup** When the **Style** property is set to this, a group of
buttons works like option buttons belonging to an option group. That is, only
one button in the button group can be selected at any given time. The selected
button appears recessed. To create a button group, buttons of type

tbrSeparator must surround the buttons in the button group. Multiple button groups can appear on a toolbar.

➤ **tbrSeparator** When the **Style** property is set to this, a vertical line separates two buttons when the toolbar's style is flat. When the toolbar's style is standard, a space about eight pixels wide replaces the vertical line.

➤ **tbrPlaceholder** When the **Style** property is set to this, a button is inserted containing nothing but whitespace. You use this button style to create a placeholder so that other control instances can be inserted on the toolbar. When creating a placeholder button, the **Width** property must be set to define the number of pixels allocated to the placeholder button.

➤ **tbrDropdown** When the **Style** property is set to this, the button works in a manner that is similar to a menu title. When it is clicked, a drop-down menu appears, and the user can then select a button from this menu. This button style is new to Visual Basic 6.0. The objects that appear on the drop-down menu are ButtonMenu objects rather than Button objects.

The first toolbar element that you will create is the File button. The File button will operate as a drop-down button. When the user clicks on the File button, three menu items will appear with captions of Open, Print, and Exit. All buttons are created and edited using the Buttons Property Page pertaining to the toolbar.

Figure 6.5 shows the Property Pages. Note that the Property Pages already contain defined buttons.

As shown in Figure 6.5, the Buttons tab of the Property Pages contains command buttons having captions of Insert Button and Remove Button. When you insert a button, that button receives a numeric index value that is one (1) greater than the currently selected numeric index value. When you remove a button, the button corresponding to the current numeric index is removed.

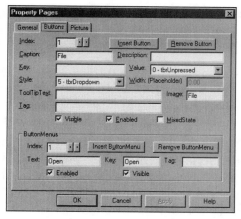

Figure 6.5 Toolbar Property Pages Buttons tab.

When you first display the Property Pages for a new toolbar control instance, all objects are disabled, with the exception of the Insert Button command button. It is enabled because a button must be created before it can be edited.

As shown in Figure 6.5, the Buttons tab on the Property Pages contains a frame having a caption of ButtonMenus. Button menus appear only when a Button's Style property is set to **tbrDropDown**. Although you can create button menus for other styles of buttons, they do not appear on the toolbar.

Syntax

> Button

6

Properties

➤ The **ButtonMenus** collection stores references to the ButtonMenu objects created on the toolbar.

➤ The **Style** property defines the style of the button.

➤ The **Value** property can be set to one of two constant values. If set to **tbrPressed,** the button appears pressed (recessed); if set to **tbrUnpressed,** the button appears normal.

➤ The **Image** property can contain either the numeric index or the string key of an image that is stored in an instance of the ImageList control associated with the toolbar.

Each Button object can contain a reference to a **ButtonMenus** collection, which in turn contains references to ButtonMenu objects. ButtonMenu objects appear as drop-down menu items on a button. Figure 6.6 depicts the relationships between the **Buttons** collection, the Button object, the **ButtonMenus** collection, and the ButtonMenu objects.

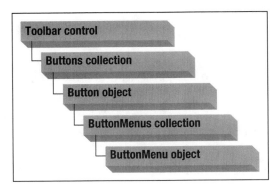

Figure 6.6   Toolbar object relationships.

As shown in Figure 6.6, one **Buttons** collection exists for the toolbar itself. Each button, in turn, can contain a reference to the **ButtonMenus** collection. Again, this collection is used only for buttons having a drop-down style.

Drop-down menu buttons are only one of the button types supported by the Toolbar control. In the ICS program, the toolbar will include other button types as well. The Up and Down buttons will be implemented as default buttons. The First and Last buttons will be implemented as checked buttons. Finally, a button group will display the country of origin for the currently selected flight.

To create a drop-down button:

1. Make sure that the Buttons tab of the Property Pages for the toolbar is active.

2. Click on Insert Button to insert a new button. This button will have a numeric index value of 1.

3. Set the **Caption** to **File** and the **Style** to **5 – tbrDropdown**.

4. Set the **Image** to **File** and the **ToolTipText** property to **Open text file**. Remember that string keys are case-sensitive.

5. In the ButtonMenus frame, click on the Insert ButtonMenu button to insert a button menu. This ButtonMenu object will have a numeric index value of 1.

6. Set the **Text** to **Open** and the **Key** to **Open**.

7. In the ButtonMenus frame, click on the Insert ButtonMenu button to insert a second button menu. This ButtonMenu object should have a numeric index of 2.

8. Set the **Text** to **Print** and the **Key** to **Print**.

9. In the ButtonMenus frame, click on the Insert ButtonMenu button to insert the third button menu. This ButtonMenu object should have a numeric index value of 3.

10. Set the **Text** to **Exit** and the **Key** to **Exit**.

11. Click on OK to apply the changes and close the Property Pages.

12. Test the program. The toolbar should appear with one button having a caption of File and a folder icon.

13. Click on the list arrow on the toolbar's File menu. The drop-down menu appears. No code will execute because you have not yet programmed the buttons.

14. End the program to return to design mode.

Now, you need to create the remaining buttons on the toolbar.

To create the remaining buttons on the toolbar:

1. Activate the Property Pages for the toolbar, and make sure that the Buttons tab is selected.

2. Click on the Insert Button command button to insert a new button. The index of the new button should have a value of 2. Set the **Key** to **Place1** and the **Style** to **4 – tbrPlaceholder**. You are creating a placeholder button.

3. Click on the Insert Button command button again to insert a button with an index value of 3. Set the **Key** to **Up**, the **Caption** to **Up**, the **Style** to **0 – tbrDefault**, and the **Image** to **Up**.

4. Insert another button with an index value of 4. Set the **Key** to **Down**, the **Caption** to **Down**, the **Style** to **0 – tbrDefault**, and the **Image** to **Down**.

5. Insert another button with an index value of 5. Set the **Key** to **Place2** and the **Style** to **4 – tbrPlaceholder**.

6. Insert another button with an index value of 6. Set the **Key** to **First**, the **Caption** to **First**, the **Style** to **1 – tbrCheck**, and the **Image** to **First**.

7. Insert another button with an index value of 7. Set the **Key** to **Last**, the **Caption** to **Last**, the **Style** to **1 – tbrCheck**, and the **Image** to **Last**.

8. Insert another button with an index value of 8. Set the **Key** to **Place3** and the **Style** to **4 – tbrPlaceholder**.

9. Insert another button with an index value of 9. Set the **Key** to **USA**, the **Caption** to **USA**, the **Style** to **2 – tbrButtonGroup**, and the **Image** to **flgUSA**.

10. Insert another button with an index value of 10. Set the **Key** to **Canada**, the **Caption** to **Canada**, the **Style** to **2 – tbrButtonGroup**, and the **Image** to **flgCanada**.

11. Insert another button with an index value of 11. Set the **Key** to **Mexico**, the **Caption** to **Mexico**, the **Style** to **2 – tbrButtonGroup**, and the **Image** to **flgMexico**.

12. Click on OK to apply the changes and close the Property Pages.

At this point, you have created all of the toolbar's buttons. You can now test the program to see the effect of the different types of buttons.

To test the toolbar:

1. Test the program.

2. Click on the First button on the toolbar. The button appears recessed when clicked because the style is set to a checked button. Click on the button again. The button is no longer recessed. Nothing will happen when you click on these buttons because you have not yet written the buttons' code.

3. The final three buttons are part of a button group. Click on the USA, Canada, and the Mexico buttons in turn. Note that only one button appears clicked at any time. Nothing will happen when you click on these buttons because you have not yet written any code for the buttons' event procedures.

4. End the program to return to design mode.

Now that you have created the toolbar's buttons, you can begin to program them. Each of the buttons appearing across the top of the toolbar is a Button object in the **Buttons** collection. The buttons that appear on the drop-down list are ButtonMenu objects in the **ButtonMenus** collection.

To reference a particular Button object, you use either the string key or the numeric index corresponding to that button. Consider the following statements to set the **Visible** property of a button to False:

```
tbrICS.Buttons("Up").Visible = False
tbrICS.Buttons(3).Visible = False
```

The first statement uses the string key to reference a button, and the second statement uses the numeric index to reference the button. Again, using string keys creates a more readable program. Both statements set the **Visible** property to False.

To reference a particular ButtonMenu object, you again reference it using a string key or a numeric index. Consider the following statements to set the **Visible** property of a ButtonMenu object to False:

```
tbrICS("File").ButtonMenus("Print").Visible = False
tbrICS(1).ButtonMenus(2).Visible = False
```

These statements make invisible the Print ButtonMenu object pertaining to the File menu. The first statement uses the string keys and the second uses the numeric indexes.

To create the most robust interface possible, most of the toolbar buttons should be inaccessible to the user when the program first starts. After the user opens a text file, your code should enable the navigational buttons. The decision to disable buttons or make them invisible is somewhat arbitrary. In this example, you will make the buttons invisible.

To change the visibility of the toolbar buttons:

1. Activate the Code window for the **Form_Load** event procedure, and enter the following statements at the end of the event procedure:

```
tbrICS.Buttons("Up").Visible = False
tbrICS.Buttons("Down").Visible = False
```

```
tbrICS.Buttons("First").Visible = False
tbrICS.Buttons("Last").Visible = False
tbrICS.Buttons("USA").Visible = False
tbrICS.Buttons("Canada").Visible = False
tbrICS.Buttons("Mexico").Visible = False
tbrICS.Buttons("Place1").Visible = False
tbrICS.Buttons("Place2").Visible = False
tbrICS.Buttons("Place3").Visible = False
```

2. Activate the Code window for the **OpenFile** general procedure, and enter the following statements:

```
mintMax = pintCounter
mintCurrent = 0
tbrICS.ButtonWidth = 659
tbrICS.Buttons("Up").Visible = True
tbrICS.Buttons("Down").Visible = True
tbrICS.Buttons("First").Visible = True
tbrICS.Buttons("Last").Visible = True
tbrICS.Buttons("USA").Visible = True
tbrICS.Buttons("Canada").Visible = True
tbrICS.Buttons("Mexico").Visible = True
tbrICS.Buttons("Place1").Visible = True
tbrICS.Buttons("Place2").Visible = True
tbrICS.Buttons("Place3").Visible = True
Call SetCurrentRecord
```

3. Test the program. When the program starts, all the toolbar buttons are invisible, except for the File button.

4. Note that unlike the completed example, the control instances on the form do not become invisible and visible. This feature has been omitted for brevity. End the program to return to design mode.

Now that you have created the buttons on the toolbar and written the code to change the visibility of the buttons, you can write the code that will execute when the user clicks on the toolbar buttons. To program the toolbar's buttons, you use two different event procedures. The **ButtonClick** event occurs when the user clicks on an ordinary button. The **ButtonMenuClick** event occurs when the user clicks on a drop-down button menu.

Syntax

Private Sub *object*_ButtonClick(ByVal Button As MSComctlLib.Button)
Private Sub *object*_ButtonMenuClick(ByVal ButtonMenu As MSComctlLib.ButtonMenu)

Dissection

➤ *object* must be an instance of the Toolbar control.

➤ The **ButtonClick** event occurs when the user clicks on an ordinary toolbar button.

➤ The **ButtonMenuClick** event occurs when the user clicks on an item on a drop-down button menu.

➤ Visual Basic passes a reference to the clicked **Button** as an argument in the **ButtonClick** event procedure.

➤ Visual Basic passes a reference to the clicked drop-down **ButtonMenu** as an argument in the **ButtonMenuClick** event procedure.

You have already created three ButtonMenu objects on the toolbar, which appear as drop-down items on the File menu. Consider the following code to respond to the **ButtonMenuClick** event procedure:

```
Private Sub tbrICS_ButtonMenuClick(ByVal ButtonMenu As _
    MSComctlLib.ButtonMenu)
    Select Case ButtonMenu.Key
        Case "Open"
            Call OpenFile
        Case "Print"
            PrintForm
        Case "Exit"
            Unload Me
    End Select
End Sub
```

Remember that you assigned a string key to each of the button menu items. The string keys are Open, Print, and Exit. You can use the **Key** property to determine which button was clicked and to write the code to perform the desired task. In the preceding example, the code calls the **OpenFile** general procedure when the user clicks on the File button. In addition, it calls the **PrintForm** statement to print the form to the default printer when the user clicks on the Print button. When the user clicks on the Exit button, the form is unloaded. This statement causes the program to exit.

To program the **ButtonMenuClick** event procedure:

1. Activate the Code window for the **tbrICS_ButtonMenuClick** event procedure, and enter the following statements:

```
Select Case ButtonMenu.Key
    Case "Open"
        Call OpenFile
    Case "Print"
        PrintForm
    Case "Exit"
        Unload Me
End Select
```

2. Test the program. On the toolbar, click on the File list arrow, and then click
   on Open. Enter the file name Chapter.06\Startup\Demo.txt, setting the
   drive designator as necessary. Click on OK. The toolbar buttons should
   become visible.

3. Click on the File list arrow, and then click on Print. An image of the form
   is sent to the default printer.

4. Click on the File list arrow, and then click on Exit. Visual Basic should
   return to design mode.

The technique to program the ordinary toolbar buttons exactly matches the
technique that you use to program the button menus. Visual Basic passes a
reference to the clicked button as an argument to the **ButtonClick** event
procedure. You must write a **Select Case** statement to determine which button
was clicked and to execute the respective code.

To program the **ButtonClick** event procedure:

1. Activate the Code window for the **tbrICS_ButtonClick** event procedure,
   and enter the following statements:

```
Select Case Button.Key
    Case "Up"
        If mintCurrent > 0 Then
            mintCurrent = mintCurrent - 1
            Call SetCurrentRecord
        End If
    Case "Down"
        If mintCurrent < mintMax Then
            mintCurrent = mintCurrent + 1
            Call SetCurrentRecord
        End If
    Case "First"
        mintCurrent = 0
        Call SetCurrentRecord
    Case "Last"
```

```
            mintCurrent = mintMax
            Call SetCurrentRecord
    End Select
```

2. Test the program. Click on the File list arrow, and then click on Open on the toolbar. When the input box appears, enter the file named Chapter.06\Startup\Demo.txt, setting the drive designator as necessary. Click on OK. Click on the Last button. The flight number should change. Click on the First button. The flight number should change again.

3. End the program to return to design mode.

The code that you just wrote to respond to the toolbar's **ButtonClick** event procedure works in much the same way as the code that you wrote to respond to the toolbar's **ButtonMenuClick** event procedure. Visual Basic passes a reference to the clicked button as an argument to the event procedure. A **Select Case** statement is built to determine which button was clicked and to execute code accordingly.

Consider the following code:

```
Case "Up"
    If mintCurrent > 0 Then
        mintCurrent = mintCurrent - 1
        Call SetCurrentRecord
    End If
```

The code for the Up button checks whether the current record is the first record. If the current record is not the first record, it is decremented by setting the value of **mintCurrent**. The code then calls the **SetCurrentRecord** procedure, which has already been created, to display the current record in the form's control instances.

```
Case "Down"
    If mintCurrent < mintMax Then
        mintCurrent = mintCurrent + 1
        Call SetCurrentRecord
    End If
```

The code for the Down button checks whether the current record is the last record. If the current record is not the last record, it is incremented and then displayed in the form's control instances by calling the **SetCurrentRecord** procedure.

Consider the following code, which pertains to the First and Last buttons:

```
Case "First"
    mintCurrent = 0
    Call SetCurrentRecord
Case "Last"
    mintCurrent = mintMax
    Call SetCurrentRecord
```

The code for the First button sets the current record to the first record and then displays it. The code for the Last button sets the current record to the last record and then displays it. To indicate when the first or last record is selected, you can write code to make the appropriate button appear recessed.

Consider the following statements, which account for the situation that occurs when the first or last record is the current record:

6

```
If mintCurrent = mintMax Then
    tbrICS.Buttons("Last").Value = tbrPressed
Else
    tbrICS.Buttons("Last").Value = tbrUnpressed
End If
If mintCurrent = 0 Then
    tbrICS.Buttons("First").Value = tbrPressed
Else
    tbrICS.Buttons("First").Value = tbrUnpressed
End If
```

These statements determine whether the current record is the first or last record and set the **Value** property of the buttons accordingly. Again, the code uses the string key to identify a particular button.

To change a button's value programmatically:

1. Activate the Code window for the **SetCurrentRecord** general procedure, and enter the following statements at the end of the procedure:

```
If mintCurrent = mintMax Then
    tbrICS.Buttons("Last").Value = tbrPressed
Else
    tbrICS.Buttons("Last").Value = tbrUnpressed
End If
If mintCurrent = 0 Then
    tbrICS.Buttons("First").Value = tbrPressed
Else
    tbrICS.Buttons("First").Value = tbrUnpressed
End If
```

2. Test the program. Open the input file named Chapter.06\Startup\ Demo.txt, setting the drive designator as necessary. When the last record is the current record, the Last toolbar button appears pressed. When the first record is the current record, the First button appears pressed.

3. End the program to return to design mode.

Now that you have created the Toolbar control instance, you can create the other control instances needed to display the information in the various Windows Common Controls that you will create on the form. Two members of the user-defined type are dates. Although you could use a TextBox control to display a date and to receive user input, the DTPicker control—which is new to Visual Basic 6.0—simplifies the management of user input involving Date data types.

Using The DTPicker Control

The DTPicker control serves three purposes. First, it displays date output in a formatted manner. By setting the properties of the control instance, you can change the format of the date value. Second, the DTPicker control allows the user a flexible means to enter input values. Third, it validates date input automatically.

The DTPicker control consists of two visible parts. The first part contains a formatted text box where the user can enter input or click on a list arrow. When the user clicks on the list arrow, the second part of the control instance appears. It consists of a calendar from which the user can enter a date. In this book, these two parts will be referred to as text view and month view, respectively.

Figure 6.7 shows an instance of the DTPicker control created on a form.

As shown in Figure 6.7, the DTPicker control contains a text portion where the user can enter a date. The list arrow at the right side of the control instance displays the calendar portion of the control. The user can click on the arrays to change the month and click on a particular day to select a specific day in that month.

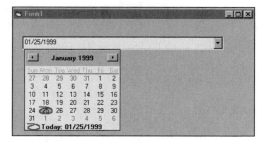

Figure 6.7 DTPicker control instance.

Syntax

DTPicker

Properties

➤ The color of the calendar portion can be configured using the **CalendarBackColor**, **CalendarForeColor**, **CalendarTitleForeColor**, and **CalendarTitleBackColor** properties.

➤ The foreground color of trailing dates (dates not in the current month) is set using the **CalendarTrailingForeColor** property.

➤ The **CheckBox** property can be either True or False. If set to True, a checkbox appears to the left of the control instance. If set to False, the checkbox does not appear. At run time, if the checkbox is not checked, the **Value** property is set to Null.

➤ The **CustomFormat** property contains a text string allowing you to customize the format appearing in the text portion of a control instance.

➤ The **DayOfWeek** property stores the selected Day of the week. The following constant values represent the days of the week: **mvwSunday**, **mvwMonday**, **mvwTuesday**, **mvwWednesday**, **mvwThursday**, **mvwFriday**, and **mvwSaturday**.

➤ You use the **Format** property to specify one of three predefined date formats. A discussion of the formats follows. In addition, you can set the **Format** property to indicate that a custom format should be used.

➤ The **MinDate** and **MaxDate** properties define the minimum and maximum allowable dates that the user can specify.

➤ The **Year**, **Month**, and **Day** properties store the selected year, month, and day, respectively. Month values range between 1 and 12. Day values range between 1 and 31.

➤ The **Value** property stores the selected date.

Events

➤ The **CloseUp** event occurs when the calendar portion of the control instance is closed.

➤ You write code for the **Format** event when using custom formats. The code in this event procedure controls which data appear in the text portion of the control instance.

➤ The **FormatSize** event occurs just before the **Format** event. It advises the control instance as to the number of characters that will be stored in a portion of the text part of the control instance.

➤ The **Validate** event occurs just before the control instance loses focus. It has the same purpose as the **Validate** event pertaining to other control instances.

When formatting an instance of the DTPicker control, you can either use one of the three predefined formats or define a custom format. The following list describes the predefined formats and indicates how the date 1/1/1999 will appear.

➤ **dtpShortDate** This constant value displays the date using the short date format defined on your system. By default, the value is 01/01/99.

➤ **dtpLongDate** This constant value displays the date using the long date format defined on your system. By default, the value is Friday, January 01, 1999.

➤ **dtpTime** This constant value displays the time instead of the date. When the time is displayed, the list arrow to the right of the control instance appears as an UpDown control.

➤ **dtpCustom** This constant value allows you to define a custom format for the control instance by setting the **CustomFormat** property's value.

The process to define custom formats is similar to the process used to define custom formats with the Format function—that is, you build a string using special format characters. Table 6.1 describes the valid format characters. Note that the format characters are case-sensitive.

Specifying a custom format is a relatively straightforward process. Consider the following code segments, which set custom formats at run time. These strings could also be set at design time using the Property Pages.

```
dtpDate.Format = dtpCustom
dtpDate.CustomFormat = "MM/dd/yyy hh:mm:ss"
dtpDate.CustomFormat = "MMMM/dddd/yyy HH:mm:ss"
```

The first format string would display a date and time in the following form:

```
01/25/1999 08:24:24
```

The second format string would display a date in the following form:

```
January / Monday /1999 08:24:24
```

To harness the power of custom formats, you must understand the concept of a callback field, the **Format** event, and the **FormatSize** event. To illustrate the purpose of these two events, consider one possible formatting option for dates.

Table 6.1   Custom formats.

Character	Definition
d	One-digit day or two-digit day
dd	Two-digit day. Single-digit days appear with a leading zero
ddd	Three-character weekday abbreviation
dddd	Full weekday name
h	One-digit or two-digit hour in 12-hour format
hh	Two-digit hour in 12-hour format. Single-digit hours appear with a leading zero
H	One-digit or two-digit hour in 24-hour format
HH	Two-digit hour in 24-hour format. Single digit values appear with a leading zero
m	One-digit or two-digit minute
mm	Two-digit minute. Single-digit minutes appear with a leading zero
M	One-digit or two-digit month
MM	Two-digit month. Single-digit months appear with a leading zero
MMM	Three-character month abbreviation
MMMM	Full month name
s	One-digit or two-digit seconds
ss	Two-digit seconds. Single-digit seconds appear with a leading zero
t	One-letter AM/PM abbreviation
tt	Two-letter AM/PM abbreviation
X	Callback field
y	One-digit year. The last digit of the year appears
yy	Two-digit year. The last two digits of the year appear
yyy	Full year. All four digits of the year appear

You have likely seen dates written in the following manner: 1st, 2nd, 3rd, and so on. Although no custom format exists to display dates in this format, you can create such a format by using the **FormatSize** and **Format** events.

When the contents of the DTPicker control instance change, the **FormatSize** event occurs, and then the **Format** event occurs. The code that you write in the **FormatSize** event sets the maximum allowable size for the formatted string. After the FormatSize event occurs, the **Format** event occurs. In this event procedure, you can write custom code to display formatted text.

The first step in this process is to define the callback string for the custom format. A callback string consists of one or more uppercase X characters. Consider the following custom format string:

```
MMMM ddXXX yyyy hh:mm:ss XXXX
```

This format string will display the month, day, year, and time. The critical part of the custom format string consists of the two callback strings "XXX" and "XXXX". When the user changes a date value, the **FormatSize** and **Format** events will occur for each of the two format strings. Each time Visual Basic calls the event procedure, it passes the callback string as an argument to the event procedures. When the user changes the current date, the **FormatSize** and **Format** events occur and Visual Basic passes the callback field as an argument to these procedures.

Syntax

     *object*_**Format**(**ByVal** *CallbackField* **As String**, *FormattedString* **As String**)

     *object*_**FormatSize**(**ByVal** *CallbackField* **As String**, *Size* **As Integer**)

Dissection

➤ *object* must be an instance of the DTPicker control.

➤ The ***CallBackField*** argument contains a text string denoting which callback field is active.

➤ In the **Format** event, you write code to set the FormatString. This string will appear in the callback field when it is displayed to the user.

➤ In the **FormatSize** event, the *Size* argument contains an **Integer** value indicating the maximum size of the formatted string. The code that you write must set this value so that the control instance allocates sufficient space to display the formatted value.

For the ICS program, you will display a suffix to the left of each day. For example, the suffix for the first day of the month is "st". The suffix for the second day of the month is "nd", and so on. The general declarations section of the form module already contains the following array declaration:

```
Private mstrDaySuffix(1 To 31) As String
```

This array contains 31 elements, each of which corresponds to a day of the month. The array is initialized in the **Form_Load** event procedure. The following code segment contains the first three statements used to initialize the first three days of the month. For brevity, the remaining statements are not listed.

```
mstrDaySuffix(1) = "st."
mstrDaySuffix(2) = "nd."
mstrDaySuffix(3) = "rd."
```

The code is straightforward. It stores the suffix corresponding to the day of the month in each element of the array.

Now consider the following event procedure to display the formatted string:

```
Private Sub dtpDate_Format(ByVal CallbackField As _
    String, FormattedString As String)
    If CallbackField = "XXX" Then
        FormattedString = mstrDaySuffix(dtpDate.Day)
    End If
    If CallbackField = "XXXX" Then
        If dtpDate.Hour >= 8 And dtpDate.Hour <= 17 Then
            FormattedString = "Peak"
        Else
            FormattedString = "Off Peak"
        End If
    End If
End Sub
```

Remember that you defined two callback strings: "XXX" and "XXXX". When the user changes the date or time at run time, Visual Basic calls this event procedure twice, once for each callback string. If the callback string is "XXX", the formatted string is set to the day suffix value. If the callback string is "XXXX", the formatted string is set to the string "Peak" or "Off Peak", depending on the time of day.

Finally, consider the code to set the size of the formatted string:

```
Private Sub dtpDate_FormatSize(ByVal CallbackField _
    As String, Size As Integers)
    If CallbackField = "XXX" Then
        Size = 3
    End If
    If CallbackField = "XXXX" Then
        If dtpDate.Hour >= 8 And dtpDate.Hour <= 17 Then
            Size = Len("Peak") + 2
        Else
            Size = Len("Off Peak") + 3
        End If
    End If
End Sub
```

This code is very important. If these statements do not appear in this event procedure, the control instance will not allocate enough space to store the formatted string. The logic of this event procedure is the same as the logic for the **Format** event procedure: the code determines the callback string and then sets the **Size** argument to the length of the format string.

If you are using Windows 95, Windows 98, or Windows NT, you can set the short date and long date format by using the Regional Settings option on the Control Panel.

In the ICS program, the two control instances will operate the same way. That is, they will display dates in the same format. Thus you will create the two control instances such that they are members of the same control array. This technique will allow both control instances to share the code that you wrote for the **Format** and **FormatSize** events.

To create an instance of the DTPicker control and set its properties:

1. Create the first instance of the DTPicker control, as shown in Figure 6.8. Note that Figure 6.8 shows the form after the creation of both control instances.

2. Set the **Name** property to dtpDate and the **Index** property to **0**.

3. Activate the General tab of the Property Pages for the control instance.

4. Set the **MinDate** to **01/01/1950** and the **MaxDate** to **01/01/2010**. Depending on the short date format setting on your computer, only the last two digits of the year may appear.

5. Set the **Format** to **3-dtpCustom** and the **CustomFormat** to **MMMM ddXXX yyy HH:mm:ss XXXX**. (The **CustomFormat** should not include the final period in the previous sentence.) Click on OK to close the Property Pages.

6. Create a second instance of the DTPicker control. Set the properties to the same values as those for the first control instance, except set the **Index** property to **1**. Click on OK to close the Property Pages.

7. Enter the following statements in the **dtpDate_Format** event procedure:

```
If CallbackField = "XXX" Then
    FormattedString = _
        mstrDaySuffix(dtpDate(Index).Day)
End If
If CallbackField = "XXXX" Then
If dtpDate(Index).Hour >= 8 And _
    dtpDate(Index).Hour <= 17 Then
        FormattedString = "Peak"
    Else
        FormattedString = "Off Peak"
    End If
End If
```

8. Enter the following statements in the **dtpDate_FormatSize** event procedure:

```
If CallbackField = "XXX" Then
    Size = 3
End If
If CallbackField = "XXXX" Then
    If dtpDate(Index).Hour >= 8 And _
        dtpDate(Index).Hour <= 17 Then
        Size = Len("Peak") + 2
    Else
        Size = Len("Off Peak") + 3
    End If
End If
```

9. Enter the following statements at the end of the **SetCurrentRecord** general procedure:

```
dtpDate(0).Value = _
    FlightRecord(mintCurrent).FlightStart
dtpDate(1).Value = _
    FlightRecord(mintCurrent).FlightEnd
```

10. Test the program. Click on the File list arrow, and then click on Open. When the input box appears, enter the file named Chapter.06\Startup\ Demo.txt, setting the drive designator as necessary. Click on OK. Change the day of the month. The date suffix should be updated when you move the focus. Change the time. When the time is between 8 and 17 (using a 24-hour clock), the string "Peak" should appear when you move the focus; otherwise, the string "Off Peak" should appear.

11. End the program to return to design mode.

The ICS program should also prevent the user from selecting an invalid combination of dates. The date and time of a flight's departure must be less than the date and time of the flight's arrival. In other words, the departure date and time must be before the arrival date and time.

To accomplish this validation task, you could use two different events to verify the validity of the date values. If you use the **Validate** event, the event does not occur until the control instance loses focus. If you use the **KeyUp** event, the event occurs each time a key is released. The ICS program will employ the **Validate** event, although the choice is somewhat arbitrary. Remember that both instances of the DTPicker control are members of a control array.

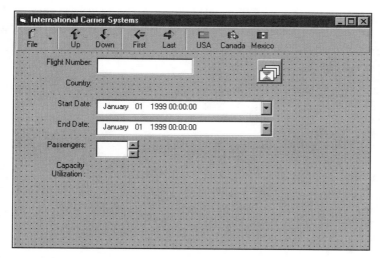

Figure 6.8 DTPicker control instances.

Consider the following code for the **Validate** event:

```
Private Sub dtpDate_Validate(Index As Integer, _
    Cancel As Boolean)
    If dtpDate(1) < dtpDate(0) Then
        Cancel = True
        Beep
    End If
End Sub
```

This code compares the starting date with the ending date. If the ending date is less than the starting date, the code cancels the **Validate** event, and an audible beep occurs. Note that the **Value** property is the default property.

To program the **Validate** event:

1. Activate the Code window for the **dtpDate_Validate** event procedure, and enter the following statements:

```
If dtpDate(1) < dtpDate(0) Then
    Cancel = True
    Beep
End If
```

2. Test the program. Open the input file, and try to enter a starting date value that is greater than the ending date. Press the Tab key to try to change the input focus. An audible beep should occur and the control instance should not lose focus.

3.   End the program to return to design mode.

In addition to allowing the user to set date values at run time, a program can modify these values with code. The following statements set the time displayed in an instance of the DTPicker control named dtpDemo:

```
dtpDemo.Hour = 8
dtpDemo.Minute = 3
dtpDemo.Second = 59
```

At this point in the program's development, the user can set the date using the list arrow and enter formatted information using the text component of the control instance.

6

More Common Controls

Using The UpDown Control

Another Windows Common Control supported by Visual Basic 6.0 is the UpDown control. The UpDown control has characteristics similar to the intrinsic scroll bar controls. In addition, it works in conjunction with a second control called a buddy control. Essentially, when the user click on the scroll buttons on an instance of the UpDown control, Visual Basic updates the contents of the buddy control instance accordingly. You commonly use the UpDown control to display the current numeric value of an UpDown control instance in a text box.

Syntax
>   UpDown

Properties

➤ The **BuddyControl** property contains the name of a control instance that will be used as the buddy control. Some controls, such as labels, cannot be used as buddies. If you try to set the **BuddyControl** property to an unsupported control type, an error will occur. Text boxes are often used as buddy controls.

➤ The **BuddyProperty** property contains the name of a property supported by the buddy control. When the user or your code updates the value of the UpDown control instance, the value of the **BuddyProperty** is updated accordingly.

➤ The **Max** and **Min** values define the range of the UpDown control instance.

➤ The **SyncBuddy** property can be True or False. If set to True, the value of the UpDown control and its buddy control are synchronized. For example, if the property settings synchronize the UpDown control with the **Text** property of a text box, the UpDown control will update the **Text** property as the user changes the value of the UpDown control.

➤ The **Increment** property defines the amount that the value will change when the user clicks on the up or down buttons.

➤ The **Value** property contains an **Integer** between the **Max** and **Min** properties.

Events

➤ The **Change** event occurs whenever the value of the UpDown control instance changes.

The critical part of using the UpDown control is understanding the relationship between the **BuddyControl** and **BuddyProperty** properties. Figure 6.9 illustrates this relationship.

As shown in Figure 6.9, when the **Change** event occurs, the user or program code updates the **BuddyControl** property. To determine which property of the **BuddyControl** will be updated, the UpDown control instance reads the **BuddyProperty**.

To provide a user with the most flexible user interface possible, you will use an instance of the UpDown control to indicate the number of passengers on the airplane. The range of possible values must be between 0 and the capacity of the flight. You will set the properties to synchronize the UpDown control instance with a text box control instance already created on the form.

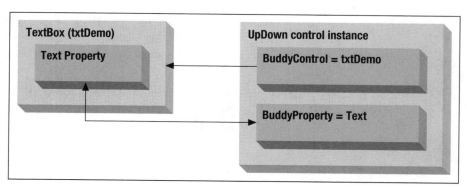

Figure 6.9   Buddy relationships.

To create an instance of the UpDown control:

1. Start Visual Basic and open the file named Chapter.06\Startup\ch6_5.vbp, if necessary. Click on the UpDown control button on the toolbox, and draw an instance of it on the form, as shown in Figure 6.10.

2. Set the **Name** property to **udPassengers**.

3. To associate the UpDown control with a text box, set the **BuddyControl** to **txtPassengers**, the **BuddyProperty** to **Text**, and the **SyncBuddy** property to **True**, if necessary.

4. Enter the following statements at the end of the **SetCurrentRecord** general procedure:

```
udPassengers.Max = FlightRecord(mintCurrent).Capacity
udPassengers.Min = 0
txtPassengers = FlightRecord(mintCurrent).Passengers
```

5. Test the program. Open the demonstration file named Chapter.06\ Startup\Demo. text, setting the drive designator as necessary. In future steps, you will be asked to open this file again, but the path name will not be given. This is done for brevity. Click on the UpDown control instance. The number of passengers in the text box should change automatically.

6. End the program to return to design mode.

Consider carefully the statements you just wrote:

```
udPassengers.Max = FlightRecord(mintCurrent).Capacity
udPassengers.Min = 0
```

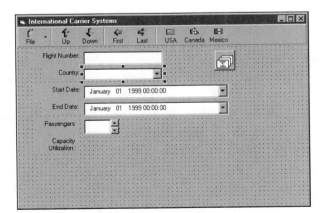

Figure 6.10   UpDown control instance.

The valid range for the UpDown control instance and the corresponding text boxes should be between 0 and the capacity of the airplane. These values must be set at run time because the capacity of each airplane may differ.

Consider the last line of code:

```
txtPassengers = FlightRecord(mintCurrent).Passengers
```

This statement initializes the value of the text box that serves as a buddy to the UpDown control instance. Note that no statement initializes the value of the UpDown control instance. This initialization is unnecessary because the UpDown control is synchronized with the text box control instance.

Next, you will use the ImageCombo control.

Using The ImageCombo Control

Visual Basic 6.0 supports another new control: the ImageCombo control. From the user's perspective, the ImageCombo control looks much like an intrinsic ComboBox control with the addition of an image appearing next to each list item. From the programmer's perspective, the ImageCombo control works much differently than its intrinsic counterpart. When you program the intrinsic ComboBox control, you set the List and ItemData properties to manage the list. This task can be performed either at design time or at run time. The ImageCombo control, however, uses a collection-based implementation to manage the list. The **ComboItems** collection contains a reference to ComboItem objects. Each ComboItem object represents an item in the list.

Syntax

ImageCombo

Properties

➤ The **ComboItems** property contains a reference to the **ComboItems** collection. The ComboItem objects in this collection represent each item in the list.

➤ The **Indentation** property contains a positive **Integer** number measured in pixels. The value represents the indentation of the objects in the control instance.

➤ The **SelectedItem** property contains a reference to the currently selected ComboItem object (item in the list).

➤ The **ImageList** property contains a reference to an ImageList control instance drawn on the form. The images in this control instance appear to the left of the items in the list portion of the ImageCombo control.

Methods

➤ The **GetFirstVisible** method returns a reference to the first visible ComboItem object in the control instance.

Events

➤ The **Click** event occurs when the user clicks on the control instance and selects an item from the list.

➤ The **DropDown** event occurs just before the drop-down list portion of the control instance appears. You typically write code for this event to add or remove items from the list.

For the ICS program, you will use an ImageCombo control to display the country of origin for each flight. Both the description of the country and an image of the country's flag will appear in the control instance.

To create an instance of the ImageCombo control:

1. Click on the ImageCombo control button in the toolbox, and create an instance of it on the form, as shown in Figure 6.11.

2. Set the **Name** property to **icCountry**. In this book, "ic" will be used as the standard prefix for the ImageCombo control.

3. Activate the General tab of the Property Pages for the control instance, and set the **ImageList** property to **ilsButtons**. You used the same ImageList control instance for the Toolbar control instance. This property could also be set at run time.

4. Click on OK to close the Property Pages.

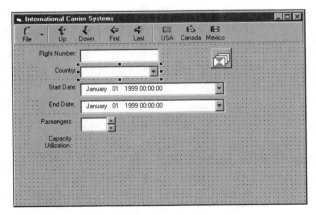

Figure 6.11   ImageCombo control instance.

This project duplicates many user interface characteristics. That is, the country of the currently selected flight appears in the toolbar and in the ImageCombo control instance. This redundancy is intentional. The goal is to show you multiple techniques by which the user can display and enter information.

Once you have created an instance of the ImageCombo control and set the **ImageList** property, you can add items to the list. Unlike with the intrinsic ComboBox control, you do not add the list items at design time. Rather, you create ComboItem objects at run time by adding new ComboItem objects to the **ComboItems** collection. The ComboItem object supports the following properties:

Syntax

ComboItem

Properties

➤ The **SelImage** property contains the string key or numeric index of an image in the ImageList control. This image appears in the ComboItem object when an item is selected.

➤ The **Indentation** property contains a positive **Integer** measured in pixels. The value represents the indentation of the ComboItem object in the control instance. Note that this property has the same name as the **Indentation** property pertaining to the ImageCombo control. It pertains to the indentation of a specific list item, rather than all items in the list.

➤ The **Selected** property contains a **Boolean** value indicating whether the ComboItem object is selected.

➤ The **Text** property contains the text that appears in the list.

➤ The **Index** and **Key** properties define the numeric index and string key, respectively, used to identify the ComboItem object in the **ComboItems** collection.

➤ The **Image** property contains the string key or numeric index of an image in the ImageList control instance bound to the ImageCombo control instance.

To add images to the ImageCombo control, you call the **Add** method pertaining to the **ComboItems** collection. The process is the same as calling the **Add** method pertaining to other collections.

Syntax

> *object*.**Add**(*Index* **As Variant**, *Key* **As Variant**, *Text* **As Variant**, *Image* **As Variant**, *SelImage* **As Variant**, *Indentation* **As Variant**) As *ComboItem*

Dissection

➤ The *object* must be a reference to the **ComboItems** collection. This reference is typically obtained from the ImageCombo control's **ComboItems** property.

➤ The **Add** method adds a new ComboItem object to the **ComboItems** collection.

➤ The *Index* and *Key* arguments specify the numeric index and string key, respectively, used to uniquely identify the ComboItem object in the collection.

➤ The *Text* argument contains a string that appears in the list portion of the ImageCombo control at run time.

➤ The *Image* argument contains the numeric index or string key of a ListImage object stored in an ImageList control. This image appears next to the text at run time.

➤ The *SelImage* argument contains the numeric index or string key of a ListImage object stored in an ImageList control instance. This image appears at run time when the item is selected.

➤ The *Indentation* argument sets the width of indentation of an item.

➤ A reference to the object added appears in ComboItem.

Code Example

```
icCountry.ComboItems.Add 1, "USA", "United States", _
    "flgUSA"
```

Code Dissection

The preceding statements add a ComboItem object to the ImageCombo control instance named icCountry. The object has a numeric index of 1 and a string key of USA. The text appearing in the control instance is "United States", and the image that will appear has a string key of "flgUSA". This value is the string key of the image in the ImageList control instance.

In the ICS project, assume that an airplane can depart from one of three countries: the United States, Canada, or Mexico. Also assume that the input text file defines the country of origin using a numeric value, such that 1 = United

States, 2=Canada, and 3 = Mexico. Given this scenario, you can add items to the ImageCombo control instance such that the numeric index of each item will correspond to one of the three countries and to the Integer value stored in the input file.

Consider the following statements to add three ComboItem objects to the ImageCombo control instance:

```
icCountry.ComboItems.Add 1, "USA", "United States", _
    "flgUSA"
icCountry.ComboItems.Add 2, "Canada", "Canada", _
    "flgCanada"
icCountry.ComboItems.Add 3, "Mexico", "Mexico", _
    "flgMexico"
```

These statements add three items to the list. The items have numeric indexes of 1, 2, and 3, respectively. For each ComboItem object added, the arguments to the **Add** method define the string key, the textual description, and the image.

When the user locates a record, the correct list item needs to be selected. Consider the following statement to accomplish this task:

```
icCountry.ComboItems(FlightRecord(mintCurrent).Country).
    _Selected = True
```

The preceding statement appears on multiple lines even though it should be entered on one line in the Code window. The statement fragment **FlightRecord (mintCurrent).Country** contains the **Integer** value of country pertaining to the selected record. This value corresponds to the string key of the ComboItem object in the **ComboItems** collection. Thus the preceding statement sets the **Selected** property of the desired ComboItem object to True.

You are now ready to add the ComboItem objects to the **ComboItems** collection and then display the appropriate object when necessary.

To add the ComboItem objects to the control instance:

1. Activate the Code window, select the **Form_Load** event procedure, and then enter the following statements at the beginning of the procedure:

```
icCountry.ComboItems.Add 1, "USA", "United States", _
    "flgUSA"
icCountry.ComboItems.Add 2, "Canada", "Canada", _
    "flgCanada"
icCountry.ComboItems.Add 3, "Mexico", "Mexico", _
    "flgMexico"
```

2. Enter the following statement at the end of the **SetCurrentRecord** general procedure. The statement should be entered on one line.

```
icCountry.ComboItems(FlightRecord(mintCurrent).
   _Country).Selected = True
```

3. Test the program. Open the demonstration file and locate different records. As you locate different records, the code that you just wrote updates the selected item in the ImageCombo control instance. Click on the ImageCombo control instance. The three countries should appear.

4. End the program to return to design mode.

The ImageCombo control has the same fundamental purpose as the intrinsic ComboBox control. It displays items from a list. The control provides two additional features: It gives the programmer a collection-based implementation of the list, and it gives the user the option of associating graphical and textual items.

The Slider control operates in a manner similar to the intrinsic scroll bar controls.

The Slider Control

The Slider control, another of the Windows Common Controls, indicates the current position within an **Integer** range. The user can change the current value of the slider by dragging the pointer. When the user drags the pointer, the Change event occurs and the **Value** property is reset. When you set the **Value** property by writing code, the control adjusts the visual pointer accordingly.

Syntax

Slider

Properties

➤ The **Max** and **Min** properties define the range of the slider.

➤ The **Orientation** property indicates whether the slider appears horizontally or vertically. If set to **ccOrientationHorizontal**, the control instance appears horizontally. If set to **ccOrientationVertical**, the control instance appears vertically.

➤ The **TextPosition** property determines the position of the ToolTip that appears as the user drags the pointer. If set to **sldAboveLeft**, the ToolTip appears above the pointer. If set to **sldBelowRight**, the ToolTip appears below the pointer. If the slider appears vertically, the ToolTip is positioned to the left of the pointer or to the right of the pointer, respectively.

➤ The **TickFrequency** property defines the number of tick marks appearing on the control instance relative to the range. As noted earlier, the **Max** and **Min** properties define the range.

➤ The **TickStyle** property defines where the tick marks appear. If the property is set to **sldBottomRight**, tick marks appear below or to the right of the pointer, depending on the orientation. If the property is set to **sldTopLeft**, tick marks appear above or to the left of the pointer. If the property is set to **sldBoth**, tick marks appear both above and below the pointer. If the property is set to **sldNone**, no tick marks appear.

➤ The **Value** property contains an **Integer** representing the current value of the slider.

Events

➤ The **Change** event occurs when the **Value** property of the slider changes.

In the ICS program, you will use an instance of the Slider control to display the capacity utilization of a particular flight. The capacity utilization depends on three values:

➤ The minimum value is always zero (an empty flight).

➤ The maximum value depends on the capacity of the airplane.

➤ The number of passengers on the flight must be between zero and the capacity of the airplane.

Each airplane may have a different capacity, so the values must be updated each time that the user locates a different record.

Consider the following statements, which update the Slider control instance when the current record is updated:

```
sldCapacity.Min = 0
sldCapacity.Max = FlightRecord(mintCurrent).Capacity
sldCapacity.Value = _
    FlightRecord(mintCurrent).Passengers
```

These statements set the lower and upper bounds of the control instance to zero and the capacity of the airplane to a number, respectively. The final statements set the current value within the range. In these statements, the information is displayed as a percentage.

You can now create an instance of the Slider control, set its properties, and update the value as the user selects different records.

To create an instance of the Slider control:

1. Click on the Slider button, and create an instance of the control, as shown in Figure 6.12.

2. Using the Properties window, set the **Name** property to **sldCapacity**.

3. Set the **TickFrequency** to **5** and the **TickStyle** to **0–sldBottomRight**.

4. Enter the following code at the end of the **SetCurrentRecord** general procedure:

```
sldCapacity.Min = 0
sldCapacity.Max = FlightRecord(mintCurrent).Capacity
sldCapacity.Value = _
    FlightRecord(mintCurrent).Passengers
```

5. Test the program and open the demonstration file. Select different records. As each record changes, the number of passengers also changes. Thus the code that you just wrote should update the current value of the Slider control instance.

6. End the program to return to design mode.

The purpose and functionality of the Slider control make it a near replacement for the scroll bar control.

Choosing between the slider control and the scroll bar control is difficult. Most programmers find that the Slider control is a suitable choice when they need a control instance to indicate a percentage.

You will now program the FlatScrollBar control. This control works much like the intrinsic vertical and horizontal scroll bar controls.

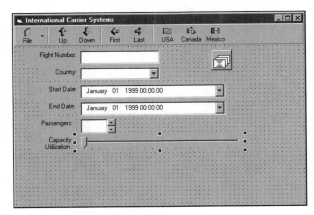

Figure 6.12   Slider control instance.

The FlatScrollBar Control

The purpose of the FlatScrollBar control is the same as that of the intrinsic vertical and horizontal scroll bars. The value of the **Max** and **Min** properties determines the range of the FlatScrollBar control. The FlatScrollBar and its intrinsic counterparts differ, however, in that the FlatScrollBar supports an **Orientation** property that causes it to appear horizontally or vertically. Thus it needs only one control type while the intrinsic scroll bars need two. The FlatScrollBar and its intrinsic counterparts also differ in appearance: the FlatScrollBar has a two-dimensional appearance and the intrinsic counterparts have a three-dimensional appearance. The standard prefix for the flat scroll bar is "fsb".

Syntax

>   FlatScrollBar

Properties

➤ The **Min** and **Max** properties define the range of the control instance.

➤ The **Value** property contains the current value of the control and must be between the **Min** and **Max** values.

➤ The **LargeChange** and **SmallChange** properties define the increment by which the value will change as the user clicks on the different regions of the control.

➤ The **Orientation** property can have one of two constant values. If set to **cc2OrientationVeritical**, the control instance appears vertically on the form. If set to **cc2OrientationHorizontal**, the control instance appears horizontally on the form.

Events

➤ The **Change** event occurs when the user changes the value of the control instance.

In the ICS program, the flat scroll bar will provide the user with another mechanism to select the current record. The implementation chosen is very simple. The code that you will write sets the **Min** and **Max** properties pertaining to the FlatScrollBar when the file is read. The **Min** property should be set to zero, and the **Max** property should be set to the number of records. When the user drags the scroll arrows on the control instance, the value is used to select the current record.

Consider the following statements:

```
fsbCurrent.Min = 0
fsbCurrent.Max = mintMax
```

This code will appear in the **OpenFile** general procedure. When the file is read, the preceding statements set the lower and upper bounds of the control instance.

Consider the following statements for the **fsbCurrent_Change** event procedure:

```
mintCurrent = fsbCurrent.Value
fsbCurrent.ToolTipText = mintCurrent
Call SetCurrentRecord
```

These statements first set the module-level variable **mintCurrent** to the current record. Next, the code resets the ToolTip. The final statement calls the general procedure to display the new current record.

You are now ready to create an instance of the FlatScrollBar control and write the necessary code to allow the user to select different records.

To use the FlatScrollBar control:

1. Create an instance of the FlatScrollBar control on the form.

2. Using the Properties window, set the **Name** property to **fsbCurrent.** Set the **Orientation** property to **0 – ccOrientationVertical**.

3. Enter the following statements in the fsbCurrent_Change event procedure:

```
mintCurrent = fsbCurrent.Value
fsbCurrent.ToolTipText = mintCurrent
Call SetCurrentRecord
```

4. Enter the following statements at the end of the **OpenFile** general procedure:

```
fsbCurrent.Min = 0
fsbCurrent.Max = mintMax
```

5. Enter the following statement at the end of the **SetCurrentRecord** general procedure:

```
fsbCurrent.Value = mintCurrent
```

6. Test the program. Open the demonstration file. Select different records using the FlatScrollBar control instance. Use the toolbar to select different records. The code that you just wrote updates the value of the FlatScrollBar control instance.

7. End the program to return to design mode.

The FlatScrollBar control provides little functionality beyond the intrinsic vertical and horizontal scroll bars. It does, however, provide a distinctive visual appearance.

Programmers use another control to display a value within a range: the ProgressBar control.

The ProgressBar Control

The ProgressBar control's purpose differs from that of the Slider control and scroll bars. The contents of the ProgressBar are typically updated by writing code to display the relative completion status of a time-consuming operation. Some operations require more than a few seconds to complete.

Communicating to the user the relative status of an operation's completion is important when the operation is a long-running operation. Many applications use progress bars to communicate with the end user. For example, Word displays a progress bar when reading or saving a file.

A program can use the progress bar to display the progress of tasks, such as opening and saving a file. Like the intrinsic status bar and its variants, the ProgressBar control supports a current position and a range.

Syntax

ProgressBar

Properties

➤ The **Alignment** property determines where the control instance appears on the form.

➤ The **Min** and **Max** properties define the range of the progress bar and have the same effect as the properties of the same name pertaining to a scroll bar.

➤ The **Orientation** property determines whether the progress bar will appear vertically or horizontally. If set to **ccOrientationHorizontal**, the control instance appears horizontally. If set to **ccOrientationVertical**, the control instance appears vertically.

➤ The **Scrolling** property determines the means by which the region of the progress bar is filled in. If set to ccScrollingStandard, the control fills blocks in its visible region to indicate the relative completion of an operation. If set to ccScrollingSmooth, the control fills in a solid bar as an operation progresses.

➤ The **Value** property identifies the current value within a range. The program sets this property to define the relative completion of an operation.

In the ICS program, you will use the progress bar to display the relative completion of the task of opening an input file. The program will use two values to update the **Value** property of the progress bar. The first value shows the relative status when the operation begins; it is always zero and indicates that no bytes have been read. The second value represents the upper bound of the range; it equals the size of the file. To determine the size of a file, the code could call the **FileLen** function, as shown below:

```
plngFileSize = FileLen(pstrFileName)
```

The preceding statement assumes that the variable **pstrFileName** contains a string. This string contains the name of the input file to be read. The FileLen function returns the size of an input file, which it stores in the variable **plngFileSize**.

Once the range has been determined, the current value must be updated. This task is considerably more difficult. As you write code to update the relative completion in the progress bar, you must consider the frequency with which the update should occur. If the value is updated too frequently, then execution time is wasted. If the value is updated too infrequently, the user will not see the progress bar updated properly. In this project, you will update the current value each time a record is read. If the input file is very large, the progress bar will likely be updated so frequently that the display contents will not change each time the **Value** property is reset. Consider the following statements:

```
If CInt(pintCounter * 60 / plngFileSize * 100) _
    <= 100 Then
    pbOpen.Value = CInt(pintCounter * 60 / _
        plngFileSize * 100)
End If
```

These statements require careful analysis. The value displayed in the progress bar is only an approximation of the number of bytes read, because the number of bytes in each record can vary slightly. The approximate size of each record is 60. The **If** statement is necessary because the progress bar's value can never exceed the maximum value (100). The standard prefix for the progress bar is "pb".

You are now ready to create and program the ProgressBar control instance.

To create an instance of the progress bar to display the relative completion of file operations:

1. Create an instance of the ProgressBar control across the bottom of the form, and set the **Name** property **to pbOpen**. Set the **Align** property to **2– vbAlignBottom**.

2. Note that the default value for the **Min** property is **0** and the default value for the **Max** property is **100**.

3. Enter the following statements at the beginning of the **OpenFile** event procedure:

```
pbOpen.Visible = True
```

4. Enter the following statements in the **OpenFile** general procedure:

```
        pintCounter = pintCounter + 1
    If CInt(pintCounter * 60 / plngFileSize * 100) _
        <= 100 Then
        pbOpen.Value = CInt(pintCounter * 60 / _
            plngFileSize * 100)
    End If
Loop
```

5. Enter the following statement at the end of the **OpenFile** general procedure:

```
pbOpen.Visible = False
```

6. Test the program. Open the demonstration file. As the code reads the file, the progress bar will update the relative completion of the task.

7. End the program to return to design mode.

You have now seen how several different types of controls can illustrate a position within a range. These controls include the UpDown, Slider, FlatScrollBar, and ProgessBar controls.

The final control type presented in this chapter has a much different purpose. The StatusBar control is used to display the status of the keyboard or current information pertaining to the program itself.

Improving The User Interface With A Status Bar

Visual Basic allows you to create forms with a status bar by using the StatusBar control. A status bar typically appears at the bottom of a form. Programmers commonly use this control to display the state of specific keys; for example, the control instance indicates whether the Caps Lock key is enabled or whether the Insert mode is on or off. If used in the database programs of Chapters 3 and 4, a status bar could have displayed the current record number, indicated whether the current record was being edited, or noted the progress of an update operation.

Figure 6.13 shows a status bar and its components.

The status bar contains regions called *panels*. The control implements each panel as a Panel object in the **Panels** collection. At design time, the programmer adds and removes panels by using the Property Pages. The Property Pages contain tabs to define the general characteristics of the status bar and the characteristics of each panel on the status bar. As with any other collection, Panel objects can be added and removed at run time using the **Add** and **Remove** methods pertaining to the **Panels** collection. The standard prefix for the StatusBar control is "sbr".

Syntax

StatusBar

Properties

➤ The **Align** property defines the placement of the status bar on the form. Typically, you align the status bar across the bottom of the form.

➤ The **Panels** property contains a reference to the **Panels** collection, which in turn stores references to each Panel object. The StatusBar control supports up to 16 panels.

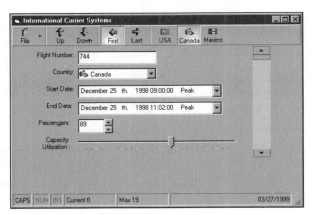

Figure 6.13   StatusBar control instance at run time.

➤ The **Style** property can be set to one of two modes. If set to the constant value **sbrSimple**, the status bar appears with one large panel encompassing the entire region of the status bar. If set to **sbrNormal** (the default), the status bar displays all Panel objects.

➤ The **SimpleText** property causes text to appear across the entire region of the status bar only when the **Style** property is set to **sbrSimple**. If the **Style** property is set to **sbrNormal**, the value is ignored.

Events

➤ The StatusBar control responds to the **Click** event like other controls, although the event seldom is used. The program's code typically manages the contents of the entire status bar.

➤ The **PanelClick** event occurs when the user clicks on a specific panel. A panel indicates status information, such as whether a field is being edited. You can write code that responds to this event, allowing your program to change the status. In this situation, the panel works much like a command button. When the **PanelClick** event occurs, Visual Basic passes a reference to the clicked panel to the event procedure.

After creating the status bar and setting the general properties, you create the individual panels and set the Panel object's properties. The **Panels** collection is a one-based collection containing a reference to each Panel object in the collection. As with most collections, a Panel object can be referenced with either a numeric index or a string key. Each Panel object supports properties to define its appearance and the size of the panel.

Syntax

Panel

Properties

➤ The **Index** and **Key** properties define the numeric index and string key, respectively, to uniquely identify the Panel object in the **Panels** collection.

➤ The **Alignment** property determines how the text is aligned inside a specific panel. Text can be left-justified, centered, or right-justified.

➤ The **Style** property defines the behavior of an individual panel. This property differs from the property of the same name pertaining to the status bar itself; it pertains to a Panel object. The **Style** property defines whether a Panel object contains text or an icon. It also is used to display the status of keyboard keys, such as the Num Lock key, the Ins key, and the Shift key.

➤ The **Bevel** property determines how the panel appears on the status bar. If set to **sbrNoBevel**, the panel appears flat on the status bar. If set to **sbrInset** or **sbrRaised**, the panel appears recessed or raised off the status bar, respectively.

➤ The **Text** property contains the text appearing inside the panel.

➤ The **Width** and **MinWidth** properties identify the size and minimum size of a panel on the status bar, respectively.

➤ The **AutoSize** property can have one of three constant values. If set to **sbrNoAutosize**, the size of the Panel object is fixed. If set to **sbrSpring**, the control adjusts the size of all panels having an **AutoSize** property of sbrSpring so that their width is equal. If set to **sbrContents,** the control adjusts the size of the panel so that the contents fit inside the panel. The size will not decrease below the **MinWidth** property when the **AutoSize** property is set to **sbrContents**.

6

A programmer commonly uses a panel on a status bar to indicate the current state of a program, such as the position within a file or the editing status of a record. For example, Microsoft Word uses the status bar to indicate the current position within a document, and Microsoft Excel uses the status bar to inform the user when it is recalculating the spreadsheet and to provide instructional tips about what to do next.

Microsoft Word and Microsoft Excel also display, in individual Panel objects, the status of specific keys. These statuses include whether the Caps Lock or Num Lock keys are pressed and whether the document is in Insert or Overwrite mode. By setting the **Style** property for a panel, the status bar will display automatically the status of these individual keyboard buttons. The valid settings for individual panels that might use the **Style** property are as follows:

➤ **sbrText** If set to this constant (the default), text and an optional bitmap appear in the panel.

➤ **sbrCaps** If set to this constant, the letters CAPS appear in the panel in bold when the Caps Lock key is enabled and are dimmed when this key is disabled.

➤ **sbrNum** If set to this constant, the letters NUM appear in the panel in bold when the Num Lock key is enabled and are dimmed when this key is disabled.

➤ **sbrIns** If set to this constant, the letters INS appear in the panel in bold when the Ins key is enabled and are dimmed when this key is disabled.

➤ **sbrScrl** If set to this constant the letters SCRL appear the panel in bold when the Scroll Lock key is enabled and are dimmed when this key is disabled.

➤ **sbrTime** If set to this constant, the current time appears in the panel.

➤ **sbrDate** If set to this constant, the current date appears in the panel.

➤ **sbrKana** If set to this constant, the string KANA appears in the panel. This setting is used for specific foreign languages.

You can use the Property Pages pertaining to the StatusBar control to set most of the design-time properties pertaining to the status bar and to the individual Panel objects.

To create a status bar and display the Panels tab of the Property Pages:

1. Create an instance of the status bar on the bottom of the form so that the status bar spans the entire width of the form. Set the **Name** property to **sbrICS**. By default, the control instance stretches across the width of the bottom of the form. Set the **Align** property to **2 – vbAlignBottom**. In the Form window, drag the staus bar so that it appears below the progress bar.

2. Activate the Property Pages for the status bar and select the Panels tab of the Property Pages. Figure 6.14 shows the Property Pages with existing panels.

As illustrated in Figure 6.14, the Panels tab of the Property Pages contains buttons to insert and remove panels. Note that each panel supports a numeric index. The scroll bars next to the **Index** property can be used to select a specific panel. You can also assign a string key to each Panel object by setting the **Key** property. When you add a panel, the new panel is inserted after the index of the currently selected panel. The Remove Panel button removes the currently selected panel. For the currently selected panel, you set the properties pertaining to that panel.

The Property Pages automatically assigns a numeric index to each Panel object. Both the string key and numeric index can be used to reference a particular Panel object in the **Panels** collection at run time.

 When inserting and deleting panels with the Panels tab of the Property Pages, the first panel (which has a numeric index value of 1) becomes the current panel. Thus you must be careful to select the correct panel when you set properties. Clicking on the Apply button will also reset the selected panel.

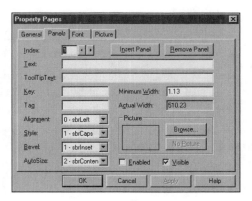

Figure 6.14   StatusBar Property Pages Panels tab.

Before setting the individual properties pertaining to a panel, consider the particulars of the panel-related properties. The StatusBar control allows the size of a panel, and the status bar itself, to be changed at run time when the form is resized. What happens to a panel when the form is resized depends on the value of the panel's **AutoSize** property.

In the ICS program, you will set the properties to resize the panels on the status bar dynamically. The panels displaying the status of the Caps Lock, Ins, and Num Lock keys will have a fixed size based upon the panel's contents. The **MinWidth** property of these panels must be explicitly set, because the default **MinWidth** property is greater than the size of the actual contents.

Another panel will display the date. You will set the **AutoSize** property so that this panel occupies the remaining space in the status bar.

In addition to displaying the status of specific keyboard keys, the status bar will display information related to the status of the current record and the total number of records.

Because the text panels will be referenced with code, you should specify a string key for both text panels. This approach will simplify the writing of the code. The three-character prefix of "pnl" denotes a Panel object.

To create the panels on the status bar:

1. Activate the Property Pages for the status bar, if necessary, and verify that the Panels tab is selected. The currently selected panel should have an index of 1.

2. Edit the first panel's properties by setting the **Style** to **1 – sbrCaps**, the **AutoSize** to **2– sbrContents**, and the **Minimum Width** to **1**.

3. Click on the Insert Panel button to insert a second panel. Use the scroll buttons to the right of the **Index** property to select panel number 2. Set the **Style** to 2 – sbrNum, the **AutoSize** to **2 – sbrContents**, and the **Minimum Width** to **1**.

4. Repeat Step 2 to insert the third panel, except set the **Style** to **3 – sbrIns**. This panel should have an **Index** value of 3.

5. Insert a panel with an Index value of **4**. Set the **Style** to **0 – sbrText**, the **AutoSize** to **3 – sbrContents**, and the **Key** to **CurrentRecord**.

6. Insert a panel with an Index value of **5**. Use the same property settings as shown in Step 5, except set the **Key** to **TotalRecords**.

7. The last panel will display the date. Create a panel with an index of 6. Set the **Style** to **6 – sbrDate**, the **AutoSize** to **1 – sbrSpring**, and the **Alignment** to **2 – sbrRight**. Click on OK to close the Property Pages.

8. Test the program. Press the Caps Lock, Num Lock, and Ins keys. As the keys are enabled and disabled, the text on the status bar appears in a normal font and then in a gray font, respectively. Also, the date is displayed at the right-hand side of the status bar.

9. End the program to return to design mode.

When you ran the program, the panels designed to show status information pertaining to the current record and the number of records displayed nothing. You must write code to display this information. Consider the following statement, which references a text panel:

```
sbrICS.Panels("CurrentRecord").Visible = False
```

The preceding statement uses the string key of a panel to set its **Visible** property to **False**, causing the panel to be invisible at run time.

In this project, you must display the current record and the maximum number of records in the status bar. The following statements accomplish this task:

```
sbrICS.Panels("CurrentRecord") = "Current " & mintCurrent
sbrICS.Panels("TotalRecords") = "Max " & mintMax
```

The preceding statements use the module-level variables **mintCurrent** and **mintMax** and concatenate them to a text string. The corresponding panel stores the values. Note that the **Value** property is not explicitly specified because it is the default property.

You now have the necessary tools to display the current record and maximum number of records in the Panel objects.

To programmatically update a Panel object:

1. Activate the Code window for the **SetCurrentRecord** general procedure, and enter the following statements at the end of the procedure:

```
sbrICS.Panels("CurrentRecord") = "Current " & mintCurrent
sbrICS.Panels("TotalRecords") = "Max " & mintMax
```

2. Test the program. Open the demonstration text file. The current record and the number of records should appear in the Panel objects. Locate different records. The current record panel in the status bar should be updated appropriately.

3. End the program to return to design mode.

 By default, the panels have a beveled style. Avoid using raised panels. They resemble command buttons, and users tend to identify such buttons as objects that they can click on to perform an action.

You have now completed the program for this chapter, which presented many options for designing a program's user interface.

CHAPTER SUMMARY

This chapter discussed several additional Windows Common Controls including the Toolbar, DTPicker, Slider, ImageCombo, FlatScrollBar, ProgressBar, UpDown, and StatusBar.

To create an instance of the Toolbar control:

➤ Create an instance of the ImageList and Toolbar controls on the form.

➤ Set the **ImageList** property of the toolbar to an instance of the ImageList control.

➤ Set the general properties of the toolbar, including the **TextAlignment**, **BorderStyle**, and **Style** properties.

➤ Create the buttons on the toolbar. Each button can display an image, or text, or both. Set the **Style** property of each button to determine its behavior.

➤ If the style is set to a drop-down button, create the ButtonMenu objects to appear on the drop-down menu. Each button menu object supports a textual description and a string key.

To program the toolbar:

➤ If a button is an ordinary button, write a **Select Case** statement to respond to the toolbar's **ButtonClick** event.

➤ If the button is a ButtonMenu, write a **Select Case** statement to respond to the toolbar's **ButtonMenuClick** event.

To use the DTPicker control:

➤ Create an instance of the DTPicker control on the form.

➤ Set the **Format** property to one of the predefined formats or use a custom format.

➤ If a custom format is being used, set the **CustomFormat** property as necessary.

➤ If the custom format uses a callback string, write code to respond to the **Format** and **FormatSize** events.

To use the UpDown control:

➤ Create an instance of the UpDown control on the form.

➤ Set the **BuddyControl** property to another control instance capable of operating as a buddy.

➤ Set the **BuddyProperty** property to a specific property of the buddy control.

➤ Set the **SyncBuddy** property to **True** to synchronize the control instance.

To use the ImageCombo control:

➤ Create an instance of the ImageCombo control on the form.

➤ Associate the control instance with an instance of the ImageList control.

➤ Call the **Add** method to add items to the list:

```
object.Add(Index As Variant, Key As Variant, Text As Variant, Image
As Variant,
SelImage As Variant, Indentation As Variant) As ComboItem
```

To use the Slider control:

➤ Set the **Min** and **Max** properties to define the range of the slider.

➤ Set the **Orientation** property to cause the control instance to appear vertically or horizontally.

➤ Set the **Value** property to define the current value of the pointer.

➤ Set the **TickFrequency** and **TickStyle** properties to determine the number and appearance of the tick marks appearing on the slider.

To use the FlatScrollBar control:

➤ Create an instance of the FlatScrollBar control on the form.

➤ Set the **Min** and **Max** properties to define the object's range.

➤ Set the **LargeChange** and **SmallChange** properties to define the amount by which the value will change when clicked by the user.

➤ Set the **Orientation** property to cause the scroll bar to appear vertically or horizontally.

➤ Write code that responds to the **Change** event.

To use the ProgressBar control:

➤ Create an instance of the ProgressBar control on the form.

➤ Set the **Align** property to determine where the control instance appears on the form.

➤ Set the **Min** and **Max** properties to determine the range of the progress bar.

➤ Set the **Scrolling** property to define how the progress bar is filled in.

➤ Set the **Value** property repeatedly as an operation progresses to fill in the progress bar.

To use the StatusBar control:

➤ Create an instance of the StatusBar control on the form.

➤ Create panels as needed to display the status of keyboard keys.

➤ Create text panels to display textual information that will change at run time.

➤ Set the size of each panel.

REVIEW QUESTIONS

1. Which of the following objects define the buttons that appear on the Toolbar control?

   a. ButtonMenu, ButtonItem

   b. ButtonMenu, Button

   c. ButtonGroup, Button, ButtonMenu

   d. MenuButton, StandardButton

   e. None of the above

2. Which of the following are valid types of toolbar buttons?

   a. Option group, separator, checked, default, placeholder

   b. Button group, separator, checked, default, placeholder

   c. Normal, separator, checked, placeholder, button group

   d. Normal, divider, checked, placeholder, button group

   e. None of the above

3. Which of the following statements pertaining to the Toolbar control is true?

   a. Buttons can display text and/or images.

   b. Other control instances can be drawn on the Toolbar control.

   c. To create a drop-down menu, you create a ButtonMenu object.

   d. All of the above.

   e. None of the above.

4. Which of the following statements pertaining to the DTPicker control is true?

   a. It consists of two parts: a text part and a calendar part.

   b. It displays a starting date and ending date.

   c. It can display a date or a time, but not both.

   d. Both a and c.

   e. All of the above.

5. Which event(s) is (are) used to format and display information related to callback strings?

   a. **CallbackString**, **CallbackStringSize**

   b. **Formatting**

   c. **FormatData**, **FormatSize**

   d. **Format**, **FormatString**

   e. None of the above

6. What CustomFormat would display the date formatted as "01/01/1999"?

   a. mm/dd/yy

   b. m/d/y

   c. MM/dd/yyy

   d. MM/DD/YYY

   e. None of the above

7. How many callback strings can be displayed in a custom format string?

    a. 1

    b. 2

    c. 1 or more

    d. 3

    e. None of the above

8. Assume that an instance of the Toolbar control named tbrQuestion exists. Write the statements to make the button having a string key of File visible. Also, write the statement to enable the button.

9. Create an event procedure that will execute when the user clicks on the buttons on the toolbar named tbrQuestion. Assume that buttons with string keys of "First", "Second", and "Third" have been defined. For each button clicked, print the string key of the button to the Immediate window.

10. Create the necessary event procedures(s) to format the callback string with one of the following three values depending on the time of day. If the time of day is between 8 A.M. and 4 P.M., display the string "Day". If the time of day is between 4 P.M. and midnight, display the string "Evening". If the time of day is between midnight and 8 A.M., display the string "Night".

11. Which of the following statements about the UpDown control is true?

    a. The control instance associated with the UpDown control is referred to as a Friend control.

    b. Multiple Friend controls can be associated with the UpDown control.

    c. The Associate property is used to synchronize an UpDown control with a Friend control.

    d. All of the above.

    e. None of the above.

12. Which of the following statements pertaining to the ImageCombo control is true?

    a. Data is stored in the **List** property.

    b. The control displays both images and text.

    c. Multiple images can appear on a single line by setting the **MultiLine** property to **True**.

    d. To change the image, you set the **Images** property pertaining to the List object.

    e. Both a and d.

13. What properties pertaining to the Slider control determine the valid range and current value?

    a. **Minimum**, **Maximum**, **Current**

    b. **Minimum**, **Maximum**, **Value**

    c. **Min**, **Max**, **Current**

    d. **Min**, **Max**, **Value**

    e. **Start**, **End**, **Current**

14. Which of the following statements about the FlatScrollBar control is true?

    a. It can fulfill the roles played by both the intrinsic vertical and horizontal scroll bar controls.

    b. You use the **Appearance** property, causing the FlatScrollBar to appear vertically or horizontally.

    c. It is an intrinsic control.

    d. All of the above

    e. None of the above

15. Which of the following characteristics do the ProgressBar, Slider, and FlatStatusBar controls have in common?

    a. They can display information vertically or horizontally.

    b. They all display a value within a range of values.

    c. Each can display a graphical image.

    d. Both a and b.

    e. All of the above.

16. What is the name of the StatusBar object used to display each element appearing on an instance of the StatusBar control?

    a. sbr

    b. StatusItem

    c. Item

    d. List

    e. Panel

17. Write the code to add an image to the ImageCombo control having a string key of "Image1", and a caption of "First Line of Text", and display the image from an ImageList control having a string key of "imgDemo".

18. Write the code to set the minimum and maximum values of the progress bar named pbQuestion to 40 and 80, respectively. Set the **Value** property such that the progress bar displays a relative completion level of 50%.

19. Write the code to display the text string "Row Count is 3" in the StatusBar panel named pnlCurrent. Assume that the name of the StatusBar control instance is sbrCurrent.

20. Write the code to disable all of the text panels on the status bar named sbrCurrent. (*Hint:* Use the Panels collection and create a For Each loop to accomplish this task.)

HANDS-ON PROJECTS

6

Project 1
In this project, you will write a program that will shuffle a deck of cards. After the cards are shuffled, the shuffled deck of cards will appear in an instance of the ImageCombo control.

a. Run the completed program named Chapter.06\Exercise\Ex1Demo.exe. Figure 6.15 shows the completed form for the program.

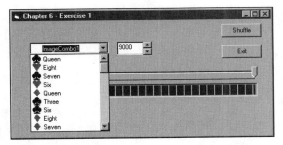

Figure 6.15   Exercise 1 Completed form.

Click on the UpDown control instance. As you click on the Up button, the value of the buddy text box increases by 1000 each time. This value indicates the number of exchanges that will be made to the deck of cards. Select a value of at least 5000, and click on the **Shuffle** command button. As the deck is shuffled, the Slider control instance and ProgressBar control instance display the relative progress being made on the task. When shuffling is complete, click on the instance of the ImageCombo control to display the cards in the order that they were shuffled. End the program.

b. Start Visual Basic, and create a new project.

c. Save the form with the name frmEx1.frm and the project with the name Ex1.vbp. Save both files in the Chapter.06\Exercise folder.

d. Add a reference to the Windows Common Controls to the project.

e. Create an instance of the ImageList control on the form. Add the following images from the Chapter.06\Exercise folder: Misc34.ico, Misc35.ico, Misc36.ico, and Misc37.ico. Set the string keys for the images to Heart, Club, Diamond, and Spade, respectively.

f. Create instances of the ImageCombo, UpDown, TextBox, Slider, and ProgressBar controls, as shown in Figure 6.15.

g. Declare a user-defined type with two elements named Suit and Card, each of type **String**.

h. Declare an array of the user-defined type with 52 elements. (Note: You can simplify the program's implementation by declaring the array with a lower bound of 1 instead of 0.)

i. Write the code to initialize the array, which should store values into the suit and card array elements. Consider the following statements to initialize the first few cards:

```
Card(1).Card = "Ace"
Card(1).Suit = "Club"
Card(2).Card = "Two"
Card(2).Suit = "Club
 . . .
Card(52).Card = "King"
Card(52).Suit = "Spade"
```

j. The difficult part of the program is to shuffle the deck of cards. To shuffle the deck of cards, you first call the Randomize function to seed the random number generator. Next, write a loop that will swap cards based upon the current value of the UpDown control instance (and corresponding buddy text box). The code in the loop should randomly select two elements from the array and then exchange the contents of those two elements. The Rnd function returns a value between 0 and 1. The following code will convert the random value into a number between 1 and 52 and store the result in the variable **pintCard**.

```
pintCard = Int(51 - 1 + 1) * Rnd + 1
```

k. Write the code to display the relative completion of the card-shuffling task in both the progress bar and the slider.

l. After the cards have been shuffled, examine each card in the array and add each element to the ImageCombo control instance. Add the items such that the suit appears as an icon, and the card appears in the textual part of the list item.

m. Test the program. Shuffle the cards. Make sure that the progress bar and slider are updated correctly. After the cards have been shuffled, click on the

ImageCombo control instance to verify that the cards appear in random order, that all of the cards are present, and that no duplicate cards exist.

n. End the program, and exit Visual Basic.

Project 2

In this project, you will use the UpDown, Slider, and StatusBar controls to experiment with color. Color is implemented using RGB (Red Green Blue) values. The color that appears on the screen is determined by the amount of each of these three colors that is included. The value of each color ranges from 0 to 255. If all three colors have a value of zero, the color is black. If all have a value of 255, the color is white. The RGB function can be used to set a color. Consider the following statement to set the background color of a shape control instance named shpOutput:

```
shpOutput.BackColor = RGB(128,128,128)
```

a. Run the completed program named Chapter.06\Exercise\Ex2Demo.exe. As shown in Figure 6.16, three instances of the UpDown control and three instances of the Slider control have been created. Select different values using each of the control instances. As you choose different values, the current value appears in the status bar at the bottom of the form, and the color appears in the shape control instance at the right of the form. Depending on the configuration of your computer and the graphics card installed, the color resolution will vary. Exit the program.

b. Start Visual Basic, and create a new project.

c. Save the form with the name frmEx2.frm and the project with the name Ex2.vbp. Save both files in the Chapter.06\Exercise folder.

d. Add the necessary Windows Common Controls to the project.

e. Create the control instances shown in Figure 6.16.

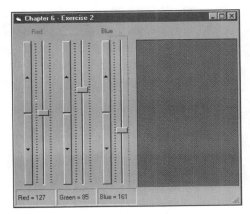

Figure 6.16   Exercise 2 Completed form.

f. The instances of the UpDown control should be synchronized with the corresponding instance of the Slider control. Set the **Min** and **Max** values for each control instance such that the valid range is between 0 and 255. Synchronize the control instances with their corresponding buddy controls.

g. Create an instance of the Shape control on the form.

h. Write the code to call the RGB function and display the resulting color in the instance of the Shape control.

i. Create an instance of the StatusBar control on the form. The status bar should have three panels, each displaying the numeric value of a component of the current RGB color.

j. Write the code to update the numeric value of the RGB color as necessary.

k. Test the program. Make sure that the control instances are synchronized properly, that the current **Integer** value of the color appears in the proper status bar panel, and that the color appears in the shape control instance.

l. Exit Visual Basic.

Project 3

In this project, you will use the DTPicker control to create a scheduling program. The scheduling program will work with 15 instances of the DTPicker control. One control instance will define the start date for a weekly schedule. The remaining 14 control instances will allow the user to set a starting and ending work time for each day of the week. As the user changes these values, Label control instances will be updated to display the number of hours worked for the day and the total number of hours for the week.

a. Run the completed program named Chapter.06\Complete\Ex3Demo.exe. Figure 6.17 shows the form for the completed program.

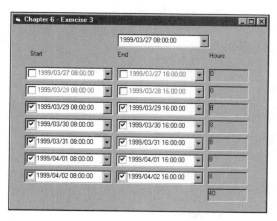

Figure 6.17   Exercise 3 Completed form.

Using the checkboxes, select and deselect starting and ending dates. The hours worked appear in the Label control instances to the right of the DTPicker control instance. Also, the total hours worked is computed. End the program.

b. Start Visual Basic, and create a new project.

c. Save the form with the name frmEx3.frm and the project with the name Ex3.vbp. Save both files in the Chapter.06\Exercise folder.

d. Add the necessary Windows Common Controls to the project.

e. Create the first instance of the DTPicker control at the top of the form. This control instance should display the current date when the form loads. Also, the control instance should display the time of day as 8:00 A.M.

f. Create the Label control instances on the form.

g. Create the remaining DTPicker control instances. How you create these control instances is critical. The left column of control instances should be implemented as a control array, and the right column of control instances should be implemented as another control array. If you do not use control arrays, the program will be significantly more complex to create.

h. Create a procedure to initialize each control instance in the control arrays. The starting date of the first control instance should be the same as the DTPicker control instance that you created in Step e. The next control instance should be incremented by one day, the next by another day, and so on. The control instances on the right side of the form should be initialized such that the time of day is eight hours later than the time for the control instance immediately to its left.

i. Write the code to validate the user input by ensuring that the ending time must be greater than the starting time.

j. Write code to update the label to the right of the ending control instance. It will contain the difference, in hours, between the ending and starting values for the day where the change took place. If both the starting and ending checkboxes are not marked, the value stored in the corresponding label should be 0.

k. Write the code that will execute whenever the value of one of the labels changes. This code should update the total hours for the week.

l. Test the program. Select different time and date values and verify that the number of hours worked functions correctly.

Project 4

In this project, you will use a database to display instances of a toolbar, a DTPicker control, and a status bar.

a. Run the completed program named Chapter.06\Exercise\Ex4Demo.exe. Figure 6.18 shows the completed form for the program. The database file named Ex4.mdb must reside in the same folder as the application for the program to work correctly.

As shown in Figure 6.18, the program contains a toolbar, instances of the DTPicker control, and a status bar. Click on the buttons on the toolbar to locate different records. The current record appears in the form's unbound control instances, and the current record number appears in the status bar at the bottom of the form. End the program.

b. Start Visual Basic, and create a new project.

c. Save the form with the name frmEx4.frm and the project with the name Ex4.vbp. Save both files in the Chapter.06\Exercise folder.

d. Add the necessary Windows Common Controls to the project.

e. This program uses unbound controls, so you must create the necessary ADO objects to establish a database connection and open a recordset. The table in the database, which is named tblCalls, contains the following fields: fldIdNumber, fldStart, and fldEnd. Write the code in the **Form_Load** event procedure to establish the connection and create a recordset.

f. Create an instance of the ImageList control on the form. The file names for the icons are Folder.02.ico, Arw01lt.ico, Arw01rt.ico, Arw01Up.ico, and Arw01Dn.ico. Set string keys as necessary for the images.

g. Create an instance of the Toolbar control on the form. The Edit menu should be implemented as a drop-down menu that has items called Add, Update, Cancel, and Delete. The remaining buttons should be implemented as default buttons.

h. Create the remaining control instances on the form.

i. Using the unbound control processing techniques introduced in Chapter 3, display the current record in the unbound control instances.

j. Write the code to locate different records as the user clicks on the buttons on the toolbar.

k. Write the code to add, change, and delete records when the user clicks on the buttons on the toolbar.

l. Create an instance of the StatusBar control on the form. Display the status of the editing keys and the current record number in the status bar.

m. Test the program. Verify that the toolbar buttons function correctly, that the records appear in the unbound control instances, and that the status bar functions correctly.

n. Exit Visual Basic.

MULTIPLE DOCUMENT INTERFACE PROGRAMMING

AFTER READING THIS CHAPTER AND COMPLETING THE EXERCISES, YOU WILL BE ABLE TO:

➤ Create a type of user interface called a multiple-document interface (MDI) program that uses multiple instances of the same form

➤ Create and destroy instances of a form at run time

➤ Manage each of the different form instances

➤ Understand the events that occur as the different forms in an MDI program are unloaded

➤ Use an instance of the CommonDialog control to provide a standard interface for the tasks of opening and saving files, selecting fonts and colors, and printing files

➤ Use a RichTextBox control to format text

CREATING A MULTIPLE-DOCUMENT INTERFACE APPLICATION

Previewing The Completed Application

The completed application uses two new controls. The first, the RichTextBox control, is a superset of the intrinsic text box. That is, it supports additional properties and methods to format and display text. The second, the CommonDialog control, provides a standard interface to open, save, and print files. It is also used to select fonts, font attributes, and font colors.

The CommonDialog displays standard dialogs allowing the user to select files to open or to save. In the past, when you opened files using Microsoft Word or Excel, you may have noticed that the user interface for the Open dialog box was identical from program to program. Visual Basic supports similar dialogs through the CommonDialog control. The code for the control exists as a Windows library that can be employed by many applications.

Unlike with the programs created in previous chapters, you will implement this program by using a multiple-document interface (MDI). MDI programs are not unique to Visual Basic—in fact, programs like Word, Excel, and Visual Basic are all MDI programs. In Word, multiple files (documents) can be open simultaneously, each appearing in a separate window. Each window appears inside the region of another window, referred to as a *parent form* or *parent window*. This program will have a similar user interface.

You can load and execute this project and use it for reference as you complete the steps in this chapter.

To preview the completed application:

1. Start Visual Basic, and open the project named Chapter.07\Complete\Ch7_ C.vbp. The project consists of two form modules: one containing the interface for the text editor, and an MDI parent form that acts as a container for the text editor form.

2. Run the program. The MDI parent form appears on the screen. Because a new file has not yet been created or an existing file opened, the form used to edit data is not displayed.

   On the form's menu bar, click on File, and then click on New to create a new file. Another form, called an MDI child form, appears inside the region of the parent form, as shown in Figure 7.1.

   Figure 7.1 shows the toolbar and menu displayed on the MDI parent form. For brevity, ToolTips have been omitted for the toolbar. The status bar appears at the bottom of the MDI parent form. At this point, one instance

Figure 7.1   Completed application.

of the MDI child form appears on the MDI parent form; this child form contains a rich text box.

3. Move the MDI child form inside the region of the MDI parent form. Notice that the visible region of the MDI child form cannot extend beyond the region of the MDI parent form. This is one of the characteristics of MDI programs.

4. In the RichTextBox control instance, enter a line of text that reads "This is a line of bold text."

5. Select the text by dragging the mouse over the sentence. On the form's menu bar, click on Format, and then click on Bold to apply the selected formatting. The selected text will appear in a bold typeface. Repeat the process for the Italic and Underline menu commands. As you apply these formatting characteristics, the buttons on the toolbar appear pressed or unpressed to indicate the current formatting attributes. The program code also updates the menu commands such that they contain either a check mark or no check mark, based on the status of the formatting characteristic.

   The toolbar buttons provide quick access to specific menu commands on the menu bar.

6. To test the toolbar, select text in the rich text box, and then click on the Bold, Italic, and Underline formatting buttons on the toolbar. These buttons have the same effects as the corresponding commands on the menu bar.

   This program uses an instance of the CommonDialog control to provide a standard interface for common functions such as opening, saving, and printing files and setting fonts. This control instance is not visible at run time, however.

7. To use the CommonDialog control instance to change the font, select some text in the rich text box, click on Format, and then click on Fonts to open the Font dialog box. Select a font and a size for the font. Click on the OK button to apply the font to the selected text.

8. The program also uses the CommonDialog control instance to save files. On the form's menu bar, click on File, and then click on Save. The Save As dialog box appears, allowing you to select a folder and file name. Select the Chapter.07\Complete folder, setting the drive designator as necessary. Enter the name Test in the File name text box, and then click on Save on the dialog box to save the file. Files can also be opened via a similar dialog box by using the File, Open menu commands.

9. Programs commonly utilize an MDI interface when the user interface must display multiple instances of the same form at the same time. In this text editor, each file that is being edited appears in a different instance of the MDI child form. To illustrate this process, click on File, and then click on New. A second form opens. It is possible to navigate between these two forms, minimize them, and close the forms independently of each other.

10. Resize the MDI parent window. You can change its size or maximize and minimize it, as necessary.

11. MDI programs support features to automatically arrange the open child forms. These functions appear on the program's Window menu. While multiple windows are open, click on Window, and then click on Cascade, Tile Horizontal, and Tile Vertical in that order. These options change the visual orientation of the different MDI child forms relative to one another.

12. Another feature of menus and MDI programs is the capability to display a list of the open MDI child forms on a menu. Click on Window, and then highlight List. The open MDI child forms are listed on the menu.

13. End the program, and then exit Visual Basic.

CHARACTERISTICS OF MDI PROGRAMS

In the programs you have developed so far in this book, you have created a single instance of a form that could appear anywhere on the screen. This type of program is called a single-document interface (SDI) program. It is also common to create multiple instances of the same form and then display those forms such that they appear inside the region of another form. These programs are called *multiple-document interface (MDI)* programs. You can use three different types of forms in an MDI program:

➤ **MDI parent** One and only one MDI parent form can be created in a project. An MDI parent form acts as a container for other forms. Other forms in the program are displayed inside the region of the MDI parent form. An MDI parent form cannot be displayed as a modal form.

➤ **MDI child** An MDI child form always appears inside the region of the MDI parent form. An MDI child form cannot be displayed as a modal form. A project may have several MDI child forms.

➤ **Standard** You can continue to use standard forms in an MDI program. Standard forms can be displayed anywhere on the screen and are not contained by the MDI parent form. You can use both MDI child forms and standard forms in an MDI program, with the standard forms being displayed as modal or modeless forms.

When you create an MDI program, the MDI parent form and its MDI child forms have unique characteristics that differ from the characteristics of standard forms. First, an MDI child form always appears inside the region of the MDI parent form. Child forms can be moved and resized, but their visible region cannot expand beyond the region of the MDI parent form. Of course, you can resize the MDI parent form itself. Depending on the desired implementation, the **BorderStyle** property of both the MDI parent and MDI child forms can be set to control whether the forms can be resized. Second, when an MDI child form is minimized, its icon appears at the bottom of the MDI parent form rather than at the bottom of the desktop. Third, when an MDI child form is maximized, the MDI child form's caption appears in brackets on the title bar of the MDI parent form. A maximized MDI child form occupies the region of the MDI parent form, rather than the entire desktop.

MDI programs can contain standard forms, although these forms typically are used as modal dialogs. The icon for a standard form in an MDI program appears on the desktop when the form is minimized. A standard form can appear anywhere on the screen. The behavior of standard forms is the same as with other programs you have created. In addition, the behavior of message boxes and input boxes does not change—that is, input boxes and message boxes are displayed as modal dialogs and can appear anywhere on the screen.

Creating the MDI interface for a program is a very simple task. First, you add an MDI parent form to the project using the Add MDI Form command on the Project menu. Because a project can have only one MDI parent form, this option becomes disabled after a MDI parent form has been added to the project. Next, you convert standard forms into MDI child forms by setting the **MDIChild** property of the desired form to **True**. In the program you will be creating for Perfect Programming Systems, the form containing the text editor will be implemented as an MDI child form.

Perfect Programming Systems sells a commercial software package consisting of several utility programs. The company will add a text editor to this package that will allow the user to edit multiple files simultaneously and to format the contents of those files.

When an MDI child form loads, it may or may not be displayed, depending on the setting of the **AutoShowChildren** property. If the **AutoShowChildren** property is set to **False**, an MDI child form will remain invisible until explicitly shown. If the property is set to **True**, the MDI child form will be made visible when loaded. Consider the following statements:

```
MDIForm1.AutoShowChildren = False
Load frmText
```

The preceding statements cause the form named **frmText** to remain hidden when loaded. The following statements cause the form to be displayed automatically:

```
MDIForm1.AutoShowChildren = True
Load frmText
```

In addition to having unique display characteristics, menus in MDI programs operate differently from those in single-document interface programs.

Menus And MDI Programs

The behavior of the menu system is one of the most significant differences between an MDI program and a standard program. In a program that incorporates only standard forms, each form can have its own set of menus, and a form's set of menus always appears at the top of the form and beneath the form's title bar. In contrast, menus for both MDI parent forms and MDI child forms appear just below the title bar of the MDI parent form. The menu that appears is the menu for the form that currently has focus. For example, if the MDI parent form has focus, its menu will appear. If an MDI child form has focus, the menu for the MDI child form will appear. If no MDI child forms are active or the MDI child form does not have a menu, then the MDI parent form's menu appears. The menus for standard forms in an MDI program appear beneath the title bar of the standard form as usual. Thus, if a program contains one MDI parent form and two different MDI child forms, three menus could exist—one for each form. Which menu appears depends on which form is active.

In the completed example, the MDI parent form menu has only three options: create a new file, open an existing file, or exit the program. The menu for the MDI child form contains the New, Open, and Exit menu commands and additional commands pertaining to the MDI child form. This technique of structuring menus for MDI parent and child forms is important. In a typical MDI program, most of the operations pertain to a specific MDI child form, which appears whenever an instance of the child form receives focus. If no MDI child forms are loaded, the MDI parent form must allow the user to create an MDI child form (load a file in this case).

Menu commands common to both the MDI parent and child forms should have the same captions. Because the two menu commands of the same name perform the same task, you, as the programmer, typically create a general procedure in either the MDI parent form or a standard module and then call the general procedure from both menu commands. Using this technique, the two different menu commands will appear to the user as one command performing the same task.

You could implement the **Open** command in Perfect Programming Systems' program in two ways. The **Click** event procedures for the **Open** commands for both forms each need to call the same general procedure. The general procedure could be placed either in the MDI parent form or in a standard module. In this text editor, you will place the code on the MDI parent form, an approach that eliminates the need to create and load another module. The code should not be placed in the MDI child form, however. To understand why, consider the situation when the program first starts. Only the MDI parent form has been loaded. If the code were placed in the MDI child form, the form would need to be loaded before the code could be executed. This arrangement is not logical.

You now will modify an existing program so that it will work as an MDI program.

To create the MDI interface:

1. Start Visual Basic, and open the project Chapter.07\Startup\Ch7_S.vbp.

2. Click on Project, and then click on Add MDI Form to add an MDI parent form to the project. Select the existing form named Chapter.07\Startup\MDIText_S.frm. Click on Open. This form already has the menu interface created. In addition to the menu interface, the form contains instances of the ImageList and Toolbar controls. Chapter 6 discussed the use of these controls. Note that the prefix for an MDI form is "MDI" rather than "frm".

3. Open the Properties window for the form named **frmText**, and set the **MDIChild** property to **True**.

4. Open the Properties window for the form named **MDIText**, and set the **AutoShowChildren** property to **True**, if necessary.

5. Click on Project, and then click on Project1 Properties. Set the Startup object (the MDI parent form) to MDIText. Click on OK to close the dialog box.

6. Test the program. An instance of the MDI parent form should appear, but the MDI child form should not. The latter form does not appear because

no statement has executed to load an instance of it. Note that Visual Basic does not load the MDI child forms automatically.

7. Exit the program to return to design mode.

This program will be implemented such that an MDI child form will not appear until a file has been opened or a new form created. Ultimately, a new form instance must be created whenever the user opens a file or creates a new document. Before programming these commands, however, a more thorough discussion of form modules is warranted.

Forms As Classes

In an MDI program, the user commonly displays multiple instances of the same MDI child form. This process is analogous to creating multiple references to the same object or creating multiple instances of the same control. You have seen how to use the **Set** statement to assign object references, and the **New** keyword was mentioned briefly as a way to create new objects explicitly. In this chapter, the **New** keyword will be used when you create multiple instance of the same form.

Remember that every object is created from a class. That is, Visual Basic defines a command button class from which command button instances are created. Each instance of a command button created on a form has properties and can respond to events. A form or form module does not really differ from a control. A form is a class. When your code loads or displays a form on the screen, Visual Basic creates an instance of the form from the underlying class. Each form in the project is a distinct class, and the name of the class is defined by the form's **Name** property. The text editor created in this chapter has two form classes: **MDIText** and **frmText**. Once an instance of the form is created, you can read and write its properties and call the methods of the form. Thus multiple instances of the same form can be created much as multiple instances of the same control can be created.

In contrast, a standard module is not a class, and you do not create instances of a standard module. Consequently, there is one—and only one—copy of the data (**Public** and **Private** variables) for a standard module. That is, one copy of the **Public** and **Private** variables in a standard module exists for the life of the program. A unique copy of the data exists for each form instance that is created, however. Consequently, if the program loads two instances of an MDI child form, two copies of the child form's data exist. Note that the previous sentence used the term "loads" rather than "becomes visible" or "displays." When a form loads, Visual Basic allocates memory for the form, and your code can access the form's properties and methods even though the form is not visible. In the Perfect Programming Systems text editor, you could display a copy of the MDI child form by calling the child form's **Show** method through the following statements:

```
Private Sub MDIForm_Load()
    frmText.Show
End Sub
```

When the MDI parent form loads, the statement in the event procedure displays the MDI child form named frmText, and the child form receives focus. Exactly what happens when the **Show** method is called is important. When a form loads, Visual Basic creates a hidden variable having the same name as the form (class) as well as an instance of the form from the underlying class. Thus, when the program starts, the MDI parent form loads, causing the **MDIForm_Load** event to occur. The code in this event procedure explicitly loads and displays the form named frmText. Visual Basic creates an instance of both forms and then declares the equivalent of a **Public** variable for each form: the variable **MDIText** of type **MDIText** and the variable **frmText** of type **frmText**, respectively. Visual Basic declares these variables because their names will change anytime you change the value of the form's **Name** property. It is as if the following variable declarations had been made:

```
Public MDIText As MDIText
Public frmText As frmText
```

One other important point needs to be made about form properties. Assume that the MDI child form (frmText) has the following general declaration:

```
Public DocumentName As String
```

If a program created multiple instances of this form, then a separate copy of the variable **DocumentName** would exist for each form instance. This concept is significant. **Public** variables in a form module are actually properties of the form and are treated just like predefined form properties such as **Name, Top**, and **Left**. To demonstrate this concept, consider the following illegal declarations in a form module named **frmText**:

```
Public Name As frmText
Public Top As Integer
```

Every form has a predefined **Name** and **Top** property. The preceding declarations will cause the following compiler error: Member Already Exists In An Object Module From Which This Object Module Derives. When you create **Public** variables in a form module, the variables are considered properties that extend the predefined properties of the form. Syntactically, you reference these variables as properties.

The technique to create multiple instances of the same form differs slightly from the technique used to create a single form instance. This difference occurs because you must create object variables to reference each form instance. To illustrate this concept, consider the following statements to create two instances of the same form. To create a new form instance, you use the **New** keyword with the **Dim** or **Set** statement. Without the **New** keyword, the variable declaration creates an object variable that references Nothing.

```
Private Sub MDIForm_Load()
    Dim frmText1 As frmText, frmText2 As frmText
    Set frmText1 = New frmText
    Set frmText2 = New frmText
    frmText1.Show
    frmText2.Show
    frmText1.Caption = "One"
    frmText2.Caption = "Two"
    frmText1.DocumentName = "Document1"
    frmText2.DocumentName = "Document2"
End Sub
```

These statements declare two object variables named **frmText1** and **frmText2** to store references to form instances created from the **frmText** class. The two **Set** statements create two form instances and cause a reference to each form instance to be stored in the two object variables. Using the object variables, you can write code to set the form's properties, call its methods, and reference the control instances on the form. In this case, calling the **Show** method for each object variable causes two MDI child forms to appear inside the region of the MDI parent form. The **Caption** property is set for each instance.

In the previous statements, the **Public** variable **DocumentName** is a property of the **frmText** form class. Interestingly, **Public Function**, and **Public Sub** procedures in form modules are treated as methods of the form class. As such, the syntax to call the method matches the syntax to call the methods of any other object. Assuming that the **MDIText** class contained a **Public Sub** procedure named **CloseFile**, you would use the following statement to call it from the MDI child form or a standard module:

```
MDIText.CloseFile
```

Note that this syntax is the same as the syntax used to call any method or to read and write a property.

You can now write the code to create multiple instances of the same form.

To create multiple instances of an MDI child form:

1. Locate the **MDIForm_Load** event procedure on the MDI parent form (MDIText), and enter the following statements:

```
Dim frmText1 As frmText, frmText2 As frmText
Set frmText1 = New frmText
Set frmText2 = New frmText
frmText1.Show
frmText2.Show
frmText1.Caption = "One"
frmText2.Caption = "Two"
```

2. Test the program. Two form instances, as shown in Figure 7.2, appear with different captions.

3. End the program to return to design mode.

Although the preceding statements illustrate the concept of multiple form instances, they have serious limitations. No provision exists for the user to create form instances dynamically. Furthermore, the statements can create only two instances of the same form. To create additional form instances, you must declare additional object variables and use the **Set** statement to create the form instances.

To create multiple instances of the same form dynamically and keep track of those form instances, you can write code to create a dynamic array. It is the responsibility of the program's code to add and delete elements from the array as new form instances are created and destroyed. Adding elements to the array is

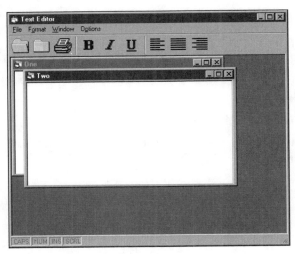

Figure 7.2 Multiple form instances.

a fairly simple task. Your code must increase the size of the array by one. Next, the code must create an instance of the form and store a reference to the form in the new array element. When the user closes a form, the form instance is destroyed, so the array element that references the form instance has no meaning. To delete the element from the array, you write code to shift the array elements. Your code must shift the array elements such that the last array element references the deleted form and then decreases the array size by one. An array of user-defined types, as follows, can simplify this process:

```
Private Type tDocType
    Active As Boolean
    frmCurrent As frmText
End Type
Private Docs() As tDocType
```

This user-defined type contains two members: a reference to the form object and a Boolean variable that indicates whether the array element is currently in use. When the user creates a form instance, you will write code so that **frmCurrent** will reference the newly created form and the Active flag will be set to True. When the user destroys the form instance, you will write code that will set **frmCurrent** to Nothing and set the Active flag to False. When the user creates a new form instance, the array can be searched to try to locate an inactive element. If one is found, the reference to the new form will be stored in an existing element. Otherwise, the size of the array would need to be increased by one. You could declare this array and the procedures to add and remove elements from the array, either in an MDI parent form or in a standard module. The process is somewhat analogous to creating your own collection.

In the Perfect Programming Systems text editor, you will declare and manage an array of MDI child form references on the MDI parent form. If you declared the array in the MDI child form, one copy of the array would exist for each loaded MDI child form, and no array would exist if no MDI child forms were loaded. Thus the array must be declared either in a standard module or in the MDI parent form.

To create an array to manage child forms:

1. Locate the general declarations section of the form module named MDIText, and enter the following statements:

```
Private Type tDoctype
        Active As Boolean
        frmCurrent As frmText
End Type
Private Docs() As tDoctype
```

2. In the MDIText form module, create the **GetFormIndex Function** procedure, and enter the following statements. This procedure is used to recycle an inactive array element or allocate a new element in the array. The function returns an **Integer** indicating the element used.

```
Private Function GetFormIndex()
    Dim pintDocCount As Integer, pintCurrent As Integer
    Dim pblnFound As Boolean
    pintDocCount = UBound(Docs)
    For pintCurrent = 1 To pintDocCount
        If Docs(pintCurrent).Active = False Then
            pblnFound = True
            Exit For
        End If
    Next
    If Not pblnFound Then
        pintCurrent = pintDocCount + 1
        ReDim Preserve Docs(pintCurrent)
    End If
    With Docs(pintCurrent)
        Set .frmCurrent = New frmText
        .frmCurrent.Tag = pintCurrent
        .frmCurrent.Show
        .Active = True
    End With
    GetFormIndex = pintCurrent
End Function
```

3. Create the **NewFile Sub** procedure on the MDI parent form; this procedure calls **GetFormIndex**. Using the index of the newly allocated form, the **Caption** property is set to the text New Document. Note that the **NewFile** procedure is declared as **Public** because it will be called by both the MDI parent form and the MDI child form. Enter the following statements:

```
Public Sub NewFile()
    Dim pintCurrentDoc As Integer
    pintCurrentDoc = GetFormIndex()
    Docs(pintCurrentDoc).frmCurrent.Caption = _
            "New Document"
End Sub
```

4. In the **mnuFileNew_Click** event procedure for the MDI parent form, enter the following statement to call the general procedure:

```
Call NewFile
```

5. In the **mnuFileNew_Click** event procedure for the MDI child form named **frmText**, enter the following statement to call the general procedure:

```
MDIText.NewFile
```

6. In the **MDIForm_Load** event procedure for the form named MDI Text, replace the existing statements with the following statement to initialize the array when the MDI parent form is first loaded.

```
ReDim Docs(0)
```

7. Test the program. On the menu bar, click on File, and then click on New. Do this several times. Notice that a new instance of the MDI child form is created each time.

8. End the program to return to design mode.

These procedures and statements require careful analysis. The **Function** procedure **GetFormIndex** performs most of the processing. It returns the index of the array element allocated to the new form. The procedure also decides whether to recycle an existing array element or to redimension the array.

```
pintDocCount = UBound(Docs)
```

The preceding statement retrieves the largest array subscript. This value is then used in the following **For** loop:

```
For pintCurrent = 1 To pintDocCount
    If Docs(pintCurrent).Active = False Then
        pblnFound = True
        Exit For
    End If
Next
```

The **For** loop examines each element in the array to determine whether an unused array element exists (that is, an element with the Active flag set to False). If an unused element is found, the code uses that element as the index into the array. In a moment, you will create the code to set this flag to False whenever a form instance is closed. The variable **pblnFound** is used to determine whether an unused array element was found, as shown in the following **If** statement:

```
If Not pblnFound Then
    pintCurrent = pintDocCount + 1
    ReDim Preserve Docs(pintCurrent)
End If
```

If the code does not find an unused element, the preceding statements create a new array element and set the new element to the current element.

```
With Docs(pintCurrent)
    Set .frmCurrent = New frmText
    .frmCurrent.Tag = pintCurrent
    .frmCurrent.Show
    .Active = True
End With
GetFormIndex = pintCurrent
```

7

The preceding statements create the new form instance and store a reference to it in the current array element. Remember that this array holds user-defined types, so the form reference is stored in the **frmCurrent** member of the type. Note that the **New** keyword causes the creation of the form instance.

The use of the **Tag** property in the previous statements will become apparent later in the chapter. For now, it is enough to say that the program uses the **Tag** property as a mechanism to identify the current form; the value of the **Tag** property is the same as the index in the array. The final two statements in the **With** block display the form and set the Active flag to True, indicating that the array element is in use and that the element references a form instance. The last statement in the procedure returns the index to the array of forms so that it can be used by the calling procedure, if necessary.

Consider the following code for the **NewFile** general procedure:

```
Dim pintCurrentDoc As Integer
pintCurrentDoc = GetFormIndex()
Docs(pintCurrentDoc).frmCurrent.Caption = _
    "New Document"
```

The **NewFile Sub** procedure calls the **GetFormIndex** function and sets the caption of the new form. This implementation could be expanded to include a number next to the text (for example, "New Document 1," "New Document 2"). The syntax that will reference the **Caption** property of the current form—**Docs(pintCurrentDoc).frmCurrent.Caption**—provides the reference to the current form. The reason for separating code into the **NewFile** and

GetFormIndex procedures is that the code you will write to open an existing file will also call the **GetFormIndex** function, but will include additional code that executes when the user specifies a file to open. The form's caption will be set to the file name instead of the constant text "New Document."

Finally, you call the **NewFile** procedure in the menu commands for both the MDI parent and child forms. The only time the menu for the MDI parent form appears is when no open MDI child forms are loaded. Otherwise, the menu for the MDI child form appears. Thus the two different Open menus will have the same effect and appear to the user as if the two commands were identical. When called from the MDI child form, the following syntax is used:

```
MDIText.NewFile
```

You must explicitly reference the MDI parent form. Otherwise, Visual Basic would not know where to look for the **NewFile** procedure. Remember that you are calling a method of the MDI parent form.

At this point, you know how to create form instances. Now you will learn how to destroy those form instances.

Destroying Form Instances

Unloading MDI parent and child forms introduces additional complexity beyond that found in a single-form application. In the Perfect Programming Systems text editor, the program keeps track of which elements in the Docs array store a reference to an active form. So, when either the user or the program code closes an instance of the MDI child form, your code must update the array accordingly. That is, the form element must reference Nothing and the Active flag should be set to False. Additionally, the program will determine whether the contents of the rich text box have changed since the file was last saved; if so, it will prompt the user to confirm that the changes should be discarded.

Creating a successful MDI program requires an understanding of the events that occur when forms are unloaded and the order in which those events take place. When an MDI child form instance or standard form instance is unloaded, two events occur for each form instance. The **QueryUnload** event occurs just before the form is unloaded. This event takes an argument, *cancel*, that, if set to **True**, cancels the subsequent **Unload** event. If the **QueryUnload** event does not set the *cancel* argument to **True**, the **Unload** event will occur.

Syntax
Private Sub Form_QueryUnload(*cancel* As Integer, *unloadmode* As Integer)
Private Sub MDIForm_QueryUnload(*cancel* As Integer, *unloadmode* As Integer)
Private Sub *object*_Unload(*cancel* As Integer)

Dissection

➤ The **QueryUnload** event occurs when an attempt is made to unload a form, typically as a result of calling the **Unload** statement.

➤ The **Unload** event occurs after the **QueryUnload** event, but only if the **QueryUnload** event was not canceled. The **Unload** event can also be canceled. It must contain a reference to an MDI parent, child, or standard form.

➤ The *cancel* argument, if set to **True**, causes subsequent **QueryUnload** or **Unload** events to be canceled.

➤ The **unloadmode** argument contains a constant indicating what caused the event to occur. For example, the event may take place because the user clicked the Close button on the Control box, Windows is shutting down, or some other cause. Refer to the **QueryUnload** event Help page for a complete list of constants.

Code Example

```
Private Sub MDIForm_QueryUnload(Cancel As Integer, _
    UnloadMode As Integer)
    If UnloadMode = vbFormControlMenu Then
        Cancel = True
    End If
End Sub
```

Code Dissection

These statements use the **UnloadMode** argument to determine whether the user clicked the Close button on the control menu to cause the event. If so, the event is canceled.

 These events occur for both the MDI parent form, when an attempt is made to unload this form, and for each instance of the MDI child form, when it is unloaded.

The **Unload** events take place in the following order when an attempt is made to unload the instance of the MDI parent form:

1. The **QueryUnload** event pertaining to the MDI parent form occurs first. This event supports the *cancel* argument. If set to *True*, all remaining **QueryUnload** and **Unload** events for both MDI parent and child forms are canceled.

2. If the **QueryUnload** event is not canceled for the MDI parent form, the **QueryUnload** event occurs for each MDI child form. This event can also be canceled. If one of the form instances sets the *cancel* argument to **True**,

no more **QueryUnload** events will occur for the MDI child forms and all **Unload** events for the MDI child and parent forms will be canceled.

3. If none of the **QueryUnload** events for the MDI child forms was canceled, the **Unload** event occurs for each MDI child form. If one MDI child form cancels the **Unload** event, the **Unload** events for all subsequent MDI child forms and the MDI parent form will be canceled.

4. The **Unload** event occurs for the MDI parent form if, and only if, none of the **QueryUnload** or **Unload** events was canceled.

In the Perfect Programming Systems text editor, the **QueryUnload** event for the MDI child forms will confirm with the user whether to discard changes for the current form. If the user does not want to discard the changes, the event will be canceled. Otherwise, the **Unload** event(s) will occur. The **Unload** event procedure for the MDI child form calls a general procedure to update the array that manages the MDI child forms. This update causes the Active flag to be set, thereby indicating that the element is not currently in use. It also causes the reference to the form to be destroyed for the proper array element. In addition, the **QueryUnload** event procedure for the MDI parent form will display a message box asking the user whether to exit the program.

To program the **QueryUnload** and **Unload** events for the MDI parent and child forms:

1. The statements in the **MDIForm_QueryUnload** event procedure will execute when an attempt is made to exit the program. The code causes a message box to appear and asks for confirmation before the program exits. If the user responds No to the message box, the event is canceled and no further attempt is made to unload any of the MDI child forms. Enter the following statements in the **MDIForm_QueryUnload** event procedure for the MDI parent form:

```
Dim pintReturn As Integer
pintReturn = MsgBox("Really Exit", vbYesNo + _
    vbQuestion)
If pintReturn = vbNo Then
    Cancel = True
End If
```

2. To cause the MDI parent form to be unloaded from either the MDI parent or child form, enter the following statement in the **mnuFileExit_Click** procedure for the MDI parent form. Enter the same statement in the **mnuFileExit_Click** event procedure for the MDI child form.

```
Unload MDIText
```

The **Form_QueryUnload** event procedure occurs when an attempt is made to close an instance of the MDI child form. It also occurs for all MDI child forms when an attempt is made to close the MDI parent form. The code uses the variable **Dirty** to determine whether the contents of the rich text box have changed. You will have the opportunity to see how the value of this variable is set. If an MDI child form instance contains unsaved changes, a message box is displayed, requesting confirmation before unloading the form. Again, the code uses the *cancel* argument to cancel the event, depending on the user's response.

3. Enter the following statements in the **Form_QueryUnload** event procedure for the MDI child form (**frmText**):

```
Dim pintReturn As Integer
If Dirty Then
    pintReturn = MsgBox("Abandon Changes", _
        vbYesNo + vbQuestion)
    If pintReturn = vbNo Then
        Cancel = True
    End If
End If
```

4. The **Form_Unload** event procedure occurs if the code did not cancel the **QueryUnload** events. The statement in the event procedure calls the **CloseFile** general procedure to make the necessary changes to the Docs array. The code in the **CloseFile** procedure sets the members of the array element such that the element does not reference an active form instance. Enter the following statement in the **Form_Unload** event procedure for the form named frmText:

```
MDIText.CloseFile Me
```

5. On the MDI parent form named MDIText, create the **CloseFile** general procedure and enter the following statements (note that the **CloseFile** procedure accepts one argument, a reference to an MDI child form):

```
Public Sub CloseFile(frm As frmText)
    Dim pintCurrent As Integer
    pintCurrent = frm.Tag
    Docs(pintCurrent).Active = False
    Unload frm
    Set Docs(pintCurrent).frmCurrent = Nothing
End Sub
```

7

6. Test the program. Create multiple instances of the MDI child forms by using the **New** command on the File menu. Change the contents of each MDI child form. Click on the **Exit** command on the File menu, which should cause the **QueryUnload** event to occur first for the MDI parent form. Click on the Yes button in the message box to continue. The **QueryUnload** event should then occur for each MDI child form.

7. Click on Yes to abandon the changes for each form. Because none of the **QueryUnload** events was canceled, the forms are unloaded and the program exits.

The code for the **QueryUnload** and **Unload** event procedures is relatively simple. A message box is displayed and, depending on the user's response, the event is or is not canceled. The code for the **CloseFile** general procedure requires careful examination. First, consider the procedure declaration:

```
Public Sub CloseFile(frm As frmText)
```

This procedure accepts one argument—"frm", a reference to the MDI child form to be unloaded. Now consider the statement to read the value of the **Tag** property for the current form:

```
pintCurrent = frm.Tag
```

Remember that you set the **Tag** property when an instance of the form was created. The value of this property contains an **Integer** representing the index in the Docs array on the MDI parent form. The statement calling the **CloseFile** procedure passes a reference to the current form as an argument to the general procedure, and the **CloseFile** procedure uses the **Tag** property to determine the desired array element.

```
Unload frm
Docs(pintCurrent).Active = False
```

The preceding statements unload the form and indicate that the array element is not in use. Remember that this value (Active) is used to reallocate an array element that is not currently in use when a new file is created or an existing file opened.

```
Set Docs(pintCurrent).frmCurrent = Nothing
```

This statement explicitly destroys the reference to the form. At this point in the program's development, your code can create form instances and destroy them. It can also keep track of the form instances. The previously presented technique for managing multiple form instances is but one option available to the programmer, however.

OTHER WAYS TO KEEP TRACK OF FORMS

In addition to using an array to manage multiple form instances, Visual Basic supports objects to help you manage the loaded forms in a program. These objects include the **Me** keyword, the **Forms** collection, and the Screen object.

The **Me** Keyword

The **Me** keyword is a global variable that represents the current instance of a class. Because a form is a class, your code can always reference the active form using the **Me** keyword. The **Me** keyword is a useful tool for passing a reference to the active form instance to a general procedure. You have seen the **Me** keyword used in previous chapters as a way to unload the current form. Consider the following event procedure, which sets the **Visible** property for all control instances on the current form to **True**:

```
Dim ctl As Control
For Each ctl in Me.Controls
    ctl.Visible = True
Next
```

The **Forms** Collection

The **Forms** collection works like the **Controls** collection. It contains a reference to each of the loaded forms. The **Forms** collection treats each instance of a form class as a separate form in the **Forms** collection. If a form has not been loaded, no entry for the form in the collection exists. Forms that are loaded and not visible can be referenced using the **Forms** collection.

This program creates several instances of the same form. Each form instance has an entry in the **Forms** collection. Iterating through the **Forms** collection is useful when the same operation should be performed for all active forms or for all active forms having the same class. In the Perfect Programming Systems text editor, a Save All function will save all unsaved files automatically. The following generic loop could be used to save the data associated with all forms having the class **frmText**:

```
Private Sub mnuFileSaveAll_Click()
    Dim frm As Form
    For Each frm In Forms
        If TypeOf frm Is frmText Then
            If frm.Caption = "New Document" Then
                SaveFile Me
            Else
                frm.rtfText.SaveFile frm.Caption
            End If
```

```
        End If
    Next
End Sub
```

This loop iterates through all the Form objects in the **Forms** collection. If the type of the form is frmText, the form may contain data that should be saved. The **Caption** property contains either the name of the file or the text "New Document" if the file has never been saved. If the file has not been saved, the **Click** event procedure calls the **SaveFile** procedure (described later in this chapter). The **If** statement uses the **TypeOf** statement to test that the form is a member of the **frmText** class. This approach prevents the **SaveFile** procedure from being called for the MDI parent form. This test is necessary because it makes no sense to save the MDI parent form, as this form does not correspond to a file.

The Screen Object

The Screen object supports properties to determine the active form instance or the active control instance. The Screen object has the following properties:

Syntax

> Screen

Properties

➤ The **ActiveForm** and **ActiveControl** properties identify the form and control instance having focus, respectively.

➤ The **Fonts** property contains an array of strings listing the fonts for the currently selected display device.

➤ The programmer typically uses the **Fonts** property with the **FontCount** property, which contains the number of fonts supported by the display device. Thus the Fonts array has index values ranging from zero (0) to FontCount minus one (-1).

➤ The programmer uses the **MouseIcon** and **MousePointer** properties to change the appearance of the mouse pointer. In addition to the Screen object, these properties affect the Form object and visible control instances that can receive focus. Refer to the MousePointer Property Help topic for a list of the valid constants representing the different mouse pointers.

The uses of the Screen object are quite varied because the object reflects the state of the program as managed by the operating system (Windows). Through the Screen object, you obtain information from Windows about which control and form instance have focus and how the mouse pointer appears on that form. Windows manages the fonts residing on the system. The fonts can be determined using the Screen object.

When using Word and other Windows programs, you may have seen a list box containing fonts, which is used to set the font of selected text. This functionality can be duplicated in a Visual Basic program by loading the available fonts into a list or combo box. Assuming that cboFonts is a valid instance of a combo box, the following **For** loop will load the available fonts into the combo box:

```
Dim pintCount As Integer
For pintCount = 0 To Screen.FontCount - 1
      cboFonts.AddItem Screen.Fonts(pintCount)
Next
```

The preceding loop iterates from zero to Screen.FontCount − 1. The variable **pintCount** is then used as an index into the Fonts array.

The Fonts array is not a collection. Thus a **For Each** loop cannot be used to examine the elements of the array.

You also can use the Screen object to change the appearance of the mouse pointer when the insertion point is positioned over a form or a particular control instance. For example, you may write code to change the appearance of the mouse pointer to an hourglass while the program is performing a lengthy operation that cannot be interrupted. Changing the cursor appearance provides a visual clue to the user that the program cannot accept input. In the Perfect Programming Systems program, reading or writing a large file may take more than a second or two, so changing the mouse pointer during these operations will improve the user interface. For a list of the valid mouse pointers, refer to the Mouse Pointer Constants Help topic. Using a progress bar to display the relative completion of loading the file would also be a suitable option.

Consider the following statements to change the appearance of the mouse pointer:

```
Private Sub cmdLong_Click()
    Screen.MousePointer = vbHourglass
    For plngCurrent = 1 To 1000000
        ' Statements
    Next
    Screen.MousePointer = vbNormal
End Sub
```

This event procedure illustrates how to change the mouse pointer in a long-running procedure. When the procedure begins, the mouse pointer is set to an hourglass; it is restored to normal when the procedure finishes.

In addition to displaying multiple instances of the same MDI child form, you can write code to arrange them on the screen.

Arranging MDI Forms

As mentioned, MDI child forms can be moved around the region of the MDI parent form. You also can write code to call the **Arrange** method pertaining to the MDI parent form to arrange the open MDI child forms or to manipulate the icons.

Syntax

> object.**Arrange** arrangement

Dissection

➤ The **Arrange** method organizes the open and iconified MDI child forms.

➤ The required *object* must be an instance of an MDI parent form.

➤ The required ***arrangement*** argument can contain one of several constants. If the argument is set to **vbCascade**, all open MDI child forms are cascaded. The constant values **vbTileHorizontal** and **vbTileVertical** cause the MDI child forms to be organized horizontally and vertically, respectively. The constant value **vbArrangeIcons** causes the minimized child forms to be arranged across the bottom of the form.

Code Example

> MDIText.Arrange vbTileHorizontal

Code Dissection

The previous statement arranges the open MDI child windows so that each occupies the width of the MDI parent window. Each MDI child window has the same vertical size.

In the text editor form, the Window menu title contains four commands to demonstrate the four possible arrangements of the MDI child forms. The code will accomplish this task by using a control array. The index of the control array elements corresponds to one of the four constant values used to define the desired arrangement. Consider the following event procedure to arrange the MDI child forms:

```
Private Sub mnuArrange_Click(Index As Integer)
    MDIText.Arrange Index
End Sub
```

This code has already been written and the menu commands have been created. You can run the program to see the effect of the different arrangements.

In addition to the previously described methods to arrange MDI child forms, Visual Basic supports a unique type of menu called a WindowList. One menu command on a menu can have the **WindowList** property set to **True**. At run time, selecting this menu displays another menu listing all loaded MDI child forms. At design time, checking the WindowList checkbox in the menu editor identifies the menu that will act as the window list menu.

To test the **Arrange** method:

1. Test the program, and create three different MDI child windows.

2. Click on Window, and then click on Tile Horizontal. The windows are tiled horizontally.

3. Click on Window, click on Tile Vertical, and then click on Cascade to see the effect of these arrangement options.

4. Minimize the MDI child forms by clicking on their Minimize buttons. Drag the icons around the MDI parent form, click on Window, and then click on Arrange Icons to arrange the icons across the bottom of the form.

5. Click on Window, and then highlight List. Notice that all MDI child form instances are displayed. Clicking on one of the commands will activate the respective form.

6. End the program to return to design mode.

This section introduced the techniques of working with MDI programs and multiple instances of the same form. These techniques of creating, destroying, and keeping track of form instances apply to every MDI program that you create.

PROGRAMMING THE RICHTEXTBOX, COMMONDIALOG, AND TOOLBAR CONTROLS

You have learned how to manage the MDI parent and child forms. Now, you will examine the specific control instances created on the forms.

Reading And Writing Files With The RichTextBox Control

At the core of the text editor in this chapter is the RichTextBox control, which is a superset of the intrinsic TextBox control that you have used previously. The RichTextBox control is an ActiveX control, so it must be added explicitly to the project before it can be used. The file richtx32.ocx stores the code for the control. The rich text box supports properties and methods to apply formatting to text, including setting fonts and font attributes.

The rich text box has a standardized file format called Rich Text Format (RTF). Embedded inside RTF files are formatting directives. The rich text box does not display these directives; rather, the control instance interprets the directives to perform a desired formatting task. Figure 7.3 shows a short RTF file with formatting directives.

As shown in Figure 7.3, directives specify the font, font size, and font attributes. The text displayed in the control instance is embedded in the directives. Fortunately, you, as the programmer, do not have to worry about these directives. Rather, the rich text box interprets these directives automatically. In addition, when formatting is applied to specific text, the rich text box stores the relevant directives in the file. The rich text box can read and write ordinary text files as well as process rich text files. The text shown in Figure 7.3 appears formatted in Figure 7.4.

One function supported by the rich text box is the capability to read and write files using two methods supported by the control. Instead of writing code to open, read or write, and then close a file, all necessary functionality is built into the RichTextBox control itself.

Syntax

> object.**LoadFile** pathname[, filetype]
> object.**SaveFile** pathname[, filetype]

Dissection

➤ The required *object* must be a valid instance of a RichTextBox control.

➤ The **LoadFile** and **SaveFile** methods read and write text and RTF files to and from a rich text box, respectively.

➤ The required *pathname* argument contains the folder and file name of the file to be read or written.

➤ The optional *filetype* argument can contain one of two constants. If set to **rtfRTF**, the control instance loads the file as an RTF file and applies the formatting directives. If set to **rtfText**, the control instance interprets the file as a plain text file. If the *filetype* argument is omitted, **rtfRTF** is assumed.

Code Example
```
rtfText.LoadFile "A:\Chapter.07\Demo.rtf"
rtfText.SaveFile "A:\Chapter.07\Demo.rtf"
```

Code Dissection

The previous statements assume that the object rtfText is a valid instance of a RichTextBox control. The standard prefix for the rich text box is "rtf." The two statements load and save the file named Demo.rtf, respectively. The control instance interprets the file as an RTF file because no **filetype** argument is specified.

Until now, you have used two techniques to read or write a file. Either the file name has been coded explicitly in the statement, as shown in the previous examples, or the user entered a path and file name in an input box. Although both of these techniques work, specifying a file name in an input box makes for a rather primitive user interface. In this chapter, you will improve the program's user interface by providing dialogs that use the same interface as do programs like Word and Excel. The control that provides this interface is called the CommonDialog control.

Opening And Saving Files With The CommonDialog Control

The CommonDialog control is an ActiveX control that allows a Visual Basic program to access the Windows library that provides a standard way to open and save files, print files, change fonts, and access the Help system. The file comdlg32.ocx contains the code for the CommonDialog control. The code in this file, in turn, calls the library routines contained in the Windows system library named comdlg32.dll. The result is a standard interface to open and save files.

The common dialog box is not a visible control. That is, the user does not click on the object drawn on the form to interact with the control instance. Rather, a dialog box appears when, at run time, your code calls the methods supported by the CommonDialog control. The standard prefix for the CommonDialog control is "cdl". Your code can display six standard dialogs, which correspond to the six different methods supported by the CommonDialog control.

Although the common dialog box supports several properties, most of these properties pertain to a specific dialog box (method). This restriction makes

```
{\rtf1\ansi\deff0\deftab720{\fonttbl{\f0\fswiss MS Sans Serif;}{\f1\froman\fcharset2 Symbol;}{\f2\fswiss MS Sans
Serif;}}
{\colortbl\red0\green0\blue0;}
\deflang1033\pard\plain\f2\fs17 This is \plain\f2\fs17\b Bold\plain\f2\fs17  text.
\par }
```

Figure 7.3   RTF file.

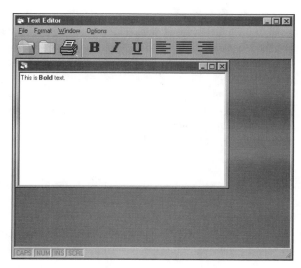

Figure 7.4   RTF file in a rich text box.

sense, as the properties related to selecting a font have nothing to do with the properties for opening a file. Few properties pertain to all dialogs.

Syntax

      CommonDialog

Properties

➤ Each dialog box has at least two command buttons. One button, which has the caption Cancel, is used to communicate to your program that the user does not want to perform the desired action. You set the **CancelError** property to control what happens when the user presses the Cancel button on the dialog box. The other button is used to indicate that the desired action should be performed.

➤ The **DialogTitle** property contains the string that appears on the title bar of the dialog box when it is displayed. If a value is not assigned explicitly to this property, the title contains a brief generic caption, such as "Open" or "Print."

➤ You set the **Flags** property with all dialogs to customize their behavior. For example, you can use different flags to prohibit the user from changing directories when the Open and Save As dialogs are displayed. Flags may also return additional information about the state of the dialog box when it was closed.

➤ The **Left** and **Top** properties determine where the dialog box appears when it is displayed.

Methods

➤ The **ShowColor** method displays the Color dialog box, which allows the user to select existing colors or define custom colors.

➤ The **ShowFont** method displays the Font dialog box, which allows the user to select fonts and font attributes such as bold, italic, and underline.

➤ The **ShowHelp** method allows your program to activate the Help system.

➤ The **ShowOpen** method displays a dialog box that allows the user to navigate through different folders to select a file to be opened.

➤ The **ShowSave** method displays a dialog box much like the Open dialog box. The dialog box allows the user to locate a folder and specify a file to be saved.

➤ The **ShowPrinter** method displays the Print dialog box, which allows the user to select a printer, number of copies to print, and other printing characteristics.

When your code calls one of the Common Dialog box methods, the corresponding dialog box appears. That is, the Print dialog box appears on the screen when the **ShowPrinter** method is called, the Save As dialog box appears when your code calls the **ShowSave** method, and so on.

> Your code can also call the Common Dialog box methods by setting the value of the **Action** property. The **Action** property provides backward compatibility with older versions of Visual Basic. Older versions of Visual Basic had limitations on their ability to call methods, so the functionality was accomplished by setting the value of a property, typically called **Action**.

The common dialog box does not actually open, save, or print files. Likewise, it does not set the fonts or colors of text explicitly. Rather, when your code displays a specific dialog box, the user selects options from the dialog box, such as a file name or a font and its attributes. When the user closes the dialog box, properties and/or flags pertaining to the dialog box are set. The code in a program must then use these properties as needed. For example, if the user should be able to change the font of a text box, you could display the Font dialog box by calling the **ShowFont** method. After the dialog box is closed, you would need to explicitly set the desired font properties of the text box based on the common dialog box's property settings. This approach must be employed for all dialogs supported by the common dialog box. That is, the common dialog box does not actually perform the desired task, but rather sets specific properties that can then be used by your program to perform that task.

Using the common dialog box to open and save files, to set fonts and colors, and to print output helps to create a user interface that is consistent with other Windows programs. Consider using this control for all these operations.

In previous chapters, you used the message box and input box dialogs to display messages and to get text from the user. In both cases, modal dialogs were used. That is, the user could not interact with the other forms in the program until the dialog box was closed. The dialogs that appear when the methods pertaining to the common dialog box are called are also modal.

To control the behavior of dialogs displayed by the CommonDialog control, you need to understand the **CancelError** property.

Understanding The **CancelError** Property

Every dialog box displayed by the CommonDialog control contains two command buttons. The user clicks on one button to indicate to the program that the desired action should be performed. The user clicks on the other button, which has "Cancel" as its caption, to signify that the task should not be performed. For example, imagine that the user wanted to open a file. In this case, your code would display the Open dialog box by calling the **ShowOpen** method. After displaying the dialog box, however, suppose the user determined that the file did not already exist or that the file could not be found. In this situation, the user would click on the Cancel button on the dialog box to indicate that a file should not be opened and that the operation should be canceled.

The behavior of the Cancel button depends on the value of the common dialog box's **CancelError** property. If the **CancelError** property is set to **True**, the CommonDialog control instance will generate a run-time error, which your program can then trap. If set to **False**, no run-time error is generated. Examine the following event procedure:

```
Private Sub Command1_Click()
On Error GoTo Cancel_Error
    cd11.CancelError = True
    cd11.ShowOpen
    ' Code to open file
    Exit Sub
Cancel_Error:
End Sub
```

This **Click** event procedure contains an error handler that simply traps the error and exits the current procedure. The first executable statement sets the **CancelError** property to **True**, causing a run-time error to occur if the user clicks on the Cancel button on the CommonDialog control instance. The **ShowOpen** method is then called. If no error occurs, the code to open the file will execute, and the event procedure will exit. Otherwise, execution will continue following the **Cancel_Error** label. Thus no attempt will be made to open a file. All dialogs supported by the CommonDialog control use this technique.

In all procedures that display a common dialog box, an error handler should be written and the **CancelError** property set to **True**. This approach is the only way that the program can be notified that the user wants to abort the current action. Imagine the user's reaction if he or she did not actually want to print a 1,000-page file, but the file prints anyway.

Now that you know how to use the **CancelError** property, you can create the code to display the Open dialog box, allowing the user to select a file to open.

Opening Files With The CommonDialog Control

The CommonDialog control supports two nearly identical dialogs: one opens a file by name, and the other saves a file by name. Programmatically, the two dialogs operate the same way. You set properties to define the initial folder, default file name, and other information, and then call a method to show the dialog box on the screen. After the code calls the method, subsequent code reads a property containing the file name specified by the user; it then uses this name to open or save the file. Figure 7.5 shows the Open dialog box.

As shown in Figure 7.5, the Open dialog box contains a list box from which to select a file and a button with which to change the current folder. The dialog box also contains buttons with which to change the current view in the list portion of the dialog box. These views are equivalent to the list and report views provided for the ListView control. The Files of type list box is used to restrict the files displayed to those having a specific file extension. Ultimately, the File name text box will hold the name of the file to be opened.

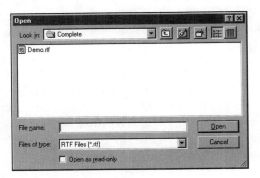

Figure 7.5   Open dialog box.

You can set the properties pertaining to an instance of the CommonDialog control by using the Property Pages or by writing code. As with other ActiveX controls, you can use the Property Pages to set the design-time properties. A Property Page tab exists for each different dialog box, with the exception of the Open and Save As dialogs. Because they are nearly identical and use the same properties, these two dialogs' properties are set using the same Property Page tab.

Consider a complex program where the common dialog box is used to open and save files of different types, and you perform other operations such as printing files and setting fonts. Your code commonly sets the properties pertaining to the specific dialog box and then calls the appropriate method to display the dialog box. Multiple forms can share this instance of the Common Dialog box control. Thus one instance of the CommonDialog control instance can be used for all operations, which reduces the amount of memory needed by the program.

When your code calls the **ShowOpen** and **ShowSave** methods, the Open and Save As dialogs are displayed.

➤ **DefaultExt property** Will set or return the default file extension for the dialog box. As you know, most file types have a default file extension. For example, text files have an extension of ".txt" and RTF files have an extension of ".rtf".

➤ **FileName property** Contains the name of the file selected by the user. The full path name, including drive, directory, and file name, is stored in this property. Setting this property before displaying the dialog box is useful for specifying a default file name.

➤ **FileTitle property** Contains the name of the file with the drive and path information removed.

➤ **Filter property** Used to control the file extensions that will be displayed in the dialog box. The **Filter** property will be discussed in more detail in this chapter.

➤ **FilterIndex property** Used in conjunction with the **Filter** property to identify the default filter. Filters are one-based. That is, the first filter has a **FilterIndex** property of one (1), the second filter has a **FilterIndex** property of two (2), and so on.

➤ **Flags property** As it pertains to the Open and Save As dialogs, this is used to determine how the user will perform directory and file selection. For example, you can use the **Flags** property to prohibit users from creating, changing, and deleting directories. You can also set the **Flags** property to allow the user to select multiple files. Refer to the Flags Property (Open, Save As Dialogs) Help topic for a more complete list of the valid flags.

➤ **InitDir property** Used to specify an initial directory to look for or to save files. If the **Flag cdlNoChangeDir** is set, the user cannot change the directory.

One of the most difficult tasks when using the **ShowOpen** method is setting the **Filter** and **FilterIndex** properties. Although not essential to displaying the Open dialog box, these properties can significantly improve the user interface by displaying only files with a specific extension. This constraint reduces clutter in the list portion of the common dialog box.

Most files have a three-character file extension to identify the file's type. For example, Jet database files have the file extension ".mdb" and Word files have the extension ".doc". Similarly, if your program uses files of a specific type, these files should have a standardized file extension. The files displayed in the common dialog box can be restricted to those having a specific extension or extensions. That is, you can create multiple filters such that the user can select one of the filters at run time. In the Perfect Programming Systems text editor, you will create filters to display text files or RTF files. A filter consists of a description, followed by a vertical bar (|), followed by the filter. Separating each filter with a vertical bar (|) creates multiple filters.

Syntax

   object.**Filter [=** description1 | filter1 | description2 | filter2 ... **]**

Dissection

➤ The *object* must be a valid instance of the CommonDialog control.

➤ The **Filter** property contains the text string that will be used as the filter.

➤ The *description* contains descriptive text that identifies the file type.

➤ The *filter* contains the three-character file extension of the filter preceded by the *. characters.

➤ Vertical bars separate filters and descriptions. Use care not to embed spaces between the vertical bars. These characters will be embedded either into the description or the filter itself, which generally is not desirable.

Code Example

```
cdlText.Filter = "Documents (*.doc)|*.doc|" & _
    "Rich Text (*.rtf)|*.rtf|All Files (*.*)|*.*"
cdlText.FilterIndex = 2
cdlText.ShowOpen
```

Code Dissection

In the preceding example, three filters are defined. The first filter displays files with the extension ".doc", the second displays files with the extension ".rtf", and the final filter displays all files in the current folder. By setting the **FilterIndex** property to two (2), the default filter is ".rtf" (the second filter). After setting the **Filter** and **FilterIndex** properties, the code calls the **ShowOpen** method to display the dialog box.

As shown in the previous filter, each description contains text followed by the file extension in parentheses [that is, (*.doc)]. This standard nomenclature for descriptions should be used so that the user is aware of the actual file extension, because the filter itself is not displayed in the dialog box. For example, consider the following filter:

```
cdlText.Filter = "Documents|*.doc|" & _
"Rich Text|*.rtf|All Files|*.*"
```

This filter does not display the file extensions as part of the filter. Also, you should usually include the *.* (All Files) filter in case the user accidentally changes the extension of a file.

The filter shown in the tip has the same effect as the filter shown in the syntax code example. The user will not see the actual file extensions displayed in the Files of type list box, however, making the interface less intuitive.

In addition to the filter, several flags pertain to the Open and Save As dialogs. You use these flags to define whether the user can navigate through the different folders or select files that do not already exist. The following flags pertain to the Open and Save As dialogs:

➤ **cdlOFNAllowMultiselect** Using Word and many other programs, the user can select multiple files in the Open dialog box. Each file selected is then opened as a separate document. If the flag **cdlOFNAllowMultiselect** is set, the common dialog box will return multiple files in the **FileName** property. The CommonDialog control lists the files such that the full path name is displayed in the string, followed by a space, followed by each of the file names separated by spaces. The programmer must then develop the code to break up the string into the individual file names and open them.

➤ **cdlOFNExplorer** By default, the common dialog box uses an interface that is similar to the Windows Explorer program. If the flag **cdlOFNExplorer** is set, the Windows Explorer style interface is used. Otherwise, an interface reminiscent of the Windows 3.1 Open File dialog box is used.

➤ **cdlOFNFileMustExist** If the flag **cdlOFNFileMustExist** is set, the user must specify an existing file. If it is not set, the user can specify files that do not exist. If the user attempts to enter a nonexistent file, the control instance displays a dialog box containing a warning message.

➤ **cdlOFNNoChangeDir** If the flag **cdlOFNNoChangeDir** is set, the user can open or save files only in the initial directory, which cannot be changed. This flag is useful when you want to restrict the user to locating and saving files to a particular folder.

➤ **cdlOFNOverwritePrompt** The flag **cdlOFNOverwritePrompt** is used by the Save As dialog box. If this flag is set, the user will be prompted if he or she specifies an existing file.

Adding the values of the different flags and storing the result in the **Flags** property is the technique used to combine flags. For example, consider the following statement:

```
cdlText.Flags = cdlOFNExplorer + cdlOFNFileMustExist
```

This statement causes the dialog box to be displayed using the Windows Explorer style interface. Also, the user must select an existing file. In the Perfect Programming Systems text editor, the common dialog box will be used to open files with the extension ".txt" or ".rtf", so the **Filter** property is set accordingly. Intuitively, if a file is being opened, it should exist. Thus the flags are set accordingly.

To open a file with the common dialog box:

1. Open the MDI parent form. Click on Project, and then click on Components to open the Components dialog box. Make sure that the Controls tab is active and that the Microsoft Common Dialog box Control 6.0 checkbox is checked. Click on OK.

2. Create an instance of the CommonDialog control on the MDI parent form. Remember that this control is not visible, so the placement of the control instance on the form is not important. Set the **Name** property to **cdlText**.

3. Locate the **OpenFile** general procedure on the MDI parent form. The statements for this procedure set the properties for the common dialog box and then display the Open dialog box. If the user does not click on the Cancel button, a new form is created using the **GetFormIndex** function (created earlier in this chapter), and the Caption is set as necessary. Change the InitDir path depending on your system configuration. Enter the following statements:

```
On Error GoTo Cancel_Error
Dim pintCurrentDoc As Integer
With cdlText
```

```
        .Flags = cdlOFNExplorer + cdlOFNPathMustExist + _
            cdlOFNFileMustExist
        .Filter = "Text Files (*.txt)|*.txt|RTF Files " & _
            "(*.rtf)|*.rtf"
        .FilterIndex = 2
        .CancelError = True
        .InitDir = "A:\Chapter.07\Startup"
        .ShowOpen
    End With
    pintCurrentDoc = GetFormIndex ()
    With Docs(pintCurrentDoc).frmCurrent
        .Caption = MDIText.cdlText.FileTitle
        .rtfText.LoadFile MDIText.cdlText.FileName
    End With
    Cancel_Error:
```

4. It should be possible to call the **OpenFile** procedure from either the MDI
   parent or child form. Locate the **mnuFileOpen_Click** event procedure in
   both the MDI parent and child forms, and enter the following statement:

   ```
   MDIText.OpenFile
   ```

5. Test the program. To test the functionality of the Cancel button, click on
   File on the form's menu bar, and then click on Open. Instead of opening a
   file, click on the Cancel button on the dialog box. The dialog box should
   close, generating a run–time error. This error is trapped by the error
   handler, so the statement to open the file will not execute.

6. On the form's menu bar, click on File, and then click on Open. The folder
   Chapter.07\Startup is the current folder because of the setting of the
   InitDir property. Click on the file named Demo.rtf, then click on the
   Open button. The RTF file opens, and text appears in the control instance.

7. End the program to return to design mode.

The statements added in the preceding steps set the filter such that text files and
rich text files having the extension ".txt" and ".rtf" can be displayed in the list
portion of the dialog box. By default, file names with the extension ".rtf" are
displayed, which is the second filter.

```
pintCurrentDoc = GetFormIndex()
With Docs(pintCurrentDoc).frmCurrent
    .Caption = MDIText.cdlText.FileTitle
    .rtfText.LoadFile MDIText.cdlText.FileName
End With
```

The preceding statements are very similar to the statements in the **NewFile** procedure. Instead of setting the **Caption** property to the constant text "New Document," the file name appears as the form's caption. The **LoadFile** method pertaining to the rich text box is then called. The file name stored in the common dialog box is used to specify which file to load.

 Whether to display the file title or the file and full path name in the title bar is a matter of choice. With long file names, however, the length of the path may not fit on a form's title bar. You should consider displaying just the title in such cases.

In addition to using the CommonDialog control to allow the user to select a file to open, you also can use it to allow the user to select a file to save.

Saving Files Using The Common Dialog Box Control

The Save As dialog box is very similar to the Open dialog box. It contains nearly the same buttons, text, and list boxes. In the Perfect Programming Systems text editor, you will use the common dialog box to save the contents of a rich text box to a file. Your code will accomplish this task by setting the necessary properties and then calling the **ShowSave** method pertaining to the CommonDialog control. Using the file specified by the user, the **SaveFile** method of the rich text box is called with the file name as an argument.

To save a file using the common dialog box:

1. Locate the **SaveFile** general procedure on the MDI parent form (MDIText), and enter the following statements (shown in bold). Change the path of InitDir, as necessary.

```
Private Sub SaveFile(frm As frmText)
On Error GoTo Cancel_Error
    With cdlText
        .Filter = "Text Files (*.txt)|*.txt|" & _
            "RTF Files (*.rtf)|*.rtf"
        .FilterIndex = 2
        .InitDir = "A:\Chapter.07\Startup"
        .ShowSave
        frm.rtfText.SaveFile .FileName
        frm.Caption = .FileName
    End With
    frm.Dirty = False
Cancel_Error:
End Sub
```

2. Enter the following statement into the **mnuFileSave_Click** event procedure on the MDI child form:

```
MDIText.SaveFile Me
```

Note that this procedure does not need to be called from the MDI parent form because when the MDI parent form's menu is displayed, no child forms (files) are open.

3. Test the program. Create a new file and enter text into the file. On the menu bar, click on File, and then click on Save. The Save As dialog box appears. Save the file using the name New File.rtf.

4. End the program to return to design mode.

The code in the **mnuFileSave_Click** event procedure is nearly identical to the code in the **mnuFileOpen_Click** event procedure. It calls the **ShowSave** method to display the Save As dialog box, however, and then calls the **SaveFile** method pertaining to the rich text box. It also resets the contents of the **Dirty** variable, indicating that the file has no unsaved changes. This variable will be set to **True** whenever the user modifies the contents of the rich text box.

Note that the **mnuFileSave_Click** event procedure accepts one argument: a reference to the form containing the data to be saved. When the code calls the **SaveFile** procedure, the statement uses the **Me** keyword as an argument to provide a reference to the active form.

In addition to using the CommonDialog control to open and save files, you can use the control to select formatting attributes.

Formatting The Contents Of A Rich Text Box

At this point, your program can open and save RTF files. The next step in the program's development is to apply formatting to the current file. The process of formatting text consists of selecting text to format and then applying a specific format to that text. The rich text box supports several properties to apply specific formatting to selected text:

➤ **SelBold**, **SelItalic**, **SelUnderline**, and **SelStrikethru** Determine whether a specific font style is applied to the currently selected text. Each property can have one of three values. If the value is **True**, the font style is applied to the selected text. If the value is **False** (the default), the font style is not applied to the selected text. If it is **Null**, the selected text contains characters with and without the formatting characteristic applied.

➤ **SelFontColor** Sets or reads the color of the selected text.

➤ **SelFontName** Sets or reads the font of the selected text.

➤ **SelFontSize** Identifies the font size of the selected text.

➤ **SelAlignment** Can have one of four constant values: **Null**, **rtfLeft**, **rtfRight**, and **rtfCenter**. These constants left-justify, right-justify, and center text. If set to **Null**, no justification is active.

➤ **RightMargin** Determines the right margin when text is right-justified or centered. The **RightMargin** property contains the number of twips from the left border of the control instance.

Each of these properties contains the value **Null** if the selected text contains different values for the same property. For example, if the selected text contained different font sizes, the **SelFontSize** property would contain the value **Null**. If the selected text contained a mixture of bold and regular typeface characters, the **SelBold** property would be **Null**. As you implement the Perfect Programming Systems program, you must decide what to do when this condition arises. For example, if the **SelBold** property was **Null** you would need to decide whether to apply or remove the boldface font. The choice is subjective, but whichever implementation you choose, be consistent. That is, if you decide to apply the attribute when the current value is **Null**, apply the attribute for all of the different properties.

In the Perfect Programming Systems text editor, three checked menu commands apply the formatting to selected text. These commands appear on the Format menu and are named **mnuFormatBold**, **mnuFormatItalic**, and **mnuFormatUnderline**.

Before creating the procedures to accomplish the formatting, a few words about the implementation are warranted. As you will see later in this chapter, the menu commands offer but one way to apply formatting. The user can also format characters using buttons on the toolbar. In addition, the user will open multiple copies of the same form at the same time. Thus you will create three procedures on the MDI parent form to apply formatting—one for the bold text, another for the italicized text, and another for the underlined text. These general procedures will be called from the **Click** event procedure for the corresponding menu command. Furthermore, the procedures will pass a reference to the current form as an argument to each procedure. The **Me** keyword contains a reference to the active form and can therefore be used to pass a form reference.

In the text editor, a formatting attribute can have one of two states. That is, the formatting attribute can be applied or not. Whenever the user changes the selected text, the value of the toolbar buttons and commands must be updated accordingly to reflect the formatting of the currently selected text. Because the user can change the formatting in a number of ways, the formatting routines, which already have been created, are separated into their own **Sub** procedures:

```
Public Sub BoldStatus(frm As Form, pbln As Boolean)
    If pbln Then
        frm.mnuFormatBold.Checked = True
        MDIText.tbrText.Buttons("Bold").Value = _
            tbrPressed
    Else
        frm.mnuFormatBold.Checked = False
        MDIText.tbrText.Buttons("Bold").Value = _
            tbrUnpressed
    End If
End Sub
```

The previous procedure sets the status of the checked menu command and the state of the toolbar button. The syntax to reference the toolbar button is the same as the syntax discussed in Chapter 6. The procedure takes two arguments: a reference to the MDI child form and a Boolean variable indicating whether the formatting attribute should be applied. Other, nearly identical, procedures named **ItalicStatus** and **UnderlineStatus** will be used to set the italic and underline formatting attributes.

To apply the formatting to the selected text:

1. Locate the **mnuFormatBold_Click** event procedure on the MDI child form, and enter the following statement:

```
MDIText.FormatBold Me
```

2. Enter the following statements in the procedures **mnuFormatItalic_Click** and **mnuFormatUnderline_Click**, respectively:

```
MDIText.FormatItalic Me
MDIText.FormatUnderline Me
```

3. Create the **FormatBold**, **FormatItalic**, and **FormatUnderline** general procedures on the MDI parent form named MDIText, and enter the following statements:

```
Public Sub FormatBold(frm As Form)
    If frm.rtfText.SelBold = True Then
        BoldStatus frm, False
        frm.rtfText.SelBold = False
    Else
        BoldStatus frm, True
        frm.rtfText.SelBold = True
    End If
```

```
End Sub

Public Sub FormatItalic(frm As Form)
    If frm.rtfText.SelItalic = True Then
        ItalicStatus frm, False
        frm.rtfText.SelItalic = False
    Else
        ItalicStatus frm, True
        frm.rtfText.SelItalic = True
    End If
End Sub

Public Sub FormatUnderline(frm As Form)
    If frm.rtfText.SelUnderline = True Then
        UnderlineStatus frm, False
        frm.rtfText.SelUnderline = False
    Else
        UnderlineStatus frm, True
        frm.rtfText.SelUnderline = True
    End If
End Sub
```

4. Test the program. Create a new document, and then enter a line of text. Select the text using the mouse. Use the Format menu and the Bold, Italic, and Underline commands to apply and remove the specified formatting.

5. End the program to return to design mode.

 In the previous example, you used the **Me** keyword as the argument to the different **Format** functions. Your code could have passed the argument using **Screen.ActiveForm**. Using the **Me** keyword, however, is considerably faster (by about 25 percent) than using **Screen.ActiveForm**.

The event procedures pass a reference to the current form to each of the general procedures as an argument. Recall from previous chapters that you can pass an object reference to a procedure. The argument name "frm" is of type Form. Form is actually a generic object type that can store a reference to any form instance.

Each general procedure has the same structure. You use an **If** statement to determine whether the style is already applied to the selected text. If so, the code removes the desired formatting. If not, the code applies the format. It also updates the command to indicate the current format by setting the **Checked** property. If the format is applied, a checkbox appears next to the command because the **Checked** property is **True**.

In addition to selecting text and applying formatting to the selected text, the checked menu commands must be updated appropriately when the selected text or the insertion point is changed. The **SelChange** event pertaining to the rich text box occurs whenever the selected text or the insertion point changes. In this event procedure, you need to call the **BoldStatus**, **ItalicStatus**, and **UnderlineStatus** procedures so that the commands will be synchronized with the selected text.

To synchronize selected text with the menu commands:

1. Enter the following statements in the **rtfText_SelChange** event procedure on the MDI child form:

```
If rtfText.SelBold = True Then
    MDIText.BoldStatus Me, True
Else
    MDIText.BoldStatus Me, False
End If
If rtfText.SelItalic = True Then
    MDIText.ItalicStatus Me, True
Else
    MDIText.ItalicStatus Me, False
End If
If rtfText.SelUnderline = True Then
    MDIText.UnderlineStatus Me, True
Else
    MDIText.UnderlineStatus Me, False
End If
```

2. Test the program. Create a new document, and then enter a line of text. Format the text with different attributes and select different text. Verify that the commands are synchronized with the selected text.

3. End the program to return to design mode.

The **SelChange** event occurs whenever the insertion point or the selected text changes. In this event procedure, the code checks the three formatting attributes to determine whether each attribute is applied. The **SelChange** event procedure then calls the corresponding general procedure to apply or remove the selected attribute.

In the Perfect Programming Systems text editor, you need to write code that will apply different fonts and font sizes to the selected text.

Working With Fonts

Before turning to the Font dialog box pertaining to the common dialog box control, a discussion of how Windows implements fonts is in order. Attached to your computer are several devices, some of which (such as the screen and printer) are output devices. Each device has unique characteristics. For example, different printers support different fonts. Programs known as *device drivers* allow these devices to communicate with one another. A *device context* is the link between a program such as Windows and the actual devices.

A unique device context exists for each printer and for the computer screen. In Visual Basic, a program obtains a reference to a device context by using the **hDC** property supported by many objects. For example, the Printer object supports the **hDC** property. Remember that a computer system can have multiple printers, and each printer is represented as a Printer object in the **Printers** Collection. Thus each printer has a device context stored in the **hDC** property of the Printer object. A form also supports the **hDC** property. The common dialog box uses the device context to determine which fonts are supported by the particular device.

The Font dialog box allows the user to select a font, a font size, and other font attributes. Like the Open and Save As dialogs, the common dialog box does not actually change the font of text. Rather, it sets properties, which you can read to set the font of text in a text box or other object. Figure 7.6 shows the Font dialog box.

As shown in Figure 7.6, selecting values from the different list boxes can set the font name, style, and size. The CommonDialog control communicates these settings to a program through the following properties that pertain to the Font dialog box:

➤ **FontBold**, **FontItalic**, **FontUnderline**, and **FontStrikethru** Identify the bold, italic, underline, and strikethrough font attributes, respectively. These properties store Boolean values.

➤ **Color** Identifies the color of the selected font. The Common Dialog box control stores this property as a **Long Integer**.

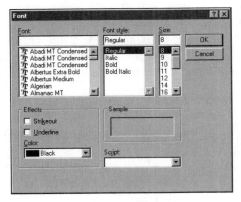

Figure 7.6 Font dialog box.

➤ **FontName** Contains the name of the selected font.

➤ **FontSize** Contains the size (in points) of the selected font.

➤ **ShowFont** This method displays the Font dialog box.

➤ **Flags** As it pertains to fonts, this property is used to determine which fonts are available and whether a font must exist for it to be selected.

➤ **Min** and **Max** Specify the smallest and largest font sizes, respectively, that can be selected in the Font dialog box.

Although the flags are optional for the Open and Save As dialogs, the type of fonts you want to use for the text editor must be specified using the **Flags** property before calling the **ShowFont** method. Otherwise, a run-time error will occur, indicating that no fonts are selected. The following list summarizes the flags pertaining to the ShowFont dialog box:

➤ **cdlCFEffects** Causes the strikethrough, underline, and color effects checkboxes to become visible and enabled. If not set, these checkboxes do not appear in the dialog box.

➤ **cdlCFPrinterFonts** Causes the dialog box to display only those fonts that apply to the currently selected printer (stored in the **hDC** property of the Printer object).

➤ **cdlCFScreenFonts** Causes the dialog box to display those fonts that apply to the screen.

➤ **cdlCFBoth** Selects both printer and screen fonts.

➤ **cdlCFLimitSize** If this flag is set, the user can select fonts only within the range of the **Max** and **Min** properties.

If you do not select a font set by using one of the flags (**cdlCFScreenFonts**, **cdlCFPrinterFonts**, or **cdlCFBoth**), a run-time error will occur.

You will use the Font dialog box to set fonts and font attributes. Because this dialog box can be used to set attributes like bold, italic, and underline, you must also format the selected text in the rich text box and update the status of the checked menu commands and toolbar. You can accomplish this task by calling the **BoldStatus**, **ItalicStatus**, or **UnderlineStatus** functions that you wrote earlier in this chapter.

To set fonts and font attributes using the common dialog box:

1. Locate the **mnuFormatFonts_Click** event procedure on the MDI child form, and enter the following statements:

```
On Error GoTo Cancel_Error
    cdlText.Flags = cdlCFScreenFonts + cdlCFEffects
    cdlText.CancelError = True
```

```
        cdlText.ShowFont
        rtfText.SelFontName = cdlText.FontName
        rtfText.SelFontSize = cdlText.FontSize
        rtfText.SelBold = cdlText.FontBold
        If cdlText.FontBold = True Then
            MDIText.BoldStatus Me, True
        Else
            MDIText.BoldStatus Me, False
        End If
        rtfText.SelItalic = cdlText.FontItalic
        If cdlText.FontItalic = True Then
            MDIText.ItalicStatus Me, True
        Else
            MDIText.ItalicStatus Me, False
        End If
        rtfText.SelUnderline = cdlText.FontUnderline
        If cdlText.FontUnderline = True Then
            MDIText.UnderlineStatus Me, True
        Else
            MDIText.UnderlineStatus Me, False
        End If
        Exit Sub
    Cancel_Error:
```

2. Test the program. Create a new document. Enter text in the document and select that text. On the form's menu bar, click on Format, and then click on Fonts. Click on different fonts and font attributes to test the procedure.

3. End the program to return to design mode.

Consider the first executable statement in this event procedure:

```
cdlText.Flags = cdlCFScreenFonts + cdlCFEffects
```

This statement sets the **Flags** argument so that the screen fonts will be displayed in the dialog box.

```
cdlText.CancelError = True
cdlText.ShowFont
```

The Font dialog box is then displayed when the **ShowFont** method is called. If the user clicks on the Cancel button, the CommonDialog control instance will generate a run–time error because the **Cancel** property is set to **True**.

```
rtfText.SelFontName = cdlText.FontName
rtfText.SelFontSize = cdlText.FontSize
```

If the user does not generate an error by pressing the Cancel button, the code applies the font, size, and typeface attributes to the selected text.

```
rtfText.SelBold = cdlText.FontBold
If cdlText.FontBold = True Then
    MDIText.BoldStatus Me, True
Else
    MDIText.BoldStatus Me, False
End If
```

The preceding statements apply the bold formatting attributes. The **If** statement then determines the value of the formatting attributes and calls the **BoldStatus** method to update the toolbar buttons and menu items as necessary. The code for the Italic and Underline attributes is almost identical.

In addition to formatting text, the RichTextBox control can justify text.

Justifying Text

The rich text box allows you to justify the text on a line. You can accomplish this task by setting the **SelAlignment** property of the rich text box to one of several constant values. If it is set to **rtfLeft**, the text is left-justified; if it is set to **rtfRight**, the text is right-justified; if it is set to **rtfCenter**, the text is centered. When you write code that right-justifies or centers the text, the right margin must be defined so that the rich text box can align the text properly. You can set the right margin through the **RightMargin** property pertaining to the rich text box. This property usually is measured in twips, just like other sizing properties. The property has already been set in the **Form_Load** event procedure for the MDI child form.

The function to set the justification will use the selected text, just like the other formatting functions you have used. It will take one argument—a string identifying the desired justification for the selected text. The code will call this function from the toolbar button code, which you will create.

To justify text in the rich text box, create the general procedure on the MDI parent form (MDIText)as follows:

```
Public Sub Justify(pstr As String)
    Select Case pstr
        Case "Left"
            Screen.ActiveForm.rtfText.SelAlignment = _
                rtfLeft
        Case "Right"
            Screen.ActiveForm.rtfText.SelAlignment = _
                rtfRight
        Case "Center"
```

```
            Screen.ActiveForm.rtfText.SelAlignment = _
                rtfCenter
      End Select
End Sub
```

These statements use a **Select Case** statement to determine the desired justification. To identify the active form, the preceding code uses the Screen.ActiveForm object. The same code could have just as easily passed the active form as an argument to the **Sub** procedure. You will test this procedure later in the next section when you program the toolbar.

Printing Output

The user uses the Print dialog box to select different printing characteristics. Again, the dialog box does not actually print a file. Instead, it sets property and flag values, which your program can examine to determine which text to print and where to print it. Figure 7.7 shows the Print dialog box.

As shown in Figure 7.7, the Print dialog box has three sections—the Printer section, the Print range section, and the Copies section. The various flags pertaining to the Print dialog box determine which buttons are enabled in these sections and which fields can be selected by the user.

As with the other dialogs, you control the Print dialog box by using both the properties and flags pertaining to the dialog box:

➤ **Copies** You set this property to determine the number of output copies to print.

➤ **FromPage** and **ToPage** Setting these properties determines the starting and ending pages to be printed, respectively.

➤ **hDC** Returns the device context.

➤ **ShowPrint** Displays the Print dialog box.

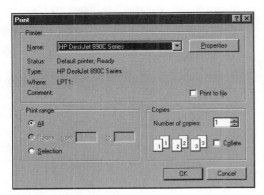

Figure 7.7   Print dialog box.

Although these properties determine the number of copies and the starting and ending pages, the flags pertaining to the Print dialog box control much of the information about what to print, where to print, and how to print. The following list summarizes the flags pertaining to the Print dialog box:

➤ **cdlPDAllPages** Controls the All Pages option button. If the flag is set, the button is selected. If it is not set, the button is not selected.

➤ **cdlPDDisablePrintToFile** By default, the Print To File checkbox is enabled. If the **cdlPDDisablePrintToFile** flag is set, the checkbox is disabled.

➤ **cdlHidePrintToFile** The Print To File checkbox can be hidden completely by setting this flag.

➤ **cdlPDNoPageNums** By default, this flag is set, which causes the option button to select specific pages and the two text boxes containing the starting and ending page number to be disabled. Clearing this flag enables the option button and text boxes. If the user selects a starting and ending page number, the CommonDialog control instance returns the values in the **StartPage** and **EndPage** properties.

➤ **cdlPDNoSelection** When this flag is set, it disables the Selection option button. The programmer typically uses this flag to allow the user to print selected text. The CommonDialog control returns the value of the Selection option button in the flag **cdlPDSelection**.

➤ **cdlPDPrintToFile**, If this flag is set, indicates that the Print to file checkbox is checked.

In practice, using the Print dialog box requires that certain flags be set before the **ShowPrinter** method is called. After calling the dialog box, the **Flags** property must be examined carefully to determine which flags are set.

To print the contents of the rich text box:

1. Create the **PrintFile** general procedure on the MDI parent form (**MDIText**), and enter the following statements:

```
Public Sub PrintFile(frm As frmText)
On Error GoTo Cancel_Error
    cdlText.CancelError = True
    cdlText.Flags = cdlPDReturnDC + cdlPDNoPageNums
    cdlText.ShowPrinter
    frm.rtfText.SelPrint cdlText.hDC
Cancel_Error:
End Sub
```

2. Locate the **mnuFilePrint_Click** event procedure on the MDI child form, and enter the following statement:

```
MDIText.PrintFile Me
```

3. Test the program. Create a new file and enter one line of text in the rich text box. On the form's menu bar, click on File, and then click on Print. Click on OK. The contents of the rich text box should print.

4. End the program to return to design mode.

The statements added in the preceding steps call the **ShowPrinter** method to display the Print dialog box and to print the contents of the RichTextBox control instance. Again, the procedure accepts one argument—a reference to the form whose contents should be printed.

```
cdlText.CancelError = True
cdlText.Flags = cdlPDReturnDC + cdlPDNoPageNums
cdlText.ShowPrinter
```

In the preceding code, the first statement causes the dialog box to generate a run-time error if the user clicks on the Cancel button. Next, the code sets the flags so that the device context will be returned by the control instance and the user cannot select specific page numbers. Finally, the code calls the **ShowPrinter** method to display the Print dialog box.

```
frm.rtfText.SelPrint cdlText.hDC
```

If the user does not click on the Cancel button, calling the **SelPrint** method causes the selected text to be printed. The **SelPrint** method takes one argument—the device context of the printer.

The final dialog box discussed in this chapter allows the user to set colors.

Changing Colors

The CommonDialog control allows the user to select colors on a palette that can, in turn, be used to change the color for an object. Like the other dialogs, the Color dialog box supports several properties:

➤ **Flags** Controls whether custom colors can be defined and dictates the initial color that appears in the dialog box.

➤ **Color** When closed, the CommonDialog control returns the selected color in the **Color** property.

➤ **ShowColor** Displays the Color dialog box.

When working with color, you should consider the target computer on which the program will run. Different computers have different color capabilities. Older display devices supporting the CGA standard can display only 16 different colors. Later standards first extended the number of colors to 256, and then to millions of colors. To represent a color, each pixel (dot on the screen) is represented by a certain number of bits. The more bits per pixel, the more colors the system can display. Current display devices use 16-, 24-, and 32-bit color, allowing for millions of different colors.

Take care that the colors you select for your program can display effectively on all computers, even those with limited color palettes. If the target computer cannot display a color you have selected, the color will be converted into one of the supported colors. This conversion does not always produce the desired results, and sometimes causes the output to be illegible.

To change the color of the selected text:

1. Locate the **mnuOptionsColor_Click** event procedure on the MDI child form, and enter the following statements:

```
On Error GoTo Cancel_Error
    MDIText.cdlText.CancelError = True
    MDIText.cdlText.ShowColor
    rtfText.SelColor = MDIText.cdlText.Color
    Exit Sub
Cancel_Error:
```

2. Test the program. Create a new file, enter text in the rich text box, and select the text. On the form's menu bar, click on Options, and then click on Color to activate the Color dialog box. Click on a different color, and then apply the color. The selected color should be applied to the selected text.

3. End the program to return to design mode.

These statements cause the Color dialog box to be displayed.

```
MDIText.cdlText.CancelError = True
MDIText.cdlText.ShowColor
```

The Color dialog box is used in the same way as the other dialogs discussed in this chapter. First, the **CancelError** property is set to **True**. Then, the dialog box is displayed.

```
rtfText.SelColor = MDIText.cdlText.Color
```

The preceding statement stores the selected color in the **Color** property of the common dialog box. This color is then applied to the selected text in the rich text box by setting the **SelColor** property.

The programming for this chapter is nearly complete. Your final task is to program the toolbar so that the buttons, when clicked, will mimic the menu commands.

Programming The Toolbar

Intuitively, you may think that a toolbar works like a menu when used in an MDI program—that is, that different toolbars appear for each form just under the menu bar. In fact, the toolbar for an MDI parent form appears just below the menu bar, if one exists. If a toolbar is created for an MDI child form, the toolbar will appear on the MDI child form rather than under the menu on the MDI parent form. As a result, when programming toolbars with MDI programs, you typically create a toolbar as an object on the MDI parent form only. Toolbars can also be used with standard forms.

Once you have created the toolbar and assigned its buttons, you must program the toolbar to respond to events when clicked. That is, you must program the **ButtonClick** event procedure just as you did in Chapter 6.

To program the **ButtonClick** event procedure:

1. Locate the **tbrText_ButtonClick** event procedure in the Code window on the MDI parent form, and enter the following statements:

```
Select Case Button.Key
    Case "Openfold"
        OpenFile
    Case "Clsdfold"
        CloseFile Screen.ActiveForm
    Case "Print"
        PrintFile Screen.ActiveForm
    Case "Bold"
        FormatBold Screen.ActiveForm
    Case "Italic"
        FormatItalic Screen.ActiveForm
    Case "Underline"
        FormatUnderline Screen.ActiveForm
    Case "Left"
        Justify "Left"
    Case "Center"
        Justify "Center"
```

```
      Case "Right"
          Justify "Right"
End Select
```

2. Test the program. Create a new file, enter text into the rich text box, and then select that text. Click on the different buttons on the toolbar to execute the general procedures corresponding to each of the commands.

3. End the program to return to design mode.

The **Select Case** statement given in the preceding steps uses the string key of the selected button to determine which button was clicked. It then calls the appropriate general procedure. The numeric index could be used as well, but the code is less readable because the numeric value does not indicate the purpose of the button. Buttons also support a **Tag** property that is ignored by Visual Basic; this tag can, however, be used to identify the button uniquely.

Understanding The Windows Clipboard

You have undoubtedly used the Windows Clipboard to copy, cut, and paste text and other types of data within a document, between documents, and between different applications. Visual Basic supports the Windows Clipboard through the Clipboard object. In this section, you will learn how to copy text to and from the Clipboard.

Most programs support three operations that use the Clipboard:

➤ **Cut** A cut operation deletes selected text from a document and places the deleted text on the Clipboard.

➤ **Copy** A copy operation copies selected text from a document and places the copied text on the Clipboard.

➤ **Paste** A paste operation copies the contents from the Clipboard to another object, such as a text box.

To perform these operations, the Clipboard object supports three methods.

Syntax

Clipboard

Methods

➤ The **Clear** method removes the existing contents from the Clipboard.

➤ The **SetText** method copies text to the Clipboard object.

➤ The **GetText** method returns the text string currently stored on the Clipboard object. The text remains on the Clipboard after this method is called. Thus repeated calls to the **GetText** method cause the same text to be retrieved from the Clipboard.

The **GetText** and **SetText** methods accept arguments to define the information copied on the Clipboard and the format of that information.

Syntax

> Clipboard.SetText *data, format*
> Clipboard.GetText (*format*)

Dissection

➤ The *data* argument, which pertains to the **SetText** method, contains the string identifying the text that is copied on the Clipboard.

➤ Text on the Clipboard can appear in different formats. The Clipboard supports both plain text and RTF. The optional **format** argument contains the format of the text being copied on the Clipboard. If the constant **vbCFRTF** is used, the methods assume that the data is in RTF format. If the constant **vbCFText** is used, the Clipboard assumes that the data is in Text format. If no format is specified, **vbCFText** is the default.

Code Example

```
Clipboard.Clear
Clipboard.SetText Text1.Text
Text1.Text = Clipboard.GetText
```

Code Dissection

Before your code performs a copy or cut operation, the contents on the Clipboard should be cleared.

You have now completed the programming for this chapter. You have seen how the CommonDialog control can improve the user interface dramatically by providing standard dialogs for common tasks. Such dialogs should be used whenever a program needs to open, save, or print files. The CommonDialog control is also useful for setting colors and fonts. In addition to working with the common dialog box, you have seen how a toolbar can augment the user interface by giving the user another way to execute common commands. These commands are usually equivalent to menu commands. Finally, you have seen how the rich text box provides extensive capabilities to format and edit text.

CHAPTER SUMMARY

In this chapter, you learned how to create MDI programs and examined the characteristics of MDI programming. The following list summarizes the general characteristics of an MDI program:

➤ An MDI program consists of one MDI parent form, one or more MDI child forms, and possibly standard forms typically used as modal dialogs.

➤ A form module is considered a class. You can create multiple instances of the same class, so you therefore can create multiple instances of the same MDI child form. Each form instance has a unique copy of its properties. **Public** variables declared in a form module are considered properties, and **Public** procedures are considered methods of the class.

➤ When unloading forms in an MDI program, the **QueryUnload** and **Unload** events occur for both the MDI parent and MDI child form instances. The **QueryUnload** event accepts two arguments. The *cancel* argument, if set to **True**, prevents subsequent **Unload** events from occurring. The **UnloadMode** argument is used to determine what caused the event to occur.

To create an MDI program:

➤ Add an MDI parent form to the project.

➤ Set the **MDIChild** property for other desired forms to **True**, thereby causing them to behave as MDI child forms.

➤ Note that standard forms can still be used in MDI programs.

➤ Set the startup object to the MDI parent form.

To create multiple instances of an MDI child form:

➤ Declare an array of object variables or user-defined types to store references to multiple form instances.

➤ Create form instances with the **New** keyword and store a reference to the newly created form in the array.

To display message boxes or obtain confirmation from the user when unloading forms:

➤ Respond to the **QueryUnload** event pertaining to the MDI form or form object.

Private Sub Form_QueryUnload(*cancel* **As Integer**, *unloadmode* **As Integer**)

Private Sub MDIForm_QueryUnload(*cancel* **As Integer**, *unloadmode* **As Integer**)

Private Sub *object*_**Unload**(*cancel* **As Integer**)

To determine the active control instance:

➤ Use the **Me** keyword.

➤ Use the **ActiveControl** property pertaining to the Screen object.

To arrange MDI child forms:

➤ Call the **Arrange** method pertaining to the MDI parent form. Use the argument **vbCascade**, **vbTileHorizontal**, or **vbTileVertical**.

To read or write a file with the RichTextBox control, call the **LoadFile** and **SaveFile** methods.

object.**LoadFile** *pathname*[, *filetype*]

object.**SaveFile** *pathname*[, *filetype*]

To format the contents of a RichTextBox control instance:

➤ Set the **SelBold**, **SelItalic**, **SelUnderline**, and **SelStrikethru** properties to **True** to apply the formatting attribute or set the respective property to **False** to remove the formatting attribute.

➤ Set the **SelFontColor** property to change the color of selected text.

➤ Set the **SelFontSize** and **SelFontName** properties to change the font size and font name, respectively.

➤ Set the **SelAlignment** property to align text.

To display Open and SaveAs dialogs using the CommonDialog control:

➤ Set the **CancelError** property to **True**, causing a run-time error to occur if the user clicks on the Cancel button.

➤ Set the **Filter** property to control the available file extensions using the following syntax:

object.**Filter** [= *description1*|*filter1*|*description2*|*filter2* ...]

➤ Call the **ShowOpen** or **ShowSave** method.

➤ Set the **Flags** property to further control the behavior and appearance of the dialog box.

➤ The file selected by the user is stored in the **FileName** property.

To display the Print dialog box:

➤ Set the **Flags** property as necessary.

➤ Call the **ShowPrint** method to display the dialog box.

To change colors using the Colors dialog box:

➤ Set the **CancelError** property to **True**.

➤ Call the **ShowColor** method.

➤ Read the value of the **Color** property, which contains a **Long Integer** value describing the selected color.

Review Questions

1. An MDI program can contain:
   a. one MDI parent form
   b. many MDI parent forms
   c. one or more MDI child forms
   d. Both a and c
   e. Both b and c

2. What is the name of the property that determines whether the MDI child forms in a program are loaded automatically?
   a. **AutoLoad**
   b. **AutoLoadChildren**
   c. **Load**
   d. **AutoShowChild**
   e. **AutoShowChildren**

3. In which order do the following events occur?
   a. **QueryUnload, Unload**
   b. **Unload, QueryUnload**
   c. **Unload, Close**
   d. **Close, QueryUnload, Unload**
   e. None of the above

4. Which of the following statements pertaining to an MDI program is true?
   a. Menus appear just below the MDI parent form's title bar.
   b. Every form in an MDI program may have a menu.
   c. Standard forms can be used in an MDI program.
   d. Message boxes and dialogs work as they do in single-document interface programs.
   e. All of the above.

5. Which of the following is a valid use of the Screen object?
   a. To determine the fonts supported by the display device
   b. To determine the number of colors supported by the display device
   c. To change the appearance of the mouse pointer
   d. Both a and c
   e. All of the above

6. Declare an array named FormsArray. Write a **For** loop that will iterate 10 times. Each time through the loop, create a new instance of the form named frmTest and store a reference to the form in the array.

7. Using the **Forms** Collection, create a **For Each** loop to unload all forms of type **frmDemo**.

8. Using the **Forms** and **Controls** Collections, write a nested **For Each** loop to print the **Name** property of all Control instances on all forms to the Immediate window.

9. Assuming that an MDI parent form named MDIParent has been created, write the necessary statements to display a message box in the **QueryUnload** event procedure that will confirm that the user really wants to exit the program. If not, the event should be canceled.

10. Write the necessary statement to arrange all MDI child forms horizontally.

11. Which of the following methods pertain to the CommonDialog control?
    a. **ShowOpen, ShowSaveFile, ShowPrint**
    b. **ShowOpen, ShowSave, ShowFont**
    c. **ShowPrinter, ShowColor**
    d. Both a and b
    e. Both b and c

12. The _____ and _____ methods pertaining to the rich text box read and write files.
    a. **Input, Output**
    b. **LoadFile, SaveFile**
    c. **Load, Save**
    d. **Read, Write**
    e. None of the above

13. If the **CancelError** property pertaining to the CommonDialog control is True, then:
    a. a run-time error will be generated by the common dialog box when the Cancel button is clicked
    b. the **Cancel** property will be set to true
    c. the event procedure will be canceled automatically
    d. All of the above
    e. None of the above

7

14. The _____ properties identify the typeface, name, and size of the selected text in a rich text box.

   a. **SelBold**, **SelItalic**, and **SelUnderline**

   b. **SelFontName** and **SelFontSize**

   c. **Bold**, **Italic**, and **Underline**

   d. Both a and b

   e. Both b and c

15. Before calling the **ShowFont** method of the common dialog box, the **Flags** property must be set to:

   a. **cdlCFScreenFonts**

   b. **cdlCFPrinterFonts**

   c. **cdlCFBoth**

   d. Any of the above

   e. None of the above

16. Assuming that an instance of the CommonDialog control named cdlOne has been created, write the code for the **cmdOpen_Click** event procedure that will display an Open dialog box with an initial directory of C:\ and a filter that will select a Jet database file having the extension .mdb. After setting the necessary properties, display the dialog box.

17. Write the statements to set the typeface of the selected text in a rich text box named **rtfCurrent** to bold, underlined, and italicized.

18. Create an event procedure named **cmdColor_Click** on that displays the Color dialog box. Create an error handler to detect whether the user clicked the Cancel button. If the user did not click on the Cancel button, set the background color of the form named Form1 to the selected color.

19. Using the Screen object, write a statement to set the **Caption** property of the command button named **cmdTest** to Test. (Hint: Use the **ActiveForm** property of the Screen object.)

20. Using the **Me** keyword, write the statements to print the caption of the form referenced by the **Me** keyword if the type of the form is frmDemo.

21. Write a **For Each** loop to print the **Name** property of each form in the **Forms** Collection.

HANDS-ON PROJECTS

Project 1

In this project, you will create an MDI program that uses a multiline text box to display ASCII files.

    a. Run the executable file named Chapter.07\Exercise\Ex1Demo.exe. Figure 7.8 shows the completed form for the exercise.

    Click on File, and then click on Open. The Open dialog box will appear. Select and open a text file residing on your system. The contents of the text file will appear in an instance of the MDI child form. Open a second file. Note that a second instance of the MDI child form is created. Click on File, and then click on Close to close one of the MDI child forms. Exit the program.

    b. Start Visual Basic, and create a new project. Set the **Name** property of the form to **frmEx1**. Save the form with the name Chapter.07\ Exercise\frmEx1.frm and the project with the name Chapter.07\ Exercise\Ex1.vbp.

    c. Add an MDI parent form to the project, and set the appropriate project properties to cause the MDI parent form to be the startup object. Set the name of the MDI parent form to MDIEdit.

    d. Set the existing form so that it operates as an MDI child form. Create a multiline text box instance with both vertical and horizontal scroll bars.

    e. For this exercise, only the MDI parent form will have a menu. There should be a File menu with three commands named Open, Close, and Exit.

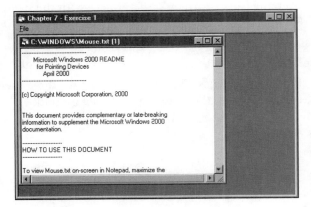

Figure 7.8   Exercise 1 completed form.

f. Create the **Open** command to display a common dialog box with the necessary filter to open text files having a file extension of ".txt". When clicked, the program should open the file, read each line, and display the file contents in the multiline text box. (*Hint:* Open and then read a sequential file using the **Open** and **Input #** statements.)

g. Create the **Close** command to close the current MDI child form.

h. Create the **Exit** command to exit the program by unloading the MDI parent form. Before exiting, the user should be prompted as to whether he or she really wants to exit the program. If the user does not, the **Unload** events should be canceled.

i. Using the techniques presented in this chapter, develop an array to manage the different instances of the MDI child forms.

j. Test the program. Open and close multiple text files. Verify that the forms are stored in the correct array element. Also verify that the file contents are read into the multiline text box properly.

k. Exit Visual Basic.

Project 2

In this project, you will use common dialogs to customize the fonts and color for all text boxes on a form. Figure 7.9 depicts the completed form.

a. Run the executable file named Chapter.07\Exercise\Ex2Demo.exe. Enter text into each of the text boxes. Using the items on the Settings menu, change the font, background color, and foreground color of the four text boxes. Exit the program.

b. Start Visual Basic, and create a new project. Set the **Name** property of the form to **frmEx2**. Save the form with the name Chapter.07\Exercise\frmEx2.frm and the project with the name Chapter.07\Exercise\Ex2.vbp.

c. Create an instance of the CommonDialog control on the form.

d. Create several text boxes on the form, as shown in Figure 7.9.

e. Create a menu named Settings. The menu should have three menu items with captions of Fonts, Foreground, and Background.

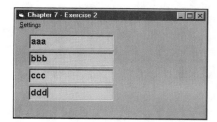

Figure 7.9 Exercise 2 completed form.

    f. Using the Font dialog box pertaining to the CommonDialog control, write the code that will allow the user to set the font for all text boxes on the form. This code should execute when the user clicks on the Fonts menu item.

    g. Use the **Controls** Collection and a **For Each** loop to examine each control instance. Inside the **For Each** loop, use the **TypeOf** keyword in an **If** statement to verify that the control instance is a text box before trying to set the fonts. Inside the **For Each** loop, set the font size, font name, and typeface attributes.

    h. Write the code for the remaining menu commands to set the foreground and background colors of the text boxes. To set the color, use the CommonDialog control instance.

    i. Use the same **For Each** structure that you used in the previous steps to verify that the type of control is a text box.

    j. Test the program by applying different colors and fonts to the text boxes.

    k. Exit Visual Basic.

Project 3

In this project, you will create an MDI program that serves a much different purpose than the one you created in this chapter. This program manages the output of machines in a production line. You will record and accumulate the number of good and defective items manufactured on each production line. Figure 7.10 depicts the completed form.

    a. Run the executable file named Chapter.07\Exercise\Ex3Demo.exe. Click on Start Machine on the Machine menu. An instance of the MDI child form will appear, displaying the number of good and

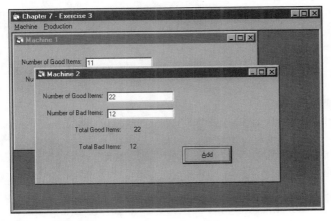

Figure 7.10   Exercise 3 completed form.

defective items. Enter a numeric value into each text box. Click on the Add button to record the changes to the accumulator for the form. Repeat the process. The total accumulators are updated. Click on Production, and then click on Display Total. The total production for all machines appears in the modal dialog box. Exit the program.

b. Create a new project, and set the **Name** property of the form to **frmEx3**. Save the form with the name Chapter.07\Exercise\ frmEx3.frm and the project with the name Chapter.07\Exercise\ Ex3.vbp.

c. Add an MDI parent form to the project. Save the MDI parent form with the name MDIEx3.frm.

d. On the MDI child form, create two text boxes in which the user will enter the number of good and defective manufactured items for a production run.

e. Create two output labels and a command button. When the command button is clicked, the program should add to the value of the output labels the current contents of the text boxes. In other words, you are creating an accumulator.

f. On the MDI parent form, create two menu commands with the captions Start Machine and Stop Machine. Both of these menu items should appear on the Machine menu. When the Start machine menu item is clicked, a new instance of the MDI child form should be created. When the Stop Machine menu item is clicked, the instance of the active MDI child form should be destroyed. Thus, when the machine is started, a new instance of the MDI child form will appear representing the newly started machine. When the machine is stopped, the corresponding form instance will be destroyed.

g. Create a menu title named Production and a menu command named Display Total to display the production output of all machines. This procedure should iterate through the **Forms** collection, examining the totals for each machine, and compute a grand total.

h. Create a third form to display the grand totals. This form should be implemented as a modal standard form. Save the form with the name frmTotal.

i. When the user clicks on the Production menu and then Display Total, the form named **frmTotal** should be displayed. The output should display the total good and defective production counts for all active machines.

j. Save and test the program. Start multiple machines. Enter production values for each machine and update the accumulators. Display the production totals for each machine.

k. Exit Visual Basic.

CHAPTER EIGHT

DESIGNING AND IMPLEMENTING COMPONENT-BASED APPLICATIONS

DESIGNING A COMPONENT-BASED PROGRAM

Previewing The Completed Application

The content and organization of this chapter differ from those of the other chapters in this book. First, this chapter presents design considerations that you can apply to create applications known as *enterprise* applications which are suitable for use throughout a large organization. Second, it discusses the use of Visual Basic to communicate with other programs that rely on existing components. The completed example uses Microsoft Excel as an existing component to perform statistical analysis on the input files.

To run the completed program and perform the hands-on steps in this chapter, Microsoft Office 97, or a newer version, must be installed on your computer.

To preview the completed application:

1. Start Visual Basic, and then load and run the completed program named Chapter.08\Complete\Ch8_C.vbp. Figure 8.1 shows the completed form for the program at run time.

2. As shown in Figure 8.1, the program contains a menu. The Open menu item allows the user to open an input file and read the data into Microsoft Excel. The Calculate menu item performs the statistical analysis on the data. When the user performs the statistical analysis, the output values appear on the control instances created on the form. The Exit menu item allows the user to exit the program.

3. Click on File, and then click on Open to display the Open dialog box. Open the file named Chapter.08\Complete\Demo.txt. Set the drive designator and path name as necessary. Click on Open to close the dialog box and open the file.

4. When the file is opened, the program code reads the input file into Microsoft Excel. Microsoft Excel does not appear on the screen, however.

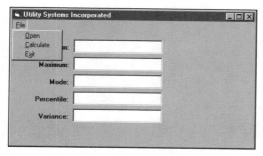

Figure 8.1 Completed form.

5. Click on File, and then click on Calculate. The program performs the statistical analysis tasks and displays the results in the form's text boxes. Note that Microsoft Excel is not visible on the screen. Rather, the completed program uses the functionality of Excel through its object interface.

6. End the program to return to design mode, and then exit Visual Basic.

Computer Programs—A Historical Perspective

Before beginning to design a component-based system, a brief historical review of computer hardware and software may help you better understand what you are doing in this chapter and why.

Both computer hardware and computer software have evolved considerably since the 1960s. The computer hardware used in the 1960s and 1970s typically consisted of mainframe computers running monolithic programs commonly referred to as *legacy systems*. All processing took place on the same physical mainframe computer.

Users typically interacted with legacy systems in one of two ways. In the first method, known as *batch processing*, input data were grouped into batches. The input data were typically stored on punched cards or magnetic tape. Each input batch was then processed and the output produced. Batch processing later gave way to online transaction processing. With this method, the user enters data at a terminal, and the mainframe computer displays the output at the same terminal. The terminal in this latter scenario is not a computer. Rather, it is simply a device that receives user input, transmits that input to the mainframe computer, and displays output from the mainframe.

Figure 8.2 illustrates the online transaction processing model of a legacy system.

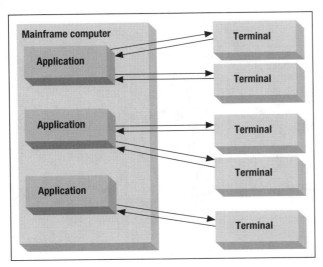

Figure 8.2 Legacy application—online transaction processing.

Although many organizations continue to use mainframe computers in enterprise applications, many organizations have replaced their mainframe systems with distributed systems. A distributed system spreads the processing tasks across multiple computers, often located in different physical locations. One type of distributed system is a client-server system. As the name indicates, in this system one computer (the client) requests services from another computer (the server). The server responds to those requests and sends information back to the client.

Consider a client-server distributed system in which the user processes data stored in a database. The software to perform the tasks is distributed across two or more physical computers. One computer is the end user's desktop workstation. This computer contains the programs to receive user input and to display output. This part of the distributed system typically includes the user interface.

Although the user requests information from the database via the client, the database physically resides on a separate computer. Thus a client's user request for data must be made to the server. Another part of the distributed system (the server) actually processes the client's request and sends the information back to the end user's program (client).

In a distributed system, developers design specific software components to perform specific tasks. Different physical computers may perform these tasks. Figure 8.3 illustrates the processing model of a distributed system.

As shown in Figure 8.3, multiple clients and a server may make up a distributed system. In this situation, the processing to perform a given task is spread across multiple computers. Data are communicated between computers via a network.

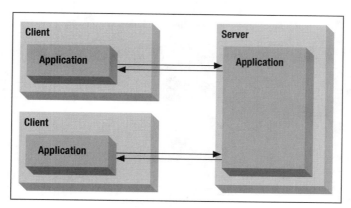

Figure 8.3 Distributed system processing.

Developing Software For A New Distributed System

Now that you know the history of distributed systems, you must consider the first step in developing the software for a new distributed system: carefully analyzing an existing system and the tasks currently performed by the users. This chapter focuses on the techniques used to design and implement a distributed system that solves the needs of business.

An application designed to run on a distributed system is often referred to as a *partitioned application*. A partitioned application consists of several parts, and each part performs a specific and well-defined task. Each part of the partitioned application is referred to as a *component*. The definition of a component is significant. Physically, a component exists as an .exe or .dll file. Programs interact with a component by means of the component's interface.

In the context of this chapter, the term *interface* does not mean the user interface. Instead, the interface of a component encompasses the properties, methods, and events supported by the component. The component hides its internal implementation from the programs that use the component. The terms *supplier* and *consumer* are often used when referring to components. A *consumer* calls upon the component to provide a service. A *supplier* (component) provides services to consumers. The interface between the consumer and supplier is often referred to as a *contract*.

By building applications from components, businesses realize several benefits:

➤ **Reusability** When programmers wrote code using legacy systems, they often wrote the same code repeatedly for different programs. By developing services based upon components, many applications can share the services provided by the same component. Thus a service can be written once and then used by several applications (consumers).

➤ **Consistency** A component has a well-known interface, which promotes consistency from application to application. In other words, a component supports a standard set of properties and methods. For example, one component can validate the input of date values and convert those values into a consistent format for all applications in the enterprise. Furthermore, if the component requires modification, all programs using that component can readily integrate those changes.

➤ **Flexibility** Code written for a legacy system ran on a single computer. When creating components for a distributed system, however, a component can be executed on the computer that is most suitable at that time for the particular task. For example, a user's workstation or the database server could execute a component.

➤ **Manageability** In recent years, computer programs have become significantly more complex, requiring large teams of programmers to develop them. By dividing a program into components, a project can be divided into smaller, more manageable tasks. This approach maximizes the efforts of the development team because individual programmers can build components for which their skills are best suited.

➤ **Maintenance** Organizations spend a large amount of time maintaining existing applications in addition to developing new ones. By breaking a program into components, each component can be maintained as an individual unit.

➤ **Cost** Programmers are able to develop programs more rapidly by sharing components and using existing components, thereby reducing development costs. Software maintenance tasks tend to decrease, as changes can be made to a single component rather than having to make similar changes to many programs.

Effectively designing and building a distributed component-based system require much more than sitting down at the computer and writing code. You need a strategy to create a system that will satisfy the needs of the users and operate effectively on networked computers. One such strategy is the three-tiered approach.

The Three-Tiered Approach

The three-tiered architectural approach to designing distributed applications is becoming increasingly popular. It divides a distributed system into three tiers or layers. Each tier makes up a functional part of an application and is known as a *service*. Consequently, the three-tiered architectural approach is often referred to as the *services model*.

The services model views an application as a group of components that fulfills consumer requests. The services model segregates development efforts into two groups. The first group of developers builds the actual components, and the second group of developers creates business solutions based on those components. A *business solution* is a component that accurately addresses and solves a specific business need or problem.

In the design and implementation phases for a component-based system, an organization must make a "build or buy decision." In making this decision, organizations must consider three options:

➤ When available, the most cost-effective approach is to use existing components to perform a particular task. In this chapter's program, you will use existing components supported by Microsoft Excel.

➤ A second option is to enhance existing components. In this scenario, existing components may handle the majority of a business need. The component must nevertheless be enhanced to completely satisfy the need.

➤ The final option is to develop new components from scratch. This choice is suitable when no existing components can be found to solve a business need.

Components in the services model are not bound to a physical platform. Rather, an organization can dynamically distribute and redistribute components across a heterogeneous computing environment. As the needs of the organization evolve, the physical location of components can be reconfigured.

In the services model, components are classified into one of three categories:

➤ **User services** Encompass the end user's view of the application. These services include the forms seen by the end user and the ways in which the end user navigates through the user interface. User services normally reside on the end user's computer (client).

➤ **Business services** Describe the business policies and generation of information from business data. For example, a business likely has a policy to grant or refuse credit to its customers based on certain criteria. Business services provide the link between user services and data services. A *business rule* is similar to a business policy or procedure. Such rules define how a business operates or how a business task is performed. If the business rule is encapsulated into a component, when the business policy or rule changes, the organization can change the code in the component accordingly. The consumers who rely on that service can immediately take advantage of the changed component (business service).

➤ **Data services** Include the definition for data storage and the method by which other programs retrieve that data. Data services are implemented as one or more databases, text files, or other file types. The data may exist on the local computer (client) or be accessed from another computer (server) via a network.

User services rely on business services, which in turn rely on data services. Figure 8.4 depicts the relationship among the three categories.

As shown in Figure 8.4, multiple applications may rely on the same business services. For example, one service may perform a simple task, such as the validation of a date. Another service may perform a much more complicated task, such as statistical analysis.

Remember that these three service layers are conceptual rather than physical. That is, each service does not describe the physical location of a computer on a

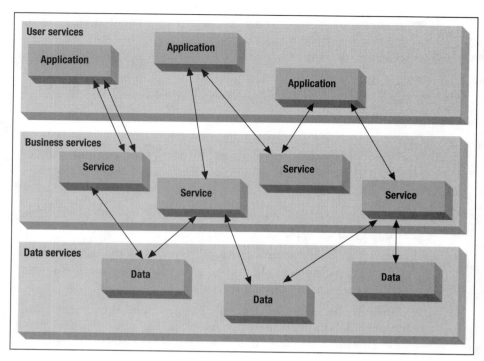

Figure 8.4 Three-tiered model.

network, but rather a logical task to be performed and the way in which that task is performed. Using the services model, you, as the programmer, view an application as a collection of services designed to solve a specific business need.

Most of the programs you have written so far in this book have relied on ActiveX controls. These controls simplify the task of program development by allowing you to take advantage of preexisting tools (components). An ActiveX control is also a component with a well-defined interface. This interface consists of the component's properties, events, and methods. The internal implementation of the component can be changed without affecting the programs that use the component, so long as the interface does not change. More importantly, as the consumer, you do not need to be aware of how the component performs its task. For instance, Microsoft could change the internal implementation of the toolbar (component), but you would not need to modify your program.

Changing Roles

In the past, the development of most legacy systems fell within the domain of an organization's central information systems department, from which users requested software development. In the services model, other organizational entities assume responsibility for certain software development tasks, and the central information systems department retains the responsibility for the computing infrastructure. Thus central information services typically develops and manages the components shared by the entire enterprise, and departments having specific needs may develop their own components, which may rely on the services provided by enterprise-based components.

In the preceding scenario, departmental components may evolve into enterprise components. Additionally, as users become more empowered, they may implement applications based upon existing components or develop their own components. Again, these components may evolve into departmental components or enterprise components over time. The key point is that the development task becomes increasingly distributed throughout the organization, and the central information systems department takes on the role of managing the components within the organization and developing key enterprise components.

Changing Technologies

The available Microsoft technologies used to implement a component-based design have evolved significantly. In the 1980s, Microsoft supported a technology known as Dynamic Data Exchange (DDE), which allowed different programs to communicate with each other. Using DDE, applications communicated by sending and receiving messages that executed commands in the other applications. In addition to executing another application's commands, DDE applications could read and write data between applications. Few applications support DDE today, and those that do usually provide such support for backward-compatibility purposes.

Following DDE, Microsoft implemented a technology known as Object Linking and Embedding (OLE) version 1.0. OLE 1.0 supported compound documents, which allowed the user to incorporate data of different formats into a single application. For example, a user could insert a Microsoft Excel spreadsheet into a Word document. From the concept of compound documents evolved OLE 2.0, which was released in 1993. OLE 2.0 was based on an extensible architecture known as the *Component Object Model (COM)*. Simply put, COM defines the standard by which objects communicate with each other. It is the foundation for component-based development on Windows-based computers.

When Microsoft originally implemented COM technology, COM ran on a single computer. Microsoft has since expanded COM to run on a variety of computers and operating systems. Distributed COM (DCOM) supports object communication over a network and is presently supported on a variety of UNIX-based computers and IBM mainframes. One reason for the success of COM and DCOM is Microsoft's licensing policy. Microsoft licenses COM to other vendors and promotes DCOM as a public Internet technology. Today, COM is the most widely used component model in the world, appearing on more than 150 million systems worldwide.

Many software tools rely on DCOM technology. These tools allow developers to easily create distributed component-based systems. The following list describes some of the software tools you can use to create distributed applications with COM and DCOM:

➤ **Microsoft Transaction Server (MTS)** MTS allows you to create COM-based servers. It provides the infrastructure for sending and receiving objects across a network. MTS manages transactions, security, and database connections. It is also well integrated with Internet Information Server and Microsoft Message Queue Server. Consequently, it is well adapted to the building of three-tier systems.

➤ **Internet Information Server (IIS)** IIS provides a component-based solution to supply reliable application services, comprehensive Web services, and integrated network services.

➤ **Active Server Pages (ASP)** An Active Server Page is an HTML file containing code written in a scripting language such as VBScript. It may also contain references to components. ASP is supported by all Microsoft Web Servers.

➤ **Microsoft Message Queue Server (MSMQ)** MSMQ provides asynchronous message queuing. It allows applications to send messages to each other without waiting for a response. MSMQ is integrated with MTS.

Although an extensive discussion of these tools is beyond the scope of this book, you should be aware that the tools described in the previous list are all well suited to implementing three-tiered applications. The preceding applications are merely a few of the many COM components and services available to the programmer.

Figure 8.5 illustrates how an application might use these tools to build a distributed application.

As shown in Figure 8.5, MTS provides the services to pull data from the database. IIS scripts, in turn, communicate with MTS and send information to remote computers via HTTP for display on a Web page. Information can also be disseminated to remote computers that employ DCOM for use by another application (consumer). Finally, MSMQ servers can disseminate information to remote computers using MSMQ services. MSMQ is suitable when no response from the client is required. To better understand these concepts, study the case of Utility Systems Incorporated, whose project you will be working on in this chapter.

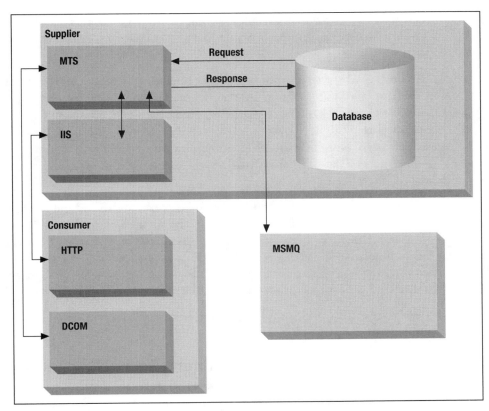

Figure 8.5   Implementation of a distributed application.

Utility Systems Incorporated (USI) supplies electricity to three western states. The company wants to update its system to analyze electrical consumption by its customers. USI uses this information to determine how much power to generate in the future. The present system is mainframe-based. The company is converting this system to one that will run on multiple personal computers.

The existing power generation system performs the following tasks:

➤ Each day, the system records, in a text file, the amount of electricity used by all of USI's customers. The text file contains one record for each minute of the day. Thus each input file contains 1,440 records. Each record contains two fields. The first field stores the date and time of day, and the second indicates the amount of power consumed.

➤ The existing system reads the input file and performs statistical analysis on it. The company uses this information to determine how much power to generate at its power plants.

➤ After computing the statistical information, the program produces a summary report.

USI wants to implement this program on personal computers. In addition, to minimize costs, the company would like to use existing software components where possible.

To illustrate these relationships, consider one possible solution to USI's business problem. The MTS component (data service) provides data to the business services component. This component could potentially produce the desired statistical results. The application layer (consumer) would display this information. Note that this chapter's application will use only existing components. That is, Microsoft Excel will supply both the business services and data services.

The task of defining OLE and COM and the exact relationship between the two are beyond the scope of this book. To implement components, however, you simply need to know that OLE objects allow you to embed objects inside other objects and that this embedding procedure allows objects to communicate with each other in a language-independent manner. That is, you can use an OLE object from any programming language that supports OLE.

Now that you have seen the tools to implement OLE components, you can proceed to design those components.

The Three Views Of Component-Based System Design

The process of designing a component-based system is divided into three phases, also referred to as *views*. The term "system" is used in this context rather than the term "application" or "program." A component-based system will likely consist of several individual programs (components), that work in unison to solve a business problem.

Designing a component-based system requires interaction between multiple individuals within an organization. Such personnel include software developers, managers, and the users themselves. All of these individuals participate in the design phase and fulfill a specific role. In this chapter, the term *design team* refers to the people who participate in the design process. The function of the design team is to define the characteristics of the implementation. Several groups must perform specific design functions:

➤ **Project management**   Is charged with obtaining information from users and ensuring that the design accurately satisfies the users' needs. This group also deals with usage scenarios, which represent the users' view of what the system should accomplish.

➤ **Program management**   Manages the design itself. This group is essentially in charge of the design process.

➤ **Development**   Will ultimately be responsible for implementing the design. This group evaluates the feasibility of the design and notes how well the design coexists with existing programs.

➤ **User education** Assesses the issues surrounding training users to interact with the new system and the effect of migrating users from an old system to a new one.

➤ **Testing and quality assurance** Verifies that the implemented system is consistent with user requirements. This team tests each new application and performs quality assurance to ensure that the implemented system works as intended.

➤ **Logistical** Examines the infrastructure issues related to the deployment of a new system.

The component-based design process has three phases:

➤ **Conceptual** In the first phase, the design team defines the conceptual view. It requires a complete understanding of the business problem to be solved and the way in which the system will solve that business problem. This stage does not involve writing code or specifying the technologies that will be used to solve the problem.

➤ **Logical** Designing the logical view requires the translation of the conceptual design into business objects, which are meaningful business terms or business processes. For example, an invoice, a customer order, and a payment are all business objects.

➤ **Physical** As the design team defines the physical design, it translates the business objects into physical components. During this phase, the development team defines which technologies will be used and specifies where individual components will be implemented.

Depending on the size and structure of an organization, one individual may assume multiple roles or several individuals may fulfill a single role. In addition, in each of the three design phases, the focus of the design should be aimed at solving a user or business need. The focus is not on software development but, rather on how a solution will solve a particular business problem.

Although the preceding list implies that the three design phases occur in a linear order, this is not the case. The conceptual design generally does progress into the logical design, which progresses into the physical design, but the design team may perform parts of each phase concurrently. Furthermore, as the design process continues, the design team may discover errors and omissions in a particular phase. For example, the design process may have reached the logical view when the design team discovers that an element of the conceptual design was omitted. In this situation, the design team should update the conceptual design as needed. The design process can then progress to the logical view.

The remainder of this section discusses each of these three design phases, beginning with the conceptual design.

Conceptual Design

In the conceptual design phase, the design team defines the system's requirements. No matter what type of system is being implemented, it should solve a particular business need or problem. As such, the business need should drive the development. If a system does not correctly solve the business need, it is worthless.

To properly understand the business problem, the design team typically develops usage scenarios. A *usage scenario* directly represents the system as viewed by the user, describing how the user will interact with the system. Usage scenarios should be designed for two different states: the current state and the future state. In many situations, the design process involves converting a monolithic legacy system (current state) to a component-based system (future state). Fully documenting the business processes involved in the existing system can help the design team understand the strengths and weaknesses of the current state. This documentation of the existing system can then serve as a foundation for creating the usage scenarios for the proposed system (future state).

Documenting the future state of the system is the key to creating an effective design. This design must incorporate the user's vision of how the software will work. It also must include each business activity that takes place as well as the data necessary to support that business activity. For example, usage scenarios for USI's desired system would likely identify the following:

➤ **Input file** To be read that contains raw statistical data

➤ **Processing** To take place on the input file

➤ **Output** Produced by the system

To produce a document that completely defines the usage scenarios, you can divide the creation of the conceptual design into six basic steps. As you view these steps, remember that usage scenarios are intended to allow the design team to document the users' view of the business solution.

1. Identify all potential users and their roles. In this step, the team defines the end users' view of the application, which involves the appearance of the system and the users' interaction with it. End users can be internal or external to the company. In this step, management also focuses on the application's adherence to business rules, business practices, and the rules of data integrity. In addition, the team defines the different needs of the different levels of management. High-level or strategic managers will likely require that the system produce information helpful in the process of strategic decision making.

2. Create user profiles. A user profile accurately represents a user in terms of both physical and psychological factors. In this phase, the perceptions and

attitudes of the users are well defined along with their work responsibilities. The design team compiles profiles from several users to fully understand the problem at hand.

3. Create business profiles. The business itself is considered a user, and different business segments may be considered to represent different users. For example, a specific department may have one set of user requirements, whereas another department may have quite different needs. Business profiles may take into account the mission of the business, its responsibilities and activities, and the number of employees.

4. Collect input. Many techniques exist to gather input from users, and each technique has its own advantages and disadvantages. Various input techniques will be discussed in more detail later in this chapter.

5. Document usage scenarios. The usage scenarios must be presented in such a way that they accurately describe the business problem and its solution. Several techniques exist to accomplish this task. For example, usage scenarios may consist of narrative text, flowcharts, and tables. The design team may also create program prototypes to help describe the business solution.

6. Validate usage scenarios. After the usage scenarios have been fully defined, they should be validated by each constituent user to ensure their correctness. As users find errors or omissions, the design team should update the usage scenarios.

The preceding list identified input collection as part of the usage scenario process. As noted there, many techniques exist to collect information from users. Unfortunately, surveys often provide limited information. Furthermore, the quality and usefulness of a survey relate directly to the quality of the survey itself; hence a poorly designed survey will generate poor results. A user survey can, however, provide a foundation for more in-depth analysis.

User interviews tend to provide a better understanding of the business problem than user surveys, but require more time and resources to carry out. The information obtained directly from a user interview tends to be more detailed than the information obtained from a survey. Furthermore, the user interview is more dynamic. The user may identify specific business problems previously not considered by the design team.

The information generated by help desks can also prove useful. This department is responsible for answering user questions as they arise. Knowing the types of questions asked and the frequency with which they arise can help the design team better understand the business problem.

Shadowing is another technique to obtain user input. Shadowing consists of passive or active user observation. In passive shadowing, the interviewer observes user activities without direct user interaction. Active shadowing combines passive observation with interaction much like that in a user interview.

The ultimate goal of the usage scenario is to define—through narrative text, structured text, prototypes, or other means—the future state of the system, as seen by the end users. As an illustration of this process, consider the example of a technician analyzing power consumption for a given day. The following paragraph illustrates a usage scenario defined in narrative text from the perspective of a single user:

I perform the following tasks to analyze the power consumption results for a specific day. I use an input file containing two columns. The first column contains the date and time of day, and the second column contains the amount of electricity consumed at that exact time. One record exists for each minute of the day. I load the data into the application and call statistical functions to calculate the minimum, maximum, mode, percentile, and variance. Once I have calculated these values, I prepare a report summarizing the information.

Typically, the design team combines narratives from multiple users into structured text, which tends to be more detailed and precise than narrative text. Structured text contains three well-defined parts:

➤ **Preconditions** Consist of circumstances that cause the event or scenario to occur.

➤ **Steps** Consist of a series of actions that take place to solve the business problem. These steps focus on the tasks carried out. They should concentrate on what happens rather than on how it happens.

➤ **Postconditions** Consist of the outcomes of the scenario.

Consider the narrative text in the previous scenario rewritten as structured text containing preconditions, steps, and postconditions:

Preconditions:

➤ Input data exist such that each file contains the power consumption values for one day. For each file, one record exists containing the power consumption values for each minute of the day.

➤ The user has access to the input file.

Steps:

1. Open the input file.
2. Select the range of values.
3. Compute the minimum and maximum data values.

4. Compute the mode on the input values.

5. Compute the 90th percentile on the input file.

6. Compute the variance on the input file.

7. Display the results.

Postconditions:

➤ The results are displayed on the terminal.

After the design team prepares the usage scenarios, they should be validated. The process of validation allows the user to review the usage scenarios to ensure that they accurately represent the business tasks. The validation phase has two goals. Ultimately, the user must agree to the usage scenario. If the user discovers errors in the scenario, the design team will need to correct the problems. In addition, the user may discover omissions in the usage scenario. Again, the design team must correct the usage scenario and revalidate it.

Multiple techniques exist to validate the usage scenarios. A walkthrough of the usage scenario is one way of performing the validation task. A second technique is to carry out the validation via role playing. Third, the design team can perform the validation task by prototyping.

The conceptual design process is not linear. That is, the design team does not complete a finite series of steps to complete the conceptual design. Instead, the conceptual design process is iterative. That is, as the design process progresses, the design team may discover that new design elements are needed, or that existing design elements are no longer relevant. In these situations, the conceptual design should be updated. This process should continue until all members of the design team agree that the conceptual design is correct.

Once the design team completes and validates the conceptual design, it can move to the second phase of the design process. This phase of the design process transforms the conceptual design into a logical design.

Logical Design

In the logical design phase, the design team migrates the conceptual design toward a physical implementation. One key part to building the logical design is to accurately define the business objects and business services. A *business service* is analogous to a business task or business process. For example, the input data representing the power consumption for a given day could be considered a business object. The statistical operations performed on that data are considered business services.

In the logical design phase, the design team should defer several parts of the system development. For example, it should not specify the technologies used to implement the system until the physical design phase begins. The following list summarizes the activities performed in the logical design phase:

➤ **Identification of business objects and business services** The conceptual design provides the basis for defining the business objects and business services. Several techniques (methodologies) exist to accomplish this task. The design team may use one of these techniques or perform a noun/verb analysis (discussed later in this section) from the usage scenarios. Consider the preceding usage scenario. The input file (noun) is a business object. Computing the minimum, maximum, and other values are considered verbs (compute).

➤ **Definition of interfaces** A business object communicates with other business objects and with the user via a programmer interface. Business objects should be as independent as possible from other business objects. That is, one business object should not rely on the services of other objects unless absolutely necessary.

➤ **Identification of dependencies between business objects** Sometimes, one business object may call or rely upon other business objects. When the design team identifies dependencies between business objects, they should be eliminated or minimized where possible so that the component will be usable by the greatest number of applications. Identifying and minimizing object dependencies is a subjective process. In some cases, the nature of business objects implies dependencies. For example, a statistical task implies the existence of (is dependent upon) an input file. When dependencies cannot be eliminated, try to organize business objects such that frequently changing objects are grouped together and relatively stable objects are grouped together. Such an organization will minimize the number of components that must be modified later.

➤ **Validation of the logical design against usage scenarios (conceptual design)** The business objects and their interfaces must be carefully examined to ensure that they accurately model the conceptual design.

➤ **Revision of the logical design** Like the conceptual design, the logical design process is typically iterative, and the full definition of business objects is not accurately defined on the first pass. Thus, after the design team completes the first attempt at the logical design, it is revisited until team members are satisfied with the design.

As mentioned, business objects are most easily identified by locating the nouns in the usage scenarios. For example, raw statistical data are considered a business object. You can identify business services by finding the verbs in the usage scenarios. If a person or other object sends or receives information to and from the system, that person or object is likely a business service.

As an illustration of a noun/verb analysis, Figure 8.6 illustrates the possible business objects and services in the statistical analysis example. Note that it is possible to first design the business objects and then the business services, or to design both concurrently.

In Figure 8.6, one business object and five business services have been defined. The power consumption object stores the physical data. It consists of one record for each minute of the day. Each record contains the minute of the day followed by the amount of power consumed during that interval. Four business services compute the mode, percentile, range, and variance based upon that data. The final business service produces a summary report.

After you define the business objects and business services, you must define their interfaces. Interfaces indicate any required preconditions and the calling conventions for each business object. One precondition might require the existence of an input file. A calling convention might be that the service to print the summary report will likely have arguments containing the resulting statistical values.

At this point in the design process, the solution remains language-independent. That is, the design team does not begin to specify whether the implementation will use Visual Basic or some other language. The design is also hardware-independent. Finally, the design does not address where individual components will execute. That is, it does not specify whether a particular component will run on a client or server.

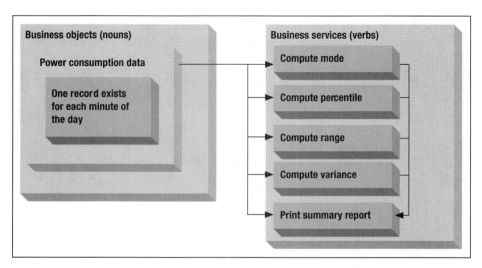

Figure 8.6 Business objects and services.

The interface for the component should be completely and accurately defined prior to its implementation. With a clearly defined interface, component developers who will use that interface can rely on its standards. In this way, the interface becomes a contract between the service (supplier) and its clients (consumer).

Once the design team completes the logical design, it validates and compares the logical design against the conceptual design to ensure correctness. This task is referred to as baselining. The following members of the design team perform the baselining task:

➤ **Product management** Compares the conceptual and logical design to verify that they are fully linked.

➤ **Program management** Assures concurrence with other project teams so that the design will fit with other enterprise applications.

➤ **Development** Analyzes the completeness of the design. Team members verify that the interfaces of each business object are fully defined and that the design accurately reflects the business objects.

➤ **User education** Analyzes usability issues. These personnel check that the navigational capabilities and user interface goals are met.

➤ **Quality assurance** Verifies that they can test the application and that the design adheres to the vision established by the user.

As the design team revises and refines the logical design, several key factors are taken into account:

➤ Some business objects or services may be found to be irrelevant. These objects or services should be eliminated.

➤ The design team may notice that two business objects share the same information or perform a similar activity. Redundant business objects should be combined.

➤ Vague or incomplete business objects should be clarified and made more concrete.

➤ Some business services must be performed as a group. In this situation, the group should be modeled as a distinct business service.

Once the design team completes the logical design and establishes the baseline, the design process moves on to the physical design phase.

Physical Design

In the physical design—the third phase of the design process—the design team fully defines which services the component will provide and how the component will encapsulate those services to form the component's interface (that is, the way a component interacts with other programs). In addition, the design team must define how each component will be packaged and deployed.

Whereas the conceptual design and logical design remain independent of any particular technology, the physical design process focuses upon defining the physical hardware and software that will actually implement the physical design. Again, the design team performs specific functions:

➤ **Product and program management** Ensure that the design is consistent with the usage scenarios.

➤ **Development** Specifies how components will be built and which services they will provide.

➤ **User education** Plans training programs.

➤ **Quality assurance** Verifies that the component design is complete and plans a testing scenario for the physical design.

➤ **Logistics** Plans for component delivery and setup.

Like the other phases of the design process, deriving the physical design involves a series of steps. Although the design team generally performs these steps in an iterative manner, it may also perform steps concurrently and revisit steps as they detect errors and omissions. If this situation occurs, then the conceptual or logical design should be corrected and a revised baseline established.

The design team performs the following tasks to define the physical design:

1. Allocate services to components

2. Perform a plan for initial component distribution

3. Specify the interface for each component

4. Implement a plan to distribute components across the network

5. Validate the physical design and that the application will perform correctly and effectively on the network

The following subsections discuss each of these steps in turn.

Allocating Services To Components
During this step, the design team uses the already-designed business objects as a template to define the actual components. Services should be separated into user, business, or data services. These services form the basis for defining components. The initial component design remains abstract at this point.

Component Distribution
At this point in the physical design process, the design team defines the relationships between supplier and consumer components. The components

that provide user services will likely run on the user's desktop machine. Data services will likely run on a remote server machine.

The component distribution phase has two parts. In the first part, the design team plans the component distribution. In the second part, the design team imposes physical constraints, such as server performance and network bandwidth. As the design team imposes these constraints, team personnel will likely allocate components to different computers. The following list describes some of the physical constraints that may require changes to a component's distribution:

➤ A server node may have insufficient processing capacity to meet the demands of the client nodes using those services.

➤ The data passed between client and server may consume excessive network bandwidth.

➤ Component dependencies that exist across network boundaries may be unacceptable in the event of network failure or the failure of a particular network node.

Several guidelines help the design team package and distribute components:

➤ Components should be distributed to the sites where they are used. This principle is referred to as *locality of reference*.

➤ Services that are dependent on each other should be implemented in the same component. Services that are not invoked together are candidates for separate components.

➤ Components should be packaged such that they have a high probability of usability by other components or consumers.

➤ You should implement components using existing components or purchased components, where possible.

A component can be very small or very large. A small component would perform a small, narrowly defined task, such as the validation of a Social Security number. This type of component tends to be reusable by many other components and have a more general purpose. Managing several small components can create problems, however, as the organization must face the task of keeping track of many more components.

Large components can perform more complex tasks. For example, a bank may implement a component to obtain and summarize the data necessary to print bank statements. In general, a component should be independent of other components and usable by other applications.

The component designer must also consider containment and aggregation. These principles determine how the interfaces of internal components are exposed to other applications. Using the principle of *containment*, the design team makes the interface of an inner component visible only through the outer component. To use the functionality of the inner component, the consumer must work with the outer component. Using the principle of *aggregation*, the design team exposes the interfaces of the inner components along with the outer components. Although containment is more commonly employed, aggregation can reduce the overhead resulting from components calling other components.

Component Interface Specification

A component's interface is a contract between a supplier and consumer. The only way for a consumer to use the services provided by a component is through this interface. The following list contains the terms of the contract or interface specification:

➤ Interface name

➤ Supported services

➤ Preconditions

➤ Postconditions

➤ Dependencies

➤ Interaction standard

Earlier, you learned about interfaces related to COM. The terms *services*, *preconditions*, *postconditions*, and *dependencies* have been discussed as well. A component may have multiple interaction standards. That is, it may interact with consumers by using stored procedures or an OLE interface. A single interaction standard, however, is preferable over multiple interaction standards. To the greatest extent possible, interaction standards should be language-independent, which means that multiple languages can call them. When considering an interaction standard, carefully consider the following requirements:

➤ The standard should support remote location and activation.

➤ The location of the component should be transparent to the clients that use the component.

➤ The component should be extensible by adding new interfaces.

➤ The developers maintaining the component should be able to replace the implementation of the component.

Network Distribution Plan

After defining the component interface and interaction standards, the design team must plan for the component's distribution across the network. A component should reside where it will be used to minimize network traffic. It must also account for expected network usage, because a component may become unusable if the network bandwidth is insufficient to process requests and return responses. In addition, the design team must consider network correctness—how components and applications interact with other components and applications. That is, the component must be able to operate reliably and correctly over a network.

After completing the design process, the design team should validate the component's physical design to ensure that it meets the user requirements and maps directly to the services defined by the business objects. Furthermore, the physical design should be validated to ensure that it will perform as expected in a networked environment. Last, the following criteria should be met:

➤ The workstation and the server must have processing capabilities sufficient to meet user requirements.

➤ The network must have bandwidth sufficient to transport data between machines.

➤ The physical design must minimize the impact of failure on a machine or on the network itself.

IMPLEMENTING THE DESIGN USING EXISTING COMPONENTS

Creating Automation Objects

In many programming situations, you do not have to create new components. Instead, you can rely upon the services of applications that expose themselves as components. For example, when you use Microsoft Word and Excel to perform word processing and spreadsheet tasks, respectively, you probably use these applications via their visual interfaces. You also can access them via their component interfaces.

Applications that support OLE automation support one or more objects. For example, Word supports Application and Document objects (among others), and Excel supports Application and Worksheet objects (among others). To create an ActiveX object in Visual Basic, you call the **CreateObject** function.

Syntax

> **CreateObject**(class, [servername])

Dissection

➤ The **CreateObject** function creates an automation object.

➤ The **class** argument contains the application name and class that the **CreateObject** function will create.

➤ The optional **servername** argument contains the name of a network server where the automation object will be created.

Code Example

```
Dim wrdCurrent As Word.Application
Dim xlCurrent As Excel.Application
Set wrdCurrent = CreateObject("Word.Application")
Set xlCurrent = CreateObject("Excel.Application")
```

Code Dissection

The first two statements declare object variables. The first object variable can store a reference to a Word Application object. The second object variable can store a reference to an Excel Application object. The third statement calls the **CreateObject** function, which creates an instance of Word, and stores a reference to that instance in the object variable **wrdCurrent**. The final statement uses the **CreateObject** function to create an instance of an Excel object and to store a reference in **xlCurrent**.

8

Before you can reference an automation object like Word or Excel, you must add a reference to the automation object using the Project References dialog box. The process is similar to the one you use to add a reference to an ActiveX control to the project.

To add a reference to an automation object:

1. Start Visual Basic, if necessary, and open the Project file named Chapter.08\Startup\Ch8_S.vbp.

2. Click on Project, and then click on References to open the References dialog box.

3. Locate the Microsoft Excel 8.0 Object Library in the list box, and select the item by clicking on the checkbox. Click on OK to add the reference to the object library, and close the dialog box. If you are using Office 2000, select the Microsoft 9.0 Object Library.

 To complete the rest of this chapter, you must have Office 97 or a later version installed on your computer. Note also that this section presumes basic literacy with Excel.

Once you have added the reference to the Excel object library, you can access its objects in the same manner that you accessed the ADO object library. That is, the object libraries contain collections, which in turn contain references to objects, which in turn contain references to other collections.

In the USI program, you will use the Excel component to import a text file and to perform statistical calculations. As this chapter is not intended to provide an in-depth analysis of the Excel object hierarchy, you will work with only a few of the supported objects. For further information, refer to the Excel developer's reference.

Before you can use the Excel objects, you must create an instance of the application with the **CreateObject** function.

To create an instance of Excel:

1. Activate the Code window for the form named frmCh8, and enter the following statement in the general declarations section of the module:

```
Private xlCurrent As Excel.Application
```

2. Select the **Form_Load** event procedure, and enter the following statements:

```
Set xlCurrent = CreateObject("Excel.Application")
xlCurrent.Visible = True
```

3. Test the program. When run, the program creates an instance of Excel. Although the user will not interact with Excel directly, by setting the **Visible** property of the application to **True**, you can see the effect of the code as you write it.

4. Close the instance of Excel. You will learn how to end this application programmatically later in the chapter. End the program to return to design mode.

Now that you have created an instance of Excel, you can program the application's objects. To access Excel programmatically, you use an object hierarchy much like ADO. Figure 8.7 illustrates the part of the Excel object hierarchy you will study in this chapter.

As shown in Figure 8.7, the **Excel Application** object is the root object. Excel disk files are stored as Workbooks. Each Workbook, in turn, contains some number of Worksheets. Range objects can be created at will to reference a cell or group of cells. Figure 8.8 shows an instance of Excel with workbooks and worksheets open.

In the first step in implementing the physical design, you create an Excel worksheet, open the input file, and read the contents of the input file into the Excel worksheet. For this step, you will use an existing component to implement the business service of opening a file.

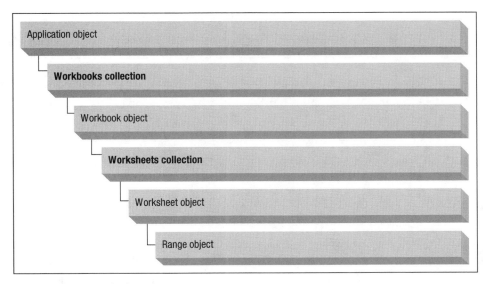

Figure 8.7   Excel objects.

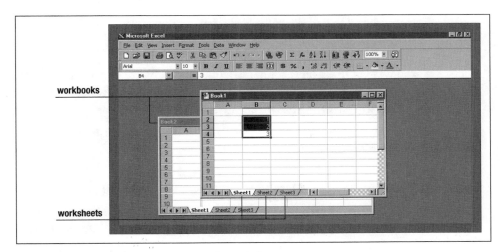

Figure 8.8   Excel workbooks and worksheets.

To create a new Workbook object and default worksheets in that workbook, you call the **Add** method pertaining to the Workbooks collection, as shown in the following statements:

```
Private xlCurrent as Excel.Application
Private wbCurrent as Excel.Workbook
Set xlCurrent = CreateObject("Excel.Application")
Set wbCurrent = xlCurrent.Workbooks.Add
```

You can also create a new worksheet by calling the **OpenText** method pertaining to the **Workbooks** collection.

Syntax

expression.**OpenText**(Filename, Origin, StartRow, DataType, TextQualifier, ConsecutiveDelimiter, Tab, Semicolon, Comma, Space, Other, OtherChar, FieldInfo)

Dissection

➤ The expression must be a reference to a **Workbooks** collection.

➤ The **OpenText** method opens a text file in a new Worksheet object.

➤ The **Filename** argument contains the name of the file to open.

➤ The **Origin** argument specifies the type of the text file. The valid constants for this argument are **xlPlatform**, **xlMacintosh**, **xlWindows**, and **xlMSDOS**.

➤ The **StartRow** argument defines the row where Excel will begin inserting text.

➤ The **DataType** argument defines the format of the text file. Use the constant **xlDelimited** for ASCII–delimited files and the constant xlFixedWidth for fixed-format files.

➤ The **TextQualifier** argument defines the delimiter surrounding text fields. Valid constants are **xlTextQualifierDoubleQuote** (which is the default value), **xlTextQualifierSingleQuote**, and **xlTextQualifierNone**.

➤ If ConsecutiveDelimiter is set to true, multiple consecutive delimiter characters will be treated as one delimiter.

➤ The optional **Tab** argument, if set to **True**, causes the Tab key to be used as the delimiter. **The DataType** must be set to **xlDelimited**.

➤ The optional **Semicolon** argument causes the semicolon character to be used as the delimiter. The **DataType** must be set to **xlDelimited**.

➤ The optional **Comma** argument causes the comma character to be used as the delimiter. The **DataType** must be set to **xlDelimited**.

➤ The optional **Space** argument causes the space character to be used as the delimiter. The **DataType** must be set to **xlDelimited**.

➤ The optional **Other** argument causes the delimiter used to be specified by the **OtherChar** argument. The **DataType** must be set to **xlDelimited**.

➤ The optional **OtherChar** specifies the delimiter character when the **Other** argument is set to **True**. If multiple characters are specified, only the first character of the string is used.

➤ The optional **FieldInfo** argument contains an array that is used to parse the individual data columns. The interpretation depends on the value of **DataType**.

Code Example

```
xlCurrent.Workbooks.OpenText" _
    FileName:="C:\a\demo.txt",Origin:=xlWindows, _
    StartRow:=1,DataType:=xlDelimited, _
    TextQualifier:=xlDoubleQuote, _
    ConsecutiveDelimiter:=False, _
    Tab:=True,Semicolon:=False,Comma:=True, _
    Space:=False,Other:=False, _
    FieldInfo:=Array(Array(1,3),Array(2,1))
```

Code Dissection

The preceding statement opens the Windows file named C:\a\demo.txt. The call to the **OpenText** method reads the file into the first row of the new worksheet. The file is ASCII–delimited with commas and double quotes surrounding the text fields. The use of the **Array** argument will be discussed next.

8

With delimited data, the **FieldInfo** argument contains an array of two–element arrays. Each two–element array specifies how Excel will convert a particular column. The first element is the column number (one-based). The second element contains one of the numbers shown in Table 8.1.

The column specifiers can appear in any order. If no column specifier for a particular column is defined, the column is parsed with the General setting. Consider the following example used in this chapter's program to read to input columns:

```
Array(Array(1, 3), Array(2, 1))
```

Table 8.1 **FieldInfo** formatting values.

Value	Meaning
1	General
2	Text
3	MDY date
4	DMY date
5	YMD date
6	MYD date
7	DYM date
8	YDM date
9	Skip the column

The preceding statement indicates that two columns will be read. The first column has a data type of **Date**, and the second column has a data type of **General**.

The **FieldInfo** argument functions differently when the source data have fixed-width columns. In this case, the first element in each two-element array specifies the position of the starting character in the column. The value is an **Integer**. Character 0 (zero) is the first character; character 1 (one) is the second character, and so on. The second element in the two-element array specifies the parse option for the column as a number between 1 and 9, as listed in the preceding table.

You can now open the input file. To accomplish this task, use the CommonDialog control. After the user specifies the file name, your code will open the text file.

To open a text file into a new worksheet:

1. Activate the Code window for the **mnuFileOpen_Click** event procedure, and enter the following statements:

```
On Error GoTo Cancel_Open
    cdl1.Filter = "Text Files|*.txt"
    cdl1.CancelError = True
    cdl1.ShowOpen
    xlCurrent.Workbooks.OpenText _
        FileName:=cdl1.FileName, _
        Origin:=xlWindows, _
        StartRow:=1, DataType:=xlDelimited, _
        TextQualifier:=xlTextQualifierDoubleQuote, _
        ConsecutiveDelimiter:=False, _
        Tab:=True, Semicolon:=False, Comma:=True, _
        Space:=False, Other:=False, _
        FieldInfo:=Array(Array(1, 3), Array(2, 1))
    xlCurrent.DisplayAlerts = False
    Exit Sub
Cancel_Open:
```

2. Test the program. Excel appears and receives focus. Minimize the Excel window. On the form's menu bar, click on File, and then click on Open. Select the file named Chapter.08\Startup\Demo.txt. Click on Open to close the dialog box and open the file. Maximize the Excel window. The text file should be loaded into Excel, as shown in Figure 8.9.

3. End the program to return to design mode.

4. Exit Excel.

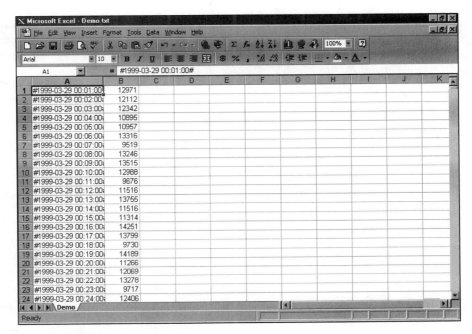

Figure 8.9   Text file in Excel.

Now that you have opened the text file, you need to learn how to reference spreadsheet cells programmatically, call Excel functions, and return the results of those functions to your Visual Basic program.

To reference a single cell or group of cells, you use the Range object. Consider the following statements to reference cells:

```
Range("A5")
Range("A5:B10")
Range("C5:D9,G9:H16")
```

The first statement references the single cell at A5. The second statement references the rectangular block of cells from A5 to B10. The final statement references multiple areas. In the USI program, you need to reference the cells in column B containing the power usage data. Because each input file has exactly the same structure, this column will always contain 1440 rows of data. Consider the following statement to call the **Mode** function on the necessary cells:

```
xlCurrent.Worksheets(1).Range("C1").Formula = _
    "=Mode(B1:B1440)"
```

This statement requires careful examination. The fragment "=Mode(B1:B1440)" stores the **Mode** function. This function takes the cells B1 through B1440 as arguments. The **Mode** function itself will be discussed in a moment. The code **xlCurrent.Worksheets(1).Range("C1").Formula** stores the string as a formula in the cell C1. The statement therefore computes the Mode of the input data and stores the result in the cell "C1".

Consider a similar statement to compute the Minimum of a list of values and store the result in the cell "C2":

```
xlCurrent.Worksheets(1).Range("C2").Formula = _
    "=Min(B1:B1440)"
```

You can call any Excel function and store the result in a cell using this technique.

At this point, you have the necessary tools to compute the statistics required by the USI program. Although Excel supports many more statistical functions than described here, you will use only five (**Min**, **Max**, **Mode**, **Percentile**, and **Variance**) to illustrate how to use Excel as a component. These functions are explained below.

The *mode* is a statistical measure of location. It returns the value appearing with the greatest frequency. For example, given the following list of numbers,

1, 2, 2, 3, 3, 3, 4

the value of the mode is 3, because the value 3 appears with the greatest frequency. If no two values in a list are repeated, the mode is undefined. That is, no value exists for the mode.

The *range* defines the minimum and maximum values within a set of data. In the previous list of numbers, the minimum is 1 and the maximum is 4. The Excel functions **Min** and **Max** compute the minimum and maximum values in a range, respectively.

The *percentile* identifies the location of values in the data set that are not necessarily central location values. This measure provides information regarding how the data items are spread over the interval, from the lowest to the highest values. In this way, percentiles indicate the dispersion or variability of the data set. To help understand the percentile function, consider the following list of power consumption numbers:

1224, 1224, 1228, 1250, 1280, 1290, 1310, 1390, 1422, 1620, 1710, 1890

Suppose you wanted to know the 90th percentile—that is, the value where at least 90 percent of the items have this value or a lesser value. The 90th percentile for this list of numbers is 1701. You will rely on the Excel component to perform the computation.

Table 8.2   Calculating the variance.

Count	Value	Mean	Squared Deviation (Value − Mean)^2
1	1224	1403.167	32,100.69
2	1224	1403.167	32,100.69
3	1228	1403.167	30,683.36
4	1250	1403.167	23,460.03
5	1280	1403.167	15,170.03
6	1290	1403.167	12,806.69
7	1310	1403.167	8680.028
8	1390	1403.167	173.3611
9	1422	1403.167	354.6944
10	1620	1403.167	47,016.69
11	1710	1403.167	94,146.69
12	1890	1403.167	237,006.7

8

Variability involves determining how data items are distributed about the mean. Again, consider the following list of numbers:

1224, 1224, 1228, 1250, 1280, 1290, 1310, 1390, 1422, 1620, 1710, 1890

You can compute the sample mean by adding all of the values together and dividing the result by the number of sample values. In the preceding list, the sum of the values is 16,838 and the list contains 12 items. The mean is therefore 16,838/12, or 1403.167.

Although the mean provides an average, it does not illustrate how the values are distributed about the average. *Variance,* however, measures the variability of deviation about the mean. The larger the variance, the greater the dispersion of values about the mean. To compute the variance, consider the values in Table 8.2.

In Table 8.2, each data value is subtracted from the mean and squared. The sum of the squared values equals 533,699.7. The variance is defined as the sum of the squared values divided by the number of values. Thus, 533,699.7/12 = 44474.97. In Excel, you can compute the variance of a sample using the **VARP** function. The following syntax discussion describes the statistical components used in this chapter. You can also use Excel Help to obtain help on these functions.

Syntax

   MIN(range)
   MAX(range)

> **MODE**(range)
> **PERCENTILE**(range,k)
> **VARP**(range)

Dissection

➤ The **MIN** function computes the smallest value in a range.

➤ The **MAX** function computes the largest value in a range.

➤ The **MODE** function computes the average value in a range.

➤ The **PERCENTILE** function finds the kth percentile within a range.

➤ The **VARP** function computes the variance based upon a population.

Code Example

```
MIN(B1:B1440)
MAX(B1:B1440)
MODE(B1:B1440)
PERCENTILE(B1:B1440,.90)
VARP(B1:B1440)
```

Code Dissection

The preceding statement fragments compute the min, max, mode, 90th percentile, and variance for the cells B1 through B1440.

You now have the necessary tools to calculate the statistical output based upon the contents of the input file.

To define the statistical component:

1. Activate the Code window for the **mnuFileCalculate_Click** event procedure, and enter the following statements:

```
xlCurrent.Worksheets(1).Range("C1").Formula = _
    "=Min(B1:B1440)"
txtMin = xlCurrent.Worksheets(1).Range("C1")

xlCurrent.Worksheets(1).Range("C2").Formula = _
    "=Max(B1:B1440)"
txtMax = xlCurrent.Worksheets(1).Range("C2")

xlCurrent.Worksheets(1).Range("C3").Formula = _
    "=Mode(B1:B1440)"
txtMode = xlCurrent.Worksheets(1).Range("C3")
```

```
xlCurrent.Worksheets(1).Range("C4").Formula = _
    "=Percentile(B1:B1440,.9)"
txtPercentile = _
xlCurrent.Worksheets(1).Range("C4")
xlCurrent.Worksheets(1).Range("C5").Formula = _
"=Varp(B1:B1440)"
txtVariance = _
    xlCurrent.Worksheets(1).Range("C5")
```

2. Remove the following line from the **Form_Load** event procedure, which will prevent Excel from becoming visible:

```
xlCurrent.Visible = True
```

3. Write the following statements in the **mnuFileExit_Click** event procedure. These statements will exit Excel and end the program.

```
xlCurrent.Quit
Unload Me
```

4. Test the program. Open the file Chapter.08\Startup\Demo.txt. Click on File, and then click on Calculate. The statistical values should appear in the form. Click on File, and then click on Exit to end the program and Excel.

5. Exit Visual Basic.

You have now completed the USI program. This section illustrated how tasks can be performed using Excel. Performing these same tasks by writing Visual Basic code would be significantly more complex.

CHAPTER SUMMARY

This chapter presented the fundamental concepts related to designing component-based programs and the benefits of using a component-based architecture to implement applications. Component-based programs tend to offer improved reusability, consistency between applications, application flexibility, and manageability. The chapter also discussed how to use existing components by referencing the object libraries contained by Microsoft Word and Microsoft Excel.

To create the conceptual design:

➤ Understand the existing application.

➤ Identify the users and their roles.

➤ Create user profiles.

➤ Create business profiles.

➤ Develop usage scenarios.

➤ Validate the usage scenarios.

To create the logical design:

➤ Identify the business objects and business services.

➤ Define interfaces.

➤ Identify dependencies between business objects.

➤ Validate the logical design against usage scenarios.

➤ Revise the logical design as necessary.

To create the physical design:

➤ Allocate services to components.

➤ Perform the initial component distribution plan.

➤ Specify the interface for each component.

➤ Plan the distribution of components across the network.

➤ Validate the physical design.

To create an automation object:

➤ Call the **CreateObject** function with the following syntax:

```
CreateObject(class, [servername])
```

To add a reference to an automation object:

➤ Activate the Project References dialog box.

➤ Locate and add the desired automation object libraries to the project.

To open a file in Excel:

➤ Call the **OpenText** method using the following syntax:

```
expression.OpenText(Filename, Origin, StartRow, DataType,
TextQualifier, ConsecutiveDelimiter, Tab, Semicolon, Comma, Space,
Other, OtherChar, FieldInfo)
```

To reference a group of cells:

➤ Use Excel's **Range** function. The **Range** function can reference a single cell, a rectangle of cells, or a group of cells.

To perform statistical analysis on a range of values using Excel:

➤ Call the **MIN**, **MAX**, **MODE**, **PERCENTILE**, and **VARP** functions having the following syntax:

MIN(range)

MAX(range)

MODE(range)

PERCENTILE(range,k)

VARP(range)

REVIEW QUESTIONS

1. Which of the following is a benefit of using components to implement programs?

   a. reusability

   b. consistency

   c. flexibility

   d. reduced cost

   e. All of the above

2. Which of the following is a member of the design team?

   a. users

   b. managers

   c. production and development teams

   d. All of the above

   e. None of the above

3. Which views make up the services model?

   a. client services, server services

   b. logical services, physical services

   c. user services, business services, data services

   d. All of the above

   e. None of the above

4. Which of the following tasks is performed in the conceptual design phase?

   a. the identification of users and their roles

   b. the development of usage scenarios

   c. the definition of business objects and services

   d. Both a and b

   e. None of the above

5. Which of the following tasks is performed in the logical design phase?

    a. the definition of business objects and services

    b. the definition of interfaces

    c. the identification of dependencies between business objects

    d. All of the above

    e. None of the above

6. Comparing the logical design against the physical design to ensure correctness is referred to as:

    a. error checking

    b. producing the physical design

    c. baselining

    d. result checking

    e. None of the above

7. The third phase of the design process is the _____ design.

    a. logical

    b. conceptual

    c. physical

    d. implementation

    e. None of the above

8. Which of the following is a guideline for packaging and distributing components?

    a. New components should be developed in favor of using existing components.

    b. The physical location of a component is not relevant.

    c. Components should be packaged such that they are usable by other components.

    d. Both a and b.

    e. None of the above.

9. Which of the following statements is true?

    a. Components can be large or small.

    b. The principles of containment and aggregation refer to how consumers can access components and subcomponents.

    c. Component dependencies should be minimized.

    d. All of the above.

    e. None of the above.

10. Which of the following statements pertaining to network component distribution is true?

   a. Network traffic should be minimized.

   b. All components should run on local clients.

   c. All components should run on remote servers.

   d. Both a and b.

   e. Both a and c.

11. Which dialog box do you use to create a reference to an automation object?

   a. the Components dialog box on the Project menu

   b. the Automation dialog box on the View menu

   c. the References dialog box on the Project menu

   d. the AddReference dialog box

   e. None of the above

12. What is the name of the function to create an automation object?

   a. **NewObject**

   b. **CreateAutomationObject**

   c. **New**

   d. **CreateObject**

   e. None of the above

13. What is the name of the Excel object to define a group of cells?

   a. Group

   b. Cells

   c. Range

   d. Block

   e. None of the above

14. Which of the following objects does Excel support?

   a. App

   b. Document

   c. Page

   d. Sheets

   e. None of the above

15. What is the name of the method to open a text file using Excel?
    a. **Open**
    b. **OpenText**
    c. **OpenFile**
    d. **Input**
    e. None of the above

16. Write a statement to create an instance of an Excel Application object and store a reference to the application in the object variable named xlCurrent.

17. Assuming that xlCurrent references an instance of the Excel application, write a statement to open the ASCII-delimited text file named A:\Demo.txt. Assume that the data should be read into the first row of the spreadsheet, that the file is comma-delimited, and that the double quote character surrounds text strings.

18. Write the statement fragment to reference the range of cells between A10 and B20.

19. Write a statement to calculate the mode of the cells from A10 to B20 and store the result in the cell C1. Use the first worksheet in the Worksheets collection.

20. Write a statement to calculate the 90th percentile of the cells from A10 to B20 and store the result in the cell C2. Use the first worksheet in the **Worksheets** collection.

HANDS-ON PROJECTS

Project 1

In this project, you will derive the conceptual, logical, and physical designs for an application given the following scenario.

> USI wants to upgrade its customer service application. This application adds new customers, determines whether a customer is required to pay a deposit based on his or her credit history, and generates work orders to connect or disconnect electrical service. The following narrative describes the process used by the customer service representative (CSR) to process requests for service connection and disconnection:
>
> When a customer requests a connection for electrical service, the CSR uses the customer database to determine whether the customer has previously received electrical service from the company. If so, and if the customer has made payments on time, he or she is not required to pay a

deposit. Otherwise, the customer must pay a $50 deposit. If the customer has never had service, he or she must pay a deposit.

If a customer exists, his or her account must be reactivated. Otherwise, the customer must be created and a new account activated. Finally, the CSR must print a work order, which is sent to a technician to either connect or disconnect electrical service. In the case of service disconnection, the CSR must deactivate the account and generate a deactivation work order.

Using any word processor, define the design for the component as follows:

a. From the previously described usage scenario, create structured text for the conceptual design.

b. From the conceptual design, derive the business objects and the business services making up the logical design.

c. Derive the physical design.

8

Project 2

In this project, you will use a financial function supported by Microsoft Excel. Depending on the processor speed of your computer, this program may produce a run-time error. This error occurs because the add-in has not finished loading when Excel tries to perform computations. Excel supports several functions in addition to those supported by Visual Basic. For example, Excel supports additional functions to compute the depreciation of an asset. In this exercise, you will use the **DB** function:

```
DB(cost,salvage,life,period,month)
```

➤ The **DB** function computes the depreciation of an asset for a specified period using the fixed-declining balance method.

➤ The **cost argument** contains the initial cost of the asset.

➤ The **salvage argument** contains the salvage value (value at the end of life) of the asset.

➤ The **life argument** contains the number of periods over which the asset will be depreciated.

➤ The **period** is the amount of time for which you want to compute the depreciation.

➤ The **month** contains the number of months in the first year (used for partial years).

    a. Run the executable program named Chapter.08\Exercise\ Ex2Demo.exe. Figure 8.10 shows the completed form for the program with both input and output values completed. Enter the input values shown in Figure 8.10. Click on the Calculate button to compute the output values. Exit the program.

b. Start Visual Basic, and create a new project. Save the form using the name Chapter.08\Exercise\frmEx2.frm and the project using the name Chapter.08\Exercise\Ex2.vbp.

c. Add a reference to the Excel 8.0 or 9.0 object library.

d. Declare an object variable to store a reference to an Excel Application object.

e. Write the statement to create an instance of an Excel Application object and store the object reference in the variable you declared in Step d.

f. The statistical function you will use is stored as an Excel add-in. Enter the following statements just after the statement to create the Excel Application instance. These statements load the add-in into the current Excel instance.

```
xlCurrent.AddIns("Analysis ToolPak").Installed _
          = False
       xlCurrent.AddIns("Analysis ToolPak").Installed _
          = True
```

g. Write the code for the **Calculate** command button. This code should store the input values in cells on the current worksheet.

h. The remaining code in the **Calculate** command button should call the **DB** function once for each depreciation period. You will likely want to create a **For** loop to perform this task. For each period, store the depreciation amount in the output text box, as shown in Figure 8.10.

i. Write the code to exit the program. This code should end the Excel instance and exit the Visual Basic program.

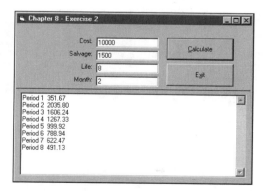

Figure 8.10   Exercise 2 Completed form.

j. Test the program. Use the values shown in Figure 8.10 for testing. Exit Visual Basic.

Project 3

In this project, you will use Excel to perform financial functions not supported by Visual Basic. Depending on the processor speed of your computer, this program may produce a run-time error. This error occurs because the add-in has not finished loading when Excel tries to perform computations. You will use two of these functions in this exercise:

```
CUMIPMT(rate, nper, pv, start_period, end_period, type)
CUMPRINC(rate, nper, pv, start_period, end_period, type)
```

➤ The **CUMIPMT** function computes the cumulative interest on some number of payments.

➤ The **CUMPRINC** function computes the cumulative principal on some number of payments.

➤ **rate** stores the interest rate.

➤ **nper** contains the number of periods

➤ **pv** contains the present value of the loan.

➤ **start_period** and **end_period** contain the starting and ending periods to examine, respectively.

➤ **type** determines when payments are made. A value of 0 indicates that payments are made at the beginning of the period and a value of 1 indicates that payments are made at the end of the period.

a. Run the executable program named Chapter.08\Exercise\ Ex3Demo.exe. Figure 8.11 shows the completed form for the program with both input and output values. Enter the input values shown in Figure 8.11. Click on the Calculate button to compute the output values. Exit the program.

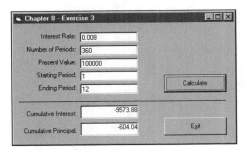

Figure 8.11 Exercise 3 Completed form.

b. Start Visual Basic, and create a new project. Save the form using the name Chapter.08\Exercise\frmEx3.frm and the project using the name Chapter.08\Exercise\Ex3.vbp.

c. Add a reference to the Excel 8.0 or 9.0 object library.

d. Declare an object variable to store a reference to an Excel Application object.

e. Write the statement to create an instance of an Excel Application object and store the object reference in the variable you declared in Step d.

f. The statistical functions you will use are stored as an Excel add-in. Enter the following statements just after the statement to create the Excel Application instance. These statements load the add-in into the current Excel instance.

```
xlCurrent.AddIns("Analysis ToolPak").Installed _
    = False
xlCurrent.AddIns("Analysis ToolPak").Installed _
    = True
```

g. Write the code for the **Calculate** command button. This code should store the input values into worksheet cells. Then, you need to call the **CUMIPMT** and **CUMPRINC** functions. Use the values you stored into the cells as arguments to the functions. Finally, read the values back into the labels on the form.

h. Make sure that Excel is not visible when the user runs the program.

i. Write the code to exit the program. This code should end the Excel instance and exit the Visual Basic program.

j. Test the program. Use the values shown in Figure 8.11 for testing. Exit Visual Basic.

CHAPTER NINE

REUSING CODE WITH CLASS MODULES

AFTER READING THIS CHAPTER AND COMPLETING THE EXCERCISES, YOU WILL BE ABLE TO:

➤ Define a class using a different type of module, called a class module

➤ Create properties for the class to define one part of the class's interface

➤ Create methods for the class to define the remainder of the class's interface

➤ Write code to create instances of the class and to call its properties and methods

➤ Compare the code in a class module with a COM object project produced by Visual Basic

➤ Create an abstract class containing an interface but no implementation

➤ Use the **Implements** statement to derive classes from the abstract class

➤ Implement polymorphism using multiple ActiveX interfaces

FUNDAMENTALS OF A CLASS MODULE

Previewing The Completed Application

In Chapter 8, you learned the essentials of component-based design and saw how to implement applications by using existing components. You saw that Microsoft Windows supports component-based programming using COM and DCOM. In this chapter, you will implement components and code to utilize those components.

The completed project for this chapter differs from the applications that you have created in previous chapters. Instead of containing a form and standard modules, it contains a form module and multiple class modules. The form, as usual, provides the visual interface for the program. The class module contains the implementation for each type of question. That is, it contains the necessary properties and methods to store and analyze the response to a question. Visual Basic stores this new type of module in the Class Modules folder in the Project Explorer, as shown in Figure 9.1.

In Figure 9.1, three class modules are defined. The **MultipleChoice** and **TrueFalse** class modules provide the implementation for the multiple choice and true/false question types, respectively. The third class module, named **Question**, is an abstract class. An abstract class defines the interface for the types of questions implemented by other classes.

The completed form in this chapter contains a very simple user interface. In practice, the user interface for the program would likely be more sophisticated, but the intent of this chapter is to demonstrate how to create and program class modules. Thus the code in the form focuses on how to use the properties and methods defined in the various class modules.

To preview the completed application:

1. Start Visual Basic, and load the Chapter.09\ Complete\Ch9_C.vbp.

Figure 9.1   Class modules in the Project Explorer.

2. Open the form module named **frmCH2C.frm.** Figure 9.2 shows the form. The form contains a command button with the caption Test Add Method. The code in this button's **Click** event procedure creates class instances (objects) from the class module. The code then calls the methods pertaining to the class to store the characteristics of a question and the responses to that question. To review the responses to the added questions, the user can click on the Test List Questions command button. The Exit button unloads the current form, ending the program. The code in the **Form_Load** event procedure creates the instances of different questions. As you analyze these procedures, you will see that the code looks much like the code you wrote to manipulate ADO and other objects in previous chapters.

3. Run the program. Click on the Test Add Method command button. This function does not produce any visible output. Instead, the command button executes the necessary code to add 10 simulated true/false questions and 10 multiple choice questions.

4. Click on the Test List Questions command button. The text box on the form displays each question and the percentage of each question response.

5. End the program, and then exit Visual Basic.

The discussions presented in this chapter, and the chapters that follow, illustrate the process of creating classes, collections, and ActiveX controls. The creation of classes and ActiveX controls is much easier to perform in Visual Basic than it is in most other languages, including C++.

An Introduction To Components

As discussed in Chapter 8, one goal of object-oriented programming is to create reusable code. You write reusable code by creating components. In Visual Basic, you implement the components you design as class modules. Other programmers can then use those components to create programs more easily.

In the past, you have created control instances, such as text boxes, to define the visual interface for a form, without considering how Visual Basic implements the text box. That is, you read and wrote properties, called methods, and wrote

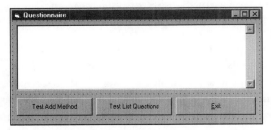

Figure 9.2 Completed form.

code in response to events. The code executing in the properties and methods displayed data, validated data, and performed other tasks in a way that was transparent to you as the programmer. You have also programmed objects such as the recordset, contained by the ADO hierarchy, without worrying about how ADO implemented the Recordset object. You, as the programmer, needed to understand only how to use the methods and properties supported by the recordset.

Writing programs that use components has many benefits:

➤ Programmer productivity improves when complex tasks can be performed without the programmer having to worry about how the component performs the task.

➤ Because a component performs a standard set of tasks, multiple programs can use the same component. As you have seen in previous chapters, any Visual Basic program can use intrinsic and ActiveX controls, ADO objects, and other objects. Each of these uses exemplifies the term *reusable code*.

➤ The internal workings of a component can be changed as long as the interface (the component's properties, methods, and events) remains constant. Thus the programmer responsible for maintaining the class module (component) can modify the implementation of the code inside the component to improve performance without disturbing the component's interface, as viewed by the programmers using it. As an example, consider a sorted list box (the **Sorted** property is set to **True**). The code inside the list box dictates how the list box internally sorts the data. The type of sort algorithm used to arrange the data could therefore be changed without affecting the programs that use the list box.

The terms *class* and *object* have been used throughout this book. A class is a template or blueprint for an object; by creating an instance of a class, you create an object that you can access programmatically. In this chapter, you will create your own classes (components) and then create objects based on those classes. The use of the terms *class* and *object* is intentional. In this chapter, you will focus on the process of creating new classes rather than on the process of creating objects from existing classes. Before creating a new class, you must understand a few key concepts and terms that form the core of object-oriented programming.

A class has a well-defined interface by which it communicates with other programs. The data and processes acting on that data constitute a class's interface. The term *interface* has the same meaning as defined in Chapter 8 in the discussion of component interfaces. The coupling of data and the processes acting on that data is referred to as *encapsulation*. In other words, class modules encapsulate data and processes, thereby forming the class's interface. In Visual

Basic, the interface of a class contains a defined set of properties and methods. An interface may also respond to events. Collectively, the properties, methods, and events form the class's interface. The interface of a class is commonly called the *exposed part*, or the public part, of the class.

In addition to a public or exposed part, every class has a private part, also known as the *hidden part*. The hidden part of a class is not visible to the programs that use the class. It does not matter how the hidden part of a class performs its tasks, so long as the exposed part does not change. The term *implementation* refers to the hidden part of a class.

A class's interface defines the protocol by which it communicates with other programs; it does not have to include an implementation. In other words, the interface of a class defines the properties and methods of the class but not what those properties and methods do. This task is left to the implementation. This concept will be discussed in more detail later in the chapter.

One component can have multiple interfaces. Consider the Recordset object as an example. The recordset's interface consists of properties to determine the status of the current record pointer and methods to locate different records. Suppose you wanted to extend the functionality of the recordset by adding a new method that would count the number of records in the recordset without having to locate the last record to obtain an accurate value. Additionally, suppose you have found a way to improve the performance of an existing method by modifying its code (hidden part). To maintain compatibility with programs that use the original interface, one component can be created with the improved code of the original methods but with two separate interfaces. Older programs would use one interface, and programs that require the extended functionality could use the other interface. The creation of two interfaces for one component ensures that the enhanced methods can be used by any program that relies on the component, regardless of which interface is used. Figure 9.3 illustrates a class with multiple interfaces.

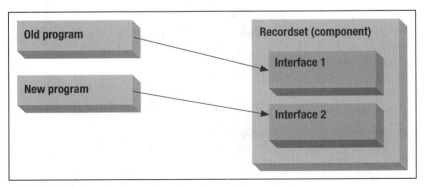

Figure 9.3   Multiple interfaces for a class.

Another concept, inheritance, also pertains to object-oriented programming. *Inheritance* is the capability of one class to use the properties and methods of an existing class. Put in other terms, classes can be derived from other classes. Again, consider the recordset example. You can set properties to create different types of recordsets, each of which has unique characteristics. For example, a Dynaset-type recordset allows data to be both read and written. A Snapshot-type recordset creates a static view of the data that cannot be changed. A Table-type recordset has characteristics that differ from those of both the Dynaset-type and Snapshot-type recordsets.

Despite their differences, these three types of recordsets share certain characteristics. Using the concept of inheritance, you could create a general class to express the properties and methods common to all three classes. The specific details of each type of recordset could be delegated to another class. In this case, a separate class for each type of recordset would exist. Each class would have properties and methods that might be unique to the class as well as other properties and methods that might be inherited from the general class.

When referring to inheritance, the term *base class* identifies the name of the class from which other classes inherit properties and methods. In addition to saying that a class can inherit properties and methods from a base class, you can say that class is derived from a base class. Figure 9.4 illustrates the concept of inheritance.

Visual Basic does not support inheritance in the same way that programming languages such as C++ do. Instead, Visual Basic implements inheritance by creating multiple interfaces for a class.

Closely related to the concept of inheritance is the notion of an abstract class. An abstract class contains no implementation. Rather, it defines only the

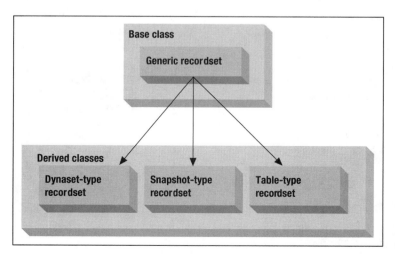

Figure 9.4 Inheritance.

interface for the class. Thus, while an abstract class defines the properties and methods for a class, it does not define what those properties or methods do. Other classes derived from the abstract class supply the actual implementation for the abstract class.

A related concept is polymorphism. When several functions (methods) share the same name, they exploit polymorphism. Again, think of the recordset example in which three types of recordsets share the same interface. Even though three different interfaces exist and each executes different code, one interface can reference the recordset by using the same object name and the same name for the respective properties and methods. Most object-oriented programming languages, such as C++, implement polymorphism using inheritance. In contrast, Visual Basic implements polymorphism using multiple interfaces for an abstract class.

The previous terms pertain to object-oriented programming in general. That is, you can apply the concepts when programming in Visual Basic, C++, or any other object-oriented programming language. Having defined these terms, you will now see how classes operate with Visual Basic and Windows.

Component Object Modules

Intrinsic controls such as the list box, ActiveX controls, and programmable objects (such as ADO) are not disparate independent classes. Furthermore, the consistent look and feel of many Windows programs is not an accident. Consistency exists because Windows defines a standard set of intrinsic controls and other classes, such as list boxes, that many different development environments can use. Whether you use C++ or Visual Basic, you ultimately reference the same underlying Windows code that implements the list box.

The list box is an intrinsic control, so the executable file produced by Visual Basic stores the code. Visual Basic does not actually implement the list box itself, however. Rather, the list box is a control provided by the Windows operating system and made available to programmers using languages such as Visual Basic or Visual C++. Thus Visual Basic merely provides an interface to the underlying ListBox control supported by Windows.

When you create an instance of an ActiveX control on a form, such as the DataGrid, the code for control is stored inside a separate file, usually with the extension of .ocx. As mentioned in previous chapters, the .ocx file must be distributed with a Visual Basic program for the program to work properly on other computers.

When you used the ADO hierarchy programmatically, you used the methods and properties pertaining to the various objects to navigate and perform operations on the data supported by those objects. All of these objects are derived from classes. Each class may have very different characteristics. For example, the list box has a visible interface, and the ADO objects do not.

ActiveX controls support Property Pages, and intrinsic Visual Basic controls do not. All these classes, however, have one feature in common—they can all operate together in the same program.

The concept of a class is not unique to Visual Basic. Rather, the Windows operating system uses classes to support object-oriented programming. When you create your own classes or ActiveX controls, Visual Basic implements those controls and classes internally using COM technology, as discussed in Chapter 8. Although a detailed explanation of the internal COM implementation is beyond the scope of this book, the basics of COM technology will help you understand why class modules work in the way that they do. As a result, you will find information about COM technology interspersed with the Visual Basic class module presentation in this chapter. This material will help you understand how the programs that you are creating operate.

Visual Basic uses ActiveX and COM technology to create all class modules. The class modules you will develop in this chapter are but one type of ActiveX component supported by Visual Basic, known as *code components*. Conceptually, the term *code component* has the same meaning as the term *component* that was defined in Chapter 8. In this chapter, you will implement the component, rather than designing it.

The Roles Of Author And Developer

Another distinction needs to be made before you create your first class module. In the previous chapters, the term *programmer* referred to a person developing a program. This definition requires refinement when used in the context of class modules (code components).

➤ The *author* is the person creating a code component (class module) or ActiveX control.

➤ The *developer* is the one who writes a program that uses a code component or ActiveX control.

In this chapter, you will assume the roles of both author and developer. When you create the code for the class module (component), you will assume the role of the author. When you write code in the form module to test the class module, you will assume the role of developer. The Visual Basic IDE allows you to take on both of these roles in the same instance of Visual Basic, thereby simplifying the debugging and testing of class module code.

Before you, as the author, can begin to implement a class module, you must understand the module's structure.

Anatomy Of A Class Module

A form module and a class module share a similar structure and syntactical rules. For example, a form module is a class, and the **Form** class supports Public variables, which are treated as properties. Class modules also support Public variables, which Visual Basic interprets as properties of the class. You can hide data in the **Form** class by declaring Private variables in a form module. You can also hide data in a class module by declaring Private variables. Furthermore, when you display or load a form, Visual Basic creates an instance of the form from the **Form** class.

You can think of a class module as a form module with no visible interface. A class module has a general declarations section containing Public and Private variable declarations. **Sub** and **Function** procedures supply the functionality for the class, just as they do for other types of modules. As in other modules, you can declare variables and procedures as either Public or Private. If you declare a variable or procedure as Public, you expose the variable or procedure; that is, other modules can reference the variable or procedure. If you declare a variable or procedure as Private, other modules cannot call it. Thus Public variables and procedures form the exposed part of the class. Private variables and procedures form the hidden part of the class and are not part of its interface. Visual Basic treats Public variables as properties of the class; it treats **Public** procedures as methods of the class. Figure 9.5 illustrates the logical components of a class module.

9

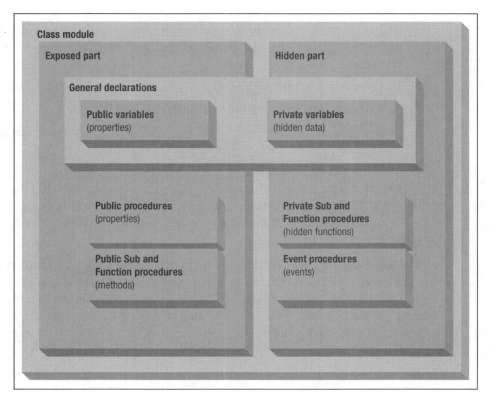

Figure 9.5 Anatomy of a class module.

When you, as the author, create class modules with multiple properties and methods, you should organize the properties and methods such that the **Property** procedures appear just after the general declarations section to improve the readability of the module. In addition, you should place the **Sub** and **Function** procedures immediately after the **Property** procedures. Within the categories of Public variables, **Property** procedures, and **Function** and **Sub** procedures, keep the modules sorted by name. When you review printed code listings, this organization of variables and modules will make it much easier to locate a procedure.

The proper naming of properties and methods will have a positive effect on the usability (interface) of the class module. The following list describes the conventions for naming these properties and methods, which are the same as those for other types of procedures:

➤ Property and method names cannot contain spaces.

➤ Use whole words, with the first letter of each word capitalized.

➤ If the name of a property or method seems too long (this length is a subjective decision), use the first syllable of a word rather than obscure abbreviations. Abbreviations are acceptable only if they are well known. For example, *qty* and *amt* are common abbreviations for the words *quantity* and *amount*, respectively. If you abbreviate a word for a property or method, abbreviate that word for all properties and methods in the class to ensure consistency.

➤ Use plural names for collections.

➤ When naming properties, use nouns such as AirplaneType.

➤ When naming methods, use a verb as the first word in the method's name, followed by a noun, such as AddAirplane.

➤ You cannot use the following as property or method names: QueryInterface, AddRef, Release, GetTypeInfoCount, GetTypeInfo, GetIDsOfNames, or Invoke. If you try to use these names, a compilation error will occur. These names are invalid because the underlying COM objects use them.

The interface for a class module requires careful design and planning. As the class's author, you should carefully consider the exposed properties and methods of the class. If the interface supports too many properties and methods, it may seem unwieldy to the developers that must use the class. Thus, before implementing a component, consider carefully the design material discussed in Chapter 8.

As the author, you also need to decide whether to implement a specific business object as a method or as a property. Consider the properties and methods of classes you have already used, such as ADO. As a general rule, if the procedure requires multiple arguments, you should implement it as a method rather than as a property. When performing an action, such as opening a recordset, you should implement the task as a method. If you are reading or writing a data value, you should generally implement the business object as a property, because a property implies the referencing of data rather than the performance of a task.

In practice, you, as the author, will create classes independently of the programs that use them. In this chapter, however, you will create the properties and methods of the class; then, using a form module, you will create object variables to reference the class. These object variables will, in turn, be used to reference the properties and methods of the class. This technique will illustrate how to create and debug class modules.

In the next chapter, you will see how to separate class modules into one project and the forms that use the class modules into another project. That is, you will separate into discrete projects the class modules developed by an author and the form modules created by a developer.

Creating A Class Module

You can create a new class module or add an existing class module to a project, just as you can with any other module file. Clicking on Project and then clicking on Add Class Module will activate the Add Class Module dialog box, which allows you to create a new class module or add an existing class module to a project. You then write code in the module's Code window in the same way as you write code for any other type of module. Because a class has no visible interface, however, no corresponding Form window exists.

Class modules appear in the Project Explorer in the Class Modules folder. A project may contain zero, one, or many class modules. Like other module files, Visual Basic stores a class module on the disk in a single text file. Class modules have the .cls file extension.

Unlike a form, which supports several properties and events, a class module supports only six predefined properties and two events. The following list describes the properties pertaining to a class module, which you can set by using the Properties window:

➤ **DataBindingBehavior** Defines whether the class can be bound to a data source.

➤ **Name** All class modules support the **Name** property. The **Name** property for a class module has the same meaning and purpose as it does for a form module. It is the name by which the developer references a class when creating object variables from that class.

➤ **DataSourceBehavior** Specifies whether an object can act as a data source for other objects.

➤ **Instancing** Determines whether other objects can create an instance of the class with the **New** keyword.

➤ **MTSTransactionMode** Used for components executed by the Microsoft Transaction Server (MTS).

➤ **Persistable** Defines whether an object can save data between one instance of the class and the next.

The **Class_Initialize** and **Class_Terminate** events occur when a Class instance is created and destroyed, respectively. Note that the **Instancing**, **MTSTransactionMode**, and **Persistable** properties only pertain to certain project types.

In the project in this chapter, you will first create the class to represent a multiple choice question. As such, the name of the class will be **MultipleChoice**. The class name conforms to the previously mentioned naming conventions because it consists of complete words with the first letter of each word capitalized.

Marketing Research, Incorporated (MRI), develops and sells software to help businesses analyze the surveys that they conduct. Each survey consists of multiple choice and true/false questions. For each survey, a business may ask a variable number of questions. Furthermore, each question may have different responses.

You will implement a prototype software package for MRI by using object-oriented component-based techniques. More specifically, an object (component) will represent each question. A developer will be able to access the properties and methods of this component to store the responses to survey questions. The component will support other methods that will summarize and perform statistical analysis on the surveys.

To add a class module to the project:

1. Start Visual Basic, if necessary, and then open the project named Chapter.09\Startup\Ch9_S1.vbp.

2. On the menu bar, click on Project, and then click on Add Class Module. Depending on the configuration of your system, the Add Class Module dialog box may appear, as shown in Figure 9.6.

   If the Add Class Module appears, make sure that the New tab is active. Click on Class Module, if necessary, and then click on the Open command button to create a new class module in the project. To open an existing class module, you can click on the Existing tab, and then use the Windows Explorer interface to locate and select the class module to open. If the dialog box does not appear, Visual Basic creates a new class module automatically. It automatically opens the Code window after creating the class.

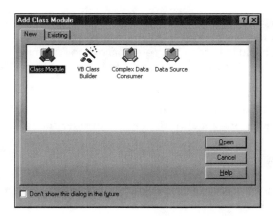

Figure 9.6   Add Class Module dialog box.

3. If the Properties window is not already open for the class module, open it by clicking on the class module in the Project Explorer, right-clicking on the mouse button, and then clicking on Properties on the pop-up menu.

4. Set the **Name** property to **MultipleChoice**. This name becomes the name of the class that will be used by the developer when creating instances of the class.

5. Save the class module on the disk by clicking on File, and then clicking on Save Class1 As. Use the name Chapter.09\Startup\MultipleChoice.cls.

As shown in Figure 9.6, the New tab of the Add Class Module dialog box supports three additional options. The author uses the VB Class Builder to help create complex object hierarchies and the **Complex Data Consumer** and **Data Source** classes to create data aware classes.

As noted earlier, class modules have no visible interface. If you click on the class module in the Project Explorer, Visual Basic disables the View Object button. As with the ADO objects you used in previous chapters, the only way for the developer to create ADO class instances and to program those objects is to do so programmatically. Objects created from class modules work in the same way. That is, the developer must use code to create an instance of the class, to set its properties, or to call its methods.

Although you can display message boxes and input boxes from a class module, the practice is uncommon. Rather, when an error occurs inside the class or information needs to be communicated outside the class, you typically use one of two other options. In the first option, the procedure in the class module raises an error. In the second option, the author implements a procedure as a **Function** procedure, which returns a value to the calling procedure. For example, if you, as the developer, tried to set a property to an

invalid value from a form module, the procedure in the class
module that was executing could raise an error. The procedure in
the form module should then contain an error handler to determine
the source of the error and specify your next action.

At this point, you have created a class. You can now declare object variables to reference the class and to create instances of the class. Consider the following statements:

```
Private Sub Form_Load()
    Dim qmc As New MultipleChoice
    Dim qmc1 As MultipleChoice
    Set qmc = qmc1
End Sub
```

These statements assume that the class named **MultipleChoice** exists. The name **MultipleChoice** represents the value stored in the **Name** property of the class itself. The first statement declares an object variable named **qmc**. Because the **New** keyword appears in the statement, the code will create an instance of the **MultipleChoice** class and store an object reference in the object variable named **qmc**. The second statement creates a second object variable, but no new object. That is, the object variable references nothing. The final statement causes both object variables to reference the same underlying object. These statements operate in the same manner as the statements you have used previously to reference control instances, form instances, and other objects.

Although you have created a class, the class does not yet support any properties or methods. In other words, it has neither an interface nor an implementation. To create the properties and methods for a class module, you must write the code for the class.

Creating The Properties Of A Class

The simplest way to create a property for a class is to declare a Public variable in a class module. A Public variable declared in a class module works like a Public variable in a form module. Because other modules can read and write the Public variable, the variable is exposed and is part of the class's interface. Assume that the following Public variable specifies the name of the question that has been declared in the **MultipleChoice** class:

```
Public Name As String
```

By declaring this variable, you create a property in the **MultipleChoice** class having the name "Name." This variable name illustrates that the variable "Name" is not the same as the class name (the value you assigned to the class via the Properties window). For example, given the previous variable declaration and the class named **MultipleChoice**, the following statements will create an instance of the class and assign a value to the **Name** property:

```
Dim qmc1 As New MultipleChoice
qmc1.Name = "How many children do you have?"
Debug.Print qmc1.Name
```

The first statement creates an object variable named **qmc1** from the **MultipleChoice** class. Because the statement contains the **New** keyword, the statement creates a new instance of the **MultipleChoice** class. The second statement then assigns a value to the **Name** property, which, in this case, is the name of the multiple choice question being asked. The assignment statement sets the value to a character string. The final statement reads the value of the property and prints its value to the Immediate window.

Assume that a survey had two questions instead of just one. Given this situation, you, as the developer, could create a second instance of the class. For example, consider the following statements:

```
Dim qmc2 As New MultipleChoice
qmc2.Name = "How many pets do you have?"
Debug.Print qmc2.Name
```

Combining these statements with the previous statements would cause two objects to be created from the **MultipleChoice** class. You can reference these objects using the object variables **qmc1** and **qmc2**.

To demonstrate the use of a property implemented with a Public variable, you will now create the **Name** property for the class, create two instances of the class, and assign a value to the **Name** property for each instance.

To create two questions and set their **Name** properties:

1. Locate the general declarations section of the class module named **MultipleChoice**, and enter the following statement. (Note that you are assuming the role of the author, as you are developing code for the component.)

   ```
   Public Name As String
   ```

2. In the form module, enter the following statements in the **cmdTestName_Click** event procedure. (Note that you are assuming the role of the developer, as you are using the component.)

   ```
   Dim qmc1 As New MultipleChoice
   Dim qmc2 As New MultipleChoice
   ```

```
qmc1.Name = "How many children do you have?"
qmc2.Name = "How many pets do you have?"
txtOut = vbNullString
txtOut = qmc1.Name & vbCrLf & qmc2.Name
```

3. Test the program. The form module appears. As shown in Figure 9.7, the form for this startup program differs from the form for the completed program. It contains buttons to test specific parts of the class module as you develop each part.

4. Click on the Test Name Property command button. The two question names should appear in the output text box, as shown in Figure 9.7.

5. Exit the program to return to design mode.

The two **Dim** statements create two instances of the **MultipleChoice** class. In other words, the current survey now contains two multiple choice questions. The two assignment statements set the **Name** properties for each of the two questions.

```
qmc1.Name = "How many children do you have?"
qmc2.Name = "How many pets do you have?"
```

The syntax to reference a property of a class instance is the same as the syntax to reference a Public variable declared in a form module. You use the object variable name, followed by a period, followed by the property you want to reference.

The final statements illustrate how to read the values of the two properties:

```
txtOut = vbNullString
txtOut = qmc1.Name & vbCrLf & qmc2.Name
```

Although implementing a property with a Public variable is suitable in some circumstances, the technique has serious limitations. To overcome the limitations of using Public variables as properties, you can implement properties

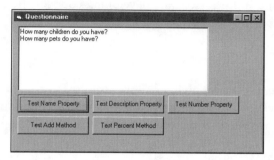

Figure 9.7 Testing the **Name** property.

by creating **Property** procedures. Choosing whether to implement a property by using a Public variable or by using **Property** procedures depends on the data stored in the property:

➤ When the value of a property cannot be validated for correctness, you should use Public variables. When the data can be validated, you, as the author, should implement **Property** procedures. The code in these procedures can validate the input when the developer sets the value of the property.

➤ You should implement **Property** procedures to create read-only properties. **Property** procedures are also required to create write-once properties. As the name implies, the value of a write-once property can be written only once. If the developer attempts to store a value in a write-once property a second time, the code in the **Property** procedure should generate a run-time error.

➤ Situations that arise when writing a value to a property should change the value of another property or update a hidden variable. You can use **Property** procedures to execute this type of code.

In addition to creating exposed data with Public variables and **Property** procedures, you may want to maintain data that is visible only inside the class. In other words, you, as the author of the class, will be able to use the data, but the developer using the class will not.

Hiding Data In The Class

You hide data in a class using the same techniques that you have used with form and standard modules: as the author, you declare a Private variable in the general declarations section of the class module. Private variable names should have the standard prefixes for variable names rather than adhering to property naming conventions, because Private variables are not properties.

The class module you are creating will ultimately store all of the responses to a question. The number of responses to any given question may vary. These requirements make a dynamic array the most suitable structure to store this data. The class, rather than the program using the class, determines how the responses are stored. Consequently, the array should be private to the class. In fact, you cannot declare a Public array in a class module. If you attempt to do so, Visual Basic will generate a syntax error. The values for the array will be Integers denoting the response, and the name or the array will be **mintValues**. The following declaration in the general declarations section of the class module creates the Private array:

```
Private mintValues() As Integer
```

You can now write the code to declare the hidden variable that will store the responses to a question.

To create a hidden variable, assume the role of the author and enter the following statement in the general declarations section of the **MultipleChoice** class module:

```
Private mintValues() As Integer
```

The **Add** method will use this variable to add responses to the question along with the other methods that analyze the responses. Note that the newly created dynamic array is hidden in the class and can be accessed only using the properties and methods that you, as the author, expose.

In addition to creating exposed and hidden data using variables, you can expose data by creating **Property** procedures.

Creating Properties With Property Procedures

Visual Basic allows the class to execute code when a property is read or written by creating **Property** procedures inside a class module. You, as the component's author, usually write **Property** procedures in pairs. One **Property** procedure executes when the developer writes code that reads the property, and the other procedure in the pair executes when the developer writes code to set the property. Reflecting this fact, **Property** procedures are often referred to as paired procedures.

In Visual Basic, the syntax of a **Property** procedure resembles the syntax of a **Sub** or **Function** procedure. Each **Property** procedure contains a procedure declaration, which can have arguments, and statements, which execute when the developer writes code that reads or writes the property. You, as the author, implement **Property** procedures using the **Property Get**, **Property Let**, and **Property Set** statements.

The syntax of a **Property Get** procedure resembles the syntax of a **Function** procedure; that is, it returns a value just as a function returns a value. You use the **Property Let** and **Property Set** statements to write properties. These properties operate in a manner similar to **Sub** procedures; they do not return a value. When a **Property** procedure assigns a value to an ordinary variable, you use the **Property Let** statement. When a **Property** procedure assigns an object reference, you use the **Property Set** statement. Conceptually, the **Property Set** statement resembles the **Set** statement used to assign object references.

The name that you give to a pair of **Property** procedures is significant. It must be the same as the name of the property. The procedure name must be exactly the same for both the **Property Let** and **Property Get** procedure pair. This naming approach violates the rule stating that procedure names must be unique. If you create a pair of **Property** procedures with different names, however, you will create two different properties—one for each name.

Syntax

[**Public** | **Private** | **Friend**] [**Static**] **Property Get** *name* [*(argumentlist)*] [**As** *type*]

    [*statements*]
    [*name* = *expression*]
    [**Exit Property**]
    [*statements*]
    [*name* = *expression*]
End Property
    [**Public** | **Private** | **Friend**] [**Static**] **Property Let** *name* [*(argumentlist)*]
    [*statements*]
    [*name* = *expression*]
    [**Exit Property**]
    [*statements*]
    [*name* = *expression*]
End Property

Dissection

➤ You declare **Property** procedures with the **Property Get** and **Property Let** statements. The **Property Get** procedure executes when the developer creates code that reads a property's value. The **Property Let** procedure executes when the developer creates code that writes a property's value.

➤ If you use the optional **Public** keyword, all other procedures in all other modules can call the **Property** procedure. That is, the property is exposed to the developer and part of the interface. If you use the optional **Private** keyword, only the procedures in the class module where the procedure is declared can call the **Property** procedure.

➤ **Friend** procedures restrict the visibility of the property between class modules in a project. Chapter 10 discusses **Friend** procedures in more detail.

➤ The values of the local variables declared in the **Property** procedure will be preserved between calls to the procedure when you use the **Static** keyword.

➤ The required *name* argument defines the name of the property and follows the standard naming conventions for property names.

➤ When setting a property requires arguments, the optional *argumentlist* allows you to pass one or more arguments to set the property.

➤ Inside the **Property** procedure, you may write any number of *statements* that execute when the developer sets the value of the property.

➤ The optional *expression* assigned to the name of the property contains the value returned when the property is read. This statement pertains only to the **Property Get** procedure.

➤ The **Exit Property** statement has the same purpose as the **Exit Sub** or **Exit Function** statements. It causes the **Property** procedure to exit before the last statement in the procedure executes.

➤ The **End Property** statement identifies the end of the **Property** procedure, just as the **End Sub** statement identifies the end of a **Sub** procedure.

When you implement **Property** procedures, you typically write code to store the value of the property in a hidden variable. This hidden variable, although global to the class, is not visible to the modules using the class. As a result, it is not part of the class's interface. When the developer writes code to set the property, the code in the **Property** procedure saves this value to the hidden variable. When the developer writes code that reads the property, the code in the **Property** procedure reads and returns the value of the hidden variable, just as a **Function** procedure returns a value.

Figure 9.8 illustrates the **Name** property you just created, implemented as a pair of **Property** procedures.

As shown in Figure 9.8, when the developer's code sets the **Name** property, the **Property Let** procedure executes, storing the value of the property in the Private variable named **mstrName**. This variable is hidden and cannot be accessed outside the class. When the developer writes code to read the **Name** property, the **Property Get** procedure executes, reading the value from the hidden variable and storing the result in the **Property** procedure name. This syntax is identical to the syntax used to return a value from a function. In this case, however, the **Property** procedure does not execute any code other than that required for manipulating the hidden variable. Thus, the property could be implemented as a Public variable.

Because a form module is considered a class, you can also create **Property** procedures in form modules.

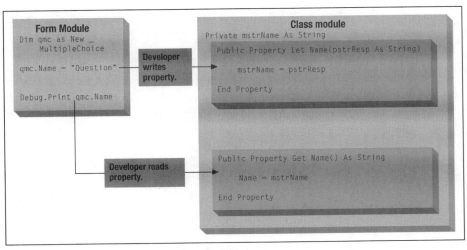

Figure 9.8   Implementation of a **Property** procedure pair.

You might think that a **Property** procedure will execute more slowly than a comparable Public variable because of the overhead required to call the procedure. This is not the case, however. When Visual Basic compiles the class into a COM object, the compiled code implements all properties internally as a pair of **Property** procedures. As a result, no internal differences exist between Public variables and **Property** procedures in a class module.

Now that you have seen the purpose of **Property** procedures, you can implement different types of properties using them.

IMPLEMENTING READ-WRITE PROPERTIES WITH PROPERTY PROCEDURES

You, as the class module author, can implement a property by creating **Property Let–Property Get** paired procedures or by creating **Property Set–Property Get** paired procedures. The **Property Let** procedure assigns a value to a property, and a **Property Set** procedure assigns a reference to an object.

You can use the **Add** Procedure dialog box to create a pair of **Property** procedures. When you set the procedure type to **Property**, the dialog box creates both a **Property Get** and **Property Let** procedure. Alternatively, you can manually enter the procedure declaration in the Code window for the desired class module.

By default, when you use the Add Procedure dialog box to create **Property** procedures, the data type of the argument in the **Property Let** procedure is a **Variant**. You should change this data type to a more specific type, if possible, to improve program performance if you know the type of data that you will store in the property.

Creating read–write properties with **Property** procedures is helpful when you need to validate the value of the property that is being set or you must perform some other operation when the property is read or written. In the MRI project, you will use a pair of **Property** procedures to implement the question name. These **Property** procedures have the same effect as a Public variable, but demonstrate the use of a hidden variable and paired **Property** procedures.

To create a read–write property with a pair of **Property** procedures:

1. Activate the Code window for the class module named **MultipleChoice**, click on Tools on the Visual Basic menu bar, and then click on **Add Procedure** to activate the Add Procedure dialog box.

2. Set the property name to **Name**, set the type to **Property**, and then click on OK.

3. Enter the following statement in the general declarations section of the class module. You will use this hidden variable to store the value of the **Name** property used by the **Property Let** and **Property Get** procedures.

```
Private mstrName As String
```

4. Remove the following statement from the general declarations section of the class module:

```
Public Name As String
```

5. Modify the **Property Let** procedure as follows:

```
Public Property Let Name(pstrResp As String)
    mstrName = pstrResp
End Property
```

6. Modify the **Property Get** procedure as follows:

```
Public Property Get Name( ) As String
    Name = mstrName
End Property
```

7. Test the program. Click on Test Name Property. It has exactly the same effect as the property implemented as a Public variable.

8. End the program to return to design mode.

The statements added in the preceding steps illustrate the technique of using **Property** procedures and a hidden variable to implement a read–write property. The **Property Let** procedure, which is called when the developer's code writes the property, stores the question name in the hidden variable **mstrName**. Conversely, when the developer's code reads the property, the **Property Get** procedure executes. The code in the **Property Get** procedure assigns the value stored in **mstrName** to the property name (**Name**). This technique is analogous to returning a value from a function.

When you implement a property, you create either a Public variable or **Property** procedures, but not both. If you create a Public variable and **Property** procedures with the same name, Visual Basic will generate a compiler error, indicating the existence of an ambiguous name.

Passing Arguments To Property Procedures

The arguments for **Property** procedures must adhere to certain characteristics. Remember that a **Property Get** procedure is a variation of a **Function** procedure—both return a value. The **Property Let** procedure is a variation of a **Sub** procedure—neither returns a value. The **Property Let** procedure requires at least one argument. In the case of a **Property** procedure, one argument is used to set the property. Intuitively, the argument in the **Property Let** procedure should have the same data type as the return value of the corresponding **Property Get** procedure. Specifically, the return value of the **Property Get** procedure must have the same data type as the last argument in the **Property Let** procedure. Consider the following invalid pair of **Property** procedures:

```
Private mintThing As Integer

Property Get Thing() As Integer
    Thing = mintThing
End Property

Property Let Thing(New_Value As Double)
    mintThing = New_Value
End Property
```

These **Property** procedures will generate a compiler error because the data type of the argument in the **Property Let** procedure is a Double, but the data type of the **Property Get** procedure is an **Integer**. In other words, these statements try to set the property to a Double when writing the property, but expect the value to be an Integer when reading the property. The data types of these two values must match exactly. For example, you cannot use a **Variant** or **Object** data type for one procedure and a more specific data type for another.

The following statements will also fail:

```
Private mintThing As Variant
Property Get Thing() As Variant
    Thing = mintThing
End Property

Property Let Thing(New_Value As Double)
    mintThing = New_Value
End Property
```

If you make this type of mistake, Visual Basic will generate a compiler error indicating that the definition of **Property** procedures for the same property is inconsistent.

IMPLEMENTING PROPERTIES WITH PARAMETERS

In the class module that you are developing for MRI, each multiple choice question has five possible responses (the letters "a" through "e"). The meaning of a response will differ from question to question. For example, the letter "a" in one question may mean "very satisfied," while the letter "a" in another question may mean "a family has no children." You, as the author, can apply different techniques to save these responses in the class instance. One possibility would be to store the five descriptions in five different Public variables (properties). For example, you could create the following properties in the class module:

```
Public Response1 As String
Public Response2 As String
. . .
Public Response5 As String
```

Given that you have declared five variables of the same data type, you might be tempted to declare an array of five elements to store the responses and to implement the property as an array, as shown in the following declaration:

```
Public Responses(5) As String
```

If you attempt to compile this statement as part of a class module, however, it will not work. Visual Basic does not support Public arrays in a class module. That is, you cannot create a property that is itself an array. As a solution to this problem, Visual Basic allows you to create **Property** procedures that require multiple arguments. One argument is typically used as an index in a Private array declared in a class module; this array is commonly referred to as a parameterized property. The hidden array (Private array) has the same purpose as the hidden variable that was used to store the **Name** property, as shown previously. Consider the following Private variable and **Property** procedures:

```
Private mstrListDescription(5) As String
Public Property Get ListDescription _
    (Index As Integer) As String
    ListDescription = mstrListDescription(Index)
End Property
Public Property Let ListDescription(Index As _
    Integer, ByVal New_Value As String)
    mstrListDescription(Index) = New_Value
End Property
```

Inside the class module, the Private variable **mstrListDescription** is an array that stores the five possible response descriptions for the question. Because each multiple choice question has five responses, the declaration defines five elements in the array. When writing code to set or to retrieve the property's value, the developer must supply additional arguments to indicate which **ListDescription** element (response) to set.

Four points need to be made about these **Property** procedures:

1. The **Property Let** procedure requires one more argument than the corresponding **Property Get** procedure. This syntax is consistent with the syntax pertaining to the arguments of **Property** procedures.

2. In the **Property Let** procedure, the argument used to set the property appears last.

3. The position of the **Index** argument is the same for both **Property** procedures; that is, the **Index** argument appears first.

4. The name of the **Index** argument must be the same for both procedures. **Property** procedures require this matching before they will work.

In this chapter's example, you will implement a one-dimensional array. Assume, however, that you wanted to implement a property that manages a two-dimensional array. In this case, you would add additional parameters, as shown in the following statements:

```
Public Property Get Grid( _
    Row As Integer, Col As Integer) As String
    ' Code to read value.
End Property

Public Property Let Grid( _
    Row As Integer, Col As Integer, _
```

```
    ByVal New_Value As String)
    ' Code to set value.
End Property
```

The previous **Property** procedures implement a two-dimensional parameterized array. The order of the **Row** and **Col** arguments must be the same for both the **Property Let** and **Property Get** procedures. Additionally, both arguments must have the same name. Another requirement exists for the list of the parameters: If the **Property Get** procedure used the word **Col** as an argument and the **Property Let** procedure used the word **Column**, a compiler error would occur, indicating that the arguments did not match.

In this chapter's program, you will implement the **ListDescription** property as a parameterized property. When reading or writing the value of this property, you will specify an Index value to indicate which element to use. You may find that the implementation of this property resembles the implementation of the **List** property pertaining to a list box. In fact, both are very similar, as you will see when you write the code that reads and writes the property.

To create a parameterized property:

1. Create the following hidden variable declaration in the general declarations section of the **MultipleChoice** class module:

   ```
   Private mstrListDescription(5) As String
   ```

2. Enter the following **Property** procedures in the **MultipleChoice** class module to read and write the **ListDescription** property. (You could also use the Add procedure dialog box, and change the arguments or enter the procedures by hand.)

   ```
   Public Property Get ListDescription _
       (Index As Integer) As String
       ListDescription = mstrListDescription(Index)
   End Property

   Public Property Let ListDescription(Index As _
       Integer, ByVal New_Value As String)
       mstrListDescription(Index) = New_Value
   End Property
   ```

3. Create the following read-only property, which will identify how many items appear in the list. Although read-only properties are discussed more fully later in this section, this procedure must be created now so that you can test the **ListDescription** property. This implementation is an

oversimplification; in reality, the program would include methods to add and delete the number of valid responses.

```
Public Property Get ListCount() As Integer
    ListCount = 5
End Property
```

4. Enter the following statements in the **cmdTestDescription_Click** event procedure in the form module to test the procedure:

```
Dim qmc1 As New MultipleChoice
Dim pintCount As Integer
qmc1.ListDescription(0) = "None"
qmc1.ListDescription(1) = "One"
qmc1.ListDescription(2) = "Two"
qmc1.ListDescription(3) = "Three to Five"
qmc1.ListDescription(4) = "More than Five"
txtOut = vbNullString
For pintCount = 0 To qmc1.ListCount - 1
    txtOut = txtOut _
        & qmc1.ListDescription(pintCount) & vbCrLf
Next
```

5. Test the program. Click on the Test Description Property command button on the form to execute the code you just wrote. The five descriptions should appear in the output text box.

6. Exit the program to return to design mode.

The code for the **ListDescription** properties was described earlier. You can compare the behavior of these **Property** procedures to the **List** property supported by a list box. The **MultipleChoice** class also supports the **ListCount** property, which determines how many items are contained in the list. This behavior is reproduced by the read-only **ListCount** property. Because the list always supports five different responses, your code sets the **ListCount** property to **5**.

As the author of the class, you could expand it so that the number of multiple choice responses varies from question to question. In this scenario, the author could implement an **Add** method requiring an argument that indicates the number of valid responses. This method would likely set the **ListCount** property to its correct value. As the author, you could also create validation code to verify that the index of the **ListDescription** property falls within a valid range—that is, from **zero (0)** to **ListCount 21**.

USING OBJECT REFERENCES IN PROPERTY PROCEDURES

In situations in which reading or writing a property assigns an object reference, you use a variation of the **Property Get** and **Property Let** procedures. When a **Property** procedure assigns an object reference, you create a **Property Get–Property Set** procedure pair instead of a **Property Get–Property Let** procedure pair. The **Property Set** procedure has the same syntax as the **Property Let** procedure, except that the former procedure assigns an object reference rather than assigning a value to a simple variable. Chapter 10 will discuss the use of **Property** procedures to assign object references.

Syntax

[**Public** | **Private** | **Friend**][**Static**] **Property Set** *name* [*(argumentlist)*]
       [*statements*]
       [*name = expression*]
       [**Exit Property**]
       [*statements*]
       [*name = expression*]
    End Property

Dissection

➤ The **Property Set** statement has exactly the same syntax as the **Property Let** statement. You use it, however, to write a property whose value is an object reference.

As you have seen with existing controls, some properties are read-write, others are read-only, and others are read-write (but can be written only once). Although the author of the class module can still use **Property** procedures to create these kinds of properties, Visual Basic supports techniques that allow you, as the class module's author, to implement read-only and write-once properties.

As a rule, if the developer using a class module attempts to perform an action that would cause an error, such as setting the value of a write-once property twice or writing a value to a read-only property, the code in the class module should raise an error. When you, as the author, raise an error in a class module, you should set the number of the error to a different value for each type of error that might be generated. The code written by the developer can then use that value to determine the type of error and figure out how to proceed. When setting the error number in a class module, you should add the value of the constant **vbObjectError** to the error code.

Read-Only Properties

Visual Basic does not support specific functions to implement read-only properties. Instead, as the author, you omit the **Property Let** procedure or create code in the **Property Let** procedure to raise an error. In the MRI project, you will create a read-only **Count** property that returns the number of responses to a question. Ultimately, its value will be calculated when the developer writes code to add responses to a question. Because the class computes the value, it does not make sense for the developer to write a value to the property.

To create a read-only property:

1. Activate the Code window for the class module named **MultipleChoice** and insert the following statement into the general declarations section:

```
Private mintCount As Integer
```

2. Insert the following **Property Get** procedure. If you used the Add Procedure dialog box, remove the **Property Let** procedure produced by the dialog box.

```
Public Property Get Count() As Integer
    Count = mintCount
End Property
```

The process you apply to implement a read-only property is similar to the process you use to implement a read-write property, except that you omit the **Property Let** procedure. In the following text, you will see how the value of the hidden variable is set as questions are added, ensuring that the hidden variable will contain the correct value whenever the property is read.

Assume that the code using the class module tried to set the value of the property using the following statement:

```
qmc1.Count = pintCurrentCount
```

This statement would generate a compiler error, indicating that the developer cannot set a value for a read-only property. This implementation makes sense because the **Count** property, when read, will return the number of responses to a question. Because this value will be computed by the code in the class module itself, the developer using the class should never set it. If you choose to implement the **Property Let** procedure and thus raise an error, the error would not occur at compile time, as shown with the previous approach. Rather, the error would occur at run time, and only if the developer executed code that tried to set the property. Because the developer causes this error, you as the author of the class, will use the compile-time approach—this way the developer receives immediate notification of a compile error

Sometimes you must create a property that should be read-write, but written only once. Such a property is called a write-once property.

Write-Once Properties

For the MRI project, you will create the **Number** property representing the question number such that once the developer sets its value, this value cannot be changed. Write-once properties are commonly employed when the respective value represents a unique index or key that should not be changed.

In this type of situation, you should create both a **Property Get** and **Property Let** procedure, but the **Property Let** procedure should raise an error if the developer tries to write the value of the property more than once. This type of error cannot be detected at design time, because the task of reading and writing properties occurs at run time. The **Property Let** procedure must, therefore, be implemented such that it raises an error if the developer makes a second attempt to set the property.

```
Public Property Let Number(ByVal pintArg As Integer)
    Static pblnInitialized As Boolean
    If pblnInitialized Then
        Err.Raise 1024 + vbObjectError
    Else
        mintNumber = pintArg
        pblnInitialized = True
    End If
End Property
```

The **Property Let** procedure contains a static variable that is used to determine whether the value of the property has already been written. If so, the procedure will raise an error. If not, the code will set the value of the hidden variable **mintNumber**, and then set the value of the local variable **pblnInitialized** to **True**. Because the variable is static, Visual Basic preserves its value between calls to the procedure. Thus, the second time the developer calls the procedure, the procedure generates a run-time error.

```
Public Property Get Number() As Integer
    Number = mintNumber
End Property
```

The corresponding **Property Get** procedure uses the same technique to read the value of a hidden variable and then store that value in the property name.

The error code 1024 was arbitrarily chosen for the error number. If a class module raises different errors for different reasons, each error should be assigned a unique error number. This approach allows the developer using your class to determine how to proceed based on the error that occurred.

To create a write-once property:

1. Activate the Code window for the class module named **MultipleChoice**, and create the following hidden variable in the general declarations section to store the value of the property:

```
Private mintNumber As Integer
```

2. Create the following **Property** procedures in the **MultipleChoice** class module:

```
Public Property Get Number() As Integer
    Number = mintNumber
End Property
Public Property Let Number(ByVal pintArg As Integer)
    Static pblnInitialized As Boolean
    If pblnInitialized Then
        Err.Raise 1024 + vbObjectError,, _
            "Cannot set write once property"
    Else
        mintNumber = pintArg
        pblnInitialized = True
    End If
End Property
```

3. Enter the following statements in the **cmdTestNumber_Click** event procedure in the form module to test the new property:

```
Dim qmc1 As New MultipleChoice
qmc1.Number = 1
qmc1.Number = 2
```

4. Test the program. Click on the Test Number Property command button. Note that the button does not produce any visible output. The first statement that sets the number will execute normally. The second assignment statement, however, will generate a run-time error. Usually, the form or standard module would contain an error handler for the procedure and determine the appropriate course of action.

5. Click on End to close the Run-time error dialog box.

The **Property Get** procedure works like the **Property Get** procedures you previously wrote. That is, your code assigns the value of a hidden variable to the property name. The **Property Let** procedure is quite different. The technique to create a write-once property uses a hidden variable—in this case, **pblnInitialized**. The first time the procedure executes, the value of this variable is **False**, so the code in the **Property Let** procedure sets the value of the hidden variable. When the code sets the value of the hidden variable, the argument **pblnInitialized** is set to **True**. If the developer writes code that calls this procedure a second time, the first part of the **If** statement will be **True**, causing the code to raise an error.

When you clicked the Test Number Property command button, Visual Basic may have entered break mode and displayed the offending statement in the form module or the class module, depending on the configuration of your system. You will see how to change this behavior so that you can debug the code in a class module.

Class Events

All class modules respond to two events: **Class_Initialize** and **Class_Terminate**. The purposes of these events are similar to those of the **Form_Initialize** and **Form_Terminate** events. This similarity is logical because a form module is a type of class.

The **Class_Initialize** event occurs when a new instance of the class is created. The author of the class commonly uses this event to initialize variables. In the MRI program, the **Class_Initialize** event will initialize the array that stores the responses to a specific question.

The **Class_Terminate** event occurs just before an instance of a class is destroyed. Typically, you write code for this event to save files or to perform other housekeeping chores before destroying the class instance.

To program the **Class_Initialize** event, locate the **Class_Initialize** event procedure for the class module and enter the following statements:

```
ReDim mintValues(0)
mintCount = 0
```

The author of the class uses the **Class_Initialize** event procedure in this class module to give an initial size to the array of responses. Remember that the variable **mintCount** is the hidden variable that stores the number of responses to a question. For this project, you create the array with no subscript, allowing it to operate as a dynamic array. The second statement assigns the value **0** to **mintCount**, indicating that no responses have been added. Although this statement is redundant because Visual Basic automatically initializes the variable to zero (0) when you create an instance of the class, explicitly assigning a value to the property illustrates the desired initial value.

In addition to implementing properties for a class, you, as the author, can write code to create methods. To implement methods, you create **Public Function** and **Public Sub** procedures in the class module. Syntactically, no differences exist between the **Function** and **Sub** procedures declared in a class module and the **Function** and **Sub** procedures implemented in other modules. Visual Basic interprets the former procedures as methods instead of as ordinary procedures, however.

You can also declare **Private**, **Function**, and **Sub** procedures in a class module. These procedures are not visible to other modules and are not part of the class's interface. Rather, they form the hidden part of the class's implementation.

Methods

As the author, you implement methods in a class module by creating **Public Function** and **Public Sub** procedures. **Function** methods return values, but **Sub** methods do not. This behavior resembles the behavior of **Function** and **Sub** procedures declared in standard modules.

For the MRI project, you will create a method to add multiple choice responses to each question. This method, named **Add**, will accept one argument—the value of the response. Assume that each multiple choice response has the same number of choices—the letters "a" through "e." Thus five possible responses exist. This setup is consistent with the behavior of the **ListResponse** property already created.

Consider the tasks to be performed by the **Add** method. Its purpose is to add one of five possible responses to a question. Logically, you should pass this value as an argument to the method. Each time that the code executes and adds a response, the array **mintValues**—which is hidden in the class—must be redimensioned to store the new value (response). The code must then store the new value in the newly created array element. Consider the following statements to accomplish this task:

```
Public Sub Add(pintResp As Integer)
      mintCount = mintCount + 1
      ReDim Preserve _
          mintValues(UBound(mintValues) + 1)
      mintValues(mintCount) = pintResp
End Sub
```

This method accepts one argument, an **Integer**. The first statement increments the value of **mintCount**, which stores the current count of responses. The code then redimensions the array, and the final statement stores the current response in the array.

Your implementation should perform an additional task to improve the robustness of the method. Because the value of a valid response is known, the method should validate the argument passed to it. If the code in the method detects an invalid response, this information should be communicated to the procedure that called the method. Two techniques exist to inform the calling procedure of an error. One technique uses a **Function** procedure that returns a value to the caller, indicating whether the operation was successful. The other technique raises an error in the procedure (method). The process to raise an error matches that employed with the **Number Property** procedure.

You should pay attention to the data type of the argument supplied to the **Add** method. You could use a simple Integer value, but you could also use enumerated types in class modules. In the MRI project, you will use an enumeration to represent the letters "a" through "e." Remember that Visual Basic does not validate the value assigned to an enumerated type. Consequently, when the code executes and writes the property, the code in the method should verify that the value contains a valid enumeration.

Class Module Enumerations

The class module you have created could use the values zero (0) through four (4) to represent the five possible letter responses to the questions. You can apply two techniques to improve the robustness of this class module, however. First, the different responses can be represented by a Public enumeration. The developer using the class can then use this enumeration when adding a response to the Question object. Second, you can create Private enumerations and hide them in the class. Consider the following enumeration and statement to add a response to the current question:

```
Public Enum Letter
    letterA = 0
    letterB = 1
    letterC = 2
    letterD = 3
    letterE = 4
End Enum

Question1.Add(letterA)
```

This enumeration allows the programmer to apply enumerated constants instead of Integer values to represent the response. It only partially solves the problem, however. Consider what would happen if the developer added a response with an invalid value, as shown in the following statement:

```
Question1.Add(99)
```

Unless the code in the **Add** method validates the response, the response would be added to the question—even though it is invalid. As you have seen, enumerations are a programming convenience and Visual Basic does not validate the value. If the developer uses an invalid Integer value as an argument to the **Add** method, an error will not occur, because the compiler does not check the validity of the enumerated value.

You can further improve the interface of the class module by verifying that the argument supplied to the **Add** method contains a valid enumeration.

To create the enumeration and validate the arguments to the **Add** method:

1. Enter the following statements in the general declarations section of the **MultipleChoice** class module:

```
Public Enum Letter
    letterA = 0
    letterB = 1
    letterC = 2
    letterD = 3
    letterE = 4
End Enum
```

2. Create the **Add** method in the **MultipleChoice** class module, using the following statements:

```
Public Sub Add(pintResp As Integer)
    Select Case pintResp
        Case Is = letterA, letterB, letterC, _
            letterD, letterE
            mintCount = mintCount + 1
            ReDim Preserve _
                mintValues(UBound(mintValues) + 1)
            mintValues(mintCount) = pintResp
            Exit Sub
    End Select
    Err.Raise vbObjectError + 1025, _
    "MultipleChoice", "Invalid Add argument."
End Sub
```

3. Enter the following statements in the **cmdTestAdd_Click** event procedure in the form module to test the method:

```
Dim qmc1 As New MultipleChoice
With qmc1
    .Add letterA
    .Add letterB
    .Add letterC
    .Add letterD
    .Add letterE
    .Add 99
End With
```

4. Test the program. Click on the Test Add Method command button. Note that the code in the event procedure produces no visible output. The first five calls to the **Add** method supply valid arguments. That is, the statements add five unique responses. The last call to the **Add** method, however, will generate a run-time error for the developer, indicating that the response is invalid. At this point, the program will not produce any output. Although the code that you just wrote in the form module adds a question, it does not print the question to the output text box.

5. Click on the End to close the Run-Time Error dialog box.

The code to add responses passes the response as an argument to the **Add** method. The **Add** method then performs two tasks. First, it determines whether the argument contains a valid enumeration. If the enumeration is valid, the code in the **Add** method performs the second task—redimensions the array containing the responses and stores the argument passed in the method in the correct array element.

The class should also determine the percentage of the total responses represented by each response. That is, the developer using the class should be able to count the number of "a," "b," "c," "d," and "e" responses to the question. The solution involves determining the count for a specific response and dividing that number by the total number of responses. As with most problems, you can apply different solutions for the implementation. Consider the possible options to implement the **ListPercent** method:

➤ When the developer writes code that calls the **ListPercent** method, the method could compute and return the percentage represented by each of the different responses. This solution offers the options of returning an array or setting the values of other properties.

➤ When the developer writes code that calls the **ListPercent** method, the method could be called with an argument indicating the response to compute. This solution provides two options for the implementation of the procedure itself. In all cases, all of the responses need to be examined. One solution, however, would maintain a single counter to count only the desired response—an **If** statement would determine whether each response is the desired one. The second approach would be to create a local array and accumulate all of the responses, regardless of which is selected. The performance difference between these two approaches is negligible because a tradeoff exists between executing the **If** statement and managing a five-element array.

For this class, you will implement the **ListPercent** method by counting all of the responses and returning only the desired response. Consider the **ListDescription** property you created earlier in the chapter. As the author of the class, you implemented it as a parameterized property, much like the **List** property used by the ListBox control. The technique to compute the percentage of a particular response works in the same way. That is, the developer specifies an argument, indicating which response to select from the list of responses. The name of the method is **ListPercent**, which clearly indicates to the developer that the property contains a list. It also makes the property name consistent with the **ListDescription** property. Consider the following statements to implement the **ListPercent** property:

```
Public Function ListPercent(pintResp As Integer) _
    As Single
    Dim pintCount As Integer
    Dim pintLetter(5) As Variant
    Dim pintTrue As Integer, pintFalse As Integer
    For pintCount = 1 To mintCount
        pintLetter(mintValues(pintCount)) = _
            pintLetter(mintValues(pintCount)) + 1
    Next
    ListPercent = pintLetter(pintResp) / mintCount
End Function
```

The **ListPercent** method contains fairly simple code. The table **pintLetter** contains five elements. The code uses each element to count a particular response to the question. That is, the count of letterA responses will be stored in element zero (0), the letterB responses in element one (1), and so on. The **For** loop examines all of the responses from response 1 to the value of **mintCount**, which is the hidden variable you declared to keep track of the number of responses. In the implementation of the program, the **ListPercent** method ignores the first element in the array containing the responses (element 0). No value is ever stored in the array element, and the element is never referenced. Instead, the statements inside the array increment the counter for the corresponding response. Once all of the responses have been examined, the method returns the percentage of the selected response by dividing the response by the total number of responses.

In reality, this method should contain code to raise an error if an invalid response was supplied as the method's argument. That particular code was omitted here for brevity.

To create the **ListPercent** method:

1. Enter the following **Function** procedure into the **MultipleChoice** class module:

```
Public Function ListPercent(pintResp As Integer) _
    As Single
    Dim pintCount As Integer
    Dim pintLetter(5) As Variant
    Dim pintTrue As Integer, pintFalse As Integer
    For pintCount = 1 To mintCount
        pintLetter(mintValues(pintCount)) = _
            pintLetter(mintValues(pintCount)) + 1
    Next
    ListPercent = pintLetter(pintResp) / mintCount
End Function
```

2. Enter the following statements in the **cmdTestPercent_Click** event procedure in the form module to test the method:

```
Dim qmc1 As New MultipleChoice
Dim pintCount As Integer
With qmc1
    .Add letterA
    .Add letterB
    .Add letterC
    .Add letterD
    .Add letterE
End With
txtOut = vbNullString
For pintCount = 0 To qmc1.ListCount - 1
    txtOut = txtOut & qmc1.ListPercent(pintCount) & _
        vbCrLf
Next
```

3. Test the program. Click on the Test Percent Method command button to test the method. The percentage of each response should be displayed in the

text box. Because you, as the developer, added five distinct responses, the percentage of each response should be 20 percent.

4. End the program to return to design mode.

This section presented the fundamental concepts employed to implement a component using a Visual Basic class module. In the current version of the MRI program, the class module contains properties and methods. Some properties are read-write properties; others are read-only properties, and still others are write-once properties. In the next section, you will improve on the simple class module created in this section.

SUPPORTING MULTIPLE QUESTION TYPES

A Behind-The-Scenes Look At Class Modules

Visual Basic hides most of the technical details of how classes work internally. In fact, you could create classes and ActiveX controls with little or no understanding of how COM operates internally. A fundamental knowledge of COM, however, may help you better understand why a class module functions as it does. Remember that Visual Basic implements class modules as COM objects. All COM objects have the following characteristics:

➤ Every COM object has one or more interfaces. Each interface contains a set of functions that define the class's implementation.

➤ The functionality of a COM object is contained in a type of dynamic link library (DLL). Any program that supports COM can access the library.

➤ Every COM object installed on a specific computer can be identified uniquely by an entry in the Windows Registry. This Registry entry is called a globally unique identifier (GUID).

The term *interface*, as previously defined, pertained to object-oriented programming and component-based design. This term has a much more specific meaning as it pertains to COM, however. Every class supports at least one interface, but every class can also support multiple interfaces. In fact, the classes you create in Visual Basic will almost always support multiple COM interfaces. When you, as the developer, create an instance of a Visual Basic class, the functions in the interfaces that will be discussed in the following paragraphs are called automatically and transparently.

Every class supports at least one interface named IUnknown. Notice that the first character of this interface's name is "I." By convention, all interface names begin with this letter. The IUnknown interface for a class contains three functions (methods). The first method is the **AddRef** method. As you have seen in previous chapters, the programmer can create multiple references to the same object. Each time you add or write code that creates an additional reference to an object, Windows calls the **AddRef** method to increment a counter defining the number of references to the object. Thus, if two object variables currently reference the same object, the reference counter for the object would be 2. Consider the following statements:

```
Dim qmcRef1 As MultipleChoice, _
    qmcRef2 As MultipleChoice
Set qmcRef1 = New MultipleChoice
```

The **Dim** statement declares two object variables of type **MultipleChoice**. Because the code does not use the **New** keyword, this statement does not create an object from the underlying class. Rather, it declares two object variables that reference **Nothing**. The **Set** statement creates an instance of the **MultipleChoice** class and assigns a reference to the class instance in the variable **qmcRef1**. Thus Windows called the **AddRef** method, which sets the reference counter for the object to 1.

```
Set qmcRef2 = qmcRef1
```

This statement assigns a second reference to the MultipleChoice object pointed to by **qmcRef1**. Thus Windows calls the **AddRef** method again, and the code in the **AddRef** method increments the reference counter to 2. Remember that Visual Basic takes care of creating the IUnknown interface when you create a class. It also calls the **AddRef** method when assignment statements create additional references to an object. The following statement causes one of the references to the object to be destroyed:

```
Set qmcRef2 = Nothing
```

When the preceding statement executes, Windows calls another method pertaining to the IUnknown interface—the **Release** method. Windows calls the **Release** method when a reference to an object is destroyed. If the reference count is greater than 1, the **Release** method decrements the reference count by 1. If the current reference count is 1, the **Release** method frees the memory and resources consumed by the object and then destroys the object. In the preceding example, when the statement sets **qmcRef2** to **Nothing**, the **Release** method decrements the reference count from 2 to 1.

```
Set qmcRef1 = Nothing
```

The preceding **Set** statement causes the reference count to become zero, which causes the object itself to be destroyed. This fact is significant because objects are not destroyed until the reference count becomes zero; that is, Windows destroys objects when no more references to the object exist.

 When you finish with an object, make sure to set all of its references to Nothing. If you fail to take this step, the memory used by the object will not be released to the system. Although this situation is not a problem with just a few objects, the effect on performance can be significant in programs that manage many objects or when a particular object itself consumes large amounts of memory.

In addition to the two functions (methods) already mentioned, the IUnknown interface supports the **QueryInterface** method. Remember that an object must have at least one interface, but can have many interfaces if desired. Classes would not be very useful if they contained only the IUnknown interface. You would be able to create references to objects, but the objects themselves would do nothing. To determine the desired interface, the IUnknown interface supports the **QueryInterface** function. Windows calls QueryInterface with arguments that identify an interface. If the object supports the interface, **QueryInterface** returns a memory address containing the code for the interface. Carefully consider what happens when the following statements execute:

```
Dim qmc1 As New MultipleChoice
Dim qmcRef As MultipleChoice
Set qmcRef = qmc1
```

In addition to IUnknown, the class supports a second interface: MultipleChoice. When a developer writes code that declares **qmc1**, Windows calls **QueryInterface** to obtain a reference to the MultipleChoice interface. It then uses this reference to call the properties and methods of the object. Additionally, Windows calls the **AddRef** method to increase the reference counter from 0 to 1. When the second **Dim** statement executes, Windows calls **QueryInterface** again to obtain a reference to the MultipleChoice interface, and the reference counter is incremented to 2.

Previous chapters of this book mentioned generic types such as Object, Form, and Control as ways to use a single object variable to reference different types of objects. Consider the following statements, which have the same effect as the previous statements, but which are implemented in a different way internally:

```
Dim qmc1 As New MultipleChoice
Dim qmcRef As Object
Set qmcRef = qmc1
```

In this example, the code declares the variable **qmcRef** as a generic Object variable that is capable of referencing any type of object. In the previous set of statements, Visual Basic could determine the interface used when the program was compiled, because the object variables specified a known interface. In the preceding code, **qmcRef** can reference any type of object. As a result, Windows cannot determine until run time which type of object is being referenced and, thus, which interface to use.

Windows supports a third interface to determine whether a class supports a specific interface: IDispatch, which is referred to as a dispatch interface. An object's dispatch interface serves no real purpose in and of itself. Rather, Windows uses a dispatch interface to determine whether an object supports a specific interface, and to identify the properties and methods that are supported by that interface.

When the preceding **Set** statement executes, Windows calls the **QueryInterface** method. Instead of obtaining a reference to the MultipleChoice interface, however, Windows uses the **QueryInterface** method to determine whether the object supports a dispatch interface (IDispatch).

Like the IUnknown interface, the IDispatch interface supports specific methods. Of particular interest are the **GetIDsOfNames** and **Invoke** methods. Windows uses the **GetIDsOfNames** method to examine the interface for the properties and methods supported by the class. For each property or method, Windows returns an Integer that represents the specific property or method. This value is called a *dispatch ID*. Whenever a property is referenced or a method is called, Windows calls the **Invoke** method to execute the method or property. Using IDispatch or the dispatch interface affects program performance, because IDispatch must determine whether a given interface exists and whether specific properties and/or methods are supported. More importantly, Windows incurs significant overhead in setting up the arguments to any methods or properties before calling the **Invoke** function.

Much more can be said about the internal workings of COM. The introduction in this chapter merely provides a foundation so that you can understand Visual Basic activities when you create class modules. As you create class modules, this information will be referred to and expanded on so that you can visualize how Visual Basic converts class modules into COM objects.

Debugging Class Modules

As you develop class modules and programs that use those modules, you, as the author, need to be aware of the various error-trapping options supported by Visual Basic. These options control what happens when run-time errors occur in class modules and other parts of a program. The debugging of an ActiveX code component is of particular importance in this chapter. It is possible for Visual Basic to enter break mode in a class module procedure even though an error handler is active. It also is possible to have the error handler in the class module perform normally and return an error code to the caller of the ActiveX code component. Figure 9.9 shows the relevant dialog box—the Options dialog box.

You use the following option buttons on the General tab of the Options dialog box to change the debugging characteristics of programs, including programs involving class modules:

➤ If you select the Break on All Errors option button, any error—whether or not an error handler is active—will cause the project to enter break mode.

➤ If you select the Break in Class Module option button, a handled error in a class module will cause the error to be trapped by the error handler and an error code to be returned to the caller. An unhandled error in a class module will generate a run-time error and Visual Basic will enter break mode.

➤ If you select the Break on Unhandled Errors option button, Visual Basic traps the error if an error handler in any procedure is active. Visual Basic enters break mode only for unhandled errors. If an unhandled error occurs in a class module, Visual Basic will enter break mode and highlight the statement in the Code window that called the class module procedure in which the error occurred, rather than entering break mode in the class module itself.

To illustrate the effect of these settings, you can again click on the Test Number Property command button. Remember that clicking on this button will cause a run-time error because Visual Basic raises an error when the code in the command button makes a second attempt to set the property.

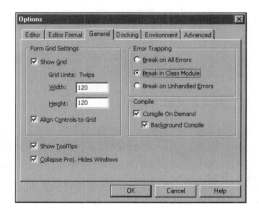

Figure 9.9   Options dialog box General tab.

To illustrate the effect of the error-trapping options:

1. If necessary, start Visual Basic and open the current program. Click on Tools, and then click on Options. Make sure that the General tab is active. Click on Break in Class Module, if necessary. Click on OK to close the dialog box.

2. Test the program. Click on Test Number Property. Again, note that the code in this command button produces no visible output. A dialog box will appear, indicating the nature of the error. Click on the Debug button. The statement that raised the error in the class module is highlighted because you specified that the program should enter break mode in the class module.

3. End the program to return to design mode.

4. To see the effect of the Break on Unhandled Errors option, repeat Step 1, but click on Break on Unhandled Errors.

5. Test the program again. Click on Test Number Property, and then click on Debug. Instead of displaying the offending line in the class module, Visual Basic enters break mode in the form module at the line that caused the error to occur.

6. End the program to return to design mode.

The choice of which debugging mode to use depends on whether you are debugging a class module, a form module, or a standard module. If you suspect that the class module produces incorrect results, use the error-trapping option Break in Class Module to help diagnose the specific cause of the error. Once you are convinced that the class module works correctly, set the option to Break on Unhandled Errors to debug the form or standard module that uses the class. Refer to Appendix A in this book for more information on this topic.

Enhancing The Class

Your class now supports properties and methods to compute the percentage of the total responses that each multiple choice answer receives. A multiple choice question is but one type of question that may be asked. In this example, your component also needs to support another type of question, which will have true/false or yes/no values. Several implementation options exist to solve this problem:

➤ You can choose an implementation that creates additional methods to store the different types of questions. For example, you could create an **Add** method, such as **AddTrueFalse** and **AddMultipleChoice**, for each type of question. This solution would require that you create additional properties, such as **CountTrueFalse** and **CountMultipleChoice**, that correspond to these methods. This cumbersome solution doubles the number of properties and methods.

➤ A second solution creates two distinct independent classes such that one class exists for each type of question. Using this solution, all of the methods and properties could have the same name, but no relationships could exist between the classes.

➤ A third solution—and the one that will be implemented in the MRI project—uses an abstract class and polymorphism to create multiple interfaces for the class. To accomplish this goal, your program will have three class modules. The first will be an abstract class that defines the interface for the other two classes but contains no implementation. The other two classes will provide the implementation for the two different types of questions. Figure 9.10 illustrates the relationship between the abstract class and the two other classes that provide the implementation.

As shown in Figure 9.10, the **Question** class is an abstract class. It merely defines the interface that will be used by the other two classes. The **MultipleChoice** and **TrueFalse** classes actually implement the abstract class. You create the abstract class by defining the same properties and methods as declared in the implemented class.

9

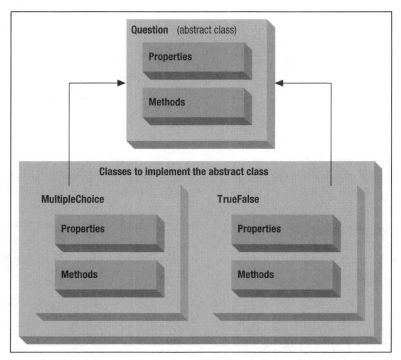

Figure 9.10   Abstract class.

Polymorphism Using The **Implements** Statement

At this point, your program supports a single class to handle multiple choice questions. The class should also handle questions that have responses such as yes/no or true/false. With this implementation, you can create additional methods and properties to support the different types of questions. That is, you can modify and expand the interface. The following properties and methods could be used to implement the new class:

➤ The **Name** property would remain unchanged because each question has a **Name**, regardless of the question type. The same is true for both the **Number** and **Count** properties.

➤ The **Add** method must be modified because the code to count the responses must know the type of response (true/false or multiple choice) that is being added. To accomplish this task, you can create two different **Add** methods, one for each type of question. If you use this approach, you must create two **Add** methods, each having a distinct name, such as **AddTrueFalse** and **AddMultipleChoice**.

➤ You would need to change the names for the **ListPercent** method.

This solution has several deficiencies. Most importantly, the interface for the class has become more cumbersome because of the additional methods. Another solution to the problem would create a second class module and implement the same methods and properties, with each having the same name. In other words, both classes would support the same interface. Using this solution, the **MultipleChoice** class would remain unchanged, and a new **TrueFalse** class could be added that has the same methods and properties. Thus, to create an instance of each class, the following statements could be used:

```
Dim qtf As New TrueFalse
Dim qmc As New MultipleChoice
```

This approach provides a consistent interface for both classes. You can think of this strategy as a simple way to implement polymorphism; that is, two different methods having the same name will execute entirely different functions. Using this approach, the two classes have nothing to do with each other. Rather, it is the responsibility of the programmer to make sure that both classes implement the same functions.

Another approach to the interface problem is to create an abstract class.

THE ABSTRACT CLASS

Before delving into this strategy for implementing the **MultipleChoice** and **TrueFalse** classes, a few words about how Visual Basic implements polymorphism are in order. C++, a well-known object-oriented programming language, supports polymorphism through inheritance. Consider the concepts of polymorphism and inheritance as they pertain to the **Question** classes you are creating. Using inheritance, you can define a general class of questions having common properties and methods—in this case, properties such as **Name** and **Number**. As you have seen, each type of question has unique characteristics. That is, the method to determine the percentage of a true or false response is different from the method used to determine the percentage of a specific multiple choice response. Using inheritance, the classes for the specific question type would use the general characteristics of the **Question** class but override the methods of the general **Question** class. That is, the **ListPercent** method would have different implementations for the **TrueFalse** and **MultipleChoice** classes, respectively.

Visual Basic does not support polymorphism through inheritance. As the MSDN Library explains, Visual Basic provides polymorphism through multiple ActiveX interfaces. The following discussion illustrates this concept.

In this section, you will implement two classes: **MultipleChoice** and **TrueFalse**. The **MultipleChoice** class will support exactly the same properties and methods as it did in the previous section. The **TrueFalse** class has already been created for you. It has the same properties and methods (interface) as the **MultipleChoice** class. That is, as the author of the class, you defined properties and methods to add responses to a question and to determine the percentage of each response. The code for the methods of the same name differs between the classes because you provide different implementations.

With **TrueFalse** and **MultipleChoice**, you now have two distinct and independent classes. Although both classes support the same properties and methods, they have nothing to do with each other. Assume that you could create one interface for the class having two separate implementations. That is, assume that you create a generic **Question** class that defines the interface for all of the different types of questions. Then, assume that two separate implementations for the two different types of questions exist. Given the classes you have already created, a **TrueFalse** implementation and a **MultipleChoice** implementation would exist.

Consider the following statements:

```
Dim qArray(1 To 2) As Question
Dim qtf1 As New TrueFalse
Dim qmc1 As New MultipleChoice
Set qArray(1) = qtf1
Set qArray(2) = qmc1
qArray(1).Name = "Question 1"
qArray(1).Add True
```

```
qArray(2).Name = "Question 2"
qArray(2).Add letterB
```

The preceding statements illustrate several important concepts. The first statement declares the array named **qArray** as the type of the abstract class (**Question**). It can store references to two types of questions (**MultipleChoice** and **TrueFalse**). The next two statements create an instance of a **TrueFalse** question and a **MultipleChoice** question, respectively. The **Set** statements create a second reference to each question via the array. Thus the first element in **qArray** references the first **TrueFalse** question, and the second element references the **MultipleChoice** question.

The assignment statements following the **Set** statements illustrate the use of the abstract class as a vehicle to set properties and to call methods. The abstract class knows which interface to use depending on the type of question. Although the code is the same as that for the **Name** method, the **Add** methods work differently for the two types of questions. The **Add** method for the MultipleChoice question has the possible values "a" through "e," and the possible values for the TrueFalse questions are true and false.

Having seen how an abstract class may be used with other classes, you can now create an abstract class and the classes that provide the implementation for that abstract class. Creating an abstract class in Visual Basic does not require a unique type of class module. Rather, you, as the author, define an abstract class by creating the properties and methods of the class and then creating no code in the **Property**, **Sub**, or **Function** procedures. That is, the purpose of the abstract class is to define the interface. Remember: Properties and methods define a class's interface.

In addition to defining the properties and methods of the abstract class, you must declare the data types of any arguments supported by those properties and methods.

To create the abstract class:

1. Start Visual Basic, if necessary, and then create a new project.

2. Add a class module to the project, and then set the **Name** property to **Question**. Save the class using the name Chapter.09\Startup\Question.cls.

3. Remove the form named **Form1** from the project.

4. Add the form named Chapter.09\Startup\frmCh9_S2.frm to the project. Using the Project Properties dialog box, make this form become the Startup form.

5. Add the class named Chapter.09\Complete\MultipleChoice.cls to the project. Make sure that you take the file from the Complete folder.

6. Add the class named Chapter.09\Complete\TrueFalse.cls to the project, and then save the project using the name Chapter.09\Startup\Ch9_S2.vbp.

7. Enter the following statements in the **Question** class module to define the interface for the abstract class:

```
Public Property Get Name() As String

End Property

Public Property Let Name(pstrResp As String)

End Property
Public Property Get ListCount() As Integer

End Property

Public Property Get ListDescription(Index As Integer) _
    As String

End Property

Public Property Let ListDescription(Index As Integer, _
    ByVal New_Value As String)

End Property

Public Property Get Number() As Integer

End Property

Public Property Let Number(ByVal pintArg As Integer)

End Property
Public Sub Add(pintResp As Variant)

End Sub

Public Function ListPercent(pintResp As Integer) _
    As Single

End Function
```

The preceding code defines the interface for the abstract class. As you can see, the class supports exactly the same properties and methods as are supported by the **MultipleChoice** class that you already created. You did not define the implementation for the abstract class, however. That is, you did not create any code in the procedures. Now that you have defined the interface for the abstract class, you can proceed to define its implementation.

IMPLEMENTING THE ABSTRACT CLASS

Once you have created the abstract class, you need to add the class modules that implement the properties and methods of the abstract class. You add the class modules such that one class module exists for each implementation. The implementation must support all of the methods and properties defined for the abstract class. Furthermore, the arguments of each property or method must be of exactly the same type.

At this point, you can modify the **MultipleChoice** class so that it implements the abstract class. This task requires that you make three changes to the class module:

➤ Each class providing the implementation for the abstract class must contain the **Implements** statement followed by the name of the abstract class that is being implemented. In the MRI project, you will implement the **MultipleChoice** and **TrueFalse** classes.

➤ You must define the names of the **Property**, **Sub**, and **Function** procedures in the implemented classes so that the procedure names have a prefix. The prefix consists of the abstract class being implemented, followed by an underscore, followed by the property or method name.

➤ The scope of the procedures that implement the properties and methods of the abstract class should be changed from Public to Private. Remember that developers will access the implemented class modules through the abstract interface.

Having noted these changes, consider the mechanics of this process in more detail.

THE IMPLEMENTS STATEMENT

In this chapter's example, the **TrueFalse** class and **MultipleChoice** class will provide the implementation for the **Question** class. To inform Visual Basic that a class module provides the implementation for an abstract class, you use the **Implements** statement in the general declarations section of the class modules that provide the implementation for the abstract class. The **Implements** statement contains the keyword (**Implements**) followed by the name of the abstract class being implemented. Thus, to tell Visual Basic that the **MultipleChoice** class provides the implementation for the abstract class named **Question**, you would use the following statement:

```
Implements Question
```

You now can add the **Implements** keyword to the **MultipleChoice** class to specify that this class implements the **Question** abstract class. The same statement is already included in the **TrueFalse** class.

To indicate that a class implements an abstract class, locate the general declarations section for the class module named **MultipleChoice**, and note that the following statement has been added just after the **Option Explicit** statement. This statement has also been added to the **TrueFalse** class.

```
Implements Question
```

Now that you have advised Visual Basic that the **MultipleChoice** and **TrueFalse** classes provide the implementation for the **Question** class, you can proceed to the second step of the process—changing the procedure names in the class.

SETTING PROCEDURE NAMES FOR THE IMPLEMENTED CLASS

When a class implements an abstract class, the names of the procedures that declare the properties and methods of the implementing class must be changed. Visual Basic requires that the procedure names be modified so that the class being implemented is specified explicitly. This task is accomplished by prefixing the property or method name with the abstract class name. The underscore (_) character separates the two names. The syntax looks much like the event procedure for a control instance. Assume that the following statements appear in the **Question** abstract class:

```
Public Property Get Number() As Integer

End Property
```

The developer accessing the class will use the names of the **Property** procedures and methods. Again, these procedures define the interface for the class. Also, assume that the following implementation is declared and defined in the **MultipleChoice** class:

```
Private Property Get Question_Number() As Integer
    Question_Number = mintNumber
End Property

Private Property Let Question_Number( _
    ByVal pintArg As Integer)
    ' Code to validate that property has not been set.
    mintNumber = pintArg
End Property
```

The only change to these **Property** procedures is the addition of the abstract class name (**Question**) to the name of the **Property** procedures. Also, because the name of the **Property Get** procedure was changed, the statement that assigns a value to the property was changed, too. This syntax is consistent with the syntax to set a function's return value. This process must be repeated for every property and method in the class module. If you try to compile the program without implementing the entire interface defined by the abstract class, a compiler error will occur. Thus this process must be performed before the project will compile.

You have one last situation to understand before the **MultipleChoice** implementation of the Question interface is complete. You declared each of the **Property** procedures and methods as Public. As such, a developer could use the class to access **MultipleChoice** questions without using the abstract Questions interface. That is, the following statement would be legal:

```
Dim qmc As New MultipleChoice,
qmc.Question_Name = "Do you have a car?"
```

This structure is not desirable because one goal of object-oriented programming is to make implementation details of the class completely transparent. Thus the final step of the conversion process is to make the procedures in the **MultipleChoice** class visible only to the abstract **Question** class. Note that this task has been completed in the **TrueFalse** and **Multiple** classes.

Making the implementation details of the class completely transparent can be accomplished by making all of the **Property**, **Sub**, and **Function** procedures that implement the methods have a Private scope. This approach may seem a bit counterintuitive. A Private variable or procedure is visible only in the module in which it is declared. The abstract class, however, can continue to access the Private properties and methods of the implementing class even though the properties and methods are Private. A developer using the class, however, cannot access these properties and methods.

You can now test the abstract class.

To test the abstract class:

1. Test the program. Click on the Test Add Method command button. Clicking on this button will produce no visible results, but the code for this button nevertheless creates questions and responses to those questions.

2. Click on the Test List Questions command button. The code in this command button analyzes the responses and prints them to the multiline text box.

3. End the program, and exit Visual Basic.

Abstract Class Initialization

Remember that the **Class_Initialize** event occurs when a developer creates an instance of the class. In this project, however, you created two classes that implement the abstract class. Thus both of the **TrueFalse** and **MultipleChoice** classes implement the abstract **Question** class. This situation creates a bit of confusion: In which class do the **Class_Initialize** and **Class_Terminate** events occur? The answer: In all of them. Given the fact that the **Class_Initialize** event occurs whenever an instance of the class is created, it makes sense that each class—even the abstract class—will raise these two events. Assume the following statements:

```
Dim q2 As New MultipleChoice
Dim q3 As New TrueFalse
Dim q1 As New Question
```

Because the **New** keyword is used for both of the first two declarations, a new instance of each class is created. Consequently, the **Class_Initialize** and **Class_Terminate** events occur for each class. The event pertains to the individual class, so different code can be placed in the event procedures to cause a different action to occur depending on the implementation.

9

CHAPTER SUMMARY

In this chapter, you have seen how to create class modules with properties and methods. A class module is like a form module without a visible interface. It has properties and methods.

To create a property in a class module:

➤ Declare a Public variable in the class module or create **Property** procedures using the following syntax:

```
[ Public | Private | Friend ] [ Static ] Property Get name [
(argumentlist) ] [ As type ]
    [ statements ]
    [ name = expression ]
    [ Exit Property ]
    [ statements ]
    [ name = expression ]
End Property
[ Public | Private | Friend ] [ Static ] Property Let name [
(argumentlist) ]
    [ statements ]
    [ name = expression ]
    [ Exit Property ]
    [statements]
```

```
        [name = expression]
    End Property
```

➤ The arguments to **Property Get** and **Property Let** procedures must be of the same type. That is, the return value of a **Property Get** procedure must be of the exact same type as the argument to the **Property Let** procedure.

To implement a read-only property:

➤ Create a **Property Get** procedure without a corresponding **Property Let** procedure.

To implement a write-once property:

➤ Declare a static Boolean variable in the **Property Let** procedure. This value is **False** the first time the **Property** procedure executes.

➤ Set this variable to **True** in the **Property** procedure the first time the procedure executes.

➤ The code in the **Property** procedure should test the value of the Boolean variable to determine if it is **True** and, if so, raise an error.

To create a method:

➤ Declare a **Public Function** procedure to create a method that returns a value.

➤ Declare a **Public Sub** procedure to create a method that does not return a value.

To create a class that supports multiple interfaces:

➤ Create an abstract class that defines the interface for the class but no implementation. That is, declare the **Property**, **Function**, and **Sub** procedures but place no code in those procedures.

➤ To create the classes that implement the abstract class, declare the actual procedures containing the code. All of the procedures declared in the abstract class must be implemented. Also, the data type of the procedures must be exactly the same.

REVIEW QUESTIONS

1. Properties are created in a class module by:
   a. declaring a Public variable
   b. creating a **Property Let–Property Get** procedure pair
   c. creating a **Property Set–Property Get** procedure pair
   d. None of the above
   e. All of the above

2. Methods are created in a class module by declaring:
   a. **Private Function** and **Private Sub** procedures
   b. **Public Function** and **Public Sub** procedures
   c. a **Method** procedure
   d. Both a and b
   e. All of the above

3. To create a read-only property, you declare a:
   a. Public variable in a class module
   b. **Property Let** procedure without a corresponding **Property Get** procedure
   c. **Property Get** procedure without a corresponding **Property Let** procedure
   d. **Property Read** procedure
   e. Both a and b

4. A Public variable is _____, and a Private variable is _____.
   a. local, global
   b. exposed, hidden
   c. hidden, exposed
   d. Both a and b
   e. None of the above

5. Which of the following statements related to **Property** procedures is true?
   a. The last argument of the **Property Set** procedure must be the same as the return value for the **Property Get** procedure.
   b. Corresponding **Property Get** and **Property Let** procedures must have the same name.
   c. The **Property Let** procedure can be omitted to implement a read-only property.
   d. All of the above
   e. None of the above

6. To create a write-once property, you:
   a. omit the **Property Let** procedure
   b. omit the **Property Get** procedure
   c. raise an error in the **Property Get** procedure if the property has already been written
   d. raise an error in the **Property Let** procedure if the property has already been written
   e. None of the above

9

7. Write the statements to declare an exposed variable (**Property**) named Exposed and a hidden variable named **mintHidden**. Both variables should be **Integer** data types.

8. Create the necessary **Property** procedures and the Private variable named **mintCounter** to implement a property named Counter having an **Integer** data type.

9. Create the necessary **Property** procedure(s) to implement a read-only property named **Key**. The value of the read-only property should be determined using a hidden variable named **mintKey**.

10. Create a write-once property named **Index** that accepts one argument, a **Long** integer. If the property has already been written, raise an error.

11. The _____ event occurs when an object is created from a class and the _____ event occurs when the object is destroyed.
    a. **Class_Load, Class_Unload**
    b. **Class_Load, Class_QueryUnload**
    c. **Class_Open, Class_Close**
    d. **Class_Begin, Class_End**
    e. **Class_Initialize, Class_Terminate**

12. An abstract class:
    a. defines an interface but no implementation
    b. is created using a class module
    c. can contain **Property**, **Function**, and **Sub** procedures
    d. has no code in the procedures
    e. All of the above

13. When you use the **Implements** statement:
    a. the argument is the name of an abstract class
    b. the statement is placed in the abstract class
    c. the statement takes no arguments
    d. All of the above
    e. None of the above

14. What is the benefit of using Class modules?
    a. code reuse
    b. improved programmer productivity
    c. ability of multiple programs to use the class
    d. All of the above
    e. None of the above

15. The class module that implements an abstract class:

    a. contains the **Implements** statement

    b. contains the same methods and properties as the abstract class

    c. has no code

    d. Both a and b

    e. Both a and c

16. Declare a Private array named **mintValues** with 10 elements that are Integers. Then create a parameterized property named **Value** using **Property** procedures. Each procedure should accept an argument to indicate the index to use in the table **mintValues**.

17. Create a method named **ElapsedMinutes** that takes no arguments and returns a **Long** integer containing the number of minutes elapsed from midnight to the current time of day.

18. Create an abstract class having an interface consisting of two properties. The first property should store a string and have the name **LastName**. The second property should store a second property having the name **IDNumber**. The data type for this property should be an **Integer**.

19. Using the properties created in Question 8, write the statements to implement the class specified in the problem. Assume the class name in Question 8 is **Employee**. The properties should be implemented such that **LastName** is a read–write property and **IDNumber** is a read–write property.

HANDS-ON PROJECTS

Project 1

Using the scenario presented in this chapter, assume that you want to create a class to support yet another type of question. The responses to this type of question contain Integer values such as a person's age, the number of years a person has lived at the same address, and so on. In other words, the valid responses to the question can be a discrete range of values. Additional methods pertaining to the class are therefore necessary. For example, a **Sum** method could be used to get the total of all responses, and an **Average** method could be used to determine the average of all responses. The average is computed by dividing the count of the responses by the sum of the responses.

    a. Run the program named Chapter.09\Exercise\Ex1Demo.exe. Figure 9.11 shows the completed form for the exercise.

b. Enter ages into the text box. Each time you enter an age, click on the Add button to add the information to the class module. When you click on the Average button, the sum and average of the ages will appear in the labels. Exit the program.

c. Start Visual Basic and create a new project, if necessary. Create a class module named **Range**.

d. Create the contol instances shown in Figure 9.11.

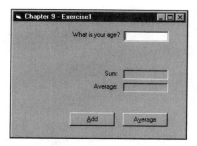

Figure 9.11   Exercise 1 Completed example.

e. Using **Property** procedures, create a read-write property named **Name**, a write-once property called **Number**, and a read-only property called **Count**.

f. Create a method named **Add** that will add a response to the question. This task can be accomplished by using a Private array and then redimensioning the array as shown earlier in this chapter. The **Add** method also should update the **Count** property using the same technique shown in this chapter.

g. Create a method named **Sum** that will add the values of all responses.

h. Create a method named **Average** that will compute the average of all responses.

i. Using a form module, create an instance of the **Range** class. Set the **Name** and **Number** properties for the new class instance. Try to set the **Number** property again to verify that the write-once property works correctly.

j. Add several responses with different Integer values to test the **Add** method.

k. After adding the responses, use the **Count** method to verify that it counts the number of responses correctly.

l. Call the **Average** method to verify that the average is computed correctly.

m. Save the project using the name Chapter.09\Exercise\Ex1.vbp, and the form using the name Chapter.09\Exercise\Ex1.frm. Use the name Chapter.09\Exercise\Range.cls for the class module.

n. Exit Visual Basic.

Project 2

Many operating systems support a program that will count the number of characters, words, and lines in a file. A word is identified as a series of characters bounded by spaces. A line is identified as a number of words terminated by a newline character. In this project, you will create a class that will determine the number of characters, words, and lines in a string.

   a. Run the program named Chapter.09\Exercise\Ex2Demo.exe. Figure 9.12 shows the completed form for the exercise.

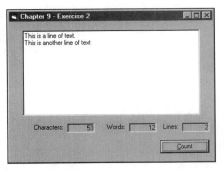

Figure 9.12   Exercise 2 Complete example.

   b. Enter two lines of text into the text box. Click on the Count button. The number of characters, words, and lines appear in the labels at the bottom of the form. Exit the program.

   c. Start Visual Basic and create a new project, if necessary. Create a read-write property to store a string. Use **CharacterString** for the property name.

   d. Create three read-only properties named **Characters**, **Words**, and **Lines**. When read, these properties should return the number of characters, words, and lines, respectively, in the character string.

   e. Consider carefully the implementation for the class. That is, use care to determine where to place the code to compute the number of characters, words, and lines. One solution is to compute each value when the property is read. Another solution is to compute the values for all of the properties whenever the value of the **CharacterString** is written.

   f. Create a form with the following objects to test the class module. A multiline text box should store the text that will be examined. Three output labels should store the count of the characters, words, and lines in the text box. A command button, when clicked, should use the class module to calculate the number of characters, lines, and words in the text box.

g. Save the project using the name Chapter.09\Exercise\Ex2.vbp, the form using the name Chapter.09\Exercise\frmEx2.frm, and the class using the name Chapter.09\Exercise\WordCount.cls.

h. Exit Visual Basic.

Project 3

In this project, you will create an abstract class and three classes that implement the abstract class. A developer of residential tract houses wants to create a class to represent the houses that are being built at a specific tract. Three different models of homes are being constructed at the tract. These models are named Barcelona, Madrid, and Rio.

a. Run the program named Chapter.09\Exercise\Ex3Demo.exe. Figure 9.13 shows the completed form for the exercise.

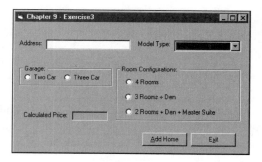

Figure 9.13 Exercise 3 Completed example.

b. Enter an address into the text box and make your model type, garage, and room configuration choices. Click on the Add Home button. The form will display your calculated price. Exit the program.

c. Start Visual Basic and create a new project, if necessary. Create an abstract class named House with the following properties and methods: **Name** (String), **GarageCount** (Integer), **Rooms** (Integer), and **Price** (Single).

d. Create three classes to implement the abstract class. Name these classes **Barcelona**, **Madrid**, and **Rio**.

e. Create the implementation for these three classes as follows: Each class should support a **Name** property to store the address of the house being built.

f. Each class should support a **GarageCount** property to store the size of the garage for the particular house. The Barcelona and Madrid houses can have either a two- or three-car garage, but the Rio house can have only a two-car garage.

g. Create another property named **Rooms** to store configurations of the house's rooms. The Barcelona can have four bedrooms, or three bedrooms and a den. The same is true for the Madrid. The Rio can have four bedrooms, three bedrooms and a den, or two bedrooms, a den, and a master suite.

h. Create a method named **Price**. The price of the home is based on a formula derived from the model and the number of cars that can fit in the garage. The base price is $120,000, $130,000, and $140,000 for the Barcelona, Madrid, and Rio options, respectively. The three-car garage option costs an additional $1500.

i. Save the class modules using the names Chapter.09\Exercise\Barcelona.cls, Chapter.09\Exercise\Madrid.cls, and Chapter.09\Exercise\Rio.cls.

j. Create a form to add houses using the techniques shown earlier in this chapter. Use your imagination to create a robust user interface to add houses and set their properties.

k. Save the form using the name Chapter.09\Exercise\frmEx3.frm and the project using the name Chapter.09\Exercise\Ex3.vbp.

l. Exit Visual Basic.

9

CHAPTER TEN

CREATING A
COLLECTION HIERARCHY

AFTER READING THIS CHAPTER AND COMPLETING THE EXERCISES, YOU WILL BE ABLE TO:

➤ Create a collection

➤ Add, delete, and locate objects in the collection using the methods pertaining to the Collection object

➤ Create an object hierarchy using a **Public** collection

➤ Create an object hierarchy using a **Private** collection

➤ Create a type of class module called a **Collection** class

➤ Improve the robustness of classes with default properties and methods

➤ Use an object called an enumerator so that a class module can support a **For Each** loop

➤ Expand the object hierarchy to include additional classes and collections

➤ Use the Class Builder utility to create a template for an object hierarchy

➤ Work with multiple projects at the same time using a project group

➤ Understand the different types of servers supported by Visual Basic

➤ Change the properties of a class module to control how the class can be used from outside the project

➤ Use the **GlobalMultiUse Instancing** property setting to create a predefined object

➤ Use underlying ADO objects to create a persistent object hierarchy based on the **Publisher** class hierarchy

IMPLEMENTING MULTIPLE CLASS MODULES

Creating A Collection Of Objects

IGX Publishing is a small publisher of technical computer books. The company requires a program that will model part of the data it maintains. This program should keep track of the employees and writers who work for IGX. In addition, it should keep track of the books created by each writer.

The implementation chosen for the completed application illustrates the use of an object hierarchy to manage data. The functionality of the object hierarchy resembles that of other hierarchies, such as ADO, that you have used previously. Figure 10.1 illustrates the object hierarchy (components) for IGX's program.

The business objects shown in Figure 10.1 model the organizational data. The component's author defined the root object called Publisher. The Publisher object supports two collections representing the employees and writers who work for the publisher. Each of these collections contains a number of Employee and Writer objects, respectively. Each writer has written a certain number of books. The component stores those books in another collection called the **Titles** collection. One **Titles** collection exists for each writer. The **Titles** collection contains Title objects to hold the individual book titles of a writer.

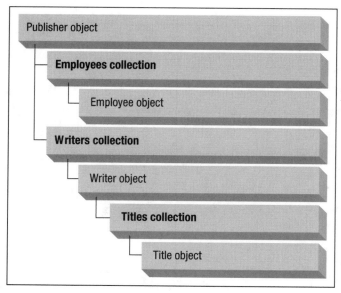

Figure 10.1 IGX object hierarchy.

You will implement each of these collections and objects as a distinct class module. The code in each collection adds and removes its corresponding objects. For example, the methods in the **Employees** collection contain the code to add and remove Employee objects to and from the **Employees** collection, respectively. Project groups, another important concept in this application, allow you, as the component's author, to develop, test, and run multiple projects in a single instance of Visual Basic. In the IGX example, one project contains the class modules that make up the component, and another project contains the forms used by the developer. Thus the developer uses one project and the author uses the other project.

In this chapter, "author" refers to the person who creates the collection hierarchy (component) in the project; this term has the same meaning as it did in Chapter 9 in the discussion of class modules. To avoid confusion in the discussions of the completed and startup programs in this chapter, the term "author" will refer solely to the creator of the collection hierarchy and the term "writer" will refer solely to the IGX writer who creates textbooks.

The project group combines these two projects so that you can develop and test them in the same Visual Basic instance. Figure 10.2 shows the Project Explorer with two projects and the modules contained in those projects. Visual Basic stores a project group as an individual file separate from the project files. The project group file stores references to the included project files and has the file extension ".vbg".

As shown in Figure 10.2, the title bar of the Project Explorer contains the name of a project group rather than a specific project. Furthermore, two types of projects appear in the project group. The first project (Ch10_C.vbp) is a Standard EXE project that can be executed by the user just like any other project. The second project is an ActiveX DLL project named POH. The name "POH" denotes the purpose of the component; it is an acronym for Publisher Object Hierarchy.

Figure 10.2   Project Explorer.

The POH project works just like the code component you created in Chapter 9. Instead of compiling the project (form and class modules) into a single .exe file, however, the class modules are grouped into a second project. You, as the component's author, compile this project into a separate executable file that a developer can add to another project by using the Project References dialog box. This process is identical to the process that you use to add a reference to a library such as ADO.

Separate class modules exist for the **Employees**, **Writers**, and **Titles** collections. These collections manage the Employee, Writer, and Title objects, respectively. In turn, these objects are implemented in the **Employee**, **Writer**, and **Title** classes. The final class is the **Publisher** class, which is the root class. In other words, the **Publisher** class appears at the top of the object hierarchy.

To preview the completed application:

1. Start Visual Basic and open the project group named Chapter.10\Complete\Ch10_C.vbg.

2. Activate the project named Ch10_C.vbp. Click on File, and then click on Print. From the dialog box, select Current Project and Code, if necessary. Click on OK to print the code for the project. When you print the code, note that Visual Basic does not print the code for the project named POH.vbp. Visual Basic will not allow you to print the code for multiple projects at once. Click on the project named POH.vbp in Project Explorer, and then print the code for this project.

3. Run the program. The form should appear as shown in Figure 10.3.

   As shown in Figure 10.3, the form contains control instances to manage the **Employees** and **Writers**. It also contains a control instance to manage the **Titles** created by a writer. In the real world, this data likely would be stored on different forms. The user interface, however, has been combined on a single form in this chapter for brevity and instructional purposes.

4. Enter name, address, city, and state information into the text boxes below the **Writers** label, and then click on the Add Writer command button. Repeat this process to add two more writers with different names. For the sake of brevity, the input is not validated. Click on the combo box below the **Writers** label and select one of the writers you just added. Note that the program automatically assigned a unique key for the writers you created.

5. In the text boxes below the **Titles** label, enter information for two books by clicking the Add Title button to add each book. Again, note that the program does not validate the input. Select different writers and add more titles. Select different writers. When you select a writer, only the titles pertaining to that writer appear in the combo box below the **Titles** label.

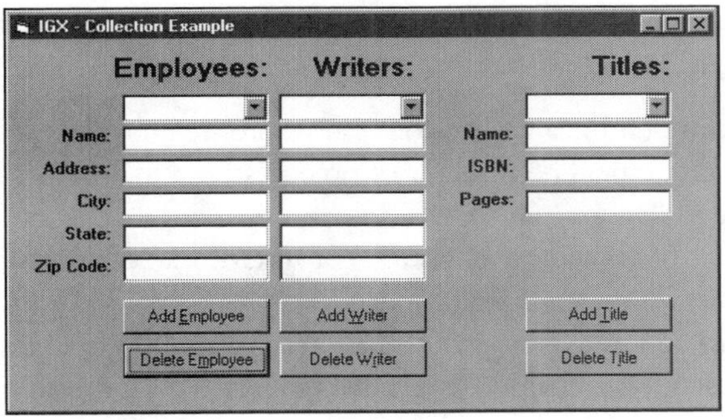

Figure 10.3   Completed program form.

In addition, the program code automatically assigns the ID number that is stored in the titles combo box.

6. Select a title and remove it. Select a writer and remove that writer's entry. Notice that when the writer is removed, all titles corresponding to the writer are removed as well.

7. The process to add, locate, and delete employees works the same as the process to add, locate, and delete writers. Add two employees. Locate an employee using the combo box. Finally, remove an employee by clicking on the Delete Employee command button.

8. End the program, and then exit Visual Basic.

Designing An Object Hierarchy

Throughout this book, you have used predefined collections. For example, you have used the collections and objects supported by the ADO hierarchy to navigate through a database. You have used collections supported by Visual Basic, including the **Forms** and **Controls** collections. Finally, you have used collections pertaining to specific controls. For example, the **ListImages** collection contains references to ListImage objects pertaining to the ImageList control.

All of these predefined collections share certain characteristics. Specifically, they support methods named **Add** and **Remove** to add and remove object references. They also support a **Count** method or property to count the number of object references in the collection. Furthermore, they support the **Item** method, which is typically the default method used to retrieve a reference to a specific object from the collection. Finally, the developer can write code to enumerate the collections using a **For Each** loop. That is, you can write a **For Each** loop, rather than a **For** loop, to examine each object referenced by the collection.

In this chapter, you will group objects (created from a class) into a collection. Collections that you create support the same methods and properties to manage objects (methods such as **Add** and **Remove**) as do the collections used by different controls and the ADO hierarchy.

User-defined collections resemble arrays in that each stores references to multiple objects, usually of the same type. The number of objects stored in an array or collection can be changed dynamically at run time. User-defined collections supply functionality beyond that of conventional arrays. For instance, a collection contains methods to add and remove objects. Using an array, you must manually redimension the array to add new elements and keep track of the elements in the array. In addition, user-defined collections typically support both a string key and a numeric index to locate a specific object in the collection. Using an array, you must code the routines to search for an element in the array.

The functionality that a user-defined collection has over an array carries a price: performance. By allocating and deallocating memory for objects, a collection may perform more slowly than a comparable array. Because Visual Basic treats each object in a user-defined collection as a Variant data type, program performance suffers, as it would with any variant reference.

You create a collection in Visual Basic from a class, just as you do with any other object. This class, known as the **Collection** class, supports the following properties and methods:

Syntax

    Collection

Properties

➤ The **Count** property returns the number of items in the collection. All collections created from the **Collection** class are one-based collections.

Methods

➤ The **Add** method adds an item to the collection. Each item must have a unique numeric index and string key, if a string key is used.

➤ The **Item** method returns a Variant containing the value of the referenced item. You write code to reference an item in a collection using either a numeric index or string key. This process is the same as the process you used previously for other collections. The **Item** method is the default method for the **Collection** class.

➤ The **Remove** method deletes an item from a collection. The method accepts an argument containing the numeric index or string key of the item to be removed.

The **Add** and **Remove** methods have the following syntax. The Item method will be discussed in a moment.

Syntax

> object.**Add** item [,key] [,before] [,after]
> object.**Remove** index

Dissection

➤ The **Add** method adds a new *item* to a collection and the **Remove** method removes an existing *item* from a collection.

➤ The required *object* argument is an object expression that evaluates to a collection object.

➤ The *item* argument is required when calling the **Add** method. You can always reference the *item* in the collection by its numeric *index*. If you specify the optional **key** argument, you can later use a string key to reference the *item* in the collection. The *key* must be unique. If you write code that attempts to add an *item* with a duplicate string key, an error will occur. As in other collections, string keys are case-sensitive.

➤ You use the optional *before* and *after* arguments to add the *item* at a specific location in the collection. The value of the argument can either be the string key or the numeric index of an existing collection member. If *before* or *after* contains an index or key that does not exist, an error will occur. You can include either *before* or *after* in the same statement. If you use the *before* argument, the *item* is added before the object referenced by the *before* argument. If you use the *after* argument, the *item* is added after the object referenced by the *after* argument.

➤ When calling the **Remove** method, you supply the required **index** argument to identify which *item* in the collection to remove. *Item* can contain an existing numeric index or the string key of an *item* to remove. If no *item* exists having the specified *index*, an error will occur.

Code Example

```
Dim Employees As New Collection
Dim pempCurrent1 As New Employee
Dim pempCurrent2 As New Employee
Employees.Add pempCurrent1, "Emp1"
Employees.Add pempCurrent2, "Emp2", "Emp1"
Employees.Remove "Emp1"
```

Code Dissection

Assume that **Employee** is an existing class. The first **Dim** statement creates a new collection named **Employees**. (Remember that collection names should be plural.) The next two **Dim** statements create two new object variables named **pempCurrent1** and **pempCurrent2**.

The first call to the **Add** method adds the object referenced by **pempCurrent1** to the collection. By default, it has a numeric index of one (1). You can also write code to reference the item using the string key "Emp1." The string key is case-sensitive, as are the string keys in most collections.

The second call to the **Add** method adds a second employee to the collection. This item is added before "Emp1" because you used the before argument. This item has a string key of "Emp2." The final statement removes "Emp1" from the collection.

Using string keys for all items in a collection negates the need to include either the before or after argument, as the developer no longer needs to be concerned with the positional placement of each item in the collection. When you implement a collection, always use a string key so that the developer using the collection can locate individual items more easily.

The singular name used for a class and the plural name used for the collection that stores a reference to the instances of the class comply with a naming convention that is not required by Visual Basic. Visual Basic also does not require that the objects in a collection have the same underlying data type. For example, the following statements are legal, assuming that **Text1** represents an instance of a TextBox control:

```
Private colMisc As New Collection
Private pempNew As New Employee
colMisc.Add Text1
colMisc.Add pempNew
```

Even though these statements are legal, they make little sense because the collection stores unrelated objects. On certain occasions, it makes sense to store references to different types of objects in the same collection. The **Controls** collection is a good example. It stores references to several types of control instances, each with a different underlying type. Although you can write code to store different object types in a collection, this practice has limited applicability.

In addition to the **Add** and **Remove** methods, the **Collection** class supports the **Item** method to locate a specific item in the collection.

Syntax

object.**Item**(index)

Dissection

➤ The required *object* must contain a valid instance of the **Collection** class.

➤ The **Item** method returns an item from the specified collection and is the default method of the **Collection** class.

➤ The required *index* must contain either the numeric index or the string key of an item in the collection. If you supply an invalid numeric index or string key, an error will occur.

Code Example

```
Employees.Item("Emp1")
        Employees.Item(1)
Employees("Emp1")
Employees(1)
```

Code Dissection

The preceding statements illustrate the syntax of the **Item** method, using both a string key and a numeric index. The first two statements explicitly reference the **Item** method. The second two statements have the same effect but take advantage of the fact that the **Item** method is the default method pertaining to the Collection object. As with other objects, taking advantage of the default method or property improves performance.

10

Collections created from the **Collection** class support the **For Each** loop, which allows you to iterate through the items in the collection. This concept is consistent with other collections that you have used. Consider the following statements:

```
Dim Employees As New Collection
Dim pempCurrent As Employee
' Code to add items to the Employees collection
For Each pempCurrent in Employees
    ' Code to reference pempCurrent
Next
```

Assuming that the **Employees** collection in the previous statements contains references to Employee objects, the **For Each** loop will iterate through the **Employees** collection. Each time through the loop, **empCurrent** will reference the next Employee object in the **Employees** collection.

Now that you have seen the Collection object and the methods pertaining to that object, you can proceed to create your first collection.

Creating A First Collection

Although you can use collections to store any type of object reference, you will most commonly use a collection to store references to objects of the same type. For example, as you saw with the ADO hierarchy, the **Commands** collection stores references to Command objects, and the **Recordsets** collection stores a reference to zero or more Recordset objects. If you create a collection and use it to store references to different types of objects, you must write code to evaluate the object's type when you retrieve an object reference from the collection. As part of the code to accomplish this task, you can use the **TypeOf** keyword in an **If** statement.

Suppose the program that you are creating for IGX Publishing operates in two modes: browse and edit. In browse mode, the text boxes should remain locked; in edit mode, they should be unlocked. One implementation solution would involve the creation of functions to lock and unlock the text boxes. These functions would set the **Locked** property of each text box to **True** or **False**, one text box at a time. Another solution would be to create a collection in which you store a reference to each of the desired text boxes. The function to lock or unlock the text boxes would then iterate through the collection. Using this technique, you can create an object variable from the **Collection** class. Then, using the **Add** method, you can add references to the text boxes to the collection. When setting the mode, you can call a function to iterate through the collection. Consider the following statements to accomplish this task:

```
Private Sub Locked(pblnLocked As Boolean)
    Dim ptxtCurrent As TextBox
    For Each ptxtCurrent In mcolControls
        ptxtCurrent.Locked = pblnLocked
    Next
End Sub
```

The **Sub** procedure **Locked** requires one argument: a Boolean value that indicates whether the text boxes should be locked or unlocked. The variable **ptxtCurrent** is declared as type **TextBox**; thus all control instances on the form must be text boxes. Next, the **For Each** loop examines each control instance on the form. Each time through the loop, **ptxtCurrent** references a control instance. The statement inside the **For Each** loop sets the value of the **Locked** property.

You now have the necessary tools and information to create a first collection for the IGX program and to add object references to the collection.

To create a collection and add object references to it:

1. Start Visual Basic, and open the project named Chapter.10\Startup\Ch10_S.vbp. Open the Form window. Figure 10.4 shows the form for this project at design time.

2. Open the Code window, and declare the following variable in the general declarations section of the form module named **frmHouses**:

```
Private mcolControls As New Collection
```

3. Enter the following statements in the **Form_Load** event procedure to add the text box references to the collection:

```
mcolControls.Add txtName
mcolControls.Add txtAddress
mcolControls.Add txtCity
mcolControls.Add txtState
mcolControls.Add txtZipCode
```

4. Create the following **Sub** procedure to iterate through the collection:

```
Private Sub Locked(pblnLocked As Boolean)
    Dim ptxtCurrent As TextBox
    For Each ptxtCurrent In mcolControls
        ptxtCurrent.Locked = pblnLocked
    Next
End Sub
```

5. On the form, create a command button, naming it **cmdLock**. Set the **Caption** to **Lock**. Enter the following statement in the **cmdLock_Click** event procedure to lock the text boxes:

```
Call Locked(True)
```

6. On the form, create another command button, naming it **cmdUnlock**. Set the **Caption** to **Unlock**. Enter the following statement in the **cmdUnlock_Click** event procedure to unlock the text boxes:

```
Call Locked(False)
```

7. Test the program. Enter values in each of the text boxes. Click on the Lock command button to lock the text boxes. Try to change the contents of one of the text boxes. It should be locked. Click on the Unlock command button to unlock the text boxes, and then verify that they are unlocked.

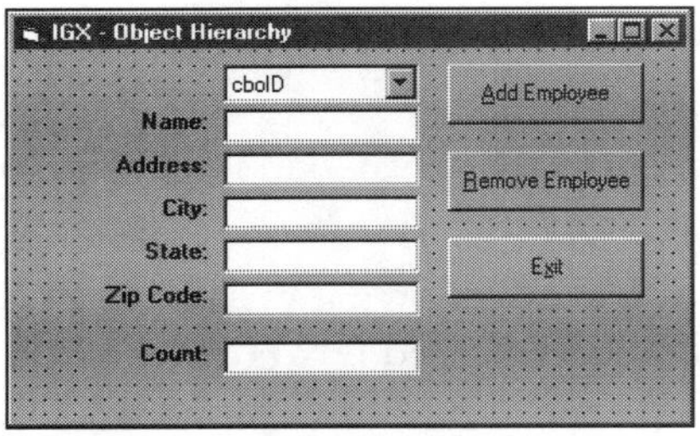

Figure 10.4 Startup form.

End the program to return to design mode.

The code in the **Locked** function requires careful analysis.

```
For Each ptxtCurrent In mcolControls
    ptxtCurrent.Locked = pblnLocked
Next
```

Similar to the process with any other collection, you can write a **For Each** loop to iterate through the individual objects in the collection. The **For Each** loop works just like the **For Each** loops you have used in the past. Each time through the loop, the object variable **ptxtCurrent** stores a reference to the next text box in the collection.

```
Dim ptxtCurrent As TextBox
```

In this code, the data type of the variable used to store the references to the individual collection members is **TextBox**, because all object references in the collection are text boxes. If you stored different types of control instances in the collection, you should have declared the object variable as Control or Object.

```
ptxtCurrent.Locked = pblnLocked
```

The code in this example accesses the properties and methods of the current text box using the variable **ptxtCurrent**, which references an instance of the TextBox control. In the preceding statement, the **Locked** property is set to **True** or **False** for the current text box. The value is stored in the variable **pblnLocked**, which is passed as an argument to the **Locked** procedure.

Now that you have created a simple collection to store references to control instances, you can begin to create collections to manage an object hierarchy.

Three Approaches To Creating An Object Hierarchy

The MSDN Library describes three approaches to creating object hierarchies: the house of straw, the house of sticks, and the house of bricks. The differences between these three approaches lie in which properties and methods that the author exposes to the developer who uses the object hierarchy. Remember that the term "author" refers to the person creating the classes that make up the object hierarchy, and the term "developer" refers to the person who uses the object hierarchy (the component).

The following list summarizes the differences between the three approaches in the implementation of the **Employees** collection:

➤ In the house of straw approach, you write code in the form module to manage the **Employees** collection. Because you, as the developer, have direct access to the **Employees** collection (form module), you can add invalid objects to the collection.

➤ In the house of sticks approach, you create the **Employees** collection and hide it inside the **Publisher** class. Inside the **Publisher** class, you create the methods to add and remove Employee objects from the collection. Because the collection remains hidden from the developer, the developer cannot add invalid objects to the collection.

➤ In the house of bricks approach, you create a separate class to manage the collection. By creating this addition, the object hierarchy will support polymorphism, which allows the methods of different collections to share the same name.

Using the Collection object and the house of straw approach, you will begin to create the object hierarchy for IGX. The first step in creating the hierarchy is creating the root class named **Publisher**. This class will contain the **Employees** collection, which will in turn will contain references to zero or more Employee objects. Figure 10.5 shows this object hierarchy.

In Figure 10.5, the Publisher object exposes a single public object—the collection named Employees. To create this public object, you declare a Public variable, just as you did in Chapter 9 to create a property in a class module. Visual Basic treats this Public variable as a property of the class.

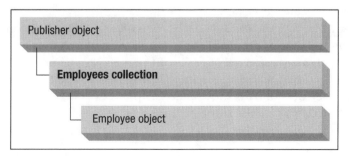

Figure 10.5   IGX object hierarchy.

To create an instance of the **Collection** class:

1. Click on Project, and then click on Add Class Module to add a new class module to the project. If the Add Class Module dialog box appears, activate the New tab, select Class Module, and then click on Open to close the dialog box.

2. Using the Properties window, set the **Name** property to **Publisher**.

3. Enter the following statement in the general declarations section of the class module:

```
Public Employees As New Collection
```

4. Save the class module using the name Chapter.10\Startup\Publisher.cls.

The code added in these steps is very simple. It creates a property named **Employees** that is itself a collection. As such, the property references an object rather than an ordinary data type such as an **Integer**. The plural name denotes that the object property is a collection. The use of the term "object property" is intentional. From the perspective of the developer, **Employees** is a property that references an object. As such, the term "object property" indicates that the property does not contain an ordinary variable, such as **Integer** or **String**. When the developer creates an instance of the **Publisher** class, this declaration will cause Visual Basic to create a new instance of the **Employees** collection. A new object is created because the **New** keyword is used.

Consider the following statements, which are found in a form module:

```
Private mpubCurrent As New Publisher

Private Sub Form_Load()
    Debug.Print mpubCurrent.Employees.Count
End Sub
```

When the new instance of the form module is created, Visual Basic allocates the memory for the module-level variables—in this case, the variable **mpubCurrent**. Because the variable declaration uses the **New** keyword, Visual Basic creates an instance of the **Publisher** class. The argument to the **Debug.Print** statement references the **Count** property pertaining to the **Employees** collection. Of course, the value is zero (0) because no items have been added to the collection. As shown, the **Employees** collection is a property of the **Publisher** class as well as an object property.

The next step in the process of creating the object hierarchy is the creation of the class that will store each employee. Each employee will be represented by an instance of the **Employee** class and, ultimately, a reference stored in the **Employees** collection. You need a mechanism to add and remove Employee objects from the **Employees** collection. Also, the **Employee** class should support properties to store the employee's name, address, city, state, and ZIP code.

To create the **Employee** class and its properties:

1. Click on Project, and then click on Add Class Module to add a new class module to the project. Depending on your configuration of Visual Basic, the Add Class Module dialog box may appear. If it does, select Class Module, and then click on the Open button to add the new class module to the project.

2. Using the Properties window, set the **Name** of the class to **Employee**.

3. In the general declarations section of the **Employee** class module, declare the following properties to represent the data pertaining to an employee:

```
Public Name As String
Public Address As String
Public City As String
Public State As String
Public ZipCode As String
```

4. Each employee will have a unique ID number. You will implement the **ID** property as a write-once property using the technique presented in Chapter 9. Enter the following statement in the general declarations section of the **Employee** class module:

```
Private mstrID As String
```

5. In the **Employee** class module, create the following **Property** procedures to implement the **ID** property. The **ID** property will correspond to the string key used to reference the employee in the **Employees** collection.

```
Public Property Get ID() As String
    ID = mstrID
End Property

Public Property Let ID(pstrID As String)
    Static pblnWritten As Boolean
    If Not pblnWritten Then
        pblnWritten = True
        mstrID = pstrID
    End If
End Property
```

10

6. Save the class module using the name Chapter.10\Startup\Employee.cls.

The **Name**, **Address**, **City**, **State**, and **ZipCode** properties in the **Employee** class store that set of information for an employee. For the sake of brevity, Public variables are used instead of **Property** procedures. Nevertheless, **Property** procedures to validate the data would be suitable for both the **State** and **ZipCode** properties. The **ID** property contains a unique identification number that cannot be changed; therefore it is implemented as a write-once property. The implementation technique is identical to the one you saw in Chapter 9.

Now that you have created the **Employees** collection and the **Employee** class, you can write the code to add Employee objects to the collection.

Adding An Employee Object To The Employees Collection

The process of adding an employee involves two distinct steps. First, your code must create a new instance of the **Employee** class and set the properties pertaining to that new instance. Then, your code must add a reference to the newly created object to the **Employees** collection. In this house of straw implementation, you, as the developer, will write the remaining code in the form module. You (as the developer) access the object hierarchy that you (as the author) have set up by creating an instance of the Publisher object, as shown in the following statement:

```
Private mpubCurrent As New Publisher
```

The following code to add an employee will appear in the **Click** event procedure for the Add Employee command button:

```
Static pintID As Integer
Dim pempCurrent As New Employee
With pempCurrent
    pintID = pintID + 1
    .ID = "e" & Format(pintID, "000")
    .Name = txtName
    .Address = txtAddress
    .City = txtCity
    .State = txtState
    .ZipCode = txtZipCode
End With
```

The preceding code keeps track of the ID number for each employee in the static variable **pintID**. The **Format** statement converts this counter (**pintID**) to a string, using the character "e" as a prefix. Each time that the procedure executes, the code increments the counter's value by one (1). The next statement creates a new instance of the **Employee** class. Thus, when the user clicks on the **Add Employee** command button, the code in the **Click** event procedure creates an instance of the **Employee** class. Inside the **With** statement, the statements generate a unique employee ID, and the values of the text boxes are stored in the properties of that particular Employee object.

Consider the following code, which adds the Employee object (**pempCurrent**) to the **Employees** collection:

```
mpubCurrent.Employees.Add pempCurrent, _
    pempCurrent.ID
```

While considering this code, remember that the **Employees** property has a data type of Collection and that you declared this collection in the **Publisher** class. To add the current Employee object, a reference to which appears in the object variable pempCurrent, your code calls the **Add** method using two arguments. The first argument contains a reference to an Employee object, and the second contains the string key that uniquely identifies the object in the collection.

In addition to adding object references to a collection, the developer must be able to retrieve those object references. You can accomplish this task by writing the following code in the **Click** event procedure for the ComboBox cboID to locate an employee in the **Employees** collection:

```
Dim pempCurrent As Employee
Set pempCurrent = mpubCurrent.Employees(cboID)
```

The preceding **Dim** statement creates an object variable to store a reference to an Employee object. When the **Add** method is called, the code you wrote adds the employee ID to the combo box. This value is the same as the string key of the item in the **Employees** collection. Thus cboID, when clicked, contains the string key of the employee in the **Employees** collection. That string key is used as the argument to the default **Item** method, which locates an employee. The following statements are therefore equivalent to one another:

```
Set pempCurrent = mpubCurrent.Employees.Item(cboID)
Set pempCurrent = mpubCurrent.Employees(cboID)
```

The next statements you will write will use the reference to the employee stored in the object variable pempCurrent to read the values from the different properties and store those values in the text boxes. You can now write the code both to add Employee objects to the **Employees** collection and to locate those objects.

To add and locate an employee:

1. Enter the following statement in the general declarations section of the **frmHouses** form module to create an instance of the **Publisher** class:

```
Private mpubCurrent As New Publisher
```

2. Enter the following statements in the **cmdAdd_Click** event procedure in the form module:

```
Static pintID As Integer
Dim pempCurrent As New Employee
With pempCurrent
    pintID = pintID + 1
    .ID = "e" & Format(pintID, "000")
    .Name = txtName
    .Address = txtAddress
    .City = txtCity
    .State = txtState
    .ZipCode = txtZipCode
End With
mpubCurrent.Employees.Add pempCurrent, _
    pempCurrent.ID
txtName = vbNullString
txtAddress = vbNullString
txtCity = vbNullString
txtState = vbNullString
txtZipCode = vbNullString
cboID.AddItem pempCurrent.ID
```

3. Enter the following statements in the **cboID_Click** event procedure:

```
Dim pempCurrent As Employee
Set pempCurrent = mpubCurrent.Employees(cboID)
With pempCurrent
    txtName = .Name
    txtAddress = .Address
    txtCity = .City
    txtState = .State
    txtZipCode = .ZipCode
End With
```

4. Test the program. Enter a name and address information in the text boxes, and then click on the Add Employee command button. Repeat the process to add two more employees.

5. Using the combo box, select one employee. The data pertaining to that employee should appear in the text boxes.

6. End the program to return to design mode.

The code in the **cmdAdd_Click** event procedure creates an instance of an Employee object, sets its properties, and then adds an object reference to the **Employees** collection. The final statements in the event procedure clear the contents of the input text boxes after adding the new Employee object. The code in the **cboID_Click** event procedure locates a reference to the desired employee and displays the information in the form's text boxes.

In addition to adding employees to the collection, the developer must be able to remove them from the collection.

Removing An Employee Object From The Employees Collection

The process of removing an employee consists of the user selecting an employee via the combo box and then clicking on a command button to remove the selected employee. Your code in the command button's **Click** event procedure must remove the selected employee from the **Employees** collection. Remember that the value in the combo box matches the string key for the corresponding Employee object in the **Employees** collection. Thus your code can use the selected item in the combo box as the argument to the collection's **Remove** method. The following code in the **cmdRemove_Click** event procedure removes the currently selected employee:

```
If cboID.ListIndex > -1 Then
    mpubCurrent.Employees.Remove (cboID)
    cboID.RemoveItem cboID.ListIndex
    txtName = vbNullString
    txtAddress = vbNullString
    txtCity = vbNullString
    txtState = vbNullString
    txtZipCode = vbNullString
End If
```

In the previous code, the **cmdRemove_Click** event procedure first checks whether an item is selected in the combo box. If an item is selected, the code in the **If** statement calls the **Remove** method pertaining to the **Employees** collection. The **Remove** method requires one argument—the numeric index or string key of the object in the collection that should be removed. To synchronize the combo box with the collection, the code removes the item from the combo box and clears the contents of the text boxes, thereby indicating that an employee is not selected.

To remove an employee from the collection:

1. Enter the following statements in the **cmdRemove_Click** event procedure for the form module:

```
If cboID.ListIndex > -1 Then
    mpubCurrent.Employees.Remove (cboID)
    cboID.RemoveItem cboID.ListIndex
    txtName = vbNullString
    txtAddress = vbNullString
    txtCity = vbNullString
    txtState = vbNullString
    txtZipCode = vbNullString
End If
```

2. Test the program. Enter the data necessary to create one employee, and then click on the Add Employee button. Select that employee from the combo box, and then click on the Remove Employee command button.

3. Click on the combo box again. The employee should be removed from the combo box and from the collection. The text boxes should contain no information, indicating that the employee no longer exists.

4. End the program to return to design mode.

In addition to adding and removing items from a collection, you can count the number of items in a collection.

Counting The Employee Objects In The Employees Collection

The **Count** property supported by the **Collection** class returns the number of items in the collection. For the IGX program, you can use the **Count** property to display the current number of Employee objects referenced by the **Employees** collection. This property must be read whenever an employee is added or removed from the **Employees** collection. You do not set explicitly the value of the **Count** property. Rather, the collection performs this task automatically as items are added and removed. Consider the following statement:

```
lblCount = mpubCurrent.Employees.Count
```

This statement counts the number of employees in the collection and stores the result in the label named **lblCount**. You can now write the code to count the number of objects in a collection.

To count the number of employees in the **Employees** collection:

1. Enter the following statement at the end of the **cmdAdd_Click** event procedure for the form module:

```
lblCount = mpubCurrent.Employees.Count
```

2. Enter the following statement at the end of the **cmdRemove_Click** event procedure for the form module:

```
lblCount = mpubCurrent.Employees.Count
```

3. Test the program. Add and remove employees from the form. As you do so, notice that the count of employees appears in the form's output label.

4. End the program to return to design mode.

As the author of a class, you should not allow the developer using the class to write code that would invalidate the object hierarchy. That is, the object hierarchy should protect itself from the developer as much as possible. Because the current version of the class contains several deficiencies and because the developer can reference the **Employees** collection directly, the developer can add invalid objects to the collection. That is, the code implements no restriction that forces the developer to add Employee objects to the **Employees** collection. As a result, the developer could attempt to add text box references, as shown in the following statement:

```
mpubCurrent.Employees.Add txtAddress
```

Furthermore, because the **Employees** collection can be referenced from anywhere in the project, any procedure can modify the collection directly. You will now write code to resolve these problems by using the MSDN Library's second approach to creating an object hierarchy—the house of sticks.

Enhancing The Class—The House Of Sticks

You can modify the object hierarchy you just created so as to significantly improve the robustness of the component. The house of sticks implementation, which hides the **Employees** collection in the **Publisher** class, prevents the developer from calling methods or setting properties that allow invalid data to be stored in the object hierarchy.

The house of sticks improvement is intended to make the **Employees** collection become private. Instead of the developer referencing the collection in the form module, you as the component's author will hide the **Employees** collection inside the **Publisher** class. Hiding the collection in the **Publisher** class has significant implications. Because the developer no longer has access to the **Employees** collection, the **Publisher** class, which hides the collection, must contain methods to add, remove, locate, and list the items (that is, the Employee objects). Thus the **Employees** collection will no longer be exposed and be part of the component's interface. By hiding the collection and implementing your own methods, you can hide the process of creating the employee ID inside the **Add** method from the developer. More importantly, because the **Publisher** class becomes responsible for adding items to the **Private** collection, the developer cannot add an invalid type of object.

When hiding a collection from the developer and creating methods and properties to emulate the properties and methods of the underlying collection, you, as the component's author, should always implement all of the methods. That is, the methods you create should supply the same functionality as the Add, Remove, Item, and Count methods pertaining to the underlying collection. Of course, you can create an even more robust collection by supplying additional methods. For the IGX project, the implementation will consist of the following methods and properties:

➤ **AddEmployee**

➤ **RemoveEmployee**

➤ **Employees** (implements the **Item** method)

➤ **CountEmployees**

Note that the method names have been changed such that the word "Employee" or "Employees" is appended to the **Add**, **Remove**, and **Count** method names. In the completed project, the **Publisher** class supports two collections: **Employees** and **Writers**. It needs to support methods for both collections. Thus the methods for the **Writers** collection will be **AddWriter**, **RemoveWriter**, and **CountWriter**. As you can see, a single method named **Add** would not work because you would have no way to distinguish which collection to use. You will solve this deficiency using the house of bricks approach later in this chapter.

The process of converting the house of straw implementation to a house of sticks implementation is relatively simple. First, you convert the **Employees** collection, which was a **Public** collection, into a **Private** collection hidden in the **Publisher** class. You will move most of the code from the form module into the **Publisher** class to implement the methods for the **Private** collection.

Next, most of the code that you previously wrote in the **Click** event procedure for the **Add Employee** command button must be moved into the **AddEmployee** method. This method will create the instance of the **Employee** class, assign a unique employee ID to the object, and then add a reference to Employee object to the **Private** collection. By creating the Employee object inside the **Publisher** class, you, as the author, hide the implementation from the developer. As a result, the developer cannot attempt to assign a duplicate employee ID or create an Employee object directly.

Consider the following statement that will appear in the general declarations section of the **Publisher** class:

```
Private mcolEmployees As New Collection
```

This statement creates a new instance of the private collection **mcolEmployees** when the developer creates an instance of the **Publisher** class. Because it is a Private variable, the developer cannot reference the private collection **mcolEmployees**. Consider the following code for the **AddEmployee** method:

```
Public Function AddEmployee() As Employee
    Static pintID As Integer
    Dim pempCurrent As New Employee
    With pempCurrent
        pintID = pintID + 1
        .ID = "e" & Format(pintID, "000")
    End With
    mcolEmployees.Add pempCurrent, pempCurrent.ID
    Set AddEmployee = pempCurrent
End Function
```

In the preceding code, the **AddEmployee** method will replace the code that you previously wrote in the command button. Although this code is very similar to the earlier version, it has a significant effect on the component. To add an employee to the collection, the developer must call the **AddEmployee** method. Thus the implementation of adding an employee becomes hidden inside the component. The final two statements in the **AddEmployee** function will change as well:

```
mcolEmployees.Add pempCurrent, pempCurrent.ID
Set AddEmployee = pempCurrent
```

Because the collection name changed, the collection name used in the **Add** method must be modified accordingly. The final statement in the

AddEmployee method is not required, but improves the developer interface. After adding a new employee, the developer will likely want to set the properties for the newly added employee. By returning a reference to this employee, the developer avoids writing code to locate the employee.

Consider the following statements in the Add Employee command buttons **Click** event, which will replace the statements you wrote to implement the house of straw approach:

```
Dim pempCurrent As Employee
Set pempCurrent = mpubCurrent.AddEmployee
pempCurrent.Name = txtName
' Statements to set the remaining properties.
```

These statements create an object variable named pempCurrent to reference the newly created Employee object. The **Set** statement assigns an object reference, so pempCurrent contains a reference to the Employee object (created and returned by the **AddEmployee** method).

Instead of removing the Employee object from the **Employees** collection in the form's option button, you, as the author, will encapsulate this task within the **RemoveEmployee** method. The **RemoveEmployee** method removes an Employee object from the hidden collection **mcolEmployees**. It requires one argument—the index or string key of the item to be removed, as shown in the following code:

```
Public Function RemoveEmployee(ByVal _
    pvntKey As Variant)
    mcolEmployees.Remove pvntKey
End Function
```

For the sake of brevity, this method does not validate the index or key; instead, it generates a run-time error if the key does not exist.

Because the **Employees** collection is hidden inside the **Publisher** class, you must explicitly create a way for the programmer to reference a specific employee in the collection. That is, you must implement a method that will perform the task of the **Item** method. The **Employees** method, shown below, serves this purpose:

```
Public Function Employees(ByVal pvntKey As Variant) _
    As Employee
    Set Employees = mcolEmployees.Item(pvntKey)
End Function
```

The preceding method duplicates the **Item** method pertaining to a collection. This **Employees** method requires one argument—the index or string key of the item in the collection to be located. This argument is passed to the **mcolEmployees** collection so as to locate the employee in the **Private** collection. For the sake of brevity, error-handling capabilities are omitted from this procedure. If you use the preceding code, the developer could use the following syntax to reference the **Employees** method:

```
Dim pempCurrent As Employee
Set pempCurrent = mpubCurrent.Employees(cboID)
```

The preceding statements declare an Employee object and store a reference to that object by using the currently selected item in the combo box.

You can now write the code to implement the house of sticks approach to creating a collection hierarchy.

To hide a collection from the developer:

1. Change the following statement in the **Publisher** class module from

   ```
   Public Employees As New Collection
   ```

   to

   ```
   Private mcolEmployees As New Collection
   ```

   This statement creates a collection to replace the **Employees** collection that you created in the house of straw implementation. Instead of being publicly available to the developer, the collection remains hidden inside the class module and is no longer part of the interface.

2. Enter the following function in the **Publisher** class module:

   ```
   Public Function AddEmployee() As Employee
       Static pintID As Integer
       Dim pempCurrent As New Employee
       With pempCurrent
           pintID = pintID + 1
           .ID = "e" & Format(pintID, "000")
       End With
       mcolEmployees.Add pempCurrent, pempCurrent.ID
       Set AddEmployee = pempCurrent
   End Function
   ```

   To the developer, this **Function** procedure will appear as a method. Remember that **Public** functions created in a class module are methods and part of the component's interface. The code adds new employees to the collection and replaces most of the code contained in the Add Employee command buttons **Click** event implemented in the house of straw scenario. It will not recycle deleted employee numbers. That is, if employee number e001 is deleted and a new employee is added, the number e001 will not be used again.

3. Enter the following **Function** procedure (method) in the **Publisher** class module to remove items from the **Employees** Collection:

```
Public Function RemoveEmployee(ByVal _
    pvntKey As Variant)
    mcolEmployees.Remove pvntKey
End Function
```

4. Enter the following **Function** procedure in the **Publisher** class module to return a reference to the collection, which effectively simulates the action of the **Item** method:

```
Public Function Employees(ByVal pvntKey As Variant) _
    As Employee
    Set Employees = mcolEmployees.Item(pvntKey)
End Function
```

5. Enter the following **Function** procedure in the **Publisher** class module to count the employees:

```
Public Function CountEmployee() As Long
    CountEmployee = mcolEmployees.Count
End Function
```

6. Modify the **cmdAdd_Click** event procedure for the form module so it contains only the following statements. Note that you must remove some lines.

```
Dim pempCurrent As Employee
Set pempCurrent = mpubCurrent.AddEmployee
With pempCurrent
    .Name = txtName
    .Address = txtAddress
    .City = txtCity
    .State = txtState
    .ZipCode = txtZipCode
End With
txtName = vbNullString
txtAddress = vbNullString
txtCity = vbNullString
txtState = vbNullString
txtZipCode = vbNullString
```

```
cboID.AddItem pempCurrent.ID
lblCount = mpubCurrent.CountEmployee
```

7. Modify the **cmdRemove_Click** event procedure for the form module so it contains only the following statements:

```
If cboID.ListIndex > -1 Then
    mpubCurrent.RemoveEmployee (cboID)
    cboID.RemoveItem cboID.ListIndex
    txtName = vbNullString
    txtAddress = vbNullString
    txtCity = vbNullString
    txtState = vbNullString
    txtZipCode = vbNullString
End If
lblCount = mpubCurrent.CountEmployee
```

8. Test the program. Add at least two employees, and then remove an employee. The program should produce exactly the same results as produced by the code in the previous version of the program. Instead of implementing the code to manage the **Employees** collection in the form, however, the collection is hidden in the **Publisher** class.

9. End the program to return to design mode.

The modifications made in the preceding steps solve the primary deficiency of the house of straw implementation by hiding the **Employees** collection in the **Publisher** class and creating methods to add, locate, and remove items from the collection explicitly. The developer can reference the **Employees** collection only through the methods defined by you, the component's author.

Although the house of sticks implementation is considerably more robust than the house of straw implementation, it has two deficiencies. First, the method names must be unique to permit the identification of a particular collection. This problem, while not enormous, does not allow for the polymorphism concept of two methods sharing the same name. That is, if the **Publisher** class contained both an **Employees** collection and a **Writers** collection, a better component interface would result if the developer could call a method named **Add** for both collections. Second, because the **Employees** collection is hidden inside the **Publisher** class, no easy way exists to iterate through the elements in the collection using a **For Each** loop. Remember, creating a robust collection requires that you provide a complete implementation. Thus your program should support all methods of a collection, including the ability to enumerate the collection using a **For Each** loop. These requirements are satisfied using the house of bricks approach.

10

Enhancing The Class—The House Of Bricks

The final improvement to the object hierarchy is implementing the
Employees collection in its own class module. This implementation is referred
to as a *collection class*. In this approach, all methods and properties to support the
collection are encapsulated in a single class, thereby improving the design of the
component. In the house of sticks solution, the method names had to be
unique for the Publisher class to support multiple collections. In the house of
bricks approach, however, when you create two separate and distinct collection
classes, the same method names can be used. Another benefit of the house of
bricks approach is that you, as the author, can enable For Each support to allow
the developer to enumerate the collection using a **For Each** loop.

The house of bricks implementation closely resembles the house of sticks
implementation in that most of the differences pertain to creating the new
Employees class and moving the code to implement the class from the
Publisher class to the new **Employees** class. The code itself remains much
the same.

The **Publisher** class, as it presently exists, contains a statement to create an
instance of the **Employees** collection. Consider the following statement in the
Publisher class:

```
Private mcolEmployees As New Collection
```

Whenever the developer creates an instance of the **Publisher** class, this statement
creates an instance of the **mcolEmployees** collection. In the completed program
for IGX, the **Publisher** class also supports a **Writers** collection. Thus the code in
the completed example creates a **Writers** collection and a **Writer** class that are
accessible to the developer. The **Writers** class would be a collection class having the
same methods as the **Employees** class you just created. The **Writer** class would
resemble the **Employee** class. The **Publisher** class then would contain the
following declarations:

```
Private mcolEmployees As New Collection
Private mcolWriters As New Collection
```

Using this approach, your component would manage both the **Employees** and
Writers from the **Publisher** class. To further improve the implementation, you
can move the management of the **Employees** collection into its own class. The
code in the new **Employees** class is nearly identical to the existing code in the
Publisher class. The primary difference is that method names such as
AddEmployee can be reduced to **Add**, because a separate class module would
be created for each collection.

To create the house of bricks:

1. Create a new class module named **Employees**. Set the **Name** property to **Employees** and save the class using the name Chapter.10\Startup\ Employees.cls.

2. Declare the following variable in the **Employees** class module to create and store a reference to the **Private** collection:

```
Private mcolEmployees As New Collection
```

3. Create the **Add Function** procedure (method) in the class module named **Employees**. Note that the code in this method is nearly identical to the code in **AddEmployee** method used in the house of sticks approach.

```
Public Function Add() As Employee
    Static pintID As Integer
    Dim pempCurrent As New Employee
    With pempCurrent
        pintID = pintID + 1
        .ID = "e" & Format(pintID, "000")
    End With
    mcolEmployees.Add pempCurrent, pempCurrent.ID
    Set Add = pempCurrent
End Function
```

4. Create the **Remove** method in the **Employees** class module:

```
Public Function Remove(ByVal pvntKey As Variant)
    mcolEmployees.Remove pvntKey
End Function
```

5. Create the **Item** method in the **Employees** class module:

```
Public Function Item(ByVal pvntKey As Variant) _
    As Employee
    Set Item = mcolEmployees.Item(pvntKey)
End Function
```

6. Create the **Count** method in the **Employees** class module:

```
Public Function Count() As Long
    Count = mcolEmployees.Count
End Function
```

7. Remove all code from the **Publisher** class module, and enter the following declaration:

```
Public Employees As New Employees
```

8. In the form module named **frmHouses**, modify **cmdAdd_Click** so that it contains only the following code:

```
Dim pempCurrent As Employee
Set pempCurrent = mpubCurrent.Employees.Add
With pempCurrent
    .Name = txtName
    .Address = txtAddress
    .City = txtCity
    .State = txtState
    .ZipCode = txtZipCode
End With
txtName = vbNullString
txtAddress = vbNullString
txtCity = vbNullString
txtState = vbNullString
txtZipCode = vbNullString
cboID.AddItem pempCurrent.ID
lblCount = mpubCurrent.Employees.Count
```

9. Modify the **cmdRemove_Click** event procedure so that it contains only the following code:

```
If cboID.ListIndex > -1 Then
    mpubCurrent.Employees.Remove (cboID)
    cboID.RemoveItem cboID.ListIndex
    txtName = vbNullString
    txtAddress = vbNullString
    txtCity = vbNullString
    txtState = vbNullString
    txtZipCode = vbNullString
End If
lblCount = mpubCurrent.Employees.Count
```

10. Modify the **cboID_Click** event procedure so that it contains only the following code:

```
Dim pempCurrent As Employee
Set pempCurrent = mpubCurrent.Employees.Item(cboID)
```

```
With pempCurrent
    txtName = .Name
    txtAddress = .Address
    txtCity = .City
    txtState = .State
    txtZipCode = .ZipCode
End With
```

11. Test the program by adding, selecting from the combo box, and deleting multiple employees. The functionality should match that shown in the house of straw and house of sticks implementations.

12. End the program to return to design mode.

To satisfy the design principles presented in this chapter, the developer should be prevented from referencing the **Employees** collection directly. You can accomplish this task by implementing the **Employees** property as a read-only property using a **Property** procedure. The technique is the same as that presented in Chapter 9.

To implement the **Employees** collection as a read-only property:

1. Remove the following statement from the **Publisher** class:

```
Public Employees As New Employees
```

2. Enter the following statement in the general declarations section of the **Publisher** class module:

```
Private mempEmployees As New Employees
```

3. Create the following **Property** procedure in the **Publisher** class module:

```
Property Get Employees() As Employees
    Set Employees = mempEmployees
End Property
```

4. Test the program. Add and remove employees. The results should be the same as before, but the developer is prevented from writing to the **Employees** property.

5. End the program to return to design mode.

You can further improve the interface for the component by defining a default property for the different various class modules.

Creating A Default Method Or Property

Most collections implement the **Item** method as their default method. Furthermore, most controls implement a default property. For example, the text box supports the **Text** property as its default. Your component, as it currently exists, does not support default methods or properties. Thus, to call the **Item** method, the developer must reference the method explicitly.

Visual Basic allows a property or method in a class module to be the default property or method. You define a property or method as the default by activating the Code window for the desired class module via the Procedure Attributes dialog box and then selecting the property or method name.

To create a default method or property:

1. Activate the Code window for the **Employees** class.

2. Click on Tools, and then click on Procedure Attributes to open the Procedure Attributes dialog box.

3. Click on the procedure Item in the Name list box, and then click on the Advanced button. The Procedure Attributes dialog box with the Advanced options is enabled, as shown in Figure 10.6.

4. In the Procedure ID list box, click on (Default).

5. Click on OK to close the dialog box and save the changes.

The change you just made causes the **Item** method to be called if the property or method is not referenced explicitly. Consider the following statements:

```
Set pempCurrent = mpubCurrent.Employees.Item(cboID)
Set pempCurrent = mpubCurrent.Employees(cboID)
```

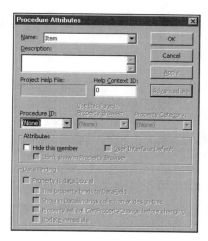

Figure 10.6   Procedure Attributes dialog box.

Before you set the default property, the second statement would have caused an error. Now, because **Item** is the default method, no error will occur.

As an alternative to activating the Procedure Attributes dialog box on the menu bar, you can accomplish the same task using the Object Browser. To create a default property using the Object Browser, click on the class in the Project/ Library list box. In the Classes list, click on the desired class. In the Members list, click on the desired member, right-click on the mouse button, and then click on Properties. The Procedure Attributes dialog box will open.

You will now modify the **Employees** collection so that it supports the enumeration with the **For Each** loop.

Enabling "For Each" Support

The **Employees** collection class that you have created supports all of the methods and properties usually supported by a collection, except for one. Remember that you can create a **For Each** loop to examine the object references in a collection, as shown in the following statements:

```
Dim pempCurrent As Employee
For Each pempCurrent in Employees
    Debug.Print pempCurrent.Name
Next
```

If the developer attempts to include this code, then she will receive an error message indicating that the object does not support this property or method. Remember that **Employees** is a class module and that the actual collection named **mcolEmployees** is hidden inside the class. As the author, you need to provide the developer with a way to enumerate the **Private** collection declared in the class module.

Although you cannot create a method to work as an enumerator in Visual Basic, you can create a link between a method in your class module and the enumerator for the **Private** collection declared in the class module. The **Collection** class supports an object called an *enumerator*. By using this object, the **For Each** loop can enumerate the items in a collection. To explain how this process works, it is necessary to return to the underlying COM objects.

Remember that classes support at least one interface named IUnknown, but usually support multiple interfaces. Also, remember that Windows does not call methods and properties by name. Instead, it uses a unique number called a Procedure ID to call each method and property. The **Collection** class supports multiple interfaces, including, of course, IUnknown. The procedure name for the enumerator is **_NewEnum**, and its Procedure ID is always 24. As the author, you can expose the enumerator to the developer using your class. You must create a method for the **Collection** class that will have the effect of calling the enumerator of the underlying collection named **mcolEmployees**.

Consider the following function to define the enumerator:

```
Public Function NewEnum() As IUnknown
    Set NewEnum = mcolEmployees.[_NewEnum]
End Function
```

This function requires careful analysis. It returns the enumerator of the IUnknown interface for the collection named **mcolEmployees**. The following statement fragment references the enumerator:

```
mcolEmployees.[_NewEnum]
```

The name **[_NewEnum]** requires a bit of explanation. Although Visual Basic does not allow method or function names to begin with a leading underscore, you can write code to reference such a method name by surrounding it with square brackets ([ ]). The leading underscore is a convention to indicate that the member is hidden and not exposed in a type library.

Given the information presented so far, you may wonder how the **For Each** loop knows that the **NewEnum** method should be called to reference the enumerator. Remember from the discussion of COM objects in Chapter 9 that every property or method has a unique identification number, called a Procedure ID, and that Visual Basic calls a property or method using this number. You can associate a specific Procedure ID with a method using the Procedure Attributes dialog box. This process is similar to setting a **Default** property. The Procedure ID for the enumerator used by the **For Each** loop is 24. Using the Procedure Attributes dialog box and setting the Procedure ID to 24 therefore represent the final step to enable For Each support. Visual Basic uses the Procedure ID rather than the name to call the method. Thus you could call the **NewEnum** function anything so long as the Procedure ID is set correctly.

To enable For Each support for a collection:

1. Enter the following statements in the **Employees** class module:

   ```
   Public Function NewEnum() As IUnknown
       Set NewEnum = mcolEmployees.[_NewEnum]
   End Function
   ```

2. Click on Tools, click on Procedure Attributes, and then select the NewEnum function from the list box, if necessary. Click on the Advanced button.

3. In the Procedure ID text box, enter the value −4, and then click on OK to save the changes and close the Procedure Attributes dialog box.

4. To test the procedure, create a command button named cmdTestEnum on the form named **frmHouses** with the caption Test Enumerator, and then enter the following statements in the command button's **Click** event procedure:

```
Dim pempCurrent As Employee
For Each pempCurrent In mpubCurrent.Employees
    Debug.Print pempCurrent.Name
Next
```

5. Test the program. Add several employees, and then click on the Test Enumerator command button to execute the **For Each** loop. The name of each employee should appear in the Immediate window.

6. End the program to return to design mode.

7. Save the project and exit Visual Basic.

As you can see, the process of using an enumerator with a **Private** collection is a rare instance where a basic knowledge of COM objects is not merely helpful, but necessary. In this case, you can see how both the IUnknown interface and the Procedure ID are used.

10

You have now completed the programming for this section. You have applied three techniques to create an object hierarchy from multiple class modules. You have also seen how to improve the robustness of a class module by including support for a default property and method and for the proper use of hidden collections.

UNDERSTANDING PROJECT TYPES

Expanding The Object Hierarchy

The object hierarchy you created earlier in this chapter is much simpler than the one shown in the completed program for IGX. Two significant differences exist between the completed application and the example you have created. First, the **Publisher** class supports two collections instead of just one. That is, the **Publisher** class supports both the **Employees** and **Writers** collections. Consider the following statements in the **Publisher** class:

```
Private mempEmployees As New Employees
Private mwriWriters As New Writers
```

```
Property Get Employees() As Employees
    Set Employees = mempEmployees
End Property

Property Get Writers() As Writers
    Set Writers = mwriWriters
End Property
```

As you can see from the preceding statements, both the **Writers** and **Employees** collections are hidden inside the **Publisher** class module. Both collections are implemented as read-only properties.

Second, the Writer object supports another collection called the **Titles** collection. This collection stores Title objects to identify the books pertaining to a writer. Consider the following declaration in the **Writer** class:

```
Private colTitles As New Titles
```

When the developer creates an instance of the **Publisher** class, an instance of the **Writer** class is created as well. When the code in the **Publisher** class creates the instance of the **Writer** class, the code in the **Writer** class in turn creates an instance of the **Titles** collection for the writer. Thus, for each writer (**Writer** class instance), a **Titles** collection will be created. The **Titles** collection, in turn, contains the necessary methods to add, remove, and reference Title objects in the **Titles** collection. The code in the **Titles** collection is nearly identical to the code in the **Writers** and **Employees** collections.

Using the techniques presented earlier in this chapter, you will now continue to expand the object hierarchy. Specifically, you will add multiple collections to an object, as shown with the **Publisher** class containing the **Writers** and **Employees** collections. In addition, you will expand the depth of the hierarchy as shown with the **Titles** collection. To help you build object hierarchies, Visual Basic supports the Class Builder utility.

Using The Class Builder Utility

As you can see, creating the collections and classes for an object hierarchy quickly can become quite tedious. Visual Basic supports a tool called the Class Builder that allows you to build a template for an object hierarchy. The Class Builder automatically creates methods for **Collection** classes. You, as the component author, can use the Class Builder utility to create the function prototypes for the properties and methods supported by an individual class.

Figure 10.7 shows the Class Builder utility with a simulated object hierarchy.

The Class Builder utility offers the greatest benefits with a new project. If used with a project having existing classes, it cannot place those classes in the object hierarchy. You must perform this task yourself by writing the code manually.

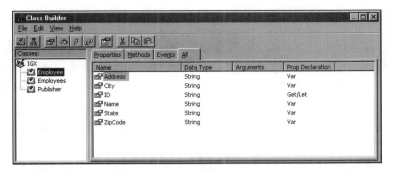

Figure 10.7   Class Builder utility.

The File menu contains options to create new collections and classes. When the Class Builder creates a new collection, the **Add**, **Remove**, **Item**, **Count**, and **NewEnum** methods are created automatically. When you create a new class, you can then establish the properties and methods for that class. The dialog boxes used to create properties and methods allow you to specify the data type of the property and state whether to implement the property as a **Property** procedure or a Public variable.

Unfortunately, most automated development tools have limitations, and the Class Builder is no exception. Although very useful, it has limitations if you supply bad input data. For example, if you try to create a property in a class and a collection of the same name in the same class, the utility may generate unpredictable results.

More About The Project

In previous chapters, you have created a Standard EXE project. This type of project usually has a visual interface (forms), although no visual interface is required. Standard EXE projects are stand-alone projects. That is, they can be run directly from the command line, Start menu, shortcut menu, or by other means.

Windows also supports files that are executable from other programs. Consider the Jet database engine. You do not execute the Jet database engine by executing it from the command line. Rather, the code executes when another program calls its methods. This type of project is known by many names, such as "library" and "server". Visual Basic supports three other project types that are used to create servers. These servers, in turn, contain components used by developers.

As the developer or author, you select the type of project and properties pertaining to the project to specify the type of executable file that Visual Basic creates when compiling the project. Consider the object hierarchy you created earlier in this chapter. An object hierarchy (component) provides a general set of services useful to many programs. Although a developer could add the class modules to the project to use them, the component's author can create a project containing only the class modules that pertain to the object hierarchy and then compile the modules into a server. The developer, in turn, can use the Components or References dialog boxes to add the new server to the project.

When you create a server, you actually create a library that any program on the computer can reference. In ActiveX terminology, this library is known as a *code component*.

When you use a code component, such as the ADO hierarchy, consider the relationship between your program and the code component. As your program runs, it calls the methods and properties supported by ADO. In other words, your program uses the services of ADO. This model of interaction between two programs commonly is referred to as a *client-server* model. In this model, your program is the client and the program that provides the ADO services is the server. When you create a class or group of classes, you can create an executable file that will behave as a server, much as in the ADO hierarchy. One characteristic of servers is their capability to support multiple clients at the same time. With ADO, you can run multiple instances of Visual Basic and multiple clients that rely on the ADO services.

As you develop a server (component), it is a good idea to create a client to test the server along the way, as you did in earlier in this chapter. The server (in this case, the **Publisher** class) can be implemented as a code component. In addition to creating the server, you must register the server to ensure that it will work correctly on the computer. To understand this concept, recall that the Windows Registry stores information about the programs residing on the computer. Consider what happens when you use the Components and References dialog boxes. The information about the different libraries and ActiveX controls is not stored inside Visual Basic, but rather in the Windows Registry. When you open the Components and References dialog boxes, Visual Basic reads this information from the Windows Registry and displays the component or controls that are registered on the system.

The object hierarchy can be compiled as a server, registered on the system, and accessed as a code component. To accomplish these tasks, you must understand two important concepts:

➤ Ultimately, the completed code component will be compiled into an executable library. From the development and testing perspective, however, it would be helpful to create two projects in one Visual Basic instance—one project containing the code component and another project to test the code component.

➤ You must understand how servers are created, what happens on the computer during the creation of a server, and what types of servers exist.

In the following sections, you will first learn how to work with multiple projects at the same time. Second, you will learn more about project files and the additional types of projects supported by Visual Basic. Finally, you will use the various project types to create servers.

Working With Project Groups

Prior to the release of Visual Basic 5.0, Visual Basic allowed you to open only one project at a time. When developing a code component, you, as both the author and as the developer, can work with multiple projects concurrently. To illustrate this capability, consider the IGX program. The class modules that implement the object hierarchy will be implemented as a code component. To facilitate testing and debugging of the code component, you can create one project for the code component (class modules) and a separate project for the form modules that use the code component.

In this scenario, Visual Basic can load and run both projects at the same time using a project group. A project group provides a mechanism to execute and debug the code contained in multiple projects concurrently. Project groups are also helpful when creating ActiveX controls, as you will see in Chapter 11. Remember that a project contains form, class, and standard modules and that each module is stored in a separate text file. The project file, in turn, contains a reference to all modules in the project. The project group, in turn, contains a reference to all projects in the project group.

10

Figure 10.8 illustrates the relationship among these files.

In Figure 10.8, the project group includes three projects. Each project, in turn, has three modules.

Before explaining the details of the types of servers and the implications that the server type has for the performance of the program, you will create a

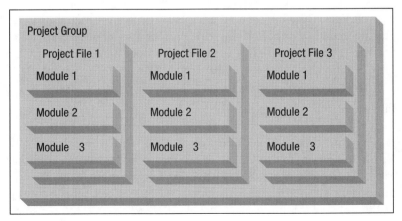

Figure 10.8 Project group.

project group, add and remove projects from the project group, and debug two projects at the same time.

Adding A Project To A Project Group

To add a project to a project group, you click on Add Project on the File menu. The Add Project dialog box appears, allowing you to add an existing project or create a new project. When you add the second project, Visual Basic automatically creates a project group. Additional options appear on the File menu, allowing you to save the project group. Project groups have names much like those of projects. That is, the name of the project group is the same as the file name on the disk. Project groups have the file extension ".vbg".

Creating a project group does not mean that you cannot open and edit the underlying projects independently. In fact, the opposite is true. Creating a project group does nothing to the underlying project files. You can still open, save, and manipulate the individual project files as if the project group did not even exist.

To remove a project from a project group, you select the project in Project Explorer, and then click on Remove Project on the File menu. The project file is not removed from the disk. Rather, it is removed from the project group, which has the effect of disassociating the project file from the project group.

For the IGX application, you will create a project group with two projects. The first project will contain the form and user interface that uses the code component. The second project will contain the class modules that make up the code component. The significance of separating the two projects will become apparent later, when you compile the code component into a server.

To create a project group:

1. Start Visual Basic, if necessary, and create a new Standard EXE project, if necessary. Remove the form named Form1. Click on Project, and then click on Add Form. Use the Existing tab to add the form named Chapter.10\ Startup\frmHouses.frm. Using the Project Properties dialog box, set the Startup Object to frmHouses. Set the project name to IGX_Client, click on OK, and then save it as Chapter.10\Startup\IGX_Client.vbp.

2. Create a second Standard EXE project by clicking on Add Project on the File menu and selecting Standard EXE in the Add Project dialog box, and then click on OK to close the dialog box. Remove the form from the project. Add class modules **Employee.cls**, **Employees.cls**, and **Publisher.cls** from the Chapter.10\Startup folder. You created these classes earlier in this chapter. Take care to add the class modules to the correct project. Using the Properties window, set the name of the second project to POH and save the project as Chapter.10\Startup\POH.vbp. After adding

Figure 10.9   Project Explorer.

the forms and class modules to the two projects, Project Explorer should look like Figure 10.9.

3. Save the project group by clicking on Save Project Group on the File menu. Set the name of the project group to Chapter.10\Startup\IGX.vbg.

The project group now contains two projects. You can include more than two projects in a project group. For example, if you were developing two code components concurrently, you could add both code components to the project group along with the client project and its forms that used the two code components. In fact, a project group can contain as many projects as necessary.

SETTING THE STARTUP PROJECT

In a single project application, you set the Startup object either to a form or the **Sub Main** procedure in a standard module. Because a project group contains multiple projects, however, you must define not only the Startup object for a project, but also the project that should execute first. You select the Startup project by right-clicking the mouse button on a project in the Project Explorer and then clicking on the Set as Startup command.

To set the Startup project:

1. Open the Project Explorer, and then click on the project named IGX_Client.

2. Right-click on the mouse button over the project, and then click on the Set as Start Up option.

3. Test the project group. You will receive a compile error indicating that the user-defined type is not defined, and part of the following line will be highlighted in the Code window:

```
Private mpubCurrent As New Publisher
```

4. Click on OK to close the dialog box.

The respective form and class modules worked when used in the single project illustrated earlier in this chapter. Suddenly, however, they do not work in a project group. Earlier in this chapter, the form could create objects from the **Publisher** class because all modules resided in the same project. Now, however, the two projects are disconnected. To make the project group work as intended, you will use knowledge about the different types of servers supported by Visual Basic, the type libraries, and the Windows Registry.

Creating A Client-Server Project Group

Getting the project group to work and configuring the POH project so that Visual Basic treats it and compiles it as a code component (server) require that you understand three distinct but intertwined topics:

➤ The use of an appropriate type of server—ActiveX DLL or ActiveX EXE

➤ The addition of a code component to a client project

➤ The setting of the **Instancing** property pertaining to class modules

Remember that the client project can no longer locate the objects in the server project containing the class modules. The client program must add the server as a code component, just as a reference to the ADO library must be added before it can be used. In this case, however, if you try to add a reference to the code component, you will find that it does not appear in the dialog box; before the Visual Basic run-time environment treats the code component as a server, you must change its project type. When you converted the project to a server, it became necessary to set another property named **Instancing** for each class module. This property controls whether a class module is visible outside the code component and whether a client can create an instance of the class.

Types Of Projects Supported By Visual Basic

In addition to Standard EXE projects, Visual Basic supports other types of projects used to create both servers and ActiveX controls. The following list describes the characteristics of these project types:

➤ ActiveX DLL and ActiveX EXE project types create programs that provide services to other programs. The servers typically cannot have a visual component, and both are considered code components. What happens when a client connects to a server varies according to whether the server is created as a DLL server or an EXE server. The difference between the two types of servers will be discussed in a moment.

➤ ActiveX control projects allow you to create ActiveX controls that developers can use in other projects and on other computers. ActiveX controls that you create have the same capabilities and characteristics as the other controls that you have used previously. That is, the developer uses the

Components dialog box to add the control to the toolbox and can then use the ActiveX control in a project.

➤ ActiveX documents have a visual interface and code like standard modules. They combine code and data in a "document" and are suitable for use with other programs such as Microsoft Binder and Web applications.

This chapter will discuss DLL and EXE servers. Chapters 11 and 12 focus on ActiveX control creation. ActiveX documents will be discussed in Chapter 13.

A Word About Executing Programs

When you run a Standard EXE file created by Visual Basic, the program is read into memory from the disk and executed. This running instance of your program is called a *process*. Imagine what would happen if you ran a second copy of the same program at the same time: Windows would load a second copy of the program and create a second process. Each process would have its own private copy of its code and data. That is, assigning a value to a variable in one process does not affect the value of the same variable in the second process. Furthermore, each process would execute different statements. For example, assume that the executing program has a long running loop. Each instance of the program would likely be at a different point in the loop. In other words, each process would have a unique execution point, known as a *thread* or *thread of execution*.

10

Another important concept is that Windows is a multitasking operating system. That is, the operating system is responsible for running multiple programs seemingly at the same time. The exact way in which Windows performs this task is beyond the scope of this book. The point to remember for the current discussion is that Windows keeps a list of all processes running on the computer.

Processes are created from many sources. When you run a program, Windows creates a process. You may have virus-checking software running in the background; it, too, is a process. As you access different libraries on the system, processes may be created. Each process can be in one of three different states. First, it can be running; that is, the code in the process can be currently executing. Second, it can be blocked; that is, it can be waiting for some external operation to complete, such as reading data from the disk. Third, a process can be idle; an idle process is capable of running but is waiting for the CPU. Windows allocates a fixed amount of CPU time to each process capable of running, giving the user the illusion that multiple programs are executing at once. In reality, Windows executes only one process at a time, but switches back and forth between programs very quickly. Computers that have multiple CPUs do not work in this way. Instead, each processor can run a separate process.

As noted earlier, Visual Basic supports ActiveX EXE servers and ActiveX DLL servers. These two types of servers are very different. Most notably, when you execute code in an ActiveX EXE server, Windows creates a new server process. When a Standard EXE file calls a function in an ActiveX EXE server, Windows creates two processes—one for the client program and another for the EXE server. Figure 10.10 illustrates such an out of process server.

Assume that the code component was compiled as an EXE server, and further assume that either of two separate client programs uses the object hierarchy in the EXE server (component). In this scenario, Windows considers each client to be a separate process. Additionally, Windows creates a separate process for each server. Conceptually, this approach is very similar to having two copies of the same Standard EXE program. Thus four distinct processes are created and managed by Windows.

When the code in a DLL server executes, Windows does not create a new process. Rather, the code is executed in the process that called the DLL server—that is, via an in process server. Figure 10.11 illustrates an in process DLL server.

In Figure 10.11, only two processes are created—one for each client. Windows does not create an additional process for the DLL server.

The following list describes the pertinent characteristics of EXE and DLL servers:

➤ EXE servers always run as out of process servers.

➤ DLL servers always run as in process servers.

➤ When a client executes an EXE server, a process must be created and the EXE server loaded into memory. As a result, it takes considerably longer initially to execute an EXE server than to execute a DLL server.

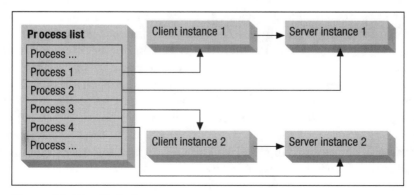

Figure 10.10 Out of process server.

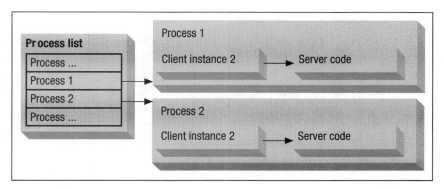

Figure 10.11 In process server.

➤ When the code in a DLL server executes, a small amount of initialization code is loaded for the component, rather than the entire module. When a program calls a method or reads or writes a property, the code for the property or method loads. Thus, in a large module that uses only a few of the properties or methods, a DLL server will provide better performance.

You use the Project Properties dialog box to specify how a project should be compiled and how it should be viewed in the Visual Basic IDE as part of a project group. When the project type is set to an ActiveX EXE or DLL server, Visual Basic enables the project as a code component for the other projects in the project group. In other words, the project will appear in the References dialog box. Several other pertinent pieces of information are specified using this dialog box. Figure 10.12 shows the Project Properties dialog box with the list of project types.

10

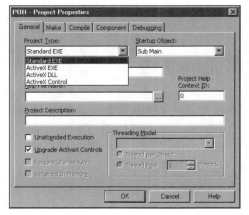

Figure 10.12 Project Properties dialog box.

The data specified in this dialog box is vital to making a code component function properly. The following list identifies the different fields of this dialog box and explains each field's significance:

➤ The Project Type list box identifies how Visual Basic compiles a program. Visual Basic can create Standard EXE files, ActiveX EXE and DLL servers, ActiveX controls, and ActiveX documents. Note that ActiveX documents do not appear in this list. ActiveX document projects must be created from the New Project dialog box. That is, an existing project cannot be converted to an ActiveX document.

➤ The Project Name text box, which is obscured in Figure 10.12, has two purposes. First, it identifies the program in the Windows Registry. Second, the project name appears in the Object Browser.

➤ The Project Description text box is used by the Object Browser for ActiveX controls and by the Components dialog box for ActiveX EXE and DLL servers. You should therefore select a meaningful description for any components you create.

➤ The Unattended Execution checkbox is valid only for certain types of servers. You use this option to create a multithreaded server. Multithreaded servers are described later in this chapter.

Although a detailed explanation of the Windows Registry is beyond the scope of this chapter, suffice it to say that code components—like the one you are creating—are made known to other programs on the system via the Windows Registry. When you compile an EXE or DLL server, Visual Basic adds your program to the Windows Registry automatically. In the IGX application, you will convert the project named POH.vbp to a DLL server (code component).

To create the code component:

1. Click on the project named POH.vbp in Project Explorer.

2. Click on POH Properties on the Project menu to activate the Project Properties dialog box. Set the Project Type to ActiveX DLL, the Project Description to Publishers Object Hierarchy, and the Startup Object to (None). Click on OK to close the dialog box. When you close the dialog box, a dialog box containing the following message should appear: Project 'Start Mode' Property Has Been Changed. Click on OK to close this dialog box.

3. Select the project named **IGX_Client** in Project Explorer.

4. Click on References on the Project menu. Using the scroll bars, locate the item named POH. You created this description for the project via the Project Properties dialog box. Check the checkbox to add a reference to the library to the project. Click on OK to close the dialog box.

5. Test the project group again. You should receive an error with the following message: No creatable Public Component Detected. You will learn how to correct this problem. Click on OK to close the dialog box.

At this point, if you were to compile the POH project, a DLL server would be created and saved on the system. Furthermore, the necessary information would be written to the Windows Registry so that the code component could be added to any project with or without a project group. Also, the information about the type library would be saved to the Windows Registry. If the code component was distributed to another computer, the Setup program would update the Windows Registry properly so the code component can be located.

If you tried to run the client project at this time, however, Visual Basic would generate an error. This problem arises because of class instancing, discussed next.

Class Instancing

In addition to the **Name** property, every class supports the **Instancing** property. As the name implies, the value of the **Instancing** property controls whether an instance of a specific class can be created from outside a project. The **Instancing** property has six possible values:

10

1. With the default **Private** option, when you create a Standard EXE project that uses class modules, it is not possible to create a code component that can be referenced by other projects. That is, the objects in the class modules are visible only to the project where those class modules exist. In other words, the class module and modules that use the class module must exist in the same project file.

2. To understand the **PublicNotCreatable** option, consider the controls in the toolbox. The TextBox and other controls are Public, meaning that they are exposed in the type library. As a result, the class is visible in the Object Browser rather than being hidden in the class. **NotCreatable** means that you cannot explicitly create a new instance of the object. The following statement will therefore generate an error, **Invalid Use Of New** keyword, if the **Instancing** property of the class module is set to **PublicNotCreatable**:

```
Dim txtCurrent As New TextBox
```

3. The **SingleUse** option pertains only to ActiveX EXE servers; it cannot be used by ActiveX DLL servers. When an object is created from a class that is declared as **SingleUse**, a new instance of the server is started for each class instance; that is, another process is created.

4. **GlobalSingleUse** is similar to the SingleUse option, but creates a global object. It is not necessary to declare an instance of the global object when the component is added to the client program. Rather, this instance is predefined.

5. Both ActiveX EXE and DLL servers can use the MultiUse option. As with the **SingleUse** option, multiple instances of the class can be created, but in the case of an ActiveX EXE server, only one instance of the server is created and shared by all processes using the server.

6. **GlobalMultiUse** is used to create global objects that can be referenced without being declared. This approach is similar to using the predefined objects supported by Visual Basic, such as the Printer, Clipboard, and Screen objects.

Consider the code component you are creating for IGX. A project that uses the code component should be able to create a new instance of the **Publisher** class. The **MultiUse** or **GlobalMultiUse** options would be suitable in this case. If the **MultiUse** option were chosen, the developer would need to explicitly create an instance of the **Publisher** class. To date you have used this technique. If the **GlobalMultiUse** option were chosen, however, then a global object variable would be created having the same name as the project name. Thus the following statements would be legal to add an employee to the **Employees** collection:

```
Dim pempCurrent As Employee
Set pempCurrent = POH.Employees.Add
```

Now consider the situation with the other two class modules. Both the **Employees** collection and the **Employee** class should be thought of as dependent objects; that is, the developer should not be able to create an instance of these objects. Thus the following two statements should cause an error:

```
Dim pempNew As New Employee
Dim pempsNew As New Employees
```

This behavior is desirable because the **Publisher** class creates an instance of the **Employees** collection when the class is initialized. Furthermore, adding and removing employees from the collection should be performed by the methods you created in the **Employees** collection class. As you have seen, however, it is useful to declare object variables to create an additional reference to an existing object. For example, the **Add** method of the **Employees** collection class creates a new instance of an Employee object and returns a reference to that instance. Thus the following statements should be legal:

```
Dim pemp As Employee, pemp2 As Employee
Dim pubCurrent As New Publisher
Set pemp = pubCurrent.Employees.Add
Set pemp2 = pemp
```

To achieve this behavior, you can use the **PublicNotCreatable** value for the **Instancing** property. In the IGX program, the **Employees** and **Employee** classes should be **PublicNotCreatable**, and the **Publisher** class should be **MultiUse**.

To set the **Instancing** property for the class modules:

1. In Project Explorer, right-click on the class module named **Employee**. Click on Properties on the pop-up menu to activate the class module. Set the **Instancing** property to **2 – PublicNotCreatable**.

2. For the **Employees** class module, set the **Instancing** property to **2 – PublicNotCreatable**.

3. For the **Publisher** class module, you should set the **Instancing** property to **5 – MultiUse**.

4. To test the **Instancing** property, run the project. Add and remove employees. The project should work as it did before.

5. End the program to return to design mode.

6. Save the program and exit Visual Basic.

Just as creating default properties for classes and collections and enabling For Each support for collections improves the component's interface, properly setting the **Instancing** property of each class module will make the program more effective.

An Introduction To Multithreading

An earlier section discussed in process and out of process servers. You can also create an ActiveX EXE server with unique characteristics that allow for the creation of a single server process. Visual Basic does not support multithreaded clients (Standard EXE files). Each process accessing the server has a unique thread of execution. That is, each client that accesses the server has its own virtual copy of the object.

Visual Basic imposes a few restrictions on multithreaded servers. First and foremost, a multithreaded server cannot contain any visual interface elements. That is, the server cannot display a form, message box, common dialog box, or any other visual element. You can create a multithreaded server by setting an option in the Project Properties dialog box. If you check the Unattended Execution checkbox, the server will compile as a multithreaded server.

Earlier in this chapter, you implemented only part of the object hierarchy illustrated in the completed program. The techniques to extend the object hierarchy are the same as those described in Chapter 9. Consider reviewing the completed program to see how a single class can support multiple collections.

CREATING A PERSISTENT COLLECTION HIERARCHY

Creating An Object Hierarchy With Persistent Data

As it presently exists, the program illustrates how to create a hierarchy of objects, but the data are not persistent. That is, the data are not stored on the disk and do not persist from one invocation of the program to another. Conceptually, solving this problem is very simple. When the developer creates an instance of the **Publisher** class, the data pertaining to the publisher must be read from the disk. Additionally, employees and writers who work for the publisher must be loaded so that the program can reference them. Furthermore, as new employees and writers are added, changed, and deleted, that information must be saved.

Consider the implementation possibilities open to the author of the class module. One option would be to read and write data to text or random files. Another option would be to use a database and implement the object hierarchy in a manner similar to the ADO hierarchy. That is, you would allow the developer to open recordsets and essentially mirror the functionality of ADO. Another possible implementation is to convert the house of bricks collection to read and write data from a database using the same hierarchy as employed in the previous sections. The developer interface for the code component is also a consideration. Implementing a collection hierarchy in this manner insulates the developer from the mechanical details of accessing the underlying data. That is, you encapsulate the data inside the component.

The implementation in this chapter will allow the developer to take advantage of persistent data that use classes similar to the ones discussed earlier. In this way, the developer can view the data for the organization without having to know about the underlying details of opening recordsets or manipulating them. Furthermore, you could change the type of database used to manage the underlying data without affecting the developer, because the data access methods are hidden inside the code component and not exposed to the developer.

To illustrate the use of persistent data, the CD includes a modified version of the partially completed program that reads data from the database when the program runs. The database itself is named IGX.mdb. Three tables in the database—tblEmployees, tblWriters, and tblTitles—have been defined to correspond to the **Employees**, **Writers**, and **Titles** collections, respectively. The records in the table are represented as objects in the respective collection. For example, each employee record in the tblEmployee table is stored as an Employee object in the **Employees** collection. In this section, you will only use tblEmployees and tblWriters.

To view the revised application:

1. Start Visual Basic and open the project group named Chapter.10\Database\IGX.vbg.

2. Print the code for both projects.

3. Test the program. Figure 10.13 shows the form at run time. In subsequent steps, you will complete the code to fill in the Writers text boxes.

4. Click on the buttons below the Employees text boxes. As you click on the buttons, different employee records are located. For the sake of brevity, the code does not check for BOF and EOF conditions, nor is the Titles table supported. You will write the code in this section to display the Writers information.

5. End the program to return to design mode.

The data-bound implementation in this example differs from the implementation that you used earlier. First, consider the class modules in the project, which are shown in Figure 10.14.

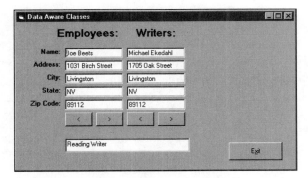

Figure 10.13   Data Aware Classes form.

Figure 10.14   Project Explorer.

As shown in Figure 10.14, only the **Publisher, Employees,** and **Writers** classes are supported. These three classes manage the object hierarchy. The code for the **Publisher** class is similar to the code shown perviously. Consider the following code in the **Publisher** class:

```
Private mempEmployees As Employees
Private mwriWriters As Writers

Public Event ReadingEmployee()
Public Event ReadingWriter()
Property Get Employees() As Employees
    RaiseEvent ReadingEmployee
    Set Employees = mempEmployees
End Property

Property Get Writers() As Writers
    RaiseEvent ReadingWriter
    Set Writers = mwriWriters
End Property

Private Sub Class_Initialize()
    Set mempEmployees = New Employees
    Set mwriWriters = New Writers
End Sub
```

The preceding code introduces two new statements. First, the **Event** statement declares events raised by the class. Second, the **RaiseEvent** keyword raises the event. The **Event** statement has the following syntax:

Syntax

[**Public**] **Event** *procedurename* [(*arglist*)]

Dissection

➤ The **Public** keyword specifies that the event is visible throughout the project.

➤ The **Event** keyword declares the event.

➤ The *procedurename* keyword specifies the name of the event and conforms to standard procedure naming conventions.

➤ The *arglist* contains the arguments that will be passed to the event when it is raised.

Code Example

```
Public Event ReadingEmployee()
Public Event ReadingWriter()
```

Code Dissection

The preceding statements declare two user-defined events, **ReadingEmployee** and **ReadingWriter**. These statements do not generate the events, but merely declare the events.

Once you have declared an event, you must write code to raise the event. The **RaiseEvent** statement generates an event declared with the **Event** statement. Note that to raise an event, the event must be declared in the same module where it is raised. The **RaiseEvent** statement has the following syntax:

Syntax

> **RaiseEvent** *eventname* [(*argumentlist*)]

Dissection

➤ The **RaiseEvent** statement generates an event. The developer can then write code to respond to the event.

➤ The *eventname* contains the name of the event to be raised. The event must be declared in the same module using the **Event** statement.

➤ The *argumentlist* contains the arguments that will be passed to the event.

10

Code Example

```
RaiseEvent ReadingEmployee
RaiseEvent ReadingWriter
```

Code Dissection

These two statements raise the **ReadingEmployee** and **ReadingWriter** events to the developer.

To ensure that the developer can respond to events, you need to declare an instance of a class module appropriately so that your code can respond to events. Consider the code you created in the previous section to create an instance of the **Publisher** class:

```
Private pubCurrent as Publisher
```

The previous declaration will not allow you to respond to any events generated by the **Publisher** class. For a program to respond to a class module event, the variable declaration must contain the **WithEvents** keyword. Consider the following statements:

```
Private WithEvents pubCurrent As Publisher
Private Sub Form_Load()
    Set pubCurrent = New Publisher
End Sub
```

These statements declare the **Publisher** class such that it will generate events and such that the developer's code can respond to those events. The statement in the **Form_Load** event procedure creates an instance of the **Publisher** class. Note that the **WithEvents** keyword cannot be used with the **New** keyword.

To illustrate how events are raised, you will write code in the **Form** module that will respond to these events.

To respond to an event from a class module:

1. Activate the Code window for the Form module named **frmBricks**.
2. In the Object list box, select pubCurrent. Note that this object appears in the list box because you declared the class "WithEvents". In the procedure list box, select the **ReadingEmployee** event, and enter the following statement:

```
txtStatus = "Reading Employee"
```

3. Select the **ReadingWriter** event, and enter the following statement:

```
txtStatus = "Reading Writer"
```

4. Test the program. Select the next employee. The text box at the bottom of the form displays the message Reading Employee.
5. End the program to return to design mode.

The event processing shown in the previous example is very simple, but nevertheless illustrates the basics of how to raise an event in a class module.

Next, you will learn how to make a class data-aware. Although the code for the **Employees** class is complete, the code for the **Writers** class is not. In this section, you will review the code for the **Employees** class and write the code for the **Writers** class.

Most of the following code should already be familiar to you, as it uses ADO and the ADO recordset. Consider the following statements in the general declarations section of the **Employees** class module:

```
Private mconCurrent As New ADODB.Connection
Private mcmdCurrent As New ADODB.Command
Private mrstEmployees As ADODB.Recordset
```

These statements create object variables to store references to ADO Connection, Command, and Recordset objects. The following code in the **Class_Initialize** event procedure creates the recordset using the same techniques discussed in Chapters 3 and 4.

```
Set mrstEmployees = New ADODB.Recordset
With DataMembers
    .Add "Employees"
End With
mconCurrent.Mode = adModeShareDenyNone
mconCurrent.ConnectionString = _
    "Provider=Microsoft.Jet.OLEDB.3.51;" & _
    "Persist Security Info=False;" & _
    "Data Source=" & App.Path & "\IGX.MDB"
mconCurrent.Open
mcmdCurrent.ActiveConnection = mconCurrent
mcmdCurrent.CommandType = adCmdText
mcmdCurrent.CommandText = "SELECT * FROM tblEmployees"
mrstEmployees.LockType = adLockOptimistic
mrstEmployees.CursorLocation = adUseClient
mrstEmployees.CursorType = adOpenKeyset
mrstEmployees.Open mcmdCurrent
mrstEmployees.MoveFirst
```

Although you could create a method and return a reference to the recordset object using that method, you have another technique available—one that involves a concept called data binding. With *data binding*, you can bind control instances, such as text boxes, directly to the recordset in the class module. To accomplish this task, you need to know about BindingCollection object. The BindingCollection object allows you to bind a data provider to a data consumer. In this example, the class module and its recordset serve as the data provider and the form module serves as the data consumer.

Syntax

BindingCollection

Properties

➤ The **DataMember** property contains a set of data to which the consumer can bind. A provider may support multiple data bindings. In this situation, you will specify multiple data members.

➤ The **DataSource** property has the same purpose as it did with bound controls in Chapter 3. It sets the data source through which the consumer is bound.

Methods

➤ The **Add** method adds a Binding object to the BindingCollection object. You can use the **Add** method to bind a control instance, such as a text box, to the data source.

To illustrate the use of the **DataBindings** collection, consider the following statements in the **Form_Load** event procedure for the form named **frmBricks**:

```
With mbndColEmployees
    .DataMember = "Employees"
    Set .DataSource = pubCurrent.Employees
End With
```

These statements use the Private variable **mbndColEmployees**, which is declared in the module as a BindingCollection object. The data member is set to the string "Employees". The significance of this string will become apparent. The next statement sets the DataSource to the **Employees** class.

Next, the **Add** method must be called to add the Binding objects to the BindingCollection object. In this example, these objects are the text boxes on the form. The **Add** method has the following syntax:

Syntax

   Object.**Add**(object, PropertyName, DataField, DataFormat, Key)

Dissection

➤ The *object* must be a reference to a BindingCollection object.

➤ The ***object*** argument contains a reference to a data consumer, such as an instance of a TextBox control.

➤ The ***PropertyName*** contains the name of the property to which the data field will be bound.

➤ The ***DataField*** argument contains the column of the data source.

➤ The ***DataFormat*** argument contains a reference to a DataFormat object or a ***DataFormat*** variable. This object or variable is used to format the data.

➤ The ***Key*** argument uniquely identifies the object in the collection.

Code Example

```
mbndColEmployees.Add txtEmpName, "Text", "fldName"
```

Code Dissection

The preceding statement assumes that the object variable **mbndColEmployees** contains a reference to a BindingCollection object. The control instance added is a text box named txtEmpName. The **Text** property is the bound property and the field bound is fldName.

The following statements in the **Form_Load** event procedure bind the text boxes pertaining to the employees:

```
With mbndColEmployees
    .Add txtEmpName, "Text", "fldName"
    .Add txtEmpAddress, "Text", "fldAddress"
    .Add txtEmpCity, "Text", "fldCity"
    .Add txtEmpState, "Text", "fldState"
    .Add txtEmpZipCode, "Text", "fldZipCode"
End With
```

In this code, each text box is bound to a field in the data source. In each case, the **Text** property is the bound property.

Two final tasks remain to complete the data binding process. First, you must modify the properties of the class module so that the class will act as a data source. Second, you must write code in another class event to bind the class to the actual data source.

Depending on the setting of a class module's **Instancing** property, additional properties become available, allowing the class to act as a data source. In the **Employees** collection class, the **DataSourceBehavior** has been set to **1 – vbDataSource**.

The second part of the process is to bind the class to the data. This task is accomplished using the **GetDataMember** event. Consider the following code in this event procedure:

```
Private Sub Class_GetDataMember(DataMember As String, _
    Data As Object)
    Set Data = mrstEmployees
End Sub
```

This event procedure binds the **Data** argument to the recordset created in the class module. Visual Basic automatically communicates this binding to the data consumer.

Although the code to bind the **Employees** class has been created, the code to bind the **Writers** class has not. You will complete this task next.

To create a data-bound class:

1. Activate the Properties window for the **Writers** class. Set the following property **DataSourceBehavior**, to **1 − vbDataSource**.

2. Activate the Code window for the **Writers** class and enter the following statements in the **Class_GetDataMember** event:

```
Set Data = mrstWriters
```

3. Create the following methods for the class:

```
Public Sub MoveNext()
    mrstWriters.MoveNext
End Sub

Public Sub MovePrevious()
    mrstWriters.MovePrevious
End Sub
```

4. Enter the following statements at the end of the **Form_Load** event procedure for the form named frmBricks:

```
With mbndColWriters
    .DataMember = "Writers"
    Set .DataSource = pubCurrent.Writers
    .Add txtWriName, "Text", "fldName"
    .Add txtWriAddress, "Text", "fldAddress"
    .Add txtWriCity, "Text", "fldCity"
    .Add txtWriState, "Text", "fldState"
    .Add txtWriZipCode, "Text", "fldZipCode"
End With
```

5. Test the program. The program should load the information for the Writers into the form's text boxes. Click on the Next (>) and Previous (<) buttons to locate the next and previous writers, respectively.

6. End the program to return to design mode. Exit Visual Basic.

You have now completed the programming for this chapter. You have seen several techniques to create nonpersistent and persistent object hierarchies.

CHAPTER SUMMARY

This chapter extended the implementation of COM components by illustrating how to create collection hierarchies and persistent object hierarchies. You also learned about additional project types used to create components.

To manage a collection:

➤ Create an instance of the Collection object.

➤ Call the **Add** method to add object references to the collection.

➤ Call the **Remove** method to remove object references from the collection.

➤ Call the **Item** method to reference an item in the collection. This method is the default and need not be explicitly specified.

➤ Read the value of the **Count** property to determine the number of items in the collection.

To create an object hierarchy using the house of straw approach:

➤ Create a class module to represent the root object.

➤ In the class module representing the root object, define **Public** collections representing the dependent child objects.

➤ For each dependent collection, create a class module corresponding to the collection.

➤ Define the properties and methods for each class.

➤ Create a form module to use the component as necessary.

To create an object hierarchy using the house of sticks approach:

➤ Create a class module for the root object.

➤ Create methods in the class representing the root object. These methods should add, delete, locate, and count the dependent objects.

➤ Hide the collections in the root object.

To create an object hierarchy using the house of bricks approach:

➤ Create a separate class module for each dependent Collection object. This class is referred to as a collection class.

➤ For each collection class, create a private collection and implement the required methods and properties to manage the collection.

➤ Create an enumerator for each collection class.

➤ Create a default property or method for each class.

To create a default method or property:

➤ Click on tools, and then click on Procedure Attributes to activate the Procedure Attributes dialog box.

➤ Select a method or property in the Name list box.

➤ Click on the Advanced button.

➤ In the procedure ID list box, click on Default.

To enable For Each support for a collection class:

➤ Enter the following code in a collection class:

```
Public Function NewEnum() As IUnknown
    Set NewEnum = privatecollection.[_NewEnum]
End Function
```

➤ Substitute the placeholder **privatecollection** with the actual collection name.

➤ Click on Tools, and then click on Procedure attributes.

➤ Select the **NewEnum** function.

➤ Set the Procedure ID to −4.

To create an ActiveX server:

➤ Set the project type to ActiveX DLL to create an in process server.

➤ Set the project type to ActiveX EXE to create an out of process server.

➤ Set the **Instancing** property for the class modules as necessary.

To create a project group:

➤ Add projects as desired. Visual Basic automatically creates a project group.

➤ Set the project type for each project as desired.

➤ Define one project in the group as the startup project by selecting the project, clicking on the right mouse button, and then selecting Set as Start Up.

REVIEW QUESTIONS

1. Which of the following methods does the **Collection** class support?
   a. **Add**
   b. **Remove**
   c. **Item**
   d. **Count**
   e. All of the above

2. Items in a collection can be referenced using a_____.
   a. numeric index
   b. string key
   c. subscript
   d. Both a and b
   e. All of the above

3. This method is the default method of the **Collection** class.
   a. **Item**
   b. **Add**
   c. **Count**
   d. **Select**
   e. **Key**

4. Which of the following statements pertaining to an enumerator is true?
   a. The **Collection** class supports an enumerator.
   b. An enumerator has a Procedure ID of −4.
   c. You can declare an enumerator object in Visual Basic.
   d. Both a and b
   e. All of the above

5. Write a statement to create a collection named **colLabels**. Add the labels named **lbl1, lbl2,** and **lbl3** to this collection. Use a string key for each item that is the same as the label name.

6. Assuming that a collection named **colButtons** has been declared and contains references to several command buttons, write a **For Each** loop to disable all buttons in the collection.

7. Write a statement to add an object named Thing to the collection named **Things** having a string key of ABC.

8. Write a statement to remove an object from the collection named **Things** having the string key of ABC.

9. Write a statement to determine the number of items in the collection named **Things** and store the result in the variable named **pintCount**.

10. List the steps involved in creating a default method or property.

11. A project group_____.

    a. replaces the project files

    b. allows multiple projects to be run in the same instance of Visual Basic

    c. is useful when developing client-server programs

    d. Both b and c

    e. None of the above

12. You can load only _____ project(s) in a project group.

    a. 1

    b. 2

    c. 3

    d. 4

    e. any number

13. Visual Basic supports ActiveX _____ project files.

    a. EXE server

    b. DLL server

    c. Control

    d. Both a and c

    e. All of the above

14. A DLL is _____ while an EXE server is _____.

    a. in process, out of process

    b. out of process, in process

    c. a thread, not a thread

    d. Both a and c

    e. Both b and c

15. To create a class such that an instance of the class can be created from another project, the **Instancing** property should be set to _____.

    a. **MultiUse**

    b. **GlobalMultiUse**

    c. **PublicNotCreatable**

    d. Both a and b

    e. All of the above

16. To create a class such that an instance of the class cannot be created from another project but an object reference can be created, the **Instancing** property should be set to _____.

    a. **MultiUse**

    b. **GlobalMultiUse**

    c. **PublicNotCreatable**

    d. Both a and b

    e. All of the above

17. Describe the steps involved in creating an enumerator for a **Private** collection.

18. Create a class module named **Thing** having the properties **Name** and **ID**. The **ID** property should be a write-once property.

19. Create a **Collection** class named **Things**. The **Things** class should implement a **Private** collection named **mcolThings**. Implement **Add**, **Remove**, **Item**, and **Count** methods for the **Private** collection that add, remove, and locate Thing objects. Also, implement an enumerator for the collection.

20. Create a new ActiveX DLL project. Set the name of the class module to **Demo**, and set the **Instancing** property such that other projects can create an instance of the class. Create a **Name** property for the class. Add a Standard EXE project to create a project group. In the Standard EXE project, create a reference to the project containing the **Demo** class. In the form for the Standard EXE project, create an instance of the **Demo** class and set the **Name** property.

10

21. Which of the following is a valid statement to declare an event?

    a. **Public Event MyEvent**

    b. **Public MyEvent**

    c. **Public MyEvent As New Event**

    d. **Public RaiseEvent**

    e. None of the above

22. What is the name of the statement to generate an event?

    a. **MainEvent**

    b. **Generate**

    c. **Event**

    d. **RaiseEvent**

    e. **GenerateEvent**

23. Which keyword do you use to declare a class module object variable reference to which the class will generate events and other modules can respond to those events?

   a. **RaiseEvent**

   b. **WithEvents**

   c. **Events**

   d. **NewEvents**

   e. None of the above

24. Which of the following properties are supported by the BindingCollection object?

   a. **RecordSource, FieldSource**

   b. **DataSource, DataField**

   c. **DataMember, DataField**

   d. **Data, Source**

   e. None of the above

25. Declare an event named **MyEvent** that accepts no arguments.

26. Write a statement to raise the event you declared in Question 25.

27. Write a statement to add the text box named txtCurrent to the BindingCollection object named bndCurrent. Use the **Text** property of the text box and assume that the data field is named fldCurrent.

HANDS-ON PROJECTS

Project 1

In this project, you will develop part of the object hierarchy shown in Figure 10.15 as well as a form to test it using the house of straw approach presented in the chapter.

   a. Run the program named Chapter10\Exercise\Ex1Demo.exe. Figure 10.16 shows the completed form.

   b. Enter information in the Name, Mail Stop, and Address fields. Click on the Add Building command button to add the information. In the combo box, select a building and click on the Remove Building command button; the selected building is removed. Note that the Iterate command button will not work in the completed executable. It prints to the Immediate window, which is not available outside the Visual Basic IDE. Exit the program.

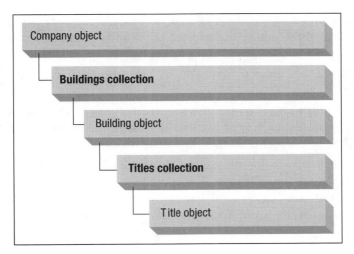

Figure 10.15   Object hierarchy.

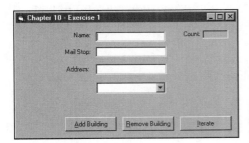

Figure 10.16   Exercise 1 Completed form.

c. Start Visual Basic and create a new project.

d. Create a class named **Building**. Create properties for the class named **Name, MailStop**, and **Address.**

e. Create a root class named **Company**. In the class module, write statements to create a collection named **Buildings** of type **Collection**.

f. In the form module, create text boxes to store the **Name, MailStop**, and **Address** properties pertaining to a building. Also, create a combo box to store a building ID.

g. In the form module, create two command buttons—one to add Building objects to the collection and a second to remove existing Building objects.

h. The **Add** command button should contain the code to add a new Building object to the **Buildings** collection. Each building should have a unique string key assigned using the same techniques presented in the chapter. When a new building is added, append the string key of the building ID to the combo box.

i. Using the selected item in the combo box, the Remove command button should remove the selected building from the collection.

j. Add the code to both the **Add** and **Remove** command buttons to display the count of the buildings in a Label control instance on the form.

k. Create a command button that will iterate through the **Buildings** collection. For each item in the collection, print the **Name** and **MailStop** properties to the Immediate window.

l. Save the classes using the names Chapter.10\Exercise\Straw\Company.cls and Chapter.10\Exercise\Straw\Building.cls, the form using the name Chapter.10\Exercise\Straw\frmStraw.frm, and the project using the name Chapter.10\Exercise\StrawEx1.vbp.

m. Exit Visual Basic.

Project 2

In this project, you will extend the object hierarchy shown in Figure 10.15 and modify the implementation to use the house of sticks implementation presented in this chapter.

a. Run the program named Chapter10\Exercise\Ex2Demo.exe. Figure 10.17 shows the completed form.

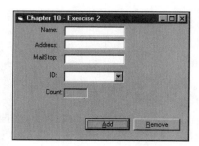

Figure 10.17 Exercise 2 Completed form.

b. The visual interface for this form is nearly identical to the visual interface for the form in Project 1. The difference in the program lies in the implementation. Test the program by adding and removing buildings. Exit the program.

c. Create a new project, or copy the project you created in Project 1.

d. Create a class module named **Company**. In the **Company** class, create a **Private** collection to store the **Buildings** collection.

e. Create an **AddBuilding** method that has the same effect as the **Add** method in Project 1.

f. Create a **RemoveBuilding** method to remove a building from the collection.

g. Create a **CountBuilding** method to count the number of buildings in the collection.

h. Create a **Buildings** method to return a specific building from the collection.

i. In the **Building** class, create Public variables to store the properties **Name**, **Address**, and **MailStop**.

j. In the **Building** class, implement the **ID** property as a write-once property.

k. Create text boxes and buttons on the form to add, remove, and locate buildings in the collection using the methods you created in the previous steps.

l. Save the classes using the names Chapter.10\Exercise\Sticks\ Building.cls and Chapter.10\Exercise\Sticks\Company.cls. Save the form using the name Chapter.10\Exercise\Sticks\frmSticks.frm and the project using the name Chapter.10\Exercise\Sticks\Ex2.vbp.

m. Exit Visual Basic.

Project 3

In this project, you will implement the entire object hierarchy shown in Figure 10.15 using the house of bricks approach, and create a project group to test the object hierarchy. Figure 10.18 shows the completed form for the program at design time. Note that a completed example is not provided for this program.

a. Create a new project.

b. Implement the **Buildings** and **Offices** collections as a **Collection** class.

c. Create **Add**, **Count**, **Remove**, and **Item** methods for both collections.

d. Enable the enumerator for both collections.

e. Create the **Building** and **Office** classes. The **Building** class should support the same properties used in Project 1. The **Office** class should support the following properties: **Name**, **Number**, and **Floor**. Both also should support a write-once **ID** property.

f. Set up the project so that the project is implemented as a DLL server.

g. Set the instancing for the class modules and collections so the developer can create only an instance of the class named **Company**. The user should be able to reference the other classes but not create an instance of them.

h. Create text boxes and buttons on the form to add, remove, and locate buildings in the collection using the methods you created in the previous steps. This form should appear as a second project.

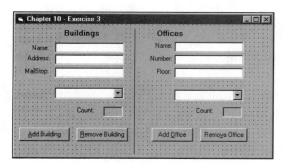

Figure 10.18 Exercise 3 Completed form.

    i. Save the form using the name Chapter.10\Exercise\Bricks\ frmBricks.frm and the project using the name Chapter.10\Exercise\ Bricks\Ex3.vbp. Use appropriate names for the class modules.

    j. Exit Visual Basic.

Project 4

In this project, you will implement an object hierarchy that, in turn, accesses the objects contained in the ADO hierarchy. In essence, you will create a layer of software that insulates the developer from the actual ADO hierarchy, using the techniques presented in the last section in this chapter. Note that this exercise does not have a completed program or figure file for reference.

    a. Create a new project group with two projects. One project should be a Standard EXE project and the other should be an ActiveX DLL server.

    b. In the ActiveX DLL server project, create a class module representing the Titles table in the database named Chapter.10\Exercise\IGA.mdb. This table has the following fields: fldName, fldISBN, fldPages, and fldID. Your class module should create a recordset based upon this table. Set the necessary properties so that the class will act as a data source.

    c. Create methods in the class to locate the next and previous records.

    d. In the form, create four text boxes to store the four fields in the Titles table. Write the necessary code to bind these control instances to the data source.

    e. Save the form using the name Chapter.10\Exercise\frmEx4.frm and the project using the name Chapter10\Exercise\Ex4.vbp.

    f. Save the class using the name Chapter.10\Exercise\Titles.cls. and the project using the name Titles.vbp.

    g. Save the project group using the name Chapter.10\Exercise\Ex4.vbg.

    h. Test the program, verifying that the data appear in the text boxes and that the two command buttons locate the next and previous records.

    i. Exit Visual Basic.

CHAPTER ELEVEN

CREATING AN
ACTIVEX CONTROL

AFTER READING THIS CHAPTER AND COMPLETING THE EXERCISES, YOU WILL BE ABLE TO:

➤ Create an ActiveX control

➤ Create a project group consisting of an ActiveX control and a Standard EXE project

➤ Understand the difference between design time and run time when creating ActiveX controls

➤ Define event responses for ActiveX controls

➤ Generate events for use by the developer

➤ Create properties for an ActiveX control

➤ Save and read properties to a form file

➤ Create properties that activate dialog boxes

➤ Create enumerated properties

➤ Create default properties

➤ Make a control data-aware so it can be used as a bound control with an instance of the ADO Data control

COMBINING A TEXT BOX AND LABEL INTO ONE CONTROL

The Basics Of ActiveX Control Creation

The completed application for this chapter is not an application in the sense of being a form with a user interface. Rather, it contains an ActiveX control that is used solely by the developer.

The end user of the program does not work with the code component. Instead, the developer, as an intermediate end user, manipulates the code component. The roles of the author and developer when creating and using ActiveX controls are the same as they were when you created and tested code components built from class modules. That is, the author creates an ActiveX control, and the developer, as an intermediate end user, uses the ActiveX control.

In this chapter, you will assume the role of both author and developer. As the author, you will develop the ActiveX control and define the properties and events used by the developer. As the developer, you will create instances of the ActiveX control on a form and test the control.

The completed application for this chapter contains an ActiveX control built from two other intrinsic controls: a text box and a label. As the author, you can use intrinsic controls, such as text boxes and existing ActiveX controls, as building blocks to create your own ActiveX control. As the developer, you can access the properties of the ActiveX control and write code that responds to events.

When you use existing controls to create your own ActiveX control, as you will do later in this chapter, you must take note of the relevant licensing issues. Most license agreements allow you to distribute in your application the .ocx file that corresponds to an ActiveX control. That is, if your program *uses* the Windows Common Controls, such as the TreeView or ListView control, you may distribute the corresponding .ocx file with your program. On the other hand, if you *create* your own ActiveX control that is based on, for example, the TreeView control, your control must "add significant and primary functionality to any redistributable" before you can legally distribute the TreeView control as part of the software you develop. Because different licensing requirements are imposed by each vendor, you should carefully examine the licensing agreement for each control use to create your own ActiveX control.

To preview the completed application:

1. Start Visual Basic. Load the project group named Chapter.11\Complete\ Ch11_C.vbg. Make sure to open the project group with the extension .vbg. Figure 11.1 shows Project Explorer for the completed application with the folders open.

Figure 11.1 Project Explorer.

In Figure 11.1, Project Explorer contains a new folder named User Controls. The **UserControl** class is the foundation of an ActiveX control. Note that this project is actually a project group. As discussed in Chapter 10, the author uses one project to create the ActiveX component (in this case, an ActiveX control). The developer uses the other project to test the ActiveX control.

2. Activate the Form window for the form named Ch11_C.frm.

3. Open the toolbox. Click on the TextBoxPlus control button in the toolbox and create a second instance of the control on the form, as shown in Figure 11.2.

4. The TextBoxPlus control supports properties just as any other control does. In the Properties window, set the **Name** property of the instance to **tbpName**, set the **Caption** property to **Name**, and remove the text from the **Text** property.

5. Activate the Code window for the form. In the Object list box, select the tbpName control instance. Activate the Procedure list box. As you can see from its contents, the control instance responds to events just as any other control instance does.

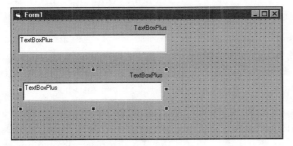

Figure 11.2 TextBoxPlus control.

6. Run the program. The TextBoxPlus control works like an ordinary text box, but it consists of both a text box and a descriptive prompt. When the text box receives focus, all characters in it are selected automatically.

7. End the program and exit Visual Basic. Do not save any of the changes.

Creating ActiveX Controls

Today, creating ActiveX controls is much easier now than it was in the past. Prior to the advent of Visual Basic 5.0, the creation of ActiveX controls required programming in C++. This requirement is no longer necessary. You now can use Visual Basic to author ActiveX controls that work just like the ActiveX controls you have used previously. You can also create Property Pages for your ActiveX controls. Visual Basic provides the author with three techniques to create an ActiveX control:

➤ **Enhancing an existing control** Involves either an existing intrinsic control, such as a text box, or an ActiveX control, such as the TreeView control. You can then add properties or methods to the new control or define additional events to which the control should respond. It also is possible to modify the behavior of existing events, properties, and methods.

➤ **Creating a control from multiple existing controls** Is much like enhancing an existing control. You add multiple instances of the same control or different controls to the ActiveX control that you are creating. For example, you could build an ActiveX control based on the TextBox and TreeView controls.

➤ **Creating a control from scratch** Is much more difficult than creating a control based on an existing control. In this book, you will not create a control from scratch.

ActiveX Terminology

The term "container" describes the relationship between a form and the control instances drawn on it. A form is the default container for control instances. The concept of a container is important for three reasons:

1. Many types of objects cannot exist by themselves. For example, if you create a simple program with a single visible object (such as a command button), you must create an instance of the command button on a form (container). The button cannot exist without its container.

2. Containers are not unique to Visual Basic. Indeed, you can develop an ActiveX control and create an instance of the control in Internet Explorer or any other program that supports COM. The important point is that a form, or Internet Explorer, can act as a container for a control.

3. A control instance and its container interact with one another. For example, a container may suggest initial properties, such as the foreground or

background color, for a control instance. Additionally, a control instance may communicate information to its container. For example, a control instance may tell the container (form) to save the value of properties so that the property settings will persist from one invocation of Visual Basic to the next. The responsibility of saving the current values of specific properties belongs to the container, not the control instance.

In all previous chapters of this book, you have used the Form window to create the form's visual interface, which is seen by the end user. The Form window is merely one type of visual designer. In this chapter you, as the author, will use another visual designer to create an ActiveX control that will be seen by the developer. When the visual designer (which closely resembles a Form window) is open, your ActiveX control is in design mode and you, as the author, can create control instances on it using controls drawn from the toolbox.

Creating ActiveX Control Objects

You use two types of modules to create ActiveX controls—User control modules and Property Page modules. Chapter 12 will discuss the creation of Property Page modules. This chapter focuses on User control modules.

With a form, the code and visual description are stored in a form module. A User control works in the same way. The code and visual description for a User control are stored in a User control module. As the author of an ActiveX control, you interact with a User control module just as you do with a form module. You, as the author, use a visual designer to develop the visual part of the ActiveX control, and you use the Code window to develop the properties and events supported by the ActiveX control. A User control module corresponds to the **UserControl** class just as a form module corresponds to the **Form** class.

The **UserControl** class is conceptually similar to a **Form** class. It employs a visual designer in the creation of the control's visual interface. An instance of the User control can respond to events just as a form does. For example, both the **Form** and **UserControl** classes respond to the **Resize** event. When the end user resizes the form, the **Resize** event occurs for the form. When the developer resizes an instance of an ActiveX control created on a form, the **Resize** event occurs for the User control.

The author defines properties and methods for the User control, which the developer later uses, via the same techniques employed to define properties and methods for code components. Specifically, to create a property, you write paired **Property** procedures; to create a method, you write **Public Function** or **Public Sub** procedures in the User control.

The container provides discrete services to the developer. Consider a developer who is creating a control instance on a form. The form might suggest default values for certain properties like colors and fonts. This information is communicated from the container, which can be a form or even Internet Explorer, to a control instance using the predefined AmbientProperties object.

The container also provides services to the author. Several properties exist that are not defined by the control itself but rather by the container (form). You do not create these properties explicitly. Instead, the container (form) supplies them. These properties are communicated between your ActiveX control and its container through the Extender object. The Extender object is predefined by the UserControl object, much in the same way that Visual Basic predefines the **Controls** collection for a particular form. You, as the developer, can therefore access the **Controls** collection to reference the control instances on a given form. As the author, you can access the properties of the Extender object to retrieve information from a container (in this case, a Visual Basic form).

As the author of a control, you have the responsibility of loading the initial properties for a control instance when the developer creates an instance of it. Consider what happens when the developer creates an instance of a text box. This instance has initial property values including font attributes and foreground and background colors. Now consider what happens when you set a design-time property for a control instance (for example, the **Text** property of a text box). When you save the form containing the text box, the property settings are saved in the form module. When you load a project, these settings then are read and applied to the control instance. As the author of a control, you use the predefined PropertyBag object to perform these tasks.

Visual Basic supports several types of projects, including the ActiveX Control project. As you saw in previous chapters when you created an ActiveX DLL or EXE server, a project group allows you to debug multiple projects concurrently. As a result, you can create the code component or ActiveX control in one project and create a program that uses the code component or ActiveX control in another project, all within the same instance of Visual Basic.

In this chapter, you will create an ActiveX control based on both a label and a text box. The ActiveX control will work just like the text box—with a few extensions. Whenever the ActiveX control receives focus, it will select all characters in the text box automatically. Also, it will display a descriptive prompt in the label just above the text box. The ActiveX control you will create in this chapter will be called the TextBoxPlus control.

Focus Management Company develops accounting applications using Visual Basic. The firm's software development staff often creates the same code to enhance the behavior of different controls. For instance, they write code to select all of the characters in a text box when that control receives focus, allowing the user to easily replace the contents of the entire field. They also create text boxes and use them in conjunction with descriptive prompts stored in the text boxes' labels. The company wants to create an ActiveX control that will support both of these features.

The process of creating an ActiveX control is similar to the process of creating a form.

To create an ActiveX control:

1. Start Visual Basic. From the CD, open the project group named Chapter.11\Startup\Ch11_S.vbg, making sure that you open the project group file (.vbg), rather than the project file (.vbp).

2. Click on Add Project on the File menu to open the Add Project dialog box, and then double-click on the ActiveX Control icon. A new project group will be created and a new ActiveX control will be added to the project.

3. Examine the Project Explorer. A new folder appears with the name User Controls. This folder contains the ActiveX controls pertaining to the new project.

4. Save the User control using the name TextBoxPlus.ctl in the Chapter.11\Startup folder. Save the project with the name SuperText.vbp.

5. Save the project group.

The files for an ActiveX control are similar structurally to the files pertaining to a form module. The code and visual component are stored in a single file with the suffix ".ctl", analogous to a form's .frm file. The .ctl file is a plain text file like an .frm file. If the ActiveX control contains graphical images, they are stored in a file with the suffix ".ctx".

When you create any ActiveX Control project, the various controls in the project (each of which is stored in a separate .ctl file) are compiled into an executable file with the extension ".ocx". An .ocx file can contain one or many different ActiveX controls. For example, the Microsoft Data List Controls are contained in a single .ocx file named MSDATLST.OCX. Every ActiveX control you create will have one User Control module. For the Focus Management program, you will create a single User control called a TextBoxPlus control. It also is possible to create a project consisting of multiple User control modules; hence multiple ActiveX controls may reside in the same .ocx file. The User control has a visual designer that works much like the Form window, and it has properties that you can set via the Properties window. It also supports properties, events, and methods in the same manner as a form module.

Although the User control supports an exhaustive list of properties, events, and methods, this section will present only the properties necessary to create a simple ActiveX control. Later in the chapter, and in subsequent chapters, additional properties, events, and methods will be introduced as they become necessary.

Syntax

> UserControl

Properties

➤ The **CanGetFocus** property contains a Boolean value indicating whether the control can receive focus when the container is in run mode.

➤ The **DefaultCancel** property allows the ActiveX control to assume the role of a Default or Cancel button. That is, the User control will support the Default and Cancel properties.

➤ The **InvisibleAtRuntime** property, if **True,** causes the ActiveX control to be invisible when the container is running. In this case, the User control will not support the **Visible** property. Otherwise, the control will support a **Visible** property, which the developer can set. Controls like CommonDialog or ImageList, for example, are not visible at run time.

➤ The **Name** property defines the name of the control. From the developer's perspective, the value of this property is the class name of the ActiveX control. It is also the name used for the control's ToolTip appearing on the toolbox. Just as the **Name** property of a form is the class name, the **Name** property of a UserControl object becomes the class name of the ActiveX control as seen by the developer.

➤ The **Public** property is a Boolean value that defines whether another application can create an instance of the control.

➤ The **ToolboxBitmap** property contains the bitmap that appears on the toolbox.

➤ The **Top**, **Left**, **Height**, and **Width** properties define the position and size of the control on its container.

You create the visual interface for an ActiveX control in much the same way that you create the visual interface for a form. You set the properties pertaining to the User control with the Properties window just as you set a form's properties, although the list of properties differs. In addition, you create control instances on the User control to define its visual interface. From your perspective as the control's author, you can set the design-time properties of each control instance using the Properties window in the same way as you do when creating control instances on a form. The control instances you create on the User control are called *constituent controls*.

To set properties for the **Usercontrol** module:

1. Click on the User control named UserControl1 in the Project Explorer, if necessary. You can use the View Code and View Object buttons to open the visual designer and Code window for the User control.

2. Click on the View Object button to open the visual designer for the User control. The visual designer looks much like the Form window.

3. Right-click on the visual designer, and select Properties on the pop-up menu.

   The Properties window is activated and set to the UserControl1 object. Conceptually, this process is analogous to opening the Properties window for a form. Just as a form—or any object, for that matter—has a **Name** property, so too does the UserControl object.

4. Set the **Name** property to **TextBoxPlus**. Set the **ToolboxBitmap** property to **Chapter.11\Startup\tbp.bmp**, setting the drive designator as necessary.

5. Close the visual designer. The new icon should appear on the toolbox.

The **UserControl** is a much different class than a form and, as such, supports different properties. At this point, your User control is similar to a blank form. You have not yet defined any event procedures for the User control, so it will not respond to any events. When you add a User control to a project, Visual Basic adds an icon to the toolbox. As the developer, you create an instance of the User control on a form just as you do for any other control. If you, as the author, leave the visual designer for the User control open, however, the control instance will appear shaded on the toolbox, indicating that the control is disabled.

Design Time Vs. Run Time

Consider the notions of design time and run time as they pertain to a project with a single form. At design time, the developer creates an instance of a control on a form using the Form window. At run time, Visual Basic automatically closes the Form window. In fact, the Form window cannot be open during run time.

When you create ActiveX controls, the concepts of design time and run time become more complex. When the developer creates an instance of a control (such as a text box or command button) on a form, Visual Basic creates a control instance from the underlying class. Compare this process to the creation of a code component. The developer creates an instance of a class by using the **New** keyword when declaring the object variable or with the **Set** statement. Even though the technique to create a class instance differs greatly from the technique to create an instance of a control, Visual Basic is performing a similar task. That is, it is creating an instance from the class.

After the developer creates a class instance, the properties of the object can be set, and the object can respond to events. For a code component, the class instance is created at run time. For a control, a control instance is created at design time.

When you create an instance of a control, such as a text box, and set the **Name** property to **txtThing**, Visual Basic responds as if the following statement had just executed. You should not attempt to enter this statement. Text boxes are not externally creatable objects and, as such, cannot be created with the **New** keyword. The only way to create a TextBox control instance is by using the toolbox.

```
Dim txtThing As New TextBox
```

This statement implies that the control instance is running—in fact, it is. When you set properties of a control instance at design time, the control instance is running. That is, it responds to events and executes code. Consider a control like the ADO Data control. When the developer sets the **RecordSource** property, the ADO Data control establishes a connection with the database by using the contents of the **ConnectionString** property. For the ADO Data control to look up the tables in a database, the ADO Data control must be running. Thus, when the developer interacts with an instance of the User control that the author created by setting the User control's properties, the control instance itself is in run mode and the Form window is in design mode.

The ActiveX controls that you create operate in the same way. When the developer creates an instance of the control in the Form window and sets its properties, the control is running. When the author creates the visual interface for the User control and the visual designer is open, the control is in design mode and cannot run. For this reason, the control is disabled (appears shaded) on the toolbox. If the author closes the User control's visual designer, the control will be enabled. Additionally, if the developer has created an instance of the control on the form, that instance will appear with diagonal lines, indicating that the control is in design mode.

In summary, a Visual Basic project group containing an ActiveX Control project and a Standard EXE project exists in one of three possible run states:

➤ If the visual designer for the user control is open, both the Standard EXE project and the ActiveX Control project are in design mode.

➤ If the visual designer for the user control is closed and the Form window is open, the Standard EXE project is in design mode but the ActiveX Control project is in run mode.

➤ If Visual Basic is in run mode, both the Standard EXE project and the User control are in run mode.

From the developer's point of view, your ActiveX control works just like any other control. That is, the developer can create an instance of the control on the form and set its properties using the Properties window.

To create an instance of the TextBoxPlus control:

1. Make sure that the visual designer for the User control is closed, and then activate the Form window.

2. Click on the TextBoxPlus control on the toolbox and create an instance of the control on the form. At this point, the TextBoxPlus control is running even though Visual Basic is in design mode. Nothing appears inside the region of the TextBoxPlus control, as you have not yet defined any constituent controls to appear in the User control.

3. Press F4 to open the Properties window, if necessary.

   You might expect that no properties would be listed in the Properties window because you, as the author, have not explicitly created any properties yet. Nevertheless, properties appear that are common to nearly every other control you have used thus far. For example, the **Top**, **Left**, **Height**, and **Width** properties appear. The source of these properties is the Extender object. The **Name** property has been set automatically to **TextBoxPlus1**, consistent with the **Name** properties of other controls that you have created. The default name for the control instance is the class name followed by a number.

4. Set the **Name** property to **tbpName**. The three-character prefix identifies the type of control, consistent with other object-naming conventions.

5. Activate the Code window for the Form module, and select the object named tbpName. Click on the Procedure list box. The Extender object defines five events: **DragDrop, DragOver, GotFocus, LostFocus**, and **Validate**.

6. To observe when the control is in design mode and when it is in run mode, activate the Code window for the User control and enter the following statement in the **UserControl_Resize** event:

```
Debug.Print UserControl.Height, UserControl.Width
```

   This statement will print the height and width of the control instance whenever the developer resizes an instance of the TextBoxPlus control.

7. When the User control is in design mode, it is not processing events. Even though Visual Basic is in design mode, however, the control may be running. Make sure that the Form window is open and that the visual designer for the User control is closed. Resize the control instance drawn on the form. As you resize the form, the **Resize** event occurs, and the current size is printed in the Immediate window. Open the Immediate window to view the changing height and width. As you can see, the control is running and responding to events.

8. Open the visual designer for the User control, and then activate the Form window. The control instance on the form appears shaded, indicating that the control itself is not running. Resize the control instance again. The current size is not printed in the Immediate window because the User control is in design mode and not responding to events.

At this point, your User control does not support even simple events, such as **Click**. That is, the developer cannot write code to respond to the **Click** event. As the author, you must expose explicitly all properties, events, and methods to the developer by creating **Public Property**, **Function**, and **Sub** procedures, except for those supplied by the Extender object.

Predefined User Control Objects

Just as the User control defines some properties and events, so too does the container. The Extender object stores these properties and events for the container. As the control's author, you do not create explicitly the Extender object. Instead, this object is predefined and created automatically when the developer creates an instance of the User control. Although many properties, such as **Height** and **Width**, have exactly the same meanings as they do for other controls, the behavior of some properties varies depending on the settings of the UserControl object.

Syntax

    Extender

Properties

➤ The **Cancel** property appears only if the UserControl object's **DefaultCancel** property is **True**.

➤ The **Default** property indicates that the ActiveX control is the default button for the container.

➤ The **Enabled** property is a read-only property that specifies whether the control supports an **Enabled** property.

➤ The **Name** property is a read-only property that contains the developer-defined name of the control.

➤ The **Parent** property is read-only at run time and contains a reference to the control's container, which typically is a form.

➤ The **TabStop** and **TabIndex** properties appear only if the **CanGetFocus** property for the UserControl object is **True**.

Events

➤ The **GotFocus** and **LostFocus** events occur only if the UserControl object's **CanGetFocus** property is True.

Not all properties listed in the Properties window come from the Extender object. The container defines another object called the AmbientProperties object. Both the AmbientProperties and Extender objects pertain to the container. Rather than being used by the developer, however, the author works with the AmbientProperties object. This object contains properties of the container that suggest default or initial values to your ActiveX control. Some containers support a more robust set of properties than others do.

Syntax

AmbientProperties

11

Properties

➤ The **BackColor** property contains the suggested interior color of the contained control.

➤ The **DisplayAsDefault** property is a Boolean value that specifies whether the control is the default control.

➤ The **DisplayName** property is a string containing the name that the control should display for itself.

➤ The **Font** property is a Font object that contains the suggested font information of the contained control. If the container does not support this property, Visual Basic supplies a default of **MS Sans Serif 8**.

➤ The **ForeColor** property contains the suggested foreground color of the contained control.

➤ The **ScaleUnits** property is a **String** data type containing the name of the coordinate units used by the container.

➤ The **ShowGrabHandles** property is a Boolean value that specifies whether the container handles the showing of grab handles. If the container does not support this property, Visual Basic supplies a default value of **True**.

➤ The **ShowHatching** property is a Boolean value that specifies whether the container handles the showing of hatching. If the container does not support this property, Visual Basic supplies a default value of **True**.

➤ The **SupportsMnemonics** property is a Boolean value that specifies whether the container handles access keys for the control. If the container does not support this property, Visual Basic supplies a default value of **False**.

➤ The **TextAlign** property is an enumeration that specifies the text alignment format. If the container does not support this property, Visual Basic supplies a default value of **0 – General Align**.

➤ The **UserMode** property is a Boolean value that specifies whether the environment is in design mode or end-user mode. If the container does not support this property, Visual Basic supplies a default value of **True**.

Constituent Controls

The easiest way to create an ActiveX control is to base it on existing controls. When you create a control instance on the User control, that control instance is considered a constituent control. In this chapter, you will build the TextBoxPlus control from two constituent controls. A constituent label will display a descriptive prompt, and a constituent text box will support input and output. Although you could create the ActiveX control from scratch, it is much easier to use the functionality of the existing label and text box and expand their features.

Before creating an instance of the User control on the form, you should understand additional details pertaining to the role of author and developer. The Focus Management example includes two projects—one for the ActiveX control created by the author and one for the project used by the developer. Although these two projects are combined into the same project group, when you work with the project named Ch11_S.vbp, you actually assume the role of the developer. When you work with the project named SuperText.vbp, you take on the role of the author.

As the ActiveX control's author, you must first create the visual interface for the User control. This process is very similar to the process of creating the visual interface for a form. You open the UserControl's visual designer. Then, using the toolbox, you create instances of the intrinsic Label and TextBox controls on the User control.

To create a constituent control:

1. Activate the visual designer for the UserControl object.

2. Create an instance of a text box on the User control visual designer, as shown in Figure 11.3.

That's it! You have just created an ActiveX control made up of a single constituent control. To use the TextBoxPlus control (assuming the role of the developer), you must close the visual designer for the User control.

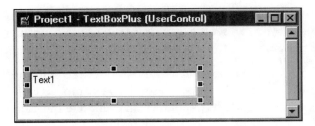

Figure 11.3   Creating the constituent text box.

Then you, as the developer, can create a new instance of the TextBoxPlus control on your form.

The UserControl object hides the events, properties, and methods of constituent controls. Thus the developer does not have access to the events and properties supported by the constituent text box.

To illustrate these hidden properties and methods, you, as the developer, will activate the Form window and view the properties and events supported by the TextBoxPlus control.

To confirm the hidden properties and events of the constituent control:

1. Close the visual designer for the User control, and then activate the Form window. Resize the control instance on the form. The text box appears on the form.

2. Open the Code window for the form, and select the tbpName object, if necessary.

3. Click on the Procedure list box. The events of the constituent text box do not appear because they are hidden from the developer.

4. Activate the Properties window for the control. Again, the properties of the constituent text box are hidden.

5. Close the Form window.

When the developer creates an instance of an ActiveX control, he or she does not directly interact with the properties of the respective constituent controls. Rather, the developer interacts with the User control using the properties, methods, and events that you, as the control's author, explicitly exposed.

As the author of an ActiveX control, you have access to all properties and methods of the constituent controls. Your ActiveX control can also respond to

11

the events generated by the various constituent controls. For example, as the ActiveX control's author, you can set the **Text** property of the constituent text box and write code that responds to events like **Change**.

For the developer, however, the properties and methods of the constituent controls are hidden. To allow the developer to set the **Text** property of the constituent text box or write code to respond to an event like the **Change** event, you, as the author, must therefore explicitly expose the property or generate the event. Figure 11.4 illustrates this concept.

As shown in Figure 11.4, the author creates **Public Property**, **Function**, and **Sub** procedures in the User control to expose properties and methods to the developer. The properties and methods of the constituent controls, however, become available only to the author.

Creating Multiple Constituent Controls

Throughout the programs in this book, you have created text boxes that have a corresponding label used as a descriptive prompt. Additionally, the name of the

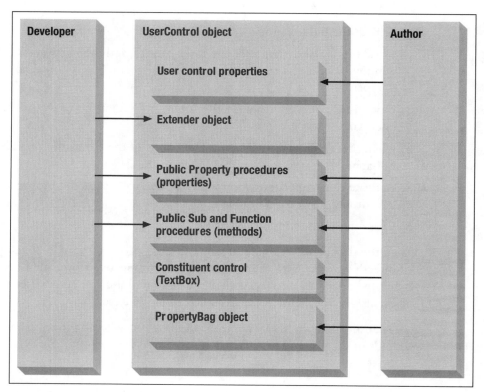

Figure 11.4   Interaction with the UserControl object.

text box has tended to closely resemble the contents of the prompt. For example, you may have a text box named txtAddress with a corresponding prompt of Address. Now you will learn how to create a constituent control made up of both a text box and a label.

To create a control with multiple constituent controls:

1. Activate the visual designer for the TextBoxPlus control.

2. Resize the control and create an instance of the label control, as shown in Figure 11.5.

3. In the Properties window for the constituent label, set the **Alignment** property to **1 – Right Justify**.

4. Close the visual designer for the User control, and then open the Form window.

5. Delete the existing control instance on the form, and then create an instance of the TextBoxPlus control, as shown in Figure 11.6.

6. Set the **Name** property of the control instance to **tbpName**.

7. Resize the control instance. The size of the constituent control will not change when the control is resized.

The names of the constituent text box and label have not been changed. As the author, you have created only one text box and label instance. As a result, you need not change the names from their default values. Remember that the developer can use the control for any purpose and that the developer will never see the names of these constituent objects.

11

At this point, your control supports only those properties and events supported by the Extender object. For your control to be useful to the developer, it should

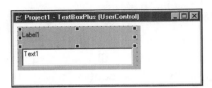

Figure 11.5   Creating the constituent label.

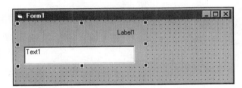

Figure 11.6   ActiveX control instance.

respond to events like **Click** and **Change**—that is, the same events supported by an ordinary text box. Also, the TextBoxPlus control should support properties that allow the developer to set properties such as the label's caption and the text of the text box. These subjects are discussed in the next section.

EVENTS, PROPERTIES, AND METHODS

At this point, your control supports (from the developer's perspective) only those properties and events supplied by the Extender object. This situation poses an interesting question. Why can the developer not set the properties of the text box and respond to its events? The answer is that you, as the control's author, must explicitly expose the properties and methods of any constituent controls to the developer. You also must write the code that will respond to events and raise events for the developer.

User Control Events

When you assume the role of the author of an ActiveX control, the concept of responding to events takes on a whole new meaning. From the perspective of the developer, the behavior of a control differs depending on whether Visual Basic is in design mode or run mode.

Consider a command button existing in the two different modes. At design time, clicking on the command button activates the control instance, allowing the developer to resize or move it. The developer can also set its properties using the Properties window. At run time, the behavior of the same control is completely different—it generates a **Click** event. If the developer has written code to respond to the **Click** event, that code will then execute.

As you may recall from earlier in the chapter, the constituent controls that make up the TextBoxPlus control are not resized when the developer resizes the control instance. From the developer's perspective, what happens during resizing of the TextBoxPlus control instance should be automatic.

As the author, you have two choices: You can implement properties that will let the developer resize the constituent controls individually, or you can create an event procedure that will resize the two constituent controls when the TextBoxPlus control is resized.

In general, the specific behavior for any constituent controls should be transparent to the developer whenever possible. In the Focus Management example, when the developer resizes the TextBoxPlus control, the constituent controls will be resized automatically.

Remember that when the developer interacts with an instance of the TextBoxPlus control, the control is running and responding to events. One event supported by the User control is the **Resize** event, which occurs as the developer resizes the control instance. It is not the same event as the **Resize** events that pertain to the constituent text box and label. These events remain hidden inside the control and are available only to the author.

When the developer resizes an instance of the TextBoxPlus control, you, as the author, must write the code to resize the constituent label and text box. You must consider several factors when the developer resizes a control instance:

➤ The width of both the constituent label and the constituent text box must be adjusted to fill the region of the control instance whenever the instance is resized.

➤ When the developer changes the height of the TextBoxPlus control instance, several implementation choices exist. One option would be to adjust the height of both the label and the text box. Another would be to use a fixed height for the label and adjust the height of the text box.

You will define the behavior of the constituent label and constituent text box so as to accomplish the following goals:

➤ The height of the label remains fixed but the height of the text box adjusts to fill the height of the TextBoxPlus control instance created on a form.

➤ The width of the constituent controls adjusts so that they fit inside the width of the TextBoxPlus control.

➤ You, as the author, will define a minimum width, prohibiting the developer from creating a TextBoxPlus control instance that is so small that the constituent controls cannot be displayed.

➤ If you set the width of the constituent text box to match the width of the User control, then the right recessed border of the constituent text box will be obscured. To solve this problem, you will use constants to define margins for the constituent control.

Consider the following statements, which you will place in the **UserControl_Resize** event. This event will occur whenever the developer resizes an instance of the control. The following statements declare the local variables used in the procedure:

```
Dim pintWidth As Integer
Dim pintTextHeight As Integer
```

The following statements execute when the developer attempts to resize the TextBoxPlus control instance. If the developer tries to resize the control

11

instance to values less than the minimum height and width, the code resizes the control instance to the minimum height and width instead.

```
If UserControl.Height <= cMinHeight Or _
    UserControl.Width < cMinWidth Then
    UserControl.Height = cMinHeight
    UserControl.Width = cMinWidth
End If
```

The following statements resize the constituent controls to match the new height and width:

```
pintWidth = UserControl.Width - cRightMargin
pintTextHeight = UserControl.Height - _
    Label1.Height - cBottomMargin
Text1.Move cLeftMargin, 280, pintWidth, _
    pintTextHeight
Label1.Move cLeftMargin, 0, pintWidth, 255
```

You can now write the code to resize the constituent controls.

To resize the constituent controls:

1. Start Visual Basic, if necessary, and then, from the CD, open the project group Ch.11\Startup\Ch11_S.vbg.

2. Activate the Code window for the User control, and enter the following statements into the general declarations section of the module. These constants will be used as the margins for the TextBoxPlus control and define the minimum height and width.

```
Private Const cTopMargin = 30
Private Const cLeftMargin = 20
Private Const cRightMargin = 80
Private Const cMinHeight = 615
Private Const cMinWidth = 1500
    Private Const cBottomMargin = 80
```

3. Remove the existing statement from the **UserControl_Resize** event procedure, and add the following code:

```
Dim pintWidth As Integer
Dim pintTextHeight As Integer
If UserControl.Height <= cMinHeight Or _
    UserControl.Width < cMinWidth Then
    UserControl.Height = cMinHeight
```

```
        UserControl.Width = cMinWidth
    End If
    pintWidth = UserControl.Width - cRightMargin
    pintTextHeight = UserControl.Height - _
        Label1.Height - cBottomMargin
    Text1.Move cLeftMargin, 280, pintWidth, _
        pintTextHeight
    Label1.Move cLeftMargin, 0, pintWidth, 255
```

4. Close the Code window and the visual designer for the TextBoxPlus control, and then open the Form window.

5. In the Form window, activate the instance of the TextBoxPlus control named tbpName, and then change its size. Because the visual designer for the User control is closed, the User control is running and will execute the code you just wrote in response to the **UserControl_Resize** event. The constituent controls should be resized so that they fill the visible region of the TextBoxPlus control.

6. Try to make the size of the control instance very small. The code in the **Resize** event prohibits the developer from making the control instance so small that the constituent controls cannot hold text.

When the developer creates or resizes an instance of the TextBoxPlus control, the **Resize** event will occur for the User control. The event also will take place when the control instance is first positioned on the form. The code in the event procedure works with the **Height** and **Width** properties of the User control. These properties contain the current height and width after the TextBoxPlus control is resized and are used as the basis for resizing the constituent controls.

Your control now responds to a design-time event, as viewed by the developer. Next, you will consider the situation in which the developer may execute code to resize a control instance at run time. If the developer created an instance of the TextBoxPlus control named tbpName on the form, the following statements could be used to resize the control instance when the form loads:

```
Private Sub Form_Load()
    tbpName.Height = 1000
    tbpName.Width = 2000
End Sub
```

As you can see from the previous example, the developer views your control much differently in run mode than in design mode. Yet, from your perspective as the control's author, the control is running.

Understanding User Control Events

From the developer's perspective, a control exhibits very different behaviors at design time and at run time. When Visual Basic toggles from design time to run time, it destroys the design-time control instances and creates the run-time control instances. Furthermore, when Visual Basic switches from run mode to design mode, the same process occurs in reverse. The run-time instances of all controls are destroyed and design-time instances of the controls are created.

A sequence of events occurs when the developer creates a control instance for the first time. When the developer creates an instance of a control based on the User control, four events occur for the User control object, in the following order:

1. The **Initialize** event occurs first when the developer draws an instance of a control on the form. At this point, the control is running and a design-time instance of the control is created. Typically, code in this event initializes the values of the control's module-level variables.

2. The **InitProperties** event occurs just after the **Initialize** event. Typically, you set the initial values for persistent properties in this event.

3. The **Resize** event occurs just after the **InitProperties** event occurs. In this event procedure, you set the size of any constituent controls as necessary.

4. Finally, the **Paint** event occurs.

When Visual Basic switches from design mode to run mode, several other events occur. These events initialize variables pertaining to the User control at run time and initialize run-time properties. These events occur in the following order. (Remember that Visual Basic destroys the design-time instance of the ActiveX control and creates a run-time instance.)

1. The **Terminate** event occurs first when the design-time instance of the User control is destroyed.

2. The **Initialize** event occurs next when the run-time instance of the User control is created.

3. The **ReadProperties** event then allows the author to read any saved properties.

4. The **Resize** and **Paint** events occur as the run-time instance of the User control is drawn on the form.

A series of events takes place when Visual Basic switches from run mode to design mode. (Remember that Visual Basic destroys the run-time control instances and creates design-time instances.)

1. The **Terminate** event occurs as the run-time instance of the User control is destroyed.

2. The **Initialize** event occurs as the design-time instance is created.

3. The **ReadProperties** event occurs next, allowing the saved design-time properties to be read.

4. The **Resize** and **Paint** events take place when the design-time instance of the control is created on the form.

Another group of events takes place when the developer closes the container in which the instance of the User control has been created. When the developer closes the Form window, Visual Basic destroys the design-time instance of the control, and the following events occur, allowing the author to save any necessary properties and perform housekeeping chores just before the destruction of the control instance:

1. The **WriteProperties** event occurs, allowing you to save any changed properties to the container.

2. The **Terminate** event occurs, just before Visual Basic destroys the design-time control instance.

A developer does not typically use a control in a project group. Rather, the developer adds a reference to the control using the References dialog box. You have used the same technique with other ActiveX controls. Ultimately, the project and its intrinsic and ActiveX controls are compiled into a Standard EXE file. For an ActiveX control, the following events occur when the user runs a Standard EXE file:

1. The **Initialize** event occurs first.

2. The **ReadProperties** event takes place next, allowing you to set the initial values for the properties.

3. The **Resize** and **Paint** events occur when Windows creates the control instance on the form.

Figure 11.7 illustrates the events that affect the User control as Visual Basic switches from design mode to run mode. First, the design-time instance of the control is destroyed. Then, Visual Basic enters run mode and creates a run-time instance of the User control.

Object Focus

Consider two events, **GotFocus** and **LostFocus**. The **GotFocus** and **LostFocus** events are supported by the constituent text box, the Extender object, and the User control. You may wonder which **GotFocus** event occurs to which object and when:

➤ One **GotFocus** event pertains to the Extender object. The container (typically the form) raises this event at run time. As the author, you do not raise this event for the developer; rather, the container raises it when a particular object receives focus.

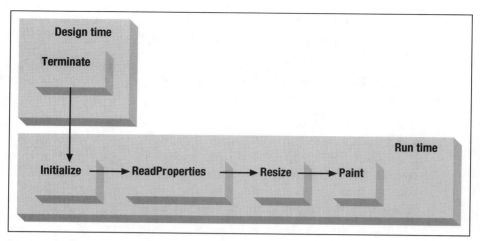

Figure 11.7 User control events.

➤ A second **GotFocus** event pertains to the User control. Only the author of the control uses this event. It occurs for the User control only if no constituent controls have been created that can receive focus.

➤ The final **GotFocus** event pertains to the constituent text box. Although this event is hidden from the developer, the author can write code for this **GotFocus** event for a constituent control.

When working with constituent controls, the term "focus" takes on a new meaning. Consider the ActiveX control you just created in your role as the author. Does the control itself receive focus or does the constituent text box receive focus? Four events pertaining to the User control deal with focus:

➤ The **EnterFocus** event occurs when the User control receives focus or a constituent control created in the User control receives focus.

➤ The **GotFocus** event occurs for the User control after the **EnterFocus** event. It takes place only if no constituent controls are defined on the User control that can receive focus. Obviously, it is a different event than the **GotFocus** event that occurs for a constituent control like a text box.

➤ The **LostFocus** event occurs when the User control loses focus. Like the **GotFocus** event, it takes place only if no constituent controls are defined on the User control that can get focus.

➤ The **ExitFocus** event occurs last, regardless of whether any constituent controls have been created on the User control.

You, as the author, will extend the functionality of the User control for the Focus Management program so that all text in the constituent text box will be selected whenever the control receives focus. You can accomplish this task in two ways. Because the constituent text box can receive focus, you can write the code in the text box's **GotFocus** event procedure. Alternatively, you can write code to respond to the User control's **EnterFocus** event procedure. The code you write can use the **SelStart** and **SelLength** properties of the constituent text box to select all of the text. To accomplish this goal, **SelStart** is set to zero (0) and **SelLength** is set to the size of the string. All characters in the string are therefore selected.

To define an event response:

1. Activate the Code window for the User control, and enter the following statements into the **GotFocus** event procedure for the constituent text box, Text1:

```
Text1.SelStart = 0
Text1.SelLength = Len(Text1)
```

2. Enter the following statement in the **LostFocus** event procedure for Text1:

```
Text1.SelLength = 0
```

3. Close the visual designer and the Code window for the User control, if they are open. Activate the Form window, and create a second TextBoxPlus instance.

4. Test the program. Enter text in the two text boxes and tab between them. The text should be selected as each text box receives focus.

5. End the program to return to design mode.

The **GotFocus** and **LostFocus** event procedures you just created pertain to the constituent text box and are hidden inside the User control.

Assuming that the developer had previously created an instance of the TextBoxPlus control named tbpName, the following procedure would be valid in the form module:

```
Private Sub tbpName_GotFocus()
    Debug.Print "tbpName GotFocus"
End Sub
```

At run time, the Extender object will raise a **GotFocus** event for the TextBoxPlus control. As the developer, you can write code to respond to this event.

When the program runs, the **GotFocus** event occurs first for the Extender object and then for the constituent control. Again, the **GotFocus** event pertaining to the constituent text box and the User control remains hidden from the developer and is available only to the author of the User control.

From the developer's perspective, your ActiveX control currently responds to the five events defined by the Extender object. It should, however, respond to events like **Click** and **Change** as well. To expose an event to the developer, you, as the author, must declare and then raise the event. You declare the event using the **Event** statement, as shown in the following syntax:

Syntax

[**Public**] **Event** *procedurename* [*(arglist)*]

Dissection

➤ The **Public** keyword identifies the scope of the event. If declared as **Public**, the event is visible throughout the project.

➤ The **Event** keyword declares an event procedure. Syntactically, you declare an event procedure in the same way that you declare any other procedure.

➤ The name of the event procedure is identified by *procedurename*. The *procedurename* must conform to the naming conventions for other procedures.

➤ The syntax for *arglist* is the same as it is for **Function** and **Sub** procedures. This list defines the name of the arguments passed to the event and the data types of those arguments.

Code Example

```
Public Event Click()
Public Event Change()
```

Code Dissection

The preceding statements declare two events named **Click** and **Change**, respectively. The statements merely declare the names of the events; they do not raise the events. Also, the events have no As Type clause because events cannot return a value. An event declaration cannot appear in a standard module.

You have created an event procedure for the constituent text box so that all of the text will be selected when the text box receives focus. Suppose that, as the author, you want the developer to have access to the **GotFocus** and **LostFocus** events. You may be tempted to create the following event declarations in your ActiveX control:

```
Public Event GotFocus()
Public Event LostFocus()
```

If you place these two declarations inside the control's general declarations section, however, a syntax error will result. The cause of the error is straightforward. The Extender object predefines the **GotFocus** and **LostFocus** events. This situation becomes clear when you, as the developer, activate the Code window for a form module and select an instance of the control as the object. Upon opening the Procedure list box, you will see the **GotFocus** and **LostFocus** events are already defined.

Once you, as the author, have declared an event, you need a mechanism to generate the event. This task is commonly referred to as *raising an event*. To raise an event, you call the **RaiseEvent** statement.

Syntax

  RaiseEvent *eventname* [(*arglist*)]

Dissection

➤ The **RaiseEvent** statement generates the event identified by *eventname*.

➤ The required *eventname* is the name of the event to be generated. It must have been declared already using an *Event* statement.

➤ The optional *arglist* contains a list of arguments that are passed to the event. In other words, the event procedure created by the developer will receive these values as arguments. Conceptually, this mechanism is the same as processing the events in any other procedure.

Code Example

```
Private Sub Text1_Click()
    RaiseEvent Click
End Sub
```

Code Dissection

The previous code would typically reside in your ActiveX control. The text box named Text1 is a constituent control. When the user clicks on the constituent text box, the **Click** event occurs for that control. The **Click** event is then raised, as seen by the developer of your ActiveX control.

Conceptually, raising an event is the reverse of responding to one. Figure 11.8 illustrates the process of raising an event.

When the end user clicks on the constituent text box at run time, the **Click** event occurs for the constituent text box. This event procedure raises the **Click** event for the developer. The code written by the developer then executes.

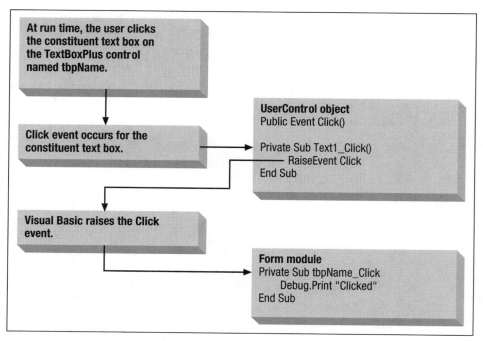

Figure 11.8 Raising an event.

With the previous event procedure now in existence, the developer can respond to the **Click** event procedure for the TextBoxPlus control. Assuming that the developer had created an instance of the TextBoxPlus control named tbpName, the following event procedure could be used to respond to the **Click** event:

```
Private Sub tbpName_Click()
    Debug.Print "I was clicked."
End Sub
```

You now have the tools required to raise an event inside your User control.

To create the code to raise an event in a User control:

1. Create the following declaration in the general declarations section of the User control named TextBoxPlus:

   ```
   Public Event Click()
   ```

2. Create the following statement in the **Text1_Click** event procedure, and then close the Code window for the User control:

   ```
   RaiseEvent Click
   ```

3. Enter the following statements in the form module:

```
Private Sub tbpName_Click()
    Debug.Print "I was clicked."
End Sub
```

4. Test the program. Click on the constituent text box part of the control instance named tbpName. The constituent text box should raise the **Click** event procedure. The event procedure **tbpName_Click** should then be raised and the text I Was Clicked. should print in the Immediate window.

5. End the program to return to design mode.

At this point, your TextBoxPlus control can raise a **Click** event. The Extender object will also raise **GotFocus** and **LostFocus** events. In reality, controls should respond to many other events. For example, the TextBoxPlus control should respond to events such as **Change**, **KeyDown**, **KeyUp**, and **KeyPress**.

Exposing Properties To The Developer

To create a property and make it available to the developer, you, as the control's author, create **Property** procedures in the User control in the same way that you created **Property** procedures for class modules. Syntactically, no difference exists between **Property** procedures created in a User control and **Property** procedures created in an ordinary class module. The difference lies in the way the developer uses the properties.

The developer can set the properties for your ActiveX control by using the Properties window at design time or by writing code, just as with any other control. You can apply four strategies to create a property:

➤ **Delegation** Exposes a property of a constituent control. It is commonly employed when you seek to build a User control from a single constituent control. For example, if the developer should be able to read and write the **Text** property of a constituent text box, you would create a pair of **Property** procedures in the User control that would read and write the **Text** property of the text box.

➤ **Aggregation** Groups properties when you build an ActiveX control from multiple constituent controls. Assume that you have created a User control from both a constituent label and a constituent text box. Also assume that when the developer sets the foreground color of the User control, the foreground color will be changed for both the constituent label and the text box. In this case, you can create a **Property** procedure named **ForeColor**. When the user reads or writes the property, the foreground colors of both constituent controls are set. In other words, the properties of both controls are aggregated into one property.

➤ **New** You can create new properties that are not supported by the constituent controls. For example, suppose you want to implement the User control with a Boolean property named **SelectAll**. When set to **True**, the User control should select all characters when the control receives focus and not select the characters when the property is **False**.

➤ **Modify** The author can modify the behavior of an existing property that is defined by a constituent control. For example, you could expose a property named **Appearance** that would change the appearance of a constituent text box but use constants that are different than the constants usually supported by the constituent text box. Use of this technique is strongly discouraged, because developers are accustomed to a property of a specific name performing a particular task.

For any given control, you may aggregate properties by creating an **Appearance** property that will set the font attribute properties for multiple controls. You may delegate the **Text** property of a constituent text box. Finally, you can create entirely new properties in the same control.

Fundamentals Of Properties

The control's container supports several properties through the Extender object. You, as the control's author, can expose other properties to the developer as needed. In previous chapters, you learned two techniques to create properties: using a Public variable and using a pair of **Property** procedures. Syntactically, you expose properties for your ActiveX control in the same way. That is, you can declare a Public variable or create **Property** procedures. As you will see shortly, however, Public variables have severe limitations when used with ActiveX controls.

As a control's author, you should consider the following features that must be supported to allow their use by the developer. These features are described from the perspective of the developer, not the author.

➤ Some properties may be available only at run time, others only at design time, and others at both design time and run time.

➤ Properties may be read-only or read-write, depending on whether the program's form module is in design mode or in run mode.

➤ You can edit design-time properties using either the Properties window or Property Pages.

➤ Some properties should have default or initial values when the developer creates a new instance of a control. Any property that can be set at design time should have a default value.

➤ Properties may be either persistent or not persistent. For example, if the developer sets a design-time property using the Properties window or

Property Pages, the value of the property should persist if the developer toggles Visual Basic between design mode and run mode. Also, the value of the property should be preserved unchanged after the developer exits Visual Basic. Properties set only at run time usually are not persistent.

The **PropertyChanged** Method

When the code in the User control changes the value of an exposed property, the container must be notified of the change so that it can update the Properties window or the control instance drawn on the form with the new value of the property. This notification does not take place automatically. Rather, when the code in your ActiveX control changes a property's value, you must call the **PropertyChanged** method pertaining to the User control. This method notifies the container that a property has been modified so that its value can be updated.

Syntax

    object.**PropertyChanged** *PropertyName*

Dissection

➤ The *object* contains a reference to a User control.

➤ The **PropertyChanged** method notifies the container that the value of the property identified by *PropertyName* has changed.

➤ The **PropertyName** must be a property created with a **Property** procedure. When the developer reads or writes the value of a Public variable, no mechanism exists to notify the container that the value of the property has changed.

Code Example

```
Public Property Let Enabled(ByVal New_Enabled _
    As Boolean)
    Text1.Enabled = New_Enabled
    PropertyChanged "Enabled"
End Property
```

Code Dissection

By calling the **PropertyChanged** method for the **Enabled** property, the container is notified whenever the value of the property changes.

It is not necessary to call the **PropertyChanged** method on properties that can be used only at run time.

Public variables should not be used to implement properties for ActiveX controls, as no way exists to notify the control's container that the value of the property has changed.

Delegating Properties

The constituent text box supports an **Enabled** property indicating whether the text box can receive focus. For the Focus Management program, you will implement the **Enabled** property using delegation. Remember, however, that the properties and events of the text box are hidden from the developer. The developer can access a property only when you, as the control's author, create a **Public Property** procedure pair in the User control.

In Visual Basic, properties you create appear automatically in the Properties window. Furthermore, depending on the property's data type, Visual Basic will display list boxes as appropriate. For example, if you create a Boolean property, Visual Basic will display the values True and False in the Value column of the Properties window. Properties with a well-defined set of values also appear in the code completion features in the Code window.

For the TextBoxPlus control, you will create a **Property** procedure pair named **Enabled.** These **Property** procedures will read or write the value of the **Enabled** property from and to the constituent text box, respectively. In other words, the **Enabled** property is delegated to the constituent text box. You also will create **Caption** and **Text** properties so that the developer can change the contents of the constituent controls. To implement the properties, you will delegate the **Caption** property to the constituent label and the **Text** property to the constituent text box. These properties should be read-write both at design time and at run time. Thus you should create both **Property Get** and **Property Let** procedures.

To create properties using delegation:

1. Enter the following **Property** procedures in the code window for the User control:

```
Public Property Get Enabled() As Boolean
    Enabled = Text1.Enabled
End Property

Public Property Let Enabled(ByVal New_Enabled _
    As Boolean)
    Text1.Enabled = New_Enabled
    PropertyChanged "Enabled"
End Property
```

```
Public Property Get Text() As String
    Text = Text1.Text
End Property

Public Property Let Text(ByVal New_Text As String)
    Text1.Text = New_Text
    PropertyChanged "Text"
End Property

Public Property Get Caption() As String
    Caption = Label1.Caption
End Property

Public Property Let Caption( _
    ByVal New_Caption As String)
    Label1.Caption = New_Caption
    PropertyChanged "Caption"
End Property
```

2. Close the visual designer and the Code window for the User control. Open the Form window, and then activate one of the TextBoxPlus objects.

3. Press F4 to open the Properties window, if necessary. Three new properties—**Caption**, **Enabled**, and **Text**—appear in the Properties window. Set the **Enabled** property to **False**. Because this property has a **Boolean** data type, the Properties window lists only the values True and False.

4. Set the values of both the **Caption** and **Text** properties to Testing. When the value of either property changes in the Properties window, the value is updated on the form. Both properties are also available at run time.

5. Enter the following statements in the **Form_Load** event procedure:

```
tbpName.Enabled = True
tbpName.Caption = "Name"
tbpName.Text = vbNullString
```

6. Test the program. The TextBoxPlus control instance tbpName should be enabled, have a caption of Name, and have no text in the constituent text box.

7. End the program to return to design mode.

The statements added in the preceding steps use delegation to implement the **Caption**, **Enabled**, and **Text** properties pertaining to the TextBoxPlus control. Remember that the properties of the constituent text box and label are hidden from the developer. Using this technique, the **Caption**, **Enabled**, and **Text Property** procedures pertaining to the User control set or read the property of the same name pertaining to the constituent text box or label.

Aggregating Properties

Aggregation works much like delegation. As an illustration of this technique, suppose you want to create a property named **FontSize** and expose the property to the developer. When the developer sets this property, your code should set the font size for the constituent text box and the label. That is, you will aggregate the **FontSize** properties for the two constituent controls.

To create properties using aggregation:

1. Enter the following **Property** procedures in the code window for the User Control:

```
Public Property Get FontSize() As Integer
    FontSize = Text1.FontSize
End Property

Public Property Let FontSize(ByVal New_Size As Integer)
    Label1.FontSize = New_Size
    Text1.FontSize = New_Size
    PropertyChanged "FontSize"
End Property
```

2. Close the visual designer and the Code window for the User control, open the Form window, and then select one of the TextBoxPlus objects.

3. In the Properties window, set the FontSize to 12. After you press the Enter key, the font size is updated for both the constituent labels and text boxes.

The preceding **Property** procedures are similar to the **Property** procedures you created in the previous steps. Instead of delegating a property to a constituent control, you aggregate the **FontSize** property from the two constituent controls. When the developer sets the **FontSize** property, the code in the **Property** procedures you created changes the value for both constituent controls.

The process for delegating or aggregating a read-only or write-once property matches the technique introduced in Chapter 9. To create a read-only property, you omit the **Property Let** procedure. To implement a write-once property, you ensure that the **Property Let** procedure contains a static Boolean variable to prevent the developer from setting the property's value more than once. Write-once and read-only properties are most commonly used with run-time properties.

Persistent Properties

Your control, as it presently exists, has a major flaw. If you set properties via the Properties window, the value will be updated on the form at design time. For example, if the developer sets the **Text** property of the TextBoxPlus control, the value is reflected in the control instance drawn on the form. If you close the Form window, or switch from design mode to run mode, the changes to the Properties window are lost. When Visual Basic switches from design time to run time, it destroys the design–time instance of the control and creates a run–time instance of the control. Unless you explicitly tell the container to retain the current value of a property (that is, to allow the property to persist), the changes will be lost. This concept is referred to as *property persistence*.

Properties set in the Properties window usually should persist between invocations of Visual Basic and between design time and run time. Consider what happens when the developer saves a form file. Visual Basic saves design-time property settings to the form file. Also, consider what happens when you run a Standard EXE project. The current design-time settings for the form and its objects are set. These settings become the initial run-time values.

Figure 11.9 illustrates a segment of a form file with the property settings for a TextBoxPlus control instance.

Note that only the properties that differ from the default property values are listed. This approach helps to reduce the size of the form file and improve performance. Think of the enormous size that a form file would have and the time that it would take to read the file if the value of every property for every control instance appeared in the form file.

The PropertyBag Object

Visual Basic neither saves design-time properties automatically when the form is closed, nor when Visual Basic switches from design time to run time, nor

```
Begin SuperText.TextBoxPlus TextBoxPlus1
         Height           =      1455
         Left             =      120
         TabIndex         =      0
         Top              =      240
         Width            =      4575
         _ExtentX         =      8070
         _ExtentY         =      2566
         ForeColor        =      16711680
         FontBold         =      0   'False
         ForeColor        =      16711680
   End
```

Figure 11.9 Form file segment.

reads the default values of properties when a control instance is created (either a design-time instance or a run-time instance). Instead, you must save and retrieve persistent properties using the PropertyBag object.

The PropertyBag object is predefined; thus you do not declare an instance of the PropertyBag object. Every User control has one—and only one—property bag. The PropertyBag object supports two methods. The **ReadProperty** method reads a property from the property bag and returns the value for the property. The **WriteProperty** method writes the value of a property to the PropertyBag object. Property values are not saved to the PropertyBag object automatically. Rather, you must explicitly save each property whose value should persist.

Syntax

object.**ReadProperty**(DataName [, DefaultValue])
object.**WriteProperty**(DataName, Value [, DefaultValue])

Dissection

➤ The **ReadProperty** method reads a property from the property bag. The **WriteProperty** method writes a property to the property bag. The **WriteProperty** method tells the container—in this case, a form module—to save the value of the specified property.

➤ The *object* must be a valid PropertyBag object.

➤ The *DataName* contains the name by which the property is referenced in the property bag. It is a string key typically having the same value as the name for the property.

➤ The *DefaultValue*, when used with the **ReadProperty** method, causes the *DefaultValue* to be returned if no value is stored in the PropertyBag object. When used with the **WriteProperty** method, it contains the default value for the property.

➤ The *Value* is the data value that is saved to the property bag.

Code Example

```
Call PropBag.WriteProperty("Enabled", _
    Text1.Enabled, True)
Text1.Enabled = PropBag.ReadProperty("Enabled", True)
```

Code Dissection

The first statement calls the property bag's **WriteProperty** method; the property to be written is the **Enabled** property. The preceding code writes the current value of the **Text1.Enabled** property to the property bag only if the value of the **Enabled** property differs from the default value, which is True. The final statement reads the value of the **Enabled** property from the property bag, if one exists. If no value is stored in the property bag, the **Enabled** property is set to **True**.

Saving properties to the property bag does not cause the properties to be saved to the form file on the disk. Instead, this saving process occurs when the developer saves the form. The container takes on the responsibility of saving a persistent property.

When using the **WriteProperty** method, you must specify a default value. If you do not, the value of the property will be written to the form file, regardless of the current setting. For example, consider the following statements:

```
Call PropBag.WriteProperty("Enabled", _
    Text1.Enabled, True)
Call PropBag.WriteProperty("Enabled", Text1.Enabled)
```

Assuming that the value of **Text1.Enabled** is **True**, the first statement will not cause the setting to be written to the form file, because the value of the property matches the default value. The second statement, however, causes the property to be written to the form file, because no default value is specified.

The **ReadProperty** method should be called when the control instance loads, and the **WriteProperty** method should be called when the control instance unloads. When the Form window is being closed or Visual Basic switches from design mode to run mode, the control instance will be unloaded. The **ReadProperties** and **WriteProperties** events occur for the User control, allowing you to retain the properties. In these event procedures, you typically call the **ReadProperty** and **WriteProperty** methods.

When the developer opens a Form window containing an instance of the ActiveX control, or Visual Basic loads a design-time instance of an ActiveX control, the **ReadProperties** event occurs. Furthermore, whenever Visual Basic switches from design time to run time, the same event occurs. You should read the values of persistent properties within this event procedure.

The **WriteProperties** event occurs whenever Visual Basic switches from design mode to run mode. It also occurs whenever the developer saves a form containing an ActiveX control. You should write the necessary code in this event procedure to save the values of persistent properties.

Syntax

> Private Sub *object*_ReadProperties(*pb* As PropertyBag)
> Private Sub *object*_WriteProperties(*pb* As PropertyBag)

Dissection

➤ *pb* is an object of variable type **PropertyBag**.

➤ The *object* must be a valid instance of a User control.

➤ The **ReadProperties** event occurs when a User control instance is loaded, allowing the author to read initial values for properties.

➤ The **WriteProperties** event occurs when an instance of the User control must be saved.

Code Example

```
Private Sub UserControl_ReadProperties( _
    PropBag As PropertyBag)
    Text1.Enabled = PropBag.ReadProperty( _
        "Enabled", True)
End Sub
Private Sub UserControl_WriteProperties( _
    PropBag As PropertyBag)
    Call PropBag.WriteProperty( _
        "Enabled", Text1.Enabled, True)
End Sub
```

Code Dissection

These two event procedures read and write the **Enabled** property from and to the property bag. The default value of the **Enabled** property is **True**.

In your ActiveX control for the Focus Management program, the **Caption**, **Enabled**, and **Text** properties you have implemented should persist whenever Visual Basic switches from design time to run time, whenever the Form window is closed, and between invocations of Visual Basic.

To create persistent properties:

1. Enter the following statements in the **UserControl_InitProperties** event procedure. This procedure will execute only the first time that the control is created. Thus the code sets the initial value for the properties.

   ```
   Text1.Text = UserControl.Name
   Label1.Caption = UserControl.Name
   ```

2. Enter the following statements in the **UserControl_ReadProperties** event procedure. This event procedure will execute each time that a control instance (either at design time or run time) is created.

```
Text1.Enabled = PropBag.ReadProperty( _
    "Enabled", True)
Label1.Caption = PropBag.ReadProperty("Caption", _
    UserControl.Name)
Text1.Text = PropBag.ReadProperty( _
    "Text", UserControl.Name)
```

3. Enter the following statements in the **UserControl_WriteProperties** event procedure:

```
Call PropBag.WriteProperty( _
    "Enabled", Text1.Enabled, True)
Call PropBag.WriteProperty("Text", Text1.Text, _
    UserControl.Name)
Call PropBag.WriteProperty("Caption", Label1.Caption, _
    UserControl.Name)
```

4. Remove the statements you wrote in the **Form_Load** event procedure.

5. Close the visual designer and the Code window for the User control. Open the Form window, select the instance named tbpName, and set the **Enabled**, **Caption**, and **Text** properties to appropriate values. Run the program and then end it. The values of the properties should persist.

6. End the program to return to design mode.

7. Save the project group.

The **Enabled**, **Text**, and **Caption** properties now are synchronized with the container. Furthermore, the values of the properties will persist when Visual Basic switches between run time and design time and between invocations of Visual Basic.

Read-Write And Read-Only Properties

As you have seen, properties can be read-only, read-write, or write-once. As the author, when creating ActiveX controls, you must determine which actions the developer can perform on a property at both run time and design time. For example, some properties should be set only at design time and other properties should be set only at run time.

To help you decide when properties should be set, consider other controls that you have used previously. For example, it makes no sense to set the ADO Data control's **Recordset** property at design time, because the ADO Data control creates the recordset at run time.

The AmbientProperties object obtains its information from the container—in this case, the form. It supports the **UserMode** property, which contains a

Boolean value indicating the state of the container. If True, then the container (in this case, Visual Basic) is in run mode; if False, the container is in design mode.

Consider the following **Property** procedures that implement a property that is read-only at run time:

```
Private mEOF as Boolean

Property Get EOF As Boolean
    EOF = mEOF
End Property
Property Let EOF()
    If AmbientProperties.UserMode Then
        Err.Raise Number:=31013, _
            Description:= _
                "Cannot write property at run time."
    End If
    EOF = mEOF
    PropertyChanged EOF
End Property
```

These statements create a Boolean variable named **mEOF**. Although not implemented in the preceding code, this property likely would be used to detect whether the state of the control had reached the end of file. For example, you might implement an ActiveX control consisting of an ADO Data control and a set of bound text boxes. Developers could then add your control to their programs without dealing with the intricacies of the interaction between the ADO Data control and bound controls.

The **Property** procedures implement a property named **EOF** that is read-only at run time. The **Property Let** procedure tests the value of the AmbientProperties object's **UserMode** property. If Visual Basic is in run mode, the code raises an error. This **Property** procedure should not be available to the developer at design time.

Creating the **Property** procedure pair ensures that the property will exist at both design time and run time. If the property has meaning only at run time, it should not appear in the Properties window. This implementation effectively hides the property from the developer at design time. The Procedure Attributes dialog box supports features that prevent the properties of your ActiveX control from appearing in the Properties window or that make a property or method become the default property or method.

The Properties window supports both an Alphabetic and Categorized tab. It also allows you to add properties that will appear in a specific, or new, category.

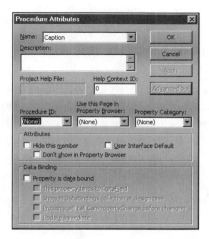

Figure 11.10   Procedure Attributes dialog box.

Figure 11.10 shows the Procedure Attributes dialog box and the settings available to manipulate the appearance of properties in the Properties window.

As shown in Figure 11.10, the Attributes section contains three checkboxes:

➤ **Hide this member** If this checkbox is checked, the property or method will not appear in either the Object Browser or the Properties window. The properties can be accessed with code, however.

➤ **User Interface Default** If this checkbox is checked, the property is highlighted in the Properties window when this window initially opens. If the object is an event, the Code window is set to the event by default when you double-click on the control. Each User control can have only one **User Interface Default** property and one **User Interface Default** event. The User Interface Default cannot be a method.

➤ **Don't show in Property Browser** If this checkbox is checked, the property will not appear in the Properties window. It will appear in the Object Browser, and the developer can continue to write code to access it.

As you create the developer interface for your control, you should consider which property, method, or event will be the most commonly used and make it into the default. Also, you should take care not to display run-time-only properties in the Properties window.

Although you can hide properties and create default properties, the properties you have created for Focus Management have a deficiency. Some properties should display a list from which the developer selects a property; other properties should display a dialog box. This situation, which typically occurs when you are setting a font or color, is the topic of the next section.

Creating Better Properties

Improving The Behavior Of The Properties Window

You undoubtedly have enjoyed the capability of the Properties window to display Properties buttons that activate dialog boxes to set colors and fonts. Usually, colors are represented by hexadecimal numbers like &H80000008&. Fortunately, you do not have to force a developer—or an end user, for that matter—to use or manipulate the numbers pertaining to colors. Instead, you can write code to support Properties buttons that open a dialog box and that set the value for a specific property pertaining to your ActiveX control.

For the Focus Management ActiveX control, you will aggregate the **ForeColor** property pertaining to the constituent label and text box controls. Instead of forcing the user to select a color by entering a hexadecimal number, your control will display a dialog box. This task is accomplished by using another data type supported by Visual Basic—**OLE_COLOR**.

Using this data type, which applies to properties that return colors, is as simple as declaring a **Property Get** procedure as the **OLE_COLOR** data type, as shown in the following **Property** procedures:

```
Public Property Get ForeColor() As OLE_COLOR
    ForeColor = Text1.ForeColor
End Property


Public Property Let ForeColor _
    (ByVal New_ForeColor As OLE_COLOR)
    Label1.ForeColor = New_ForeColor
    Text1.ForeColor = New_ForeColor
    PropertyChanged "ForeColor"
End Property
```

In this example, the **ForeColor Property Get** procedure has a data type of **OLE_COLOR**. When it executes, the **Property** procedure will display a dialog box allowing the user to select a color. The color selected by the user will be returned by the **Property** procedure as a Long Integer.

To create properties using the **OLE_COLOR** data type:

1. Start Visual Basic, if necessary, and then, from the CD, open the project group Ch.11\Startup\Ch11_S.vbg.

2. Create the following four **Property** procedures in the UserControl object:

   ```
   Public Property Get ForeColor() As OLE_COLOR
       ForeColor = Text1.ForeColor
   End Property
   ```

```
Public Property Let ForeColor( _
    ByVal New_ForeColor As OLE_COLOR)
    Label1.ForeColor = New_ForeColor
    Text1.ForeColor = New_ForeColor
    PropertyChanged "ForeColor"
End Property

Public Property Get BackColor() As OLE_COLOR
    BackColor = Text1.BackColor
End Property

Public Property Let BackColor( _
    ByVal New_BackColor As OLE_COLOR)
    Label1.BackColor = New_BackColor
    Text1.BackColor = New_BackColor
    PropertyChanged "BackColor"
End Property
```

3. Enter the following statements at the end of the
   UserControl_WriteProperties event procedure:

```
Call PropBag.WriteProperty("BackColor", _
    UserControl.BackColor, &H8000000F)
Call PropBag.WriteProperty("ForeColor", _
    Label1.ForeColor, &H80000012)
```

4. Enter the following statements at the end of the
   UserControl_ReadProperties event procedure:

```
Text1.BackColor = PropBag.ReadProperty _
    ("BackColor", &H8000000F)
Label1.BackColor = PropBag.ReadProperty _
    ("BackColor", &H8000000F)
Text1.ForeColor = PropBag.ReadProperty _
    ("ForeColor", &H80000012)
Label1.ForeColor = PropBag.ReadProperty _
    ("ForeColor", &H80000012)
```

5. Close the visual designer and the Code window for the User control, and
   then activate the Form window. Set the **ForeColor** and **BackColor**
   properties for an instance of the TextBoxPlus object. As you change the
   properties, note that the foreground and background colors of the
   constituent controls change accordingly.

The code that you just wrote uses the aggregation technique to implement the **ForeColor** and **BackColor** properties. It is very similar to the code that you wrote to aggregate the **FontSize** property earlier. The most notable difference is that you used the **OLE_COLOR** data type to display a dialog box to set the value. The values for the default property consist of the actual hexadecimal values for the property. The easiest way to determine such a value is to create a control instance, set the value to the desired color, and then copy the value to the event procedure.

Enumerated Properties

In addition to using the OLE data types, you can use enumerations for properties. Two different types of enumerations are possible: enumerations supported by an object's type library or user-defined enumerations.

To view the enumerations supported by the type library, use the Object Browser. Visual Basic offers several predefined enumerations. For each of these enumerations, the suffix "Constants" appears in the classes section of the Object Browser. If you click on the enumerated constant in the Object Browser, the description window will indicate that it is an enumeration.

Suppose you want to expose the text box's **MousePointer** property, which typically is represented by an enumeration in the Properties window, by using the following statements:

```
Public Property Get MousePointer() _
    As MousePointerConstants
    ' Statements to change the mouse pointer.
End Property
Public Property Let MousePointer( _
    ByVal NewPointer As MousePointerConstants)
    ' Statements to change the mouse pointer.
End Property
```

These **Property** procedures have the enumerated type **MousePointerConstants**. The applicable mouse pointer constants will therefore be displayed automatically in the Properties window.

As with all enumerated constants, Visual Basic does not prevent you from assigning an invalid value to the property. For example, consider the following statements:

```
Private Sub TextBoxPlus1_Click()
    TextBoxPlus1.MousePointer = 999
End Sub
```

The statement in the event procedure will generate a run-time error because the property value is invalid. To prevent the run-time error, the **Property Let** procedure could validate the value to verify that the constant is valid. This process is relatively intricate. At design time, the developer will see the enumerated constant in the Properties window. At run time, however, the developer can set the property using code.

It would be reasonable for the **Property Let** procedure to raise an error if the developer assigned an invalid value to the property. If no error is raised, the developer will not know that the property was set to an invalid value. This omission could lead to a hard-to-find error.

To use the enumerated mouse pointers:

1. Create the following **Property** procedures for the User Control:

```
Public Property Get MousePointer() _
    As MousePointerConstants
    MousePointer = Text1.MousePointer
End Property

Public Property Let MousePointer( _
    ByVal NewPointer As MousePointerConstants)
    Text1.MousePointer = NewPointer
    PropertyChanged "MousePointer"
End Property
```

2. Enter the following statement at the end of the **UserControl_ReadProperties** event:

```
Text1.MousePointer = PropBag.ReadProperty( _
    "MousePointer", 0)
```

3. Enter the following statement at the end of the **UserControl_WriteProperties** event:

```
Call PropBag.WriteProperty("MousePointer", _
    Text1.MousePointer, 0)
```

4. Close the visual designer for the User control and activate the Form window. Activate the Properties window for the TextBoxPlus control instance, and select the **MousePointer** property. The list of valid properties should appear in a list box.

11

In addition to using predefined enumerations, you can create your own enumerations, expose them in a type library, and make them available in the Properties window.

User-Defined Enumerations

To enumerate a property, you create a user-defined enumeration in the User control, and then create the **Property** procedure pairs such that the **Property Get** procedure returns the enumerated type and the **Property Let** procedure takes an argument of the enumerated type.

In the next steps, you will supply multiple formats to incorporate different font colors and attributes. This type of functionality is suitable in situations in which you want developers to use one of a few standardized styles.

To create a property having an enumerated type:

1. Enter the following statements in the general declarations section of the User control:

```
Enum tbpAttention
    tbpLight = 0
    tbpNormal = 1
    tbpDark = 2
End Enum
Private mAttention As tbpAttention
```

2. Create the following **Property Get** and **Property Let** procedures:

```
Public Property Get Attention() As tbpAttention
    Attention = mAttention
End Property

Public Property Let Attention( _
    New_Attention As tbpAttention)
    Select Case New_Attention
        Case tbpLight
            Text1.FontBold = False
            Text1.ForeColor = vbBlue
        Case tbpNormal
            Text1.FontBold = False
            Text1.ForeColor = vbBlack
        Case tbpDark
            Text1.FontBold = True
            Text1.ForeColor = vbBlack
    End Select
    mAttention = New_Attention
```

```
        PropertyChanged "Attention"
    End Property
```

3. Enter the following statement at the end of the **UserControl_ReadProperties** event:

```
Text1.FontBold = PropBag.ReadProperty( _
    "Attention", tbpNormal)
```

4. Enter the following statement at the end of the **UserControl_WriteProperties** event:

```
Call PropBag.WriteProperty("Attention", mAttention)
```

5. Activate the Code window for the **Form_Load** event procedure, and enter the statement shown in Figure 11.11. The Auto List Members box displays the legal options for the setting. Select tbpDark.

The code to create the **Attention** property is straightforward. The argument to the **Property Let** procedure has a data type of **tbpAttention**—the same data type as that of the return value of the **Property Get** procedure. The module-level variable **mAttention** stores the value of the property. To ensure that the property will persist, the properties are written to the property bag. This example exploits the concept of aggregating properties.

Creating Data-Aware Controls

As a superset of an ordinary text box, you can provide the developer with the ability to make the control become a data-aware control.

In previous chapters, you bound controls to a data source. You performed this task at design time by first setting the properties of the ADO Data control and then setting the **DataSource** property to bind other control instances to an instance of the ADO Data control. Visual Basic allows you to perform this task dynamically at run time. You cannot, however, bind the Intrinsic Data control or the Remote Data control at run time.

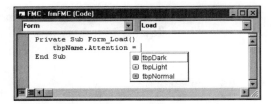

Figure 11.11   Auto List Members.

Two properties control data binding:

➤ The **DataBindingBehavior** property determines whether an object can be bound to a data source. This property can have one of three constant values. If set to **0 – vbNone**, the control cannot be bound to a data source. If set to **1 – vbSimpleBound**, the control can be bound to a field in a data source. If set to **2 – vbComplexBound**, the control can be bound to an entire row source (recordset).

➤ The **DataSourceBehavior** property determines whether an object can act as a source for data.

Creating a data-aware control is quite simple. The following list summarizes the steps involved in the creation of a data-aware control:

1. Use the Procedure Attributes dialog box to set the data-binding characteristics.

2. Inside the **Change** event procedure of the constituent control, call the **PropertyChanged** method. This method provides the link between your control and the ADO Data control. It allows the ADO Data control to update the database whenever the value of the control changes.

3. The **CanPropertyChange** method, which pertains to the User control, is typically used in a **Property Let** procedure of a constituent control to verify that the value of the property can be changed.

To make a control become a data-aware control:

1. Open the Code window for the TextBoxPlus control. Click on Tools, click on Procedure Attributes, and then click on the Advanced button. Select Text from the Name drop-down list. In the Data Binding section, check Property Is Data Bound. The remaining checkboxes in the frame may already be enabled. Check all of these checkboxes, if necessary. Click on OK to close the dialog box.

2. Activate the Code window for the TextBoxPlus control, and then enter the following statement in the **Text1_Change** event:

```
PropertyChanged "Text"
```

3. In the case of a bound text box, the **Text** property is bound to an instance of the ADO Data control. Modify the following **Property** procedure so that it matches the code below:

```
Public Property Let Text(ByVal New_Text As String)
    If CanPropertyChange("Text") Then
        Text1.Text() = New_Text
```

```
        PropertyChanged "Text"
    End If
End Property
```

4. Close the Code window and the visual designer for the User Control. Activate the Form window, and select an instance of the TextBoxPlus object. The **DataField** and **DataSource** properties appear automatically in the Properties window. You can bind the control to an ADO Data control just as you would bind any other control.

Using The ActiveX Control Interface Wizard

So far, you have exposed only a subset of the properties that the TextBoxPlus control should support. The developer cannot create a multiline text box, for example. Furthermore, the control supports only the **Click** and **Change** events. As a result, your control cannot generate events to support a keyboard handler. A well-designed and well-implemented ActiveX control should fully support the properties and events of the constituent controls.

The process of delegating the different properties usually supported by the text box is a tedious process. Fortunately, Visual Basic includes a wizard that will help you delegate and aggregate properties.

The Visual Basic ActiveX Control Interface Wizard aids you in exposing the properties, methods, and events for a control. It can help aggregate and delegate properties. The Wizard has four dialog boxes:

> The Select Interface Members dialog box allows you to select a list of events, methods, and properties that should be exposed for your control.

> The Create Custom Interface Members dialog box allows you to create properties, events, and methods not listed in the Select Interface Members dialog box.

> The Set Mapping dialog box allows you to delegate properties to constituent controls.

> The Set Attributes dialog box allows you to define the run-time and design-time behavior of properties (for example, read-only, read-write). You also can assign default values to properties in this dialog box.

The code created by the wizard takes advantage of the techniques presented in this chapter to delegate properties and create persistent properties. Although it cannot write all code for a control, the wizard provides a great foundation from which to start. It relieves you of much of the burden of mapping all the common properties manually.

CHAPTER SUMMARY

This chapter presented the fundamental techniques to create an ActiveX control. In Visual Basic, you create an ActiveX control in much the same way as you would create any other program. You use a visual designer to create the interface for the control and the Code window to write code for the control. Typically, you create a control from existing controls.

To create an ActiveX control:

➤ Create an ActiveX control project. For debugging purposes, this project is typically part of a project group.

➤ Create the desired constituent controls in the ActiveX control.

➤ Delegate or aggregate the properties of the constituent controls as necessary.

➤ Declare the events to which the control should respond.

To create a property for an ActiveX control:

➤ Declare **Property** procedures for the control.

➤ Use delegation or aggregation with constituent controls.

To declare and raise an event in an ActiveX control:

➤ Declare the event using the **Event** keyword:

```
[ Public ] Event procedurename [ (arglist) ]
```

➤ Raise the event using the following syntax:

```
RaiseEvent eventname [(arglist)]
```

To advise a control's container that the value of a property has changed, call the **PropertyChanged** method:

```
object.PropertyChanged PropertyName
```

To create a persistent property:

➤ Read and write properties to the PropertyBag object using the following methods:

```
object.ReadProperty(DataName [, DefaultValue] )
object.WriteProperty(DataName, Value [, DefaultValue] )
```

REVIEW QUESTIONS

1. Which of the following sets of objects is used to make an ActiveX control?
   a. UserControl, Ambient, Extended, PropertyBag
   b. UserControl, AmbientProperties, Extender, PropertyBag
   c. Control, AmbientProperties, Extender, PropertyBag
   d. Control, AmbientProperties, Extended, PropertyBag
   e. None of the above

2. Which of the following techniques can you use to create an ActiveX control?
   a. enhance an existing control
   b. use multiple constituent controls
   c. use the control designer
   d. Both a and b
   e. All of the above

3. Which of the following statements pertaining to ActiveX control creation is true?
   a. You create a project of type Control.
   b. The code for the control is stored in a module having the type of ActiveX control.
   c. You create the visual interface using the Form window.
   d. All of the above.
   e. None of the above.

4. When you compile an ActiveX control, the file created has a suffix of
   _____:
   a. .ctl
   b. .ocx
   c. .vbp
   d. .vbg
   e. None of the above

5. Which of the following is true when the developer sets design-time properties for an ActiveX control?
   a. Visual Basic is in design mode.
   b. The control is in design mode.
   c. The control is in run mode.
   d. Both a and b.
   e. Both a and c.

6. Which of the following is true when the author sets properties for a User control?

   a. Visual Basic is in design mode.

   b. The control is in design mode.

   c. The control is in run mode.

   d. Both a and b.

   e. Both a and .c

7. An intrinsic or ActiveX control that is created on a User control is called a _____ .

   a. base control

   b. visible control

   c. constituent control

   d. text box

   e. label

8. Which of the following statements is true about constituent controls?

   a. Their properties and methods are hidden from the developer.

   b. Their properties and methods are visible to the developer.

   c. Their events are visible to the developer.

   d. Both a and c.

   e. Both b and c.

9. Which of the following properties is supported by the User control?

   a. **DefaultCancel**

   b. **Name**

   c. **CanGetFocus**

   d. None of the above

   e. All of the above

10. Create an event procedure that will execute when the user resizes the User control. The code in the event procedure should print the size of a constituent text box named txtOne in the visible region of the text box.

11. What is the correct order of events that occurs when a control is drawn on a form for the first time?

   a. **Initialize, InitProperties, Resize, Paint**

   b. **Initialize, InitProperties, Resize, Paint. Terminate**

   c. **Terminate, Initialize, InitProperties, Resize, Paint**

   d. **Initialize, ReadProperties, Resize, Paint**

   e. None of the above

12. To generate an event in your control that is visible to the developer, you must:

    a. declare the event procedure using the **Event** keyword

    b. use the **Declare** statement

    c. raise the event procedure

    d. Both a and b

    e. Both a and c

13. Which method do you use to inform the container that the value of a property has been updated?

    a. **Change**

    b. **Changed**

    c. **PropertyChange**

    d. **PropertyChanged**

    e. **Property**

14. Which two methods do you call to read and write properties from the PropertyBag?

    a. **ReadProperty, WriteProperty**

    b. **ReadProperties, WriteProperties**

    c. **ReadPropertyBag, WritePropertyBag**

    d. **Property Let, Property Get**

    e. None of the above

15. How do you prevent a property defined in a User control from appearing in the Properties window?

    a. Set the **Visible** property of the UserControl object to **False**.

    b. Set the **Enabled** property of the UserControl object to **False**.

    c. Use the Procedure Attributes dialog box.

    d. Use the Tools Options menu.

    e. None of the above.

16. The _____ property is used by the control to determine whether Visual Basic is in run mode or design mode.

17. The _____ event for the UserControl object occurs once, when the control instance is created on the form.

18. Write a statement to declare an event procedure named **Click**. The event procedures should not accept any arguments. Write the statement to raise the **Click** event you declared when the constituent command button named **cmdButton** is clicked.

11

19. Create **Property** procedures to delegate the **MultiLine** property of a constituent text box named txtLong to the developer.

20. Create **Property** procedures to aggregate the **Min** property for three constituent scroll bars named hsb1, hsb2, and hsb3.

21. What data type do you use for a **Property** procedure to display a color dialog box?

    a. **Color**

    b. **vbColor**

    c. **OLE_COLOR**

    d. **OLE_DATA**

    e. None of the above

22. Which of the following statements about enumerated properties is true?

    a. Visual Basic offers several predefined enumerations.

    b. You can declare enumerations.

    c. The enumerated constants appear in the Properties window.

    d. All of the above.

    e. None of the above.

23. How do you create an enumerated property?

    a. Use the Object Browser.

    b. Declare **Property** procedures having an enumerated data type.

    c. Use the **Enumeration** keyword.

    d. Any of the above.

    e. None of the above.

24. What is the name of the property that determines whether an object can be bound to a data source?

    a. **DataSourceBehavior**

    b. **DataBinding**

    c. **DataBindingBehavior**

    d. **DataBehavior**

    e. None of the above

HANDS-ON PROJECTS

Project 1

In this project, you will create a control made from four constituent controls—a scroll bar and three labels. When the user changes the value of the scroll bar, the current value will be displayed in one of the labels. When the user changes the maximum or minimum property of the control, the values of the two other labels should be updated. Figure 11.12 shows an instance of the control created on a form.

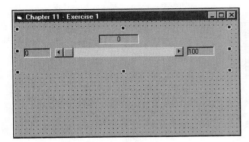

Figure 11.12   Exercise 1.

a. Start Visual Basic, if necessary. Create a new project, and set the **Name** property of the form to **frmEx1**. Save the form using the name Chapter.11\Exercise\frmEx1.frm and the project using the name Chapter.11\Exercise\Ex1.vbp. This form will be used to test the control.

b. Add a second project (ActiveX control) and create a project group. Save the control with the name ScrollBarPlus.

c. Add a constituent scroll bar and three labels to the ActiveX control. The three labels will display the maximum, minimum, and current values of the scroll bar.

d. Delegate the scroll bar's **Max, Min, Value, SmallChange**, and **LargeChange** properties.

e. Make the properties that you delegated in the previous step become persistent.

f. Expose the scroll bar's **Click** and **Change** events.

g. Write the code in the ActiveX control to update the value label whenever the user changes the current value of the scroll bar.

h. Write the code in the ActiveX control to update the maximum and minimum labels whenever the developer or user changes the **Max** and **Min** properties, respectively.

11

i. Test the program by creating an instance of the ActiveX control on the form.

j. Make the control a data-aware control.

k. Exit Visual Basic.

Project 2

In this project, you will create a control made from three constituent controls—two command buttons and a label. The label will display a number. The two command buttons will increment or decrement the number stored in the label. Figure 11.13 shows an instance of the control created on a form.

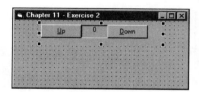

Figure 11.13 Exercise 2.

a. Start Visual Basic, if necessary. Create a new project, and set the **Name** property of the form to **frmEx2**. Save the form using the name Chapter.11\Exercise\frmEx2.frm and the project using the name Chapter.11\Exercise\Ex2.vbp.

b. Add a second project and create a project group. Save the control with the name UpDownBox.

c. Add a label and two command buttons to the ActiveX control.

d. Write the code to increment the value of the label when the user clicks on the Up command button and to decrement the label when the user clicks on the Down command button.

e. Create two properties named **Min** and **Max**. The value of the label cannot exceed these values.

f. Expose the necessary events so that the user can click on the buttons.

g. Whenever the value of the label changes, the program should generate a **Change** event. Create this **Change** event, which should pass one argument, an Integer, containing the value of the label.

h. Test the program. Create an instance of the control on the form. Set the **Min** and **Max** properties. Click on the command buttons to verify that the value of the label is updated correctly and that the **Change** event works properly.

i. Exit Visual Basic.

Project 3

In this project, you will create a control that will display one item in a list of items. Each time the control is clicked, it will display the next item in the list. If the last item in the list is the current item, then the first item in the list should be displayed. Figure 11.14 shows an instance of the control created on a form.

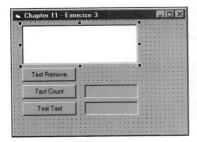

Figure 11.14   Exercise 3.

a. Start Visual Basic, if necessary. Create a new project, and set the **Name** property of the form to **frmEx3**. Save the form using the name Chapter.11\Exercise\frmEx3.frm and the project using the name Chapter.11\Exercise\Ex3.vbp.

b. Add a second project and create a project group. Save the control with the name CircularList.

c. Add a Label control to the ActiveX control.

d. Create a method named **AddItem** that will add an item to the list. Internally, you should implement the list as either an array or a **Private** collection. Implement the **Remove** and **Item** methods and a **Count** property.

e. Expose a **Click** event so that when the user clicks on the constituent label, the next item in the list is displayed. If the last item in the list is selected, display the first item.

f. Expose a **Text** property that returns the text of the currently selected list item. This property should be read–only at run time.

g. Expose the **BackColor** and **ForeColor** properties. Use the **OLE_COLOR** data type.

h. Test the program. Create an instance of the control. Call the **AddItem** method several times to populate the list. Click on the control at run time to verify that the list is updated correctly.

i. Exit Visual Basic.

11

Project 4

In this project, you will create an ActiveX control built from two constituent list boxes and five command buttons. Figure 11.15 shows an instance of the control created on the form.

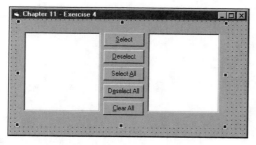

Figure 11.15 Exercise 4.

In your completed code, when the user clicks on the Select command button, the currently selected item in the first list box should move to the second list box. When the Deselect command button is clicked, the selected item in the second list box should move to the first list box. The Select All command button should move all items in the first list box to the second list box. The Deselect All command button should move all items from the second list box to the first list box. The Clear All button removes all items from both lists. Such a control would be useful for selecting fields in a database or names from a list, for example.

   a. Start Visual Basic, if necessary. Create a new project, and set the **Name** property of the form to **frmEx4**. Save the form using the name Chapter.11\Exercise\frmEx4.frm and the project using the name Chapter.11\Exercise\Ex4.vbp.

   b. Add a second project (ActiveX control) and create a project group. Save the control with the name SelectList.

   c. Create the required list boxes and command buttons in the control.

   d. Delegate the first list box's **Add**, **Clear**, and **RemoveItem** methods. Delegate the List and **Count** properties.

   e. Create a property named **SelectedList**, which is really the **List** property of the second list box.

   f. Create a method named **ClearAll** to clear the contents of both list boxes.

   g. Test the program. Create an instance of the ActiveX control on the form. Add items to the first list box. Select and deselect items.

   h. Exit Visual Basic.

CHAPTER TWELVE

EXTENDING ACTIVEX CONTROL FEATURES

AFTER READING THIS CHAPTER AND COMPLETING THE EXERCISES, YOU WILL BE ABLE TO:

- ➤ Create ActiveX controls that support Property Pages
- ➤ Use standard Property Pages defined by Visual Basic
- ➤ Create user-defined Property Pages
- ➤ Synchronize Property Page settings with properties defined in the User control
- ➤ Debug an ActiveX control
- ➤ Set up the Calendar control so that it can be downloaded to a Web browser over the Internet
- ➤ License a control
- ➤ Handle the issues surrounding control security

Adding Internet Support And Property Pages To An ActiveX Control

Adding Property Pages To An ActiveX Control

The completed application for this chapter is an ActiveX control that implements a visual calendar with several features. Figure 12.1 shows the visual interface for the calendar.

As shown in Figure 12.1, the Calendar control contains two combo boxes. The user can select the month and the year using these combo boxes, and the calendar is updated accordingly. When the Calendar control first loads at run-time, the month and year are set automatically to the current month and year.

The calendar contains labels to identify the day of the week. Below the labels, a control array of text boxes displays the different dates. The Calendar control supports the following features:

➤ It displays dates such that the first day of the week can be either Sunday or Monday.

➤ When the user selects a month or a year, the days in the calendar are updated accordingly.

➤ The developer can change the foreground and background colors of both weekdays and weekend days.

In this chapter, you will not write the code to implement the Calendar control. This task has already been completed for you. Instead, you, as the author, will write the code to implement Property Pages for the control and to enable the control to operate with a Web browser. The structure of the User control matches that of the User control you created in Chapter 11. The project also

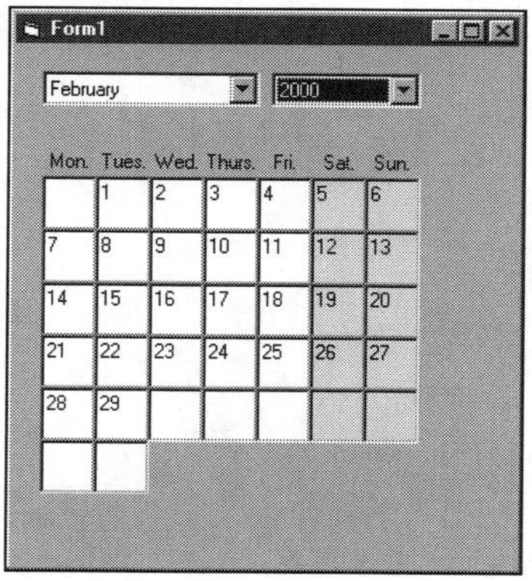

Figure 12.1   Calendar visual interface.

requires you to assume the roles of the author and the developer, just as you did in Chapters 10 and 11. As the author, you will develop Property Pages for the Calendar control. As the developer, you will create an instance of the Calendar control on a form for testing purposes.

Extensive Controls is a software publisher that develops ActiveX controls used by other software developers. The company creates ActiveX controls for use both by Visual Basic and by Web browsers. Currently, the company is developing a visual calendar control. To support the features usually supplied by other ActiveX controls, you will add Property Pages to this calendar (a control) and compile it so that it can be downloaded from the Internet and displayed in a Web browser.

The constituent text boxes, combo boxes, and labels are hidden from the developer and available only to the control's author. The exposed properties allow the developer to set the range of years in the combo box, to define which day appears as the first day of the week, and to set colors for weekdays and weekends. The following list describes the exposed properties of the Calendar control:

➤ The **StartDay** property is an enumerated type with possible values of Sunday and Monday. If set to **Sunday**, Sunday appears as the first day of the week and Saturday appears as the last day of the week. If set to **Monday**, Monday appears as the first day of the week and Sunday appears as the last day of the week.

➤ The **StartYear** property provides the first year that is displayed in the year combo box.

➤ The **EndYear** property provides the last year that is displayed in the year combo box.

➤ The **WeekDayForeColor** and **WeekDayBackColor** properties define the foreground and background colors for weekdays (Monday through Friday), respectively.

➤ The **WeekEndForeColor** and **WeekEndBackColor** properties define the foreground and background colors for weekend days (Saturday and Sunday), respectively.

In Chapter 11, you implemented properties by either aggregating or delegating the properties pertaining to the various constituent controls. The **Property** procedures in this chapter are far more complex and interrelated. In this section, you will open the completed application and explore its features. Each part of the completed application will then be discussed in detail.

To preview the completed application:

1. Start Visual Basic. Once it's running, load the project group named Chapter.12\ Complete\Ch12_C.vbg. Make sure to open the project group file, rather

than the project file. A message may appear indicating that the file Cal.ocx is not registered because the control has not been registered on your computer. Click on Yes to continue loading the project.

2. Open the Project Explorer.

Figure 12.2 shows the Project Explorer with the folders of the completed program expanded.

As shown, the Project Explorer contains a new category of modules called Property Pages. As the author of an ActiveX control, you will use this module type to create a tab in the set of Property Pages.

3. Open the Form window, and create an instance of the Calendar control on the form. Right-click on the instance of the Calendar control, and select Properties. This control supports Property Pages, unlike the control you created in Chapter 11.

The Property Pages contain two tabs. The developer will use the General tab to set common properties for a control instance and the Color tab to set the foreground and background colors of weekdays and weekend days.

4. Select the General tab, if necessary, and set StartDay to Monday. Set StartYear to 1950 and EndYear to 2050. Click on the Apply button on the Property Pages to commit the changes. When you commit the changes, note that the first day of the week displayed in the Calendar control instance appears as Monday. Figure 12.3 shows the Property Pages for the Calendar control.

5. Activate the Color tab, if necessary. This tab lists four properties related to colors: **WeekDayForeColor**, **WeekDayBackColor**, **WeekEndForeColor**, and **WeekEndBackColor**. In the Color Set, select Standard Colors, if neccessary. Select each of these properties, change the colors, and then click on the Apply button. Your actions apply the colors to the Calendar control instance on the form.

6. Close the Property Pages, and then run the program. Click on different months and years in the combo boxes. The calendar is updated accordingly.

Figure 12.2   Project Explorer.

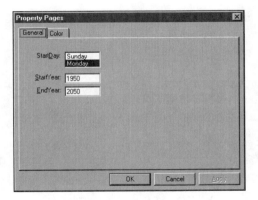

Figure 12.3   Property Pages.

7. End the program to return to design mode.

8. Exit Visual Basic without saving any changes.

This control can also be displayed on a Web page. In that situation, Internet Explorer can act as the control's container.

To display a control on a Web page:

1. Start Internet Explorer. Internet Explorer 5.0 is included on the CD accompanying this book.

2. Select Chapter.12\Dist\Cal.HTM as the address. Make sure to include the letter of the drive that contains your data files. The calendar will appear in the Web browser, as shown in Figure 12.4.

Figure 12.4   Calendar displayed in Internet Explorer.

3. Select different years and months. The calendar is updated accordingly, just as it was when it appeared on a Visual Basic form.

4. Exit Internet Explorer.

In the completed program for Extensive Controls, you saw both Visual Basic and Internet Explorer act as containers for the Calendar control. This distinction is an important one.

The following text summarizes the code for the Calendar control. For a complete description of the Calendar control's implementation, refer to the commented code in the completed application.

A control array of text boxes stores the days of the month. The control array has a lower bound (a first index) of one (1) rather than zero (0). This approach simplifies the code required to store the first day in the first text box. Several events will cause the contents of the constituent text boxes to be updated. First, whenever the user selects a different month or year, the text box contents must be updated. Also, if the developer changes the **StartDay** property, the text boxes must be updated so that the calendar begins on the correct day. The **InitDayNumbers** procedure resets the days in the Calendar control with the following code:

```
If IsNumeric(cboYear.Text) Then
    pintYear = CInt(cboYear.Text)
Else
    pintYear = Year(Date)
End If
pintMonth = cboMonth.ItemData(cboMonth.ListIndex)
pintDay = 1
pdatCurrent = DateSerial(pintYear, pintMonth, pintDay)
pintDaysInMonth = GetDaysInMonth(pintMonth)
```

These statements first determine the selected year by using the **Text** property of the combo box named **cboYear**. If the user has not selected a year in the combo box, the procedure uses the current year. The code in the control detects the current month through the **ItemData** property of the month combo box. The first month (January) has an **ItemData** value of one (1), February has an **ItemData** value of two (2), and so on. The day is set to one (1). The **DateSerial** function uses the year, month, and day to derive the date, storing this value in the variable **pdatCurrent**.

Next, the **Function** procedure named **GetDaysInMonth** determines the number of days in the month. This procedure takes one argument, an **Integer** representing the selected month. It returns the number of days in the month.

The code in the **GetDaysInMonth** procedure uses an enumerated type that contains a constant value for each month in the year. This value is the number of days in that particular month.

A Boolean function, named **IsLeap**, determines whether the selected year is a leap year. This function contains the following code:

```
Private Function IsLeap(pintYear As Integer) As Boolean
    If (pintYear Mod 4 = 0) And _
        ((pintYear Mod 100 <> 0) Or _
        (pintYear Mod 400 = 0)) Then
        IsLeap = True
    Else
        IsLeap = False
    End If
End Function
```

This function utilizes a well-known formula for determining whether a year is a leap year: If a year is divisible by 4, but not by 100, the year is a leap year; if the year is divisible by 400, the year is a leap year.

```
pintWeekDayOffset = WeekDay(pdatCurrent) - 1
```

The previous statement appears in the **InitDayNumbers** procedure and accounts for the fact that the first day of the month may fall on any day of the week. If the first day of the month is Sunday, the value (1) should be stored in the first text box in the control array. If the first day of the month is Monday, however, the value (1) should be stored in the second text box and the first text box should be empty (assuming that the user sets the start date to Sunday). The program uses the variable **pintWeekDayOffset** to determine which text box stores the first day of the month. If **pintWeekDayOffset** is Sunday and the first day of the week is Sunday, then **WeekDay(pdatCurrent)** returns one (1) and the value one (1) is subtracted from this value. Thus, if the first day of the week is Sunday, the offset is zero (0). The next code segments will use this offset.

The code presented so far has computed part of the information necessary to display the calendar. In the next step, the code displays the values (dates) in the calendar's text boxes by using three **For** loops.

The control array **txtDay** contains 37 elements numbered from 1 to 37 to accommodate months that contain 31 days and that start on a Saturday (assuming that the user selected Sunday as the start day). The first **For** loop clears the contents of the initial text boxes. For example, if the first day of the month is Tuesday, the first two text boxes (Sunday, Monday) should be blank.

12

```
For pintCurrentText = 1 To pintWeekDayOffset
    txtDay(pintCurrentText) = vbNullString
Next
```

The second **For** loop stores the day values in the text boxes:

```
For pintCurrentText = (1 + pintWeekDayOffset) _
    To pintDaysInMonth + pintWeekDayOffset
    txtDay(pintCurrentText) = _
        pintCurrentText - pintWeekDayOffset
Next
```

The variable **pintWeekDayOffset** adjusts which control array element contains the first day. If the first day of the week is Sunday, the **pintWeekDayOffset** variable contains the value zero (0). Thus the value one (1) would be stored in the first element of the control array. **GetDaysInMonth** computes the value **pintDaysInMonth**, which is then added to the offset to determine how many values will be stored in the text boxes.

The last **For** loop performs the same task as the first For loop, but clears the contents of the remaining text boxes:

```
For pintCurrentText = pintDaysInMonth + _
    pintWeekDayOffset + 1 To 37
    txtDay(pintCurrentText) = vbNullString
Next
```

Setting the foreground and background colors is a difficult task, because the first day of the week can be either Sunday or Monday. The code to set these properties must therefore determine the first day of the week and then set the color of the appropriate text boxes in the control array.

Consider the following code to set the background color of the text boxes for weekend days:

```
Private Sub SetWeekEndBackColor(pColor As OLE_COLOR)
    Dim pintCurrent As Integer
    If mintStartDay = Sunday Then
        For pintCurrent = 1 To 36 Step 7
            txtDay(pintCurrent).BackColor = pColor
        Next
        For pintCurrent = 7 To 36 Step 7
            txtDay(pintCurrent).BackColor = pColor
        Next
    Else
        For pintCurrent = 6 To 36 Step 7
```

```
            txtDay(pintCurrent).BackColor = pColor
        Next
        For pintCurrent = 7 To 36 Step 7
            txtDay(pintCurrent).BackColor = pColor
        Next
        txtDay(36).BackColor = mWeekDayBackColor
    End If
End Sub
```

The **If** statement determines whether the variable **mintStartDay** (the first day of the week) is Sunday or Monday. If it is Sunday, the first text box displays Sunday, the second displays Monday, and so on. If the first day is Monday, Sunday appears as the last day of the week.

Two **For** loops exist for each part of the **If** statement. The first **For** loop sets the color of one weekend day, and the second **For** loop sets the color for the other weekend day. The **For** loops in the conditions differ only in their initial values. Two other procedures set the foreground and background colors for the weekdays. Commented code for these procedures appears in the completed example program.

Having reviewed the code for the calendar control, you now can use the control on a form to review both the developer interface and the user interface.

Creating Property Pages

As you have seen, ActiveX controls typically support Property Pages so that the developer can set the design-time properties of the control. Property Pages allow for an infinitely customizable developer interface for setting properties. Furthermore, although Visual Basic allows you to set properties through the Properties window, not all containers support the Properties window as a mechanism to set properties. In these cases, the only way to set properties is via Property Pages.

Implementing Property Pages for a control does not preclude the developer from using the Properties window to set the same properties. Some properties, however, are too complex to be set through the Properties window. Consider the **ListImages** property pertaining to the ImageList control. As the developer, when you interact with the Images tab on the Property Pages, the underlying code creates ListImage objects in the **ListImages** collection. In contrast, no entry exists in the Properties window to define ListImage objects or the **ListImages** collection.

Consider another point regarding ActiveX controls that support Property Pages. When you, as the author, define Property Pages for an ActiveX control, the code reads and writes the value of the properties defined in the User control. In addition, when you, as the author, build an ActiveX control from one or more constituent controls, the properties, events, and methods of the constituent control are hidden from the developer. These hidden properties and events are not exposed to the Property Pages either. Instead, only the Public properties declared in the User control are exposed to the Property Pages.

Figure 12.5 illustrates the relationship between the Property Pages and the control that uses them.

As shown in Figure 12.5, the exposed properties in the UserControl can be set via either the Properties window or the Property Pages. Neither has access to the hidden data stored in the constituent controls. This approach is consistent with the strategy employed with the ActiveX control that you created in Chapter 11.

Visual Basic treats each tab of the Property Pages as a single **Property Page** module with a file extension of ".pag". In other words, a tab on the Property Pages is a Property Page. Property Pages support both a visual designer and a corresponding code module. Visual Basic stores any graphical images in a corresponding file with the extension of ".pgx". This approach is consistent with that undertaken with other visible objects such as **Form** and **UserControl** modules.

You might expect that a single **Property Page** module would define all of the tabs that make up the Property Pages. This is not the case, however. Rather, each module corresponds to an individual tab (Property Page) on the control's Property Pages.

Like other components you have developed, Property Pages should have a standardized interface. In this case, the term *interface* refers to the developer interface rather than the user interface, because the developer—rather than the

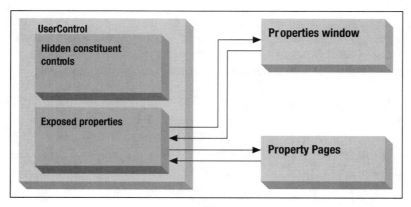

Figure 12.5   Property Page relationships.

user—works with the Property Pages. As a general rule, Property Pages should have the following characteristics:

➤ When initially displayed, the first tab should receive focus.

➤ All fields should support an access key. The letter "A" cannot be used as an access key because it is used by the Apply button.

➤ Use a standard size for all Property Pages.

➤ When using a label as a descriptive prompt, set the caption of the label to the property name. This convention helps the developer identify the property when writing code. Also, set an access key for each label that you create.

➤ When a property stores an enumerated type, use a list box or combo box for selection. Also, the value in the list box should have the same name as the enumerated type.

➤ When a User control supports multiple Property Page tabs, you, as the control's author, must decide which tab will support which property. Properties having a similar purpose or function should appear on the same tab.

➤ Standard page tabs should appear as the last tab.

➤ Avoid displaying dialog boxes.

➤ Avoid graphics that serve no purpose. The Property Pages should be as simple and fast as possible.

12

Most Property Pages consist of multiple Property Page tabs. When this situation occurs, one Property Page tab with the caption General should exist as the first tab in the series. Because an OCX file can contain multiple ActiveX controls and because you can use one Property Page tab for all or most of the ActiveX controls in the OCX file, the properties common to the multiple ActiveX controls should appear on the General tab.

The process for creating the visual interface for a Property Page is similar to the process for creating the visual interface for a User control or form: You draw intrinsic and other ActiveX constituent controls on the visual designer for the Property Page. The events and methods of the constituent controls in a Property Page are hidden from the developer. When the developer opens the Property Pages for the ActiveX control, the active Property Page is in run mode. As the author, when you have the visual designer for a **Property Page** module open, the Property Page is in design mode. This concept is consistent with the use of run and design modes during the creation of the User control.

Standard Property Pages

Property Pages can have two types of tabs: standard and user defined. Standard tabs set properties containing colors and fonts. User-defined tabs set properties that store strings and numbers and perform complex operations to set properties. Visual Basic defines four types of standard tabs corresponding to four well-defined property types:

➤ The **StandardFont** Property Page is used by the developer to set font attributes, such as font name and size, and font effects, such as bold, italic, and underline.

➤ The **StandardColor** Property Page sets colors.

➤ The **StandardPicture** Property Page assigns pictures to properties.

➤ The **StandardDataFormat** Property Page applies standard numeric and date formats when data binding is used.

Properties having a data type of **OLE_COLOR** automatically appear on the StandardColor Property Page. Properties having a data type of **Font** appear on the StandardFont Property Page, and properties having a data type of **Picture** appear on the StandardPicture Property Page.

A **Property Page** module is not associated with a particular User control simply because it exists in the same project as the User control. Rather, the User control's **PropertyPages** property defines the association. As an illustration of this fact, consider an ActiveX project with multiple ActiveX controls. Assume that the author defined three tabs as common to all ActiveX controls and other tabs as unique to specific ActiveX controls. The User control supports a property named **PropertyPages**, which contains an array of strings. Conceptually, the **PropertyPages** property operates much like the ListBox's **List** property, which also contains an array of strings. Each string in the array represents a specific Property Page that is displayed on a control's Property Pages. The collective list of **Property Page** modules makes up the Property Pages for a particular ActiveX control.

Figure 12.6 shows the relationship between a UserControl object and its associated **Property Page** modules.

In Figure 12.6, the ActiveX control project has two separate User controls. Both of these controls share a General tab. Only the second User control uses the second tab of the Property Pages, however.

When you set the UserControl's **PropertyPages** property, Visual Basic displays the Connect Property Pages dialog box, as shown in Figure 12.7.

In this dialog box, you define which Property Page tabs will be associated with a particular ActiveX control and the order in which each tab will appear on the

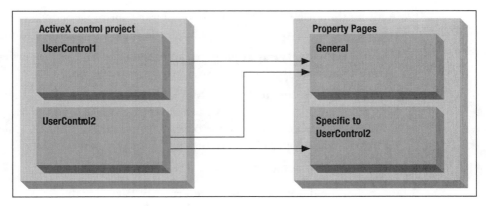

Figure 12.6   UserControl / Property Page relationship.

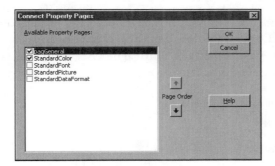

Figure 12.7   Connect Property Pages dialog box.

12

Property Pages. The four standard tabs of the Property Pages always appear in the dialog box. Any other **Property Pages** modules that are added to the project will appear as well. In Figure 12.7, for example, the **Property Page** module **pagGeneral** appears.

To associate a particular **Property Page** module with a User control, you check the box found to the left of the Property Page. The Page Order arrows on the dialog box allow you to set the order of the tabs. The order of the items displayed in the Available Property Pages list box defines the order of the Property Pages.

After you (as the author) associate Property Pages with an ActiveX control, the developer can activate the Property Pages by using a pop-up menu or by using the (**Custom**) property in the Properties window.

To associate standard Property Page tabs with a User control:

1. Start Visual Basic. Then load the Chapter.12\Startup\Ch12_S.vbg. project group.

2. Activate the Properties window for the User control named Calendar.ctl. (Remember that you are now assuming the role of the control's author.)

3. Select the **PropertyPages** property, and then click on the Properties button to activate the Connect Property Pages dialog box.

4. Check the checkbox next to the **StandardColor** property, and then click on OK to save the changes and close the dialog box. You have now associated the **StandardColor** Property Page with the ActiveX Calendar control; the developer can therefore display the Property Pages.

5. Close the visual designer for the UserControl object.

When you, as the developer, display the Property Pages for the ActiveX control, you do not have to write code to explicitly display the individual tabs. Instead, this functionality is built into the Property Pages themselves.

As noted earlier, the Calendar control supports four properties related to color. These properties are **WeekDayForeColor**, **WeekDayBackColor**, **WeekEndForeColor**, and **WeekEndBackColor**. The User control already contains the following **Property** procedures for the UserControl object:

```
Property Let WeekDayForeColor(pColor As OLE_COLOR)
    mWeekDayForeColor = pColor
    SetWeekDayForeColor pColor
    PropertyChanged WeekDayForeColor
End Property

Property Get WeekDayForeColor() As OLE_COLOR
    WeekDayForeColor = mWeekDayForeColor
End Property

' The code for the other three color properties
' is nearly identical.
```

These properties have the data type of **OLE_COLOR**. The data type of the StandardColor Property Page also is **OLE_COLOR**. When the developer opens the StandardColor Property Page, all four properties of the User control having the data type of **OLE_COLOR** appear in the Properties section of the Property Page. If you created a fifth property, **Shading**, of type **OLE_COLOR**, it would also appear in the list. The variable **mWeekDayForeColor** is a hidden variable used to store the current value of the property.

The StandardFont Property Page works like the StandardColor Property Page, except that it lists the properties declared as type **Font**. Similarly, the StandardPicture Property Page displays all properties of type **Picture**.

To see the effect of these **Standard** properties, you can test the Property Pages and set colors.

To use the StandardColor Property Page:

1. Activate the Form window, if necessary. Create an instance of the Calendar control on the form. Right-click on the Calendar object, and then select Properties from the pop-up menu. The Property Pages should appear, as shown in Figure 12.8.

2. The four properties shown in Figure 12.8 appear in the StandardColor Property Page because **Property** procedures in the User control declared these properties as type **OLE_COLOR**. As the control's author, you do not add these properties explicitly. Rather, Visual Basic performs this task automatically. Select the Standard Colors Color Set.

3. Select the **WeekDayForeColor** property, and then change the color. Repeat this process for the other three properties. Apply the changes, and then close the Property Pages. The colors that you changed will appear in the ActiveX Calendar control instance created on the form.

4. Close the form window.

The StandardColor Property Page performs many tasks for you transparently. When the Property Pages are displayed, the Property Page automatically reads each of the four separate properties and invokes the corresponding **Property Get** procedures in the **User control** module. The current setting (color) is then displayed to the left of the property. Whenever you click on the Apply button or select a different property, the StandardColor Property Page automatically calls the corresponding **Property Let** procedure with the new property setting. For a standard Property Page such as Color, this process takes place automatically. When you create a user-defined **Property Page** module, however, you must explicitly read the current value for a specific property into the **Property Page** module and explicitly save any changes.

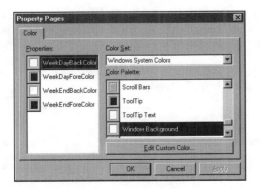

Figure 12.8   StandardColor Property Page.

User-Defined Property Page Modules

In addition to a standard Property Page tab, you can add one or more user-defined Property Page tabs to the Property Pages for a project, just as you would add any other module. After adding the module, you can create constituent control instances on it in the same way that you developed constituent controls to define the interface for a User control. A project can have as many Property Page tabs, and corresponding modules, in the Property Pages as necessary.

Syntax

> PropertyPage

Events

➤ Property Pages are not modal, so the developer can change the number of selected control instances at any time. For instance, whenever the developer changes the selected control instances and then opens the Property Pages, the **SelectedControls** property should be read to determine which control instances currently are selected and the Active Property Page updated accordingly. The **SelectionChanged** event performs this task.

➤ Every Property Page has OK, Apply, and Cancel buttons. The **ApplyChanges** event occurs when the developer clicks on either the OK button or the Apply button. In this event procedure, the ActiveX control's author writes code to save the changed properties back to the User control. When the developer clicks on the OK button, the Property Pages close after the **ApplyChanges** event procedure is completed. Clicking on the Apply button does not close the Property Pages. When the developer clicks on the Cancel button, the Property Pages close and the **ApplyChanges** event does not occur.

➤ When the developer clicks on the Properties button in the Properties window, the **EditProperty** event occurs, allowing the author to move the cursor to the correct control instance on the Property Page. To assign a specific Property Page to a property, you use the Procedure Attributes dialog box.

➤ The **Initialize** event occurs when the Property Page displays on the screen. It takes place before the **SelectionChanged** event.

Properties

➤ The value of the **Caption** property appears on the Property Page tab.

➤ The **StandardSize** property can have one of three values. If set to the default of zero (0), the object determines the size of the Property Page. If set to one (1), small, the Property Page is 101 pixels high by 375 pixels wide. If set to two (2), large, the Property Page is 179 pixels high by 375 pixels wide.

➤ The **Changed** property is a runtime property that indicates whether one of the properties in the Property Page has changed. Setting this property to True or False enables or disables,

➤ The **SelectedControls** property is a collection containing a reference to all control instances currently selected by the developer. Visual Basic updates this property when the developer selects or deselects a control instance on the form.

A Property Page resembles a User control in many ways. Like the User control, it supports events that occur when the Property Page loads. These events are hidden from the developer and exposed to the author. As with a User control, constituent controls make up the Property Page. The events and properties of these constituent controls are also hidden from the developer.

To create a user-defined Property Page:

1. Make sure that the project named Cal is active. If the Standard EXE project is active, the Property Page will be added only to the module containing the form.

2. Click on Project, and then click on Add Property Page. The Add Property Page dialog box may or may not appear, depending on the settings on the Environment tab of the Options submenu on your computer. If the Add Property Page dialog box appears, select the New tab, click on Property Page, and then click on the Open button. The Property Page should be added to the project and the visual designer should open.

   Like all other module files, a Property Page has a disk file name and a **Name** property. As the author, you use the **Name** property to associate a Property Page with an ActiveX control.

3. Open the Properties window, if necessary, for the newly added Property Page. Set the **Name** property to **pagGeneral**.

4. Set the **Caption** property to **General**. This caption will appear on the tab when the developer accesses the Calendar control's Property Pages.

5. Save the file using the name pagGeneral.pag in the Chapter.12\Startup folder.

6. At this point, the Property Page resembles an empty form or User control. You now must add the control instances that the developer will use to set the properties. Create the control instances as shown in Figure 12.9.

   As shown in Figure 12.9, three descriptive labels serve as prompts. Each label has an access key. A constituent list box and two constituent text boxes exist to receive input focus.

12

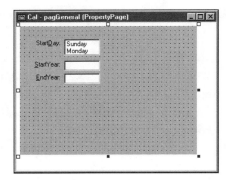

Figure 12.9   Creating the Property Page.

7. Set the **Name** property of the list box to **lstStartDay**, and then store the values Sunday and Monday in the **List** property. Set the **Name** properties of the two text boxes to **txtStartYear** and **txtEndYear**, respectively. Remove the text from the **Text** property for both text boxes.

8. Close the visual designer for the Property Page. Activate the visual designer for the User control, and then open the Properties window, if necessary. Activate the **PropertyPages** property, and click on the List button to activate the Connect Property Pages dialog box.

9. Add the General Property Page named pagGeneral so that it will appear on the Calendar control. Use the Page Order buttons to ensure that the General Property Page appears first.

10. Click on OK to save the changes and close the dialog box.

In this set of steps, you created a single user-defined Property Page. A User control can support as many Property Page tabs as needed. Each Property Page tab, however, is a separate module and therefore has its own code in the **SelectedControls** and **ApplyChanges** event procedures.

Consider the access key defined for the three labels. As you know, a label cannot receive input focus. Interestingly, when you use an access key with a label, the next object in the Tab order is the object that will receive focus when the user selects the label's access key. To make the access keys work properly, you must set the Tab order of both the labels and the corresponding list and text boxes.

To enable the access keys:

1. Activate the visual designer for the General tab of the Property Pages, and then open the Properties window.

2. Set the **TabIndex** property of the first label to 0 and the **TabIndex** property of the list box to 1.

3. Set the **TabIndex** property of the second label to 2 and the **TabIndex** property of the txtStartYear text box to 3.

4. Set the **TabIndex** property of the last label to 4 and the **TabIndex** property of the txtEndYear text box to 5.

5. Activate the Form window. Test the Property Page. To verify that the access keys work correctly, press Alt+D, Alt+S, and Alt+E to activate the **StartDay**, **StartYear**, and **EndYear** properties, respectively.

6. Click on Cancel to close the Property Pages.

As the developer, you can activate the General Property Page for the Calendar control. Presently, however, the General Property Page and the User control instance do not communicate. Because the Property Pages are merely a means to set the underlying properties of the Calendar control, you must write the necessary code to communicate property settings between the Calendar control instance and the Property Pages.

When the developer first activates the Property Pages for an ActiveX control, the initial values should appear in the control instances on the Property Page tab that has focus. Assuming that the User control possesses a **Caption** property that has a value, the initial value of the caption on the Property Page should contain the same value. When the developer changes the value of a constituent control on a Property Page, the code that the author wrote must explicitly set the value of the actual property in the User control.

When the developer activates a Property Page, the **SelectionChanged** event occurs for the corresponding **Property Page** module. This event procedure should contain code to copy specific properties from the User control to the visible objects on the active Property Page. When the developer applies changes, you, as the author, must write code that explicitly saves the current values of each supported property into the corresponding ActiveX control.

The preceding scenario presents a problem—namely, the developer can select multiple control instances before activating the Property Pages. The developer can also change which control instances are selected because Property Pages are modeless. If the developer selects multiple control instances, you, as the author, must determine the proper course of action when a specific property value differs between control instances. The **SelectionChanged** event also occurs whenever the developer selects different control instances from those initially chosen.

To keep track of the actions of the developer as he or she selects different control instances, a **Property Page** module supports the **SelectedControls** property. Just as the **Controls** collection contains a reference to each control instance created on a form, the **SelectedControls** collection contains a reference to each ActiveX control instance currently selected by the developer. If only one control instance is active, the **SelectedControls** collection contains one reference. The **SelectedControls** collection is a zero-based collection.

Consider the code for the **SelectionChanged** event to read the **StartYear** property of an underlying User control:

```
Private Sub PropertyPage_SelectionChanged()
    txtStartYear = SelectedControls(0).StartYear
End Sub
```

This event procedure executes whenever the developer selects different control instances on the form.

Because this Property Page is bound to a specific type of control, only controls of type Calendar can be stored in the **SelectedControls** collection. Consequently, the only properties you can read and write using the Property Pages are those properties exposed by the Calendar control itself.

The scenario in the previous paragraph assumes that the developer can select only one control instance at a time. The following statement references the currently selected User control:

```
txtStartYear = SelectedControls(0).StartYear
```

The Calendar User control supports the **StartYear** property, so the code **SelectedControls(0).StartYear** refers to the **StartYear** property supported by the Calendar control. The value is stored in the **Text** property of the text box named txtStartYear in the **Property Page** module named **pagGeneral**.

In the code developed in the remainder of this section, you will assume that the developer selects only one control instance at a time. Later in the chapter, you will learn how to work with multiple selected control instances.

To load the initial property values into the Property Page named pagGeneral:

1. Activate the Code window for the **Property Page** module named **pagGeneral**.

2. Enter the following statements in the **PropertyPage_SelectionChanged** event procedure:

```
txtStartYear = SelectedControls(0).StartYear
txtEndYear = SelectedControls(0).EndYear
If SelectedControls(0).StartDay = Sunday Then
    lstStartDay.ListIndex = 0
Else
    lstStartDay.ListIndex = 1
End If
Changed = False
```

3. Close the Code window and the visual designer for the **Property Page** module, and then open the Form window.

4. Activate the Properties window for the Calendar object instance created on the Form window, and then set StartYear to 1995.

5. Activate the Property Pages, and then select the General tab of the Property Pages. StartYear appears on the tab.

6. Close the Property Pages.

The statements created in the preceding steps set the initial values for the three properties supported by the General Property Page. They also assume that only one Calendar control instance is selected at a time. **SelectedControls(0)** references this control instance.

Consider the following code:

```
txtStartYear = SelectedControls(0).StartYear
txtEndYear = SelectedControls(0).EndYear
```

In these statements, the **StartYear** property pertaining to the User control is read and stored in the text box named txtStartYear. When the code in the **SelectionChanged** event reads the property, the **StartYear Property Get** procedure declared in the UserControl object executes. The second statement performs the same task with the ending year.

Consider the following code:

```
If SelectedControls(0).StartDay = Sunday Then
    lstStartDay.ListIndex = 0
Else
    lstStartDay.ListIndex = 1
End If
Changed = False
```

In the preceding statements, the property **StartDay** is an enumerated type. Previously, when you used an enumerated type with the Properties window, the Properties window displayed a list of the valid enumerations. The same is not true with a **Property Page** module, however. In that case, you loaded the valid enumerations at design time. You must therefore set explicitly the selected item in the list box to the current value of the property.

The final statement in the procedure sets the **Changed** property to **False**. This action causes the Property Page to be marked as clean (no pending changes exist), which disables the Apply button.

12

At this point, the code for the **SelectionChanged** event reads the default properties when the developer activates the Property Pages. The next step in the development of the Property Pages is to determine when the value of a property has changed and to write the modified property value back to the User control.

To successfully accomplish this step, you must remember that every Property Page contains OK, Cancel, and Apply buttons. When the developer first displays a Property Page, the Apply button is disabled; the other two buttons are enabled. When the developer clicks on one of these buttons, your code must advise the active Property Page that a property has changed and set the **Changed** property to True. The Apply button is then enabled. When the user clicks on the Apply button, the **ApplyChanges** event occurs, allowing your code to save the changes back to the selected User control instance. After this event occurs, the **Changed** property is set to False and the Apply button becomes disabled again.

Although the **Changed** property identifies that one or more properties have changed, it does not keep track of which properties have changed. This task is your responsibility as the control's author.

Two implementation choices exist to save changed properties. First, you can create a module-level Boolean variable for each property. Whenever the value of a specific property changes, your code sets the **Changed** property to True and sets the value of the Boolean variable corresponding to the property to True. Then, in the **ApplyChanges** event, you save only those properties that actually have changed by checking the value of the Boolean variable pertaining to a specific property.

Second, you can choose not to keep track of which properties have changed, but rather save all properties back to the User control when the **ApplyChanges** event occurs. This option should be used when the Property Page contains just a few properties. For the Extensive Controls project, you will use this approach because you need to save only three properties.

To write the properties back to the User control:

1. Activate the Code window for the **Property Page** module named **pagGeneral** and create the following event procedures:

```
Private Sub lstStartDay_Click()
    Changed = True
End Sub

Private Sub txtEndYear_Change()
    Changed = True
End Sub
```

```
Private Sub txtStartYear_Change()
    Changed = True
End Sub
```

2. Enter the following code in the **PropertyPage_ApplyChanges** event procedure:

```
If IsNumeric(txtStartYear) And _
    IsNumeric(txtEndYear) Then
    SelectedControls(0).StartYear = txtStartYear
    SelectedControls(0).EndYear = txtEndYear
Else
    MsgBox "Start and End years must be numeric", _
        vbInformation & vbOKOnly
End If
If lstStartDay.ListIndex = 0 Then
    SelectedControls(0).StartDay = Sunday
Else
    SelectedControls(0).StartDay = Monday
End If
```

3. Close the code window for the Property Page, and then open the Form window.

4. Activate the Property Pages for the Calendar control instance, and then change the value of the **StartDay**, **StartYear**, and **EndYear** properties. Click on the OK button to save the changes and close the Property Pages.

5. Test the program. The **StartDay** property is updated. Select a year. The range of years in the combo box is bound by the start and end years you just defined.

6. End the program to return to design mode.

Whenever the contents of either constituent text box change, the **Change** event occurs for the constituent text box, and the code in the **Change** event procedure for the text box sets the **Changed** property (pertaining to the Property Page named pagGeneral) to True. The **Change** events for the constituent controls are hidden from the developer.

When the developer clicks on either the OK or Apply button, the **ApplyChanges** event occurs and the code in the **ApplyChanges** event procedure executes. You, as the author, do not have to write code to set the **Changed** property to **False**; the event procedure itself handles this task automatically.

12

Consider the following code:

```
If IsNumeric(txtStartYear) And IsNumeric(txtEndYear) Then
    SelectedControls(0).StartYear = txtStartYear
    SelectedControls(0).EndYear = txtEndYear
    . . .
```

These statements validate whether both **Start Year** and **End Year** contain numeric values. If they do not contain numeric values, the code displays a message box advising the developer of the error condition.

```
If lstStartDay.ListIndex = 0 Then
    SelectedControls(0).StartDay = Sunday
Else
    SelectedControls(0).StartDay = Monday
End If
```

The preceding statements determine which item in the list box is selected and set the **StartDay** property accordingly. When this code executes, the **StartDay Property Let** procedure in the User control executes. The code in the **Property Let** procedure actually updates the control instances that display the days. After the **ApplyChanges** event is complete, the Property Page automatically sets the **Changed** property to **False**, thereby disabling the Apply button.

In this program, the code does not attempt to determine which property has changed. As a result, all of the properties must be saved. Also, this program assumes that the developer selects only one control instance at a time. If the developer selected multiple control instances, the property would be saved only for the first control instance in the **SelectedControls** collection. The next section deals with the situation in which multiple control instances are selected concurrently.

Multiple Selected Controls

When the developer selects multiple control instances concurrently, you, as the author, have several situations to handle. For instance, how you set the properties for multiple selected control instances depends largely on the purposes of those properties. Imagine that the developer has selected several control instances. Your code must determine which initial caption, if any, should appear in the Property Page when the developer displays it. If all of the captions are identical, the choice is simple. If the captions are not all the same, you could display no caption at all, indicating no initial value, or you could display the caption of the first selected control instance.

These choices seem relatively simple. A more serious problem occurs, however, when you must write the changed caption back to multiple selected control instances. To solve this problem, you can choose from two logical implementations.

First, you can write the same caption back to all selected control instances. In this implementation, you simply create a **For Each** loop to iterate through all selected control instances and write the appropriate property for each selected control instance, as shown in the following code:

```
Private Sub PropertyPage_ApplyChanges()
    Dim pobjCurrent As Object
    For Each pobjCurrent In SelectedControls
        pobjCurrent.Caption = txtCaption
    Next
End Sub
```

These statements iterate through the **SelectedControls** collection. Each time through the **For Each** loop, **pobjCurrent** references one of the selected control instances. The code in the **ApplyChanges** event procedure sets the property to the contents of the text box (**txtCaption**). The **Dim** statement declares the variable as type **Object**. Although you might think that you could declare the variable as type **Control**, doing so would cause an error.

Second, you can implement the **Property Page** module so that it allows the developer to select a control instance and to set properties for each selected control instance independently. This solution requires considerably more code than the first option does. Conceptually, this behavior is much like the behavior of the standard Property Page types. Instead of selecting a property for a specific control instance, however, you create a list box containing the selected control instances. The developer would then select a control instance and apply the changes for a specific property.

Debugging ActiveX Controls

Because ActiveX controls run as in process components, debugging such a control is much like debugging an ActiveX DLL project. To debug an ActiveX control, you create a project group. One project in the group is used to test the ActiveX control. The other project contains the ActiveX control(s) and associated Property Pages.

You can set breakpoints, as needed, to test the ActiveX control or Property Pages. When Visual Basic reaches a breakpoint, it will enter break mode and the line in either the control or the tab of the Property Pages will be displayed.

To demonstrate this process, you will set breakpoints in both the User control and the Property Pages for the Extensive Controls project to see the events that occur as the developer sets the values of various properties.

To debug an ActiveX control:

1. Activate the Code window for the User control, and then set a breakpoint at the first executable statement in the **StartDay Property Let** procedure. Refer to Appendix A if you are not familiar with setting breakpoints.

```
mintStartDay = eDay
```

2. Set a breakpoint at the first executable statement in the **StartDay Property Get** procedure:

```
StartDay = mintStartDay
```

3. Activate the Code window for the **Property Page** module named **pagGeneral**, select the **lstStartDay_Click** event procedure, and then set a breakpoint at the following statement:

```
Changed = True
```

4. Close the code window for the Property Page. As the developer, open the Form window, right-click on the Calendar control instance, and then select Properties from the shortcut menu to activate the Property Pages. The Property Pages are not displayed. Rather, your action activates the Code window for the User control and highlights the following statement in the Property Get procedure:

```
StartDay = mintStartDay
```

This code executes because the Property Pages executed a statement that tried to read the property.

As you click on the Start button, Visual Basic executes the code in either your ActiveX control or in the Property Page. You can debug this code, print values in the Immediate window, and perform other debugging tasks, just as you could with a form.

Enabling A Control For Use On The Internet

Using ActiveX Controls On The Web

Visual Basic supports ActiveX controls that can be used by Web browsers such as Internet Explorer. Now you will learn how to create a simple Web page, embed an ActiveX control on a Web page, and use an ActiveX control (created in Visual Basic) with Internet Explorer. The first step, however, is to take note of a few caveats:

➤ Internet Explorer 4.0 or 5.0 must be installed on the system. Other browsers, such as Netscape, will not work in these examples.

➤ You do not need an Internet connection to complete the hands-on steps in this chapter. Internet Explorer can display local documents without connecting the computer to the Internet.

The Web consists of clients and servers. Web clients include browsers like Internet Explorer and Netscape. They run on the client computer and display pages supplied by Web servers. When you display a document in Internet Explorer, you are displaying a Web page. This page may exist on the local computer (that is, the computer running Internet Explorer) or somewhere on the Internet.

Every Web page has a Uniform Resource Locator (URL). If you have used the Web, you have undoubtedly seen that a URL that looks similar to the following:

```
http://www.coriolis.com
```

A URL has two parts. The first part defines the protocol to use, and the second part identifies a file or location (that is, the server). Web documents (pages) are written in a language called the Hypertext Markup Language (HTML). The protocol used to transfer an HTML document from the server to the client is the Hypertext Transfer Protocol (HTTP).

Consider the following valid URLs:

```
http://www.coriolis.com
ftp://ftp.coriolis.com
file:\\A:\Chapter.12\Dist\Cal.htm
```

The first URL uses HTTP as the protocol. The second uses the File Transfer Protocol (FTP). The final URL is more interesting and will be used in this chapter. Because a Web browser such as Internet Explorer can display a Web page on the client computer as well as a page on the Web, the Web browser can recognize a Web page on the floppy drive in the folder A:\Chapter.12\Dist.

All URLs have the following syntax:

Syntax
method://server[:port]/file

Dissection

➤ The method indicates which protocol to use. Valid protocols include HTTP, FTP, News, and file.

➤ The server represents the Internet host that supports the method (protocol).

➤ Most methods communicate over a well-defined port. For testing purposes, however, a server can use a different port. To use that port, you specify the port address in the URL.

➤ The file argument contains the file to be transmitted.

This chapter covers only HTTP. Chapter 14 discusses FTP.

Static And Dynamic Web Pages

Web pages can be classified into two categories: static and dynamic. Static Web pages contain text and graphics and hyperlinks to other Web pages. The user cannot interact with them to perform common business tasks, such as looking up data in a database. A static Web page cannot contain ActiveX controls either. Static Web pages do not execute any code; they just display information.

Dynamic Web pages, on the other hand, offer a great deal more flexibility. They can display ActiveX controls. The ActiveX controls, in turn, can execute code. In this section, you will learn how to use an ActiveX control on a Web page, thereby creating a dynamic Web page. To accomplish this task, a brief introduction of the HTML programming language is in order.

A Very Brief Introduction To HTML

For all of its vast capabilities, the HTML language itself includes only two types of elements—tags and data. HTML documents are made up of tags, which are code that directs the browser to perform a task. Tags are embedded inside brackets (that is, **<TAG>**). Data, as the name implies, provides the information for the Web page. Data is not enclosed in brackets.

HTML is an interpreted language, so you do not compile an HTML page into an executable file. Rather, the Web browser reads the text file, interprets the tags, and displays the Web page. The HTML language is not case-sensitive.

The following code segment illustrates a complete, although simple, HTML document:

```
<HTML>
This is a line of text
</HTML>
```

In this code segment, the **<HTML>** and **</HTML>** tags mark the beginning and end of the document, respectively. The document contains one line of text that will be displayed on the page.

Another HTML tag is the **<TITLE>** tag, which specifies the document title. The text in the **<TITLE>** tag will appear on the Internet Explorer title bar. For example, to add a title to the page, you could use the following code:

```
<HTML>
<TITLE>
Calendar
</TITLE>
This is a line of text
</HTML>
```

HTML supports extensive formatting capabilities. The following list summarizes some of its formatting tags:

➤ The **<B>** tag sets the text in a bold typeface.

➤ The **<I>** tag sets the text in an italic typeface.

➤ The **<TT>** tag specifies a monospace Courier font.

➤ The **<P>** tag specifies a paragraph boundary.

➤ The **<HR>** tag draws a horizontal line on the page.

The following code segment illustrates the use of these tags:

```
<HTML>
<B>This is a line of bold text</B>
<I>This is a line of italic text</I>
</HTML>
```

The preceding code prints two lines of text—the first in a bold typeface and the second in an italic typeface.

Tags can be nested inside each other. Nesting tags is useful if you want to display a bold italic font, for example. The following statements display a line of text in a bold font. Embedded in that bold text is italicized bold text.

```
<B>This is a line of bold <I>italic</I> text</B>
```

Documents can also have headers. Headers are used much in the same way as an outline. The header tags **<H1>** through **<H6>** define headers. The following code segment illustrates the use of headers:

```
<H1>Heading1</H1>
<H2>Heading2</H2>
<H3>Heading3</H3>
```

12

One commonly used tag is the anchor tag, which creates links to other Web documents. The following statement illustrates the use of the anchor tag:

```
<A Href="http://www.coriolis.com">"Jump to The Coriolis Group"
```

The anchor tag contains a reference (**Href**) to another Web site (**http://www. course.com**).

These tags are but a few of the many tags supported by the HTML language. For instance, HTML also supports tags to create tables and figures.

Many programs will help you write HTML. In fact, Word 97 can save documents as HTML documents.

To create an HTML document:

1. Start WordPad or Notepad, and then enter the following text:

```
<HTML>
<TITLE>Calendar</TITLE>
<H1>Sample HTML file</H1>
<P>This is a sample HTML file with a link to the The Coriolis Group
Web site.
</P>
<A Href="http://www.coriolis.com">"Jump to The Coriolis Group"
</HTML>
```

2. Save the file as a text file using the name Chapter.12\Startup\Demo.htm. Exit the word processor.

3. Start Windows Explorer, and locate the Chapter.12\Startup folder. Double-click on the Demo.htm file. Internet Explorer starts, and the Web page displays.

4. Click on the underlined text Jump To The Coriolis Group. This link will not work unless your computer is connected to the Internet.

5. Exit Internet Explorer, and close Windows Explorer.

The HTML code you just wrote contains a title that is displayed on the Internet Explorer title bar. It also contains one heading—a paragraph of text. The anchor creates a link to The Coriolis Group's Web site.

HTML also defines tags to manage images and lists. This chapter's HTML discussion focuses on the use of an **<OBJECT>** tag to include an ActiveX control on a Web page. For more information on the HTML language, check the Microsoft Web site or any of the numerous books available on this topic.

<OBJECT> *Tags*

After this brief introduction to HTML, you are now ready to insert ActiveX controls into an HTML document by using the **<OBJECT>** tag. The **<OBJECT>** tag, which is new to version 3.0 of HTML, allows you to encapsulate an ActiveX control (or other type of object) inside a Web page (HTML document).

When you insert an ActiveX control in a Web page, you insert only a reference to the control. The actual control resides in a file separate from the Web page itself. The following example illustrates an **<OBJECT>** tag:

```
<HTML>
<OBJECT ID="Calendar"
    WIDTH=341
    HEIGHT=290
    CLASSID="CLSID:28B10CDB-97C8-11D1-ADD6-444553540000"
    CODEBASE="Calendar.CAB#version=1,0,0,0"
</OBJECT>
</HTML>
```

The **<OBJECT>** tag has many parts. The **ID** contains the name of the control. The **HEIGHT** and **WIDTH** set the height and width of the control in the container, which, in this case, is Internet Explorer.   In addition, every control registered on the system has a unique **CLASSID**. When Internet Explorer detects an **<OBJECT>** tag, it attempts to load the control on the local machine by first searching the Windows Registry for the **CLASSID**. If the control is found, Internet Explorer loads it on the local machine. If the control is not found, Internet Explorer loads the control from a remote server.

If a control has already been downloaded and you, as the author, upgrade the control, the version of the control on the remote machine will be out of date; it should therefore be downloaded again. To determine whether the control is out of date, Internet Explorer uses the **CODEBASE** parameter. This parameter contains the name of the file (control) to retrieve along with the version information pertaining to the control. If the version of the control on the machine is older than the version specified in the **CODEBASE** argument, Internet Explorer downloads the control.

Distributing An ActiveX Control

Now that you have built a complete ActiveX control, you must learn how to deploy it for use by other developers. Two basic options exist for distributing an ActiveX control: distribution as a compiled component and distribution of the source code. Each option has advantages and disadvantages.

When you distribute a control as a compiled component:

➤ The implementation of the control is hidden from the developer. Thus the implementation is confidential.

➤ Developers cannot change the implementation of the control.

➤ The distribution process is simplified, because you can distribute new features and bug fixes to the developers using your control.

When you distribute a control as source code:

➤ You do not distribute an OCX file with the control.

➤ The control is compiled into the application. Thus the developer does not need to worry whether the application will work with future control versions.

➤ The entire application must be recompiled to fix any errors in the control.

➤ If multiple applications use the control, each application will have a larger size because the code is compiled into the application.

Creating an ActiveX control and compiling it into an OCX file does not make the control available for downloading on the Web. The control must also be compiled and converted into a special type of file known as a *cabinet* or (CAB) file. Chapter 17 discusses cabinet files in more detail.

Consider the ActiveX controls you have created and used to this point. Most of these controls have dependencies—that is, support files that are necessary for the control to run. These support files are usually DLL files. The references appear in a part of the CAB file called an INF (information file).

The INF file has two purposes: It identifies the dependencies, and it contains a reference to a site where the dependent files can be downloaded. As the control's author, you have two choices for downloading dependent files. First, you can specify a site that you own for downloading. This option requires that you have the necessary files on a server available for downloading. Second, Microsoft allows dependent files to be downloaded from its Web site. This approach is usually the better choice, as Microsoft keeps these files up to date. Furthermore, it puts less strain on your Web server.

Licensing A Control

As an ActiveX control's author, you can prevent unauthorized use of the control by including a license key with it. When a developer tries to create a design-time instance of a control that you authored and the control requires a license key, Visual Basic uses the Windows Registry to verify that the license key exists and is correct. How you license a control depends on whether the control is built for standard distribution (with an OCX file) or for distribution over the Internet.

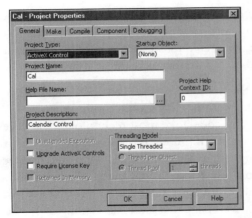

Figure 12.10   Project Properties dialog box.

Licensing a control for standard distribution is very simple. The Project Properties dialog box, shown in Figure 12.10, contains a checkbox on the General tab named Require License Key. If this box is checked, the developer must have a valid license key to create a design-time instance of the control. Creating a run-time instance of the control does not involve license keys.

Creating a license key for a control that will be distributed on the Internet requires two steps. First, you must create a license package (LPK) file. Second, you must create a reference to the licensing package file on the Web page. To develop a license file, you use the Project Properties dialog box to require a license key and to compile the project.

After adding licensing support to the control, you use the License Package Authoring tool to create the license package file. The Tools\Lpk_Tool folder on the Visual Basic CD-ROM contains this file, which allows you to select the controls that you want to license. After selecting the desired controls, you save the license information to the LPK file. You must then modify the **<OBJECT>** tag in the Web page to reference the license package file.

When the ActiveX control is installed, the Setup program typically writes the license information to the Windows Registry. Because the license key is stored in the Windows Registry, Visual Basic does not need or use the license package file. Thus, to test the LPK file, you first must remove the key from the Windows Registry.

Control Security

You are undoubtedly aware of the threat posed by viruses and the importance of keeping them out of your computer. The first viruses were spread from computer to computer using floppy disks as people shared tainted programs from unknown origins. When these programs were run, they generally would perform some malicious (or at least irritating) act on your computer. When the first personal computers were connected to the Internet, downloading a file and executing it sometimes caused the computer to contract a virus.

Because of their static nature, the first Web pages were not sources of viruses. These Web pages displayed information and possibly had links to other Web sites, but they did not execute any code. Like most technologies, however, the Web and Web browsers have become infinitely more sophisticated over time. Browsers now support scripting languages that allow a Web page to execute code. More importantly, a Web browser can download a control that executes inside the browser on the local computer. Thus a computer can now potentially contract a virus by displaying a Web page that executes code.

When a browser downloads an ActiveX control and executes it on a computer, a security risk exists. For instance, if a malicious control author placed code in a control to remove all of the files on your computer, and you then downloaded the control and executed it, your computer's data would disappear. As an ActiveX control author, you must assure the developer that a control is safe and free from viruses or other unexpected side effects.

Two radically different approaches to solving this security dilemma exist. The first approach, which is used by the Java scripting language, is often called the *sandbox* approach. The term reflects the fact that the code executes in a "sandbox" and cannot get out. With this approach, the language itself prohibits a control from harming the destination computer. In the sandbox approach, an intermediate language executes the code in the control. This language prevents potential harmful activities, such as writing to the disk or calling operating system functions. It also prevents the control from accessing the memory of other procedures.

The second approach—and the one used by ActiveX controls—is called the *trust me* approach. With this approach, a control is deemed safe because some authority has said the control is safe and you believe that statement. The first step in the execution of the trust me approach is the creation of a control that is safe and free from harmful side effects. The second and more important part of the process is called *signing*. This topic is discussed next.

Obtaining A Digital Signature

A digital signature verifies the identity of the software publisher and assures the integrity of that software from the publisher to the end user. A digital signature neither prevents the inclusion of errors in code nor blocks viruses from occurring. Rather, it proves that the control's purported author is really the author. You must then decide whether to trust in the author's integrity and credibility.

Although the digital signature authenticates the identity of the author, it does not guarantee that person's credibility. Grantors of digital signatures, however, do verify businesses and their financial worthiness. Furthermore, to have a digital signature, you must make legal and binding promises to create virus-free controls. Digital signatures work because of the integrity and accountability of the software publisher.

Adding a digital signature to your control is a two-step process:

1. You must apply for a digital signature from a certificate authority (CA).

2. Once you have received a digital signature, you must sign your controls.

A certificate authority (CA) is an institution, such as VeriSign, that grants certificates. As a software publisher, you would apply to VeriSign (or another CA) for a certificate (digital signature). As part of the application, you, as the software publisher, provide positive identification about your company. You must pledge not to distribute a program that is known to have viruses or that contains code that would harm the user's machine. The CA will check the financial standing of your company using a Dun and Bradstreet rating. Once the CA has determined that your company is authentic, you will receive a digital signature.

A digital signature relies on a technology called *public key cryptography*. A digital signature has two keys: a public key and a private key. As a control's author, you supply the private key to your control. This private key is secret and known only to the author. The only way to decode the private key is using the public key. In this example, the public key would be known to anyone who uses your control. The user of your control can be assured of the control's authenticity because the public key should successfully decode the private key.

From an implementation perspective, you sign a control using the ActiveX Software Development Kit (SDK). This kit can be downloaded from www.microsoft.com. To sign the files, you run the Signcode.exe program included in the SDK. Any type of file can be signed, although digital signing typically used with CAB files.

Another security issue that arises with scripting relates to the fact that your control may support features to remove and modify files. If, for example, you created a control that used features of a constituent CommonDialog control to manage and potentially remove files, your control is unsafe for scripting because an erroneous script could potentially damage the computer.

You can apply one of two levels of safety to a control to guarantee that it will not damage the user's computer. If a control is marked safe for initialization, then you guarantee that when a Web browser loads the control, the control will not corrupt the end user's system. In addition, the control must not corrupt the system when it is displayed by a Web page that you did not create. If a control is marked safe for scripting, a Web developer cannot write scripts using the control that will corrupt the end user's system.

Now that you understand the issues surrounding control distribution, you can prepare the Exclusive Controls control for distribution.

The Property Page Wizard

Visual Basic supports a tool called the Property Page Wizard to help you create Property Pages. The Property Page Wizard can attach standard Property Pages to a User control. It can also help you to create a new user-defined Property Page. To create a user-defined Property Page, you specify the properties pertaining to the User control that should appear on the Property Page. Visual Basic will then create the necessary label and text box control instances to support those properties.

The Property Page Wizard is not without limitations, however. It cannot create control instances for properties having specific data types. For example, if a property has an enumeration as its data type, the Property Page Wizard will ignore the property.

The Package And Deployment Wizard

The Package and Deployment Wizard prepares applications for distribution or for deployment. The collection of files that you deploy is referred to as a *package*. A package contains all of the files necessary to deploy a program to the end user. The Package and Deployment Wizard contains the options required to create a package representing a distributable program.

The Package and Deployment Wizard is not part of the Visual Basic IDE. Rather, it is a standalone program that you run independently of Visual Basic. As with any other wizard, you interact with the Package and Deployment Wizard by completing a series of dialog boxes. Figure 12.11 shows the Package and Deployment Wizard.

The Package and Deployment Wizard contains a list box in which you select a project to deploy. It also contains three command buttons:

➤ The Package command button allows you to prepare a project for distribution.

➤ The Deploy command button allows you to send a package to a distribution site.

➤ When you deploy a package, the information pertaining to the package is stored in a script. The Manage Scripts command button allows you to rename, delete, and duplicate these scripts.

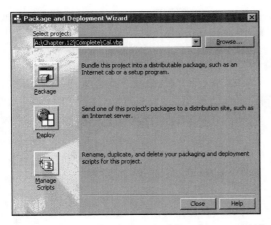

Figure 12.11   Package and Deployment Wizard.

In this chapter, you will use the Package and Deployment Wizard to build a package that is distributable over the Internet. Chapter 17 discusses the Package and Deployment Wizard in more detail.

To build a Internet-distributable package:

1. Make sure that Visual Basic is not running.

2. On the Windows Start menu, select Programs, Microsoft Visual Basic 6.0, Microsoft Visual Basic 6.0 Tools, and then click on Package and Deployment Wizard. The Package and Deployment Wizard should appear.

3. Next, you must select the Visual Basic project that you want to deploy. Click on the Browse command button to locate a project. Select the project named Chapter.12\Complete\Cal.vbp. If you have not used the Package and Deployment Wizard before, the list box to the left of the Browse command button will be blank. Otherwise, it will contain a list of deployed projects.

4. Click on the Package command button. The wizard will examine the project. Its exact behavior will differ depending on whether you have previously compiled the project and whether the executable file is newer than the project file. If you have not previously compiled the project, the dialog box shown in Figure 12.12 will appear.

Figure 12.12   Package and Deployment Wizard dialog box.

5. If the dialog box shown in Figure 12.12 appears, click on Compile to compile the project. Visual Basic will compile the project. The Packaging Script dialog box may then appear. It allows you to create a new script or select an existing script. If this dialog box appears, select (None) from the Packaging script list box, and click on Next to activate the Package Type dialog box, as shown in Figure 12.13.

6. As shown in Figure 12.13, the wizard supports three types of packages. Because you want to build an Internet-distributable package, click on the Internet Package option, and then click on the Next button to display the Package Folder dialog box, as shown in Figure 12.14.

7. The package folder indicates where the wizard will write the deployment files. Select the folder, Chapter.12\Deploy, which contains no files, and click on the Next button.

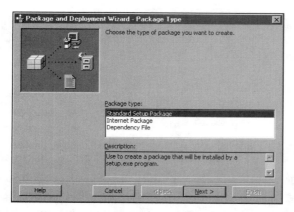

Figure 12.13   Package Type dialog box.

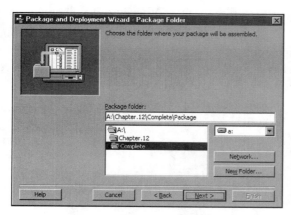

Figure 12.14   Package Folder dialog box.

8. Because this project contains Property Pages, a dialog box may appear indicating that you must distribute a DLL for the Property Pages to work properly. Click on Yes to close the dialog box.

9. The next dialog box to appear is the Included Files dialog box, which lists the included files that will be distributed. Click on Next to accept the default options.

10. The File Source dialog box specifies runtime cabinet files and their locations. Click on Next to accept the default options.

11. Next, the Safety Settings dialog box appears. In this dialog box, you specify whether your control is safe for scripting or safe for initialization. The default values are No for both options. To accept the default options, click on Next to display the Finished dialog box. Click on Finish to build the package.

12. The wizard will display a dialog box as it creates the CAB files. When the wizard is finished, the Packaging Report dialog box appears. Click on Close to close the dialog box.

13. Click on Close to exit the Package and Deployment Wizard.

The Package and Deployment Wizard creates both the CAB file and a sample HTML document containing the <**OBJECT**> tag. At this point, you can run your ActiveX Calendar control inside a Web browser.

Setting up an Internet Web server is beyond the scope of this book. You can see how your Calendar control will function inside a Web browser, however, by starting Internet Explorer and loading the HTML document created by the Package and Deployment Wizard. The code segment in Figure 12.15 shows the HTML document produced by the Package and Deployment Wizard.

The HTML document is written in the Setup folder you specified. It contains a comment related to licensing. It also contains the necessary <**OBJECT**> tag to load the control.

To load an ActiveX control in a Web browser:

1. Locate the Chapter.12\Deploy folder using Windows Explorer. The file named Cal.HTM should appear. Double-click on Cal.HTM. Internet Explorer should be activated, and the Calendar control should appear, as shown in Figure 12.16.

2. Click on different months and years, noting that the control works as it did in the Form window.

3. Exit Internet Explorer and close Windows Explorer.

```
<!   If any of the controls on this page require licensing, you must
     create a license package file. Run LPK_TOOL.EXE to create the
     required LPK file. LPK_TOOL.EXE can be found on the ActiveX SDK,
     http://www.microsoft.com/intdev/sdk/sdk.htm. If you have the Visual
     Basic 6.0 CD, it can also be found in the /Tools/LPK_TOOL directory.
     The following is an example of the Object tag:
<OBJECT  CLASSID="clsid:5220cb21-c88d-11cf-b347-00aa00a28331">
     <PARAM NAME="LPKPath"   VALUE="LPKfilename.LPK">
</OBJECT>
--><OBJECT ID="Calendar"CLASSID="CLSID:7C041793-F5BE-11D2-A633-EEF745BB9633"
CODEBASE="Cal.CAB#version=1,0,0,0"></OBJECT>
<HTML>
<HEAD>
<TITLE>Cal.CAB</TITLE>
</HEAD>
<BODY>
<!-- If  any of the controls of this page require licensing, you must
     create a license package file. Run LPK_TOOL.EXE to create the
     required LPK file. LPK_TOOL.EXE can be found on the ActiveX SDK,
     http://www.microsoft.com/intdev/sdk/sdk.htm. If you have the Visual
     Basic 6.0 CD, it can also be found in the \Tools\LPK_TOOL directory.

     The following is an example of the Object tag:

<OBJECT CLASSID="clasid:5220cb21-c88d-11cf-b347-00aa00a28331">
     >PARAM NAME="LPKPath" VALUE="LPKfilename.LPK">
</OBJECT>
-->

<OBJECT ID="Calendar"
CLASSID="CLSID:7C41793-F5BE-11D2-A633-EEF745BB9633"
CODEBASE="Cal.CAB#version=1,0,0,0">
</OBJECT>
</BODY>
</HTML>
```

Figure 12.15　HTML code.

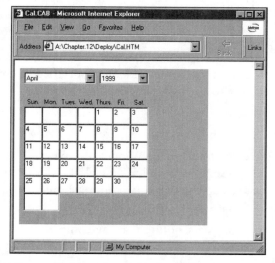

Figure 12.16　The Calendar control in Internet Explorer.

CHAPTER SUMMARY

In this chapter, you learned how to attach Property Pages to an ActiveX control and to enable the downloading of controls over the Internet. Property Pages come in two types: standard and user-defined. A standard Property Page is used with properties having a data type of **Font**, **OLE_COLOR**, or **Picture**. All properties having the same type as the standard Property Page are displayed on the Property Page. For example, if a User control exposed four properties of type **OLE_COLOR**, then those four properties would appear in the standard Color Property Page.

To add a standard Property Page to a User control:

➤ Activate the Properties window for the **User control** module.

➤ Select the **PropertyPages** property, and click on the Properties button.

➤ On the Property Pages dialog box, select the standard pages that should appear. Use the arrow buttons to change the order of the pages.

To add a user-defined Property Page to a User control:

➤ Select the desired ActiveX control project.

➤ Click on Project, and then click on Add Property Page. If the Add Property Page dialog box appears, click on the Property Page option to add a new Property page.

➤ Create the desired control instances on the Property Page. Set access keys for the descriptive labels. The name of a descriptive label should match the name of the corresponding property.

➤ Activate the Properties window for the **User control** module.

➤ Select the **PropertyPages** property, and click on the Properties button.

➤ Add the new Property Page to the list of Property Pages, and reorder the pages as necessary.

To store initial values into a Property Page when displayed by the developer:

➤ Respond to the **SelectionChanged** event procedure.

➤ The code in the **SelectionChanged** event procedure should use the **SelectedControls** collection to read the property values.

➤ Set the **Changed** property to False.

To indicate that a property has changed:

➤ Set the value of the **Changed** property on the Property Page to **True**.

To apply changes to the User control:

➤ Respond to the **ApplyChanges** event on the Property Page.

➤ The code in the **ApplyChanges** event should read the values of the constituent controls on the Property Page and store the values to the **SelectedControls** collection.

To debug an ActiveX control or Property Page:

➤ Create a project group containing a Standard EXE project and an ActiveX control project.

➤ Set breakpoints in the User control and **PropertyPage** modules, as necessary.

To distribute an ActiveX control for deployment on the Web:

➤ Start the Package and Deployment Wizard.

➤ Click on the Package button to build the package.

➤ Select the Internet Package package type.

➤ Select the folder where the package will be deployed.

REVIEW QUESTIONS

1. Which of the following statements pertaining to the style of a Property Page is true?

   a. All properties should have an access key.

   b. The caption for a property should be the same as a property's name.

   c. Properties should be grouped on the same page based on their function.

   d. None of the above.

   e. All of the above.

2. What are the data types supported by the standard tabs of the Property Pages?

   a. **OLE_COLOR, Font, Picture**

   b. **OLE_COLOR, Font, Pictures**

   c. **Colors, Fonts, Pictures**

   d. **Color, Font, Picture**

   e. None of the above

3. What are the names of the four standard tabs of the Property Pages?
   a. OLE_COLOR, Font, Picture, Data
   b. Color, Font, Picture, Data
   c. StandardColor, StandardFont, StandardPicture, StandardDataFormat
   d. None of the above
   e. All of the above

4. What event occurs in a **Property Page** module when the user selects a different control instance?
   a. **SelectedControl**
   b. **SelectedControls**
   c. **SelectionChanged**
   d. **Update**
   e. **Edit**

5. Which event occurs when the user clicks on the Apply or OK button on a tab in the Property Pages?
   a. **Change**
   b. **OK**
   c. **ApplyChanges**
   d. **Select**
   e. **Update**

6. Which property do you set to alert a **Property Page** module that a value has been updated?
   a. **Change**
   b. **Changed**
   c. **Updated**
   d. **Update**
   e. None of the above

7. How do you associate specific Property Page with a User control?
   a. Use the Object Browser.
   b. Add a Property Page to the project.
   c. Set the **PropertyPages** property for the form.
   d. Set the **PropertyPages** property for the User control.
   e. Use the Project Properties dialog box.

8. Which method do you use to inform the container that the value of a property has been updated?

   a. **Change**

   b. **Changed**

   c. **PropertyChange**

   d. **PropertyChanged**

   e. **Property**

9. When the developer selects different control instances, the _____ collection on the **Property Page** module contains a reference to the control instances.

   a. **Objects**

   b. **Control**

   c. **SelectedControl**

   d. **Controls**

   e. **SelectedControls**

For Questions 10 through 12, assume that a User control named SuperText exists and that the control has a General tab on the Property Pages.

10. Create the event procedure to load the first selected control instance in a text box on the Property Page named txtContents. Assume that you are reading the **Contents** property for the selected control.

11. Create the event procedure to save the property you read in Question 10.

12. Create the event procedure to notify the Property Page that the contents of the text box named txtContents have changed.

13. Assuming that several control instances are selected, write a **For Each** loop to save the text in the text box named txtContents on the Property Page to the **Contents** property of the User control.

14. Which of the following is an invalid URL?

   a. **http://www.microsoft.com**

   b. **ftp://ftp.microsoft.com**

   c. **file:\\A:\Demo.html**

   d. None of the above is valid

   e. All of the above are valid

15. Which of the following statements is true regarding Web pages?
    a. Static Web pages do not execute code.
    b. Dynamic Web pages execute code.
    c. Dynamic Web pages can execute ActiveX controls.
    d. Both b and c.
    e. All of the above.

16. Which of the following is a valid HTML tag?
    a. **\<HTML\>**
    b. **\<OBJECT\>**
    c. **\<TITLE\>**
    d. Both a and b
    e. All of the above

17. Which tag is used in an HTML document to download a control?
    a. **\<LINK\>**
    b. **\<HREF\>**
    c. **\<CONTROL\>**
    d. **\<OBJECT\>**
    e. **\<ACTIVEX\>**

18. To create a downloadable control, you _____.
    a. change the project type to Internet control
    b. use Internet Explorer
    c. use the Package and Deployment Wizard
    d. compile the program in Visual Basic
    e. None of the above

19. Which of the following statements is true regarding a digital signature?
    a. It guarantees the credibility of the control's author.
    b. It authenticates that the control's author really is the author.
    c. It uses a public key and a private key.
    d. Both b and c.
    e. None of the above.

20. Which of the following is a valid safety option for a control?

    a. safe for initialization

    b. safe for scripting

    c. safe for running

    d. Both a and b

    e. All of the above

HANDS-ON PROJECTS

Project 1

In this project, you will develop an ActiveX control and then create Property Pages for the control. Figure 12.17 shows the user-defined Property Page you will create.

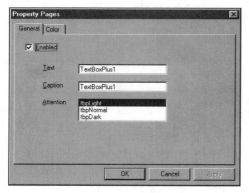

Figure 12.17 Exercise 1 Completed Property Page.

a. Start Visual Basic. Create a new project, and set the **Name** property of the form to frmEx1. Save the form using the name Chapter.12\Exercise\frmEx1.frm and the project using the name Chapter.12\Exercise\Ex1.vbp.

b. Using the TextBoxPlus control created in Chapter 11, add the ActiveX control project and create a project group.

c. Create a user-defined Property Page named General. Set the caption of the Property Page to General.

d. Add a checkbox to the General Property Page. This checkbox should be used to support the **Enabled** property of the TextBoxPlus control.

e. Add two text boxes to the Property Page. One text box should support the **Caption** property and the other should support the **Text** property.

f. Create a list box to support the **Attention** property. Remember that this property is an enumerated type. The list box should display the valid enumerated types.

g. Create a StandardColor Page to display **OLE_COLOR** properties.

h. Test the project group.

i. Exit Visual Basic.

Project 2

In this project, you will expand the Calendar control created in this chapter. Figure 12.18 shows a completed Property Page for the control.

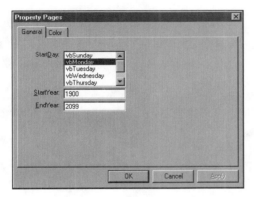

Figure 12.18   Exercise 2 Completed Property Page.

12

a. Start Visual Basic. Create a new project, and set the **Name** property of the form to frmEx2. Save the form using the name Chapter.12\Exercise\frmEx2.frm and the project using the name Chapter.12\Exercise\Ex2.vbp.

b. Create a project group, and add the Calendar control from this chapter to the project.

c. Modify the control and the Property Page so that the first day of the week can be any day, instead of just Sunday or Monday.

d. Validate the **StartYear** and **EndYear** properties on the Property Page so that the starting year must be greater than the ending year. Display a message box if an error occurs.

e. Test the program.

f. Exit Visual Basic.

Project 3

In this project, you will use the control created in Project 2 and make the control downloadable over the Internet.

a. Using the Package and Deployment Wizard, complete the dialog boxes to create a downloadable control.

b. Create or modify an HTML document as needed to display the control in a Web browser.

c. Test the control.

d. Exit the program.

CHAPTER THIRTEEN

ActiveX Documents

AFTER READING THIS CHAPTER AND COMPLETING THE EXERCISES, YOU WILL BE ABLE TO:

➤ Create an ActiveX document project

➤ Site the document in Internet Explorer used as a container

➤ Create persistent properties for an ActiveX document

➤ Create event procedures to navigate between different ActiveX documents

➤ Use the Microsoft Office Binder application

➤ Add documents to a binder and navigate between binder documents

➤ Modify an ActiveX document so that it can support multiple containers

Creating An ActiveX Document Project

Before you preview the completed applications for this chapter, you need to be aware of two caveats. The applications in this chapter do not run as standalone programs. That is, you do not view the visual interface at runtime using a Visual Basic window. Instead, you use another application, called a container application, to view the project. You will use two containers in this chapter: Internet Explorer and Office Binder. To complete the exercises in this chapter, you must have both Internet Explorer and Office Binder installed on your computer. Office Binder is part of Microsoft Office. You must therefore have a licensed copy of Microsoft Office to use Office Binder.

Mid Pacific Bank originates loans to customers across the United States. To better serve its customers and branch offices, Mid Pacific Bank is exploring emerging technologies that will allow the company to develop applications usable both over the Internet and on standalone computers. The bank wants a prototype that will illustrate how such a program might work.

To preview the completed application:

1. Start Visual Basic. Setting the drive designator as necessary, load the project named Chapter.13\Complete\Ch13_C.vbp.

2. Open the Project Explorer, if necessary. The project is of a different type than you have seen previously; it is an ActiveX Document DLL. You can view the project type by examining the Project Properties dialog box. In addition, the project contains a new type of module—an ActiveX document module. Mid Pacific Bank's project includes two separate documents: docApply and docLoan.

3. Run the program. When you run the program, Visual Basic will enter run mode, Internet Explorer will start, and, depending on the configuration of your computer, the File Download dialog box may appear. This dialog box warns you that you are downloading a file and executing foreign code on your computer. If the dialog box appears, click on Open This File From Its Current Location, and then click on OK. Unless you request otherwise, the dialog box appears to warn you of the possible security risks of executing downloaded programs.

4. Internet Explorer starts and displays the document shown in Figure 13.1.

5. Using the scroll bars, scroll to the bottom of the document, and then click on the Loan Payment button. Clicking on this button causes Internet Explorer to display the other document in the project. (Again, the File Download dialog box may appear, requesting that you open the file from its current location or save the file to disk.)

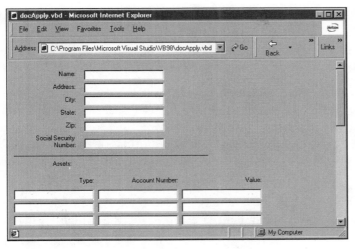

Figure 13.1   Completed program in Internet Explorer.

6. Default values are supplied for the loan amount, term, and interest rate. Click on Calculate on the Loan menu to calculate the payment of the loan.

7. Exit Internet Explorer, and then exit Visual Basic. Do not save any changes to the program.

The Role Of ActiveX Documents

ActiveX controls and ActiveX documents rely on COM technology for communication. You have seen two different containers that support ActiveX controls: a Visual Basic form and Internet Explorer. It is important to remember that an ActiveX control cannot exist by itself, but rather is executed from a container. In this regard, ActiveX documents are very similar to ActiveX controls because ActiveX documents must execute from a container as well.

ActiveX document technology evolved from a proprietary Windows technology that was initially used by the Microsoft Office Binder application to collect and group the data from different Microsoft Office applications. Internet Explorer also supports ActiveX document technology. As a result, you can include ActiveX documents on a Web page, just as you can include an ActiveX control instance. Datacentric technology allows users to work with information rather than concentrating on the programs that manipulate that information. ActiveX documents exploit this type of datacentric technology.

An ActiveX document project differs slightly from a project made up of multiple Visual Basic forms. A Visual Basic project consisting of forms runs in a standalone mode. That is, the form acts as the container for the control instances created on it, but the program containing the form is run directly by the user. Users do not run ActiveX document projects directly, however. Instead, another container, such as Internet Explorer, manages and displays ActiveX documents.

ActiveX Document Design Guidelines

An ActiveX document can be displayed only inside a container. Three containers support ActiveX documents: Internet Explorer, Office Binder, and the Visual Basic development environment.

The notion of multiple containers is significant. Different containers may not support the same features. For example, when a Visual Basic project contains a User control, the container (in this case, a form) supports the Extender object and its properties as a way to communicate information between the User control module and the container. Other containers might not support these same properties, and some containers may support different properties.

When creating ActiveX documents, you need to be aware of design considerations, ActiveX document limitations, and the containers that may use your document. For instance, the code in your document must determine the container in which the document is being displayed and execute the correct methods pertaining to that container. In addition, the methods to navigate from one document to another in Office Binder are different than those employed by Internet Explorer.

When designing an ActiveX document, you must remember that containers such as Internet Explorer and Office Binder all have their own menus. Your ActiveX document may also have a menu. When Internet Explorer displays an ActiveX document, the menu pertaining to the ActiveX document does not appear on the document itself. Rather, the menu is integrated into the menu of the container application (Internet Explorer). Because the user of your ActiveX document may not recognize the source or purpose of the application, you should create an About menu command to display an About box identifying the ActiveX document application to the user.

Because an ActiveX document project is an ActiveX component, you can create it as either an in-process component (DLL) or an out-of-process component (EXE). As a general rule, in-process components offer better performance than out-of-process components. You cannot, however, display a modeless dialog box (form) from an in-process component (DLL).

Because different types of containers support different properties and methods to manage an underlying ActiveX document, the presentation of the ActiveX document material will be coupled tightly with the respective container. The first section of this chapter discusses the use of Internet Explorer as the container, and the second section discusses the use of Office Binder as the container.

In this chapter, you will create ActiveX documents and display them in a container application on the same computer. In the real world, it is more likely that an ActiveX document would be downloaded from the Internet.

Creating An ActiveX Document

From Visual Basic's perspective, an ActiveX document is just another type of module. The module is stored in two files. A file with the extension .dob stores the visual interface and code part of the document, and a file with the extension .dox stores any graphical images. These file suffixes are analogous to the suffixes used by .frm and .frx files.

At the core of an ActiveX document lies the UserDocument object, which is similar to the UserControl object pertaining to an ActiveX control. It supports events that occur when a container creates an instance of the UserDocument. It also supports properties that can be made persistent by saving property values to the PropertyBag object.

Syntax

UserDocument

Properties

➤ The **Hyperlink** property returns a reference to a Hyperlink object. You use the Hyperlink object when Internet Explorer is the container application. It contains methods to locate URLs.

➤ You use the **ContinuousScroll** property when the document will not fit in the visible region of the container. If this property is False, the container repaints the document when the user releases the mouse button. If it is True, the container repaints the document as the user moves the scroll bar.

➤ The **MinHeight** and **MinWidth** properties establish the minimum height and width for the document, respectively.

➤ The **ViewportHeight**, **ViewportLeft**, **ViewportTop**, and **ViewportWidth** properties return the position and size of the container's Viewport. These properties are read-only at runtime.

Events

➤ Container applications download ActiveX documents asynchronously. When the downloading of a document is complete, the **AsyncReadComplete** event occurs.

➤ The **Initialize** event occurs whenever a container creates an instance of an ActiveX document.

➤ The **InitProperties** event occurs after the **Initialize** event when the document is sited on its container.

➤ The **ReadProperties** event occurs after the **Initialize** event and only for an already-saved document.

➤ The **Terminate** event occurs just before a container destroys the ActiveX document instance.

➤ The **Show** event occurs when the user opens an already-sited ActiveX document. It also occurs when the user clicks the Forward or Back buttons on Internet Explorer.

➤ The **Hide** event occurs before the **Terminate** event takes place, when Internet Explorer terminates, or when the user navigates to a different document.

Methods

➤ Calling the **AsyncRead** method begins an asynchronous read from a source. The source can be a file or URL.

➤ The **CancelAsyncRead** method cancels a request made by the **AsyncRead** method.

➤ The **SetViewport** method sets the left and top coordinates of the UserDocument object that will be visible in the container's Viewport.

The process of creating an ActiveX document is almost the same as the process of creating a form or other visible object. You use controls on the toolbox to create control instances on the visual designer for the UserDocument object. In the Mid Pacific Bank example, you will develop a program to compute the monthly payment for a loan. The user will supply input values to specify the amount, term, and interest rate for the loan.

To create an ActiveX document project:

1. Start Visual Basic, if necessary, and then click on New Project on the File menu if the New Project dialog box does not appear. On the New Project dialog box, click on ActiveX Document Dll and then click on Open. Visual Basic creates the project, and the User Documents module category appears in Project Explorer.

2. Open the visual designer for the default UserDocument object and open the Properties window, if necessary. Set the **Name** property to **docLoan**.

3. Save the project. Save the document as Chapter.13\Startup\docLoan.dob and save the project as Chapter.13\Startup\Ch13_S.vbp. Set the drive designator as necessary.

An ActiveX document is similar to a form in many ways. For example, the user interacts with the control instances created on the User document. The User document can display forms and dialog boxes. In addition, it can have menus.

ActiveX Document Menus

ActiveX document menus appear on the menu bar of the container rather than on the menu bar of the document. In fact, an ActiveX document has no menu bar. Most containers (Internet Explorer and Office Binder) have their own menus, and the menu for an ActiveX document you create becomes integrated with the menu of the container application.

The **NegotiatePosition** property defines how the menu of the ActiveX document will be integrated into the container's menu. Only menu titles are negotiable (can be integrated). Menus can be negotiated in four different ways:

➤ **0 – None (Default)** The menu will not appear on the container's menu bar.

➤ **1 – Left** The menu appears on the left side of the container's menu bar. In the case of Internet Explorer, this menu will appear after the File menu.

➤ **2 – Middle** The menu appears in the center of the container's menu bar.

➤ **3 – Right** The menu appears on the right side of the container's menu bar.

To illustrate menu negotiation between an ActiveX document and its container, you will create a menu for the UserDocument object. The commands on this menu will respond to a **Click** event in exactly the same way that a menu command responds for a form. That is, when the user clicks a menu command, Windows generates a **Click** event, and the code in the corresponding event procedure executes.

To illustrate these concepts, you will create a simple menu that will negotiate with Internet Explorer's menu. One menu command will compute the results of the loan, another will save the current loan information, and a third will display an About box.

To create a menu for a UserDocument object:

1. Activate the visual designer for the UserDocument object, if necessary. The visual designer looks like the visual designer for an ActiveX control and is activated by clicking on the View Object button on the Project Explorer.

2. Click on Tools on the Visual Basic menu bar, and then click on Menu Editor. Next, you will create the menu shown in Figure 13.2.

3. As shown in Figure 13.2, two menu titles contain the captions Loan and Help. Set the **Name** property of these titles to **mnuLoan** and **mnuHelp**, respectively. Set the **NegotiatePosition** property to **3 – Right** for both menu titles.

13

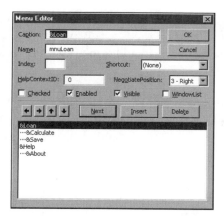

Figure 13.2 ActiveX document menu.

4. The menu titles contain menu commands with the captions Calculate, Save, and About. Set the **Name** property of these menus to **mnuLoanCalculate**, **mnuLoanSave**, and **mnuHelpAbout**, respectively.

5. Click OK to close the Menu Editor. The menu bar does not appear in the ActiveX document visual designer.

6. Add the About form by clicking on Add Form on the Project menu, and then add the existing form named Chapter.13\Startup\frmAbout.frm.

7. In the Code window for the ActiveX document, create the following event procedure to display the About form as a modal form:

```
Private  Sub mnuHelpAbout_Click()
    frmAbout.Show vbModal
End Sub
```

This code will display a modal form when the user clicks the About command on the Help menu. Although you have used menus to display forms previously, the menu on the container has a much different appearance. As you will see, the Loan and Help menus will be integrated in the menu of the container.

As the next step in the process, you will create the objects on the User document and write the code for the menu commands. The user interacts with the control instances created on a User document in the same way as he or she would interact with control instances created on a form.

To create the objects on the User document:

1. Create the control instances on the User document, as shown in Figure 13.3, setting the captions as necessary. These control instances consist of four labels used as prompts, three text boxes to store the loan amount, term, and interest rate, and an output label to store the payment. Set the **Name**

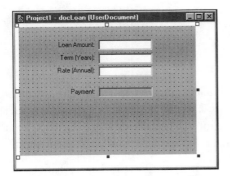

Figure 13.3   UserDocument visual designer.

property of the text boxes to **txtLoanAmount**, **txtTerm**, and **txtRate**, respectively. Set the name of the output label to **lblPayment**.

2. For each text box, set the **Text** property to an empty string. For the label named **lblPayment**, set the **BorderStyle** property to **1 − Fixed Single** and the **Caption** property to an empty string.

3. You activate the Code window for a User document in the same way as you do for a form. Select the docLoan User document in the Project Explorer and click on the View Code button. Declare the following variables in the general declarations of the User document code module:

```
Private msngLoanAmount As Single
Private mintTermYears As Integer
Private mintTermMonths As Integer
Private msngRateYears As Single
Private msngRateMonths As Single
```

These variables will store hidden information pertaining to properties.

4. Enter the following code in the event procedure named **mnuLoanCalculate_Click** to calculate the payment on a loan:

```
Dim psngPayment As Single
If IsNumeric(txtLoanAmount) And IsNumeric(txtTerm) _
    And IsNumeric(txtRate) Then
    msngLoanAmount = CSng(txtLoanAmount)
    mintTermYears = CInt(txtTerm)
    msngRateYears = CSng(txtRate)
    mintTermMonths = mintTermYears * 12
    msngRateMonths = msngRateYears / 12
    psngPayment = Pmt(msngRateMonths, _
        mintTermMonths, txtLoanAmount)
    lblPayment = Format(psngPayment, "Currency")
```

1Ǝ

```
        Else
            Call MsgBox("Invalid input", vbInformation + _
                vbOKOnly)
        End If
```

The variable declarations you just created convert and store the validated input from the input text boxes. Later, you will use them to create hidden variables that will be used by Property procedures. The implementation matches the one you used when you created your own ActiveX control and class modules.

The code to compute the loan payment first validates the input fields. If the data are valid, it computes the loan payment. The computations to calculate the payment convert the term of the loan and interest rate to express the values in months instead of years. The code then stores the converted values in the variables **mintTermMonths** and **msngRateMonths**. Next, it calls the **Pmt** function to compute the loan payment amount. If the input data are invalid, the code displays a modal dialog box (message box). In a DLL or EXE document, you can display modal dialog boxes as necessary; you cannot, however, display modeless forms from an ActiveX Document DLL project.

At this point, you have created a very basic ActiveX document. If you ran the program, however, you would not see a visible window inside Visual Basic because ActiveX documents are not standalone applications. Rather, you would see them displayed inside a container such as Internet Explorer.

Executing An ActiveX Document

A control instance cannot exist by itself. Instead, the developer creates a control instance on a form, and the form acts as a container. This process is called *siting*. When a control instance is sited on a form, the control's properties and methods become available to the container. In other words, the developer can set the properties of the control instance and write code in the Code window to respond to the events.

The concept of siting extends beyond ActiveX controls. In Visual Basic, you create control instances on the User document. The User document does not become visible at runtime until it is sited on a container, just as a control instance does not become visible until it is sited on a form.

Several activities occur when an ActiveX document is sited on its container:

➤ The **Parent** property supported by the ActiveX document contains a reference to the container—usually a reference to Internet Explorer or Office Binder.

➤ The properties supported by the ActiveX document become available to the container.

➤ ActiveX documents support persistent properties though their containers. The **InitProperties** and **ReadProperties** events occur just as they do for ActiveX controls. You can write code to respond to these events. Such code typically reads and writes persistent properties from and to the PropertyBag object.

The process of testing an ActiveX document differs dramatically from the process of testing ActiveX controls and code components. Although you create and edit the design-time User document in Visual Basic, you cannot view the running document from Visual Basic. Rather, you must start an instance of a container application, such as Internet Explorer, and load the document into the container's Viewport. Fortunately, Visual Basic performs this task automatically.

Before you learn how to load an ActiveX document into a container application, you should know that an ActiveX document project will compile into either a DLL or EXE server that will likely contain multiple User documents. Visual Basic creates a document file (VBD file) for each User document in the project. Each VBD file is tightly coupled with the accompanying DLL or EXE file. The location of each file is significant. When you compile the document into a DLL or EXE file, the accompanying VBD file is written to the same directory as the project. When you distribute the project, you need to distribute the DLL files as well as the VBD files.

When you run an ActiveX document project inside the Visual Basic IDE, however, Visual Basic creates the corresponding VBD file in the directory where Visual Basic is installed, which may vary from computer to computer. If a project included two UserDocument objects, for example, Visual Basic would create two VBD files. In addition, when the project runs, Visual Basic creates temporary entry in the Windows Registry so that other programs, such as Office Binder, can locate the document. When you toggle from run mode to design mode, Visual Basic will destroy the temporary copy of the VBD file.

If you have created an association for the file type, you can run the VBD file by clicking on it. Note that VBD files can be associated only with Internet Explorer or Office Binder. When you run an ActiveX document project inside the Visual Basic development environment, the VBD file is created in the root directory of the Visual Basic development environment. By default, the path name for Visual Basic is C:\Program Files\Microsoft Visual Studio\VB98.

Testing The Document
The following steps display a document in a container and test it interactively with the Visual Basic runtime environment:

1. Run the Visual Basic document project, which causes the VBD file to be written in the Visual Basic installation directory.

2. Visual Basic will start Internet Explorer as the container application and load the VBD file.

3. If necessary, start the container application.

4. Load the VBD file in the container. For example, to load the VBD file in Internet Explorer, you enter the file name in the Address list box.

Significant differences exist between debugging an ActiveX document and debugging a Standard EXE project. Although you can set breakpoints in the ActiveX document, run the project, and then enter break mode, ending the program in Visual Basic will typically generate errors in the container application. These errors occur because when Visual Basic enters run mode, it creates the VBD file only temporarily. When Visual Basic switches between run mode and break mode, the contents of the VBD file persist. When Visual Basic enters design mode, however, it destroys the corresponding VBD file with the temporary entry in the Windows Registry. As a result, the container application cannot locate the document. Visual Basic can detect whether a container such as Internet Explorer is referencing the file and can display a message to alert the user that the document is in use.

Because Visual Basic allows you to toggle back and forth between run and break mode, you can set breakpoints, examine the values of variables and properties, and perform any other debugging tasks. You cannot, however, make changes that will require Visual Basic to enter design mode without affecting the container application. In this situation, you must rerun the program and reload the VBD file from the container application.

The visible area of the container application where the ActiveX document is displayed is called the Viewport. If the ActiveX document will not fit in the Viewport, the container will display scroll bars allowing the user to navigate to different parts of the document.

To display (site) an ActiveX document in Internet Explorer:

1. Test the program. The Project Properties dialog box may appear. If it does, make sure that the Start component option button is selected, and then click on OK to close the dialog box.

2. Depending on the configuration of your system, the File Download dialog box may appear, requesting that you choose how Internet Explorer should execute the file. Click Open This File From Its Current Location, and then click on OK to close the dialog box and display the document in Internet Explorer.

3. Enter the following information in the text boxes: a loan amount of 100000 for 30 years at 10 percent (.10). Using the commands pertaining to the ActiveX document that are integrated on the menu bar for Internet

Explorer, click on Calculate on the Loan menu. The code you wrote in the User document calculates and displays the result, which is a payment of $877.57.

4. Activate Visual Basic, and then end the loan program. A warning message, as shown in Figure 13.4, indicates that a container presently is using the application. Click No to continue running the program.

5. Activate Internet Explorer, and then exit the loan program.

6. Activate Visual Basic, and then end the loan program. Because the container is no longer using your application, the warning message does not appear.

If you end the loan program without first closing the container application that is using the document, an error likely will occur in the container because it can no longer reference the VBD file. The error may be severe enough that the container will exit. The actual behavior will vary depending on the container and its version.

Lifetime Of An ActiveX Document

In many ways, an ActiveX document is similar to a form; in other ways, it works more like the UserControl object used to create ActiveX controls. When examining an ActiveX document runtime instance, you must take into account the container application. When Internet Explorer loads an ActiveX document for the first time, a set of events pertaining to initialization occurs. Because Internet Explorer maintains a cache of documents, however, these events do not always take place as the user moves back and forth between ActiveX documents, because one or both documents can remain in the cache and be loaded from that cache. Loading from the cache circumvents the initialization events. Nevertheless, specific events will always occur each time that a container displays or hides a document.

Consider the following sequence of events that occurs as the user navigates between one document and another using Internet Explorer:

➤ When Internet Explorer loads a document for the first time, the **Initialize** and **InitProperties** events occur, in that order. Next, the **Show** event occurs.

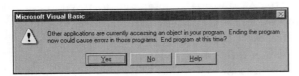

Figure 13.4   Warning message.

➤ When Internet Explorer loads a document that has been saved, the **Initialize** and **ReadProperties** events occur, in that order. Next, the **Show** event occurs.

➤ When navigating between cached documents, only the **Show** event occurs.

➤ The **Hide** event occurs when the container navigates to another document.

➤ When the container removes the document from the cache, the **Terminate** event occurs.

To illustrate the use of the **InitProperties** event, you will assign initial values to the input text boxes the first time Internet Explorer loads the VBD file.

To initialize the UserDocument object:

1. Enter the following statements in the **UserDocument_InitProperties** event procedure of docLoan:

```
txtLoanAmount = 100000
txtTerm = 30
txtRate = 0.1
```

2. Test the program. Internet Explorer loads the VBD file, and the text boxes assume initial values because of the statements in the **InitProperties** event procedure.

3. Exit Internet Explorer and, in Visual Basic, end the loan program.

At this point, the three text boxes contain initial values. You can also make these values persist between invocations of Internet Explorer.

Persistent Properties

When working with properties, an ActiveX document functions much like an ActiveX control. You define properties by creating **Property Get** and **Property Let** procedures. A container can initialize properties when it creates an instance of the User document. To make properties persistent, you respond to the **ReadProperties** and **WriteProperties** events to read data from and store data in the PropertyBag object, respectively.

When you created an ActiveX control, the container (form window) saved the persistent properties into the form file that used the control. The actual task of saving the form file to disk and reading the form file (module) was the responsibility of the container rather than the control itself. Your ActiveX control told the container that a property should be persistent through the PropertyBag object, and it informed the container that the value of a particular property had changed.

The same process occurs when an ActiveX document is displayed inside a container such as Internet Explorer, because the VBD file is not an executable file but rather is an OLE structured storage. OLE uses this type of file to combine data with program information.

To illustrate the use of persistent properties, you will allow the user of the Mid Pacific Bank program to save the input parameters of the current loan to disk. When the ActiveX document reloads, the values will be read and displayed in the appropriate document fields. This task involves defining the three properties for the three input values, writing those properties to the PropertyBag before destroying the document, and reading them when a container creates an instance of the document.

To create persistent properties:

1. Create the following **Property** procedures in the UserDocument object named docLoan:

```
Property Let LoanAmount(psngAmount As Single)
    msngLoanAmount = psngAmount
    LoanAmount = msngLoanAmount
End Property

Property Get LoanAmount() As Single
    LoanAmount = msngLoanAmount
End Property

Property Let TermYears(psngAmount As Single)
    mintTermYears = psngAmount
    TermYears = mintTermYears
End Property

Property Get TermYears() As Single
    TermYears = mintTermYears
End Property

Property Let RateYears(psngAmount As Single)
    msngRateYears = psngAmount
    RateYears = msngRateYears
End Property

Property Get RateYears() As Single
    RateYears = msngRateYears
End Property
```

13

2. Enter the following statements in the **UserDocument_ReadProperties** event procedure for docLoan:

```
msngLoanAmount = PropBag.ReadProperty("LoanAmount")
mintTermYears = PropBag.ReadProperty("TermYears")
msngRateYears = PropBag.ReadProperty("RateYears")
txtLoanAmount = msngLoanAmount
txtTerm = mintTermYears
txtRate = msngRateYears
```

3. Enter the following statement in the **UserDocument_WriteProperties** event for docLoan:

```
PropBag.WriteProperty "LoanAmount", CSng(txtLoanAmount)
PropBag.WriteProperty "TermYears", CInt(txtTerm)
PropBag.WriteProperty "RateYears", CSng(txtRate)
```

4. Enter the following statements in the **mnuLoanSave_Click** event procedure:

```
UserDocument.PropertyChanged "LoanAmount"
UserDocument.PropertyChanged "TermYears"
UserDocument.PropertyChanged "RateYears"
```

5. Test the program. Internet Explorer starts and displays the VBD file. Change the contents of each of the three text boxes, and then click on Save on the Loan menu. This action notifies Internet Explorer that the properties have changed.

6. Try to exit Internet Explorer. The dialog box shown in Figure 13.5 appears.

7. Click Yes to save the changes, and Internet Explorer will exit. Do not end the program in Visual Basic.

8. Start Internet Explorer again and reload the VBD file. Remember that Visual Basic temporarily creates the docLoan.vbd file in the default Visual Basic folder, typically C:\Program Files\Microsoft Visual Studio\VB98. Note that the changes persist from one invocation to the next.

9. Close Internet Explorer, and end the program in Visual Basic.

Figure 13.5   Save changes message.

As you can see from the interaction between Internet Explorer and your ActiveX document, Internet Explorer (the container) saves the persistent properties rather than the User document itself. These changes are saved to the VBD file. It also should be evident that once the container has saved a document, the **ReadProperties** event occurs instead of the **InitProperties** event. Remember, the **InitProperties** event contained code to set the initial input values for the document. The code in the **ReadProperties** event contains code to read the values of already-saved properties. Had the **InitProperties** event occurred, the values of the input text boxes would have contained the initial values rather than the changed values.

The technique used to implement the three properties and make them persistent is the same as the one used to make ActiveX control properties persistent in Chapter 11. The **Property** procedures **LoanAmount**, **TermYears**, and **RateYears** implement the three read–write properties. To inform the container that a property has been changed, you write code that calls the **PropertyChanged** event with one argument—a string containing the name of the property. The **ReadProperties** and **WriteProperties** events occur for the User document just as they did for an ActiveX control.

Not all containers support the PropertyBag object. Presently, only Internet Explorer and Office Binder do so. To implement persistent properties without the PropertyBag object, you must read and write text files.

Multiple ActiveX Document Applications

Just as many projects consist of multiple forms, ActiveX document applications often include several User document modules. Three significant differences exist between a Standard EXE project and an ActiveX document project:

➤ Standard EXE projects have a known beginning. That is, the developer can control which form appears first in an application.

➤ The user of a form-based application navigates from one form to another by clicking on buttons that explicitly display different forms, typically by your code calling the form's **Show** method. The user of your ActiveX document project can display any document at any time, just as he or she can activate any document on the Web in any order by selecting its URL, even if the document was intended to be displayed in a particular order relative to other documents.

➤ The methods to navigate between documents depend on the container in which the application is sited. Internet Explorer uses the **NavigateTo** method pertaining to the Hyperlink object, and the Microsoft Office Binder application uses sections in a binder.

Internet Explorer Navigation

To navigate between User documents, you can also use command buttons and write code that executes in response to the button's **Click** events. These buttons do not prevent the user from explicitly referencing a specific document. They merely provide an additional means of navigation.

To locate a different ActiveX document or URL, you use the methods pertaining to the Hyperlink object.

Syntax

  object.**GoBack**
  object.**GoForward**
  object.**NavigateTo Target** [, Location [, FrameName]]/

Dissection

➤ The **object** must be a valid instance of the Hyperlink object.

➤ The **GoBack** method locates the previous URL.

➤ The **GoForward** method locates the next URL.

➤ The **NavigateTo** method locates a specific URL specified by **Target** and **Location**.

➤ The **Target** must contain a valid URL to access. If the **Target** is invalid, an error will occur, which you can trap.

➤ The **Location** is the location within the **Target** URL to which to jump.

➤ If the URL contains frames, the **FrameName** argument specifies the frame within the URL.

Code Example

```
UserDocument.Hyperlink.GoBack
UserDocument.Hyperlink.GoForward
UserDocument.Hyperlink.NavigateTo _
    cstrPath & "docApply.vbd"
```

Code Dissection

The first two statements use the Hyperlink object to locate the previous and next URLs, respectively. The final statement locates a specific URL—the ActiveX document stored in the VBD file named docApply.vbd. These statements assume that Internet Explorer is the container application. They also assume that the variable **cstrPath** contains the full path name of the document docApply.vbd.

To use this concept with the program for Mid Pacific Bank, assume that the payment calculation form is merely one of several services that the bank wants to make available to its customers. In addition, the bank would like to provide users with the option of completing a preliminary loan application that will ultimately be sent to a customer services representative. The process of navigating between documents is the same, regardless of the particular document's contents. Thus you will create a second User document that will contain a prototype for what would eventually be expanded into a loan application form. In addition, you will enhance the existing payment calculation form so that the user can navigate from one document to another, and you will write code to locate the previous and next documents in the container's cache.

ActiveX document projects support standard modules. You can create general procedures and declare variables in a standard module just as you have in other programs. In the example for Mid Pacific Bank, the user will navigate between two ActiveX documents stored on the local machine. To reduce typing, your code will store the path name of the Visual Basic root directory as a constant in a standard module.

A second ActiveX document, which contains a prototype for a loan application, has been created for you. In the chapter's program, nothing is done with any data entered by the user, because the purpose of the form is to illustrate navigation between documents.

To perform document navigation using the Hyperlink object:

1. Add a standard module to the project. Setting the drive designator as necessary, save it as Chapter.13\Startup\Standard.bas. Enter the following statement in the module, changing the path name as necessary if you have installed Visual Basic in a different folder:

```
Public Const cstrPath = _
    "C:\Program Files\Microsoft Visual Studio\VB98\"
```

2. Save the standard module. On the UserDocument form named docLoan, create three command buttons, as shown in Figure 13.6.

3. Set the captions as shown in Figure 13.6, and then set the **Name** properties of the buttons to **cmdBack**, **cmdForward**, and **cmdApply**, respectively.

4. Click Add User Document on the Project menu, select the Existing tab, and then double-click on the existing UserDocument object named docApply.dob from the Chapter.13\Startup folder. This document contains the same user interface as the document you used in the completed example.

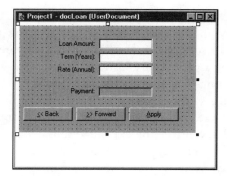

Figure 13.6 UserDocument command buttons.

5. Click References on the Project menu, and then click on the Microsoft Binder 8.0 Object Library checkbox. You will use these objects to reference the Office Binder and its objects later in this chapter. Click OK to close the dialog box.

6. On both UserDocument objects, enter the following code in the **cmdBack_Click** and **cmdForward_Click** event procedures as follows:

```
Private Sub cmdBack_Click()
On Error GoTo NoBack
    UserDocument.Hyperlink.GoBack
    Exit Sub
NoBack:
End Sub

Private Sub cmdForward_Click()
On Error GoTo NoForward
    UserDocument.Hyperlink.GoForward
    Exit Sub
NoForward:
End Sub
```

7. On the UserDocument object named docLoan, enter the following statement in the **cmdApply_Click** event procedure:

```
UserDocument.Hyperlink.NavigateTo _
    cstrPath & "docApply.vbd"
```

8. On the UserDocument object named docApply, enter the following statement in the **cmdLoan_Click** event procedure:

```
UserDocument.Hyperlink.NavigateTo _
    cstrPath & "docLoan.vbd"
```

9. Test the program. Internet Explorer starts and loads the file named docLoan. Click Apply, which causes the loan application document to be loaded and displayed. Click the Back command button and then the Forward command button to locate the previous and next documents, respectively.

10. Exit Internet Explorer and, in Visual Basic, end the program.

These statements illustrate the methods supported by the Hyperlink object. The constant declaration makes the path name of the Visual Basic document files available to the rest of the program.

Consider the following code:

```
On Error GoTo NoBack
    UserDocument.Hyperlink.GoBack
    Exit Sub
NoBack:
```

The preceding statements execute when the user clicks the Back button. Syntactically, the UserDocument object's Hyperlink property contains a reference to a Hyperlink object. The **GoBack** method pertaining to the Hyperlink object locates the previous URL. Both the **cmdBack_Click** and **cmdForward_Click** event procedures implement an error handler. If no previous or next document exists in the document history, a runtime error occurs, which the event procedures trap.

The syntax of the **NavigateTo** method is straightforward:

```
UserDocument.Hyperlink.NavigateTo _
    cstrPath & "docApply.vbd"
```

The **NavigateTo** method accepts one argument—a URL to locate. In this example, concatenating the path name of Visual Basic to the name of the document file defines the **URL** argument.

Controlling Navigation

The solution you just implemented allows the user to navigate from one document to another, but it does not prevent the user from displaying documents in an unintended order. In some applications, this scenario is not a problem. Consider, however, a situation in which a Mid Pacific Bank customer should see a disclaimer document (UserDocument) before accessing the other documents. Although ActiveX documents themselves do not provide this functionality, you can declare a global object variable in a standard module to solve the problem.

Assume that the UserDocument project contains the following declaration:

```
Public gdocInit As Object
```

Remember that a global variable references Nothing until an object has been assigned to it. Thus, when the startup or disclaimer document displays, an assignment statement can store a reference to the startup object. To accomplish this task, you place code in the **Click** event procedure, as shown in the following statements:

```
Private Sub Command1_Click()
    Set gdocInit = Me
    UserDocument.Hyperlink.NavigateTo _
        cstrPath & "docLoan.vbd"
End Sub
```

Each of the other User documents needs statements to determine whether the user activated the startup object. You can accomplish this task by having code in the User document check whether the global variable references a valid object or Nothing, as shown in the following statements:

```
Private Sub UserDocument_Show()
    If gdocInit Is Nothing Then
        UserDocument.Hyperlink.NavigateTo _
            cstrPath & "docInit.vbd"
    End If
End Sub
```

Understanding The Viewport

Because another application (container) displays an ActiveX document, the user can arbitrarily resize the container at any time. The Viewport is the visible area of the container application that displays the ActiveX document. By default, scroll bars will appear if the ActiveX document will not fit in the visible region of the Viewport.

In the Mid Pacific Bank example, the loan application form will not fit in the region of the Viewport. A vertical scroll bar therefore appears, allowing the user to scroll through the document. As the user enters data into the various text boxes, however, he or she will eventually tab to a text box that is not visible in the Viewport, and the container will not automatically scroll to make the text box with focus visible. This situation may confuse the user of your program, because the insertion point will seemingly disappear.

To solve this problem, you can write code that calls the **SetViewport** method to ensure that the object with focus remains visible in the Viewport.

Syntax

object.SetViewport left, top

Dissection

➤ The **object** must be an instance of the UserDocument object.

➤ The **SetViewport** method sets the left and top coordinates of the Viewport.

➤ The required **left** argument contains the left coordinate of the UserDocument object.

➤ The required **top** argument contains the top coordinate of the UserDocument object.

Code Example

```
UserDocument.SetViewport 0, txtApply(Index).Top
```

Code Dissection

This statement positions the ActiveX document in the Viewport such that the top of the Viewport displays the text box that currently has focus. **txtApply** is assumed to be a control array of text boxes, and Index contains the text box that currently has focus.

You can use the previous statement in the **GotFocus** event for each text box in the ActiveX document to cause the text box that currently has focus to appear in the Viewport.

13

To control the Viewport:

1. Enter the following statement in the **txtApply_GotFocus** event procedure for docApply:

```
UserDocument.SetViewport 0, txtApply(Index).Top
```

2. Test the program. Visual Basic and Internet Explorer load the document named docLoan. Click the Apply command button to display the document named docApply. Press the Tab key repeatedly, noticing that the text box with focus appears at the top of the Viewport.

3. Exit Internet Explorer and, in Visual Basic, end the program.

In this section, you have seen how an ActiveX document interacts with Internet Explorer as a container. In the next section, you will see how to use the Office Binder application as a container.

Using The Office Binder As An ActiveX Document Container

Office Binder As A Container

In this section, you will learn how to display an ActiveX document using Office Binder as a container. Office Binder is a container application that displays and organizes other documents.

The Office Binder application groups Microsoft Office data files, including Word documents, Excel spreadsheets, PowerPoint presentations, and ActiveX documents created by Visual Basic. Figure 13.7 shows the Office Binder application with three documents—a Word document, an Excel spreadsheet, and a Visual Basic ActiveX document.

As shown in Figure 13.7, Office Binder has two panes. The left pane lists the documents that are part of the current binder. In the vernacular of Office Binder, each document constitutes a section. Only one section can be visible and active at any given time. Office Binder negotiates menus between the contained application in the same manner as Internet Explorer does. That is, when a section is active, the Office Binder menu displays the menu of the contained application. For example, the Word 97 menus appear when a Word document is active.

The Internet Explorer container and the Officer Binder container manage ActiveX documents differently. When the container is Internet Explorer, your code must perform document navigation using the methods of the Hyperlink object. Office Binder, however, does not support the Hyperlink object. Consequently, if multiple containers will display an ActiveX document, you must determine which container is displaying the document and call the appropriate methods supported by that container.

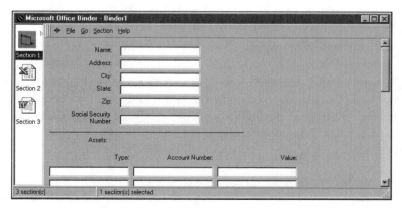

Figure 13.7 Microsoft Office Binder.

Introducing The Microsoft Office Binder

As the Microsoft Office Binder program is relatively new, you may have not used it to group ActiveX documents. The key to understanding Office Binder is knowing that each document—whether a Word document, an Excel spreadsheet, or an ActiveX document created with Visual Basic—is considered a section. Sections can be added and removed as necessary.

To preview the Office Binder application:

1. Start Microsoft Office Binder. Depending on how the Microsoft Office software was installed, Office Binder may or may not be present on your system. It typically appears on the Start menu with the other Microsoft Office applications.

2. Click Add on the Section menu to add a new section to the current binder. A dialog box may appear asking you to create a template folder. If it does appear, click on Yes. The available document types and the tabs that appear will vary depending upon the configuration of your system.

3. The Add Section dialog box lists the document types that can be added to the current binder; the appearance of the items on the General tab will depend on which view is selected. Click the Blank Document icon, and then click on OK. A new Word document is inserted in the current binder.

4. Click Add on the Section menu to add a second section to the current binder. Click the Microsoft Excel Worksheet icon, and then click on OK to add a second section to the current binder.

5. To toggle between one section and another, click on the section listed in the left pane of the current binder.

6. Click Close on the File menu to exit Office Binder. Office Binder will prompt you to save the current binder file. Click No in the dialog box.

By itself, Office Binder does very little. Instead, it serves to organize, display, and manage other documents.

Determining The Container

In its present form, the code in your program supports only Internet Explorer as the container. In this section, you will supply additional functionality to ensure that the User document code will support Office Binder as a container as well.

The first step toward providing this functionality is determining the current container in which the document is running (sited). You can write code to accomplish this task by using the **Parent** property pertaining to the UserDocument object. This property returns a string variable that indicates the container.

13

Consider the following statements:

```
Dim gstrContainer As String
gstrContainer = TypeName(UserDocument.Parent)
```

The statement fragment **UserDocument.Parent** returns a reference to the UserDocument object's container. The **TypeName** function returns a string that describes the type of a variable or object. The following list identifies the strings returned by the **TypeName** function for various containers:

➤ Internet Explorer version 3.0 has a **TypeName** of **IWebBrowserApp**.

➤ Internet Explorer versions 4.0 and 5.0 have a TypeName of IWebBrowser2.

➤ Office Binder has a TypeName of Section.

The code for all navigational buttons must be modified to determine the type of container. Depending on the type of container, the code will call different methods, as shown in the following **Select Case** statement:

```
Dim gstrContainer as String
Select Case gstrContainer
    Case "IWebBrowser2", "IWebBrowserApp"
        UserDocument.Hyperlink.GoBack
    Case "Section"
        ' Navigational code for the Binder
    Case Else
        Call MsgBox("Container not supported.")
End Select
```

This **Select Case** statement will have the same structure for all navigational buttons on the two documents. If the container is a version of Internet Explorer, the code will call the methods of the Hyperlink object. If the container is a version of Office Binder, different methods will be called to locate a specific section in the binder.

Accessing Office Binder Programmatically

The techniques to access the methods and properties of Office Binder resemble the techniques you used to manage **ADO** collections and objects. Figure 13.8 illustrates part of the Office Binder object hierarchy.

As shown in Figure 13.8, the Office Binder object is the root object containing the **Sections** collection. Every document is considered a Section object in the **Sections** collection. The **Sections** collection is a one-based collection, which supports methods to add and remove individual Section objects to and from the collection.

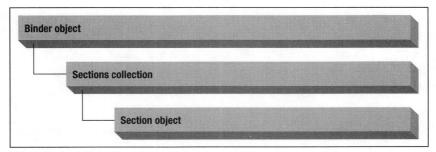

Figure 13.8 Binder objects.

To access the objects pertaining to Office Binder, you must add a reference to the object library. The process is the same as that used to add a reference to the ADO objects or to any other object library. You click on References on the Project menu, and then add the Microsoft Binder 8.0 Object Library.

The reference to an instance of the binder is made through the UserDocument object.

Referencing the root Office Binder object from the Visual Basic ActiveX document is a bit contorted. Consider the following statements:

```
Dim secCurrent As Section
Set secCurrent = UserDocument.Parent
```

These statements return the section of the current object (in this case, your ActiveX document), but do not reference the Binder object itself. The Binder object is considered the parent of a section. Thus, to reference the Binder object, you would use the following statements:

```
Dim bndCurrent As Binder
Set bndCurrent = UserDocument.Parent.Parent
```

In the Mid Pacific Bank example, you want similar functionality for the navigational buttons, regardless of the container. Whether Office Binder or Internet Explorer is the container, the Back button should locate the previous document, the Forward button should locate the next document, and the Loan and Apply buttons should display the Loan and Apply documents, respectively.

To create this functionality for both containers, you must learn a few of the methods and properties supported by the Office Binder.

13

Syntax

Binder

Properties

➤ The **ActiveSection** property identifies the Section object that currently has focus.

➤ The **Name** property is a string containing the name of the Section object.

➤ The **Sections** property contains a reference to the **Sections** collection. This collection, in turn, contains a reference to the loaded Section objects.

Methods

➤ The **Close** method closes the current binder.

➤ The **Open** method opens a new binder.

➤ The **Save** method saves the current binder.

Tightly coupled with the Office Binder object is the Section object. The Section object supports properties and methods that apply to the specific sections in the binder.

Syntax

Section

Properties

➤ The **Name** property contains the name of the Section object, excluding the path name.

➤ The **Path** property contains the fully qualified path name of the Section object.

➤ The **Parent** property contains a reference to the Parent object of the Section object—typically, the Office Binder object itself.

➤ The **Type** property contains the OLE class name of the Section object.

Methods

➤ The **Activate** method activates a Section object, causing the Section object to receive focus.

➤ The **Copy** method duplicates a Section object.

➤ The **Delete** method deletes a Section object.

In the Mid Pacific Bank program, the Back button will locate the previous Section object in the **Sections** collection. This task requires that your code determine the current Section object and then activate the previous one. The following code illustrates one possible implementation:

```
With UserDocument.Parent.Parent
    For pintCurrent = 2 To .Sections.Count
        If .Sections(pintCurrent).Name = _
            .ActiveSection.Name Then
            Set secCurrent = _
                .Sections(pintCurrent - 1)
            secCurrent.Activate
        End If
    Next
End With
```

The code fragment **UserDocument.Parent.Parent** references the binder, and the **For** loop examines each Section object in the **Sections** collection. In addition, the starting value in the **For** loop is 2 instead of 1 (the first element in the collection). If the first Section object is active, the statements in the **For** loop will never execute and the Back button will do nothing.

This code is merely one possible implementation, as it would also be reasonable to locate the last Section object if the first Section object was currently active. That is, clicking on the Back button would loop around the Section objects indefinitely. In addition, inside the **If** statement, the code would compare the **Name** property of the ActiveSection with the current item in the collection. When they were the same, the code could determine and activate the previous Section object by calling the **Activate** method on the Section object.

A similar loop can be written to program the Forward navigation button:

```
With UserDocument.Parent.Parent
    For pintCurrent = 1 To .Sections.Count - 1
        If .Sections(pintCurrent).Name = _
            .ActiveSection.Name Then
            Set secCurrent = _
                .Sections(pintCurrent + 1)
            secCurrent.Activate
        End If
    Next
End With
```

This code differs little from the previous **For** loop. In this case, the loop does not examine the last item in the collection. That is, if the last item is active, the Forward button will do nothing when clicked.

You now can modify the code for the Forward and Back buttons to accommodate both Internet Explorer and Office Binder.

To create navigational code to support multiple containers:

1. Create the following global variable in the standard module for the project:

```
Public gstrContainer As String
```

2. Enter the following statements in the **UserDocument_Show** event procedure for both User documents. These statements determine the name of the container that is siting the document.

```
If gstrContainer = vbNullString Then
    gstrContainer = TypeName(UserDocument.Parent)
End If
```

3. Modify the code in the **cmdForward_Click** event procedures for both User documents so that they contain the following statements.

```
On Error GoTo NoForward
    Dim secCurrent As Section
    Dim pintCurrent As Integer

    Select Case gstrContainer
        Case "IWebBrowser2"
            UserDocument.Hyperlink.GoForward
        Case "Section"
            With UserDocument.Parent.Parent
                For pintCurrent = 1 To _
                    .Sections.Count - 1
                    If .Sections(pintCurrent).Name = _
                        .ActiveSection.Name Then
                        Set secCurrent = _
                            .Sections(pintCurrent + 1)
                            secCurrent.Activate
                    End If
                Next
            End With
        Case Else
            Call MsgBox("Container not supported.")
    End Select
    Exit Sub
NoForward:
```

4. Modify the code in the **cmdBack_Click** event procedures for both User documents so they contain the following statements.

```
On Error GoTo NoBack
    Dim secCurrent As Section
    Dim pintCurrent As Integer
    Select Case gstrContainer
        Case "IWebBrowser2"
            UserDocument.Hyperlink.GoBack
        Case "Section"
            With UserDocument.Parent.Parent
                For pintCurrent = 2 To .Sections.Count
                    If .Sections(pintCurrent).Name = _
                        .ActiveSection.Name Then
                        Set secCurrent = _
                            .Sections(pintCurrent - 1)
                            secCurrent.Activate
                    End If
                Next
            End With
        Case Else
            Call MsgBox("Container not supported.")
    End Select
    Exit Sub
NoBack:
```

The code in the **Show** event procedure is the same for both modules:

```
If gstrContainer = vbNullString Then
    gstrContainer = TypeName(UserDocument.Parent)
End If
```

If the string describing the container application has never been set, the code determines the container by reading the type name of the UserDocument's Parent object. In the case of Office Binder, the result is the string "Section". You wrote the code in the **Show** event rather than the **Initialize** event. If you wrote the code in the **Initialize** event, the program would not work because the document is not yet sited on its container when the Initialize event occurs.

The **cmdBack_Click** and **cmdForward_Click** event procedures have very similar code. In both cases, the variable **gstrContainer** stores the string describing the container application. If the container application is Internet Explorer, the procedure uses the Hyperlink object, as shown in earlier in this chapter. If the container is Office Binder, the Back button executes the following code to change the current Section object:

```
With UserDocument.Parent.Parent
    For pintCurrent = 2 To.Sections.Count
        If .Sections(pintCurrent).Name = _
            .ActiveSection.Name Then
            Set secCurrent = .Sections(pintCurrent - 1)
            secCurrent.Activate
        End If
    Next
End With
```

The **With** statement provides a reference to the Binder object. The **For** loop examines the second through the last Section objects. For each Section object examined, the code compares the name of the Section object with the name of the active Section object (stored in the **ActiveSection** property of the Binder object). If they are the same, the statements in the **If** block cause the variable **secCurrent** to reference the previous Section object. The code then calls the **Activate** method to activate the desired Section object.

The code to locate a different document is a bit more complicated, because the desired document may or may not be an active Section object in the binder. In the Mid Pacific Bank example, the implementation of the program will ensure that a new Section object is added if the document type has not yet been added. If the document type already exists in the **Sections** collection, however, the code will set that document to be the active document. This task requires that you learn how to determine the document type and to add new documents.

The **Type** property supported by the Section object contains a string that identifies the class name of the document. For ActiveX documents, this name consists of the name of the project, followed by a period (.), followed by the name of the document. The following statement fragments indicate the fully qualified names for the two ActiveX documents in this project:

```
MPBLoan.docApply
MPBLoan.docLoan
```

If a Section object is not loaded, it must be added to the **Sections** collection. To accomplish this task, you call the **Add** method pertaining to the **Sections** collection.

Syntax

expression.Add(Type, FileName, Before, After)

Dissection

➤ The **expression** must contain a reference to the **Sections** collection.

➤ The **Add** method adds a new Section object to the collection.

➤ The **Type** argument contains the class name of the Section object to be created.

➤ The **FileName** argument contains the file name of the Section object to create. In the case of an ActiveX document, the file name can be the .vbd file on the disk.

➤ The **Before** and **After** arguments can contain a reference to a Section object. If the **Before** argument is specified, the method adds the new Section object before the current Section object. If the **After** argument is specified, the method adds the new Section object after the current Section object.

Code Example

```
UserDocument.Parent.Parent.Sections.Add _
    "MBPLoan.docApply"
```

Code Dissection

The preceding statement adds the ActiveX document having the class name MPBLoan.docApply to the current binder.

13

To locate a specific document using Office Binder as a container:

1. Replace the code in the **cmdApply_Click** event procedure for the docLoan UserDocument object with the following statements:

```
Dim secCurrent As Section
Select Case gstrContainer
    Case "IWebBrowser2"
        UserDocument.Hyperlink.NavigateTo _
            cstrPath & "docApply.vbd"
    Case "Section"
        With UserDocument.Parent.Parent
            For Each secCurrent In .Sections
                If secCurrent.Type = _
```

```
                              "MPBLoan.docApply" Then
                              secCurrent.Activate
                              Exit Sub
                          End If
                  Next
                  .Sections.Add _
                              "MPBLoan.docApply"
              End With
          Case Else
              Call MsgBox("Container not supported.")
      End Select
```

2. Replace the code in the **cmdLoan_Click** event procedure for the
   docApply UserDocument object with the following statements:

```
Dim secCurrent As Section
Select Case gstrContainer
    Case "IWebBrowser2"
        UserDocument.Hyperlink.NavigateTo _
            cstrPath & "docApply.vbd"
    Case "Section"
        With UserDocument.Parent.Parent
            For Each secCurrent In .Sections
                If secCurrent.Type _
                    = "MPBLoan.docLoan" Then
                    secCurrent.Activate
                    Exit Sub
                End If
            Next
                .Sections.Add _
                    "MPBLoan.docLoan"
        End With
    Case Else
        Call MsgBox("Container not supported.")
End Select
```

These event procedures have a structure that is similar to that of the Back and
Forward navigational procedures. Both use a **Select Case** statement to
determine the container and to execute different statements, based on the
container. The statements to locate or add a new Section object require careful
examination.

```
With UserDocument.Parent.Parent
    For Each secCurrent In .Sections
        If secCurrent.Type = "MPBLoan.docLoan" Then
            secCurrent.Activate
```

```
        Exit Sub
    End If
Next
    .Sections.Add _
        "MPBLoan.docLoan"
End With
```

The **With** statement provides the reference to the Office Binder object. The **For** loop examines each Section object in the **Sections** collection to determine whether a Section object having the correct class has been loaded. If the code finds the Section object, it activates the object and the event procedure exits. If the code does not find the Section object, it adds the object to the collection by calling the **Add** method.

Testing Office Binder

The easiest way to test the Mid Pacific Bank application is to compile it into an Automation server so that it is properly registered on the system. As you will see in a moment, Office Binder uses the information in the Registry to determine which types of documents it can load.

To compile the project:

1. Click Project, and then click on Project1 Properties. On the General tab of the Project Properties dialog box, set the Project Name to MPBLoan. Click OK.

2. Close all Visual Basic windows except Project Explorer. Save the project.

3. Click Make Ch13_S.dll on the File menu.

4. Save the DLL in the Chapter.13\Startup folder, with the default name. These steps register the DLL server on the system. You now can start the Office Binder application and load the different documents.

5. Start Office Binder.

6. Click Add on the Section menu to activate the Add Section dialog box, and then click on List view.

7. Click MPBLoan.docApply, and then click on OK to add the Section object. The document will appear in Office Binder just as it appeared in Internet Explorer.

8. Scroll to the bottom of the document, and then click on Loan Payment. The loan document will appear in a new Section object.

9. Click the Forward and Back buttons to navigate between the two documents.

10. Exit Office Binder, but do not save the changes.

11. Exit Visual Basic.

As you can see, the documents appear in Office Binder just as they do in Internet Explorer. The only real difference relates to the methods used for navigation.

CHAPTER SUMMARY

This chapter presented the fundamental techniques used to manage ActiveX documents with multiple containers.

To create an ActiveX document project:

➤ Create a new ActiveX Document DLL or EXE project.

➤ Add User document modules as necessary, representing each document to be displayed in a container.

➤ Create menus for each User document module. These menus will be integrated with the container based upon the setting of the **NegotiatePosition** property.

➤ Create the text and navigational control instances as necessary.

➤ Test the program by running it. Internet Explorer will automatically act as the project's container.

To initialize properties for a User document:

➤ Set the properties of constituent controls in the **InitProperties** event procedure.

To create persistent properties:

➤ Read and write data from and to the PropertyBag object using the **ReadProperty** and **WriteProperty** methods. Call these methods from the **ReadProperties** and **WriteProperties** events, respectively.

To navigate between documents when Internet Explorer is the container:

➤ Call the following navigational methods:

```
object.GoBack
object.GoForward
object.NavigateTo Target [, Location [, FrameName]]/
```

To change the visible portion of the Viewport:

➤ Call the SetViewport method:

```
object.SetViewport left, top
```

REVIEW QUESTIONS

1. Which of the following statements about menus, as they pertain to ActiveX documents, is true?
   a. The menus for an ActiveX document appear on the menu for the container rather than on the document itself.
   b. The use of the **NegotiatePosition** property controls how menus are integrated with the container.
   c. ActiveX documents do not support menus.
   d. Both a and b.
   e. All of the above.

2. Which of the following statements regarding ActiveX Document DLL projects is true?
   a. They can display modal forms.
   b. They can display modeless forms.
   c. They can display dialog boxes.
   d. Both a and c
   e. Both b and c

3. The interaction between the menus on an ActiveX document and the container's program is referred to as _____.
   a. combination menus
   b. compatible menus
   c. menu synchronization
   d. menu negotiation
   e. None of the above

4. Which of the following is a valid file extension for files pertaining to an ActiveX document?
   a. .doc
   b. .dox
   c. .vbd
   d. Both a and b
   e. All of the above

5. The events pertaining to an ActiveX document occur in which order?

   a. **Initialize, InitProperties, Show**

   b. **Initialize, ReadProperties, Show**

   c. **Initialize, Load, Show**

   d. Both a and b

   e. Both b and c

6. Which of the following methods is supported by the Hyperlink object?

   a. **GoBack**

   b. **Link**

   c. **Jump**

   d. Both a and b

   e. All of the above

7. Write the statements to navigate forward to a "next" document. The statements you write should check whether Internet Explorer is the current container.

8. Write the statements to locate the URL named Chapter.13\Question\docDemo. Assume that Internet Explorer is the current container.

9. Write the statement to locate the coordinates 0,0 in the Viewport.

10. Which of the following is a valid container application for ActiveX documents?

   a. Office Binder

   b. Internet Explorer

   c. Word

   d. Both a and b

   e. All of the above

11. The individual documents stored in the binder are called _____.

   a. Hyperlinks

   b. Page objects

   c. ADO objects

   d. Section objects

   e. Document objects

12. Office Binder can display and group _____ documents.

    a. Word

    b. ActiveX

    c. Excel

    d. Both a and b

    e. All of the above

13. The **Type** property as it pertains to a Section object contains _____.

    a. the file name of the Section object

    b. an Integer

    c. the OLE class name of the Section object

    d. None of the above

    e. All of the above

14. What is the name of the method used to set the position of an ActiveX document in the Viewport?

    a. **SetViewport**

    b. **Top**

    c. **Left**

    d. **Viewport**

    e. None of the above

15. Which of the following is a valid string for the Internet Explorer and Office Binder containers?

    a. IWebBrowser2

    b. IWebBrowserApp

    c. Section

    d. Both a and b

    e. All of the above

13

16. Create an event procedure that will set the Viewport to the top-left corner of an ActiveX document when the command button named cmdHome is clicked.

17. Write the statement to determine the container of a UserDocument object. Store the string in the variable named **gstrDemo**.

18. With the UserDocument objects as a reference, write the statement to reference an Office Binder object and to store the reference in the object variable named **bndCurrent**.

19. Write a **For Each** loop to print the **Type** (class name) of all Section objects in the binder. Use the UserDocument object to obtain a reference to the binder.

HANDS-ON PROJECTS

Project 1

In this project, you will create an ActiveX document project that can be displayed by Internet Explorer.

a. Create a new project ActiveX Document DLL named Chapter.13\Exercise\Ex1.vbp.

b. Create three ActiveX documents named docIE1, docIE2, and docIE3.

c. On each ActiveX document, create four command buttons. The first two buttons should locate the previous and next documents. Make sure to create an error handler in case no previous or next document exists.

d. The second two command buttons should locate the other two documents. That is, the two command buttons on the docIE2 should locate docIE1 and docIE3, respectively.

e. Test the program. Start Internet Explorer and test the navigational methods of the three forms. Close Internet Explorer, end the program, and exit Visual Basic.

Project 2

In this project, you will create an ActiveX document project that can be used by Office Binder.

a. Create a new project ActiveX Document DLL named Chapter.13\Exercise\Ex2.vbp.

b. Create three ActiveX documents named docBind1, docBind2, and docBind3.

c. On each ActiveX document, create four command buttons. The first two buttons should locate the previous and next documents in the **Sections** collection. The second two command buttons should activate the other two documents. That is, the two command buttons on the docBind2 should activate docBind1 and docBind3, respectively.

d. Compile the project into an ActiveX DLL server and set the project name to Exercise2.

e. Start Office Binder. Add each of the three documents to the current binder and test the navigational command buttons. Close Office Binder, end the program, and exit Visual Basic.

Project 3

In this project, you will create an ActiveX document project that can be used by both Internet Explorer and Office Binder.

a. Create a new project ActiveX Document DLL named Chapter.13\ Exercise\Ex3.vbp.

b. Create three ActiveX documents named docBind1, docBind2, and docBind3.

c. On each ActiveX document, create four command buttons. The first two buttons should locate the previous and next documents. You must write code to determine the current container and, based on that information, call the appropriate navigational methods.

d. Create the second two command buttons, which should activate the other two documents.

e. Set the project name to Exercise3. Change the documents named in Step b to docIEBind1, docIEBind2, and docIEBind3.

Test the program using both Internet Explorer and Office Binder as containers. After each test, close the respective container, end the program, and then exit Visual Basic.

CHAPTER FOURTEEN

USING INTERNET CONTROLS

AFTER READING THIS CHAPTER AND COMPLETING THE EXERCISES, YOU WILL BE ABLE TO:

➤ Use various Internet technologies

➤ Learn about the protocols used to communicate over the Internet

➤ Establish a connection to the Internet using the Winsock control

➤ Send an electronic mail message with the Simple Mail Transfer Protocol (SMTP)

➤ Communicate with the Internet using the Internet Transfer control

➤ Create an FTP client capable of navigating through the files on an Internet server and downloading files from that server

WORKING WITH SMTP AND FTP

Sending Mail Using The Winsock Control And The Simple Mail Transfer Protocol

To use the completed program and to complete the exercises in this chapter, your computer must have a connection to the Internet because the programs send electronic mail messages through and download files from the Internet. In addition, you must have a valid electronic mail address.

MFD Productions wants to enable its applications for use on the Internet. Specifically, the company wants a program that will allow a user to send a mail message over the Internet without having to access or start another program. It also wants a program that will allow users to transfer files using the File Transfer Protocol (FTP).

The completed application in this chapter consists of two separate programs that share a common thread. Both are client applications that rely upon the services of the Internet. The first application sends electronic mail, and the second transfers files using the File Transfer Protocol (FTP).

To preview the completed application:

1. Start Visual Basic, and load the project named Chapter.14\Complete\Ch14_C.vbp. The project consists of three forms. The first form contains two command buttons that display the other two forms. The second form sends email, and the third form displays files available through FTP and downloads them.

   As shown in Figure 14.1, the form contains fields to enter both the sender's and receiver's email addresses. It also contains a field to identify the computer that processes your mail. Although the sender and mail host usually are configured on a per-computer basis, the solution used in this chapter allows the program to run without knowing the particulars of your Internet provider. The form also contains a multiline text box to store the mail message itself and a text box that shows a log of the commands exchanged between two computers as the program processes the mail message.

2. Run the program, and then click on the Winsock/Email command button. The form to send an email message appears. The second form is shown in Figure 14.1.

3. Establish a connection to your Internet provider. The steps to accomplish this task will vary depending on how your computer connects to the Internet.

4. Enter your email address in the From and To text boxes. In the Host text box, enter the host name of the computer that accepts mail for you. If you

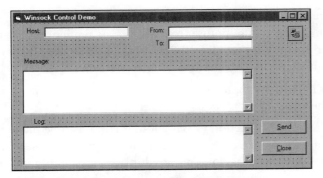

Figure 14.1   Completed Winsock form.

do not know this name of this computer, check with your Internet provider or the administrator for your computer. Alternatively, you can use the following address for the email provider: VBmail.AccessNV.com.

Access Nevada, an Internet provider, provides electronic mail forwarding services for use with this book. Before using this address, read the usage restrictions found on the Copyright page in this book.

5. In the Message text box, enter some text. This text forms the body of the email message. Click on Send. As the program establishes the necessary connection and sends the mail message, a log of the messages sent and the responses received from the remote computer appear in the text box at the bottom of the form.

6. After a few minutes, check your email to see whether the message was delivered. The time it takes to deliver the message will vary depending on your Internet provider.

7. End the program.

The second part of the MFD Productions program implements an FTP client using the TreeView control. Chapter 6 covered programming the TreeView control. FTP servers have a hierarchical directory and file organization similar to those of both the Windows and UNIX file systems. As a result, the TreeView control is well suited to displaying this information.

To test the FTP client:

1. Start the program, making sure that you are still connected to the Internet.

2. Click on the Internet Transfer Control/FTP button to activate the FTP form.

3. In the Address text box, use the default FTP address of ftp.microsoft.com, and then click on the Connect button. The program makes a request to the FTP site and a list of the files in the root directory is downloaded. Be patient. Depending on the speed of your Internet connection and the load

on the remote site, the request may take a minute or two. The completed program changes the mouse pointer to an hourglass while it processes the request. When the task is complete, the program lists the files in the TreeView control instance, as shown in Figure 14.2.

Some listings have a trailing forward slash (/), indicating that the listing is a directory rather than a file.

4. Click on a directory. This action causes another request to be made to display the contents of that directory. When the program receives the contents of the directory, the contents are displayed as children of the selected node. Thus the organization of the files in the TreeView control matches the organization of the files on the FTP server. If the directory is empty, nothing will happen.

5. To download a file, click on a listing that is not a directory.

6. The program displays a dialog box asking where the file should be saved. Many of the files are quite large; consider downloading the file named disclaimer.txt. Specify the Chapter.14\Complete folder, and then click on Save.

7. End the program, and then exit Visual Basic.

If you are familiar with the Internet, this next section will likely be a review for you. This section has two goals: to provide enough detail to help you create Visual Basic programs that can access various Internet services and to give you a general understanding of how those services work.

An Introduction To The Internet

The success of the Internet did not happen by accident. Starting from the initial research funded by the Defense Advanced Research Projects Agency (DARPA), a set of network standards has been developed that allow heterogeneous and geographically distant computers to communicate.

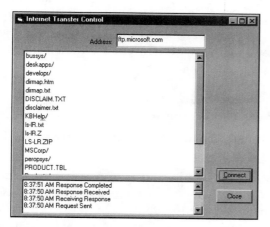

Figure 14.2   Completed FTP form.

These network standards, or protocols as they often are called, are commonly referred to as the Internet protocol suite or TCP/IP. They hide the low-level details of the communication from computer to computer and are responsible for sending information from one computer to another. As an analogy, consider what happens when you mail a letter. You put an address on a letter, put it in a mailbox, and it gets delivered. Neither you nor the intended recipient needs to know about the delivery process, the path taken by the letter, or the specific technologies used to deliver the letter. Much like the network standards, the post office hides these details from you.

Internet Numbers And IP Numbers

Just as the postal service delivers a letter to a unique address, each computer connected to the Internet has a unique address called the Internet number or IP number. An Internet number is a 32-bit number divided into four octets. Thus a number like 131.216.39.3 is a valid Internet number. Because IP numbers are not intuitive, computers on the Internet also have names. These names are hierarchical, being organized into domains and subdomains. Most computers are categorized into the following primary domains:

➤ Commercial organizations are in the com domain.

➤ Governmental entities are in the gov domain.

➤ Educational institutions are in the edu domain.

➤ General organizations have a domain of org.

➤ Network organizations have a domain of net.

Within these primary categories, domains and subdomains uniquely identify a computer on the Internet. Names are written such that each domain or subdomain is separated by a dot (.). Names appear from the most specific to the most general, as shown in the following list:

➤ microsoft.com

➤ west.engineering.sun.com

➤ West.Engineering.Sun.Com

An address can have any number of subdomains, which are not case-sensitive. Thus the last two names in the above list are equivalent.

TCP/IP

Although TCP/IP appears as a single acronym, TCP and IP are actually two different protocols. This chapter does not attempt to define the mechanics of how TCP/IP works. Some background will be useful, however, as you develop programs that utilize the services provided by the Internet.

Consider the following formal definitions of the Internet protocols:

➤ IP is an unreliable, connectionless, packet delivery service.

➤ TCP is a connected, reliable, data transport service.

➤ UDP is an application-level, unreliable, packet delivery service.

Now consider the role played by each Internet protocol. Data are sent across the Internet in units called *packets*. IP sends such packets from the source computer to its destination by transmitting each packet of information, which is commonly called an *IP datagram*. The protocol does not establish a connection with a remote computer; therefore, it is *connectionless*. IP also does not verify that the destination actually received the packet; therefore, it is *unreliable*. Finally, IP does not verify that messages made up of multiple packets were received in the correct order. Remember: All IP does is send packets from one computer to another.

Given these facts, you may wonder why IP is of any use. If you cannot send a message from one computer to another and guarantee that it will arrive, then what good is it? The answer lies in TCP. TCP is a higher-level protocol than IP. As IP packets arrive at a computer, TCP reassembles the packets into the proper order and determines whether any packets were lost during transmission. If a packet was lost, TCP automatically requests that the packet be resent. This protocol therefore provides the reliability not provided by IP.

Another protocol closely related to IP is the User Datagram Protocol (UDP), which provides the mechanism for applications to send IP datagrams from a source to a destination. UDP is used for application programs that do not require the receiver to acknowledge the arrival of the datagram.

Figure 14.3 illustrates the relationships among TCP, IP, and UDP.

As shown in Figure 14.3, TCP and UDP are independent protocols that both rely on the services of IP.

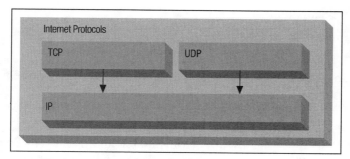

Figure 14.3   TCP/IP and UDP.

The TCP/IP protocols do not care about the contents of the data inside a packet. That is, the data in a packet could take the form of a mail message, or the packet could contain parts of a file being downloaded using FTP. Likewise, TCP/IP does not care about the type of data being sent. That is, the data could contain ASCII characters or binary data.

Internet Services

Intertwined with TCP/IP are several services that make up the suite of Internet services. If you have ever used the Internet, you have used these services. If you have read documents using the Web, you have used the Hypertext Transfer Protocol (HTTP) to transfer Web pages from a remote computer to your computer. If you have downloaded a file, you have used the File Transfer Protocol (FTP) to transfer the file. If you have sent an electronic mail message, your email program relied on the Simple Mail Transfer Protocol (SMTP) to deliver the message. Each of these three protocols is a distinct service. Web browsers, because of their sophisticated interfaces, cause these individual services to appear as a single application.

Services on the Internet can be categorized roughly as either low-level or high-level services. The following list summarizes a few of the more significant low-level services provided by the Internet:

➤ **Nameservice** When you refer to a host by a name like ftp.course.com, that name is translated into an IP number such as 35.17.12.128.

➤ **Routing** This low-level service determines the path taken to deliver packets from the source to the destination. As the Internet transfers a packet between its source and destination, the packet may travel through many different hardware components.

➤ **Address resolution** Although computers have an IP number, the devices have a physical address in addition to an IP address. The Address Resolution Protocol (ARP) maps IP addresses to physical addresses.

These low-level protocols are largely transparent to application developers. As discussed later in the chapter, you, as the developer, can use Visual Basic to establish a connection to a remote host using either the name of the host or its IP number. As the application developer, you do not need to be concerned about how the host name gets translated into an IP number or be aware of the route (path) taken to deliver the information.

As an application developer, you can take advantage of the Internet's high-level services to send mail, transfer files, and perform other tasks. The following list summarizes some of these services:

➤ Email uses SMTP to deliver a message from the source computer to its destination.

➤ File transfer uses FTP to upload and download files from one computer to another.

➤ Web pages are transferred using HTTP.

Each of these high-level services also relies on TCP/IP to work. Figure 14.4 illustrates the relationships of these high-level services to the underlying TCP/IP protocols.

As shown in Figure 14.4, the SMTP, FTP, and HTTP services all rely on a TCP connection. TCP, in turn, relies on IP.

Implementing Internet Services

The first computers to use the Internet were based on UNIX. Any program that wanted to make a connection to the Internet would do so via a *socket*, which is an endpoint for communication.

To further illustrate a socket, imagine that you write books at home for a publisher. You must communicate with the publisher, who is at one end of the country, and with your editor, who is located somewhere else. In this situation, three entities communicate: you, the publisher, and the editor. Each has a physical address; each address is analogous to an Internet site.

Assume that these three parties communicate by telephone and by fax, and that each office has two telephone lines—one for the telephone (voice) and one for the fax machine. If a fax is sent over the voice line, the person sending the fax will hear an unintelligible, garbled mess and the person receiving the telephone call will hear an almost deafening beep. If you attempt to make a voice connection on a fax line, the fax machine will hear an unintelligible, garbled mess. While each scenario uses the same low-level protocol (the telephone line), the high-level protocol differs for the two services, as shown in Figure 14.5.

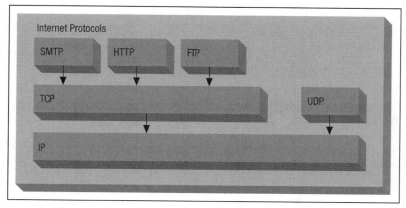

Figure 14.4   Internet services.

As shown in Figure 14.5, each physical address is analogous to a computer (host) on the Internet. Each site has two different sockets or endpoints of communication—one for voice and one for data. Although both sockets use the same type of low-level protocol (the telephone line), the two work with completely different high-level protocols (voice or fax).

This model of different protocols can be extended to the Internet. Consider the two high-level protocols, SMTP and FTP. The servers that process incoming requests listen for these requests at a specific port, and each port is identified by a distinct Integer number. SMTP servers listen at port number 25, for example. If you try to send a mail message using SMTP to the FTP port, FTP will not understand the message. The Internet functions because services like FTP and SMTP agree to communicate over the same well-defined and consistent port numbers. Returning to the telephone example, the fax machine and voice lines have different telephone numbers or ports.

All programs that work with sockets share the following characteristics:

➤ They must have an IP address.

➤ They must identify a specific port.

➤ They must specify a connection type. In the context of Visual Basic, this characteristic means that you must specify whether to use TCP or UDP.

In Visual Basic, you program sockets using the Winsock control. The Winsock control is an ActiveX control and must therefore be added to the project. Like the CommonDialog control, it is invisible at run time. The user does not interact with

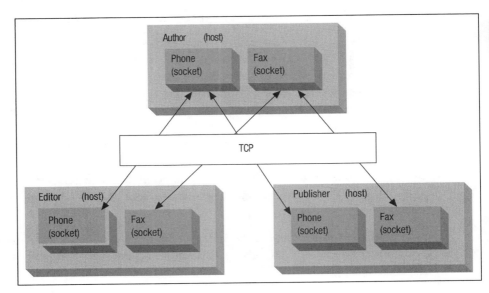

Figure 14.5 Sockets.

the Winsock control. Instead, you, as the programmer, use its properties and methods by writing code. The standard prefix used for the Winsock control is "sok".

The Winsock Control

The Microsoft Winsock control implements both TCP and UDP and handles, by means of its methods and properties, many of the details necessary for communication via these protocols.

The Winsock control itself neither sends a mail message nor transfers a file. Instead, it merely establishes a connection between two computers. Your program is responsible for sending the messages to the remote computer and processing any responses from the remote computer.

When you access the services of the Internet, a client-server relationship commonly exists between the two connected computers. For example, when you download a file from the Internet, your computer is the client and the remote computer is the server. In this model, the server always listens for requests from the client. When the server receives a request for a connection, it establishes a connection with the client. The client and server exchange messages until the conversation is complete; at that point, the connection ends. The server then waits for another connection request from another client.

This above scenario is somewhat of an oversimplification, as most servers can accept several requests from different clients at the same time. The term "message" here means data sent from one computer to another; it does not imply a specific type of message. You should take care not to confuse the generic term "message" with a more specific use like "electronic mail message."

To use the Winsock control, you must set the necessary properties to establish a connection. Once this connection is established, the source and destination computers exchange messages. After the exchange of messages ends, the connection closes. This process can be illustrated with an analogy—a telephone call. The telephone is an endpoint of communication. To make a telephone call, one endpoint (the source) tries to establish a connection with the other endpoint (the destination). Once the connection is established (you reach someone at the other end), the source and destination send and receive messages (you talk back and forth). At some point, the connection terminates and the socket awaits another incoming message; that is, you hang up the telephone and wait for it to ring again.

The Winsock control supports both properties to determine which computers will communicate and methods to send outbound messages and process inbound messages.

Syntax

> Winsock

Properties

➤ The read-only **LocalHostName** property contains the name of the local machine.

➤ The read-only **LocalIP** property contains the IP number of the local machine.

➤ The **LocalPort** property is a read-write property indicating the port from which the client sends data.

➤ The **Protocol** property can be set to one of two constants. If set to **0 – sckTCPProtocol** (the default), the Winsock control uses the TCP protocol for communication. If set to **1 – sckUDPProtocol**, the UDP protocol is used.

➤ The **RemoteHost** property can contain either the name of the remote host or its IP number.

➤ The read-only **RemoteHostIP** property contains the IP number of the remote host after a connection has been made.

➤ The **RemotePort** property contains the number of the port corresponding to the service that the client wants to use—for example, SMTP (25).

➤ The read-only **State** property identifies the current state of the socket. Unique states indicate whether the socket is attempting a connection, the socket is connected, or the socket is closing a connection.

Events

➤ The **Close** event occurs when the remote computer terminates an established connection. Your program should respond to this event by calling the **Close** method.

➤ The **Connect** event occurs when a connection is first established between the client and server.

➤ The **ConnectionRequest** event occurs when a remote computer requests a connection from your computer. This event applies only to server programs.

➤ When new data arrive from the remote computer, the Winsock control stores the information in the input queue, and the **DataArrival** event occurs. Typically, you call the **GetData** method to move the data from the input queue into a string in your program.

14

➤ When you call a method such as **Connect**, the request may fail for several reasons. The **Error** event occurs whenever the request cannot be satisfied.

➤ When sending a message to a remote computer (typically using the **SendData** method), the **SendComplete** event occurs after the message has been sent.

➤ The **SendProgress** event is useful for sending large messages. It contains arguments to identify the number of bytes already sent and the number of bytes still to be transmitted.

Methods

➤ The **Close** method closes an open socket. Calling this method has the effect of breaking an established connection.

➤ The **Connect** method establishes a connection to a remote computer. You must set the **RemoteHost**, **RemotePort**, and **Protocol** properties before calling this method.

➤ When the remote host sends data to the local computer, the Winsock control stores the data in a buffer called the input queue. The **GetData** method moves data from this buffer into a **Variant** or **String** variable.

➤ Used only for TCP connections, the **PeekData** method allows you to view the contents of the input queue without removing the existing contents.

➤ The **SendData** method sends a text or binary message to a remote computer.

➤ To implement a server, you use the **Accept**, **Bind**, and **Listen** methods.

To begin your work on the MFD Productions program, you will first establish a connection to a remote computer, and then expand the program to send a mail message. Thus you will use the SMTP service. Before you can establish a communication link, however, you must define the computer to which you want to talk. This task involves setting the **RemoteHost**, **Protocol**, and **RemotePort** properties. Because the protocol used to send and receive mail messages relies on TCP rather than UDP, you should set the protocol to TCP. The remote host can be set to either the IP number or the name of the remote host. If you use a name, the Winsock control translates it into an IP number. Finally, you must specify the port. The generally accepted port for SMTP is 25. Last, because an email message consists of multiple parts, you must send—as separate pieces—the sender's email address, the recipient's address, and the body of the mail message. To keep track of where the message is in the process at any given time, you will use a variable named **State** to monitor the current state of the mail transaction.

To establish a connection with a remote computer:

1. Start Visual Basic, and then load the project for the chapter. It is named Chapter.14\Startup\Ch14_S.vbp.

2. Use the Components dialog box to make sure that the Microsoft Internet Controls and the Internet Transfer Control 6.0 have been added to the project. You will use the Internet Transfer control in the next section of this chapter.

3. Create an instance of the Winsock control on the form named frmSok. Set the **Name** property of the control instance to sokSMTP.

4. Enter the following statements in the **cmdSend_Click** event procedure:

```
If mblnInProgress = True Then
    Exit Sub
End If
sokSMTP.Protocol = sckTCPProtocol
sokSMTP.RemoteHost = txtHost
sokSMTP.RemotePort = 25
sokSMTP.Connect
mblnInProgress = True
State = Connect
```

5. Enter the following statement in the **sokSMTP_Connect** event procedure. This statement displays a message in the text box indicating that a connection has been established.

```
txtLog = "Connected"
```

6. Test the program. Establish a connection to the Internet. Click on the Winsock/Email button. Enter the name of the host that agrees to process your mail in the Host text box, and then click on the Send command button. You can use the address VBMail.AccessNV.com if you are unsure of your Internet provider's email host. When the Winsock control establishes a connection to the Internet, the message "Connected" should appear in the text box at the bottom of the form.

7. End the program to return to design mode. Terminate the Internet connection.

The statements in the **cmdSend_Click** event procedure attempt to establish a TCP connection with the remote host on port 25 (the SMTP port). This host is identified by the value stored in the text box named txtHost. If the connection is successful, the **Connect** event occurs. If the request is unsuccessful, however, the **Error** event occurs, indicating that a connection could not be established.

14

If the **Connect** event occurs, the code tests the module-level variable **mblnInProgress** to see whether its value is True. The code uses this variable to determine whether a mail message is in progress; if so, the procedure ends. Because establishing a connection is the first step in sending a message, the Boolean variable is set to True at the end of the procedure. Other procedures will set this variable as necessary to indicate when the transmission of a message is complete.

The Error Event

The **Error** event occurs when the Winsock control detects an error.

Syntax

*object*_**Error**(*number* **As Integer**, *Description* **As String**, *Scode* **As Long**, *Source* **As String**, *HelpFile* **As String**, *HelpContext* **As Long**, *CancelDisplay* **As Boolean**)

Dissection

➤ The *object* must contain an instance of the Winsock control.

➤ The **Error** event occurs whenever a TCP or IP error occurs.

➤ The *number* argument contains an Integer to identify the source of the error. For a complete list of these values, refer to the "Error Event" Help page pertaining to the Winsock control.

➤ The *Description* argument contains a textual description of the error.

➤ The *Source* argument describes the source of the error. This value typically contains the project name that generated the error.

➤ The *HelpFile* and *HelpContext* arguments identify the Help file contents of a Help page to be displayed.

➤ By default, Visual Basic will display a message box when the **Error** event occurs. Setting the *CancelDisplay* property to **True** will prevent the message box from appearing.

Failure of the Winsock control to locate a host is one common source of errors. In this example, you will display any error message in the Status text box.

To respond to the **Error** event:

1. Enter the following statements in the **sokSMTP_Error** event procedure:

```
Select Case Number
    Case sckHostNotFound, sckHostNotFoundTryAgain
```

```
          txtLog = Number & " " & Description
End Select
sokSMTP.Close
mblnInProgress = False
```

2. Test the program. Establish a connection to the Internet. Click on the Winsock/Email button. Enter the host named notesgw.course.coz (an invalid host name). Click on the Send button. After a moment, a message will appear in the Status text box, indicating that the host could not be located.

3. End the program to return to design mode. Terminate the Internet connection.

The Winsock control raises the **Error** event whenever an error occurs. This event contains arguments to identify the error number and its description. Your code can use this value to inform the user about the cause of the error or to determine whether it makes sense to continue processing. This **Select Case** statement could be easily expanded to process the other possible errors. In addition to displaying the error message, the code in the **Error** event procedure calls the **Close** method pertaining to the Winsock control to terminate the connection.

The final statement in the event procedure is as follows:

```
mblnInProgress = False
```

The module-level variable identifies whether a mail transaction is in progress. Checking the value of this variable in the **cmdSend_Click** event procedure will prevent the user from trying to send a second mail message while the first message is still being transmitted. This variable will be set and its value tested throughout the program.

At this point, you can make a connection to a remote computer and detect whether an error occurred. You can also send and receive messages. Your program, however, needs to manipulate the contents of those messages. To learn how to accomplish this task, you must first learn the basics of SMTP. SMTP is but one of many Internet standards.

Internet Standards (RFCs)

The Internet connects computers that use different hardware and software. You can work with many different client computers from various manufacturers to access the Internet. These clients may run different operating systems. A computer running Windows, for example, can send a message to another computer without knowing the type of hardware or software that the remote computer is running.

This communication is possible because Internet services, such as SMTP, conform to a well-defined and widely adopted standard. Regardless of the computer hardware and software, every computer agrees to transfer mail using the SMTP service, for instance. FTP and HTTP also use well-defined, widely accepted standards.

Standards for Internet services are specified in Request for Comments (RFC), which are identified by unique numbers. For instance, RFC 821 defines SMTP. RFCs can be readily downloaded from the Internet.

SMTP

The SMTP model involves two-way connected communication between a sender and receiver. In this example, your program is the sender. The receiver is the computer (Internet provider) that accepts your messages for delivery. The sender generates commands, which are transmitted to the receiver. The receiver acknowledges each command sent and indicates whether it was successful. Your program, as the sender, is the client, and the receiver is the server.

In this section, you will use SMTP as a vehicle to illustrate the use of the Winsock control. Only the most fundamental commands pertaining to the creation of an SMTP client are presented here.

Consider the process of sending an email message as a transaction having the following four steps:

1. The first step is an acknowledgment between the sender and receiver.
2. The second step identifies the sender.
3. The third step identifies the receiver.
4. The final step sends the contents or body of the message.

All SMTP commands use the same generic syntax. A command consists of a three- or four-character command name, followed by data that must be terminated with a carriage return (**vbCrLf**). Although SMTP commands are not case sensitive, this book will adopt the convention of capitalizing all SMTP commands. Email addresses are also not case sensitive.

As the commands in the previous numbered list execute, an SMTP server (the remote computer, in this case) keeps track of the transaction's state. The state of the mail message is significant because if your code does not send the commands in the proper order, errors will occur. If you send an incorrect command to an SMTP server, the server will return a message indicating that it could not successfully process the command.

You may expect that this scenario (an STMP error) would cause the Winsock control to raise an error, but it does not. The Winsock control raises the **Error** event only when it detects a TCP error. A TCP error occurs because a connection with the SMTP server cannot be established or because the connection has been lost. An SMTP error, on the other hand, is a textual message indicating that the SMTP server cannot process the command. Thus TCP and the Winsock control do not produce an error. As your code sends messages to SMTP and receives responses, it must also interpret those responses, determine whether an error has occurred, and decide whether it makes sense to continue.

Each time you send a command to an SMTP server, the server processes the command and generates a response. This response takes the form of a textual message containing two parts—a three-digit number identifying the response and a textual description.

After your client program makes a connection with an SMTP server, the first step in sending a mail message is to send the **HELO** command. The **HELO** command identifies the sending and receiving computers. It sets the initial state, indicating that no transaction is in progress. If the **HELO** command is successful, the SMTP server sends a return code of 250.

After transmitting the **HELO** command, your code must send the **MAIL FROM** command. The **MAIL FROM** command identifies the sender and has the syntax shown in the following statement fragment:

```
MAIL FROM: Ekedahl@Course.com
```

This statement tells the SMTP server (receiver) that a mail transaction is beginning and identifies the sender of the mail message. Angled brackets (< >) enclose the email address of the sender. In this sample statement, the sender has an email address of Ekedahl@Course.com.

If the **MAIL FROM** command is valid, the server sends a return code of 250. The **RCPT TO** command—the next step in the transaction—has the following syntax:

```
RCPT TO: Kate@Course.com
```

This statement informs the receiver (SMTP server) of the intended recipient of the mail message. If the name of the recipient is valid, the SMTP server sends a return code of 250. A return code of 550 indicates that the request failed. The syntax used is the same as that employed with the **MAIL FROM** command. Angled brackets enclose the recipient's email address.

Some mail servers may perform forwarding. That is, you may specify a recipient who is not on the receiving machine. For example, imagine that you send a

14

message to "Joe@beets.com" to the server at Course.com. The server at Course.com must determine whether it will forward the mail to beets.com. This configuration can vary among SMTP servers. The SMTP server at VBMail@AccessNV.com has agreed to forward mail for use with the exercises in this book. To transmit mail to multiple recipients, you send multiple **RCPT TO** commands—one for each intended recipient.

The third step in the process is to send the body of the message using the **DATA** command. The **DATA** command takes no arguments. If this command is successful, the SMTP server sends a return code of 354. Next, you send the text of the message. You then terminate the **DATA** command by sending a carriage return followed by a period (.), followed by another carriage return.

The following statements illustrate a complete mail transaction. In this transaction, the "S" in the first column indicates the sender's message and the "R" indicates the response from the receiver.

```
S HELO
R #250#GREETINGS
S MAIL FROM:<Ekedahl@Course.com>
R 250 OK
S RCPT TO: <Kate@Course.com>
R 250 OK
S DATA
R 354 Start mail input; end with <CrLf>.<CrLf>
S A first mail message.
S Michael V. Ekedahl
S <CrLf>.<CrLf>
R 250 OK
```

This complete transaction sends a mail message from Ekedahl@Course.com to Kate@Course.com. The data of the message contains two lines—"A first mail message." and the name "Michael V. Ekedahl." The message is terminated with a period (.) on a line by itself.

In summary, sending a mail message involves two-way communication between the sender (your computer) and the receiver (the remote computer). The first step is to send a message to acknowledge yourself. The receiver gets this message and replies with an acknowledgment. You then proceed through the remaining steps in the transaction by identifying the sender of the message, the receiver of the message, and the data contained in the message.

To keep track of the current state of the transaction, your program uses an enumerated type containing the possible states of this simple mail message. The following code segment illustrates the enumerated type used to identify the states of a mail transaction. In this program, the states proceed from the first to the last member of the enumerated type.

```
Private Enum EState
    Connect
    Helo
    MailFrom
    SendTo
    Data
    MessageData
    EndMessage
End Enum
```

In the preceding code, the initial state is the **Connect** state. It indicates that the program has connected to the server, but that a mail transaction is not in progress. The next three states are used for the **HELO** initialization state and to indicate that the **MAIL FROM** and **RCPT TO** commands have been sent. The **Data** and **MessageData** states denote when the **DATA** command has started and when the sending of data is complete, respectively. The final state, **EndMessage**, indicates that the mail message transaction has completed.

To send a TCP message to a receiver, you call the **SendData** method pertaining to the Winsock control.

Syntax
> *object*.**SendData** *data*

Dissection

➤ The *object* must be a valid instance of the Winsock control.

➤ The **SendData** method sends a message to the connected host. If the Winsock control has not established a connection, it will raise the **Error** event.

➤ The **SendData** method can send either textual or binary *data*. If textual data are sent, a string should be used. If binary data are sent, a byte array should be used. Mail messages always use textual data.

Code Example

```
sokSMTP.SendData "HELO VBMail.AccessNV.com" & vbCrLf
```

Code Dissection
This code sends the HELO message and identifies the local host as VBMail.AccessNV.com. The string is terminated explicitly with a carriage return. If it was not terminated with a carriage return character, SMTP would not recognize the string as a complete command.

14

The MFD Productions program needs to send the **HELO** command to the SMTP server when a connection is made. You must add the respective code to the **Connect** event procedure.

To send an SMTP **HELO** command:

Enter the following statements in the **sokSMTP_Connect** event procedure:

```
txtLog = "Connected"
State = Connect
sokSMTP.SendData "HELO " & txtHost & vbCrLf
mblnInProgress = True
```

These statements reset the state of the mail transaction to indicate that a transaction is in progress. The **SendData** method sends a **HELO** command to the server. The server name is contained in the text box named txtHost. If the host does not exist, the Winsock control will raise an **Error** event.

Processing Incoming Data

When the client program receives a message from the remote site, the Winsock control generates the **DataArrival** event. Your client program must respond to this event and determine the receiver's response. Remember that the Winsock control merely passes TCP messages on to your program; the code in your program must actually process the contents of those messages. In this example, the TCP messages consist of SMTP commands and responses.

Syntax

> *object*_**DataArrival** (*bytesTotal* **As Long**)

Dissection

➤ The *object* must be a valid instance of the Winsock control.

➤ Each time data arrive from the remote host, the **DataArrival** event occurs.

➤ The *bytesTotal* argument indicates how many bytes have been received from the remote host.

When data arrive from the remote host (SMTP server) and the **DataArrival** event occurs, the data are stored in an input queue. This queue is a temporary storage area from which your program must move the data. The Winsock control moves data from the input queue into a variable in your program by using the **GetData** method.

Syntax

> object.**GetData** data, [type,] [maxLen]

Dissection

➤ The *object* must be an instance of the Winsock control.

➤ The **GetData** method reads a fixed number of bytes from the input queue into a program variable.

➤ The *data* argument contains a variable that stores the data moved from the input queue. The data type of this variable will depend on the value of the *type* argument.

➤ The optional *type* argument identifies how the data in the input queue are interpreted. Under SMTP, all data should be interpreted as strings.

➤ The optional *maxLen* argument identifies the maximum number of bytes to read. If this argument is less than the total number of bytes in the input queue, the method will return the error code 10040.

Code Example

```
sokSMTP.GetData strBuffer, vbString
```

Code Dissection

This statement retrieves the data stored in the input queue and stores it in the string variable **strBuffer**. The data are interpreted as a **String** data type.

For the MFD Productions program, you already sent the **HELO** command when the connection to the remote host was established. The SMTP server will therefore receive the message. The server will then generate a reply. You will write code that will read this reply by calling the **GetData** method in the **DataArrival** event. Pay attention to the sequence of events that is occurring. You send a message to the server and wait for a reply. When you receive a reply, you get the data from the input queue, process it, and then send another message. This process continues until the conversation is complete. This process represents a message loop.

To program a message loop:

1. Enter the following statements in the **sokSMTP_DataArrival** event procedure to read the data from the input queue and to reset the current state:

```
Dim pblnStatus As Boolean
Dim pstrBuffer As String
```

14

```
Select Case State
    Case Connect
        sokSMTP.GetData pstrBuffer, vbString
        pblnStatus = _
        CheckResponse(pstrBuffer, "220")
        If pblnStatus = True Then
            txtLog = Time & " " & pstrBuffer & _
                vbCrLf & txtLog
            State = State + 1
        Else
            sokSMTP.Close
            State = 0
        End If
End Select
```

2. Test the program. Establish an Internet connection. Click on the Winsock/ Email button. In the Host text box, enter the host name of the computer that accepts mail for you. If you do not know its name, check with your Internet provider or the administrator of your computer. Alternatively, you can use the following address for the email provider: VBmail.AccessNV.com. Click on Send to send the message. When the **DataArrival** event receives the data, the code in the event procedure stores the response from the HELO message in the Log text box.

3. End the program to return to design mode. Terminate the Internet connection.

The **SendData** command causes the statements in the **sokSMTP_DataArrival** event procedure to process the data sent by the remote server. The retrieved data are stored in the variable named **pstrBuffer**. This code appends this value (stored in **pstrBuffer**) to the text box representing the log of messages sent from the remote SMTP server.

The following statement increments the **State** variable:

```
State = State + 1
```

This statement updates the current state of the mail transaction. The initial state was Connect. After the variable is incremented, the state has the value of Helo, indicating that the **HELO** command has been processed.

The procedure also calls the **CheckResponse** function. This function takes two arguments—the expected response and the actual response returned by the server. The procedure, which has already been created, contains the following code:

```
Private Function CheckResponse(pstrGot, pstrExpect) _
    As Boolean
```

```
        Dim pstrResp As String
        pstrResp = Mid(pstrGot, 1, 3)
        If StrComp(pstrResp, pstrExpect) = 0 Then
            CheckResponse = True
        Else
            CheckResponse = False
        End If
End Function
```

In the preceding code, the procedure compares the first three characters of the SMTP response with the expected response. If they match, the function returns True; otherwise, it returns False. If the function returns True, the code increments the state and the response is added to the Log text box. If an error occurred, the connection closes and the state is reset to zero (0).

Completing the transaction—in other words, sending the remaining parts of the mail message—involves sending the **MAIL FROM** and **RCPT TO** commands, transmitting the body of the message, and then closing the connection. This task can be accomplished by sending the necessary data, processing the response, and updating the state by incrementing the State variable.

To complete the mail transaction:

1. Enter the following statements in the **sokSMTP_DataArrival** event procedure:

```
    Select Case State
        Case Connect
            sokSMTP.GetData pstrBuffer, vbString
            pblnStatus = _
                CheckResponse(pstrBuffer, "220")
            If pblnStatus = True Then
                txtLog = Time & " " & pstrBuffer & _
                    vbCrLf & txtLog.Text
                State = State + 1
            Else
                sokSMTP.Close
                State = 0
            End If
        Case Helo
            sokSMTP.GetData pstrBuffer, vbString
            pblnStatus = _
                CheckResponse(pstrBuffer, "250")
            If pblnStatus = True Then
                txtLog = Time & " " & pstrBuffer & _
                    vbCrLf & txtLog
                sokSMTP.SendData "MAIL FROM:" & _
```

14

```
                        txtMailFrom & vbCrLf
                State = State + 1
            Else
                sokSMTP.Close
                State = 0
                mblnInProgress = False
                Exit Sub
            End If
        Case MailFrom
            sokSMTP.GetData pstrBuffer, vbString
            pblnStatus = _
                CheckResponse(pstrBuffer, "250")
            If pblnStatus = True Then
                txtLog = Time & " " & pstrBuffer & _
                    vbCrLf & txtLog
                sokSMTP.SendData "RCPT TO:" & _
                    txtRecvTo & vbCrLf
                State = State + 1
            Else
                sokSMTP.Close
                State = 0
                mblnInProgress = False
                Exit Sub
            End If
        Case SendTo
            sokSMTP.GetData pstrBuffer, vbString
            txtLog = Time & " " & pstrBuffer & _
                vbCrLf & txtLog
            sokSMTP.SendData "DATA" & vbCrLf
            State = State + 1
        Case Data
            sokSMTP.GetData pstrBuffer, vbString
            txtLog = Time & " " & pstrBuffer & _
                vbCrLf & txtLog
            sokSMTP.SendData txtMessage & vbCrLf & _
                "." & vbCrLf
            State = State + 1
        Case MessageData
            sokSMTP.GetData pstrBuffer, vbString
            txtLog = Time & " " & pstrBuffer & _
                vbCrLf & txtLog
            sokSMTP.Close
            State = State + 1
            mblnInProgress = False
    End Select
```

2. Test the program. Establish an Internet connection. Click on the Winsock/Email command button. In the Host text box, enter the host name of the computer that accepts mail for you. If you do not know its name, check with your Internet provider or the administrator of your computer. Alternatively, you can use the following address for the email provider: VBmail.AccessNV.com. Click on the Send command button. The program will connect to the server, send the **HELO** command, and continue sending the remaining SMTP commands until the mail message is delivered.

3. End the program. Terminate the Internet connection.

The statements added in the preceding steps process each of the transactions generated by the remote server. Although you could implement this program in different ways, the implementation chosen here responds to the **DataArrival** event by processing the data received by the server and sending a message representing the next part of the transaction.

Consider the following code:

```
Case Helo
    sokSMTP.GetData pstrBuffer, vbString
    pblnStatus = CheckResponse(pstrBuffer, "250")
    If pblnStatus = True Then
        txtLog = Time & " " & pstrBuffer & _
            vbCrLf & txtLog
        sokSMTP.SendData "MAIL FROM:" & _
            txtMailFrom & vbCrLf
        State = State + 1
    Else
        sokSMTP.Close
        State = 0
        mblnInProgress = False
        Exit Sub
    End If
```

In the preceding code, the program enters the Helo state after the Connect state. It retrieves the server's response from the **HELO** command and verifies it. If the expected response is received, the Log text box is updated, the **MAIL FROM** command is sent, and the state is updated. If an unexpected response is received, the connection ends.

After the Helo state, the program enters the MailFrom state. In this state, the response is validated. If the code detects the desired response, it sends the **RCPT TO** command. The remaining states are used to send the **DATA** command and the message.

The Winsock control is not limited to exchanging information using SMTP. With the techniques you just learned, you could use the Winsock control to implement an FTP client or server. In this situation, you would set the host and port as you did previously. Instead of processing SMTP commands, however, your code would process FTP commands. You would write code to implement the protocols in the same way as well. The commands and responses, however, would differ. Fortunately, you do not have to implement an FTP client yourself. The Internet Transfer control implements this protocol for you.

Transferring Files With The Internet Transfer Control

The Internet Transfer Control

In the previous section, you used the Winsock control to establish a connection to the Internet and to process an email transaction between a client and a server. Although you could also use the Winsock control to establish a connection with an FTP server to download files, the Internet Transfer control can simplify the process.

As you saw in the previous section, TCP is layered on top of IP; the various Internet services are, in turn, layered on top of TCP. In a similar manner, you can envision the Internet Transfer control as being layered on top of the Winsock control. With the Internet Transfer control, you do not have to explicitly specify the host name and service (port) that you want to use. Instead, you specify a Uniform Resource Locator (URL). Using the information given in the URL, the Internet Transfer control will establish the connection. In this chapter's program, you will use the Internet Transfer control to create an FTP client.

Syntax

>   Internet Transfer

Events

➤ As the server processes requests, the **StateChanged** event occurs to indicate the current state of the connection. The state is identified by a constant value.

Methods

➤ The **Cancel** method will cancel any pending request and close the open connection.

➤ When the Internet Transfer control receives data from a server, it places the data into a buffer (input queue). The **GetChunk** method moves the data out of this buffer.

➤ The **GetHeader** method is used only with HTTP. It retrieves the header text from an HTTP file.

➤ The **Execute** method requests a service from the remote computer. For example, the **Execute** method can initiate an FTP session or download a file.

➤ The **OpenURL** method opens an HTML document.

Properties

➤ The **Password** property contains the password that will be sent to log on to a remote computer.

➤ The **Protocol** property specifies which Internet protocol to use. If set to **icFTP**, the File Transfer Protocol is used. If set to **icHTTP**, the Hypertext Transfer Protocol is used. Both the **OpenURL** and **Execute** methods modify the value of the **Protocol** property.

➤ The **RemoteHost** property contains either the name or the IP address of the remote host. You do not set the port explicitly as you do when using the Winsock control. Instead, the Internet Transfer control handles this task automatically.

➤ The **RequestTimeout** property indicates the number of seconds allowed to complete a request. If your code uses the **Execute** method to make a request, a timeout will cause the **StateChanged** event to occur with an icError error code. If it uses the **OpenURL** method, an error will occur.

➤ The Internet Transfer control sets the **ResponseCode** property whenever the **StateChanged** event occurs. It contains the numeric value of the response from the remote server.

➤ The **ResponseInfo** property contains the textual description corresponding to the response identified by the **ResponseCode** property.

➤ The **StillExecuting** property contains a Boolean value indicating whether the Internet Transfer control is busy processing a server request. The Internet Transfer control does not respond to events while the **StillExecuting** property is **True**.

➤ The **URL** property contains the URL used by the **Execute** and **OpenURL** methods.

➤ Your code uses the **UserName** property in conjunction with the **Password** property to specify the user name on the remote host.

14

The Internet Transfer control can send requests to an FTP server or to an HTTP server. When you must access these two services, the Internet Transfer control is the logical choice because the control itself handles several details concerning the underlying FTP or HTTP protocols.

Synchronous Vs. Asynchronous Transmission

Before you try to use the Internet Transfer control, a word about transmission modes is in order. In fact, the term "transmission mode" is too specific, because the following concepts pertain to how any procedure or method executes.

The following terms describe the execution of any command:

➤ **Synchronous** That is, execution of the command must be complete before the next command begins to execute. From the perspective of executing a Visual Basic statement that calls a **Function** procedure or method, the **Function** procedure or method must execute and return a value before the next statement executes. From the perspective of the Internet Transfer control, a request to download a file from the Internet must complete before the client can make another file download request.

➤ **Asynchronous** That is, a statement will start executing a command and then begin executing other commands regardless of whether the first command has completed. From the perspective of executing a Visual Basic statement, you may execute several statements that affect the appearance of the form and its control instances on the screen. You can continue to execute statements while Windows processes tasks that you already have requested. From the perspective of the Internet Transfer control, you may execute a statement that makes a request from a server. Visual Basic will continue to execute other statements in your program, even though the first request for service from the Internet has not yet been completed.

The Internet Transfer control uses either the synchronous or asynchronous transmission mode depending on whether you use the **OpenURL** or **Execute** method. The **OpenURL** method uses synchronous transmission, which means that the request must complete before the next statement will execute. The **Execute** method uses asynchronous transmission, which means that a statement that requests FTP services does not need to be complete before the next statement will execute. To illustrate asynchronous methods, consider the following statements:

```
itt1.Execute "FTP://" & txtAddress, "DIR /*"
itt1.Execute "FTP://" & txtAddress, _
    "Get localfile remotefile"
```

The preceding statements make two requests. The first statement attempts to establish a connection with an FTP server, and the second statement tries to download a specific file. If you execute these statements, your program likely will generate a run-time error because the second statement will try to retrieve the file before the first statement, which establishes the connection, has completed. Thus, when using the FTP service, your program must not make requests while another request is pending; otherwise, an error will occur.

Implementing An FTP Client

FTP transfers files across the Internet from one computer to another and is a client-server protocol much in the same way that SMTP is a client-server protocol. Whenever you download a file from a remote computer to your computer, the remote computer acts as the FTP server and your computer acts as the FTP client.

The first step in making an FTP request is authentication. To download a file from an FTP server, the FTP server usually requires that you specify both a login and a password. By convention, most publicly accessible FTP servers permit access using a well-known login and password. This login name is "anonymous" (hence the name "anonymous FTP"); the agreed-upon password is the electronic mail address of the client user.

When using anonymous FTP, you, as the client, are restricted to performing only certain actions. Because you are not a privileged user, you can look at and download files, but you cannot write files to the server or change the contents of existing files.

Implementing The File Transfer Protocol

As a developer, you need to recognize several facts surrounding the creation of an FTP client to transfer files across the Internet. For instance, files can be of different types. The default file type—ASCII—is supported by all FTP implementations. In addition, most FTP implementations support image, or binary, files. Binary files are transferred as a series of contiguous bytes. Also, FTP uses a connected server to process requests, just as SMTP does. Requests are sent from the client to the server in the form of commands, much as commands are sent to an SMTP server. The notion of a transaction or state does not apply in the same sense as it does with an SMTP server, because each command is treated as a distinct unit in FTP.

When using the Internet Transfer control to access FTP, you can envision the Internet Transfer control as being layered on top of FTP. On the one hand, it simplifies the process of transferring a file. On the other hand, you do not have access to all underlying commands supported by FTP itself. To access these commands, you must use the Winsock control and then send requests and process the responses using the same techniques as you employed with SMTP.

The following list summarizes some of the FTP commands supported by the Internet Transfer control:

➤ **CD** Changes the current working directory.

➤ **DIR** Lists files on a remote computer.

➤ **GET** and **RECV** Are equivalent. Both retrieve a file from the remote computer.

➤ **LS** Lists files on the remote computer.

You can use these commands when you are an authenticated user or when you use anonymous FTP. Other commands, listed below, can be executed only if the user has privileges on the remote computer:

➤ **DELETE** Removes a file from the remote computer.

➤ **MKDIR** Creates a new directory on the remote computer.

➤ **SEND** and **PUT** Send a file from the local computer to the remote computer.

➤ **RENAME** Changes the name of a file on the remote computer.

To execute FTP commands using the Internet Transfer control, you embed the command and its arguments inside the operation argument of the **Execute** method.

Syntax

      object.**Execute** url, operation, data, requestHeaders

---

Dissection

➤ The *object* must be a valid instance of the Internet Transfer control.

➤ The **Execute** method sends the command stored in *operation* to the specified *url*.

➤ The optional *url* argument specifies the Internet address of the remote server where the request will execute.

➤ The optional *operation* argument, when used with FTP, indicates which action to perform. These operations include downloading or uploading files and changing or listing directories.

➤ The optional *data* argument is used for certain operations that take arguments. For example, the CD command takes one argument—a directory name. In this case, the directory name is specified in the *data* argument.

➤ The optional *requestHeaders* argument sends additional header information to the remote server.

Code Example

```
itt1.Execute "ftp://ftp.course.com" "DIR"
```

Code Dissection

This statement establishes a connection with the host named ftp.course.com using FTP. Using the *operation* argument, it executes the **DIR** command on the remote server. The Internet Transfer control stores the response from this request in the input queue until the **GetChunk** method retrieves the data.

If you are already familiar with FTP, you will notice that the syntax of the previous statement differs from that of FTP commands. If you have worked with the UNIX or DOS shell to perform FTP, you probably have typed a statement like:

```
ftp ftp.course.com
```

This statement establishes an interactive FTP connection with the host ftp.course.com. The syntax of the **Execute** method is much different, however—it includes a URL. The first part of the URL (ftp://) specifies which protocol to use and the second part indicates the location (host). The Internet Transfer control is designed to download HTML documents as well as provide FTP services. Consequently, the **Execute** method uses a URL syntax to specify a Web site.

Once a connection has been established, you can execute FTP commands to look at the directories on a remote computer and to transfer files. To process these FTP commands, the program calls the **Execute** method pertaining to the Internet Transfer control.

As you work on this task, remember that the **Execute** method runs asynchronously. As a result, your program will continue to execute statements while an FTP request is pending. If you call the **Execute** method to make another request while a request is pending, the Internet Transfer control will generate an error, indicating that a request is still being executed—each request must be completed before the next request can begin to execute.

In the MFD Productions program, the user will enter an Internet address in the Address text box and click on the Connect command button to establish a connection with the remote FTP server. The user must be prevented from making another request, however, until that connection request has completed. To prevent such as error, the program should check the **StillExecuting** property, which is True if a pending request exists and False otherwise, before attempting to execute another FTP request.

You now can write the code to request a connection with a remote FTP server.

To establish an FTP connection using the Internet Transfer control:

1. Create an instance of the Internet Transfer control on the form named frmITC (note that the ToolTip for the control is Inet), and then set the **Name** property to **itt1**.

2. Enter the following statements in the **cmdConnect_Click** event procedure on frmITC:

```
On Error Resume Next
    If itt1.StillExecuting Then
        Exit Sub
    Else
        itt1.Execute "FTP://" & txtAddress, _
            "DIR /*"
    End If
```

These statements verify that no request is pending by checking the value of the **StillExecuting** property. The operation argument tells the FTP server to get a directory listing of the root directory.

At this point, you have written the necessary code to retrieve a directory listing from the remote computer. As yet, you have not written the necessary code to display the information returned from the FTP server. To accomplish this task, you must be able to detect when the request is complete and to process the data returned by the request.

Fortunately, as you send requests to the Internet Transfer control using the **Execute** method, the control keeps track of the progress of that request. Every time the status of the request changes, the **StateChanged** event occurs. The **StateChanged** event takes one argument—an **Integer** containing the current state of the request. For the MFD Productions program, you will write code for the following states:

➤ When a request is being sent, the state should be set to the constant **icRequesting**.

➤ If the request generates a response that returns data like a **DIR** or **LS** command, the state is set to icResponseCompleted.

➤ Some requests do not return any data. For example, if you try to retrieve the contents of an empty directory, the state should be set to icResponseReceived rather than icResponseCompleted.

In addition to executing a command asynchronously with the **Execute** method, you can use the **OpenURL** method to execute a command synchronously. The purposes of the **Execute** and **OpenURL** methods are nearly identical. The **OpenURL** method returns data in the form of an HTML document. As a result, a document downloaded using this method can be viewed with a Web browser like Internet Explorer.

Processing Responses From The Internet Transfer Control

Processing data sent from the server using the Internet Transfer control is similar to the technique used with the Winsock control; that is, the data are read into an input queue. You then must copy the data from the input queue and store it in your program. In the MFD Productions program, when the **DIR** statement reads the directory, the data must be copied from the input queue into a program string. The program then can process this string. Data read as a result of calling the **Execute** method are retrieved into the program by calling the **GetChunk** method.

Syntax

   object.**GetChunk**(*size* [,*datatype*])

Dissection

➤ The *object* must be an instance of the Internet Transfer control.

➤ The **GetChunk** method reads the number of bytes from the input queue.

➤ The required *size* argument determines the number of bytes to read.

➤ The optional *datatype* argument determines whether the data will be interpreted as a string or as an array of bytes.

Code Example

```
Dim pstrRecv as String
pstrRecv = itt1.GetChunk(1024, icString)
```

Code Dissection

These statements read, at most, 1024 characters from the input queue into the string named pstrRecv.

In this chapter's program, you can use the **StateChanged** event to advise the user of the program's progress and to change the insertion point so that the user will be aware that a request currently is executing.

To program the **StateChanged** event:

1. Enter the following statement in the **itt1_StateChanged** event procedure on the form frmITC:

```
On Error Resume Next
    Dim pstrRecv As String
```

```
Dim pstrTemp As String
Select Case State
    Case icRequesting
        Screen.MousePointer = vbHourglass
    Case icResponseReceived
        Screen.MousePointer = vbNormal
    Case icError
        PrintLog icError
    Case icResponseCompleted
        pstrRecv = itt1.GetChunk(1024, icString)
        LoadNodes pstrRecv
    Screen.MousePointer = vbNormal
End Select
PrintLog State
```

2. Test the program. Then establish a connection with the Internet, and click on the Internet Transfer Control/FTP command button. Accept the default address (**ftp.microsoft.com**) shown in the Address text box, and then click on Connect.

   As the request executes, the Internet Transfer control moves through various states. These state transitions appear in the Log text box at the bottom of the form. The statements added in Step 1 change the mouse pointer to an hourglass while a request is pending and return the mouse pointer to normal when the request completes. When the state changes, the **PrintLog Sub** procedure is called to write a log message into the multiline text box at the bottom of the form. The log messages may help you, as the programmer, to visualize the events taking place and the different state transitions occurring as requests are made and then satisfied.

3. End the program to return to design mode. Terminate the Internet connection.

The icResponseCompleted state contains the important code in this procedure:

```
pstrRecv = itt1.GetChunk(1024, icString)
LoadNodes pstrRecv
Screen.MousePointer = vbNormal
```

The **GetChunk** method reads the data from the input queue. At most, 1024 characters are read. If the input queue contains more than 1024 characters, the remaining data will be ignored and will remain in the input queue. You could improve this procedure by writing a **For** loop and examining the length of the string returned. If the length of the string is less than the number of bytes requested, then all the data have been read.

The string contains a directory listing of the FTP server's root directory. Almost all FTP servers return the directory listing in a well-defined format. Each directory has a trailing forward slash (/); ordinary files do not. Each directory or file is separated by a carriage return and linefeed sequence. Each directory or file is stored in a node in the TreeView control instance.

Consider the following statements in the previously created **LoadNodes** general procedure:

```
Private Sub LoadNodes(pstr As String)
    Dim pstrTemp As String
    Dim pintCurrent As Integer
    Dim pintLast As Integer
    Static pblnInit As Integer
    pintLast = 1
    For pintCurrent = 1 To Len(pstr) - 2
        Debug.Print (Asc(Mid(pstr, pintCurrent, 1)))
        If Asc(Mid(pstr, pintCurrent, 1)) = 13 Then
            pstrTemp = Mid(pstr, pintLast, _
                pintCurrent - pintLast)
            If Not pblnInit Then
                tvwFTP.Nodes.Add , , , pstrTemp
            Else
                tvwFTP.Nodes.Add mnodCurrent, _
                    tvwChild, , pstrTemp
                mnodCurrent.Expanded = True
            End If
            pintLast = pintCurrent + 2
        End If
    Next
    pblnInit = True
End Sub
```

This procedure examines the input string and breaks it into the individual directory and file entries. It accomplishes this task by locating the carriage return characters in the string. Each time it detects a carriage return, the **Mid** function copies a part of the string. In turn, this substring is added to the text of a new node. The static variable **pblnInit** determines whether this occasion marks the first time the procedure has been called. In other words, it determines whether the root directory is being examined. If it is, then the code in the procedure adds the nodes as top-level nodes. If it is not, then a child node was clicked; this node is referenced in the module-level variable **mnodCurrent**. The new nodes are subsequently added as children of the node that was clicked.

The following code has already been written in the **PrintLog** procedure:

```
Private Sub PrintLog(pintState As Integer)
    Dim pstrState As String
```

```
    Select Case pintState
        Case icNone
 *          pstrState = "None"
            . . .
        Case icResponseCompleted
            pstrState = "Response completed"
    End Select
    txtLog = Time & " " & pstrState & vbCrLf & txtLog
End Sub
```

The preceding code is very simple. The procedure takes one argument—the state of the Internet Transfer control. This value inserts a message in the Log text box containing the current time and the state of the control. This chapter uses this level of logging to illustrate the state transitions that occur to the Internet Transfer control.

At this point, your program will display the files and directories in the FTP server's root directory. Most servers have many levels of directories, however. In the current version of the MFD Productions program, these directories are displayed as nodes in the TreeView control instance. When the user clicks on one of these nodes, one of two actions should occur:

➤ If the node is a directory, another request should be made to the FTP server, and the directories and files in that directory should appear in the TreeView control as children.

➤ If the node is a file, the file should be downloaded from the FTP server to the local computer.

The forward slash character (/) indicates that the entry is a directory rather than an ordinary file. Thus, when the user clicks on a node, your code should check the last character in the node's **Text** property. If it is a file, the file should be downloaded. Otherwise, the files in that directory should be listed and added as children of the current node.

To determine the file type, enter the following statements in the **tvwFTP_NodeClick** event procedure in the form frmITC:

```
Dim pstrFile As String
Set mnodCurrent = Node
pstrFile = mnodCurrent.Text
If Mid(pstrFile, Len(pstrFile), 1) = "/" Then
    GetDir Node
Else
    GetFile Node
End If
```

This procedure assumes that the last character of a directory name contains a forward slash. If this situation is **True**, the **GetDir** procedure is called. If not, the entry is an ordinary file and the **GetFile** procedure is called.

You tested the **StillExecuting** property when the Connect command button was clicked to prevent another request from being made while the prior request was still pending. Both the **GetDir** and **GetFile** procedures should perform the same check because the user could click on a directory, thereby causing the **GetDir** procedure to execute. While the request is being satisfied, the user could click on another directory or file name, which would cause an error. Another solution is to lock specific control instances while a request is pending.

```
If mnodCurrent.Children = 0 Then
    itt1.Execute "FTP://" & txtAddress, _
    "dir " & pnod.FullPath & "/*"
End If
```

The **If** statement checks the value of the current node's **Children** property to see whether the node currently has children. If the node has children, the directory already has been read from the server and should not be read again. The other option would be to delete all child nodes and make the request again. Although this approach would refresh the server directory, it is likely that the request is unnecessary and will just delay the user from obtaining a response.

The **GetFile** procedure uses a different operation (the *operation* argument) for the **Execute** method. This time, a **GET** operation is performed.

```
itt1.Execute "FTP://" & txtAddress, _
    "GET " & pnod.FullPath & " " & cdlInet.filename
```

The **GET** operation takes two arguments. The first argument—the name of the remote file—can be found by obtaining the full path of the node in the TreeView control instance. Note that the path separator pertaining to the TreeView control must be set to an empty string "" because the paths already are embedded in the file names displayed in the nodes.

To download a file:

1. Create the **GetDir** procedure in the form named frmITC, and insert the following statements:

```
Private Sub GetDir(pnod As Node)
    If itt1.StillExecuting Then
        Exit Sub
    Else
```

14

```
        If mnodCurrent.Children = 0 Then
            itt1.Execute "FTP://" & txtAddress, _
                "DIR " & pnod.FullPath & "/*"
        End If
    End If
End Sub
```

2. Create the **GetFile** procedure and insert the following statements:

```
Private Sub GetFile(pnod As Node)
On Error GoTo CancelError
    If itt1.StillExecuting Then
        Exit Sub
    Else
        cdlInet.FileName = pnod.Text
        cdlInet.ShowSave
    itt1.Execute "FTP://" & txtAddress, _
        "GET " & pnod.FullPath & " " & _
            cdlInet.FileName
    End If
    Exit Sub
CancelError:
End Sub
```

3. Test the program. Establish a connection to the Internet. Click on the Internet Transfer Control/FTP command button. Accept the default ftp.microsoft.com by clicking on the Connect command button and then wait for the root directory to be downloaded. Click on a directory (an entry with a trailing slash). This action causes another request to be made from the server and the contents of that directory to be downloaded.

4. Click on a file that is not a directory. The CommonDialog control will be activated, allowing you to download a file. Enter a file name, and then save the file in the Chapter 14\Startup folder to begin the download process. (Consider downloading Disclaim.txt.)

5. End the program to return to design mode. Terminate the Internet connection.

The **GetDir** general procedure first tests whether the current node has any children. If it does, the program should not reread the child directory; otherwise, the child directory is read. The general procedure does not deal with the response from the FTP server. The **StateChanged** event procedure that retrieves the data returned handles this issue.

If the current node is a file rather than a directory, the code in the **GetFile** procedure executes. It calls the **Execute** method to make an FTP request, just as the other procedures you have called have done. This request is a request to download a file, however. The code in the **GetFile** procedure code calls the **Execute** method, a technique you have seen before. Nevertheless, the *operation* argument is much different, because the code performs a **GET** operation to download data from the remote server. The **GET** operation takes two arguments—the file to be downloaded from the remote server and the file to be stored on the local disk.

Network Timeouts

One problem that can occur with programs that access a network is network timeout. This problem arises when you send a request to the server but the server never sends a response. You can control how long your program will wait for a server response by setting the **RequestTimeout** property of the Internet Transfer control. As the developer, you need to decide what is a reasonable amount of time to wait for a server response. Determining this value is subjective. If the value is too small, the program may not behave as desired when the Internet or your network provider is busy. If the interval is too long, the user may not be aware that the server is no longer available and may continue waiting.

The **RequestTimeout** property contains an Integer value indicating the number of seconds to wait before either raising an error, in the case of the **OpenURL** method, or raising the **StateChanged** event, in the case of the **Execute** method. By default, the value of the **RequestTimeout** property is 60 (60 seconds).

Chapter Summary

In this chapter, you have seen how to implement an Internet client that accesses the services supplied by Internet servers.

To establish a connection using the Winsock control:

➤ Set the **Protocol** property as necessary.

➤ Set the **RemoteHost** property to the name of the remote host.

➤ Set the **RemovePort** property to the appropriate Integer number for the service.

➤ Call the **Connect** method.

➤ Call the **SendData** method to send a message to a server.

➤ Respond to the **DataArrival** event to process server responses. In the **DataArrival** event, call the **GetData** method to retrieve data from the input queue.

➤ Respond to the **Error** event as necessary when the Winsock control generates an error.

To perform FTP requests using the Internet Transfer control:

➤ Call the **Execute** method to make a request to the remote server.

➤ In the **StateChanged** event, call the **GetChunk** method to retrieve data from the remote server.

REVIEW QUESTIONS

1. Which of the following protocols does the Winsock control support?
   a. IP/UDP
   b. TCP/IP
   c. TCP/UDP
   d. All of the above
   e. None of the above

2. What is the well-defined port number used by SMTP?
   a. 10
   b. 25
   c. 30
   d. 35
   e. 40

3. Which of the following are low-level Internet services?
   a. SMTP
   b. FTP
   c. Nameservice
   d. All of the above
   e. None of the above

4. Which of the following statements about SMTP is true?
   a. Commands are not case-sensitive.
   b. Mail addresses are not case-sensitive.
   c. Commands are terminated with a carriage return/linefeed sequence.
   d. All of the above.
   e. None of the above.

5. Which of the following is a valid SMTP command?

   a. **MAIL TO**

   b. **RECV FROM**

   c. **MAIL FROM**

   d. **SEND**

   e. **RECEIVE**

6. The _____ method transmits data to a remote host and the _____ method retrieves data from the input queue.

   a. **DataSend, DataGet**

   b. **Write, Read**

   c. **SendData, GetData**

   d. **Output, Input**

   e. None of the above

7. When does the Winsock control's **Error** event occur?

   a. when an invalid SMTP response is received

   b. when a TCP error occurs

   c. when an IP error occurs

   d. Both b and c

   e. All of the above

8. Write the statements to connect to the host named mail.microsoft.com using a Winsock control named sokMail. Use the SMTP port.

9. Write the statement to send the **HELO** SMTP command to the host named mail.microsoft.com using the Winsock control named sokSMTP.

10. Create the event procedure to store incoming data from the Winsock control named sokSMTP. Store the incoming data in the string variable named **pstrBuffer**.

11. Which of the following protocols is supported by the Internet Transfer control?

    a. TCP/IP

    b. TCP/UDP

    c. FTP/HTTP

    d. FTP/TCP

    e. FTP/IP

14

12. Which of the following statements about transmission modes is true?

    a. Synchronous transmission means that the execution of a command must be completed before the next command executes.

    b. Asynchronous transmission means that the execution of commands can continue, even though the execution of a previous command has not been completed.

    c. Synchronous transmission is faster than asynchronous transmission.

    d. Both a and b.

    e. All of the above.

13. Which of the following is a valid anonymous FTP command?

    a. **LS**

    b. **LIST**

    c. **DIRECTORY**

    d. **WRITE**

    e. **READ**

14. Which of the following is a valid privileged FTP command?

    a. **RMDIR**

    b. **RENAME**

    c. **PUT**

    d. None of the above

    e. All of the above

15. Which of the following statements about the Internet Transfer control's **StateChanged** event is true?

    a. The **StateChanged** event occurs as a request is made and then completed.

    b. The **StateChanged** event raises the **Error** event.

    c. When a request is made, the current state is Requested.

    d. All of the above.

    e. None of the above.

16. To send an FTP command using the Internet Transfer control, you call the _____ method.

    a. **FTP**

    b. **Execute**

    c. **Write**

    d. **SendData**

    e. **SendMessage**

17. To copy data from the input queue to a variable in your program using the Internet Transfer control, you call the _____ method.

   a. **GetData**

   b. **Read**

   c. **GetChunk**

   d. **GetInfo**

   e. **Input**

18. Assuming an Internet Transfer control named ittFTP has been created, write the statements to execute the URL to connect to the FTP site named ftp.microsoft.com and then list the files in the root directory. Make sure that a request is not currently being executed.

19. Assuming that an Internet Transfer control named ittFTP has been created, write the statements to download the file named 1s-RW.txt from the FTP server named ftp.microsoft.com. Save the file in the folder named A:\ls.txt.

20. Write the statement(s) to retrieve the response from the Internet Transfer control named ittFTP, and store the response in the string variable named **pstrFTP**.

21. Write the statement to change the timeout of an Internet Transfer control named ittFTP to 2 minutes in a program's **Form_Load** event procedure.

HANDS-ON PROJECTS

Project 1

In this project, you will create a program to send mail messages. Instead of sending a message to a single recipient, however, the program will send messages to multiple recipients.

   a. Run the executable file named Chapter.14\Exercise\Ex1Demo.exe. The form that appears contains a list box from which you can select an email address. Note that the mail addresses shown are not valid and are provided for demonstration purposes only. Check the boxes next to each name and then try to send a mail message to all recipients. Exit the program.

   b. Start Visual Basic. Create a new project, and set the **Name** property of the form to **frmEx1**. Save the form using the name Chapter.14\Exercise\frmEx1.frm and the project using the name Chapter.14\Exercise\Ex1.vbp.

   c. Create an instance of the Winsock control on the form.

d. Create text boxes to store the host name (of the mail server) and the return address of the mail message. Also, create a text box to store the message itself.

e. Create a checked list box (the **Style** property of the list box is set to **CheckBox**). Add email addresses of people you know to that list box.

f. Create a command button named Send. When clicked, the program should try to send an email message to each selected recipient. The process is identical to the one presented in this chapter with one exception—instead of using the **RCPT TO** command once, the command must be called for each selected person in the list box. Thus you should create a **For** loop to examine all elements in the list box, determine whether the item is selected, and then add the recipient.

g. Test the program. The mail message should be sent to the multiple recipients. Exit Visual Basic.

Project 2

In this project, you will use the techniques presented in this chapter to create an FTP client. This program will use both the ListView and TreeView controls. Directories will be displayed in the TreeView control and ordinary files will be displayed in the ListView control.

a. Run the executable file named Chapter.14\Exercise\Ex2Demo.exe. Establish a connection to the Internet. Enter ftp.microsoft.com as the host name. Click on the Connect command button. Directories appear in the TreeView control instance and ordinary files appear in the ListView control instance. Exit the program.

b. Start Visual Basic. Create a new project, and set the **Name** property of the form to **frmEx2**. Save the form using the name Chapter.14\Exercise\ frmEx2.frm and the project using the name Chapter.14\Exercise\Ex2.vbp.

c. Create a ListView, TreeView, and Internet Transfer control on the form.

d. Create a text box so that the user can enter an FTP address. Create a command button that, when clicked, establishes a connection with the server.

e. Instead of displaying all entries in a TreeView control as described in this chapter, display directory entries in the TreeView control and display file names in the ListView control.

f. When the user clicks on a node in the TreeView control, connect to the server and download the directory. Directories should appear as children of the node that was clicked. Regular files should appear in the ListView control.

g. Test the program. Make sure that the files and directories appear in the correct control. Exit Visual Basic.

CHAPTER FIFTEEN

DHTML AND HTML HELP

AFTER READING THIS CHAPTER AND COMPLETING THE EXERCISES, YOU WILL BE ABLE TO:

➤ Discover the purpose of a Dynamic HTML (DHTML) application

➤ Modify an existing Web page to operate as a DHTML page

➤ Add programmable elements to a DHTML page

➤ Understand the DHTML object model

➤ Compile a DHTML application

➤ Install HTML Help

➤ Create a Help project

➤ Add topic pages to a project

➤ Add a table of contents to the Help project

➤ Add an index to the Help project

➤ Compile the Help project

➤ Access help from a Visual Basic application

➤ Develop context-sensitive help

Developing Help And Dynamic Web Pages For Intranets

Developing A Dynamic HTML Application

This chapter contains two completed applications. The first illustrates a technique to create interactive Web pages using Dynamic HTML (DHTML). The second illustrates how to deploy the Help system with an application. You will preview the second application later in this chatper. To complete both sections in the chapter, you must have Internet Explorer 5.0 installed on your computer. To perform the steps in the last half of the chapter, you must have HTML Help Workshop installed on your computer.

To preview the first completed application:

1. Start Visual Basic. This chapter's project consists of a new type of module called a DHTML page. Furthermore, the project type represents a new type of project: a DHTML project. Load the file named Chapter.15\Complete\Dhtml\Ch15_C.vbp.

2. Run the program. This type of project uses Internet Explorer as its container. The initial document displayed contains the closing cost estimation page, as shown in Figure 15.1.

3. In the combo box, select the value $125,000. In the Estimated Down Payment text box, enter a value of 20000. Click on the Calculate button to compute the output values. These values appear at the bottom of the page. To calculate the payment, the code calls the **Pmt** function. This function returns a negative number. You may need to use the scroll bars to locate the output, depending on the size of the Internet Explorer window.

4. At the bottom of the page, the text Click To View Our Home Page appears. The words Home Page form a hyperlink. Click on the hyperlink (the text Home Page) to view the other DHTML page making up the application. Note that the second page contains minimal text; its purpose is simply to demonstrate the use of a hyperlink.

5. Exit Internet Explorer.

6. In Visual Basic, end the program.

7. Exit Visual Basic.

This chapter assumes that you are familiar with the basic elements of HTML, including heading and paragraph tags. As this chapter is not intended to serve as a tutorial on HTML, only the most basic language elements will be discussed and used. You can create much more sophisticated DHTML documents than the ones discussed in this chapter.

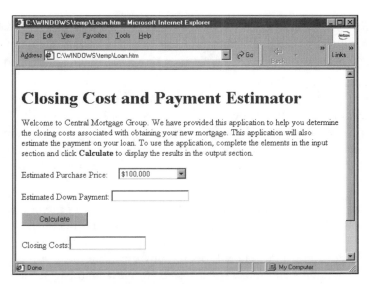

Figure 15.1   Internet Explorer displaying DHTML page.

Dynamic HTML

The HTML language was initially used primarily by scientific and educational institutions to display static information. One major benefit of HTML is that the language is platform-independent. That is, you can display the same HTML page on a computer running Windows, UNIX, or any other operating system by using any browser.

The first versions of HTML had several limitations. The first HTML pages were static, and the end user had little or no control over the page once the browser rendered it. As the focus of HTML shifted from the educational world into the commercial world, the language evolved considerably. The advent of scripting and applets gave Web browsers the ability to execute code contained in Web pages. This feature allowed Web pages to become dynamic rather than static.

The first uses of scripting and applets ran on HTML servers. Thus the server took responsibility for changing the content of the HTML page. At this point in HTML's development, the client still could not modify the content or appearance of an HTML page dynamically. The advent of DHTML, however, changed that paradigm.

To improve HTML, Microsoft introduced a revolutionary Internet technology (initially code-named Trident) that encapsulated HTML into an object model including all of the HTML elements. By encapsulating HTML into an object model, you, as the developer, gain programmatic access to all of the components making up an HTML page. In addition, this expanded HTML model supports client-side scripting. That is, Internet Explorer can run scripts on the client

15

without making server requests. These scripts can change content, apply formatting, and execute any other code.

To understand HTML and DHTML scripting, you need to know how Internet Explorer and the HTML object model work. Internet Explorer comprises a group of components. A small container program named IEXPLORE.EXE provides a frame to the WebBrowser object named SHDOCVW.DLL. This object, in turn, provides basic browser features such as navigation, refreshing pages, and printing. It does not display HTML pages, however. Rather, it acts as an ActiveX document container. This container, in turn, loads an ActiveX document server that interprets the desired URL.

This separation of responsibilities has significance. By making the document viewer independent of the browser itself, Internet Explorer becomes document-independent. Specifically, Internet Explorer can handle many types of documents in addition to HTML documents. For example, it can display both Word documents and Excel spreadsheets. To view Web pages, Internet Explorer uses the HTML viewer named MSHTML.DLL. This program is also an ActiveX document server. To view other documents, like Word or Excel documents, Internet Explorer employs a different viewer.

You can apply two techniques to build Web applications with Visual Basic: Internet Information Server (IIS) and Dynamic HTML (DHTML). These applications provide Web services in different ways. IIS applications perform their processing on the server, whereas DHTML applications carry out their processing on the client. Processing data on the client rather than the server reduces server and network contention. Because the browser refreshes DHTML pages from the client rather than the server, performance tends to improve. DHTML applications also allow you to leverage your Visual Basic knowledge to create event-driven Web pages. Although the HTML viewer can interpret and display HTML documents, it is not able to execute code. To execute code, the HTML viewer relies upon the services of a scripting engine. For example, to run Visual Basic scripts, the viewer uses VBSCRIPT.DLL; to execute JavaScript, it uses JSCRIPT.DLL. The scripting engine takes the responsibility for executing any and all code.

The Dynamic HTML object model relies upon seven objects and one collection, as shown in Figure 15.2.

As shown in Figure 15.2, the Window object is the root object; it represents the browser's window. Like any object, the Window object supports events, properties, and methods. It also supports the remaining objects in the hierarchy. In DHTML, you use the BaseWindow object to programmatically reference the underlying Window object. The Window object contains the following collections and objects:

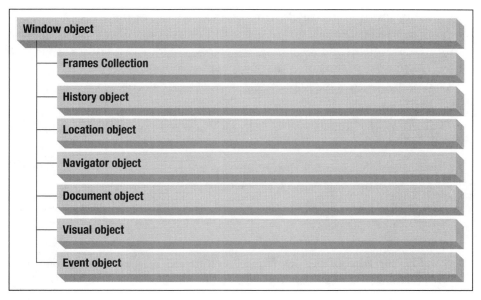

Figure 15.2 DHTML object model.

➤ **Frames collection** Provides a reference to those frames. (Most currently used browsers support Frames.)

➤ **History object** Supports methods allowing navigation through the browser's history list. It also supports properties providing access to the current URL.

➤ **Location object** Represents the current URL. It supports a method to reload the current URL and to provide information about the current URL.

➤ **Navigator object** Provides information about the current browser, including the browser's name and its version. You use this object to perform different actions based upon the type and version of the browser. It is useful because all browsers may not support the same capabilities.

➤ **Document object** Represents the Web page currently displayed in the window. The Document object represents each element on the Web page using a group of collections and other objects.

➤ **Visual object** Provides information about the screen and its display capabilities.

➤ **Event object** Supports properties associated with the current event, such as a mouse click. It also provides support for canceling an event.

As mentioned, the Document object represents the Web pages displayed on the browser. This object contains a reference to numerous collections and other

15

objects representing elements on the page. As the programmer, you have complete access to these objects and collections, so you can dynamically change the contents and formatting of the page. Figure 15.3 illustrates the collections and objects pertaining to the Document object.

➤ **All collection** Contains a reference to all of the elements in the object hierarchy.

➤ **Links collection** Stores a reference to Link objects. One Link object exists for each anchor tab containing an HREF attribute.

➤ **Anchors collection** Contains a reference to the Anchor objects. One Anchor object exists for each <A> tag.

➤ **Images collection** and corresponding **Image object** Return a reference to the images on the page. (A DHTML document may contain one or more images.)

➤ **Forms collection** Contains references to Form objects. The primary purpose of a Form object is the submission of a form to a remote site.

➤ **Applets collection** As the name implies, provides a reference to all Applet objects in the page.

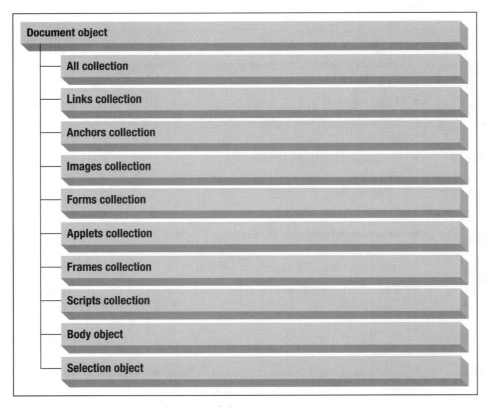

Figure 15.3 Document object model.

➤ **Frames collections** Represent the frames making up the document.

➤ **Scripts collection** Contains a reference to all scripts used by the Web page. These scripts may be written in different scripting languages.

➤ **Body object** Provides access to the textual content of the Web page.

➤ **Selection object** Contains the text currently selected by the end user.

Each of these objects is available to you as the DHTML application programmer.

DHTML Application Structure

DHTML applications can be used with Internet Explorer 4 or 5 to display documents from an intranet. Dynamic HTML is a superset of the HTML language. A DHTML application consists of one or more DHTML pages; each DHTML page can execute Visual Basic code and respond to events. The following list describes the parts of a DHTML application:

➤ A DHTML application contains a project file, just like any other Visual Basic application.

➤ An application consists of one or more DHTML pages, rather than forms. When compiled, the code for the application is stored in a DLL library. Visual Basic stores the source code for a DHTML page in a file having the extension ".dsr". The page may also have a corresponding .dsx file that contains binary information.

➤ You create the visual interface from elements rather than from controls. Furthermore, you use a different visual designer (the DHTML page designer) rather than the Form window.

➤ In addition to using the msvbm60.dll run-time library, DHTML applications require the use of the Internet Explorer browser library.

➤ You create Visual Basic code to handle events. Visual Basic compiles this code into a DLL file that runs as an in-process component inside Internet Explorer. Unlike with an ordinary HTML page, the user cannot view the code.

15

To create a new DHTML application, you first create a DHTML project. You then can develop new DHTML pages and add existing DHTML or HTML pages to the project.

To create a DHTML project:

1. Start Visual Basic, and activate the New Project dialog box, if necessary. Double-click on the DHTML Application project type to create the new project. Visual Basic creates a new project with a standard module and a DHTML module.

2. In the Project Explorer, open the Designers folder and double-click on DHTMLPage1 to open the DHTML page designer.

When you create a new DHTML project, Visual Basic automatically creates a blank DHTML page. To define the content for the DHTML page, you must create the HTML text and buttons that will appear on the page. You have two options for designing the content of the HTML page. You can use an editor capable of writing HTML files, or you can use yet another visual designer.

The DHTML page designer allows you to edit existing DHTML documents and to create new ones. Figure 15.4 shows the DHTML page designer with a blank DHTML document.

As shown in Figure 15.4, the DHTML designer contains two panes. The left pane lists the HTML sections and control instances (members) found on the page. The listing is hierarchical because HTML tags can be nested. The right pane shows the visual interface for the DHTML document as it will appear in a browser. Just as with the Form window, you create elements in the right pane.

You are not restricted to creating HTML documents in the DHTML page designer, however. You can develop HTML documents using any tool that writes HTML, including Microsoft Word, Microsoft FrontPage, and many others. Although you can use other tools to create HTML, these tools do not typically support the DHTML extensions. Thus, although you can create basic HTML documents using other tools, you must work with the DHTML designer to create the visual elements, such as buttons, in your document and to write code for those buttons.

Like any other module, a DHTML page consists of a visible part and an accompanying code. You use the Code window to create this code for the DHTML module.

By default, a DHTML page supports three objects:

➤ **BaseWindow** Contains a reference to the browser window and displays the Document object.

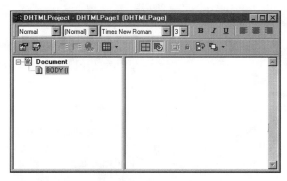

Figure 15.4 DHTML page designer.

➤ **Document** Contains a reference to the HTML page viewed by the end user in a Web browser. You use the Document object and its supported events to access the DHTML object model. This object contains a reference to the DHTMLPage object.

➤ **DHTMLPage** Is a run-time component that establishes the connection between the Visual Basic run-time environment and the DHTML object model. This object provides support for events such as **Load**, **Initialize**, and **Terminate**. Note that the DHTMLPage object cannot be referenced through the Document object.

As with any other module, you can create code in the Code window to set properties and to respond to events generated by these objects.

The DHTMLPage object manages the Web page while it is running. The DHTML Page object supports a sequence of events as the page loads and unloads. These events are similar to the events supported by a form:

1. The **Initialize** event occurs first when a Web browser begins to load the DHTML page. When the **Initialize** event occurs, the browser may not have loaded the remaining objects on the page. Thus you should not attempt to reference properties for other elements on the page in this event.

2. The **Load** event occurs after the **Initialize** event. When this event occurs depends on whether the page is loaded asynchronously or synchronously. If the page is loaded asynchronously, the **Load** event occurs after the creation of the first element on the page. If the page is loaded synchronously, the **Load** event occurs after the creation of all elements.

3. The **Unload** event occurs when the end user navigates to another page or closes the application. During this event, the elements on the page still exist.

4. The **Terminate** event occurs just before the destruction of the page. When this event occurs, the elements on the page no longer exist.

15

Unlike other projects, Visual Basic can save DHTML pages in different ways.

First, you can save the DHTML page within the designer file. Although this option allows other developers working on the project to easily view and edit the page, you cannot edit it with an external editor. That is, you cannot use an application such as Microsoft FrontPage or a simple editor such as Notepad to edit the HTML document when the page is saved in the designer file.

Alternatively, you can save a page to an external location. Using this method, the DTHML designer creates a reference to an external HTML file. Although this option allows you to edit the file from an external editor, moving the file to a different location or computer will make the reference invalid.

Both of these options apply only while you are developing the application. Once you compile the application, Visual Basic generates a DLL file and external HTML files.

Because this book is not intended as a comprehensive discussion of HTML, you will insert an existing HTML document into the project and modify it to operate as a DHTML application.

To add a DHTML document to an application:

1. In the Project Explorer, open the Designers folder, if necessary.

2. Right-click on the page named DHTMLPage1, and click on Remove DHTMLPage1. If a dialog box appears asking whether you want to save changes to the listed files, click on No. You will not use the empty file in this project.

3. Click on Project, and then click on Add DHTML Page to activate the DHTMLPage1 Properties dialog box. Your responses in this dialog box will determine how Visual Basic saves the document. You can save the file either inside the designer file or as an external HTML document. Click on the Save HTML In An External File: Option button. Click on Open to open an existing HTML file. Select the file named Chapter.15\Startup\Dhtml \Loan.htm, and then click on the Open button.

4. On the Properties dialog box, click on OK. The DHTML Page designer opens, displaying the existing document.

5. To add the second DHTML page in the project, click on Project, and then click on Add DHTML Page. Click on the Save HTML In An External File: Option button. Click on Open to open an existing DTHML file. Select the file named Chapter.15\Startup\Dhtml\Home.htm, and then click on the Open button. On the Properties dialog box, click on OK.

6. Open the Visual Designer for the page named DTHMLPage1, if necessary. Figure 15.5 shows the completed DHTML page with all folders open.

7. To open and close a folder, you click on the plus or minus sign located to the left of the folder. Click on the plus sign to the left of the Document object to display the objects contained by the document.

Carefully examine the left pane of the DHTML page designer. This pane of the designer displays, in a hierarchical manner, the elements of the HTML page. As shown in Figure 15.5, the root object is the Document object. The Document object, in turn, contains several elements, including headings and paragraphs. At this point, the document you inserted has characteristics like those of other HTML documents. In the remainder of this section, you will modify and enhance the document so that it will compute the closing costs for a mortgage and estimate a mortgage payment. For brevity, you will not validate any of the input fields.

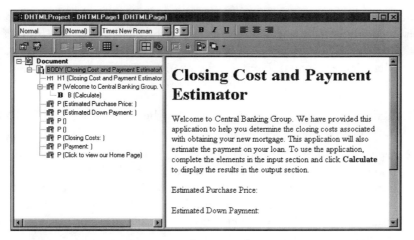

Figure 15.5   DHTML page in the page designer.

You create buttons and text boxes in a DHTML document in the same way that you create buttons and text boxes on a form. That is, you click on controls in the toolbox and create instances of them in the DHTML document. DHTML uses a different terminology than a form-based application, however. The term *element* replaces the term *control*, and the term *attribute* replaces the term *property*.

DHTML elements are similar in purpose to intrinsic controls, but they differ from their intrinsic counterparts in that they support different properties and methods and respond to different events. For example, DHTML elements use the **id** attribute instead of the **Name** property. The following list describes some of the more commonly used DHTML elements and their purposes:

➤ **Button** Is similar to a command button. When clicked, it responds to the **onclick** event.

➤ **Checkbox** Is similar to the CheckBox control.

➤ **Option** Is similar to an option button.

➤ **Select** Is similar to an intrinsic combo box. When clicked, the element responds to the **onclick** event.

➤ **TextField** Is similar to a text box. This input-output element is used to retrieve and display text.

➤ **TextArea** Works much like a multiline text box.

➤ **Hyperlink** Creates text or an image that, when clicked, allows the user to jump to another page.

When you create elements on a DHTML document, you must be aware of a concept called positioning. You can position an element in one of two ways. With absolute positioning, you position the element relative to the body of the document. An absolute positioned element therefore appears where you place it on the document. With relative positioning, the element appears in the flow of the document. For example, if you create an element and position it relative to text, that element would flow with the relative text.

To create a Select element:

1. Activate the DHTML page designer for the page named DHTMLPage1. In the left pane of the page designer, open all folders.

2. Open the toolbox, if necessary. In the toolbox, click on the HTML button, if necessary, to display the DHTML elements. Click on the Select Element button on the toolbar, move the mouse to the right of the text Estimated Purchase Price, and then draw an instance of the element. Unlike other visual designers, the mouse cursor does not change to a crosshair when you are creating the element.

3. Look in the left pane. Note that the Select element that you just created appears relative to the last item on the page. That is, the item is relative to the document and appears at the end of the document structure.

4. Right–click on the Select element you just created, and then click on the Absolute Position menu item to remove the check mark. Drag the Select element to the right of the Estimated Purchase Price text. As you perform this task, note that the element moves in the hierarchy to appear as a subelement of the Estimate Purchase Price paragraph.

5. Right–click on the object that you just created, and then click on Properties. The Property Pages for the element appear.

   Defining the properties for a Select element differs significantly from defining the properties for an intrinsic combo box. In this case, the Property Pages display text boxes to store the text that appears in the visible portion of the select element and a corresponding value.

6. In the Text box, enter a value of $100,000; in the Value text box, enter a value of 100000. Click on Insert to insert a new item in the list. Enter a Text value of $125,000 and a value of 125000. Click on the Insert button again. Repeat this process to insert two more list items with values of 150000 and 175000.

7. Click on OK to close the Property Pages.

8. Press F4 to activate the Properties window for the element. Set the (**Id**) attribute to selPurchasePrice. You must set the (**Id**) attribute to execute code for the element.

The next field you will create is a text field. In this text field, the user will enter the amount of the down payment. For brevity, you will not validate the input values. Although a text field element works like the intrinsic TextBox control, it has different attributes:

➤ **Boolean disabled** Indicates whether the text field is enabled or disabled.

➤ **value** Defines the text appearing in the text field.

➤ **readOnly** Controls whether the user can enter text in the text field.

To create a Text field:

1. On the toolbox, click on the TextField button. Create a text field on the DHTML page to the right of the Estimated Down Payment text.

2. Right-click on the text field and make sure that Absolute Position is not checked.

3. Move the text field you just created so that it appears to the right of the Estimated Down Payment text and as a child of the Estimated Down Payment paragraph in the left pane of the DHTML page designer.

4. Activate the Properties window for the text field element that you just created.

5. Set the (**Id**) attribute to **txtDownPayment**.

6. Remove the text from the value attribute.

7. Create two more text fields next to the Closing Costs and Payment. Set the (**Id**) attributes for these text fields to **txtClosingCosts** and **txtPayment**, respectively. Turn off absolute positioning, and make sure that the text fields appear to the right of the appropriate text. Remove the text from the value attribute. Finally, set the **readOnly** attribute to **True** for both text fields.

The next element you will create on the DHTML page is the Button element. When clicked, this element will execute code to compute the output values. The Button element works like the CommandButton control. Again, the attribute names of the button element differ from the property names corresponding to the CommandButton control:

➤ **accessKey** Contains a single character used to define an access key for the button.

➤ **value** Stores the text that appears in the button.

In this example, you will use a Button element to calculate the output values when the user clicks on the button. Again, this button has the same purpose as a command button on a form.

To create a Button element:

1. In the toolbox, click on the Button Element button.

2. Create an instance of the element on the DHTML page designer.

15

3. Turn off absolute positioning and anchor the element to the blank paragraph between the line Estimated Down Payment: and the line Closing Costs.

4. Set the (**Id**) attribute to **cmdCalculate**, and set the **value** attribute to **Calculate**.

5. Set the **accessKey** attribute to **C**.

Now that you have created the elements on the DHTML page, you can test the project for the first time. The process of testing a DHTML project differs from the process of testing a form-based application, because DTHML projects use Internet Explorer as a run-time container. Furthermore, when you run a DHTML project for the first time, the Project properties dialog box appears, asking how you want to start the project. The default option is to run a DTHML page. The Project properties dialog box also allows you to execute another program or indicate a specific URL to be run in a browser. In this example, you will run the DHTML component that you just created.

To test the DHTML application:

1. Test the program. The Project Properties dialog box appears.

2. The default option Start component should be selected. Make sure that DHTMLPage1 is selected in the adjacent list box.

3. Click on OK to run the program.

4. The DHTMLPage appears in Internet Explorer. Click on the Select element to the right of the Estimated Purchase Price text. A drop-down list should appear. At this point, the elements that you created do nothing because you have not yet created any event procedures.

5. Exit Internet Explorer.

6. In Visual Basic, end the program to return to design mode.

Your application, as it presently exists, is merely a user interface. That is, the elements perform no actions. You define event responses for elements in the same way as you define event responses for the intrinsic control instances you create on a form—you create event procedures.

Understanding The DHTML Event Model

Since the first chapter of this book, you have written code that executes in response to events. For example, a command button responds to a **Click** event. In a form-based project, each event must have its own unique event handler. That is, unique event procedures must exist for each object. Two objects (unless they are members of control arrays) cannot share the same event procedures. Event handlers in DHTML applications, however, function differently—event handlers are hierarchical. The following steps outline the sequence of events that occurs in a DHTML application:

1. As you have seen with all other programs, when the user clicks on a button or performs some other action, an event occurs. This event may occur to an element because the user moved the mouse over the element, moved the mouse off the element, or clicked the element.

2. If you have created an event handler (event procedure) for that element, its code will execute. This process is the same as you have seen with typical form-based applications.

3. In a form-based application, the event process ends at this point. In a DHTML project, however, after the event fires for the affected element, the event is passed to the parent element for processing. This process is known as event bubbling.

4. The process of event bubbling continues until the event reaches the Document object or the event is canceled.

5. A default action occurs. It is independent of event bubbling. To stop the default action from occurring, you must cancel it.

The events supported by DHTML elements differ from the events supported by Visual Basic controls. The following list summarizes selected events supported by most DHTML elements:

➤ **onclick** and **ondoubleclick** Occur when the user clicks and double-clicks the mouse on an element, respectively.

➤ **onmousedown** Occurs when the user clicks the mouse on an element. When the user releases the mouse, the **onmouseup** event occurs.

➤ **onmousemove** Occurs when the user moves the mouse pointer over an element.

➤ **onmouseout** Occurs when the user moves the mouse pointer off an element.

➤ **onmouseover** Occurs when the user moves the mouse pointer into an element.

In addition to supporting mouse events, HTML documents support three keyboard events:

➤ **onkeypress** Occurs when the user presses and releases a key.

➤ **onkeydown** Occurs when the user presses a key. Only one event will occur even if the user holds down the key.

➤ **onkeyup** Occurs when the user releases a key.

15

At this point in the program's development, you have created the elements on the DHTML page, but you have not yet written any code to execute as the user interacts with those elements. The code to compute the closing costs has been simplified for brevity. The closing costs are calculated at 2.3 percent of the loan amount. The code to compute the payments assumes an interest rate of 0.08 percent per month for 30 years. In reality, these values would likely change at run time.

You create an event procedure for a DHTML element in the same way as you create the code for any other event procedure. Remember, however, that event names for DHTML elements differ from the events supported by similar intrinsic controls.

To create event responses in the Code window for the DTHML page:

1. In the DHTML page designer for the DHTML page named DHTMLPage1, double-click on the cmdCalculate button element to activate the Code window. Select the **onclick** event procedure for the cmdCalculate button element, if necessary.

2. Enter the following statements in the event procedure:

```
Dim psngClosing As Single
Dim psngPayment As Single
Dim psngLoanAmount As Single
psngLoanAmount = selPurchasePrice.Value - _
    txtDownPayment.Value
psngClosing = psngLoanAmount * 0.023
txtClosingCosts.Value = psngClosing
psngPayment = Pmt(0.008, 360, psngLoanAmount)
txtPayment.Value = Format(psngPayment, "Fixed")
```

The preceding code is quite simple. It declares local variables to store the intermediate results of the various calculations. Your code computes the loan amount by subtracting the down payment from the purchase price. Next, you compute the closing costs by multiplying the loan amount by 0.023 (2.3 percent). To compute the payment, you call the **Pmt** function and store the result in an output text field.

Now that you have created the code for the button element, you can test the program.

To test the onclick event procedure:

1. Test the program. The DHTML page appears in Internet Explorer.

2. Select a purchase price of $150,000. Enter a down payment of 30000.

3. Click on the Calculate button.

4. The calculated results appear in the output text elements. You may need to use the scroll bars to display the output values.

5. Exit Internet Explorer.

6. End the program to return to design mode.

So far, you have used the DHTML project type and DHTML designer to create a fully functional DTHML page. Although you can create much more complex DHTML pages, you can apply the basic techniques illustrated here to create dynamic elements on any page.

Setting Element Styles

When using intrinsic controls, you set properties, including **ForeColor** and **BackColor**, to change the appearance of a particular control instance. To change the position or format of an element, however, you use a much different technique. Each type of element supports an object named Style that defines all possible styles for the element type. For example, nearly all elements support the following formatting styles. Note that these styles are merely a few of the many styles supported.

➤ **backgroundColor** and **foregroundColor** Set and retrieve the background and foreground colors of the element, respectively. The MSDN Library contains a list of valid strings defining colors.

➤ **borderStyle** Defines the element's left, right, top, and bottom borders. The values can be set to the strings none, solid, double, groove, ridge, inset, or outset. You can set the top, left, bottom, and right borders using the borderTop, borderLeft, borderBottom, and borderRight styles, respectively.

➤ **textAlign** You set the **textAlign** style to define the alignment of the text in the element. Valid values are the strings left, right, center, and justify.

➤ **height**, **left**, **top**, and **width** Determine the position and size of the element on the page.

➤ **visibility** Indicates whether an element will be visible.

To illustrate how to use a run-time style, you will change the foreground color of the selected object named **selPurchasePrice** when the user passes the mouse pointer over the element. To accomplish this task, you can write code in response to the onmouseover and onmouseout events:

```
Private Sub selPurchasePrice_onmouseout()
    selPurchasePrice.Style.backgroundColor = "IVORY"
End Sub

Private Sub selPurchasePrice_onmouseover()
    selPurchasePrice.Style.backgroundColor = "AQUA"
End Sub
```

15

The preceding event procedures resemble the event procedures you have created for intrinsic controls. They differ in two ways, however. First, the event names differ. Second, the statements use the Style object to set the background colors.

To set the style for an element:

1. Activate the Code window for the DHTML page named DHTMLPage1.

2. Activate the **selPurchasePrice_onmouseout** event procedure, and enter the following statement:

```
selPurchasePrice.Style.backgroundColor = _
    "IVORY"
```

3. Activate the **selPurchasePrice_onmouseover** event procedure, and enter the following statement:

```
selPurchasePrice.Style.backgroundColor = _
    "AQUA"
```

4. Test the program. When you run the program, the DHTML page appears inside Internet Explorer and Internet Explorer receives focus. Move the mouse pointer over the Select element and click on the list arrow. The drop-down list appears with an aqua-colored background. Select an object; the background color returns to ivory.

5. Exit Internet Explorer.

6. In Visual Basic, end the program to return to design mode.

In a DTHML document, each element need not have its own event procedure to respond to a particular event. Instead, events bubble. Using this paradigm, if an event handler does not exist for a particular element, the parent object will be checked for an event handler, then its parent, and so on, until either an event handler is found or the hierarchy is exhausted.

Consider the Central Banking Group program. Central Banking Group originates home loans and provides other banking services at its branch offices around the United States. The company wants to provide its employees and customers with the ability to estimate the costs associated with originating a home loan. Because most of their customers and employees are familiar with Internet Explorer, Central Banking Group would like to deploy this system such that the users can compute the loan costs through this Web browser. In addition, the company wants the ability to deploy Help systems with its applications and have the systems contain elements common to all Help systems. These elements include a table of contents, an index, and context-sensitive help.

Assume that each element on the DTHML page should appear with an aqua background color when the mouse pointer is positioned over the element, and that the elements should have an ivory background color when the mouse is not positioned over the elements. In a traditional form-based application, you would create event procedures for each intrinsic control instance created on the form to accomplish this task. Because of event bubbling, however, the task becomes much easier for DHTML pages.

To take advantage of event bubbling, you need to understand how to reference the current event and the element that caused the event. The DHTMLPage object supports a property named DHTMLEvent, which contains a reference to the currently running event. This object supports several properties that allow you to manage the event.

Syntax

> Event

Properties

➤ The **AltKey** property returns the state of the Alt key. If the value is **True**, the user held down the Alt key when the event occurred. If it is **False**, the user did not hold down the Alt key.

➤ The **Button** property indicates which mouse button was pressed by the user.

➤ The **CancelBubble** property stops events from cascading (bubbling up through the object hierarchy).

➤ The **SrcElement** property contains a reference to the element that fired the event.

➤ The **Type** property indicates the name of the event.

15

To illustrate the use of the Event object, assume that you wanted each element to appear in a different color than the other elements when the mouse is positioned over the element. One technique you can use to accomplish this task is to set the backgroundColor style in the **onmouseout** and **onmouseover** events for each element you created on the DHTMLPage. In this example, this approach is not a problem because the page contains only a few elements. Nevertheless, you can significantly reduce the amount of coding required by taking advantage of event bubbling.

In event bubbling, the event occurs first for the element that caused the event. It then occurs to each element in the HTML hierarchy. As the Document object exists at the top of the DHTML hierarchy, writing code in the event procedures for the Document object will execute code for all elements created on the DHTML page. Consider the **onmouseout** and **onmouseover** event procedures pertaining to the Document object:

```
Private Sub Document_onmouseout()
    DHTMLPage.DHTMLEvent.srcElement. _
        Style.backgroundColor = "IVORY"
End Sub
Private Sub Document_onmouseover()
    DHTMLPage.DHTMLEvent.srcElement. _
        Style.backgroundColor = "AQUA"
End Sub
```

These event procedures will execute each time the mouse passes over and off an element, regardless of the element. To determine which element caused the event, the event procedure contains the following statement fragment to reference the element:

```
DHTMLPage.DHTMLEvent.srcElement
```

Using this reference, the procedure sets the background color of the element that generated the event.

To program a bubbling event:

1. Activate the Code window for the DHTMLPage named DHTMLPage1, and enter the following statement in the **Document_onmouseout** event procedure:

```
DHTMLPage.DHTMLEvent.srcElement. _
    Style.backgroundColor = "IVORY"
```

2. In the **Document_onmouseover** event procedure, enter the following statement:

```
DHTMLPage.DHTMLEvent.srcElement. _
    Style.backgroundColor = "AQUA"
```

3. Test the program. Internet Explorer appears and receives focus. Move the mouse over the various elements making up the DHTML page. As the mouse moves over each element, the foreground and background colors change. Note that the colors change for all elements, including the textual paragraphs on the page and the page itself. Be sure to move the mouse over the text parts of the page and the buttons. Note that the colors change for these elements as well.

4. Exit Internet Explorer.

5. In Visual Basic, end the program to return to design mode.

The program as it presently exists has two deficiencies. First, suppose that you did not want the textual components to change color as the user passes the mouse over these elements. Second, suppose that you did not want the button to change color. Several techniques exist to solve these problems. Remember that you assigned a value to the **id** attribute for all of the elements (Textfield, Select, and Button) that you created on the DHTML page. The remaining elements have no value assigned to the **id** attribute. Thus you can add an **If** statement to the event procedures to determine whether the **id** attribute contains a value. If it does not, then you should not apply formatting to the element.

Consider the following expansion of the event procedures to account for the **id** property of each element:

```
Private Sub Document_onmouseout()
    If DHTMLPage.DHTMLEvent.srcElement.id <> _
        vbNullString Then
        DHTMLPage.DHTMLEvent.srcElement. _
            Style.backgroundColor = "IVORY"
    End If
End Sub
Private Sub Document_onmouseover()
    If DHTMLPage.DHTMLEvent.srcElement.id <> _
        vbNullString Then
        DHTMLPage.DHTMLEvent.srcElement. _
            Style.backgroundColor = "AQUA"
    End If
End Sub
```

The preceding statements check the **id** attribute of the element that caused the event to occur. If this attribute is blank, then the **If** statement is False and the code that sets the background color is not executed. Otherwise, the code sets the color of the element that caused the event to occur.

To program a bubbling event:

1. Activate the Code window for the DHTMLPage named DHTMLPage1, and enter the following statements in the **Document_onmouseout** event procedure:

```
If DHTMLPage.DHTMLEvent.srcElement.id <> _
    vbNullString Then
    DHTMLPage.DHTMLEvent.srcElement. _
        Style.backgroundColor = "IVORY"
End If
```

2. Activate the Code window for the **Document_onmouseover** event procedure, and enter the following statements:

```
If DHTMLPage.DHTMLEvent.srcElement.id <> _
    vbNullString Then
    DHTMLPage.DHTMLEvent.srcElement. _
        Style.backgroundColor = "AQUA"
End If
```

3. Test the program. Internet Explorer appears and receives focus. Move the mouse over the DHTML page. As you move the mouse over each element containing a value for the id attributes, the foreground and background colors change. Be sure to move the mouse pointer over the text parts of the page. Note that the colors for these elements no longer change. Move the mouse pointer across the Calculate button. Note that its color does change. Because this element has a value in its **id** attribute, the code in the event bubble sets the foreground color. You will remedy this deficiency in the next set of steps. Note that this program is very simple and not robust. For example, clicking the Refresh button in Internet Explorer will cause an error. Clicking other buttons may cause additional errors.

4. Exit Internet Explorer.

5. In Visual Basic, end the program to return to design mode.

The code that you wrote solves part of the problem. That is, it no longer sets the background color for the text elements. Nevertheless, one deficiency remains. At this point, the code continues to set the background color for the button because this element has a value set for the **id** attribute. Two possibilities exist to solve this problem. First, you could modify the event procedures that you just wrote to account for the button. Second, you could cancel the event bubbling for the button.

Consider the following statements to cancel the event bubble for the button named cmdCalculate:

```
Private Sub cmdCalculate_onmouseout()
    DHTMLEvent.cancelBubble = True
End Sub

Private Sub cmdCalculate_onmouseover()
    DHTMLEvent.cancelBubble = True
End Sub
```

In the preceding event procedures, the DHTMLEvent object contains a reference to the current event. Thus, when the code sets cancelBubble to True, the event is canceled and no longer passed to the Document object. Thus the background color for this element will not change.

To cancel an event bubble:

1. Activate the Code window for the DHTMLPage named DHTMLPage1, and enter the following statement in the **cmdCalculate_onmouseout** event procedure:

```
DHTMLEvent.cancelBubble = True
```

2. Enter the following statement in the **cmdCalculate_onmouseover** event procedure:

```
DHTMLEvent.cancelBubble = True
```

3. Test the program. Move the mouse over the Calculate button element. The color no longer changes because the code that you just wrote cancels the event bubble.

4. Exit Internet Explorer.

5. In Visual Basic, end the program to return to design mode.

The preceding code uses the **id** attribute and the type of element to determine when to format an element. This technique is merely one approach that you can use to process bubbling events. As another option, you can check for the element type or the name of the **id** attribute to determine whether to cancel the bubble.

Navigating Through DHTML Applications

DHTML applications can consist of multiple HTML pages. You may therefore want to provide the user with the capability to navigate to different DHTML pages in your application or to different Web sites. DHTML supports two navigation techniques:

➤ You can program a hyperlink to locate a specific page.

➤ You can program a button that calls the **Navigate** method pertaining to the BaseWindow object.

Hyperlinks are familiar to most Web users. Typically, a hyperlink appears underlined and in a different color. When the user clicks on the hyperlink, the browser displays the page referenced by the hyperlink. You create a hyperlink in a DHTML page by performing the following steps:

1. In the DHTML page designer, select the text that should appear as the link.

2. Click on the Make Selection Into Link button.

3. Right-click on the selected text and then click on Properties.

4. In the Property Pages, specify the link to be created.

The DHTML application for Central Banking Group consists of two pages. The first page contains the closing cost estimator, and the second page contains the home page. For brevity, the home page contains minimal text. Its purpose is to demonstrate navigation between DHTML documents.

To create a link to another document:

1. Activate the DHTML designer for the page named DHTMLPage1, and scroll to the bottom of the page.

2. On the line that reads Click To View Our Home Page, select the text Home Page.

3. Click on the Make Selection Into Link button on the toolbar of the DHTML page designer. The text appears underlined.

4. Right-click on the selected text, and then click on Properties from the pop-up menu. The Property Pages appear, as shown in Figure 15.6.

5. Click on the Browse button to activate the Open dialog box. Select the file named Home.htm, in the folder named Chapter.15\Startup\Dhtml, and then click on the Open button. The document appears in the Link text box. Click on OK to close the Property Pages.

6. Test the program. In Internet Explorer, scroll to the bottom of the document and click on the underlined text you defined as a link. The home page appears in the browser.

7. Exit Internet Explorer.

8. End the program in Visual Basic.

After you have created your DHTML document, you must compile and deploy it.

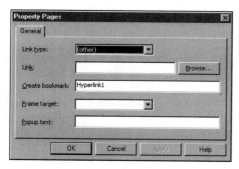

Figure 15.6 Property Pages.

Compiling The DHTML Project

You compile and deploy a DHTML project in the same way as you compile any other project. When you compile a DHTML project, Visual Basic builds a .dll file containing the code that you wrote for the program's elements.

To compile the DHTML project:

1. Click on File, and then click on Make DHTMLProject.dll. If the file already exists, Visual Basic will prompt you before overwriting the file. Click on OK in the Make Project dialog box.

2. Test the program by starting Internet Explorer and loading the file named Chapter.15\Startup\Dhtml\Loan.htm. The document appears inside Internet Explorer.

3. Exit Internet Explorer.

4. Exit Visual Basic.

HTML Help

Previewing The Completed Application

The purpose of this section is not to develop the application itself, but rather to see how an application can utilize a Help system. Thus the completed application contains multiple forms containing buttons and simple text.

To preview the completed application:

1. Start Visual Basic, if necessary, and after it is running, run the program named Chapter.15\Complete\Help\Ch15_C.vbp. Note that the application performs no processing. Its only purpose is to demonstrate how to develop a Help system for an application.

2. Press F1 to display the Help system. The Help window appears with two panes, as shown in Figure 15.7. The left pane contains tabs to display a table of contents or index. The right pane displays the Help topic associated with the selected contents or index entry.

3. Click on the plus sign located to the left of the Welcome folder to expand it. Click on each topic appearing in the folder. As you click on each topic, it appears in the right pane.

4. Click on the Index tab above the left pane. In the left pane, double-click on each topic pertaining to each index entry to display it.

5. Click on the Close button in the title bar of the Help window to exit the Help system.

6. In Visual Basic, end the program to return to design mode.

7. Exit Visual Basic.

15

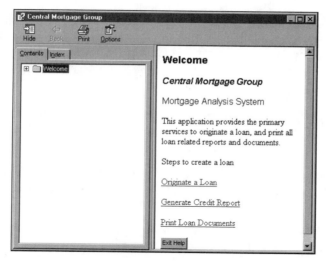

Figure 15.7   Help system.

Introducing HTML Help

Traditional Help systems implemented for Windows 95 and Windows NT utilized Win32Help. These Help files could display an index, display a table of contents, or search for keywords. Ultimately, the Help system displays a Help document (topic). Although Win32Help continues to be supported and widely used, Microsoft has replaced the traditional Help system with a new generation of software named HTML Help. HTML Help takes advantage of many components of Internet Explorer to display Help information. Thus Help files can now run scripts, including those developed in Microsoft Visual Basic Script. The HTML Help system consists of several components:

➤ HTML Help Workshop is a stand-alone program that you use to create the Help system for an application.

➤ The HTML Help ActiveX control adds navigation features and supports pop-up topics and other features to create a robust Help application.

➤ The HTML Help Image Editor allows you to create screen shots and edit them for use in your Help system.

➤ The HTML Help Java Applet is another control that you can insert into HTML files for browsers that support Java.

➤ The program hh.exe runs the compiled Help application.

Microsoft, which created these tools, supplies them with Visual Basic and Visual Studio. In addition to using HTML Help Workshop, you can elect to work with third-party Help authoring tools. These tools provide an easier-to-use interface as you create Help files.

Installing HTML Help Workshop

HTML Help files are independent of Visual Basic. Thus you do not use the Visual Basic IDE to create and edit an HTML Help project. Instead, you use HTML Help Workshop, which is a stand-alone program. Depending on the Visual Basic installation options you selected, HTML Help Workshop may not be installed on your computer. Furthermore, several versions of HTML Help Workshop exist, and the version that you have may vary depending on when you purchased Visual Basic. At the time of this printing, HTML Help Workshop version 1.21 was the most current version. It can be downloaded from Microsoft. As this version contains numerous enhancements and bug fixes, you should download and install the most current software. The steps in this book were developed and tested using version 1.21. If HTML Help software is not installed on your computer, complete the following steps to install the software.

To install HTML Help Workshop:

1. From the downloaded file from Microsoft, run the file HtmlHelp.exe.

2. Accept the license agreement to continue.

3. Click on Next to begin installing HTML Help Workshop. In the Select Destination Folder dialog box, select the default folder or select a different folder depending on your system configuration. Click on Next to display the Choose Type of Setup dialog box.

4. In the Choose Type of Setup dialog box, select Complete, if necessary, to install all necessary components, and then click on Next to display the Select Program Item Group dialog box.

5. Accept the default options or specify a different program group. Click on Next to activate the Personalize HTML Help Workshop dialog box.

6. Enter your name, and then click on Next to activate and install the setup files.

7. When the installation is complete, a dialog box will appear. Click on OK to complete the installation.

HTML Help Workshop is now available for use.

Structure Of A Help System

You build a Help system for a project by using HTML Help Workshop. Like a Visual Basic project, an HTML Help project includes several files:

➤ Topic files represent the content in a Help system. They contain the text that appears on the Web page. Topic files are HTML documents having a suffix of ".htm".

➤ Links to graphics and multimedia files are stored in Graphics files.

➤ The table of contents for a Help system is stored in a separate Table of Contents file. Table of Contents files have the suffix ".hhc."

➤ A searchable index is stored in an Index file. Index files have the suffix ".hhk".

➤ A reference to the previously listed files is stored in the Help system's Project file. Help Project files have the suffix ".hhp."

You can use HTML Help Workshop to edit each of these file types. As you edit the various files constituting the Help system, you can compile and test them.

Creating An HTML Help System

The order in which you create your Help system is subjective. You can develop the HTML topic files first, and then create the index and table of contents for those files. Alternatively, you can create each part interactively as you develop the Help system. As with any program you develop, however, proper design is important. For example, the table of contents should be organized along functional boundaries and reference all pertinent topics in the Help system. Furthermore, creating the index is also important. All significant keywords should be listed in the index.

The first step in creating an HTML Help project is to complete the dialog boxes in the New Project Wizard. This wizard allows you to create new projects and insert existing components (table of contents, index, and topic files) into the new project.

Creating Topic files is a matter of writing HTML documents. As this book is not intended to serve as a tutorial on HTML, you will add existing topic files (HTML documents) to the project. You will provide HTML tags, however, to create links to other documents and to display buttons on the pages. Links and buttons are common features of HTML Help documents. The Topic files used in this project were created using Word 97 and saved as HTML documents. Of course, you can use many different editors to create HTML documents. Which one you select is a matter of professional choice.

If you later create new Topic files, you can use the Topic files dialog box to add those new topics to the Help system. In addition, you can select a file in the dialog box and click on the Remove button to disassociate the Topic file from the project. Note that the Topic file is not removed from the disk; instead, the reference is merely removed from the Topic file.

To create a new Help project:

1. HTML Help Workshop should be available from the Start menu. Its location will vary depending on where you installed the software. Start HTML Help Workshop.

2. Click on File, and then click on New to create a new Help project.

3. When the New dialog box appears asking you what type of file to create, click on Project, and then click on OK to activate the New Project Wizard.

4. The New Project dialog box contains a check box allowing you to convert an existing WinHelp project into an HTML Help project. Because you will not convert an existing project, do not click on this check box. Click on Next to activate the Destination dialog box.

5. The Destination dialog box allows you to specify where HTML Help Workshop should create the files. Click on the Browse button to open the Open dialog box. Select the folder Chapter.15\Startup\Help and enter the file name Ch15. Click on the Open button. The file name appears in the text box on the Destination dialog box. Click on Next to activate the Existing Files dialog box.

6. The Existing Files dialog box allows you to add existing files to the project. In this example, the HTML files have been partially completed, but the table of contents and the index have not. Check the HTML files (.htm) check box, and then click on the Next button.

7. The HTML Files dialog box appears. Using this dialog box, you can add existing HTML files to your Help system. Click on the Add button to add existing files to the application. Again, the Open dialog box appears, allowing you to add the existing files.

8. Select the files named Credit.htm, Origin.htm, Print.htm, and Welcome.htm.

9. Click on the Open button. The four files you selected should appear in the HTML file dialog box. Although these HTML files were created for you, you could have just as easily created them yourself by using any editor that supports HTML.

10. Click on Next to activate the Finish dialog box.

11. Click on Finish to create the Help project.

After the wizard builds the project, HTML Help Workshop appears with tabs allowing you to manage the project, as shown in Figure 15.8.

As shown in Figure 15.8, the left pane consists of three tabs:

➤ **Project** Lists the configuration settings and files that make up the project.

➤ **Contents** Allows you to create and edit the table of contents associated with the Help project.

➤ **Index** Allows you to create and edit the index associated with the Help project.

Buttons appear to the left of each tab. The buttons that appear will vary based on which tab you have selected.

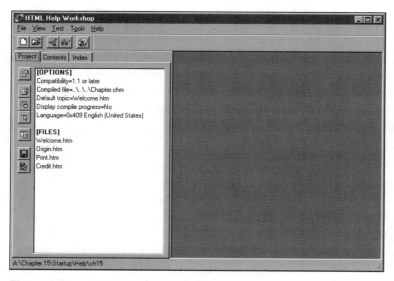

Figure 15.8   HTML Help Workshop.

A Help project consists of sections, some of which may not exist depending on the project. Figure 15.8 shows a project with two sections: the [OPTIONS] section and the [FILES] section. The options section contains general settings pertaining to the project. You define most of these settings using the Options dialog box. The following list summarizes selected properties that you can set through this dialog box:

➤ **Title**   Contains a text string. The text appears in the title bar of the compiled Help file.

➤ **Compiled file**   Contains the path and file name of the compiled Help file.

➤ **Default file**   Contains the name of the HTML file that will appear whenever the user activates the Help system. Note that you can also display specific files as needed to provide context-sensitive help.

Each of these settings will create an entry in the [OPTIONS] section of the project.

To set the Help project options:

1. Make sure that the Project tab is active, and then click on the Change Project Options button to activate the Options dialog box.

2. Make sure that the General tab is active. Set the **Title** to Central Banking Group. This name will appear in the title bar of the compiled Help application.

3. Activate the Files tab. Set the **Compiled file** property to Chapter.15\ Startup\ Help\Ch15.chm, setting the drive designator as necessary.

4. Click on OK to close the dialog box.

You can also set options to optimize the performance of your Help system. In addition, you can specify compatibility options that will make your HTML Help system work with previous HTML Help versions.

At this point, you have defined the HTML pages that will appear in your Help application and specified the general configuration options pertaining to the application. Next, you will define the topics that will appear on the Index tab when the user displays the Help system.

Defining The Table Of Contents

Now that you have added the Topic files to the document, you can create the table of contents that will allow the user to locate those topics. This table of contents has the same purpose as the table of contents for a book. That is, it contains a hierarchical list of topics. Each HTML Help project contains a Table of Contents file with the suffix ".hhc." Note that an HTML Help project does not require that a Table of Contents file be present.

By default, a Table of Contents file consists of a number of folders, which can be organized hierarchically, and pages. You use the buttons on the left side of HTML Help Workshop to edit the table of contents.

To manage the table of contents for a Help system, you activate the Contents tab. The buttons that appear to the left of the Contents tab allow you to insert and edit headings and insert pages. The following list describes the buttons and their purposes:

➤ **Contents Properties** Activates a dialog box that you use to set the general properties pertaining to the table of contents. These properties specify the font, colors, the icons that appear in the table of contents, and the styles.

➤ **Insert A Heading** Inserts a heading entry. By default, this type of entry appears as either an open or closed folder.

➤ **Insert A Page** Adds a reference to a topic page.

➤ **Edit Selection** Allows you to edit the currently selected heading or page reference.

➤ **Delete Selection** Will delete an entry. You select the heading or page in the table of contents, and then click on the button.

➤ **Move Selection Up** and **Move Selection Down** Move the currently selected item up and down, respectively, in the table of contents.

➤ **Move Selection Right** and **Move Selection Left** Increase and decrease the level of indenting for the currently selected heading or page, respectively. Thus these buttons change the level of the entry (indenting) in the table of contents hierarchy.

15

➤ **View HTML Source** Click on the View HTML Source button (after selecting the topic) to view the HTML source code referenced by the topic.

➤ **Save File** Saves the table of contents.

Because the Help system for the Central Banking Group application is quite small, all of the entries on the table of contents will fit on the screen. Consider, however, the table of contents for large applications like Word or Visual Basic. These Help applications contain hundreds or even thousands of entries. As you design the table of contents for a large application, you should organize primary topics into folders. Each folder can support subfolders, which in turn can have additional folders. The primary folders are analogous to chapters in a book, with the subfolders being analogous to sections in a chapter. Each of these folders may support pages that, in turn, display Help topics.

In the small application given in this section, you will create a single folder with four topics. Although most Help systems support many more entries, the same process is used to define the table of contents.

To define the table of contents:

1. In HTML Help Workshop, activate the Contents tab. Because you have not yet created a table of contents for the Help system, a dialog box appears asking whether you want to create a new contents file or open an existing one.

2. Click on the Create A New Contents File Option button, if necessary, and then click on OK to create a new table of contents.

3. The Save As dialog box appears, asking you to assign a name to the new Table of Contents file. Use the default name, and then click on the Save button to create the table of contents and activate the Contents tab in HTML Help workshop. At this point, the table of contents is empty.

4. Click on the Insert A Heading button to display the Table of Contents Entry dialog box, as shown in Figure 15.9.

As shown in Figure 15.9, each entry has a title which will appear in the table of contents.

Each entry in the table of contents can display a URL link to an HTML document. To create an entry using the Table of Contents Entry dialog box, you enter a title in the Entry title text box, and then click on the Add button. HTML Help Workshop activates another dialog box, allowing you to select the path name of the Help file or a URL. When the user runs the project, HTML Help will display the URL when the user selects the title in the table of contents.

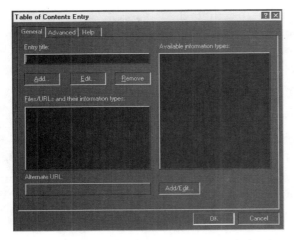

Figure 15.9   Table of Contents Entry dialog box.

To add a URL to the table of contents and view the HTML source:

1. In the Entry title text box, enter Welcome. The user will see this entry in the table of contents.

2. Click on the Add button to activate the Path or URL dialog box. Because you have already added the HTML files that constitute the project, these documents will appear in the HTML title dialog box. In the HTML titles section, click on Welcome, and then click on OK to close the dialog box.

3. The HTML file that you added appears in the Table of Contents Entry dialog box. Click on OK to close the dialog box and to add the table of contents entry. The new entry appears in the Contents tab of HTML Help Workshop.

In addition to inserting headings, you can also insert pages into the table of contents. Although the process followed is the same, the icon in the table of contents differs.

To add page entries:

1. Make sure that the Welcome heading is highlighted in the Contents tab.

2. Click on the Insert A Page button. A dialog box appears, asking: Do You Want To Insert This Entry At The Beginning Of The Table Of Contents? If you click on Yes, the new entry will appear before the Welcome entry. Click on No to insert the page after the Welcome entry.

3. The Table of Contents Entry dialog box appears again. Enter the text "Credit Report" in the Entry title text box.

4. Click on the Add button to activate the Path or URL dialog box. In the HTML titles list box, click on Credit, and then click on the OK button to close the dialog box. In the Table of Contents Entry dialog box, click on OK to close the dialog box and add the entry.

5. You need to add two more pages to the table of contents. Click on the Insert A Page button to add another page to the table of contents. Set the entry title to Print Loan Documents. Click on Add to activate the Path or URL dialog box, and select the HTML file Print. Click on OK to close the dialog box. Click on OK to close the Table of Contents Entry dialog box.

6. To add the last table of contents entry, click on the Insert A Page button. Set the entry title to Originate a loan. Click on Add to activate the Path or URL dialog box, and select the HTML file Origin. Click on OK to close the dialog box. Click on OK to close the Table of Contents Entry dialog box. At this point, the Contents tab should look like the one shown in Figure 15.10.

In addition to using the table of contents to locate Help information, most Help systems support an alphabetic index. You will create that index next.

Defining The Index

An Index file has the same purpose as an index found in the back of a book. That is, it provides an alphabetized listing of keywords and page references to them. A well-designed index can significantly improve any Help system. As you develop an index, use care to select keywords that the user will find meaningful. On the other hand, take care not to clutter the index with words that most users will typically understand.

The process of building the index is similar to the process used to create the table of contents. In fact, the dialog boxes for both tasks are nearly identical.

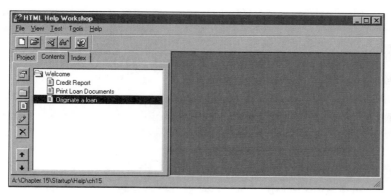

Figure 15.10 Contents tab.

To create the Index file:

1. Click on the Index tab in HTML Help Workshop. Because you have not yet associated an index with the Help system, the Index Not Specified dialog box appears, asking if you want to create a new index file or open an existing one.

2. Select the Create A New Index File Option button, if necessary, and click on OK to activate the Save As dialog box. Use the default file named Index.hhk, and then click on Save to continue. HTML Help workshop activates the Index tab. At this point, the index is empty.

3. Click on the Insert A Keyword button to activate the Index Entry dialog box. This dialog box is nearly identical to the dialog box that you used to add table of contents entries.

4. Enter "Credit Report" as the keyword, and then click on the Add button to activate the Path or URL dialog box. You used the same dialog box to associate a table of contents entry with an HTML page.

5. Select the HTML file named Credit, and then click on OK to close the dialog box. Click on OK to close the Index Entry dialog box.

6. You will add two more index entries to the index. Click on the Insert A Keyword button again to insert another index entry. HTML Help Workshop displays a dialog box asking if you want to insert this entry at the beginning of the index. Click on No to add the entry after the one you just created.

7. In the Index Entry dialog box, enter "Originate Loan" as the keyword, and then click on the Add button to activate the Path or URL dialog box.

8. Select the HTML title named Origin, and then click on OK to close the dialog box. Click on OK to close the Index Entry dialog box.

9. To add the final entry to the index, click on the Insert A Keyword button again. Enter a keyword of "Print Loan Documents". Click on the Add button to activate the Path or URL dialog box. Select the HTML title Print. Click on OK to close the dialog box.

10. Click on OK in the Index Entry dialog box to close it.

At this point, you have defined the HTML files making up your Help application and defined both the index and table of contents. Next, you will compile the Help application to see how it will appear to the user.

Compiling The Help System

Once you have defined the table of contents, index, and the topic pages to be displayed, you can compile the Help system and test it. When you compile the Help system, HTML Help Workshop treats all files as input files and creates an output file with the extension ".chm."

To compile the HTML Help system:

1. Click on File, and then click on Compile. The Create a compiled file dialog box appears. Specify the file named Chapter.15\Startup\Help\Ch15, setting the drive designator as necessary.

2. Check the box named Automatically Display Compiled Help File When Done to display the HTML Help application.

3. Click on Compile. Depending on whether you have saved the project since making changes to it, a dialog box may appear asking whether to save the changes. If this dialog box appears, click on Yes. A window appears as HTML Help Workshop compiles the application. When the compilation is complete, a log appears in the right pane of HTML Help Workshop. Depending on the version of HTML Workshop that you are running, the compiled help file might not appear automatically. If it does not, complete Step 4.

4. To test the compiled Help file, activate Windows Explorer. Locate the folder named Chapter.15\Startup\Help. Double-click on the file Ch15.chm. The title you specified should appear in the title bar of the Help file. Additionally, both the Contents and Index tabs appear.

5. Click on the Index tab. The three keywords you specified should appear. Double-click on each of these keywords. When you double-click on each keyword, the document corresponding to that keyword should appear in the right pane of the Help document.

6. Click on the Contents tab. Click on the plus sign next to the Welcome folder, if necessary, to display the three items. Click on each of the items to display the corresponding page.

7. Click on the Close button in the title bar to end the application.

At this point in the development of your Help system, you have defined the pages, the table of contents, and the index. The table of contents and index offer two ways that the user can navigate through the topics in your Help application. In addition to these two navigational techniques, you can create links on HTML pages to display other documents. You can also add buttons to your HTML pages to perform specific tasks.

Adding Links To The HTML Pages

As you are likely aware, HTML supports hyperlinks. When a user clicks on a hyperlink, HTML displays the page referenced by that hyperlink. In the Central Banking Group example, you will modify the Welcome page to display links to the three other pages. Creating a hyperlink is not actually a function of HTML Help Workshop, but rather a function of the HTML language itself. Thus, to create a hyperlink, you activate the necessary HTML page and enter the hyperlink.

To create hyperlinks:

1. In HTML Help Workshop, activate the Project tab. In the [FILES] section, double-click on the file Welcome.htm. HTML Help Workshop opens the HTML document in a window in the right pane. Enter the following text in the file:

```
<P>Steps to create a loan</P>
<P><A HREF="Origin.htm">Originate a Loan</A></P>
<P><A HREF="Credit.htm">Generate Credit Report</A></P>
<P><A HREF="Print.htm">Print Loan Documents</A></P>
```

2. On the menu bar, click on File, and then click on Save File to save the HTML document.

3. Click on the Close button on the file to close it.

Now when the user runs the HTML Help application, the document will appear with links to other documents.

In addition to creating links, you can place buttons on documents to perform specific actions. The user can click on these buttons to display related topics, close the application, and perform other tasks. To create a button, you use the HTML Help ActiveX control.

Using The HTML Help ActiveX Control

The HTML Help ActiveX control allows you to insert HTML tags into your documents without writing the tags manually. The control will add several types of tags. In this section, you will create a tag to close the Help application. In practice, you would likely use much more complex related topics than those developed in this short example.

To create a Close button in an HTML document:

1. Activate the Project tab in HTML Help Workshop, if necessary.

2. In the [FILES] section, double-click on the file named Welcome.htm.

3. Scroll to the end of the document, and position the cursor just before the </HTML> tag at the end of the document.

4. Click on the HTML Help ActiveX control button to activate the HTML Help ActiveX Control Commands dialog box, as shown in Figure 15.11.

5. In the Specify the command list box, select Close Window.

6. Click on Next to display the Display Type dialog box. The default option is to display the command as a button. The Hidden option is used for scripting. In this chapter, you will not use scripting. Click on Next to accept the default option and to display the Button Options dialog box.

7. You can display text, bitmaps, or icons on buttons. In this example, you will display a textual message. Enter "Exit Help" in the Text box, and then click on Next to display the Finish dialog box.

8. Click on the Finish button to add the new HTML tag to the HTML file.

9. Click on File, and then click on Save File to save the modified file. Click on the Close button on the HTML file to close it.

You have completed another milestone in the development of your HTML Help file—you have added hyperlinks and added a button to one of the pages. To see the effect of these changes, you will again compile the application and test it.

To compile and test the HTML Help application:

1. In HTML Help Workshop, click on File and then click on Compile to compile the application.

2. In the Create a compiled file dialog box, click on Compile to compile the project.

3. Close the log file in the right pane of HTML Help Workshop. Depending on the HTML Help version, the compiled help file might not appear. If the Help system opens automatically skip Step 4.

4. To test the compiled Help file, activate Windows Explorer. Locate the folder named Chapter.15\Startup\Help, setting the drive designator as necessary. Double-click on the file Ch15.chm.

5. Note that the newly added links appear on the Welcome page. Also, the Exit Help button appears at the bottom of the page. Click on the Exit Help button to end the Help application.

Your Help system is almost complete. Users will not run your Help system by selecting the file from Windows Explorer, however. Rather, they will likely gain access to Help from your Visual Basic application.

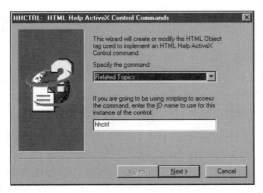

Figure 15.11   HTML Help ActiveX Control Commands dialog box.

In addition to displaying a Help file from an application, most systems support context-sensitive help. That is, when the user presses the F1 key or clicks on the Help button on a form, the Help topic pertaining to that form should appear automatically. Developing context-sensitive help is a two-stage process. First, you must alter the Help system itself. Second, you must modify the Visual Basic application.

You will modify your Help application so that it will support context-sensitive help. Then you will modify the Visual Basic application to display the appropriate Help topic.

Creating A Context-Sensitive Help File

Creating a context-sensitive help file requires that you assign a unique ID, called a Map, to each Help topic that should be context-sensitive. Defining the Map IDs involves creating a Map file. The following code segment illustrates the Map file that you will create for this application:

```
#define IDH_WELCOME 99
#define IDH_ORIGINATE 100
#define IDH_CREDIT 200
#define IDH_PRINT 300
```

A Map file has a well-defined syntax. One line exists in the file for each topic that should be context-sensitive. Thus the preceding code defines four context-sensitive topics. Each line has the same syntax. The first part contains the word **#define**. The second part consists of a unique constant, and the third part consists of a unique Integer value. You will use the Integer value in your Visual Basic program.

If you are familiar with the C programming language, you may notice that the preceding code segment looks identical to a C header file. If fact, both have the same syntax.

To create the Map file:

1. Start Notepad, and enter the following text in a new file:

   ```
   #define IDH_WELCOME 99
   #define IDH_ORIGINATE 100
   #define IDH_CREDIT 200
   #define IDH_PRINT 300
   ```

2. Save the file using the name Chapter.15\Startup\Help\Context.h, setting the drive designator as necessary. Be sure to change the Save as type option

to All Files(*.*), or Notepad will add a ".txt" suffix to the file. Enclose the file name Context.h in quotes.

3. Exit Notepad.

In addition to creating the Map file, you must associate the constants you defined with particular HTML pages. You accomplish this task by creating an alias using HTML Help Workshop.

To define the Map and create the aliases:

1. In HTML Help Workshop, make sure that the Project tab is active.

2. Click on the HtmlHelp API Information button. The HtmlHelp API information dialog box appears, as shown in Figure 15.12.

3. First, you will add to this project the Map that you created in the previous project steps. On the Map tab, click on the Header File button. The Include file dialog box appears. Click on Browse, and select the file Context.h that you created in the previous steps. Click on Open to associate the Map file with the project.

4. Click on OK to close the Include File dialog box.

5. Click on the Alias tab.

6. Click on the Add button to activate the Alias dialog box, as shown in Figure 15.13. In this tab, you will map the constants you defined to the HTML topic files.

7. In the text box at the top of the form, enter the constant name **IDH_ORIGINATE**.

8. In the Use it to refer to this HTML file list box, select Origin.htm.

9. Click on OK to add the alias.

Figure 15.12   HtmlHelp API information dialog box.

Figure 15.13   Alias dialog box.

10. Now you must add the remaining three aliases. Click on the Add button again. Add the constant **IDH_CREDIT**, and set the HTML file to Credit.htm. Click on OK to add the alias.

11. Click on the Add button again. Add the constant **IDH_PRINT**, and set the HTML file to Print.htm. Click on OK to add the alias.

12. Click on the Add button again. Add the constant **IDH_WELCOME**, and set the HTML file to Welcome.htm. Click on OK to add the alias. In the HtmlHelp API information dialog box, click on OK to close the dialog box.

13. Note that the project file now includes the aliases and the Map. Click on File, and then click on Save Project to save the project file. Click on File, and then click on Compile to compile the project. In the Create a compiled file dialog box, click on Compile.

The Help system is now complete. Your only remaining task is to link the Visual Basic program to the project.

Connecting The Help System To The Program

Now that you have created the Help system, you can connect it to your Visual Basic program. Visual Basic allows you to display an application's Help system and specific topics based on the form or control instance with focus. Two properties allow your program to establish a connection with a Help system and display particular Help topics:

➤ **HelpFile** As it pertains to the App object, specifies the name of the Help file used by your application. It contains the full path name of the compiled Help file created through Help Workshop or HTML Help Workshop. You can set this property at run time or at design time using the Project properties dialog box.

➤ **HelpContextID** Pertains to most objects and displays context-sensitive help for the control instances in your application.

15

To identify a Help file with an application:

1. Start Visual Basic. After you have it running, load the project file named Chapter.15\Startup\ Help\Ch15_S.vbp. Because the purpose of this section is to demonstrate how to display Help files, this project has been designed to include multiple forms. When you complete the program, pressing the F1 key will display the Help pertaining to that form.

2. Activate the form named **frmCh15_S.frm**. Enter the following statement in the **Form_Load** event procedure. This statement assumes that the Help file appears in the same folder as your application.

```
App.HelpFile = App.Path & "\Ch15.chm"
```

3. Test the program. When the main form appears, press the F1 key to display the Help system. By setting the **App.Helpfile** property, Visual Basic can display the Help file with your program.

4. End the program to return to design mode. Close the Help system.

Because you set the **HelpFile** property pertaining to the App object, your program will display the Help system whenever the user presses the F1 key. At this point, however, you have made no provision to display a particular Help topic when a specific form is active.

To display a particular Help topic when a specific form or control instance is active, you assign a value to the **HelpContextID** property pertaining to the form or control instance. The value of the **HelpContextID** is the same as the value that you defined for the particular topic in the Map file.

To create context-sensitive help:

1. Activate the Properties window for the form named frmCh15, and set the **HelpContextID** property to **99**.

2. Activate the Properties window for the form named frmCred, and set the **HelpContextID** property to **200**.

3. Activate the Properties window for the form named frmDocs, and set the **HelpContextID** property to **300**.

4. Activate the Properties window for the form named frmOrig, and set the **HelpContextID** property to **100**.

5. Test the program.

6. Click on the Originate A Loan button on the form. Press F1 to display the context-sensitive help. The appropriate Help topic appears in the Help window.

7. Click on the Exit button on the form.

8. Repeat Step 6 for the other command buttons. When you press the F1 key for the form having focus, the appropriate context-sensitive help should appear.

9. Close the Help system.

10. Exit the program.

In this example, you defined only four context IDs. Most Help systems would likely have many more.

Developing What's This Help

Another form of context-sensitive help that your program can supply to the user is What's This Help, also known as help pop-ups. The user accesses this type of Help by clicking on a question mark in the title bar of the form. This action activates What's This Help, and the mouse pointer changes to a question mark. The user can then move the question mark over the form or a particular control instance and click on the left mouse button; which causes the Help system to display a pop-up containing the relevant Help topic. Although, Visual Basic does not directly provide support for displaying Help pop-ups with HTML Help, you can perform this task by using facilities supported by the Windows operating system. To accomplish this task, you need to be aware of two concepts:

➤ The first concept, called subclassing, allows your program to perform non-default processing for Windows messages. Windows sends messages to forms and control instances. Through subclassing, you can perform specific processing for specific messages before those messages are handled by the window.

➤ The other concept relates to the Windows API. Windows contains functions available to the Visual Basic programmer. Although the Windows API is discussed in detail in Chapter 16, it is introduced in this chapter only to support Help pop-ups.

15

Windows sends messages to your forms; Visual Basic can respond to these messages by executing code in event procedures. On the other hand, Visual Basic does not support events to respond to the HTML Help messages. Thus your program must intercept certain Windows messages before they are passed to your Visual Basic form—a concept known as subclassing. If you frequently perform subclassing from Visual Basic, third-party controls are available to help you perform this task. For this section's example, code has been provided to perform the subclassing for you. The code that performs the subclassing appears in the standard module named **Context.bas**. The first part of this standard module contains constant and function declarations to make specific Windows functions available to the program.

A function named **LoadIDTopics** loads the Help topic IDs pertaining to a particular form. This function builds an array containing references to the control instances on the form and their corresponding topic ID values. The functions **ContextSubClass** and **SubClass** provide the actual subclassing. The commented code in the **Context.bas Standard** module contains comments describing how the subclassing works.

Consider the following code in the main form to prepare to display Help pop-ups:

```
Private Sub Form_Load()
    App.HelpFile = App.Path & "\Ch15.chm"
    Call LoadIDTopics(Me, idTopics())
    Call SubClass(Me)
End Sub
```

When the form loads, this code calls the **LoadIDTopics** function with two arguments. The first argument contains a reference to the form, and the second contains a reference to the array named **idTopics**. This function will load the **WhatsThisHelpID** property and a reference to the corresponding control instance for each control instance on the form. The final statement calls the procedure to subclass the form.

In this example, the subclassing causes Windows to call a function as HTML Help messages are received. You must create two procedures in the form to display the context-sensitive help. Consider the following **General** procedures in the form module:

```
Public Sub ContextMenu(hWndControl As Long)
    Call HtmlHelp(hWndControl, App.HelpFile & _
        "::/popup.txt", HH_TP_HELP_CONTEXTMENU, _
        idTopics(0))
End Sub
Public Sub ContextHelp(hWndControl As Long)
    Call HtmlHelp(hWndControl, App.HelpFile & _
        "::/popup.txt", HH_TP_HELP_WM_HELP, _
        idTopics(0))
End Sub
```

As Windows generates HTML messages, the code in the subclassing modules intercepts these messages and calls the two preceding functions. The **ContextMenu** and **ContextHelp** functions, in turn, call the **HtmlHelp** function to display the pop-up.

In addition to developing the subclassing procedures, you must define the text pop-ups in HTML Help Workshop. Each text pop-up consists of two parts. The first part is a header file that looks identical to a Map file. The header file used in this chapter consists of the following code:

```
#define IDH_POPUP_ORIGINATE 1000
#define IDH_POPUP_CREDITREPORT 1010
#define IDH_POPUP_PRINT 1020
#define IDH_POPUP_EXIT  1030
```

The second part of the text pop-up is a Topic file containing the Help pop-ups.

Consider the following code:

```
.topic IDH_POPUP_ORIGINATE
Click to originate a Loan.
.topic IDH_POPUP_CREDITREPORT
Click to evaluate client's credit worthiness.
.topic IDH_POPUP_PRINT
Print Loan Document.
.topic IDH_POPUP_EXIT
End the Program.
```

The Topic file has a simple format. The word .topic followed by a constant identifies a particular Help topic. After the topic line, you enter the text that should appear in the pop-up. The preceding code defines four topics, with the constant for each topic corresponding to a constant in the header file.

The final task you must perform is to set the necessary properties so that a form will display What's This Help. The following list describes these properties:

➤ For the form, set the **MinButton** and **MaxButton** properties to **False**. Also, set the **WhatsThisButton** and **WhatsThisHelp** properties to **True**.

➤ For each control instance that will display What's This Help, set the **WhatsThisHelpID** property to an Integer value. This Integer value corresponds to the integer value stored in the header file.

You can now perform the steps to support Help pop-ups.

To create text pop-ups:

1. In HTML Help Workshop, click on the HtmlHelpAPI Information button and activate the Text Pop-ups tab.

2. Click on Header File to activate the Include File dialog box. Click on Browse, and locate the file named Chapter.15\Startup\Help\Popup.h. Click on Open to select the file. In the Include File dialog box, click on OK to add the header file.

3. Click on Text File to activate the Include File dialog box. Click on Browse, and locate the file named Chapter.15\Startup\Help\Popup.txt. Click on

Open to select the file. In the Include File dialog box, click on OK to add the text file. Click on OK to close the HtmlHelpAPI information dialog box.

4. Save the project, and recompile the Help file.

The remaining steps must be performed in Visual Basic. They add the subclassing module, create the necessary procedures in the form, and set the **Help** properties.

To display Help pop-ups from Visual Basic:

1. Add the standard module named Chapter.15\Startup\Help\Context.bas to the project.

2. Add the class module named **clsSubContext** to the project.

3. Enter the following statement in the general declarations section of the form named frmCh15:

```
Private idTopics( )As HH_IDPAIR
```

4. Enter the following statements in the **Form_Load** event procedure for the form named frmCh15:

```
App.HelpFile = App.Path & "\Ch15.chm"
Call LoadIDTopics(Me, idTopics())
Call SubClass(Me)
```

5. Create the following procedures in the form module:

```
Public Sub ContextMenu(hWndControl As Long)
    Call HtmlHelp(hWndControl, App.HelpFile & _
        "::/popup.txt", HH_TP_HELP_CONTEXTMENU, _
        idTopics(0))
End Sub
Public Sub ContextHelp(hWndControl As Long)
    Call HtmlHelp(hWndControl, App.HelpFile & _
        "::/popup.txt", HH_TP_HELP_WM_HELP, _
        idTopics(0))
End Sub
```

6. Activate the Properties window for the form named frmCh15.

7. Next, set the **MinButton** and **MaxButton** properties to **False**. Then, set the **WhatsThisButton** and **WhatsThisHelp** properties to **True**.

8. Set the **WhatsThisHelpID** property for the command buttons as follows: cmdOriginate = 1000, cmdCredit = 1010, cmdPrint = 1020, and cmdExit to 1030.

9. Test the program. When it is run, a question mark should appear in the title bar for the main form. Click on this question mark. Move the icon to the Originate A Loan command button, and click on the button. The pop-up should appear.

10. End the program to return to design mode.

11. Exit Visual Basic.

You have now completed the programming for this section. Although this section presented the essential aspects of creating a Help system, you can, of course, create much more robust and complex Help systems.

CHAPTER SUMMARY

This chapter has presented two discrete topics: the creation of DHTML documents, and the creation of an HTML Help system for an application.

To create a DHTML project:

➤ Activate the New project window, and double-click on the DHTML application project type. Visual Basic creates the project with a blank DHTML page.

➤ Add existing HTML documents to the project as necessary.

➤ Create elements on the DHTML documents to perform the desired tasks.

➤ Compile the project.

To create an element:

➤ Activate the DHTML designer for the desired page.

➤ Click on the desired element on the toolbox.

➤ Create an instance of the element on the DHTML page.

➤ Activate the Properties window for the newly created element.

➤ Set the **id** attribute.

➤ Activate the Code window for the element and create the event responses as desired.

To set the style for an element:

➤ Select an event procedure in the Code window.

➤ Write the statements to set the style for the desired object.

To cancel an event bubble:

➤ Use the DHTMLEvent object to reference the element you want to cancel.

➤ Set the **cancelBubble** property to **True**.

To navigate to another DHTML page:

➤ In the DHTML page designer, select the text that should become the hyperlink.

➤ Click on the Make selection into link button.

➤ Right-click on the selected text, and select Properties from the pop-up menu.

➤ In the Property Pages, click on the Browse button and select the HTML page to which you want to link.

To create a new Help system:

➤ Start HTML Help Workshop.

➤ Click on File, and then click on New. When the New dialog box appears, click on Project and then click on OK to activate the New Project Wizard.

➤ In the New Project Wizard, convert an existing Win32Help project if desired.

➤ In the next dialog box, select any existing index, table of contents, or HTML files that should be added to the project.

➤ Save the project.

To define the table of contents for a Help project:

➤ Create a new Table of Contents file.

➤ Insert contents entries for headings and pages as desired.

➤ For each heading or page, add a reference to the corresponding HTML page.

To define the index for a Help project:

➤ Create a new Index file.

➤ Create the keywords and topics corresponding to those keywords.

To use the HTML Help ActiveX control:

➤ Open the desired HTML document.

➤ Highlight the position where the tag should appear.

➤ Click on the HTML Help ActiveX control.

➤ When the dialog box appears, select the command you want to execute.

To create a context-sensitive help file:

➤ Create a Map file with constants and integer values. Each value must be unique.

➤ Create aliases for the project. These aliases should correspond to the entries in the Map file. Each alias should list the constant and the corresponding HTML page to be displayed.

To connect the Help system to the program:

➤ Set the **HelpFile** property pertaining to the App object.

➤ For each form or control instance needed to support context-sensitive help, set the **HelpContextID** to a valid Map in the Help file.

REVIEW QUESTIONS

1. Which of the following objects does DHTML support?
   a. DHTMLPage, DHTMLDocument
   b. DHTMLPage, InternetExplorer, DHTMLDocument
   c. Page, InternetExplorer
   d. DHTMLPage, BaseWindow, Document
   e. None of the above

2. Which of the following are valid HTML elements?
   a. CommandButton, SelectBox, TextBox
   b. Button, Select, TextField
   c. Button, Select, Text
   d. All of the above
   e. None of the above

3. Which events are supported by most elements?
   a. **Click, MouseUp, MouseDown**
   b. **ElementClick, ElementMouseUp, ElementMouseDown**
   c. **Reposition, MoveUp, MoveDown**
   d. **onclick, onmouseup, onmousedown**
   e. None of the above

15

4. What is the name of the object used to define the formatting characteristics of an element?

   a. Format

   b. FormatElement

   c. Style

   d. Fonts

   e. None of the above

5. Which of the following statements pertaining to event bubbling is true?

   a. You create a procedure named bubble to define an event bubble.

   b. You write code in response to the bubble event.

   c. You call the Bubble function to create a bubble.

   d. All of the above.

   e. None of the above.

6. How do you navigate to another DHTML document?

   a. Call the **Jump** method.

   b. Use a hyperlink.

   c. Call the **Navigate** method.

   d. Both b and c.

   e. None of the above.

7. Which of the following statements pertaining to compiling a DHTML project is true?

   a. Visual Basic builds a DLL file.

   b. HTML documents are embedded into a DLL file.

   c. One DLL file is created for each DHTML page.

   d. All of the above.

   e. None of the above.

8. Create an event procedure that will set the background color of the Select element named selQuestion to "WHITE" when the user clicks on the element.

9. Create an event procedure for the Document object that executes when the user clicks on any element. The event procedure should set the foreground color to "RED."

10. Write a statement to cancel the current event bubble.

11. Which of the following Help component files is valid?

    a. Description

    b. Glossary

    c. Embedded

    d. All of the above

    e. None of the above

12. Which of the following statements pertaining to creating a new Help project is true?

    a. You can convert an existing Win32help project.

    b. You can insert existing HTML files.

    c. You can insert existing Index and Table of Contents files.

    d. All of the above.

    e. None of the above.

13. Which of the following statements pertaining to a table of contents is true?

    a. It consists of elements.

    b. The Table of Contents file has a suffix of ".toc".

    c. The table of contents is stored inside the project file.

    d. Every project must have at least one table of contents.

    e. None of the above.

14. Which of the following statements pertaining to an index is true?

    a. Keywords map to HTML pages.

    b. The suffix for an Index file is ".idx."

    c. HTML Help Workshop creates the index automatically.

    d. All of the above.

    e. None of the above.

15. What happens when you compile a Help project?

    a. The project is compiled into an .exe file.

    b. The project is compiled into a .chm file.

    c. The project is compiled into a .dll file.

    d. HTML Help projects are not compiled.

    e. None of the above.

15

16. What is the purpose of the HTML Help ActiveX control?

   a. to create a table of contents

   b. to create an index

   c. to add buttons to an HTML page

   d. All of the above

   e. None of the above

17. Which properties do you use to display Help from an application?

   a. **HelpFile, HelpContextID**

   b. **Help, HelpFileName**

   c. **HelpID, HelpFileID**

   d. All of the above

   e. None of the above

18. Which of the following statements about context-sensitive help is true?

   a. You must define a Map file.

   b. You must define aliases.

   c. You set the alias property in a Visual Basic program.

   d. Both a and b.

   e. All of the above.

19. Write a statement that will set the Help file for the application you developed in the last half of the chapter to A:\Question\Question.chm.

HANDS-ON PROJECTS

Project 1

In this project, you will create a DHTML project consisting of a single page that will convert units of measure.

   a. Start Internet Explorer, and load the document named Ex1.htm. This document contains the template text that you will use to create your document. Exit Internet Explorer.

   b. Start Visual Basic, and create a new DHTML project. Save the project using the name Chapter.15\Exercise\Ex1.vbp.

   c. Create two select elements. In each, store the following values: feet, inches, millimeters, centimeters, and meters.

   d. Create a text field on the form. The user will enter a value in this field.

   e. Create another text field to display the converted output value.

f. Create a Button element on the form. When the user clicks on the Button element, the program code should convert the value in the input text field from the selected unit of measure in the first Select element to the selected unit of measure in the second Select element. Display the results in the output text field. Note that there are 2.54 centimeters per inch.

g. Change the background color for the text field and Select elements of a different color when the mouse passes over the element. Use event bubbling to accomplish this task.

h. Save and test the project. Make sure that the values are converted properly and that the background color changes correctly.

i. Exit Visual Basic.

Project 2

In this project, you will create a Help system for a program and a demonstration program to test the help system.

a. Start HTML Help workshop, and create a new project. Save the project using the name Chapter.15\Exercise\Ex2.hhp.

b. Add three HTML pages to the project: Raw, Prod, and Finished. Assume that this application is for a manufacturing business and that the three pages describe the raw materials, production process, and finished products.

c. Create a table of contents for each of the three pages.

d. Create an index for each of the three pages.

e. Perform the necessary tasks so that each page can be displayed as context-sensitive help from a Visual Basic program.

f. Using the HTML Help ActiveX control, create a button on each page to exit the Help system.

g. Compile the Help system.

h. Create a Visual Basic program with multiple forms to test the Help project.

15

CHAPTER SIXTEEN

UNDERSTANDING THE WINDOWS APPLICATION PROGRAMMING INTERFACE

AFTER READING THIS CHAPTER AND COMPLETING THE EXERCISES, YOU WILL BE ABLE TO:

➤ Save the current configuration of a program in the Windows Registry

➤ Read specific Windows Registry settings to configure a program

➤ Manipulate the Windows Registry using the RegEdit program

➤ Learn about the characteristics of Windows Dynamic Link Libraries

➤ Expose a function declared in a DLL to a Visual Basic program

➤ Call a DLL function

➤ Understand the implications of passing different data types to DLL functions

➤ Perform asynchronous notification using events and callbacks

EXPANDING THE POWER OF VISUAL BASIC BY CALLING DLL FUNCTIONS

Programming The Windows Registry

This chapter provides an introduction to reading and writing information from and to the Windows Registry and calling specific functions supported by the Windows operating system.

These functions are typically referred to as DLL functions. Presenting all of the functions supported by Windows is beyond the scope of this book. This chapter therefore describes only a few Windows functions that a typical Visual Basic programmer may find useful.

The completed application for this chapter calls various DLL functions. It is not a fully functional application. Rather, the functions that are implemented in the completed application appear so that you can see how they call underlying Windows DLL functions.

Geological Services Corporation (GSC) develops programs in Visual Basic. The company wants the File menus of its programs to display a list of recently opened files. GSC also requires program capabilities not supported by Visual Basic, including functions to cause a specific form to always appear as the topmost form and functions to create temporary files. Finally, the company wants programs to execute methods asynchronously.

To preview the completed application:

1. Start Visual Basic. Figure 16.1 shows the main form for the project. Load the project named Chapter.16\Complete\CallBack\Ch16_C.vbp.

2. Run the program. Figure 16.1 shows the form at run time.

3. Click on the Show Topmost Form command button. The Top dialog box should appear as a modal dialog box that cannot be obscured. Try to obscure the dialog box by activating another window and moving that window over the visible region of the dialog box. The Top dialog box will always appear as the topmost window. The program code accomplishes this task by calling a Windows DLL that changes the characteristics of a particular form.

4. Close the form by clicking on the Close button.

5. Click on Open on the File menu of the form, select a file name in the common dialog box, and then click on Open. The prototype program does not actually open the files, so it does not matter which file you select. Repeat the process four times, opening a different file each time. Click on

Exit on the File menu to exit the program. The **Form_Unload** event procedure executes and writes the list of recently opened files to the Windows Registry.

6. Run the program again, and then click on File. The program reads the list of recently opened files from the Windows Registry and then displays them on the File menu. Press the Esc key.

7. Click on File, and then click on Make Temporary. Activate the Immediate window. The code in the menu command calls a procedure to generate a unique temporary file name. The code prints this file name to the Immediate window.

8. Click on the Shell button. The Open dialog box appears. Locate an .exe file on your computer, select it, and then click on the Open button. The code in the command button's **Click** event procedure executes the program. Exit the executable program you ran, if necessary.

9. Click on the Callback command button. This button uses a Windows DLL procedure to implement a timer. The text "Timer" appears in the Immediate window.

10. In the Notification frame, enter the value 10000050 in the Start text box and the value 10000100 in the End text box, and then click on the Calculate button. The code uses a class module and asynchronous processing to display a message indicating whether a number is prime. Although the result of the processing is visible, the processing itself remains hidden.

11. End the program and exit Visual Basic.

Although the actions carried out by the completed program may seem trivial, they cannot be accomplished by calling Visual Basic statements or intrinsic functions. Instead, these commands interact with the Windows Registry and call functions that are part of the Windows application programming interface (API).

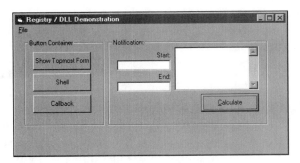

Figure 16.1 Completed application.

Introducing The Windows Registry

Before you begin to program the Windows Registry, a strong word of caution is in order. The Windows Registry maintains information vital for your computer's operation. If you accidentally delete critical Windows Registry information, your system will likely become corrupted and will not boot. Furthermore, existing programs installed on your computer will not work correctly. You should therefore consider preparing a Windows emergency disk or backing up your system so that you can recover from accidental system corruption. Also, use caution when performing the steps in this section, especially when using the RegEdit program, and follow the steps exactly.

A robust program should save configuration information about itself when the program exits. Common configuration data may include a list of files recently opened by the user or the position of various windows on the screen. The GSC completed program reads configuration data when the user runs the program and saves it when the program exits.

Furthermore, programs must make themselves known to the system. As you have seen in previous chapters, ActiveX controls and DLL components are registered on the system using the Windows Registry. In previous chapters, Visual Basic caused the information contained in the Windows Registry to be stored there. In this section, you will store information of your own choosing in the Windows Registry. In this chapter, the term *Registry*—rather than *Windows Registry*—will be used for the sake of brevity.

The Registry stores configuration information for specific programs in a hierarchical database. It stores information from the different .ini files pertaining to a specific application in one central location. In addition, the Registry identifies all installed hardware and peripherals as well as all software currently installed on the computer. It also maintains information pertaining to particular programs.

Windows divides the Registry data into two files. System.dat contains the Registry itself. User.dat contains the information pertaining to the users on the system. Windows stores backup copies of these files in System.da0 and User.da0. If the Registry becomes corrupted, Windows will re-create the Registry information from the backup files.

The Registry is hierarchical, much in the same way that the Windows file system is hierarchical. In fact, the program used to edit the Registry, called RegEdit, has an interface very similar to Windows Explorer. Registry information is organized into trees and subtrees. A tree or subtree resembles a folder in Windows Explorer. A tree or subtree holds Keys that contain data. The keys and their corresponding data are similar to the files displayed by Windows Explorer. Figure 16.2 shows the RegEdit program displaying the primary trees in the Registry.

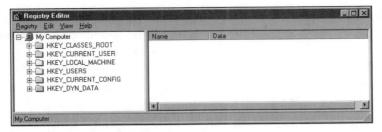

Figure 16.2   Registry Editor.

As shown in Figure 16.2, the Registry contains six primary trees. In this chapter, the capitalization used for Registry tree and subtree entries will be consistent with the style conventions of RegEdit. If you view different books on the Registry, you soon will discover that they differ on their capitalization conventions.

➤ **HKEY_CLASSES_ROOT** Points to a subtree of HKEY_LOCAL_MACHINE and defines software settings.

➤ **HKEY_CURRENT_USER** Contains the user profile for the user currently logged on the system.

➤ **HKEY_LOCAL_MACHINE** Contains the configuration of the local computer. It has subtrees to list the hardware and software installed on the computer.

➤ **HKEY_USERS** Maintains user profile information about the various users on the system.

➤ **HKEY_CURRENT_CONFIG** Points to the current system configuration in the collection of configurations stored in HKEY_LOCAL_MACHINE\Config.

➤ **HKEY_DYN_DATA** Stores information in RAM. This Registry area holds information that must be modified and retrieved faster than is possible by reading from and writing to the disk.

These six trees look much like folders in Windows Explorer. Using Registry terminology, the terms *tree* and *subtree* replace the terms *folder* and *subfolder*. A tree or subtree is not a physical file but rather a way of organizing Registry information. A tree can contain zero or more subtrees, which in turn can contain zero or more subtrees, and so on.

A key/value pair represents data in the Registry. The key identifies a particular item of data in a subtree. The value contains the data pertaining to that key. You can think of keys as equivalent to strings and data values as equivalent to variants. Any type of information can be stored as the value associated with a key.

16

Registry Functions

Visual Basic supports functions that operate on the Registry. The **GetSetting** function returns a string containing the value of a specific Registry entry, and the **SaveSetting** function saves a key and its value to the Registry. Both the **GetSetting** and **SaveSetting** functions save data in the following Registry section: HKEY_USERS\.Default\Software\VB and VBA Program Settings. To read and write data from and to other Registry locations, you must revert to DLL functions. In this section, you will use the **GetSetting** and **SaveSetting** functions.

Syntax

> GetSetting(**appname**, **section**, **key** [, **default**])
> SaveSetting(**appname**, **section**, **key**, **setting**)

Dissection

➤ The **GetSetting** function reads a setting from the Registry. This setting is a unique combination of an application name, a section, and a key. If no valid entry exists for the **appname**, **section**, and **key**, and no **default** value is specified, **GetSetting** returns an empty string. It returns the value for the unique **key** if a value is found and the **default** value if no value is found.

➤ The **SaveSetting** function writes a setting to the Registry. If a value already exists for the **appname**, **section**, and **key**, the value is overwritten. If the **key** does not yet exist, the **key**, the corresponding **section**, and the **appname** are added as necessary.

➤ The required **appname** argument contains the name of the application or project. This value must be a string.

➤ The required **section** refers to a subtree of **appname**.

➤ The required **key** contains the unique key used to look up the value in the Registry. If no value exists for the specific key, **GetSetting** returns the value of **default**. Otherwise, **GetSetting** returns an empty string.

➤ The required **setting** argument contains the value to set when using the **SaveSetting** function.

Code Example

```
mintFiles = GetSetting(App.Title, "Files", _
    "FileCount", 10)
SaveSetting App.Title, "Files", "FileCount", "10"
```

Code Dissection

In the previous code, the **GetSetting** function attempts to read the **FileCount** key in the section named Files for the application specified by App.Title. If a value exists, the **GetSetting** function returns the value in mintFiles. If a value does not exist, **GetSetting** returns the default value 10. The **SaveSetting** function stores the value 10 for the same Registry entry specified by the **GetSetting** function.

One common use of the Registry is to display, on the File menu, a list of the files recently opened by a program. In the completed program for GSC, this process is fairly simple. When the form loads, the code in the **Form_Load** event procedure reads a list of the last five file names from the Registry and adds them to a control array of menu commands. When the user opens files, the most recently opened file appears first on the menu and the least recently opened file appears last. If the list already contains five files, then the least recently opened file should disappear from the list; that is, the list of recent files should not grow indefinitely. When the user exits the program, the **Form_Unload** event procedure saves the current list of files to the Registry so that the list can be reloaded the next time the program is run.

This chapter's program is a prototype, however, in that it does not actually process any of the open files. That is, the GSC program uses the common dialog box to select a file to open, but it neither opens nor performs any actions on the selected file. It merely illustrates how to read and write information from and to the Registry.

To read and write information from and to the Registry:

1. Start Visual Basic, if necessary, and then load the project named Chapter.16\Startup\Event\Ch16_S.vbp.

2. Activate the Code window for the **Form_Load** event procedure for the form named frmCh16, and then enter the following statements:

```
Dim pintCount As Integer
Dim pstrFile As String
For pintCount = 1 To cMaxMenu
    pstrFile = GetSetting(App.Title, _
        "Files", "File" & CStr(pintCount))
    If pstrFile = vbNullString Then
        Exit Sub
    End If
    Load mnuFileList(mnuFileList.UBound + 1)
    mnuFileList(mnuFileList.UBound).Caption = _
        pstrFile
    mnuFileList(mnuFileList.UBound).Visible = _
        True
Next
```

16

3. For the same form, activate the Code window for the **Form_Unload** event procedure, and then enter the following statements:

```
Dim pintMax As Integer
Dim pintCurrent As Integer
pintMax = mnuFileList.UBound
For pintCurrent = 1 To pintMax
    SaveSetting App.Title, "Files", "File" & _
        CStr(pintCurrent), _
        mnuFileList(pintCurrent).Caption
Next
```

4. On the same form, enter the following statements in the **mnuFileOpen_Click** event procedure:

```
On Error GoTo CancelError
    Dim pintMax As Integer, pintCurrent As Integer
    Dim pintPrevious As Integer
    cdl1.ShowOpen
    pintMax = mnuFileList.UBound
    If pintMax < cMaxMenu Then
        pintMax = pintMax + 1
        Load mnuFileList(pintMax)
        mnuFileList(pintMax).Caption = _
            mnuFileList(pintMax - 1).Caption
    End If
    pintCurrent = pintMax
    pintPrevious = pintMax - 1
    Do While pintPrevious >= 0
        mnuFileList(pintCurrent).Caption = _
            mnuFileList(pintPrevious).Caption
        pintCurrent = pintCurrent - 1
        pintPrevious = pintPrevious - 1
    Loop
    mnuFileList(1).Caption = cdl1.FileName
    Exit Sub
CancelError:
```

5. Test the program. Click on the File menu and then click on Open to display the Open dialog box. Note that the files you opened in the completed example appear in the File menu because both programs use the same Registry keys.

6. Select a file, and then click on Open.

7. Repeat Steps 5 and 6 several times. This code does not actually open the file. Instead, it merely stores a list of current files in the Registry.

8. Click on Exit on the File menu. Do not click on the End button on the Visual Basic toolbar. If you do, the **Form_Unload** event will not occur and the current file list will not be written to the Registry.

9. Run the program again, and then click on the File menu. The file list should appear containing the files that you opened previously.

10. End the program to return to design mode.

The preceding code requires careful analysis. When you run the program, the **Form_Load** event occurs. The code in this event procedure attempts to read the list of the most recently opened files from the Registry. When the **Form_Unload** event occurs, the code in the event procedure writes the list of recently opened files back to the Registry. If this is the first time the user has run the program, no recent files exist in the Registry. Even so, the constant **cMaxMenu** contains the constant value five (5), which is the maximum number of files to list, and the statements inside the **For** loop attempt to load the full path of the last five files opened.

```
pstrFile = GetSetting(App.Title, _
    "Files", "File" & CStr(pintCount))
```

The **GetSetting** function uses App. Title (the **Title** property of the App object) to identify the application. In this example, the literal value "Files" is used for the section. Remember that this statement executes inside a **For** loop. As such, **pintCount** contains an Integer ranging from one (1) to five (5). The code converts this value to a string and concatenates the string to the literal value "File" to define the keys. Thus the keys are File1, File2, File3, and so on. If the call to **GetSetting** succeeds, the key, section, and title all exist, and the call to the **SaveSetting** function stores the value in **pstrFile**.

```
If pstrFile = vbNullString Then
    Exit Sub
End If
```

If the call fails, the code stores an empty string in **pstrFile**. If no file is found, the procedure exits, as shown in the preceding statements. If a file is found, the following statements execute:

```
Load mnuFileList(mnuFileList.UBound + 1)
mnuFileList(mnuFileList.UBound).Caption = pstrFile
mnuFileList(mnuFileList.UBound).Visible = True
```

Remember that the **Load** statement increases the number of elements contained in a control array. The implementation chosen in this example is a bit tricky. The menu named mnuFileList was created as a control array using the Menu Editor. The control array has one element with a separator bar as its

16

caption. When a recent file is found in the Registry, the code calls the **Load** statement to increase the size of the mnuFileList control array by one (1). It then sets the caption of the new element to the file name returned by **GetSetting**; it also sets the **Visible** property to **True**. You, as the programmer, can use this technique to manage a recent file list.

The code created in the preceding steps uses the **Form_Unload** event procedure to save the list of current files in the Registry. The first statement determines the number of elements in the control array. Element 0 contains the separator bar. Elements 1 through 5, if they exist, contain the list of recently opened files. Thus the **For** loop iterates between one (1) and the number of current files. The call to the **SaveSetting** function writes the contents of the current control array element (current file) to the same section of the Registry used for the **GetSetting** function.

Consider the following code:

```
SaveSetting App.Title, "Files", "File" & _
    CStr(pintCurrent), _
    mnuFileList(pintCurrent).Caption
```

App. Title and "Files" identify the application and section in the Registry, respectively. The preceding code determines the file number (Registry key) by concatenating an Integer value to the literal string "File". The code stores this value in the caption of the current element in the control array.

The **Open** command does nothing with the Registry itself. Instead, it merely manages the control array containing the recent list of files.

Viewing The Registry Using RegEdit

At this point, it would be difficult to examine the values in the Registry to see whether the calls to the **SaveSetting** and **GetSetting** functions are working correctly. Fortunately, the RegEdit (short for Registry Editor) program allows you to add, change, and delete entries in the Registry manually. RegEdit displays the hierarchy of Registry entries much in the same way that Windows Explorer displays a hierarchy of files. Figure 16.3 shows the Registry Editor with selected trees and subtrees open.

As you can see in Figure 16.3, the interface for the Registry Editor looks like the interface for Windows Explorer. Although the interface is similar, the data have a much different meaning and purpose. As shown in Figure 16.3, a Software subkey appears. Inside the Software subkey, another subkey named VB and VBA Program Settings appears. Inside that subkey, still another subkey appears for the project you are developing. That subkey, in turn, contains a Files subkey listing the recently saved files. The list portion of the Registry Editor displays the keys for the recently opened files and the values corresponding to those keys.

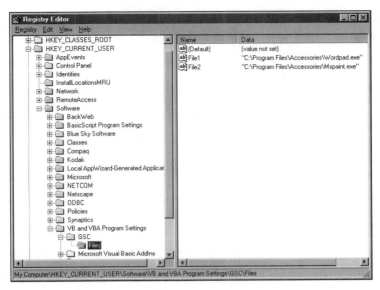

Figure 16.3   Registry subtrees.

In Figure 16.3, only two recently opened files appear. When you activate the Registry Editor on your computer, the number of subtrees shown will likely differ as your computer will have different software installed.

Rather than explaining the details of each and every Registry entry, you first will see how to view the Registry settings that you saved in the previous steps.

To locate an entry in the Registry:

1. On the Start menu, click on Run, enter the file name RegEdit to start the Registry Editor, and then click on OK. (RegEdit usually is not available on the Programs menu so as to hide the program from general users.) Click on Find on the Edit menu to display the Find dialog box, as shown in Figure 16.4.

2. Click on the checkbox options as shown in Figure 16.4. Enter the text "GSC" in the Find what text box, and then click on Find Next. A dialog box appears while RegEdit searches for the entry.

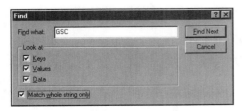

Figure 16.4   Find dialog box.

3. In the Registry Editor, open the folder named GSC, and then click on the Files folder. The keys and data files for the files you most recently opened should appear in the Registry Editor.

RegEdit also allows you to add new keys, modify existing keys, and delete keys. The Edit menu contains a Modify option that allows you to change the value of the selected key. To remove a key, you can select the key name and then click on Remove on the Edit menu.

To edit and remove keys from the Registry:

1. Click on the key named File1, and then click on Modify on the Edit menu to activate the Edit String dialog box.

2. Change the name of the file (Value data) to any name of your choosing. Click on OK to close the dialog box.

3. Run the Visual Basic program. Click on the File menu. The changes you made to the Registry should appear in the listing on the File menu. End the program.

4. Click on the Files subtree in the Registry Editor, and then delete it by pressing the Delete key. A dialog box will appear, asking you to confirm the deletion. Click on Yes. Exit RegEdit.

5. In Visual Basic, run the program. No files should appear in the listing on the File menu because the entries were removed from the Registry.

6. End the program to return to design mode.

In addition to deleting Registry entries using RegEdit, you also can delete them using Visual Basic.

Deleting Registry Entries

The **DeleteSetting** function removes a specific key/value pair from the Registry. It can also delete the key/value pairs for an entire section or for all the Registry settings pertaining to an application.

Syntax

DeleteSetting(**appname**, **section**[, **key**])

Dissection

➤ The required **appname** argument contains the name of the application stored in the Registry.

➤ The required **section** argument identifies a section of the application.

➤ The optional **key** argument identifies a specific key value in the **section**. If the **key** is omitted, the entire section is removed.

Code Example

```
DeleteSetting App.Title, "Files", "File1"
DeleteSetting App.Title, "Files"
DeleteSetting App.Title
```

Code Dissection

The first call to the **DeleteSetting** function removes the key and value for the File1 key in the Files section of the application App.Title. The second call removes the entire Files section, and the third call removes all settings for the application.

Using these Visual Basic functions, you can access only a small part of the Registry. One benefit of this limitation is that Visual Basic prevents you from changing a Registry entry that might cause other programs on the system to stop working.

Registering A Server

When you created ActiveX controls and ActiveX DLL servers, Visual Basic automatically added the necessary information pertaining to those servers to the Registry. You could therefore create project groups to debug and test your DLLs and ActiveX control projects because, when a project is run from the Visual Basic IDE, Visual Basic temporarily registers the server.

You can, however, register a server manually using the RegSvr32.exe utility. A copy of this utility appears in the Windows or Windows\System folder. You can also find the RegSvr32 utility on the Visual Basic CD-ROM. You call the RegSvr32.exe program from the MS-DOS prompt or the Run dialog box accessed from the Start menu. The command has a very simple syntax.

```
RegSvr32 Demo.dll
RegSvr32 /u Demo.dll
```

16

The first statement registers the component named Demo.dll, and the second statement removes the Registry entry for the program named Demo.dll from the Registry.

Remote Component Registration

In addition to accessing **COM** modules (code components) on a local machine, Visual Basic supports distributed COM (DCOM) and Remote Automation so as to work with components on a remote machine. When a program operates with code components on remote machines, you can register those components by using a tool called the Remote Automation Connection Manager (RACM). RACM is a stand-alone program typically found in the

VB\Clisvr folder. Note that this facility is included only in the Enterprise version of Visual Basic.

The Basics Of Windows Dynamic Link Libraries

Dynamic Link Library Defined

Throughout this book, you have written programs consisting entirely of Visual Basic statements. Visual Basic simplifies the development of programs by encapsulating the functionality of various Windows objects into an integrated development environment.

Windows makes its functionality available to other programming languages by providing those programming languages with the ability to use the application programming interface (API) (or Windows API). The functions pertaining to the Windows API are stored in Dynamic Link Libraries (DLLs).

Before discussing the details of accessing the Windows API through a DLL, a few words about program compilation and linking may prove helpful regarding how Windows DLLs work. Windows and most other operating systems encapsulate the code for common functions into a library. When you compile a program, the compiler translates language statements into some form of executable file. The first step in the compilation process is translation. In this stage, the compiler translates source language statements into a form understood by the computer hardware. These statements will likely make references to library routines stored in another file. The second step in the compilation process is to copy those library routines from the library into the executable file itself. The process of establishing a reference to a procedure in a library is called *linking*.

One technique to link programs is called *static linking*. With static linking, the compiler copies the necessary code from the library into the executable file. For example, if you call the **Format** function, the compiler will copy all code written to implement that function into your executable program. Figure 16.5 illustrates the process of static linking.

Static linking had a serious deficiency. Most programs written utilize the same functions. For example, nearly every Visual Basic program you write calls the Format and string conversion functions. Thus every program written stores a copy of these same functions in its executable file on the disk. This linking technique makes each program much larger than it would be if the program itself could just call a function that resided in a common library. Furthermore, storing several copies of the same function wastes disk space.

Another form of linking, called *dynamic linking*, was introduced to overcome the flaws of static linking. With dynamic linking, one copy of a specific library procedure is stored in a single file. Consider what happens when you run a program that uses a function (like **Format**) in a dynamically linked library.

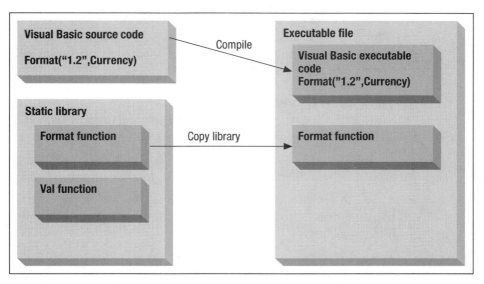

Figure 16.5   Static linking.

Instead of the code for the **Format** function being copied into your program's executable file, the compiler creates a reference in your program that allows the executable file to find the file and function in the library containing the code for the **Format** function. The term *dynamic linking* reflects the fact that programs are linked to various libraries dynamically at run time rather than statically at compile time.

Figure 16.6 illustrates a dynamically linked program.

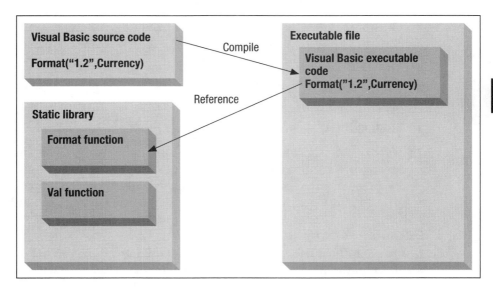

Figure 16.6   Dynamic linking.

Windows DLLs, as the name implies, are dynamically linked. To call a DLL procedure from a Visual Basic program, you must tell Visual Basic the name of the library and the name of the function you want to call. Your program stores a reference to the library and a function in that library.

Referencing A Dynamic Link Library

From Visual Basic, you can access the hundreds of procedures stored in the DLLs defined by Windows. Calling Windows DLL functions offers several benefits:

➤ Some tasks are difficult, if not impossible, to perform using Visual Basic.

➤ Although you may be familiar with the capabilities supported by Visual Basic controls, you can expand the functionality of many controls by calling DLL procedures.

➤ The procedures in a DLL are typically optimized for performance.

Many DLLs are components of the Windows operating system. Each DLL contains a set of procedures you can call at run time. These procedures perform tasks such as updating windows, reading and writing information from and to the disk, and so on. You call DLL procedures much in the same way that you call intrinsic Visual Basic procedures. To use a DLL procedure in a Visual Basic program, you follow two steps:

1. You make the name and arguments of the DLL procedure known to the Visual Basic program.

2. You call the DLL procedure as needed.

The following DLLs defined by Windows have particular importance:

➤ **Comdlg32.dll** Contains the library functions for the CommonDialog control. The Visual Basic CommonDialog control calls these functions.

➤ **GDI32.dll** Contains functions to perform graphical and drawing operations.

➤ **Kernel32.dll** Contains functions to perform tasks closely related to the operating system.

➤ **Shell32.dll** Contains functions to access the Windows shell.

➤ **User32.dll** Contains functions to manage windows. You can also access the functions pertaining to intrinsic controls such as text and list boxes. Remember that an intrinsic control, such as a text box, is not specific to Visual Basic, but rather is common to the Windows operating system.

Declaring A DLL Procedure

Before your Visual Basic program can call a DLL procedure, you must declare the name of the Windows library, the procedure name, and the arguments required by the procedure by using the **Declare** statement.

Syntax

[**Public** | **Private**] Declare Sub name Lib "libname" [**Alias** "aliasname"]
[([arglist])]
[**Public** | **Private**] Declare Function name Lib "libname" [**Alias** "aliasname"] [([arglist])] [**As type**]

Dissection

➤ The optional **Public** and **Private** statements declare procedures that are visible to all other procedures in all modules and that are visible in the module where the procedure is declared, respectively. They have the same meaning as when you declare Visual Basic functions and procedures. Declared procedures are **Public** by default. You can use a **Declare** statement with the **Public** keyword only in a standard .bas module. DLLs declared in a form, or any type of class module, must be **Private**.

➤ The **Declare** statement associates a DLL procedure with a Visual Basic program so that the program can access the DLL procedure.

➤ The **Sub** keyword indicates that the DLL procedure does not return a value. The **Function** keyword indicates that the DLL procedure does return a value. Either the **Function** or **Sub** keyword must be included.

➤ The meaning of the required **name** argument depends on whether you use the **Alias** keyword. If you omit the **Alias** keyword, **name** represents both the name of the procedure within the DLL and the name of the procedure as it is known to your Visual Basic program. Note that DLL procedure names are case-sensitive, unlike ordinary Visual Basic procedure names.

➤ The required **Lib** and **libname** arguments specify the library containing the DLL procedure.

➤ The **Alias** keyword indicates that the procedure being called has another name in the DLL. Aliases are useful when the DLL procedure name has the same name as a Visual Basic keyword. You also can use the **Alias** keyword when a DLL procedure has the same name as a **Public** variable, a constant, or any other procedure in the same scope. In addition, an alias is useful if the Visual Basic naming conventions disallow the use of any characters in the DLL procedure name.

➤ The optional **aliasname** contains the name of the procedure in the DLL.

➤ The optional **arglist** contains a list of arguments that are passed to the procedure when it is called.

➤ The optional **type** argument contains the data type of the value returned by a DLL **Function** procedure. This value may be a **Byte**, **Boolean**, **Integer**, **Long**, **Currency**, **Single**, **Double**, **Date**, **String** (variable length only), or **Variant**. It can also be a user-defined or object type.

16

Code Example

```
Declare Function SetWindowPos Lib "user32" _
    (ByVal hwnd As Long, _
    ByVal hWndInsertAfter As Long, _
    ByVal x As Long, _
    ByVal y As Long, _
    ByVal cx As Long, _
    ByVal cy As Long, _
    ByVal wFlags As Long) As Long
```

Code Dissection

The previous statement declares the Windows DLL procedure named **SetWindowPos** so that your Visual Basic program can use it. This DLL procedure resides in the User32.dll library. The procedure takes seven arguments, all passed by value, and returns a **Long Integer** data type. The purpose of this DLL function and the meaning of the various arguments will be discussed later in the section.

Note the case of the User32 library name and the **hwnd** argument. In the preceding syntax, both words appear in all lowercase characters, even though the file name on the disk appears as User32.dll and most objects refer to the **hwnd** property as **hWnd**. The capitalization used for DLL procedure names follows the capitalization conventions used by the API Text Viewer.

Although you could declare a DLL procedure on a single line, this book will take the approach of using continuation lines to declare a DLL procedure to improve readability.

Creating Aliases

As noted in the discussion of the syntax for the **Declare** statement, a DLL procedure may contain the **Alias** keyword. An alias defines a name for a DLL procedure that differs from the actual procedure name stored in the DLL.

Visual Basic requires the use of aliases because some DLL procedures have names that are not legal Visual Basic names. For example, many DLL procedures contain a leading underscore or a hyphen embedded in the procedure name. Aliases also prove useful when a DLL procedure has the same name as a Visual Basic intrinsic function. In addition, you can use aliases to provide shorthand names for DLL procedures.

Another common use for aliases is to rename a DLL procedure because its name conflicts with a Visual Basic statement or function. For example, Visual Basic supports a function named **Beep** that will generate an audible beep. The

Windows DLL kernel32.dll also contains a procedure named **Beep**. Consider the following statements:

```
Private Declare Function Beep Lib "kernel32" _
    (ByVal dwFreq As Long, _
    ByVal dwDuration As Long) As Long
Private Sub Command1_Click()
    Beep
End Sub
```

The previous code has a problem. The **Declare** statement makes the Windows DLL **Beep** function available to your program. Assume that the code in the command button's **Click** event procedure intended to call the Visual Basic **Beep** function. The name of the DLL procedure **Beep** overrides the intrinsic Visual Basic **Beep** function. As a result, the number of arguments in the Visual Basic **Beep** function does not match the expected number of arguments in the DLL procedure, which will produce a compiler error. To solve this problem, you must create an alias for the DLL **Beep** procedure, as shown in the following statements:

```
Private Declare Function BeepWin32 Lib "kernel32" _
    Alias "Beep" _
    (ByVal dwFreq As Long, _
    ByVal dwDuration As Long) As Long

Private Sub Command1_Click()
    Dim pLng As Long
    pLng = BeepWin32(0, 0)
End Sub
```

The preceding statements resolve the problem by creating an alias named BeepWin32 to call the DLL Beep function. Because your Visual Basic program recognizes the function as BeepWin32, the code in the command button was changed to call the DLL Beep function and the function was changed to contain the necessary arguments.

16

Locating A DLL Procedure

The first step in using DLL procedures is learning the DLL procedures that Windows exposes to the Visual Basic programmer, the return values of those procedures, and the arguments required by them. Conceptually, the process is the same as defining the arguments and the return value for Visual Basic functions. DLLs and Windows, however, are much more particular about the accuracy of the data types used by both DLL arguments and the return value of DLL functions.

The API Text Viewer provides a list of the constants, function declarations, and data types needed to call a particular DLL. To use the API Text Viewer, you select items from the Available Items list box, which causes them to appear in the Selected Items list box. Once you have selected the desired constants, function declarations, and data types, you click on the Copy button to copy the items to the Windows Clipboard. You then paste the Clipboard data into a module in your program. If, as you develop your program, you realize that you forgot to add a particular DLL procedure, you can reactivate the API Text Viewer, select additional items, copy them to the Clipboard, and add them to the desired module file.

The API information is typically stored in the file named Win32API.txt, which usually appears in the WinAPI folder in the Visual Basic root directory. This file may not exist, however, depending on the Visual Basic installation options chosen.

 If you frequently use DLLs in your programs, you can convert the Win32API.txt file into a database file that will be readable by the Jet Engine. The default database file name is Win32API.mdb; it is generally written to the same folder as the file Win32API.txt. You convert the text file to a database file by activating the API Text Viewer, clicking on Load Text File on the File menu, and then clicking on Convert Text to Database on the File menu. Once the conversion to a database file is complete, the API Viewer can open the new file.

In this section, you will call the following DLL functions:

➤ **GetTempFileNameA**

➤ **GetTempPathA**

➤ **SetWindowPos**

➤ **SetTimer**

➤ **KillTimer**

You now can use the API Text Viewer to view the necessary constants and **Declare** statements so that you can add them to your program. Note that these constants and **Declare** statements have already been added to the standard module for GSC's project.

To view the Win32API.txt file:

1. Start the API Text Viewer either on the Start menu or the Add-Ins menu from the Visual Basic menu bar. Note that you may need to use the Add-In Manager to load the API Text Viewer.

2. Click on Load Text File on the File menu.

3. Click on the file Common\Tools\WinAPI\Win32API.txt, and then click on the Open button. The root Visual Basic directory is usually found in the folder \Program Files\Microsoft Visual Studio. (The full path on your machine may differ depending on your installation.)

4. A message box may appear, asking if you want to convert the text file to a database file to improve performance. If you intend to use the API Text Viewer often, click on Yes, and select a name for the database, as prompted.

5. In the API Type list box, click on Declares, if necessary. The **Declare** statements for all DLL functions will appear in the Available Items list box.

6. In the Available Items list box, click on the DLLs named **GetTempFileName** and **GetTempPath**, clicking on Add after clicking on each item. The items should appear as shown in Figure 16.7.

7. Click on Copy to copy the items to the Windows Clipboard. These items could then be pasted to any Visual Basic module. This action is not necessary, however, because the code in the startup program already contains the DLL declarations in the standard module named **API.bas**.

8. Exit the API Text Viewer.

Before calling these DLL procedures, you should consider your program design. Imagine that you have created a large program with several forms. Assume that many of these forms require the services of several common DLL procedures. With such a scenario, you have several implementation options from which to choose:

➤ You could declare the DLL procedures with the **Private** keyword in each form module. The code in the form module then would call the DLL directly.

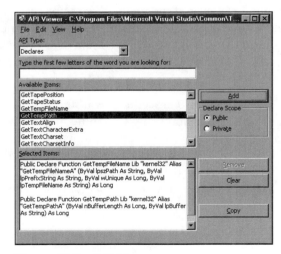

Figure 16.7   API Viewer.

➤ You could declare each DLL procedure as **Public** in a standard module. This solution allows the DLL procedure to be declared only once. Each form or other module then could call the DLL procedure directly.

➤ The third approach is to create a *wrapper procedure*. Using this technique, you create a standard module and declare each of the DLL procedures used by the program in that standard module. Instead of calling the DLL procedures directly from other forms and modules, however, you create another procedure in the standard module, called a *wrapper procedure*. The wrapper procedure, in turn, calls the underlying DLL procedure or procedures. This technique frees the developer from worrying about the technical details of calling the various DLL procedures.

Programming DLLs requires much more than simply learning a list of DLL functions and their arguments. Because DLLs access the functions pertaining to the Windows operating system, you must understand the underlying Windows concepts related to these types of DLL procedures.

One important concept is the window. (In the discussion that follows, the term *operating system* refers to the Windows operating system.) The operating system views every form, and nearly every control instance on a form, as a unique window. The operating system assigns a unique Long Integer number called a *window handle* to each window; this window handle is stored in the **hWnd** property of a particular form or control instance. Labels, lines, and shapes are not windows and therefore do not support an **hWnd** property.

Many operating system functions (DLL procedures) require an argument consisting of the window to which you are referring. To illustrate how this process works, suppose that you want to create a dialog box that will always appear on top of all other windows, even if the window does not have focus. This ability may be useful for displaying a dialog box that notifies the user of a very important error condition that should not be overlooked. You may also want to display a floating toolbar that should never be hidden (obscured by another window).

Before attempting to declare and call DLL procedures, you should know that much of the Windows operating system and many DLL functions are written in the C or C++ programming languages. That is, the DLL functions you call were written in C. C (or C++) and Visual Basic do not share the same data types. Table 16.1 describes some of the C data types and the equivalent Visual Basic data types that should be used as the arguments to a DLL procedure.

Not only do the data types have significance when passing arguments to DLL procedures, but you must also consider how to pass those arguments to DLL procedures.

Table 16.1   C data types versus Visual Basic data types.

C Data Type	Visual Basic Data Type
ATOM	ByVal variable As Integer
BOOL	ByVal variable As Long
CHAR	ByVal variable As Byte
LONG	ByVal variable As Long
LPSTR,LPCSTR	ByVal variable As String
NULL	ByVal variable As Long
SHORT	ByVal variable As Integer

Using **ByVal** And **ByRef** Arguments In DLL Procedures

In Visual Basic, all function arguments are passed either by reference (the default) or by value. For data types like **Integer**, **Float**, and **Boolean**, passing an argument by reference means that the procedure receives the memory address of the variable, rather than the data itself. Many DLL procedures expect their arguments to be passed by value, however. Thus the **Declare** statement should always contain the **ByVal** or **ByRef** keyword for each argument so that your code will correctly pass the arguments to the DLL.

Although the data types **Long**, **Integer**, and **Single** pass a memory address when the argument is declared with the **ByRef** keyword, and the same data types pass data when the **ByVal** keyword is used, strings work much differently. When passing a string variable by value (using the **ByVal** keyword), Visual Basic passes the memory address of the first data byte in the argument. When passing a string variable by reference, the argument consists of a memory address where another memory address is stored. In Visual Basic, you nearly always pass strings by value to DLL functions.

When declaring DLL procedures, you must ensure that the declaration correctly defines how each argument is passed. If a DLL expects an argument to be passed **ByVal** and your code passes it **ByRef**, the DLL will receive incorrect information and errors will occur.

Calling A DLL

The **SetWindowPos** DLL procedure changes the size of a window, its position, or its ZOrder relative to other windows. This function has the following type declaration in Win32API.txt.

Syntax

Declare Function SetWindowPos Lib "user32" Alias "SetWindowPos" (ByVal **hwnd** As Long, ByVal **hWndInsertAfter** As Long, ByVal **x** As Long, ByVal **y** As Long, ByVal **cx** As Long, ByVal **cy** As Long, ByVal **wFlags** As Long) As Long

Dissection

➤ The user32.dll library contains the **SetWindowPos** function. This function changes the size, position, and ZOrder of a window.

➤ The **hwnd** argument contains a **Long Integer** data type representing a window handle. You typically obtain this value by reading the **hWnd** property of a form or control instance.

➤ The **hWndInsertAfter** argument specifies the window that will precede the window referenced by **hWnd** in the ZOrder. Several valid constants for this argument exist. **HWND_BOTTOM** causes the window to appear at the bottom of the ZOrder. **HWND_NOTOPMOST** causes the window to appear above all non-topmost windows. **HWND_TOP** places the window at the top of the ZOrder.

➤ The **x** and **y** properties specify the left side and top of the window, respectively.

➤ The **cx** and **cy** arguments specify the new width and height of the window, respectively.

➤ The **wFlags** argument contains the flags that specify various sizing and positioning characteristics of the window. The flag **SWP_NOMOVE** retains the current position of the window. The flag **SWP_NOSIZE** retains the current size of the window. Many other flags exist to control the window's behavior.

For the GSC program, you will create a function that will cause a form to appear as the topmost window when the form is displayed.

To make a window appear as the topmost window:

1. Create the following wrapper procedure in the standard module named **API** to hide the DLL from the programmer. The **Declare** statement for the **SetWindowPos** function has already been placed in the standard module.

```
Public Sub SetTop(frm As Form)
    Dim plngFlags As Long, plngResult As Long
    plngFlags = SWP_NOSIZE Or SWP_NOMOVE
    frm.Show
    plngResult = SetWindowPos(frm.hWnd, _
        HWND_TOPMOST, 0, 0, 0, 0, plngFlags)
End Sub
```

2. In the form named **frmCh16**, enter the following statement in the **cmdShowTop_Click** event procedure:

```
Call SetTop(frmTop)
```

3. Test the program. Click on the Show Topmost Form command button. The dialog box should appear with the text "Top" in the title bar. Try to obscure the dialog box. It should always appear as the topmost window.

4. Click on the Close button to close the form, and then end the program.

The **SetTop** procedure accepts one argument—a reference to a form. The following statement sets the necessary flags to ignore the size and position arguments:

```
plngFlags = SWP_NOSIZE Or SWP_NOMOVE
```

The DLL procedure will use the settings of the form's **Height, Width,** and positioning properties to determine the size and position of the form on the screen.

Consider the following code:

```
plngResult = SetWindowPos(frm.hWnd, _
    HWND_TOPMOST, 0, 0, 0, 0, plngFlags)
```

The preceding statement uses the window handle of the form (stored in the **hWnd** property) as the first argument. The second argument contains the constant value **HWND_TOPMOST**, which causes the form to appear as the topmost form. Because the flags are set to **SWP_NOSIZE** and **SWP_NOMOVE**, the **SetWindowPos** DLL uses the form's positional properties to determine the size and position of the form on the screen.

The technique used to display a form as a topmost form illustrates the use of a wrapper procedure. A programmer can call the **SetTop** procedure without worrying about the details of calling the **SetWindowPos** DLL.

Managing Temporary Files

Applications commonly need to create and destroy temporary files. These files typically remain transparent to the user of your program. Although you could create an arbitrary empty file, your program should verify that the file name does not already exist. Fortunately, Windows supports DLL procedures that allow you to control the folders where temporary files are stored and to obtain a temporary file name that is guaranteed to be unique—the **GetTempPath** and **GetTempFileName** DLL procedures perform these tasks. Before using these two procedures, however, you must be able to write code that passes strings as arguments to DLL procedures.

Passing Strings To DLL Procedures

Passing a string as a DLL procedure argument requires that you understand the operation of string arguments, the difference between the Visual Basic representation of a string and the C representation of a string, and the concept of a pointer. You must also be familiar with the concepts of passing arguments by reference and by value.

In general, strings are represented in one of two ways. Internally, Windows 95 and Windows 98 DLLs process strings using the **LPSTR C** data type. This value is a 32-bit pointer to an ASCII character string. Windows NT internally supports two character sets: UNICODE, which requires two bytes for each character, and ASCII, which requires one byte for each character. The difficulty arises because Visual Basic internally manipulates strings as UNICODE.

To resolve this discrepancy, Windows DLL procedures that manipulate strings exist in two versions: one to process UNICODE characters and another to process ASCII characters. Consider the following possible **Declare** statements for the **GetTempPath** function:

```
Declare Function GetTempPath Lib "kernel32" _
    Alias "GetTempPathA" _
    (ByVal nBufferLength As Long, _
    ByVal lpBuffer As String) As Long
Declare Function GetTempPath Lib "kernel32" _
    Alias "GetTempPathW" _
    (ByVal nBufferLength As Long, _
    ByVal lpBuffer As String) As Long
```

These two **Declare** statements are identical with one exception—each has a different value for the **Alias** argument. When you call the DLL from Visual Basic, the function name **GetTempPath** will be used. In the first **Declare** statement, however, the actual function name in the Windows DLL is **GetTempPathA**. **GetTempPathA** specifies the ASCII version of the function. In the second **Declare** statement, the function name is **GetTempPathW**. **GetTempPathW** specifies the UNICODE version of the function. The character "W" as the suffix stems from the word "Wide."

In Visual Basic, you generally should use the ASCII version of string functions rather than the UNICODE version, as Windows 95 and 98 support only the ASCII versions. Windows NT supports both the ASCII and UNICODE versions. Thus, you should use the UNICODE version only if you are confident that the users of your program will run it only on the Windows NT platform.

When passing strings to a DLL procedure, you always pass the string argument **ByVal** rather than **ByRef**. Your code does not pass the string itself. Rather, it passes the memory address of the first character of the string. One problem that can arise when passing strings to a DLL procedure occurs when the DLL procedure modifies the contents of the string argument. Consider the following Visual Basic function and function call:

```
Public Sub GetDateString(ByRef pstrValue As String)
    pstrValue = Date()
End Sub

Dim pstrDateString As String
Call GetDateString(pstrDateString)
```

While nonsensical, this **Sub** procedure and the call to the **Sub** procedure illustrate a very important point: **pstrDateString** contains no characters when it is declared. The procedure call therefore passes the empty string to the **Sub** procedure **GetDateString**. Inside that procedure, the code increases the size of the string so as to store the string representation of the current date.

When you pass a string to a DLL procedure, this technique will not work. DLL procedures cannot increase the size of a string argument. Thus, if you fail to allocate enough space for the DLL to store the data in the string, the DLL procedure will not increase the size of the string. Instead, it will overwrite memory that is used by another variable. As a result, the data in your program may become corrupted or Visual Basic may crash. Two solutions to this problem exist:

➤ You can use variable-length strings. When applying this solution, the string passed to the DLL must be large enough to hold the string returned by the DLL. The Visual Basic String function stores a repeating character in the string; which in effect defines an explicit size for the string.

➤ You can use fixed-length strings.

To illustrate these two techniques, consider the following string declarations and statements:

```
Dim pstrFixed As String * 255
Dim pstrVariable As String
pstrVariable = String(255, Chr(0))
```

The first statement declares a 255-character fixed-length string. The second and third statements together create a 255-character variable-length string containing null bytes; thus both strings are 255 characters in length. A DLL procedure using this string can store as many as 255 characters in the string without generating an error.

Visual Basic stores strings differently from the way that Visual C and C++ store them. The C language stores strings as consecutive ASCII characters. A special character called a *null byte* always terminates the string. The constant **vbNullString** represents a null byte. Alternatively, you can store a null byte in a string by using the **Chr** function with the argument zero (0). The following statements create a string containing a null byte as the first character:

```
Dim pstrNull As String * 255
pstrNull = Chr(0)
```

When a DLL expects a string as an argument, it may be necessary to pass a **null string** (a string containing only a null byte). This task requires you to store only a null byte in the string and to pass it as an argument. The easiest way to accomplish this task is to use the constant **vbNullString** when passing the argument. You cannot use an empty string as identified by the following statements:

```
Dim pstrEmpty As String
pstrEmpty = ""
```

After examining the basic mechanics of passing string arguments to a DLL procedure, you are now ready to use string arguments in the **GetTempPathA** and **GetTempFileNameA** functions.

Syntax

Declare Function GetTempPath Lib "kernel32" Alias "GetTempPathA" (ByVal **nBufferLength** As Long, ByVal **lpBuffer** As String) As Long

---

Dissection

➤ The DLL function **GetTempPathA** will retrieve the full path, including the drive designator for the directory where Windows creates temporary files.

➤ The **nBufferLength** contains a Long Integer that defines the length of the character buffer (**lpBuffer**) used to store the temporary file path.

➤ The **lpBuffer** argument contains the address of the string variable that stores the path of the temporary directory. If the function completes successfully, the value returned will indicate the number of characters copied to the string named **lpBuffer**. If the function fails for any reason, the value zero (0) will be returned.

➤ The **TMP** and **TEMP** environment variables determine the setting of **lpBuffer**. If **TMP** is defined, **lpBuffer** contains the value of **TMP**. If **TMP** is not defined but **TEMP** is defined, **lpBuffer** contains the value of **TEMP**.

If neither variable is defined, the function returns the full path of the current directory.

The **GetTempFileNameA** function has the following syntax.

Syntax
Declare Function GetTempFileName Lib "kernel32" Alias "GetTempFileNameA" (ByVal **lpszPath** As String, ByVal **lpPrefixString** As String, ByVal **wUnique** As Long, ByVal **lpTempFileName** As String) As Long

Dissection

➤ The **GetTempFileNameA** function creates either a temporary file or a name for a temporary file.

➤ The argument **lpszPath** contains the full path where the temporary file will be created. You determine this value by calling the **GetTempPathA** function.

➤ The **lpPrefixString** contains a string-character prefix. **GetTempFileNameA** uses the first three characters of the string as the prefix of the file name. This string must be a null-terminated string.

➤ The **wUnique** flag is an **Integer** that the **GetTempFileNameA** function converts to a hexadecimal number so as to derive a file name. If the value of **wUnique** is zero (0), the hexadecimal string is derived from the system date. Windows guarantees that the file name does not already exist on the system. If this value is not zero (0), it is converted to a hexadecimal string and used as the basis for the temporary file name. Windows does not test whether the file exists.

➤ The **lpTempFileName** argument contains the memory address of the string where the function will store the temporary file name.

➤ If successful, **GetTempFileNameA** returns a unique numeric value that is used in the temporary file name. If the function fails, it returns the value zero (0).

To illustrate the use of these two functions and the dangers of processing strings with DLL arguments, you will create a **Public** function procedure (wrapper procedure) in the standard module named **API.bas** that ultimately will call these two DLL procedures. This procedure will allow a developer to call a Visual Basic function that will create a temporary file name so that the developer need not worry about the details of calling a DLL procedure. Because these two

DLLs have already been declared in the standard module, the next step is to create a **Public** general procedure that will call these DLLs.

Consider the following statements:

```
Public Function GetTempFile() As String
    Dim pstrPrefix As String * 4
    Dim pstrPath As String * 255
    Dim pstrFileName As String * 1024
    Dim pintSize As Integer
    Dim plngSize As Long
    pstrPrefix = "VBT" & Chr(0)
    pintSize = GetTempPathA(255, pstrPath)
    plngSize = GetTempFileNameA(pstrPath, _
        pstrPrefix, 0, pstrFileName)
    GetTempFile = pstrFileName
End Function
```

The preceding statements create a wrapper procedure named **GetTempFile**. This procedure defines the length for the string arguments. It then calls the **GetTempPathA** and **GetTempFileNameA** DLL functions.

Consider the following statement to declare the variable **pstrFileName**, which stores the path of the temporary directory, and the syntax to call the **GetTempFile** function:

```
Dim pstrFileName As String * 255
pstrFileName = GetTempFile()
```

The preceding statements declare **pstrFileName** and call the wrapper function **GetTempFile**.

As a programmer, you often copy data from an original file that is opened in a temporary file. This approach ensures that the original contents of the original file can be restored if the file becomes corrupted or the user makes some error from which he or she cannot recover. For example, in a data-processing program, you may want to copy a particular database file to a temporary file before opening the database.

To create a temporary file:

1. Create the following procedure in the standard module named **API.bas**:

```
Public Function GetTempFile() As String
    Dim pstrPrefix As String * 4
    Dim pstrPath As String * 255
    Dim pstrFileName As String * 1024
    Dim pintSize As Integer
```

```
      Dim plngSize As Long
      pstrPrefix = "VBT" & Chr(0)
      pintSize = GetTempPath(255, pstrPath)
      plngSize = GetTempFileName(pstrPath, _
          pstrPrefix, 0, pstrFileName)
      GetTempFile = pstrFileName
   End Function
```

2. Enter the following statements in the **mnuFileMakeTemporary_Click** event procedure on the main form named **frmCh16**:

```
Dim pstrFileName As String
pstrFileName = GetTempFile()
Debug.Print pstrFileName
```

3. Test the program. Click on File, and then click on Make Temporary. The code in the **Click** event procedure prints the temporary file name to the Immediate window. Open the Immediate window to verify that the file name appears.

4. End the program to return to design mode.

In addition to problems that may occur when passing strings to DLL procedures, complexities arise when passing properties.

Passing Properties

Passing property values to a DLL procedure is very similar to passing variables. When passing properties that contain strings, however, you cannot pass the property directly in a DLL argument. For example, suppose you wanted to store the path of the Windows temporary directory in an object such as a text box. You may be tempted to enter the following statements:

```
Dim pstrTempPath As String * 255
pintSize = GetTempPath(255, Text1.Text)
```

The preceding statements will not work, however. Because your code must pass strings to a DLL procedure by value, and because these statements cause a pointer to be passed containing an address of the first character of the string, you must use another technique. To use a string property as an argument in a DLL call, you must create a temporary variable to store the string, and then write code to read and write the variable, as shown in the following statements:

```
Dim pstrTempPath As String * 255
pstrTempPath = Text1
pintSize = GetTempPath(255, pstrTempPath)
```

As the Visual Basic programmer, you can exploit another feature of DLLs called a *callback*.

Callback Functions

As an introduction to the concept of a callback function, consider the ways in which you know how to call a **Function** or **Sub** procedure in Visual Basic:

➤ You can call a **Function** or **Sub** procedure explicitly by writing a Visual Basic statement to call it. Although the syntax used differs slightly for standard and class modules, the result is the same: The **Function** or **Sub** procedure executes in direct response to being called from a statement that you wrote.

➤ You can create an event procedure that executes in response to some event. Windows generates an event that, in turn, causes the code in the event procedure to execute. You do not call the event procedure explicitly. Rather, the event procedure executes automatically in response to some Windows-generated event.

➤ When you created an ActiveX control, as the author, you could write code to raise an event. This approach would cause Visual Basic to respond to an event procedure written by a developer.

Another way to call a function is via a callback. Creating a callback function in Visual Basic is no different than creating any other Visual Basic function. What changes is how that function is called. To create a callback function, you register a Visual Basic procedure to a Windows DLL function. When Windows fires a specific event, it will execute the newly registered Visual Basic callback function.

To understand the mechanics of a callback procedure, you will create a simple callback function that illustrates a completely new technique to implement a well-known task. You have likely used the Timer control in forms. You can also implement a timer through callbacks by using the **SetTimer** and **KillTimer** functions.

Syntax

Declare Function SetTimer Lib "user32" Alias "SetTimer" (ByVal **hwnd** As Long, ByVal **nIDEvent** As Long, ByVal **uElapse** As Long, ByVal **lpTimerFunc** As Long) As Long Declare Function KillTimer Lib "user32" Alias "KillTimer" (ByVal **hwnd** As Long, ByVal **nIdEvent** As Long) As Long

---

Dissection

➤ The **SetTimer** function creates a timer with a specified timeout value. The **KillTimer** function destroys a particular timer created by the **SetTimer** function.

➤ The **hwnd** argument associates a timer with a particular window.

➤ The functions use the **nIDEvent** argument only if the **hwnd** argument is not null. This argument also specifies a timer identifier.

➤ The **uElapse** argument specifies the timeout value in milliseconds.

➤ The **lpTimerFunc** argument specifies the function that will execute when **uElapse** reaches the timeout value.

To create a callback timer, you must learn about **AddressOf** keyword. As its name implies, this keyword is used to pass the address of a procedure or variable. The **AddressOf** keyword passes the address of a callback procedure to a Windows DLL function. To illustrate the use of the **AddressOf** keyword, you will create a wrapper function that a developer can call to set the timer.

Consider the following wrapper function to set the timer:

```
Public Function SetDLLTimer(plngTime As Long, _
    objCurrent As Object) As Long
    Set mobjCurrent = objCurrent
    SetDLLTimer = SetTimer(0, 0, plngTimer, _
        AddressOf TimerProc)
End Function
```

The developer will call the **SetDLLTimer** function with two arguments. The first argument contains the number of milliseconds that will elapse before the timeout value occurs. The second argument consists of an object reference; it contains the form or class module that contains another (as yet unspecified) function that will execute before the timer fires.

The code in the function performs two tasks. First, it saves the object reference in the module-level variable **mobjCurrent**. Second, the function calls the underlying **SetTimer** DLL procedure. No **hWnd** or **nIDEvent** arguments are specified. The third argument contains the value of the timeout. The fourth argument is significant. Consider the statement fragment for this argument:

```
AddressOf TimerProc
```

This statement fragment passes the memory address of the procedure named **TimerProc**. By calling the **SetTimer** function, the wrapper procedure creates a timer and registers the procedure named **TimerProc**. When the timeout period expires, Windows will call the procedure **TimerProc** automatically. Thus **TimerProc** is a callback procedure.

When Windows calls the **TimerProc** callback procedure, it does so with specific arguments. Consider the code for this procedure:

```
Private Function TimerProc(ByVal hWnd As Long, _
    plngMsg As Long, ByVal plngTimerID As Long, _
    ByVal plngTime As Long) As Long
On Error Resume Next
    Call KillTimer(0, plngTimerID)
    mobjCurrent.DllTimer
```

In this example, only the **plngTimerID** argument is used. This argument contains a Long Integer that uniquely identifies the timer. The **TimerProc** procedure uses this value to destroy the timer by calling the **KillTimer** function. Thus, in this example's implementation, the timer is created, the timeout occurs once, and the timer is destroyed.

Consider the final statement in the procedure:

```
mobjCurrent.DllTimer
```

Remember that the developer calls the **SetDLLTimer** procedure with an argument containing a reference to a form or class module. The preceding statement calls a method named **DLLTimer** that is contained by that form or class module. Thus the developer can write code in the **DLLTimer** procedure that will execute when the timeout period occurs.

Consider the following procedures in the form module:

```
Private Sub cmdCallback_Click()
    SetDLLTimer 10, Me
End Sub

Public Sub DllTimer()
    Debug.Print "Timer"
End Sub
```

When the user clicks the cmdCallback button, the code in the button's event procedure calls the **SetDLLTimer** wrapper procedure, sets the timeout period to 10 milliseconds, and passes a reference to the current form. When the timeout period expires, Windows calls the **TimerProc** callback procedure, which in turn calls the **DLLTimer** procedure. Figure 16.8 illustrates the flow of execution in this process.

The code in the standard module has already been created for you. To test the callback procedure, you will call the wrapper function and write the procedure that executes when the timeout period expires.

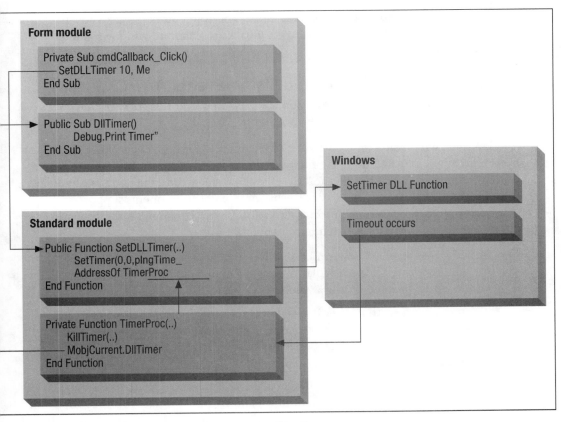

Figure 16.8   Callback procedure—execution flow.

To use a callback function:

1. Enter the following statement in the **cmdCallback_Click** event procedure of frmCh16:

```
SetDllTimer 10, Me
```

2. Create the following procedure in the form:

```
Public Sub DLLTimer()
    Debug.Print "Timer"
End Sub
```

3. Test the program. Click on the Callback command button. The text "Timer" should appear in the Immediate window.

4. End the program to return to design mode.

The preceding example is but one illustration of how you might take advantage of Windows callbacks. You can also use callbacks to examine windows and to perform many other tasks.

Asynchronous Notification Using Events And Callbacks

The topic of asynchronous notification is presented in this section of the chapter because of its relationship to Windows callback procedures.

Consider two possible outcomes of calling a method from a client. First, the client may be blocked until the method returns. That is, the code in the client cannot execute while the method executes; in other words, the code executes synchronously. Second, as you have seen, some code components support asynchronous processing. For example, as you saw in Chapter 14, the Internet Transfer control can process requests asynchronously.

The benefit of asynchronous processing is that a client can continue to execute code while waiting for a particular method to complete. The following list identifies some possible uses of asynchronous processing:

➤ You can work with ADO objects asynchronously. Thus, when you are working with remote databases, code in the client continues to execute while an ADO object processes an asynchronous request.

➤ Many methods requiring significant processing time are suitable candidates for asynchronous processing. Code in the client can continue to execute while the time-consuming method executes.

➤ Requests made over a network are suitable asynchronous-processing candidates.

Asynchronous processing poses a set of problems that must be handled from the perspective of both the code component (created by the author) and the client (created by the developer):

➤ The client may require status information on the relative completion of the asynchronous task.

➤ The client generally needs to know when the component (method) completes the task.

To satisfy these requirements, you can supply clients with asynchronous notification from code components by using two techniques:

➤ You can create components that provide notification to clients by raising events.

➤ You can create components that provide notification to clients by implementing callbacks.

In this section, you will use both techniques to solve the same problem.

Asynchronous Notification Using Events

The business problem used in this chapter illustrates asynchronous processing with a long-running operation. The code component used in the GSC program computes prime numbers. The existing class module supports the following methods:

➤ The **Add** method adds a number to a list. Its purpose is similar to that of the **Add** method pertaining to any collection. Another method will determine whether each number in the list is prime.

➤ The **Count** method returns the number of items in the list.

➤ The **List** method takes one argument—an index into the list of numbers—and returns a number from the list.

➤ The **ListPrime** method takes one argument—index into the list of numbers—and returns a Boolean value indicating whether the corresponding number is prime.

➤ The **Calculate** method examines each number in the list and determines whether it is prime.

Although the startup program contains complete code for the preceding methods, it does not contain all of the code needed to perform asynchronous processing. You will modify the program to perform asynchronous processing using events. To accomplish this goal, you must make the following enhancements to the component and to the client that will use the component:

1. You will define the notifications because, in this example, the component will notify the client each time that the component (**Calculate** method) determines whether a number is prime. Also, the component will notify the client when it has examined the entire list of prime numbers.

2. For each notification, you must declare an event in the component and raise that event as necessary.

3. In the client, the class instance must be declared "**WithEvents**."

4. In the client, you must write code to respond to the events (notifications) supported by the class module.

The process to declare the events and raise them from the component is similar to the process you used to expose events in an ActiveX control. Consider the following statements in the class module to declare the two events:

```
Public Event PrimeEvent(plngCurrent As Long, _
    pblnPrime As Boolean)
Public Event PrimeComplete()
```

The preceding statements declare events named **PrimeEvent** and **PrimeComplete**. The first statement (event) takes two arguments. The first argument contains a number, and the second contains a Boolean value indicating whether the number is prime.

In addition to declaring the events, the code component must raise the event at the appropriate time. In this example, the component should raise the **PrimeEvent** event whenever it determines whether a number is prime. It should also raise the **PrimeComplete** event when it finishes analyzing the list of prime numbers. Thus **PrimeEvent** provides status notification, and **PrimeComplete** provides completion notification. Consider the statements to perform this task:

```
For plngCount = 1 to mlngCount
    plngPrime = mPrimes(plngCount).Number
    For plngCurrent = 2 to plngPrime -1
        ' Code to determine prime number.
    Next
    RaiseEvent PrimeEvent(mPrimes(plngCount).Number, _
        mPrimes(plngCount).IsPrime)
Next
RaiseEvent PrimeComplete
```

The preceding code contains two **For** loops. The outer loop examines each number in the list of numbers. The inner **For** loop examines a specific number to determine whether it is prime. This code to determine whether a number is prime was omitted from the preceding code segment for the sake of brevity. Refer to the completed program for an analysis of this code. After examining the number, the code raises **PrimeEvent**. After all numbers have been examined, the code raises **PrimeComplete**. In the form module, you must write code to respond to these events.

To perform asynchronous notifications using events:

1. Activate the Code window for the class module named **Prime**, and declare the following procedure in the general declarations section of the module:

```
Public Event PrimeEvent(plngCurrent As Long, _
    pblnPrime As Boolean)
Public Event PrimeComplete()
```

2. In the general declarations section of the form module named **frmCh16**, modify the following statement

```
Private pclsPrime As Prime
```

so that it reads

```
Private WithEvents pclsPrime As Prime
```

3. Enter the following statements, in the **Calculate** function of the **Prime** class module:

```
For plngCount = 1 To mlngCount
    plngPrime = mPrimes(plngCount).Number
    For plngCurrent = 2 to plngPrime -1
          . . .
    Next
    RaiseEvent PrimeEvent(mPrimes(plngCount).Number, _
        MPrimes(plngCount).IsPrime)
Next
RaiseEvent PrimeComplete
```

4. Activate the Code window for the form module named **frmCh16**, and create the following two event procedures:

```
Private Sub pclsPrime_PrimeComplete()
    txtOut = txtOut & vbCrLf & "Complete"
End Sub
Private Sub pclsPrime_PrimeEvent( _
    plngCurrent As Long, pblnPrime As Boolean)
    txtOut = txtOut & cStr(plngCurrent) & " " & _
        CStr(pblnPrime) & vbCrLf
End Sub
```

5. Test the program. In the Start and End text boxes, enter a range of numbers for the program to evaluate, and then click on the Calculate button. Each time the method evaluates a number, the **PrimeEvent** event is raised and your code prints the number and an indicator of whether it is prime to the output text box. When the method is complete, the code prints the text "Complete" to the text box.

6. End the program, save your work, and exit Visual Basic.

In addition to performing asynchronous notifications using events, you can perform the same task using callback methods.

Asynchronous Notification Using Callbacks

Performing asynchronous notification using callbacks is more complex than performing the same task using events. As the component's author, you must create an abstract class containing the callback procedure declarations. As the developer, you must write code that implements the abstract class. To perform asynchronous notification using callbacks, you perform the following steps:

1. Define the notifications to perform.

2. Create a type library containing the interface. You can create a type library either by defining an abstract class or by using the MkTypLib utility.

3. Write code to call the appropriate callback methods.

4. As the developer, create a public class that implements the interface defined by the author in the preceding steps. You must implement all methods defined by the interface.

For the GSC program, you will implement the same two notifications with callbacks that you implemented previously with events. The first step in the process is to define the interface (abstract class). Consider the following code in the **IPrimeNotify** class:

```
Public Sub PrimeReady(plngCurrent As Long, _
    PblnPrime as Boolean)
End Sub

Public Sub PrimeComplete()
End Sub
```

The preceding **Sub** procedures define the interface for the notification class. It is an abstract class, so the code defines the interface but no implementation.

Next, you must modify the **Prime** class to execute the callbacks. Consider the following statement in the general declarations section of the **Prime** class:

```
Public mipn As IPrimeNotify
```

This statement declares an object variable to reference the abstract class. Your code will use this variable to execute the callback procedures.

Consider the following code in the **Calculate** method:

```
For plngCount = 1 to mlngCount
    plngPrime = mPrimes(plngCount).Number
    For plngCurrent = 2 to plngPrime -1
        ' Code to determine prime number
    Next
    mipn.PrimeReady mPrimes(plngCount).Number, _
        mPrimes(plngCount).IsPrime
Next
mipn.PrimeComplete
```

The preceding statements call the notification callbacks. The placement of these statements matches the placement that you used when you utilized events to provide notification. Instead of raising events, however, these statements call the methods **PrimeReady** and **PrimeComplete**, both of which must be implemented in a class created by the developer.

The developer accomplishes the final part of the process. He or she must create a class that implements the methods of the abstract class. Whenever you implement an abstract class, remember that you must implement all of the properties and methods.

Consider the following code in the **PrimeNotify** class:

```
Private Sub iPrimeNotify_PrimeReady (plngCurrent) _
      As Long, pblnPrime As Boolean)
      frmCh16.txtOut = frmCh16.txtOut & _
          CStr(plngCurrent) & " " & CStr(pblnPrime) _
          & vbCrLf
End Sub

Private Sub iPrimeNotify_PrimeComplete()
    frmCh16.txtOut = frmCh16.txtOut & vbCrLf & _
        "Complete"
End Sub
```

These statements execute when they are called by the **Calculate** method in the **Prime** Class. The two methods implement the methods of the **IprimeNotify** abstract class.

To perform asynchronous notification using callbacks:

1. Start Visual Basic. After Visual Basic is running, open the project named Chapter.16\Startup\ Callback\Ch16_S.vbp.

2. Activate the Code window for the **Prime** class, and modify the **Calculate** method so that it contains the following statements:

```
. . .
For plngCount = 1 to mlngCount
    plngPrime = mPrimes(plngCount).Number
    For plngCurrent = 2 to plngPrime -1
        . . .
    Next
    mipn.PrimeReady mPrimes(plngCount).Number, _
        mPrimes(plngCount).IsPrime
Next
mipn.PrimeComplete
```

3. Create the following procedures in the **IprimeNotify** class to define the interface:

```
Public Sub PrimeReady(plngCurrent _
      As Long, pblnPrime As Boolean)
    End Sub
```

16

```
Public Sub PrimeComplete()
End Sub
```

4. Create the following procedures in the **PrimeNotify** class to implement the abstract class:

```
Private Sub iPrimeNotify_PrimeReady(plngCurrent _
    As Long, pblnPrime As Boolean)
    frmCh16.txtOut = frmCh16.txtOut & _
        CStr(plngCurrent) & " " & CStr(pblnPrime) _
        & vbCrLf
End Sub

Private Sub iPrimeNotify_PrimeComplete()
    frmCh16.txtOut = frmCh16.txtOut & vbCrLf & _
        "Complete"
End Sub
```

5. Test the program. Enter starting and ending numbers in the text boxes on the main form, and then click on the Calculate button. The program should work as it did before. Instead of using events, however, this code utilizes callback methods.

6. End the program to return to design mode.

Executing Other Programs

In some circumstances, a program may need to call another executable program. For example, suppose you create a complex program consisting of several executable files. Each of these .exe files is a stand-alone executable. You could create another program consisting of only a toolbar. Each button on the toolbar would be used to start one of the different executable programs. Conceptually, this approach is similar to having the Microsoft Office toolbar remain visible on the screen. The buttons on the toolbar execute the individual Microsoft Office programs. You can use the **Shell** function to execute a program from Visual Basic.

Syntax

    Shell(**pathname**[,**windowstyle**])

Dissection

➤ The **pathname** argument must contain the full path, including the drive designator, of the file to execute.

➤ The optional **windowstyle** argument can contain a constant value indicating how the window will appear to the user when it is opened. If set to the constant **vbHide**, the window remains hidden. If set to

vbNormalFocus, the new window receives focus and appears with its original size and position. The constants **vbMinimizedFocus** and **vbMaximizedFocus** cause the window to be displayed as an icon and maximized, respectively. The constants **vbNormalNoFocus** and **vbMinimizedNoFocus** cause the active window to remain active and the new window not to receive focus, respectively.

Code Example

```
Dim pintID As Long
pintID = Shell("C:\demo.exe", vbNormalFocus)
```

Code Dissection

This code attempts to execute the executable file named Demo.exe located in the root directory of drive C. If the file does not exist, an error will be returned. The window displayed by the executable program will appear with normal focus.

The **Shell** command has many uses. In this example, you will create a general-purpose application of the **Shell** function allowing the user to select an .exe file through the CommonDialog control. The selected file then executes.

To execute a program with the **Shell** function:

1. In the Code window for the form named **frmCh16**, enter the following statements in the **cmdShell_Click** event procedure:

```
On Error Resume Next
    Dim pintID As Long
    cd11.Filter = "Executable files (*.exe)|*.exe"
    cd11.ShowOpen
    pintID = Shell(cd11.filename, vbNormalFocus)
```

2. Test the program. Click on the Shell command button, and then select an executable file. Open the file. The **Shell** statement should execute the selected file. Exit any programs or dialog boxes that the executable file may have run or opened.

3. End the program to return to design mode.

4. Exit Visual Basic.

The statements created in the preceding steps are very simple. The user, using the CommonDialog control, selects a file name. The **FileName** argument is passed to the **Shell** function for execution. The constant **vbNormalFocus** is used so the window will receive focus and be restored to its normal size and position.

16

CHAPTER SUMMARY

To read and write Registry information:

➤ Call the **GetSetting** and **SaveSetting** functions.

```
GetSetting(appname, section, key[, default])
SaveSetting(appname, section, key, setting)
```

To remove a Registry entry:

➤ Call the **DeleteSetting** function.

```
DeleteSetting(appname, section[, key])
```

To change the position or characteristics of a window using a DLL:

➤ Call the **SetWindowPos** procedure.

```
Declare Function SetWindowPos Lib "user32" Alias "SetWindowPos"
(ByVal hWnd As Long, ByVal hWndInsertAfter As Long, ByVal x As Long,
ByVal y As Long, ByVal cx As Long, ByVal cy As Long, ByVal wFlags As
Long) As Long
```

To get the path name that Windows uses for temporary files and generate a temporary file name:

➤ Call the **GetTempPathA** or **GetTempFileNameA** DLL functions.

```
Declare Function GetTempPath Lib "kernel32" Alias "GetTempPathA"
(ByVal nBufferLength As Long, ByVal        lpBuffer As String) As Long
```

```
Declare Function GetTempFileName Lib "kernel32" Alias
"GetTempFileNameA" (ByVal lpszPath As String, ByVal
lpPrefixString As String, ByVal wUnique As Long, ByVal
lpTempFileName As String) As Long
```

To create a timer with a DLL:

➤ Create a wrapper procedure to call the **SetTimer** function.

```
Declare Function SetTimer Lib "user32" Alias "SetTimer" (ByVal hWnd
As Long, ByVal nIDEvent As Long, ByVal uElapse As Long, ByVal
lpTimerFunc As Long) As Long
```

➤ In the **TimerProc**, call the **KillTimer** function.

```
Declare Function KillTimer Lib "user32" Alias "KillTimer" (ByVal
hwnd As Long, ByVal nIDEvent As Long) As Long
```

To implement asynchronous notification using events:

➤ Define the notifications.

➤ For each notification, declare an event in the component and raise that event as necessary.

➤ In the client, declare the class instance "**WithEvents**."

➤ In the client, write code to respond to the events (notifications) supported by the class module.

To implement asynchronous notification using callbacks:

➤ Define the notifications to perform.

➤ Create a type library containing the interface. You can create a type library either by defining an abstract class or by using the MkTypLib utility.

➤ Write code to call the appropriate callback methods.

➤ As the developer, create a public class that implements the interface created by the author in the preceding steps. You must implement all of the methods defined by the interface.

To execute another program from Visual Basic:

➤ Call the **Shell** function.

```
Shell(pathname[,windowstyle])
```

REVIEW QUESTIONS

1. Which of the following statements pertaining to the Registry is true?
   a. The Registry is hierarchical.
   b. Values are stored in the Registry as strings.
   c. Each entry in the Registry is a file.
   d. Both a and b.
   e. All of the above.

2. Which of the following is a valid tree in the Registry?
   a. HKEY_LOCAL_MACHINE
   b. HKEY_USERS
   c. HKEY_CURRENT_CONFIG
   d. All of the above
   e. None of the above

16

3. The _____ function will read a setting from the Registry, and the _____ function will write a value to the Registry.

   a. **ReadSetting, WriteSetting**

   b. **GetSetting**, **SaveSetting**

   c. **GetRegEnt**, **SaveRegEnt**

   d. **Read, Write**

   e. None of the above

4. The Visual Basic statements that manipulate the Registry store information in which subtree?

   a. VB and VBA Program Settings

   b. Visual Basic

   c. Settings

   d. Program Files

   e. Program Settings

5. You can use the Registry Editor to _____.

   a. add entries to the Registry

   b. change the values corresponding to a particular Registry key

   c. delete entries from the Registry

   d. All of the above

   e. None of the above

6. What is the name of the program used to register a server?

   a. RegServer

   b. Regsvr

   c. RegEdit

   d. Register

   e. None of the above

7. Write the code to read the Registry value for the application named Demo, the section named Position, and the key named Top.

8. Write a statement to write the value 150 to the Registry setting defined in the previous section.

9. Write a statement to delete the Registry setting having an application name of Demo, the section named Position, and a key named Left.

10. Write the code to delete all of the Registry entries for the application named Demo.

11. Which of the following types of linking is valid?

    a. common

    b. static

    c. dynamic

    d. Both a and b

    e. Both b and c

12. Which of the following statements regarding the declaration of DLL procedures is false?

    a. A **Declare** statement can exist in a standard module.

    b. A **Declare** statement can exist in a form module.

    c. The **Alias** keyword is used to call a DLL by a different name.

    d. The **Lib** keyword contains the name of the Windows library.

    e. All of the above.

13. Which of the following elements is listed by API Text Viewer?

    a. constants

    b. function declarations

    c. types

    d. Both a and b

    e. All of the above

14. What are the names of the two DLL procedures used to obtain the temporary directory and create a temporary file?

    a. **GetTempPathA, GetTempFileNameA**

    b. **GetTmpPathA, GetTmpFileNameA**

    c. **GetTempDirA, GetTempFileA**

    d. **GetTempDir, GetTempFile**

    e. None of the above

16

15. When passing string properties to a DLL procedure, you must use:

    a. the **AddressOf** keyword

    b. a temporary variable to store the property

    c. the **PropertyConvert** function

    d. Both a and b

    e. Both a and c

16. A callback function is:

   a. written in Visual Basic

   b. called by a Windows DLL

   c. not possible using Visual Basic

   d. All of the above

   e. None of the above

17. Which of the following statements is true about performing asynchronous processing using events?

   a. You must create an event procedure for each event that will be raised.

   b. The developer must write code to respond to the events that are raised.

   c. You create a callback function.

   d. Both a and b.

   e. All of the above.

18. Which of the following statements is true about performing asynchronous processing using callbacks?

   a. You must create an abstract class to define the callback procedures.

   b. Callback procedures are executed by means of an event.

   c. You use the **Callback** statement to generate the callback.

   d. All of the above.

   e. None of the above.

19. Write a statement to call the executable file named Demo.exe in the root directory of drive C.

20. Write a statement to raise the event named **AllFinished**, which accepts no arguments.

HANDS-ON PROJECTS

Project 1

In this project, you will save information to the Registry when a program exits and read information when the program starts. Many programs save the current condition of open windows when a program closes and then restore the window to the same condition when the program starts.

   a. Run the executable file named Chapter.16\Exercise\Ex1Demo.exe. Click on the command buttons on the forms so that all three forms in the program are open. On one of the forms, click on the Exit button to end the program and write the information to the Registry. Run the program again. The size and position of the forms are restored based on the information read from the Registry. The forms therefore open as they existed just before you exited the program. End the program.

b. Start Visual Basic. Create a new project, and set the **Name** property of the form to **frmEx1Main**. Save the form using the name Chapter.16\ Exercise\frmEx1Main.frm and the project using the name Chapter.16\Exercise\Ex1.vbp. This form should be the Startup form for the program.

c. Create two additional forms named frmEx1Sub1 and frmEx1Sub2. On each form, create three command buttons. Two of the command buttons should set the focus to the other two forms. For example, on **frmEx1Main**, one command button should display frmEx1Sub1, and the other should display frmEx1Sub2.

d. Ensure that one of the command buttons on each form exits the program.

e. Whenever the user exits the program (by calling the Exit command button on one of the forms), a general procedure should be called to write the current condition of the open forms. This information should include the position of each form. Consider the following implementation. Delete the information pertaining to the current state of the program from the Registry. Create a **For Each** loop in this general procedure to examine the **Forms** collection. For each form, save the size- and position-related properties to a section in the Registry.

f. When the user starts the program, a procedure should execute that reads the contents of the Registry and restores the contents of the program to the state it was in when the program closed.

g. Test the program. Make sure that the program saves and restores the information properly. End the program. Exit Visual Basic.

Project 2

In this project, you will use the Registry and the **Shell** function to execute programs and keep a list of recently executed programs.

16

a. Run the executable file named Chapter.16\Exercise\Ex2Demo.exe. On the menu bar, click on File, and then click on Execute. The Open dialog box appears. Locate an executable file on the disk. Select the file, and click on Open to run it. In the Visual Basic program, click on the File menu again. The file that you just executed appears in the recently opened file list. Exit both programs.

b. Start Visual Basic. Create a new project, and set the **Name** property of the form to **frmEx2**. Save the form using the name Chapter.16\Exercise\ frmEx2.frm and the project using the name Chapter.16\Exercise\Ex2.vbp.

c. On the form, create a menu named File.

d. On the File menu, create a menu item named Execute that, when clicked, will display a CommonDialog control.

e. Using the file returned by the CommonDialog, execute the **Shell** function to execute the file.

f. Using the technique presented in the chapter, create a menu control array in which the first element has a separator bar as its caption. This control array should appear at the end of the File menu.

g. When the user clicks the Execute menu and just before executing the command, add the command to the control array.

h. When the form unloads, write the list of recently executed files to the Registry.

i. When the form loads, read the list of recently executed files from the registry. Note that the program should list a maximum of 10 files.

j. Test the program. Execute various files. Make sure that the recent file list is updated correctly. End the program and restart it. Make sure that the recent file list is restored correctly. End the program. Exit Visual Basic.

Project 3

In this project, you will work with asynchronous events using the same techniques presented in the chapter. This program, instead of calculating prime numbers, will calculate Fibonacci sequences. A Fibonacci sequence is the sequence of integers 0, 1, 1, 2, 3, 5, 8, 13, 21, 34.... in which each element in the sequence is the sum of the two preceding elements.

a. Run the executable file named Chapter.16\Exercise\Ex3Demo.exe. Enter the number 44 in the sequence text box. Click on Calculate. The Fibonacci sequence appears in the list box. Exit the program.

b. Start Visual Basic. Create a new project, and set the **Name** property of the form to **frmEx3**. Save the form using the name Chapter.16\Exercise\ frmEx3.frm and the project using the name Chapter.16\Exercise\Ex3.vbp.

c. Create objects on the form to match those in the complete program that you tested in Step a.

d. Create a class module for the form. Save and name it Chapter.16\Exercise\ Ex3.cls.

e. In the class module, declare two events named **FibEvent** and **FibComplete**. The **FibEvent** event should accept a **Long Integer** argument representing the current Fibonacci number in the sequence.

f. Create a method named **Calculate** that accepts one argument: the count of numbers in the sequence. Use the following code to compute the Fibonacci sequence:

```
Dim plngLoFib As Long
Dim plngHiFib As Long
Dim plngTemp As Long
Dim plngCurrent As Long
plngLoFib = 0
plngHiFib = 1
For plngCurrent = 2 to plngFib
    plngTemp = plngLoFib
    plngLoFib = plngHiFib
    plngHiFib = plngTemp + plngLoFib
Next
```

g. Write the code to raise the **FibEvent** event each time that the code derives a new number in the sequence.

h. Write the code to raise the **FibComplete** event when the entire sequence is evaluated.

i. In the form module, create the necessary event responses to display the current number in the sequence each time that the **FibComplete** event is raised.

j. In the form module, display the text "Complete" in the list box when the sequence finishes.

k. Test the program to verify that the events are raised properly. Exit Visual Basic.

Project 4

In this project, you will work with asynchronous callbacks using the same techniques presented in the chapter to implement the Fibonacci sequence.

a. Start Visual Basic. Create a new project, and set the **Name** property of the form to **frmEx4**. Save the form using the name Chapter.16\Exercise\ frmEx4.frm and the project using the name Chapter.16\Exercise\Ex4.vbp.

b. Create objects on the form to match those in the complete program that you tested in Project 3.

c. Create a class module for the form. Save and name it Chapter.16\Exercise\Ex4.cls.

d. Implement the same Fibonacci sequence that you implemented in Project 3. This time, however, use callbacks instead of events.

e. Test the program. The program should operate identically to the program in Project 3.

f. Exit Visual Basic.

16

CHAPTER SEVENTEEN

PROGRAM DEPLOYMENT AND MAINTENANCE

AFTER READING THIS CHAPTER AND COMPLETING THE EXERCISES, YOU WILL BE ABLE TO:

➤ Compile programs into executable files

➤ Understand the types of executable files supported by Visual Basic

➤ Understand the options available to optimize a program

➤ Conditionally compile code into a program

➤ Catalog and organize components using Visual Component Manager

➤ Add components to Visual Component Manager

➤ Identify components so that developers can easily locate them

➤ Create packages intended for deployment on floppy disks and CD-ROMs

➤ Learn how to deploy packages to a network

➤ Learn how to deploy packages to the World Wide Web

➤ Deploy different types of packages

CREATING A PROGRAM FOR DISTRIBUTION

The Visual Basic Compiler

This section does not focus on the application itself. Rather, it discusses the decisions you must make about compiling a Visual Basic program and describes how to compile a program to achieve peak performance. The code you will use in this section is computationally intensive, which will allow you to observe the performance effects of the various program compilation options. The completed application determines whether a number is a prime number. The code is similar to the code used in Chapter 16.

Scientific Applications develops and sells engineering software. Because the company's software is computationally intensive, its programs must be optimized for peak performance. In addition, the company develops a vast array of software based on reusable components; it therefore needs an efficient mechanism to organize existing components and to make other developers aware of the components that have already been created. Finally, Scientific Applications must deploy its software using traditional distribution media, including floppy disks and CD-ROMs. The company must also deploy its software over networks and the Web.

To preview the completed application:

1. Start Visual Basic, and load Chapter.17\Complete\Ch17_C.vbp. Set the drive designator as necessary. Figure 17.1 shows the main form at run time with calculated output. As shown in Figure 17.1, the program contains two text boxes with captions of Start and End, respectively. These values represent the lower and upper bounds of a range of numbers. For each Long Integer within this range, the program will determine whether the number is a prime number. If it is, the program will print the number. In Figure 17.1, the values in the text boxes specify a range of numbers between 10,000,000 and 10,000,200. For each number in that range, the code tests whether the number is a prime number. If so, the code displays it in the multiline text box at the bottom of the form. The left column of the text box displays the number of seconds that it takes to determine whether a specific number is prime.

2. Run the program. Enter the value 10000000 in the Start text box, enter the value 10000200 in the End text box, and then click on the Calculate button. The prime numbers within this range will appear as shown in Figure 17.1. The time to calculate the prime numbers will vary depending on the speed of your computer.

3. End the program by clicking on the Exit button.

4. Exit Visual Basic.

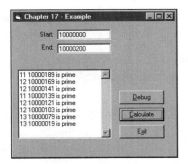

Figure 17.1   Main form at run time.

As you know, the process of translating language statements (in this case, Visual Basic statements) into an executable program is called *compilation*. Visual Basic can compile a program into two types of executable files:

➤ The first type of file is called *p-code*. When you compile a program into p-code, the p-code file produced by Visual Basic cannot run on its own. Rather, a p-code file is an interpreted file. When Windows executes a p-code file, the Visual Basic run-time library interprets the statements in the file, translates them into an executable form, and then executes them.

➤ The other type of executable file produced by Visual Basic is called *native code*. A native code executable file does not require the same services provided by the Visual Basic run-time library for p-code. In general, executing Visual Basic statements that are compiled into native code occurs more rapidly than executing the same statements compiled into p-code.

The choice of whether to compile a program into p-code or native code depends on the nature of the program itself. As noted, native code generally runs faster than p-code. Several factors, such as whether your program is computationally intensive, may lead to a minimal performance difference. The following list summarizes these factors and circumstances:

➤ Programs that spend most of their time inside form modules, performing tasks such as responding to events and processing character input and output, will benefit little from being compiled into native code.

➤ Programs that manipulate objects extensively will not benefit from compilation into native code. For example, if the bulk of the program statements read and write object properties or call methods, program performance will improve only marginally by compiling it to native code.

➤ The performance of p-code and native code is about the same when calling DLL functions. This parity occurs because most of the execution time is spent inside the DLL, and the overhead to call a DLL function is roughly the same for both native code and p-code.

17

The Compile tab on the Project Properties dialog box, shown in Figure 17.2, contains several options to define how Visual Basic will compile a project.

As shown in Figure 17.2, you can compile a program into either p-code or native code. When compiling a program into native code, Visual Basic can perform several optimizations:

➤ In general, a tradeoff exists between code size (the size of the executable file produced by the compiler) and the speed of the executable file. If you select Optimize for Fast Code, the compiler will optimize the executable file for speed rather than size. If you select Optimize for Small Code, the compiler will optimize the executable file for size rather than speed.

➤ The No Optimization option causes Visual Basic to perform no optimization on the executable file.

➤ The Favor Pentium Pro(™) option causes programs that are executed on a Pentium Pro processor to run faster if this option is selected. If the program runs on other types of processors, however, its performance will deteriorate.

➤ You use the Create Symbolic Debug Info option when the executable file will be debugged by another program, such as Visual C++. This chapter does not discuss how to debug Visual Basic programs in other languages.

Most of today's systems have large disks. As such, most users likely will prefer a faster program to a smaller program that runs more slowly. Furthermore, a program compiled to native code will almost always run faster than a program compiled to p-code. In some cases, however, the performance improvement will be minimal.

As shown in Figure 17.2, the Compile tab contains a button having a caption of Advanced Optimizations. Clicking on the Advanced Optimizations button

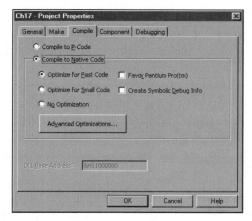

Figure 17.2 Compile tab.

activates the Advanced Optimizations dialog box, which contains an additional set of options that can improve the performance of a computationally intensive program.

> The Advanced Optimizations dialog box contains optimization options that should be used with great caution. Checking any of these options will cause the executable file to ignore common tests that verify the correctness of both array references and arithmetic operations. Omitting these "sanity checks" may cause programs to crash or produce incorrect results.

The Assume No Aliasing checkbox informs the compiler that the program does not use aliases. Aliasing occurs when a program uses multiple names to refer to the same variable or memory location. Aliasing commonly occurs when using arguments that are passed by reference, as shown in the following code segment:

```
Dim gintY As Integer
Sub Foo(ByRef pintX As Integer)
    pintX=5
    gintY=6
End Sub

Sub Main
    Foo gintY
End Sub
```

The preceding code references the memory address used by the global variable named **gintY** by two different names. Inside the **Sub** procedure, the argument **pintX** points to the same memory address used by the global variable named **gintY**. In this case, **pintX** and **gintY** are aliases to the same memory location. In this example, if you checked the Assume No Aliasing checkbox, the compiled program would produce incorrect results.

Each time you write a statement that reads or writes data from or to an array, Visual Basic checks that the statement references a valid array element. That is, Visual Basic checks that the value of any subscripts used exist between the lower and upper bounds of the array dimension. If the array subscript does not lie within the bounds of the array, Visual Basic will, by default, generate a run-time error. When you check Remove Array Bounds Checks, the code in the executable program does not verify that array subscripts are valid. Although eliminating this sanity check improves program performance, code that references an invalid array element can generate invalid results or the program may crash.

As an example of this problem, consider an array in which you declared 10 elements. Assume also that you have written a statement to store a value in the eleventh array element, which does not exist. If you remove the array bound checking, your code will compute a memory address for this nonexistent element and store a value in that memory address. Another variable likely uses this memory address. Because the contents of the memory address have been corrupted, the value of this other variable is invalid.

Each time you perform integer arithmetic on a value, Visual Basic checks that the variable's value lies within the range of the underlying data type; it will generate a run-time error in the event of numeric overflow or underflow. For example, the largest positive number that an **Integer** data type can store is 32,767 and the largest negative number for an Integer is −32,768. Attempting to store a number outside this range will cause an overflow or underflow condition. Adding 1 to 32,767 will cause an overflow condition; subtracting 1 from −32,768 will cause an underflow condition. By default, a run-time error will occur in these circumstances because the code in the executable program checks for underflow or overflow. If you check the Remove Integer Overflow Checks checkbox, the executable code produced by the compiler will not perform these checks.

As an example, consider the following statements:

```
Dim pintBad As Integer
pintBad = 32767
pintBad = pintBad + 1
txtBad = pintBad
```

The **Integer** variable **pintBad** contains the maximum valid value for an Integer number (32767). By default, adding 1 to this number will generate a run-time error. If you check the Remove Integer Overflow Checks checkbox, a run-time error will not occur in the compiled executable, and the value −32768 will be stored in the text box named txtBad. The reason −32768 is stored in the variable stems from the way that the computer performs integer arithmetic.

In addition to performing overflow and underflow checks on Integer values, by default, the executable code makes similar checks on floating-point values. By default, if a numeric overflow or underflow condition occurs when the executable program evaluates a floating-point expression, your code will generate a run-time error. If you mark the Remove Floating Point Error Checks checkbox, no run-time error will occur and the program will likely produce incorrect results. The situation is very similar to the one you saw with the Integer overflow.

The Allow Unrounded Floating Point Operations checkbox causes floating-point operations not to be rounded. Although using unrounded floating-point operations may improve the performance of the program, it will maintain arithmetic expressions to a much lower precision. This fact becomes significant when comparing two floating-point numbers in an **If** statement. Because of the extended precision and the way that computers perform floating-point arithmetic, two values you may expect to be the same might differ by a very small amount.

The final option—the Remove Safe Pentium(™) FDIV Checks—pertains to some of the first Pentium processors created. These processors had a bug, known as the FDIV bug, that would occasionally produce incorrect results. By default, the Visual Basic compiler will produce code to avoid this bug. If you mark this checkbox, the compiler will not generate the proper code and certain Pentium processors may produce incorrect results in rare situations.

You will compile the Scientific Applications prime number calculator using different compilation options to see the effect on program performance. The code used in the program is not discussed in this chapter because the prime number generator uses nearly the same code as that employed in Chapter 16. This code creates a computationally intensive routine that will take more than a few seconds to run.

As a consequence, the executable program produced by compiling the program to native code should run considerably faster than the same program compiled to p-code. Note that the executable files will also run faster than running the same program inside the Visual Basic IDE.

To test the different compilation options:

1. Start Visual Basic. Load the project named Chapter.17\Startup\ Ch17_S.vbp.

2. Activate the Project Properties dialog box. Select the Compile tab, and then select the Compile to P-Code option button, if necessary. Click OK to close the dialog box. On the File menu, click on Make Ch17_P.exe, and save the executable file as Chapter.17\Startup\Ch17_P.exe, setting the drive designator as necessary. Click OK to compile the program.

3. Compile the program again, this time to native code, by using the Compile tab in the Project Properties dialog box, selecting the Compile to Native Code option, and optimizing the program for Fast Code. Save the executable file as Chapter.17\Startup\Ch17_N.exe.

4. Run each of the programs outside the Visual Basic IDE, using starting and ending values of 10000000 and 10000200, respectively. The elapsed time to compute each prime number appears in the first column of the multiline text box. Because the program is computationally intensive, the native code version should run much faster than the p-code version. Both versions should run faster than the code runs inside the Visual Basic IDE.

17

Table 17.1 Execution speed.

Number	Elapsed Seconds (Native Code)	Elapsed Seconds (p-code)	Elapsed Seconds (IDE)
10000189	2	8	12
10000169	3	8	12
10000141	2	8	12
10000139	2	8	12
10000121	3	8	12

Table 17.1 shows the computation times when the program was compiled on a 450 MHz Pentium with sufficient memory such that the program did not have to be swapped to disk. Although your timings may differ depending on the speed of your computer, you should see a similar performance difference between native code and interpreted code.

As shown in Table 17.1, the native code performs between three and four times faster than the p-code version. Because this program is computationally intensive, it maximizes the benefit of compiling to native code. As mentioned earlier, code that consists mostly of DLL calls or form management will benefit much less from compiling a program to native code.

Conditional Compilation

Conditional compilation has nothing to do with program compilation from the perspective of optimization. Instead, it allows specific statements to be included or excluded from an executable file.

Just as you can use an **If** statement to execute different code depending on some condition, so too you can use another form of an **If** statement to determine whether specific statements in a program are compiled into the executable program. This concept is referred to as *conditional compilation*. Conditional compilation uses constants, literal values, and the following form of an **If** statement:

Syntax

      #If *expression* **Then**
        statements
      [**#ElseIf** *expression-n* **Then**
        [*elseifstatements*]]
      [**#Else**
        [*elsestatements*]]
      #End If

Dissection

➤ The required *expression* can contain constants, literal values, and operators. It must evaluate to True or False, just like the other form of an **If** statement.

➤ The required *statements* contain the Visual Basic statements that are included in the executable file if the *expression* is True.

➤ Like an ordinary **If** statement, the **#If** statement can contain zero or more **#ElseIf** clauses and an optional **#Else** clause.

➤ The **#End If** statement marks the end of the **#If** block.

Code Example

```
#If (cDebugLevel = 1) Then
    Debug.Print "Basic Debugging"
#ElseIf (cDebugLevel = 2) Then
    Debug.Print "Extended Debugging"
#End If
```

Code Dissection

The previous statements test the constant value **cDebugLevel** to determine whether its value is 1 or 2. If the value is 1, the code prints the value "Basic Debugging" in the Immediate window. If the value is 2, the code prints the value "Extended Debugging" in the Immediate window. If the constant has a different value, then nothing is printed in the Immediate window. In reality, you would print the values of pertinent program variables to the Immediate window or log file.

Several reasons exist to use conditional compilation:

➤ **Debugging** As you develop large programs, you may frequently insert **Debug.Print** statements into a program to trace the flow of execution and examine the values of variables. After the program works correctly, you may remove these statements from the final product. Rather than removing these statements, however, you can conditionally compile the debugging code into the debugging executable and exclude it from the finished product. With this approach, if you detect a bug in your code, you can enable the debugging code without having to recreate it.

➤ **Multiple configurations** In another scenario, assume that you are developing a software product where the user must obtain a license to specific parts of the program—something analogous to the Visual Basic Learning Edition, Professional Edition, or Enterprise Edition. In such a situation, you can conditionally compile code in modules to enable or disable specific functions.

17

➤ **Custom configurations**   In a final scenario, suppose you have developed a Visual Basic program, but a few customers require customizations. Rather than maintaining different programs (software versions) for each customer, you can conditionally compile customized code for each customer that needs it but omit the customizations for other customers. You, as the developer, then need to maintain only a single copy of the source code for a program.

To define the values for the constants used in conditional compilation, you use the Conditional Compilation Argument on the Make tab of the Project Properties dialog box. To define a constant, you specify the constant name followed by an equals sign (=), followed by a value. You specify multiple constants by separating each declaration by a full colon (:), as shown in the following code:

```
cDebugLevel = 1
cDebugLevel = 1 : cOther = 3
```

The first statement declares a constant named **cDebugLevel** having a value of 1. The second statement declares two constants named **cDebugLevel** and **cOther**, respectively. The first has a value of 1, and the second has a value of 3. The second statement illustrates how you can specify multiple constant value pairs. The following example, though simple, further illustrates how conditional compilation can be used in a program.

To compile code conditionally:

1. Enter the following statements into the **cmdDebug_Click** event procedure on the form named frmCh17:

```
#If (cDebugLevel = 1) Then
    Debug.Print "Basic Debugging."
#ElseIf (cDebugLevel = 2) Then
    Debug.Print "Extended Debugging."
#End If
```

2. Activate the Project Properties dialog box, and then click on the Make tab.

3. In the Conditional Compilation Arguments text box, enter the following line:

```
cDebugLevel = 1
```

4. Click OK to accept the compiler option and close the dialog box.

5. Test the program. Click the Debug command button. The text string Basic Debugging should be printed to the Immediate window. End the program to return to design mode.

6. Activate the Project Properties dialog box, and then click on the Make tab. Change the Conditional Compilation argument to the following statement, and then click on OK:

```
cDebugLevel = 2
```

7. Test the program again. Click the Debug command button. The text string Extended Debugging should be printed to the Immediate window.

8. End the program, save your project, and then Exit Visual Basic.

These statements illustrate a simple use of conditional compilation. As programs become more complex, you may define several different conditional compilation constants to control the statements that the compiler includes in an executable file.

As a last note, remember that Visual Basic supports two predefined constants. The constant **#Win16** has a value of True on 16-bit systems (Windows 3.1) and a value of False on 32-bit systems. The constant **#Win32** has a value of False on 16-bit systems (Windows 3.1) and a value of True on 32-bit systems. Trying to define these constants will generate an error.

Visual Component Manager

The Purpose Of Visual Component Manager

When applying component-based techniques, an organization may create hundreds or thousands of components usable by many applications and developers. These components must be stored and cataloged. Furthermore, developers need to be able to locate components quickly and effectively. Visual Component Manager satisfies these needs by allowing developers to register, locate, and share reusable components. Supported components include Visual Basic project types and Visual Basic program elements, such as forms or class modules. Visual Component Manager also supports components created in other languages and binary components.

You access Visual Component Manager from Visual Basic by means of an add-in. This add-in must be installed and loaded before you can use Visual Component Manager from Visual Basic.

To verify that Visual Component manager is installed and loaded:

1. Start Visual Basic, if necessary, and create a new Standard EXE project.

2. On the menu bar, click on Add-Ins, and then click on Add-In Manager to activate the Add-In Manager dialog box.

3. Using the scroll bars, if necessary, locate Visual Component Manager 6.0 in the Available Add-Ins list. If the Load Behavior column contains the text

"Startup / Loaded," Visual Component Manager is ready for use. If this text does not appear, select the line from the Available Add-Ins list. In the Load Behavior frame, check the Loaded/Unloaded and Load On Startup checkboxes. Click OK to close the dialog box and load the add-in.

Once Visual Basic has loaded and started Visual Component Manager, it is ready for use. How you store components in Visual Component Manager depends on the needs of the organization and the developers using the components.

Organization Of Visual Component Manager

Visual Component Manager stores components in either Access or SQL Server databases. It supports multiple databases that can be open concurrently; each database is called a *repository*. Each repository, in turn, contains folders and subfolders used to catalog and organize information. Inside the folders and subfolders, a repository contains items. Items make up the components stored in a repository. An organization could have enterprise repositories, departmental repositories, and workgroup repositories, each storing different groups of components (items).

For the Scientific Applications programs, you will examine the structure of the default database (repository), retrieve and store items from and to the default repository, and create a new repository.

You store and retrieve information from Visual Component Manager repositories through an interface consisting of three panes:

➤ **Explorer**   Displays a hierarchical view of the currently loaded database. Each database appears with folders and subfolders. The interface is similar to the left pane used in Windows Explorer.

➤ **Contents**   Displays the folders and items for the currently selected folder in the explorer pane.

➤ **Properties**   Lists the attributes of the currently selected folder or item appearing in the contents pane. The information displayed includes descriptive text and keywords used to identify the folder or item.

By default, when you install Visual Component Manager, the program also installs a default repository named Local Database. This default repository contains a limited set of templates. From this default repository, you can add, modify, and retrieve folders, subfolders, and items.

To start Visual Component Manager and examine its interface:

1. Start Visual Basic and, if necessary, create a new project.

2. Activate Visual Component Manager by clicking on View, and then clicking on Visual Component Manager. Visual Component Manager should appear. If VCM has never been used, a dialog box may appear asking if you want to import the VB templates. Click Yes.

3. By default, the database is installed with default folders and some demonstration projects. Click the plus sign to the left of the Local Database folder to display the subfolders. The subfolder Visual Basic should appear, among others. Double-click on the Visual Basic subfolder, and then double-click on Projects to display the contents of the Projects folder, as shown in Figure 17.3.

Figure 17.3 shows the projects folder (contents pane) with six projects. The properties for the selected project named CtlsAdd appear in the properties pane. You can think of these projects as being comparable to templates. One use of Visual Component Manager is to store templates for projects or forms.

You can use templates and other components stored in Visual Component Manager either by copying components into existing projects or by creating entirely new projects from templates stored in the database.

To copy a project (template) from Visual Component Manager:

1. Click the project named CtlsAdd to select it, and then right-click on it.

2. In the pop-up menu, click on Open. The Select Folder dialog box should appear. The Select Folder dialog box allows you to select the drive and folder to which the Visual Component Manager will copy and create a new project. Using this dialog box, you can also create new folders or access network folders.

3. Using the Drives and Folders list boxes, select a folder on your hard disk. Click the New Folder button, create a new folder named New in the Select Folder dialog box, and then click on OK to create a new project.

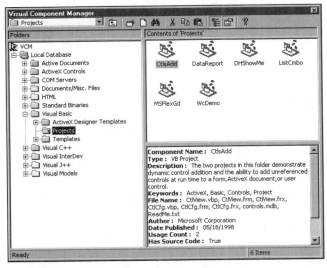

Figure 17.3   Visual Component Manager.

Visual Component Manager copies the new project to the selected folder and loads it into the current instance of Visual Basic. This template program adds control instances dynamically to a form. Although merely a sample application, it illustrates how to create a template project from a project stored in Visual Component Manager.

4. Close Visual Component Manager, and then exit Visual Basic. Do not save any changes to the project, as you will not use this template project further in this chapter.

The retrieval of existing templates from Visual Component Manager constitutes only one example of the roles fulfilled by Visual Component Manager. You can store the source code for forms, ActiveX controls, and other components as described in the following list. You can also store binary components. Visual Component Manager supports the following types of components (items):

➤ ActiveX controls having an extension of .ocx

➤ ActiveX documents having an extension of .vbd

➤ Class modules having an extension of .cls

➤ COM servers having an extension of .dll or .exe

➤ COM libraries having an extension of .dll

➤ Form templates, MDI form templates, menu templates, and control set templates having an extension of .frm

➤ Property Pages templates having an extension of .pag

➤ Standard binary files having an extension of .dll or .exe

➤ User control templates having an extension of .ctl

➤ Visual Basic projects and Visual Basic sample projects having an extension of .vbp

➤ Visual Basic project groups having an extension of .vbg

Visual Component Manager also supports other language projects, including Visual J++ projects, Java classes, Java applets, HTML files, and Visual Model files.

When you store a component (item) in Visual Component Manager, you publish it. You can publish almost any Visual Basic programming element. For example, you can publish class modules, standard forms, and form templates. To publish an item, you copy that item (form, ActiveX control, component) from the disk into a Visual Component Manager repository.

Publishing A Component

When you first create a repository (or use the default repository for the first time), it is almost empty. Visual Component manager adds a few sample Visual Basic projects to help you get started. As you saw in Figure 17.3, the empty repository contains a number of default folders. In these folders, you can create other folders to organize components. These folders can, in turn, contain subfolders, which can also contain their own subfolders. In these subfolders, you publish components.

To publish a component, you use a wizard that guides you through the process. You can start the wizard in three ways:

1. In Windows Explorer, you can select a component and drag it to a folder in the Visual Component Manager.

2. In the Visual Basic Project Explorer, you can select the project, right-click on the mouse, and select Publish Component from the pop-up menu.

3. You can select a folder in Visual Component Manager, and click on New component on the shortcut menu.

Any of these techniques will activate the Visual Component Manager Publish Wizard. This wizard allows you to publish any type of component in the repository. The Wizard consists of seven dialog boxes:

➤ **Introduction** Contains an introductory screen. You can turn this dialog box off, if desired.

➤ **Select a Repository/Folder** Allows you to select the repository and the folder in that repository to which you want to publish the component. It also allows you to define the Item name by which the project will be known.

➤ **Title and Properties** Allows you to give the component a name, identify files, set the type of component, and supply various options.

➤ **More Properties** Allows you to supply a description for the component along with keywords that will help developers locate the component.

➤ **Select Additional File(s)** Allows you to select all files that make up the component. You can add files to and remove files from this list.

➤ **COM registration** Allows you to define the components to register. (Most binary components must be registered before they are available to use.)

➤ **Finished** Appears after you complete these dialog boxes.

In the first example, which involves the Publish Wizard, you will publish a form template. The first dialog box you must complete is the Title and Properties dialog box. In this dialog box, you specify the name of the component and general properties pertaining to the component:

➤ The value you supply in the Component Name field will appear in the contents pane of Visual Component Manager to identify the component.

➤ The Primary File Name list box contains the primary name of the file.

➤ You use the Type list box to define the type of item you are publishing. The types appearing in this list box will vary based on the file extension of the primary file name.

➤ The Author text box contains the name of the author who is publishing the component.

➤ The dialog box contains four checkboxes describing the support files that are published with the component. These support files include sample code, documentation, source code, and help files.

No matter which type of component you publish, you always use the Publish Wizard to publish it. In the next set of steps, you will publish a dialog box by completing a series of steps that define the location in the repository where the dialog box will be published and that supply information allowing the developer to locate the dialog box. This dialog box will serve as a standard login dialog box to be used throughout the organization. Thus developers will add this dialog box (form) to each of their projects.

To start the Publish Wizard and define the title and properties:

1. Start Visual Basic, and load the project named Chapter.17\Vcm\Dialog.vbp. This project contains a single form intended for use as a standard login dialog box.

2. In the Project Explorer, open the Forms folder, and then select the form named frmLogin. Right-click on the name of the folder to activate the pop-up menu. On the pop-up menu, click on Publish Component. The Publish Wizard should start, allowing you to publish the component in a Visual Component Manager repository.

3. If the Introduction screen appears, click on Next to display the Select a Repository/Folder dialog box. By checking the appropriate checkbox, you can inhibit this introductory dialog box from appearing in the future. In the Select a Repository/Folder dialog box, you must select the repository and folder/subfolder within that repository where Visual Component Manager will publish the component. When you first install Visual Component Manager, it creates a default local database (repository) containing a group of default folders and subfolders. Depending on the configuration of your system, this local database may be the only database created. The text box making up most of the form displays repository folders and subfolders hierarchically. You store components (items) in these folders and subfolders.

4. In the combo box, double-click on the Local Database repository to select the default local database. The folders in the local database should appear in the text area.

5. Double-click on the Visual Basic folder. Visual Component Manager opens the folders and displays the subfolders. Double-click on Templates, and then

double-click on Forms. Figure 17.4 shows the Repository/Folder dialog box with the combo box open so that you can see the hierarchy of folders.

6. In the New Item Name text box, enter a name of Standard Login. Developers will see this descriptive name as they search for the component you published. Click Next to display the Title and Properties dialog box.

In the Title and Properties dialog box, you specify several pieces of information that will allow the developer to locate your component in the repositories. You should therefore provide accurate descriptive names for each item of information to simplify the process of component location. The following list identifies the fields in this dialog box and the purpose of those fields.

➤ The Component name will appear in the contents pane, allowing the developer to locate and identify the component.

➤ The Primary File Name text box identifies the primary file for a component. For a project, the primary file is typically a project file. For an ActiveX control, the primary file is likely an .ocx file. In this example, the primary file will be the form file.

➤ The Type list box allows you to specify the type of the component you are publishing. Accurately specifying the type has significance because Visual Component Manager performs different actions depending on the type of component. A developer can also use the component type as a search parameter in an effort to locate the component. In this example, the type will be a Visual Basic form template.

➤ You use the Author list box to specify the developer or author of the component.

➤ Four checkboxes appear at the bottom of the dialog box. They identify types of additional support files that you will publish along with the component. These files include sample code, documentation, source code,

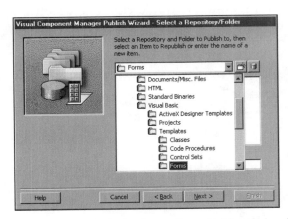

Figure 17.4   Select a Repository/Folder dialog box.

and help files. A developer can also search for components based upon these entries.

In addition to the Title and Properties dialog box, the More Properties dialog box contains a multiline text box and a list box. In the multiline text box, you supply a description for the component you are publishing. In the Keywords list box, you add keywords that other developers will use to locate that component. Use care to provide a clear and accurate description of the component, as the information entered in this dialog box can help the developer to more easily locate the component you are registering.

You will now describe the title and properties related to your component.

To describe a component:

1. In the Title and Properties dialog box, make sure that the Component Name is set to Standard Login.

2. Accept the default name for the Primary File Name. It is the name of the file that will be registered in the repository.

3. Make sure the Type is set to VB Form Template.

4. Enter your name as the Author. Because you will provide supplemental documentation for the component that you are registering, click on the Documentation checkbox at the bottom of the form.

5. Click on Next to activate the More Properties dialog box.

6. In the Description text box, enter the following text: "Standard dialog to obtain user login information". As you will see in the following steps, the developer can use this description to search for this component.

7. Just as a description will help a developer locate your component, so too will well-chosen keywords. Developers locate components using keywords, just as you use keywords to locate topics in a Help system. Click on the Add button to add new keywords to aid a developer in identifying the component. The Item Keywords dialog box should appear, as shown in Figure 17.5.

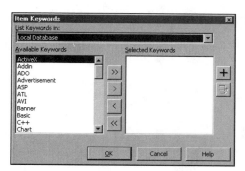

Figure 17.5 Item Keywords dialog box.

As shown in Figure 17.5, the Item Keywords dialog box contains two list boxes. One contains a list of available keywords, and the other displays the selected keywords. Visual Component Manager stores a list of keywords for each repository (database). You can use an existing keyword to describe a component, add new keywords, or modify existing keywords.

To add keywords to describe a component:

1. In the Item Keywords dialog box, click on the plus sign to open the Add a Keyword dialog box. In this dialog box, enter the keyword "Login", and then click on OK to close the dialog box and add the keyword. The new keyword should appear in the Selected Keywords list box.

2. Add a second keyword named Dialog. Click on OK to close the Item Keywords dialog box. The newly added keywords should appear in the Keywords list box on the More Properties dialog box.

3. Click on Next to activate the Select Additional File(s) dialog box.

In the Select Additional File(s) dialog box, you can publish files related to your component. These files may include documentation pertaining to your component or any other related information you want to publish. In this example, you will publish a simple ReadMe file with the component.

To publish related files with a component:

1. Click on the Add Files button to activate the Add File dialog box. This dialog box allows you to select a file from the disk to publish with your component. You can publish as many files as desired with your component.

2. In the Add File dialog box, select the file named Chapter.17\Vcm\Readme.txt, setting the drive designator as necessary, and then click on Open to add the file to the list of published files. When a developer retrieves the component form file, the readme file you stored with the component will be retrieved as well. Click on Next to display the COM registration dialog box.

After you have selected the files to publish, the COM registration dialog box appears. In this dialog box, you specify the files that will require COM registration on a remote computer. For example, if you are publishing an .ocx file, that component must be registered to run on a remote computer. For Scientific Applications' example, your published component is a source Visual Basic form file; component registration is therefore unnecessary. In general, binary files must be registered.

To specify the files requiring registration:

1. In this example, you are publishing a form file. A developer will incorporate this source file into a Visual Basic project. You do not need to register the

component in this case. If you are publishing an .ocx file or certain other binary file types, however, you must advise Visual Component Manager so that the component will be properly registered when used by a developer on a remote computer. Click on Next to accept the default options and to activate the Finished dialog box.

2. Click on Finish to publish the component.

When you published your components and associated readme file, the two files were stored in the VisualBasic\Templates\Forms subfolder. In addition to storing components in existing folders and subfolders, you can create folders and subfolders that pertain to the components of a specific organization. The process of adding and removing folders and subfolders is similar to the process of adding and removing folders using Windows Explorer.

To illustrate the process, you will create and destroy a subfolder in the repository. You will create a subfolder named SA, denoting Scientific Applications.

To create and destroy repository subfolders:

1. Reactivate Visual Component Manager, if necessary.

2. In the explorer pane, click on the Local Database folder. Right-click on the folder to activate the pop-up menu. On the pop-up menu, highlight New, and then select Folder.

3. Visual Component Manager creates a new folder as a child of the Local Database folder just as Windows Explorer creates child folders. The folder becomes active and selected. You can rename this folder, move it, and remove it, just as you can in Windows Explorer. Name the folder SA, and then press Enter.

4. To illustrate the deletion process, right-click on the new folder you just created. Select Delete. A dialog box will appear, requesting your confirmation. Click on Yes to delete the folder.

You can add, edit, and delete folders, subfolders, and items to suit your needs. As you will see later in the section, you can create additional databases (repositories) as well. In addition to storing information in Visual Component Manager repositories, developers must be able to easily locate information stored in those repositories.

Locating Components

Successfully publishing components requires that you supply meaningful descriptions and keys so that other developers will notice your components. Developers have several options to locate components. They can search for components by their type, by keywords, or by description. The more well-organized your published components, the more easily a developer can locate them.

To locate a component, you click on the Find Item(s) button on Visual Component Manager to activate the Find dialog box, as shown in Figure 17.6.

As shown in Figure 17.6, the Find dialog box contains three tabs:

> **Description** In the Description tab, you can locate a published component by its description, by keywords, or by file type. You used the same criteria when you specified the properties for the component.

> **History** In the History tab, you can locate a published component based on the person who published the component, when the component was published, or when the component was last used.

> **Related Files** In the Related Files tab, you can locate components that have certain types of related support files or specific items.

To illustrate how to locate a component, you will use different means to locate your just-published component. You will search for this component based upon different criteria.

To locate a published component by keyword:

1. In Visual Component Manager, click on the Find Item(s) button to activate the Find dialog box. Make sure that the Description tab is active.

2. Click on the Select From Keyword List button to the right of the Containing Text dialog box to activate the Item Keywords dialog box. You used the same dialog box to add keywords in earlier steps in this section.

3. In the Available Keywords list box, select the keyword "dialog". You specified this keyword when you published the component.

4. Click on the greater than sign (>) to select the keyword, and then click on OK to close the dialog box.

5. Click on the Find Now button to search for the component matching the criteria you specified. The component(s) matching the criteria you specified should appear in the list view at the bottom of the form.

6. Close the dialog box. Exit Visual Component Manager.

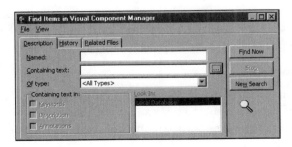

Figure 17.6   Find dialog box

Once you, as a developer, have located a component, you can use it. That is, you can add the component to an existing project or create a new project using the component.

Adding Components To A Project

Once you have located a desired component, you can add it to a project. Accomplishing this task is as simple as selecting the desired component in the contents pane or clicking on the right mouse button and then selecting Add To Project from the pop-up menu. The component will be copied from the Visual Component Manager database into your project.

To add a component to a project:

1. Create a new Visual Basic project.

2. Activate Visual Component Manager by clicking on View on the Visual Basic menu bar, and then clicking on Visual Component Manager.

3. You can locate the standard dialog box you created earlier by either clicking on the Find button or navigating through the folders in the explorer pane. Using the explorer pane, open the Local Database folder, and then open the Visual Basic folder. Open the Templates folder, and then open the Forms folder. The Standard Login dialog box should appear in the contents pane.

4. Right-click on the Standard Login dialog box in the contents pane, and then click on Add To Project. The component (form) should be added to your new project, as shown in Project Explorer.

In addition to performing operations on the local repository, you can create other databases to serve the needs of your organization.

Creating Additional Repositories

You use Visual Component Manager to create additional repositories, open them, and close them. You can open multiple repository entries concurrently. To create a new repository, you select the root VCM entry in the explorer pane, click on the right mouse button, and select Repository from the pop-up menu. From the pop-up menu, you can either create a new repository or open an existing one. Repositories may be stored on local disks or on the network.

To create a new repository:

1. Activate Visual Component Manager, if necessary. Note that depending on the configuration of your computer, you may not be able to create additional repositories. If the Repository menu does not appear, you cannot complete the following steps.

2. Select the root VCM entry at the top of the explorer pane. Right-click on the mouse to activate the pop-up menu, highlight Repository, and then click on New to activate the Select Database Type dialog box.

3. Visual Component Manager supports both Microsoft Access and SQL Server database types. Note that you must have SQL Server installed to create an SQL Server database. Make sure that Microsoft Access Database (MDB) is selected, and, then click on OK to activate the Create Access Type Database dialog box.

4. In this dialog box, you specify where Visual Component Manager should create the database. Create a new folder on your hard disk named VCMDemo using the path of your choice. Set the file name to Demo.mdb. Click on Save.

5. Once you have created this new repository, you can store components in it just as you stored components in the default repository.

6. Exit Visual Basic.

Visual Component Manager creates a new database with the same structure (folders and subfolders) used for the local database.

The Package And Deployment Wizard

Introducing The Package And Deployment Wizard

In previous chapters, you used the Package and Deployment Wizard to perform specific tasks. In this section, you will learn more about the wizard. You can use the Package and Deployment Wizard to perform the following tasks:

➤ Create a Setup program that will install an application

➤ Deploy desktop applications using floppy disks or CD-ROMs

➤ Deploy desktop applications on the Web

➤ Deploy desktop applications over a network

➤ Provide support for uninstalling an application

➤ Deploy application updates

After creating a Visual Basic application, you must prepare the application for distribution to other computers. This process is referred to as *deployment*. As a user, you typically install an application by running a Setup program. You may run this program from floppy disks, via CD-ROM, or over the network. Furthermore, you may also install software from the Web. This section will examine each of these deployment options.

17

Floppy Disk And CD-ROM Deployment

The traditional means of deploying software is via floppy disks and CD-ROMs. The user installs a software package by running a Setup program from either of these two distribution media. The Setup program typically performs several tasks:

➤ It copies the program to the destination computer's hard disk.

➤ Files necessary to run the program, called dependent files, are copied to the destination computer.

➤ The Setup program updates the Registry.

➤ The Setup program updates the Start menu.

Whether you create a floppy disk or CD-ROM distribution, you will complete almost exactly the same series of steps using the Package and Deployment Wizard. As its name indicates, the Package and Deployment Wizard performs two discrete tasks. The first task is to create the package. During this phase, the Package and Deployment Wizard collects all files pertaining to the application into a single location. The second task is to deploy the package. In the deployment phase, you actually deploy the package to the distribution media.

The following list outlines the necessary steps to build the package:

1. Start the Package and Deployment Wizard. Make sure that the project you want to deploy is not loaded in Visual Basic.

2. Select the project to deploy.

3. Compile the project, if necessary.

4. The Package and Deployment Wizard allows you to create two types of packages for Standard EXE projects: Standard Setup Packages and Dependency Files. You create a Standard Setup Package for a package designed to be installed by the Setup.exe program. For certain project types, including ActiveX controls, and ActiveX documents, you can create an Internet package type—that is, a package type deployed on the Internet.

5. Select the folder where the package will be built. The Package and Deployment Wizard will assemble the package in this folder. The folder should be empty, as the Package and Deployment Wizard may overwrite an existing file there.

6. The Package and Deployment Wizard displays a list of files to be included in the project. Select the desired files, add any other files needed, and remove unnecessary files.

7. The Package and Deployment Wizard groups the files into a cabinet (or CAB) file. Cabinet files are discussed more fully later in this chapter. When deploying a project to floppy disks, you create multiple CAB files. Each file

should be the same size as the floppy disk. When deploying an application to CD-ROM, you create a single CAB file.

8. Supply an installation title for the project. The Setup program will display this title on its initial dialog box.

9. Specify where the project should appear on the Start menu. You can change the project group and the program name using this option.

10. Define the install locations. These locations determine where the software will be installed on the destination computer.

11. Identify any shared files. Shared files are those files used by multiple applications. If a single application is removed, the shared file(s) should not be deleted until all programs using the shared file have been removed.

To illustrate how to use the Package and Deployment Wizard, you will create a floppy disk-based deployment for a completed project.

To build a package:

1. Make sure that Visual Basic is not running. If it is running and the project you intend to deploy is loaded, then the Package and Deployment Wizard cannot compile the project.

2. On the Startup menu, select Programs, then Microsoft Visual Basic 6.0, then Microsoft Visual Basic 6.0 Tools, and then Package and Deployment Wizard to start the Package and Deployment Wizard. In the main dialog box, click on the Browse button and select the project named Chapter.17\Dist\Tree.vbp, setting the drive designator as necessary. Click on Open. It is the same project used as the completed program in Chapter 5. This project was selected because it contains dependent files and a database file that you must add to the package manually.

3. Click on the Package button in the Package and Deployment Wizard to begin creating the package.

4. This project has not been compiled yet. The Package and Deployment Wizard analyzes the project file to verify that the compiled program is more recent than the project file. If the project has not been compiled or the executable file is outdated, a dialog box will appear asking whether you want to search for the executable file or recompile it. Click on Compile to compile the file. The wizard displays a dialog box while the file compiles.

17

5. The Package and Deployment Wizard stores the package information in a script file. You can reuse this script file to deploy the package again. The Packaging Script dialog box may not appear if no packages have been built on your computer. If the Packaging Script dialog box appears, select (None) as the packaging script to use. This choice causes the wizard to create a new packaging script. The Package Type dialog box should appear.

6. You use the Package Type dialog box to specify the kind of package you want to create. The Standard Setup Package type creates a package that will be deployed to other computers. The Dependency File package type creates a file that lists the files required for your program to run on the destination computer. Other package types may appear depending on the type of project involved. Select the Standard Setup Package type, and then click on the Next button to activate the Package Folder dialog box.

7. In Package Folder dialog box, you specify the folder where the Package and Deployment Wizard will assemble the files making up the package. You should select an empty folder. If you use a folder containing files, the Package and Deployment Wizard may overwrite those files. Select your hard drive, and click on the New Folder button. In the New Folder dialog box, enter the folder name TreePackage, and then click on OK to create the folder. Click on the Next button to display the Included Files dialog box.

8. Depending on your system's configuration, a dialog box may appear indicating the dependency information is missing for the file named MSADO20.TLB. This dialog box appears because the Package and Deployment Wizard cannot detect whether this file requires other files. Click on OK to close the dialog box. In the Included Files dialog box, you specify the support files required for the application to run on the destination computer. These support files typically consist of OCX files, DLL files, and other files. The MSCOMCTL.OCX file contains the code for the Windows Common Controls. The user will run the SETUP.EXE file to install the software. The SETUP1.EXE project is used by the Setup program. STUNST.EXE contains the program to uninstall the software. The remaining files represent the executable program and the Visual Basic run-time library.

9. In addition to the dependent files detected by the Package and Deployment Wizard, you also deploy the database file corresponding to the application. Because the database file is not referenced in the project file, the wizard cannot detect this dependency. Thus you must add the database file manually. In the Included Files dialog box, click on Add to activate the Add File dialog box. In the Files of type list box, select All files. Select the file name ETC.mdb, and then click on Open to add the dependent file to your distribution. The file should appear in the Files list. Click on Next to select the files. The Cab Options dialog box opens.

10. In the Cab Options dialog box, you specify whether to create a single cab file or multiple cab files. When creating a floppy disk-based distribution, you use multiple cab files. When creating a CD-ROM installation, you use a single cab file. In this example, you will create a floppy disk distribution. Select Multiple Cabs, and make sure the Cab size is set to 1.44 MB (assuming that you are using high-density floppies). Click on Next to display the Installation Title dialog box.

11. In the Installation Title dialog box, you define the title that the user will see when running the Setup program. Set the Installation Title to Organizational Hierarchy. Click on Next to display the Start Menu Items dialog box.

12. You use the Start Menu Items dialog box to define where your application will appear on the Start menu. Using this dialog box, you can change both the name of the project group and the name of the item. You can also create new project groups and items. Click on the Next button to accept the default options. The Install Locations dialog box opens.

13. Most frequently, the Setup program determines where to install files by means of macros. These macros define the location of the Windows system directory and the default locations for applications. Accept the default options, and then click on the Next button to display the Shared files dialog box.

14. In the Shared Files dialog box, you specify any files in the application that will be shared by other applications. A file that is marked as shared will not be removed until all other files that use the application are removed as well. Because other applications will not share this program, do not check the ETC.exe checkbox. Click on Next to display the Finished dialog box.

15. In the Finished dialog box, you specify a script name. This script name helps you remember the parameters specified to build the package. Thus, if you rebuild the package, you can load the script without specifying all of the options again. Set the script name to Tree Package, and then click on the Finish button.

16. The Package and Deployment Wizard displays a dialog box while it builds the CAB files. When complete, the wizard displays the Packaging Report dialog box. You can either save the report or close the dialog box. Click on Close to close the dialog box without saving the report.

At this point in the process, you have built the package. One more task remains, however—you must deploy the Package. The Package and Deployment Wizard also provides this service. To deploy a package, you perform the following general steps:

1. Select the package to deploy.

2. Select the deployment method. The Package and Deployment Wizard can deploy packages to floppy disks, a folder, or the Web. The dialog boxes that appear after this dialog box depend on the deployment method chosen.

3. Select the floppy drive or folder where you want to deploy the package.

4. Assign a name to the deployment script.

In this example, you will create a floppy disk distribution. To complete the following steps, you will need two blank floppy disks.

17

To create a floppy disk-based distribution:

1. In the Package and Deployment Wizard, click on the Deploy button to activate the Deployment script dialog box. This dialog box may not appear, depending on whether you have previously deployed any packages. Click on Next to activate the Package to Deploy dialog box.

2. The Package to Deploy dialog box allows you to select a package script. This script is the same script file you specified when creating the package. Make sure that Tree Package is selected, and then click on Next to activate the Deployment Method dialog box.

3. In this example, you will deploy the program to floppy disks. Make sure that the Deployment method is set to Floppy Disks, and then click on the Next button to display the Floppy Drive dialog box.

4. In the Floppy Drive dialog box, you specify the floppy drive to which the Setup and CAB files will be copied. You can also specify whether to format the disks before copying the data. Select the floppy drive on your computer that you want to use. If your disks are not formatted, check the Format Before Copying checkbox. Click on Next to activate the Finished dialog box.

5. In the Finished dialog box, you assign a name to the deployment script. You can reuse this script if you later deploy this package. Enter the name "Tree Deployment", and then click on Finish to begin deploying the package.

6. A dialog box will appear, requesting that you insert the first blank floppy disk. Insert the first blank disk, and then click on OK to begin the deployment process. The wizard will begin copying data to the floppy. After the wizard has filled the disk, it will ask you to insert a second floppy disk. Insert the second disk when requested, and then click on OK to continue. When complete, the wizard displays a dialog box containing a report of the files copied. Click on Close to close the report without saving it.

7. Exit the Package and Deployment Wizard.

To illustrate how the user will see your package, you will install it. This process is the same one used to install any other software.

To install the deployed package:

1. Insert the first deployment floppy disk.

2. Click on Start and then Run on the Start menu to run a program. In the dialog box, type A:\Setup, and then click on OK. The Setup program begins by copying the files to a temporary folder on the disk. After copying the files from the first disk, you will be requested to change disks. Insert the second disk when requested to do so.

3. After the files have been copied, the Setup program will appear. The caption Organizational Hierarchy Setup appears. This caption is the same as

the installation title you specified when building the package. Click on OK to begin installing the package.

4. Another dialog box will appear, asking where you want to install the files. Click on the button on the dialog box to install the program in the default location.

5. Another dialog box appears, allowing you to select a program group. You can use the suggested program group or create a new one. Click on Continue to select the default program group. Setup displays a progress bar as it installs the files. When complete, another dialog box indicates that the installation was successful. Click on OK.

6. To test the installation, locate the Organizational Hierarchy option on the Start menu and click on it. The program should start.

7. Exit the program.

In addition to installing programs, users frequently want to remove programs from the system. The Package and Deployment Wizard provides support for this task. You remove programs by means of the Control Panel.

To remove a program:

1. Activate the Control Panel and double-click on Add/Remove Programs.

2. The Add/Remove Programs Properties dialog box appears. In the list box, select Organizational Hierarchy, and then click on the Add/Remove button. The Setup program will again appear and display a dialog box requesting that you confirm the deletion. Click on Yes to remove the program and its files. Note that the ADO file is marked as a shared file. Click on Keep so as not to remove this file.

3. Click on OK, and then click on OK again to close the Add/Remove Programs dialog box. Close the Control Panel.

4. Attempt to locate the program on the Start menu. Notice that it no longer appears.

In addition to deploying packages to CD-ROMs and floppy disks, you can deploy packages to a network. The process to deploy an application to a network is the same as the process to deploy a package to CD-ROM. You can also deploy certain types of packages to the Web.

17

Deploying Packages To The Web

The following list describes the types of packages suitable for Web deployment:

➤ ActiveX controls intended to be displayed on a Web page

➤ ActiveX EXE or DLL files designed to run on a Web client or Web server

➤ ActiveX documents displayed on a Web page

When you deploy packages destined for the Web, you must address three important issues. Many of these topics were discussed in earlier chapters.

➤ Controls and other programs you develop for Web deployment should have a digital signature. A digital signature allows the user to verify the contents of a file and make sure that a responsible source generated the file.

➤ Safety settings assure the user that a component will not harm the computer. These safety settings denote whether a component is safe for initialization and/or safe for scripting.

➤ When you place a component on the Web, anyone can download it. Thus, if you want to protect a component from unauthorized distribution, you must license the component.

Preparing A Digital Signature

By default, most Web browsers, including Internet Explorer, require that software have a digital signature before the software will be downloaded. You can apply digital signatures to EXE, CAB, DLL, OCX, and VBD files. Because you will deploy most components as cab files, you generally must apply the digital signature only to the CAB files. If you deploy components without CAB files, however, the component should also be signed.

To apply a digital signature, you use Authenticode technology. Authenticode performs two tasks to provide accountability. First, it verifies that the publisher for a software component is indeed the publisher of that component. Second, it assures the user that a third party has not altered the component.

Authenticode achieves these two goals by using public key cryptography. A digital signature consists of two keys: a public key and a private key. These keys encrypt and decrypt digitally signed files. The following steps describe the Authenticode process:

1. When the developer of a component signs a file, Authenticode calculates the number of bytes in the file. This technology uses a private key to encrypt this number, which is stored in the file to be distributed.

2. When the user attempts to download and install the file, the user's computer also calculates the number of bytes in the file. The numbers must match before the file will be considered authentic.

3. To assure the user that the source of the component is indeed the company that created the component, the browser uses the public key to determine which certification authority supplied the digital signature. The browser also determines the source identity.

4. The certificate authority verifies the source identity and issues a certificate. This certificate contains the source's name encrypted with a private key.

5. The browser uses the private key to decrypt the encrypted file.

6. If the first five steps are successful, the installation will proceed.

To apply a digital signature to a component, you must have the Authenticode software installed. You can download this software from the ActiveX Software Development Kit at Microsoft's Web site. In addition, you must obtain a certificate. You obtain a digital signature from a certificate authority, such as Verisign. When Verisign issues a certificate, it is imperative that you keep this certificate secure. If an unauthorized entity were to obtain the certificate, that entity could effectively sign files as if it were you.

Establishing Safety Settings

Each component that you supply for downloading should be assigned safety settings to assure the user that the component will not harm his or her computer. Components can be marked as safe for initialization or safe for scripting.

By marking a control as safe for initialization, you guarantee that the control will not perform any actions on the end user's computer. When you mark a control as safe for initialization, initialization parameters cannot be used to write or change either Registry entries or INI files. Note that a control that is marked safe for initialization does not guarantee the accuracy of the methods or properties pertaining to the control.

By marking a control as safe for scripting, you assure the user that a script cannot cause the control to damage the user's computer. These controls also must not be able to obtain unauthorized information. For example, the control should not be able to identify personal information about the user and disseminate that information.

Just because a control has been marked as safe for scripting and safe for initialization, it does not necessarily mean that the control itself is safe to use. A malicious control author could mark a control both safe for scripting and initialization even though the control may perform a malicious act on the system. In this situation, however, the control author could be held criminally liable for his or her actions. When you deploy a package using the Package and Deployment Wizard, you can mark a control safe for scripting and/or safe for initialization. Another technique involves the use of the IObjectSafety interface. The IObjectSafety interface is not discussed in this book.

Component Licensing

You are undoubtedly aware of the issue of software piracy. In essence, a software pirate runs software for which he or she has not obtained a license. When you distribute a component as part of a Web page, any users who download the Web

17

page have access to the component. Thus the user could potentially take that component and use it in his or her own applications, even though you never intended this type of use. To prevent unauthorized use of controls included with your Web pages, you can license your controls. This goal is accomplished using a license package file (or LPK file).

To implement licensing, each control that requires a license has an associated license string. License strings are stored in LPK files. When an HTML page uses a control that requires licensing, an LPK file must exist containing the license string for the control. Note that a single LPK file can be shared by multiple controls and hence by multiple pages.

A license file has two parts. First, it should contain a copyright notice to deter individuals from copying the file and, as such, violating the license. Second, you must embed an object called a *license manager* in the HTML page that is responsible for downloading your ActiveX controls. To do so, you create an OBJECT tag that references the LPK file pertaining to your ActiveX control. The Package and Deployment Wizard will perform these two tasks automatically.

Preparing An ActiveX Control For Web Deployment

In this section, you will deploy the calendar control originally created in Chapter 12 such that it can be downloaded from the Web. You will perform this task using the Package and Deployment Wizard. As the Package and Deployment Wizard performs several tasks automatically, a review of the tasks being performed will help you understand this process. Creating a component for download involves two critical files:

➤ The cabinet (CAB) file contains the files for the component and any support files necessary for the component to work correctly. Cabinet files are similar to files produced by programs like the zip utility. That is, individual files are compressed and cataloged into a single file.

➤ Inside the cabinet file, another file with the suffix of .inf must be included. This file contains directives that the browser uses to download and install the component.

Microsoft originally used cabinet files so as to compress its software that was distributed on disks. The intent was to minimize the number of disks supplied with a product. The format of a CAB file matches the format of a ZIP file. Although the Package and Deployment Wizard manages and builds the CAB files for you, you can also modify the contents of CAB files by using the Cabarc program. This utility allows you to add and remove individual files from a CAB file and to specify how those files should be added. For example, you can include or exclude directory names from files as they are added to the CAB file.

In addition to the CAB file, the Package and Deployment Wizard creates an INF file that describes the contents of the CAB files and specifies how to install them. The format of the INF file matches the format of an INI file. The file contains section names in brackets followed by key/value pairs. The following code segment shows the first few lines of an INF file:

```
[version]
signature="$CHICAGO$"
AdvancedINF=2.0
```

The signature tag in the INF file indicates that this file is compatible with Windows 95, 98, and NT. The AdvancedINF tag specifies the version of the Advpack.dll that Internet Explorer must use to process the INF file.

In addition to the version section, the INF file contains several other sections:

➤ The [Add.Code] section maps specific files to subsections, typically of the same name. In these subsections, key/value pairs contain related information about the file, including its version and instructions for its extraction.

➤ The [SourceDiskFiles] section identifies which disk contains a particular file. In the case of a single CAB file, the value of each associated CAB file is 1. When multiple cabinet files are used, the number indicates which CAB file on which floppy disk contains a particular file.

➤ The [RegisterFiles] section lists the files in the CAB file that require registration.

You can customize a package by using the CabArc utility and modifying the contents of the INF file.

To package a control for Web deployment:

1. Reinsert your Student Disk into the A: drive, if necessary.

2. Make sure that the Package and Deployment Wizard is running.

3. Use the Browse button and select the project named Chapter.17\Inet\Cal.vbp, setting the drive designator as necessary.

4. Click on Package to begin creating the package. Because no compiled version of the control resides on the disk, a dialog box will appear asking you to compile the executable file named Cal.ocx. Click on Compile to compile the control. A dialog box will appear while the wizard performs the compilation.

5. After the control is compiled, the Packaging script dialog box may appear. If it does, enter the name "MyCalendar" in the dialog box. You can reuse this packaging script in the future if you later rebuild the package. Click on Next to continue.

17

6. The Package Type dialog box will appear. Because the type of executable file is suitable for Internet deployment, another option appears in the Package Type list box, with the caption of Internet Package. Select Internet Package, if necessary, and then click on Next to continue.

7. In the Package Folder dialog box, you specify where the wizard should build your package. You should select an empty folder or create a new one, as the wizard may overwrite existing files. Select a new folder on your hard disk named InetPackage, and then click on OK to close the New Folder dialog box. Click on Next to continue.

8. A dialog box will appear indicating that you must include the Property Page DLL if the control will be used in a development environment other than Visual Basic. Because your distribution is designed only for users to create run-time instances of the control, click on No in this dialog box.

9. In the Included Files dialog box, the Package and Deployment Wizard displays the files required for the component to execute properly. These files will be included in the CAB file produced by the wizard. In addition to the files suggested by the wizard, you can click on the Add button to include any other support files, such as additional documentation, Help files, or any other file type. Use the default files suggested by the wizard, and then click on Next to display the File Source dialog box.

10. Specific dependency files can be included into the cabinet file produced by the Package and Deployment Wizard. In addition, you can exclude specific files, ensuring that they will instead be downloaded when needed from either Microsoft's Web site or another Web site of your choosing. By specifying that a file should be downloaded from another source, you reduce the size of your cabinet file. Furthermore, by downloading specific ActiveX and other components from Microsoft's Web site, you are assured of getting the most current component version. By default, the calendar control you are packaging will be included in the CAB file. The dependent VB6 Runtime library will be downloaded from Microsoft's Web site. To accept the default options, click on Next.

11. In the Safety Settings dialog box, you indicate whether the script is safe for scripting and/or safe for initialization. Because you did not create this control, you should not deploy it as safe unless you carefully verify its status. Thus you should accept the default options indicating that the script is not safe, and then click on Next to continue the deployment.

12. In the Finish dialog box, you can assign a name to the script used to package the control. Set the Script name to MyCalendar, if necessary, and then click on Finish.

13. The wizard builds the package and creates a packaging report. Click on Close to close the Packaging Report dialog box.

If you examine the files produced to build the package (stored in the package folder), you will see that two files were written to the package folder you specified, and that the wizard created a folder named Support. The following files appear in the package folder:

➤ The file Cal.cab contains the CAB file ultimately used for deployment.

➤ The file Cal.HTM contains an HTML document to extract the OCX file from the CAB file.

➤ The Support folder contains the files necessary to rebuild the .cab file.

The deployment part of the Package and Component Wizard uses all of these files to deploy the package.

The Support folder contains a copy of the OCX and INF files used to build the CAB file. In addition, it contains a batch file you can use to re-create the CAB file, if necessary. You must re-create the CAB file if you make changes to the INF file.

Deploying The Package

Once you have created a package for Internet distribution, you can deploy it in one of two ways: by publishing the package directly to a Web server or by distributing the package to a folder on the local disk or network. In this example, you will deploy the application to a folder. You can deploy the package to the Web only if you have the necessary access privileges to publish components on Web servers. The process of deploying an Internet application to a folder is similar to the process of deploying an EXE package to a floppy disk or CD-ROM—you again use the Package and Deployment Wizard.

To deploy an Internet Package:

1. Make sure that the Package and Deployment Wizard is active. Click on the Deploy button to begin deploying a package. The wizard may display the Deployment Script dialog box, allowing you to select an existing deployment script. This option means that you can deploy a previously deployed package without having to re-create all of the input parameters. In the Deployment Script list box, select (None), and then click on Next to continue.

2. In the Package to Deploy dialog box, you select a previously created package to deploy. In this example, you will deploy the package you created in the previous steps. Select, if necessary, the package named MyCalendar, and then click on Next to continue.

3. In the Deployment Method dialog box, you select how you want to deploy the package. The Package and Deployment Wizard displays a list of deployment methods that varies according to the type of package. Because

17

you have created an Internet package, you can publish the package to the Web or deploy it to a folder. Select the Folder option, and then click on Next to continue.

4. In the Folder dialog box, you specify the local or network folder where the package will be deployed. Select your hard drive letter, click on the New Folder button, and then create a new folder named CalDeploy on the hard disk. Set the path as necessary. Click on Next to display the finished dialog box. Click on Finish to deploy the package.

5. Click on Close.

6. Exit the Package and Deployment Wizard.

If you analyze the contents of the files produced when you deployed the package, you will find that the CAB file and the corresponding HTML file were copied to the deployment folder you specified. You can deploy these files to the Web.

Understanding Application Updates

As you develop components, you may find that—no matter how well you design them—requests will arise for enhancements. Some enhancements may require changes to an existing interface. As you create new components with changed or improved interfaces, however, you must consider their effects on existing applications. For example, if you add an argument to a component's method, you risk breaking the programs that use the component's method. The version compatibility features of Visual Basic allow you to enhance a component without creating problems in the existing applications that use the component. You control compatibility using the Component tab on the Project Properties dialog box. Three version compatibility options exist:

➤ **No Compatibility** With the No Compatibility option, each time you compile a new version of the component, Visual Basic generates new class IDs and type library information. Thus no relationship exists between the current version of the component and previous versions.

➤ **Project Compatability** With the Project Compatibility option, the component's type library is preserved. Test projects will therefore continue to work properly with existing programs.

➤ **Binary Compatability** The Binary Compatibility option is used to make a component compatible with older versions.

If you do not want to maintain compatibility between two versions of the same component, select the No Compatibility option. In addition, you must change both the file name of the component and the project name on the Project Properties dialog box. This approach ensures that the new component will have a new type library name and unique programmatic IDs.

If you are developing a new component, select the Project Compatibility option. This choice preserves the type library information and allows you to avoid resetting the references from test projects to component projects.

When you are creating new versions of existing components, use the Binary Compatibility mode. With this option, applications compiled with earlier versions of a component will work with new versions of the component. In addition, Visual Basic will preserve the class ID and interface ID of the previous component version and create a new class ID and interface ID for the new version. Both the new and the old programs can use the same component. If you make changes to a component and specify binary compatibility, Visual Basic will warn you of possible incompatible changes.

CHAPTER SUMMARY

This book has presented the necessary topics to create full-featured desktop business applications using Visual Basic. It also has discussed how to create reusable code using components, and how to organize those components using Visual Component Manager. While each chapter presented a specific topic such as database programming or using the Windows Common Controls, you can combine the topics presented in each chapter to design, plan, and implement large-scale applications.

A Visual Basic project has a specific type and is made up of one or more modules also of specific types. You can combine as many modules as you desire to build an application. As you create general-purpose modules or components, you can organize them using Visual Component Manager. These components can then be reused in other programs as necessary.

Database processing is an important part of most business applications. The ADO object model presented in this book forms the building blocks for both local and distributed database applications. To create ADO-based programs, you can use the ADO Data control, access ADO programmatically, or use a combination of both techniques. In addition, the DataList, DataCombo, and DataGrid controls will help you build the visual elements of ADO programs.

Controls are an important part of building the user interface for a Visual Basic program. This book has discussed the intrinsic controls, Windows Common Controls, Common Dialog control, and many others. While important, these controls are only a small subset of the controls available to the Visual Basic programmer. In addition to these controls, many other controls are distributed with Visual Basic. Furthermore, you can purchase additional controls from vendors other than Microsoft. These third party controls extend the power of Visual Basic. When using controls, use care to choose the most appropriate control for the task.

Component-based programming is the key to creating reusable code. Visual Basic allows you to create class modules and develop object hierarchies using class modules. Furthermore, you can also develop your own ActiveX controls and ActiveX documents. All of these components are based on COM technology. As you design programs, carefully analyze the problem to be solved and decide how the problem can be translated into business objects and business services. Then implement those objects and services as components, to allow for code reuse.

As today's applications must interact with the Internet, this book has discussed the various Visual Basic tools that allow you to build Internet applications. A few of these tools are DHTML applications, ActiveX controls, and ActiveX documents. The Internet Transfer control and Winsock control also allow you to build Internet-enabled applications.

Visual Basic is not an island. Rather, the Visual Basic environment allows you to build applications that rely upon the services provided by Windows. You can access the Registry from Visual Basic and gain access to the Windows operating system using DLLs.

The final chapter of the book discussed how to compile programs to obtain peak performance and deploy those programs to a network, to floppy disks or CD-ROMs, and to the Web.

In conclusion, much more could be said about Visual Basic. This book has given the reader a rich toolchest from which to build applications. As you develop more and larger applications, you will undoubtedly apply other tools and find unique ways to use them.

REVIEW QUESTIONS

1. Which of the following statements is true?
   a. Visual Basic can compile files to p-code.
   b. Visual Basic can compile files to native code.
   c. Optimization may be performed on native code.
   d. All of the above.
   e. None of the above.

2. In general, _____.
   a. native code runs more rapidly then p-code
   b. native code runs more slowly than p-code
   c. the performance of native code is roughly the same as that of p-code
   d. turning off array bounds checking will degrade performance
   e. All of the above

3. Which of the following statements is true?

   a. Code that manipulates objects extensively will benefit from being compiled to native code.

   b. The performance of DLL calls will improve by compiling a program to native code.

   c. Native code can be optimized for either size or speed.

   d. All of the above.

   e. None of the above.

4. What will happen when you remove integer and floating-point arithmetic checks, and a numeric underflow or overflow error then occurs?

   a. Visual Basic will crash.

   b. The executable program will generate a run–time error.

   c. The code will produce invalid results.

   d. All of the above.

   e. None of the above.

5. What statements do you use to perform conditional compilation?

   a. **Conditional**

   b. **#Conditional**

   c. **#If, #Then #End If**

   d. **If, Then, End If**

   e. None of the above

6. Which of the following reasons for using conditional compilation is valid?

   a. to improve the performance of a program

   b. as an alternative to using **If** statements

   c. because conditional statements execute more rapidly than other statements

   d. All of the above

   e. None of the above

7. Write the statement(s) to print the string "Option 2" to the Immediate window if the constant **cDebugLevel** is equal to 8. Use conditional compilation to accomplish this task.

8. Write the statement(s) to print the values of the variables **pintX**, **pintY**, and **pintZ** if the constant **cDebugLevel** is set to 2. If the constant is set to 1, print the values of **pintX** and **pintY** only. If the value of the constant is something else, do not print anything.

9. Which of the following statements pertaining to Visual Component Manager is true?

    a. The purpose of Visual Component Manager is the same as the purpose of Visual Source Safe.

    b. Visual Component Manager can manage only Visual Basic projects.

    c. You access Visual Component Manager by means of an add-in.

    d. All of the above.

    e. None of the above.

10. The database where Visual Component Manager stores information is called a(n) _____.

    a. entity

    b. location

    c. repository

    d. storage

    e. None of the above

11. What type of database does Visual Component Manager support?

    a. Oracle

    b. SQL Server

    c. Access

    d. Both b and c

    e. All of the above

12. What is the term used to describe the process of storing a component in Visual Component Manager?

    a. register

    b. publish

    c. store

    d. inform

    e. None of the above

13. Which of the following statements pertaining to storage of information in Visual Component Manager is true?

    a. You should provide a descriptive name and keywords for the components published.

    b. You can store Help files and other support files with the components you publish.

    c. You can publish source and binary files.

    d. All of the above.

    e. None of the above.

14. Components stored in Visual Component Manager are stored in _____.

    a. registry entries

    b. folders and subfolders

    c. Windows Explorer

    d. encoded files

    e. None of the above

15. Which of the following statements is true?

    a. All components are registered on one database.

    b. Visual Component Manager supports multiple databases.

    c. You must manually create a default database during the installation of Visual Component Manager.

    d. Only one database can be open at a time.

    e. None of the above.

16. Which of the following statements regarding the default database created by Visual Component Manager is true?

    a. It contains default folders and subfolders.

    b. It contains a reference to other databases.

    c. The default database is empty when created.

    d. Visual Component Manager does not create a default database.

    e. None of the above.

17. Which of the following destinations is valid for deploying packages?

    a. CD–ROM

    b. the Web

    c. floppy disks

    d. network

    e. All of the above

18. Which of the following statements pertaining to deploying software to floppy disks is true?

    a. You typically use a single CAB file.

    b. You typically use multiple CAB files.

    c. Floppy disk distributions do not use CAB files.

    d. Floppy disk distributions use fd files.

    e. None of the above.

17

19. Which of the following is a valid type of package?
    a. EXE packages
    b. control packages
    c. ActiveX packages
    d. All of the above
    e. None of the above

20. To create a floppy disk–based installation, you should create a _____.
    a. Dependency file
    b. Standard Setup package
    c. floppy package
    d. disk package
    e. None of the above

21. Which of the following statements about a package is true?
    a. It contains dependency information.
    b. It contains all files necessary for the program to run.
    c. It contains a Setup program.
    d. All of the above.
    e. None of the above.

22. Which of the following statements pertaining to package deployment is true?
    a. You can deploy packages to floppy disks, CD–ROM, or the Web.
    b. Any type of package can be deployed to the Web.
    c. Web deployment does not use CAB files.
    d. All of the above.
    e. None of the above.

23. Which of the following project types is suitable for Web deployment?
    a. Active X controls
    b. ActiveX documents
    c. Standard EXE files
    d. Both a and b
    e. All of the above

24. Which of the following statements about a digital signature is true?
    a. It contains a digitized version of the author's signature.
    b. Digital signatures use public key cryptology.
    c. Internet Explorer does not support digital signatures.
    d. All of the above.
    e. None of the above.

25. Which of the following safety settings is valid?
    a. safe for initialization
    b. safe for scripting
    c. safe for running
    d. Both a and b
    e. Both a and c

26. What is the purpose of a component license?
    a. to register a control on a remote system
    b. to prevent unauthorized use of a downloaded control
    c. to identify the author of the control
    d. components do not support licenses
    e. None of the above

HANDS-ON PROJECTS

Project 1

In this project, you will create a project that performs a time-consuming operation. Using this project, you will experiment with various compilation options to evaluate the effect on program performance. You will also use conditional compilation to see how to insert debugging code into a project.

  a. Start Visual Basic, and create a new project. Save the form using the name Chapter.17\Exercise\frmEx1.frm and the project using the name Chapter.17\Exercise\Ex1.vbp.

  b. Create two arrays of 100,000 elements of type **Long**. In the first array, initialize all values so that the contents of the array elements are the same as their subscripts. Initialize the second array so that the content of each element is the same as the content of the corresponding element in the first array multiplied by 2.

  c. Compile the program to both p-code and native code, and then run the executable programs. Record the time it takes to execute each version.

17

d. Compile the program to native code again, but this time, select each of the different optimization options. Record the execution time for each option.

e. Using the Advanced Optimizations dialog box, remove the error checks and recompile the program. Test the executable file to see the effect on performance, if any.

f. Insert debugging code to save the values of the arrays to a file after they are initialized. The debugging code should use conditional compilation.

g. Save the program.

Project 2

In this project, you will use Visual Component Manager to publish components and check those components out of Visual Component Manager.

a. Start Visual Basic, and create a new project named Chapter.17\Exercise\ VCMDemo.vbp.

b. Using Visual Component Manager, locate the component named ListCmbo and add it to a new project named Chapter.17\Exercise\ ListCmbo.vbp.

c. Examine the project file and save it.

d. Create another new project named Chapter.17\Exercise\Utility.vbp.

e. In the new project, create a second form module to be used as a splash screen. Save the form using the name Chapter.17\Exercise\ frmEx2Splash.frm.

f. Create a standard module named Chapter.17\Exercise\Utility.bas.

g. Activate Visual Component Manager. Create a new folder in the local database named Exercise Utilities. In that folder, publish both of your components (frmEx2Splash.frm and Utility.bas). Be sure to supply descriptive names and keywords for each component.

Project 3

In this project, you will publish a component for floppy disk deployment.

a. The folder Chapter.17\Exercise\Std contains a project named Ch7_C.vbp. It is the same program used in Chapter 7. In this exercise, you will package and deploy the Standard EXE file.

b. Using the Package and Deployment Wizard, create a package file for the control. You should use a standard package type. Create the package with multiple cab files so that it can be deployed to floppy disks.

c. After creating the package, deploy it to floppy disks.

Project 4

In this project, you will publish a component for Internet-based development.

a. The folder Chapter.17\Exercise\Inet contains a project named SuperText.vbp. It is the same text box control you created in Chapter 11. In this exercise, you will package and deploy the control.

b. Using the Package and Deployment Wizard, create a package file for the control. You should create an Internet package type. Create the package such that you identify that it is neither safe for initialization nor safe for scripting.

c. After you have created the package, deploy the package to a folder.

DEBUGGING

TECHNIQUES FOR RESOLVING ERRORS IN A VISUAL BASIC PROGRAM

Identifying Programming Errors

Only rarely will you write a program that works perfectly the first time. You have likely discovered that locating and correcting programming errors can be a time-consuming and tedious process. Such programming errors can be classified as one of three types: syntax, run-time, and logic.

➤ **Syntax error** Occurs when you write a statement that Visual Basic cannot understand because the statement violates the rules of the Visual Basic language. For example, you may misspell a keyword or try to reference a property that a particular project does not support.

➤ **Run-time error** Occurs when a program is executing. Run-time errors can occur for many reasons. For example, Visual Basic may evaluate an expression, inadvertently causing a numeric overflow or underflow error to occur. You can trap all run-time errors using error handlers.

➤ **Logic error** Occurs when the program does not perform as intended and produces incorrect results. Logic errors may or may not generate run-time errors.

The distinction between logic and run-time errors is not always clear. A logic error would occur if you intended to add two numbers together but instead wrote statements to multiply them. When the program executes, the multiplication might generate an overflow run-time error. In this case, the logic error causes a run-time error.

Fortunately, regardless of whether you have created a logic error, a run-time error, or a combination of the two, the tools provided by the Visual Basic IDE can make detecting and correcting the errors much simpler. Using these tools to identify programming errors is known as *debugging*.

Preparing A Program For Debugging

Visual Basic checks for syntax errors when it compiles a program. How Visual Basic compiles a program and how it handles errors depends on the settings in the Options dialog box. You activate the Options dialog box from the Tools menu. Because the settings in this dialog box are saved to the Visual Basic environment, you should verify that they are correct for the project to be debugged.

Figure A.1 shows the General tab on the Options dialog box. The Error Trapping and Compile frames on this dialog box pertain to debugging.

As shown in Figure A.1, the Compile section contains two checkboxes:

➤ **Compile On Demand** If you check the Compile On Demand checkbox, Visual Basic compiles the current procedure and analyzes it for syntax errors just before executing the procedure. In this situation, Visual Basic compiles a procedure only when it is called for the first time; thus it will not find the syntax errors in a project until all procedures in the project execute. While you are writing and testing programs, checking this box will allow your programs to execute much more rapidly because Visual Basic does not compile the entire project prior to executing it. If you do not check the Compile On Demand checkbox, Visual Basic checks the syntax of an entire program before the program begins executing.

➤ **Background Compile** If you check the Background Compile checkbox, Visual Basic will compile a program while the computer is idle during run time. The Background Compile checkbox option can improve execution speed the first time that procedures execute. This option is available only when the Compile On Demand checkbox is checked.

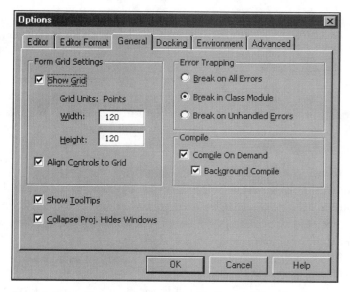

Figure A.1   General tab on the Options dialog box.

The way that Visual Basic handles run-time errors depends on settings in the Error Trapping section in the Options dialog box. These options become important when you are debugging class modules, error handlers, and project groups. The three options in this section control the behavior of Visual Basic when a run-time error occurs:

➤ **Break On All Errors** When you select the Break On All Errors option, any run-time error will cause Visual Basic to enter break mode and highlight the offending statement in the module where the error occurred, regardless of the type of module.

➤ **Break In Class Module** When you select the Break In Class Module option, errors in class modules that are not handled by an On Error statement cause Visual Basic to enter break mode and highlight the offending statement in the Code window.

➤ **Break On Unhandled Errors** The Break On Unhandled Errors option causes Visual Basic to enter break mode when a run-time error that is not handled by an On Error statement occurs.

To illustrate the effect of these options, the sample program that you will debug contains a class module (DLL server) and a Standard EXE project with three command buttons. Using each error-trapping option, Visual Basic will generate an overflow error (a run-time error) when the program code attempts to multiply two Integer numbers that produce a result greater than 32,767. When and where Visual Basic generates the errors depend on your selection of the error-setting options. Because the focus of this program is simply to learn about error trapping, the code is nonsensical and simple and the errors are obvious.

Consider the following code, which is contained in the **Mult** method of the class module named **clsDebug**:

```
Public Function Mult(pintArg1 As Integer, _
    pintArg2 As Integer) As Integer
        Mult = pintArg1 * pintArg2
EndfFunction
```

The Break Mode command button on the form contains code to create an instance of the class and to call the **Mult** function with arguments that will generate a run-time error. It also contains code to perform the same multiplication operation in the **Click** event procedure for the button itself:

```
Private Sub cmdBreakMode_Click()
On Error Resume Next
    Dim pintResult As Integer
    Dim d As New clsDebug
    pintResult = 32000 * 32000
```

```
        pintResult = d.Mult(32000, 32000)
        Exit Sub
cmdError:
        Debug.Print Err.Number
        Debug.Print Err.Description
End Sub
```

The preceding code performs the same multiplication operation in both the command button's **Click** event procedure and the class module. One statement will cause a run-time error in the command button's **Click** event procedure. The other will generate a run-time error in the class module.

To examine the error-trapping options:

1. Start Visual Basic, and open the project group Appendix.A\Complete\Debug.vbg. Set the drive designator as necessary. On the menu bar, click on Tools, and then click on Options. On the General tab in the Options dialog box, click on the Break on All Errors option button in the Error Trapping section. Click on OK to close the dialog box.

2. Test the program. Click on the Break Mode command button. The overflow error message appears, as shown in Figure A.2.

3. Click on Debug to highlight the statement that caused the overflow error, shown in the following statement:

```
pintResult = 32000 * 32000
```

This error occurred in the command button's **Click** event procedure, even though the code in the **Click** event procedure contained an error handler. Had you clicked one of the other option buttons in the Error Trapping section, the run-time error would have been trapped by the error handler, and execution would have continued.

4. End the program to return to design mode.

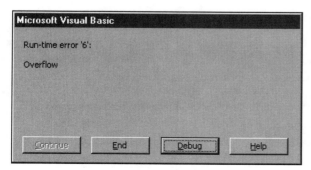

Figure A.2 Overflow error message.

5. On the menu bar, click on Tools, and then click on Options. On the General tab in the Options dialog box, click on Break In Class Module, click on OK, and then test the program as you did before. This time, the following statement, which caused the error, appears in the class module:

```
Mult = pintArg1 * pintArg2
```

The organization of the code in the **Click** event procedure ensures that the call to the **Mult** method in the class module appears after the attempt to multiply the same numbers in the event procedure. The error handler therefore trapped the error that occurred in the previous set of steps. Because you clicked Break In Class Module, however, Visual Basic raises the unhandled error in the class module.

6. End the program to return to design mode.

7. On the menu bar, click on Tools, and then click on Options. On the General tab in the Options dialog box, click on Break On Unhandled Errors, click on OK, and then test the program as you did before. This time, the program does not generate a run-time error. In this situation, Visual Basic raises an error in the class module. It returns the error code to the calling procedure—in this case the **Click** event procedure for the command button. The code in the event procedure then handles the error in the class module.

8. End the program to return to design mode.

The error-trapping mode that you use depends on the code to be debugged. For example, if you believe that a class module (component) is working correctly, you probably do not want to trap the errors in that module. Instead, the class module should return any errors to the client using the class. You will therefore choose the Break In Class Module option. On the other hand, sometimes you may want to test your error handlers to see whether they are working as expected. In this situation, the Break On All Errors option button will prove useful. If you want to test your program and handle errors in the same way that the code will handle errors when run by the user, select the Break On Unhandled Errors option. In all cases, remember that these debugging tools are just that—tools. You undoubtedly will find your own preferred method of using them.

Visual Basic Debugging Tools

In the previous steps, you saw how to use error-trapping settings to trap run-time errors in modules. These options work only when an error in your code actually generates a run-time error. Other types of problems, however, do not generate trappable run-time errors. In this section, you will learn how to anticipate and control these types of errors by using the Visual Basic debugging tools and debugging windows.

Visual Basic debugging tools consist of commands that allow you to suspend temporarily the execution of your program by entering break mode and then tracing the execution of statements and procedures. You can execute each statement in the program line by line, suspending execution when a specific statement is reached or the value of a variable or object changes. Suspending execution when a statement is reached is called setting a breakpoint.

The debugging windows consist of the Immediate, Watches, and Locals windows. Whenever you suspend the execution of your program, you do so to identify a particular problem. This task involves examining the values of the variables and object properties in your program to see whether they contain the correct data. You can analyze the contents of variables and objects through the Immediate, Watches, and Locals windows. To locate and fix run-time and logic errors in your program, you use the debugging commands in conjunction with these windows.

Tracing Program Execution

When a program produces incorrect results, but you are not sure why, it is often helpful to step through the statements in a program. Several commands allow you to follow the execution of your program:

➤ **Step Into button** Causes one statement to execute, after which Visual Basic enters break mode. If the statement is a procedure call, the procedure declaration for the procedure that will be executed next is highlighted in the Code window.

➤ **Step Over button** Has the same effect as the Step Into button unless the statement is a procedure call. If the statement is a procedure call, however, Visual Basic executes all of the statements in the procedure and then enters break mode just before executing the statement following the procedure call.

➤ **Step Out button** When clicked, causes Visual Basic to execute all remaining statements in the current procedure.

You typically use the Step Into button to suspend execution after each statement in a procedure so as to detect an error in that procedure. The Step Over button allows you to execute all statements in a procedure and suspend execution from the statement following that procedure. Finally, you use the Step Out button to complete the execution of a procedure when you have identified the error in that procedure.

In addition, you can suspend execution at any time by clicking on the Break button at run time. As well as stepping through every statement in every procedure in a program, you can step through parts of a program or pause the program and continue executing statements one at a time. This capability allows you to avoid tracing through the procedures that you know work correctly. Finally, you can alter the flow of execution during break mode by clicking on a statement in the Code window, clicking on Debug, and then clicking on Set Next Statement.

To illustrate the ways that you can step through a program, this section contains an example that allows you to locate a specific module containing an error and to locate the code that is causing the error. This simple example uses only three procedures.

 As you debug programs, you may find it useful to display the Debug toolbar and use its buttons to perform debugging tasks. To display the Debug toolbar, click View on the menu bar, select Toolbars, and then check the Debug option.

In this example, the code computes the area of a rectangle (length * width) and the volume of a three-dimensional cube (length * width * height):

```
Private Sub cmdTrace_Click()
    Dim pintArea As Integer
    Dim pintVolume As Long
    pintArea = Area(txtLength, txtWidth)
    pintVolume = Volume(pintArea, txtHeight)
    txtVolume = pintVolume
End Sub
Private Function Area(l As Integer, w As Integer)
    Area = l * w
End Function
' The following statement contains the logic error.
Private Function Volume(a As Integer, h As Integer)
    Volume = a / h
End Function
```

The preceding code calculates the area of a rectangle by multiplying the length of the rectangle by its width. The result is then used as an argument in the call to the Volume function. The Volume function, however, contains a logic error. Instead of multiplying the area by the height, it divides the area by the height. You can use the various execution tracing techniques to examine the execution flow of this program.

To trace a program's execution flow:

1. Press the F8 key to start the program. At this point, the program is running but no statement is executing. The program is waiting for an event to occur.

2. Enter the values 1, 2, and 3, as the length, width, and height, respectively, and then click on the Trace command button.

3. The event procedure named **cmdTrace_Click** is highlighted in the Code window, indicating that the procedure is next to execute.

4. Press the F8 key again. The following statement is highlighted because it is the next statement to execute:

```
pintArea = Area(txtLength, txtWidth)
```

5. Move the insertion point over the arguments named **txtLength** and **txtWidth**. Note that a ToolTip appears containing the current value of these two arguments. This technique is a quick way to discover the current value of a property or variable.

6. Press the F8 key again to execute the statement. The function is called and the **Function** procedure named Area is highlighted, indicating that this procedure is ready to execute.

7. Continue to press the F8 key. You will see the Area function execute and return, and then the Volume function called. Eventually, no statement appears highlighted in the Code window. At this point, Visual Basic is not executing a statement but rather is waiting for an event to occur.

8. End the program to return to design mode.

You also can step over a function procedure when it is working correctly.

To step over a **Function** or **Sub** procedure:

1. Start the program by pressing the F8 key. Enter values for the length, width, and height again, and then click on the Trace command button. Press the F8 key to highlight the following statement and then press the Shift+F8 keys to step over it:

```
pintArea = Area(txtLength, txtWidth)
```

2. The function executes. The next statement that will execute is the call to the Volume function.

3. End the program to return to design mode.

Although stepping through all the statements in a program is useful, it has serious limitations. Imagine that you had to execute 10,000 statements to reach the location where you suspect a problem exists. In this situation, a better tactic would be to tell Visual Basic to suspend execution when it reaches a particular statement and, from that point, to examine the executing statements one at a time. You can accomplish this goal by setting a breakpoint.

Setting Breakpoints

A breakpoint is a program line at which you specify that the program should suspend its execution and enter break mode. You can set breakpoints only on statements containing executable code; you cannot set a breakpoint on a line containing a variable declaration.

To set a breakpoint, you locate a statement in the Code window and then either click on the Toggle Breakpoint button on the Debugging toolbar (which is available only when the Code window is active) or press the F9 key. Breakpoints do not persist between invocations of Visual Basic. Thus, if you have several breakpoints set for a particular debugging session, they will disappear the next time you start Visual Basic.

You can also set a breakpoint by clicking in the left margin of the Code window that contains an executable statement. This action highlights the line and sets the breakpoint. Click in the margin to the left of the highlighted line again to remove the breakpoint.

When you set a breakpoint on a line, the line will appear in a highlighted color. To clear a breakpoint, click on the line in the program where a breakpoint is set, and then click on the Toggle Breakpoint button. When you run the program and Visual Basic reaches the statement containing the breakpoint, Visual Basic suspends execution of the program and enters break mode just before executing the statement containing the breakpoint. Once in break mode, you can use the Immediate window and the Step Into or Step Over buttons to find problems in the code. For example, if you have determined that a function, such as Pmt, produces incorrect results, you might set a breakpoint just before the function is called; you can then examine the values of the arguments to determine which one is incorrect.

To set a breakpoint:

1. Activate the Code window for the form module.

2. Set a breakpoint on the following line in the **cmdTrace_Click** event procedure:

```
pintArea = Area(txtLength, txtWidth)
```

3. Test the program. Enter values for the length, width, and height, and then click on the Trace command button. The program will enter break mode just before executing the statement.

4. End the program to return to design mode.

The same process is used to create and destroy all breakpoints. You can create as many or as few breakpoints as necessary. Again, you should decide where to set a breakpoint and how many breakpoints to set based on the debugging task at hand.

Using The Immediate Window

Programmers use the Immediate window to examine the values of variables and object properties as well as to change those values. You can use the Immediate window in three ways:

➤ You can call the **Debug.Print** method in a program. When you call this method, Visual Basic prints the method's arguments in the Immediate window.

➤ You can type **Print** statements directly in the Immediate window to examine values of variables and object properties in the program. Note, however, that you can type statements in the Immediate window only while a program is in break mode or design mode.

➤ You can execute a procedure by typing its name and arguments in the Immediate window.

In the following example, you will use the Immediate window to examine the value of variables and to call a function explicitly.

To display values in the Immediate window:

1. Start the program. Enter values for the length, width, and height, and then click on the Trace command button. The breakpoint you set in the previous steps should be highlighted.

2. Click on Immediate Window on the View menu to open the Immediate window, if necessary. Enter the following statement into the Immediate window, and then press the Enter key:

```
Print txtLength
```

The value you entered for the length will appear in the Immediate window.

3. Enter the following assignment statement in the Immediate window, and then press the Enter key:

```
txtArea = Area(10,10)
```

Visual Basic calls the Area function and stores the result in the text box named txtArea. As you can see, you can execute assignment statements in the Immediate window, just as the statement has been entered in your code. This capability can help you to test whether a particular function is working correctly.

4. End the program to return to design mode. Remove the breakpoint.

Again, when to use the Immediate window to display the value of variables and properties is a matter of professional choice.

Using The Watches Window

Although they are similar to breakpoints, watch expressions allow you to suspend execution when a condition is True or when the value of an object or variable changes. As with breakpoints, you can create, change, or delete watch expressions while a program is in design mode or break mode. Also as with breakpoints, Visual Basic does not preserve watch expressions after you close a project or exit Visual Basic. The more watch expressions you define, the more slowly your program will execute, because Visual Basic must check each watch expression for every statement that executes. Thus, when you debug a program, use watch expressions sparingly.

You use the Add Watch dialog box, shown in Figure A.3, to add a watch expression to a project.

The Add Watch dialog box contains three sections:

➤ **Expression** You enter the expression that Visual Basic should evaluate in the Expression text box. The watch expression can be a variable, a property, or a procedure call. To avoid typographical errors, you can copy the expression or variable from the Code window using the Copy and Paste commands.

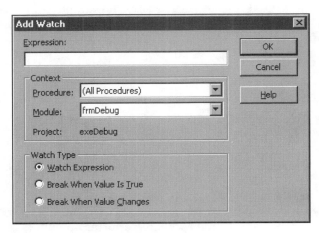

Figure A.3   Add Watch dialog box.

➤ **Context** The Context section sets the scope of the expression to watch. This section is useful if variables of the same name appear in different procedures. Module refers to the form or other module in your project that should be watched. The Project label is useful when you are debugging multiple projects; it indicates the project that is being watched.

➤ **Watch Type** The Watch Type section instructs Visual Basic about how to respond to the watch expression. If you select the Watch Expression option button, Visual Basic displays the value of the expression in the Watches window, but the program will not enter break mode when the expression becomes True or changes. You should consider selecting the Watch Expression option button if you need to print the value of a variable frequently when you reach a breakpoint. In addition, this option allows you to trace the value of a variable when you are using the Step Into button to watch the contents of a variable in detail. If you select the Break When Value Is True option button, Visual Basic enters break mode whenever the expression is True. If you select the Break When Value Changes option button, Visual Basic enters break mode whenever a statement changes the value of the watch expression.

As an illustration of the usefulness of a watch expression, consider a **Do** loop that iterates hundreds or thousands of times. In this situation, setting a breakpoint in the loop may not be effective for debugging because you would need to resume execution each time through the loop. A watch expression may prove more useful, however, because Visual Basic will not suspend execution each time through the loop.

In the sample program for this appendix, the command button with the caption Watch contains the following code in its **Click** event procedure. This code consists of nested **For** loops to initialize a 100-by-100 two-dimensional array.

```
Private Sub cmdWatch_Click()
    Dim pintArray(100, 100)
    Dim pintX As Integer
    Dim pintY As Integer
    For pintX = 0 To 99
        For pintY = 0 To 99
            pintArray(pintX, pintY) = 10
        Next
    Next
End Sub
```

In this example, you will set different watch expressions to trace the execution of the event procedure. Note that this procedure performs no useful task, but merely illustrates a long-running loop.

To set and use watch expressions:

1. Click on Add Watch on the Debug menu to activate the Add Watch dialog box.

2. Enter the expression pintX = 84 in the Expression text box, and then click on the Break When Value Is True option button in the Watch Type section. Set the module to **frmDebug** and the procedure to **cmdWatch_Click**. Click on OK to add the watch expression.

3. Open the Add Watch dialog box again. Enter the expression "pintY" in the Expression text box, and then click on the Watch Expression option button in the Watch Type section, if necessary. Set the module to **frmDebug** and the procedure to **cmdWatch_Click**. Click on OK.

4. If necessary, click on Watch Window on the View menu to activate the Watches window, as shown in Figure A.4. Note that Figure A.4 shows the Watches window while the program is running.

5. Test the program. Click on the Watch command button. Visual Basic will suspend execution as the values of the watch expressions change.

6. End the program to return to design mode. Exit Visual Basic.

Setting watch expressions is particularly useful when you know that a particular variable contains an incorrect value. In this situation, you should set a watch expression that will occur when the value of a particular variable changes.

Using The Locals Window

The Locals window displays the local variables pertaining to the currently executing procedure. As the current procedure changes from one procedure to another, Visual Basic updates the window to show the local variables pertaining to the new procedure. Figure A.5 shows the Locals window.

In Figure A.5, the currently executing procedure is cmdTrace_Click. It contains two local variables named pintArea and pintVolume. You can change the values of these variables by clicking on the Value column and changing each variable's values.

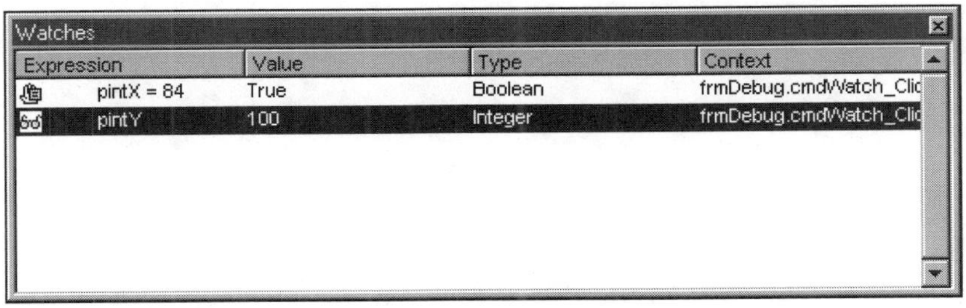

Watches				
Expression	Value	Type	Context	
pintX = 84	True	Boolean	frmDebug.cmdWatch_Clic	
pintY	100	Integer	frmDebug.cmdWatch_Clic	

Figure A.4   Watches window.

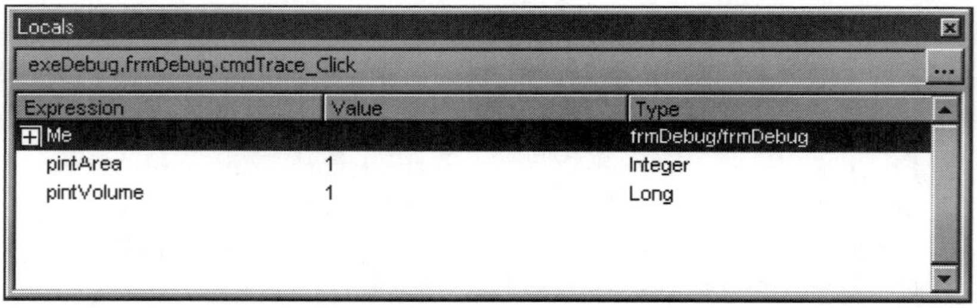

Figure A.5 Locals window.

When debugging a large program, you will likely use a combination of breakpoints and watches to locate and correct problems. You will probably step through each statement in a specific procedure when you have isolated a problem to a particular procedure. No right answer exists to the debugging problem, however. As you develop more and larger programs, you will likely find your own style when using these tools.

MAPPING *MCSD VISUAL BASIC 6 DESKTOP* TO CERTIFICATION EXAM 70-176

Deriving the Physical design

Objectives	Section	Chapter
Assess the potential impact of the logical design on performance, maintainability, extensibility, and availability	The Three-Tiered Approach Logical Design	8
	An Introduction to Components	9
Design Visual Basic components to access data from a database.	Developing Software For A New Distributed System	8
Design the properties, methods and events of components.	Physical Design	8
	Anatomy Of A Class Module	9
	Designing An Object Hierarchy	10

Establishing the Development environment

Objectives	Section	Chapter
Establish the environment for source code version control	Configuring Visual SourceSafe	1
Install and configure Visual Basic for developing desktop applications.	Installing Visual Basic	1

Implementing Navigational design

Objectives	Section	Chapter
Dynamically modify the appearance of a menu		2
Add a pop-up menu to an application	Adding A Pop-Up Menu To An Application	2
Create an application that adds and deletes menus at run time.		2
Add controls to forms.	The Label Control	1
Set properties for controls.	Understanding Properties Using The Properties Window	1
Assign code to a control to respond to an event.	Responding To An Event The Code Window	1

Creating data input forms and dialog boxes

Objectives	Section	Chapter
Display and manipulate data by using custom controls. Controls include TreeView, ListView, ImageList, Toolbar, and StatusBar	Introducing The Windows Common Controls	5
	Storing Images In The ImageList Control	
	Introduction To Drill-Down Interfaces	
	The TreeView Control	
	The ListView Control	
	Improving The User Interface With The Toolbar Control	6
	Improving The User Interface With A Status Bar	
	Programming The Toolbar	7
Create an application that adds and deletes controls at run time		2
Use the Controls collection to manipulate controls at run time.	Collections	2
	Other Ways To Keep Track Of Forms	7
Use the Forms collection to manipulate forms at run time. The Forms Collection		7

Writing code that validates user input

Objectives	Section	Chapter
Create an application that verifies data entered at the field level and the form level by a user.	Understanding Mouse And Keyboard Events	2
		3
	Validating Field Input	3
	Validating Changes In The DataGrid Control	4
Create an application that enables or disables controls based upon input in fields.		2
		3

Writing code that processes data entered on a form

Objectives	Section	Chapter
Given a scenario, add code to the appropriate form event. Evens include Initialize, Terminate, Load, Unload, QueryUnload, Activate, and Deactivate.	The Basics Of Form Events	2
	Destroying Form Instances	7
Add an ActiveX control to the toolbox.	Introducing ActiveX Controls	3
Create a Web page by using the DHTML Page Designer to dynamically change attributes of elements, change content, change styles, and position elements.	Dynamic HTML	15

(continued)

Writing code that processes data entered on a form *(continued)*

Objectives	Section	Chapter
Use data binding to display and manipulate data from a data source	Creating A Class Module	9
	Creating An Object Hierarchy With Persistent Data	10

Instatiating and invoke a COM component

Objectives	Section	Chapter
Create a Visual Basic client application that uses a COM component.	Creating Automation Objects	8
Create a Visual Basic application that handles events from a COM component.	Asynchronous Notification Using Events	16
Create callback procedures to enable processing between COM components and Visual Basic client applications.	Callback Functions Asynchronous Notification Using Callbacks	16

Implementing online user assistance in a desktop application

Objectives	Section	Chapter
Set appropriate properties to enable user assistance. Help properties include **HelpFile**, **HelpContextID**, and **WhatsThisHelp**.	Connecting The Help System To The Program Developing What's This Help	15
Create HTML Help for an application	HTML Help	15
Implement messages from a server component to a user interface.	Implementing the File Transfer Protocol Network Timeouts	14

Implementing error handling for the user interface in desktop applications

Objectives	Section	Chapter
Identify and Trap run time errors.	Creating An Error Handler Handling Database Errors Understanding The CancelError Property	2 4 7
Handle inline errors.	Creating An Error Handler	2

Creating and managing COM components

Objectives	Section	Chapter
Create a COM component that implements business rules or logic. Components include Dlls, ActiveX controls, and active documents. (ActiveX documents.)	An Introduction To Components Anatomy Of A Class Module Creating A Class Module	9
Create ActiveX controls.	Creating ActiveX Controls Constituent Controls Creating Better Properties	11

(continued)

Creating and managing COM components *(continued)*

Objectives	Section	Chapter
Create an ActiveX control that exposes properties.	Exposing Properties To The Developer	11
	Delegating Properties	
	Aggregating Properties	
Use control events to save and load persistent properties.	User Control Events	11
	Understanding User Control Events	
	Persistent Properties	13
Test and debug an ActiveX control.	Debugging ActiveX Controls	12
Create and enable property pages for an ActiveXcontrol.	Creating Property Pages	12
Enable the data binding capabilities of an ActiveX control.	Creating Data Aware Controls	11
Create an ActiveX control that is a data source.	Creating Data Aware Controls	11

Creating an active document

Objectives	Section	Chapter
Use code within an active document to interact with a container application.	ActiveX Document Menus	13
	Determining The Container	
	Accessing Office Binder Programmatically	
Navigate to other active documents.	Multiple ActiveX Document Applications	13
Debug a COM client written in Visual Basic	Debugging Class Modules	9
	Appendix A Debugging	A
Compile a project with class modules into a COM component.	More About The Project	10
Implement an object model within a COM component.	Creating A Collection Hierarchy	10
Set properties to control the instancing of a class within a COM component.	Class Instancing	10
Use Visual Component Manager to manage components.	Visual Component Manager	17
Register and unregister a COM	Register A Server	16

Creating data services

Objectives	Section	Chapter
Access and manipulate a data source by using ADO and the ADO Data control.	A Conceptual Overview Of ActiveX Data Objects And OLE DB	3
	The ADO Data Control	
	Creating Bound Controls	
	The Recordset Object	
	Using The Recordset Object To Manipulate Data	

Testing the solution

Objectives	Section	Chapter
Given a scenario, select the appropriate compiler options.	The Visual Basic Compiler	17
Control an application by using conditional compilation.	Conditional Compilation	17
Set watch expressions during program execution.	Using The Watches Window	A

Monitoring the value of expressions and variables by using the Immediate window

Objectives	Section	Chapter
Use the Immediate window to check or change values.	Using The Immediate Window	A
Use the Locals window to check or change values.	Using The Locals Window	A

Implementing project groups to support the development and debugging process

Objectives	Section	Chapter
Debug DLLs in process.	Debugging Class Modules	9
Test and debug a control in process.	Debugging ActiveX Controls	12
Given a scenario, define the scope of a watch variable.	Using The Watches Window	A

Deploying an application

Objectives	Section	Chapter
Use the Package and Deployment Wizard to create a setup program that installs a desktop application, registers COM components, and allows for uninstall	The Package And Deployment Wizard	17
Plan and implement floppy disk–based deployment or compact disc–based deployment for a desktop application.	Floppy Disk And CD-Rom deployment	17
Plan and Implement Web-Based deployment for a desktop application	The Package And Deployment Wizard Deploying Packages To The Web	12 17
Plan and Implement network–based deployment for a desktop application	Introducing The Package And Deployment Wizard	17

Maintaining and supporting an application

Objectives	Section	Chapter
Fix errors, and take measures to prevent future errors.	Appendix A	A
Deploy application updates for desktop applications.	Understanding Application Updates	17

MCSD Requirements*

Core

Choose 1 from the desktop applications development group	
Exam 70-016	Designing and Implementing Desktop Applications with Microsoft Visual C++ 6.0
Exam 70-176	Designing and Implementing Desktop Applications with Microsoft Visual Basic 6.0
Choose 1 from the distributed applications development group	
Exam 70-015	Designing and Implementing Distributed Applications with Microsoft Visual C++ 6.0
Exam 70-175	Designing and Implementing Distributed Applications with Microsoft Visual Basic 6.0
This solution architecture exam is required	
Exam 70-100	Analyzing Requirements and Defining Solution Architectures

Elective

Choose 1 from this group	
Exam 70-015	Designing and Implementing Distributed Applications with Microsoft Visual C++ 6.0
Exam 70-016	Designing and Implementing Desktop Applications with Microsoft Visual C++ 6.0
Exam 70-029	Designing and Implementing Databases with Microsoft SQL Server 7.0
Exam 70-024	Developing Applications with C++ Using the Microsoft Foundation Class Library
Exam 70-025	Implementing OLE in Microsoft Foundation Class Applications
Exam 70-055	Designing and Implementing Web Sites with Microsoft FrontPage 98
Exam 70-057	Designing and Implementing Commerce Solutions with Microsoft Site Server 3.0, Commerce Edition
Exam 70-165	Developing Applications with Microsoft Visual Basic 5.0
	OR
Exam 70-175	Designing and Implementing Distributed Applications with Microsoft Visual Basic 6.0
	OR
Exam 70-176	Designing and Implementing Desktop Applications with Microsoft Visual Basic 6.0
Exam 70-069	Application Development with Microsoft Access for Windows 95 and the Microsoft Access Developer's Toolkit
Exam 70-091	Designing and Implementing Solutions with Microsoft Office 2000 and Microsoft Visual Basic for Applications
Exam 70-152	Designing and Implementing Web Solutions with Microsoft Visual InterDev 6.0

* This is not a complete listing—you can still be tested on some earlier versions of these products. However, we have tried to include the most recent versions so that you may test on these versions and thus be certified longer. We have not included any tests that are scheduled to be retired.

The MCSD program is being expanded to include FoxPro and Visual J++. However, these tests are not yet available and no test numbers have been assigned.

Core exams that can also be used as elective exams can be counted only once toward certification. The same test cannot be used as both a core and elective exam.

INDEX

W